Canadian Labour Policy and Politics

Canadian
LABOUR POLICY
and POLITICS

EDITED BY

John Peters and Don Wells

UBCPress · Vancouver · Toronto

31 30 29 28 27 26 25 24 23 22   5 4 3 2 1

Printed in Canada on FSC-certified ancient-forest-free paper (100% post-consumer recycled) that is processed chlorine- and acid-free.

Library and Archives Canada Cataloguing in Publication

Title: Canadian labour policy and politics / edited by John Peters and Don Wells.

Names: Peters, John, 1963- editor. | Wells, Don, 1946- editor.

Description: Includes bibliographical references and index.

Identifiers: Canadiana (print) 20220407843 | Canadiana (ebook) 2022040786X | ISBN 9780774866057 (softcover) | ISBN 9780774866101 (PDF) | ISBN 9780774866156 (EPUB)

Subjects: LCSH: Labor policy—Canada.

Classification: LCC HD8106.5 .C346 2022 | DDC 331.0971—dc23

Canadä

UBC Press gratefully acknowledges the financial support for our publishing program of the Government of Canada (through the Canada Book Fund), the Canada Council for the Arts, and the British Columbia Arts Council.

This book has been published with the help of a grant from the Canadian Federation for the Humanities and Social Sciences, through the Awards to Scholarly Publications Program, using funds provided by the Social Sciences and Humanities Research Council of Canada.

Printed and bound in Canada by Friesens
Set in Gilam and Ramilas by Artegraphica Design Co.
Copy editor: Camilla Blakeley
Proofreader: Andrew Wilmot
Indexer: Noeline Bridge
Cover designer: Will Brown

UBC Press
The University of British Columbia
2029 West Mall
Vancouver, BC V6T 1Z2
www.ubcpress.ca

Contents

Acknowledgments

BOOKS ARE ALWAYS collective efforts, and *Canadian Labour Policy and Politics* would not have been possible without the support from the outset of our colleagues and friends, our students and families. All the contributors willingly gave insight, encouragement, and friendship as we moved the project forward. Their patience and encouragement helped us to see this collection - far too long in the making - through to the end, and to produce a comprehensive, accessible, and insightful resource for students, educators, activists, and other readers in the years to come.

We are greatly indebted to David Mitchell for his tireless editing, as well as to Daria Levac for taking the lead in revising the notes, preparing the manuscript, and more. We also thank the reviewers for their insightful and generous comments, which sharpened our ideas. Randy Schmidt at UBC Press was consistently enthusiastic about the project from the beginning, and we thank him for his care and comments.

Special thanks is extended to Camilla Blakeley, whose careful and incredibly sharp and judicious editing of the manuscript has done so much to make this book a much clearer and more cohesive whole. And many thanks to Meagan Dyer and the production staff at UBC Press for keeping us on track and for their patient attention to detail. Finally, we are very appreciative of the support of the United Steelworkers Canada, and of Ken Neumann and Marty Warren, who have graciously helped support this publication.

Don Wells thanks friends and colleagues for working so hard to write such accessible, superb chapters for this book. Don is also grateful to many activists in the labour movement for their advice and insights. Among them were fellow workers from his time at the Ford assembly plant in Oakville and at Dofasco's (now ArcelorMittal Dofasco's) steel complex in Hamilton, both in Ontario. They taught him not only how to be an autoworker and a steelworker but also much about the culture and politics of solidarity at work. Don also thanks friends and students at McMaster University for their personal support and solidarity over many years, and for their important, inspiring contributions to education, work, and politics. Don is grateful, as always and profoundly, to Ruth Frager, Ariela Frager-Wells, and Benjamin Frager-Wells, for their abiding love, wisdom, insights, patience, and sense of humour.

John Peters would like to express his gratitude to Angela Carter for her support and intellectual energy. Both are essential in tackling inequality and the climate crisis, and both are needed on a daily basis to provide assurance that things can be different - and will be much better.

Canadian Labour Policy and Politics

Introduction

IT IS 2020. JENS, who is twenty-five, and Anna, who is twenty-three, are recent social science university graduates. They live in a rent-controlled apartment in Copenhagen, Denmark. They have no student debt, and their two-year-old daughter is in a high-quality daycare just down the street and for which there are no fees. At the start of the coronavirus pandemic, in March, Anna had recently returned to her retail job after eighteen months off with good maternity benefits. She and Jens were both temporarily laid off from their jobs when the pandemic hit, and their daycare closed. Both continued to be paid. Many public outdoor facilities remained open, so they took the time to enjoy the outdoors and split their time looking after their daughter – as did many other parents in their neighbourhood.

By mid-April, both had returned to work, though primarily from home. And they were able to go back to nearly full-time hours because their daycare reopened with several precautionary measures, including smaller groups and more handwashing. Both remain worried about the long-term effects of the virus on Denmark and other European countries. Neither is worried about their safety or their short-term future.

Jessica lives in Vancouver, Canada. She is twenty-three and also a recent social science university graduate. She attended the University of British Columbia and did well in her studies, but with the pandemic she has become very anxious about her future. She had been working two poorly paid part-time jobs and was considering returning to university or going to college for another degree. When the pandemic began, she was immediately laid off from her retail job. After six months, she has still not been called back to work as her employer has shifted to online sales only. Her partner, Marta, who is twenty-eight, is also a university graduate and is working three jobs with no safety equipment and little physical distancing.

They live with two others in a small two-bedroom apartment in Vancouver that costs them $2,400 a month. Each has big student debts – Jessica owes almost $26,000, Marta more than $35,000. Neither has been able to find a job that would allow her to use her academic skills and abilities. And neither has the time needed to search for a better job, especially with the pandemic still ongoing and the limited number of jobs available.

Marta is considering moving back to live with her parents in New Westminster to save money, but she would have to commute more than two hours in to work in Vancouver, and her mother has serious health conditions that make both of them nervous about the danger of infection. Jessica would like to move to a less costly city with Marta, but their student debt payments and the difficulty of finding jobs and an affordable apartment are discouraging hurdles. Their dream of starting a family soon seems even more unrealistic. The few childcare spots normally available in Vancouver have dwindled because of concerns about the virus.

Marta and Jessica initially relied on the **Canada Emergency Response Benefit (CERB)**, but they worry whether they will have enough income to live on at the end of this program. Both are very concerned about what their futures hold. Neither has any confidence in making plans for the next few months or the coming year.

AS THIS COMPOSITE sketch demonstrates, everyday life differed dramatically in Canada and Denmark with the onset of the COVID-19 pandemic , even though both have advanced, rich economies. *Canadian Labour Policy and Politics* asks why.

In providing answers, this book explores how labour law and social and economic policies are intensifying the polarization between **good jobs** and **bad jobs**. It examines the reasons behind decreasing labour market regulation and why so many people are living in poverty despite being employed. And it asks what progressive policies Canada could enact to develop greater economic equality and political inclusiveness while ensuring a green recovery in the wake of the pandemic.

The answers to all these questions are complicated, to be sure. But a key reason Canadians like Jessica and Marta are so worried about their futures is because business interests and the rich have systematically remade Canadian politics and reoriented power and policy to meet their own needs. Over the past few decades, one of the most striking features of politics in Canada has been the growing scope and influence of business and wealthy elites. Just as distinctive is how many elected officials have been pulled toward the positions of economic elites, leaving many workers ever further behind. The

reasons behind these trends are straightforward, and the combined impact has been potent.

Increasingly, powerful business and financial interests have successfully shifted public policy and labour laws away from promoting the collective prosperity of the many and toward the profits of the few. At the same time, the ability of unions and progressive civil society actors and advocacy groups to influence politics and to protect themselves and their families has declined. The consequences have been profound.

In theory, a liberal democracy, such as Canada's, is supposed to create pressures for politicians to listen to popular majorities. However, as governments in Canada and other more market-oriented liberal democracies (such as in the United States and the United Kingdom) have turned their ear mainly to the priorities of dominant business interests and the rich, the voices of workers have been muted, and the labour laws and public policies that are supposed to help workers have been undermined or eroded. It is this intensifying cycle of strengthening business influence – alongside the weakening of democracy and the decline in workers' power – that is key to explaining why so many Canadians face growing difficulties both on and off the job today.

PUBLIC POLICY IN A COVID-19 WORLD

To make matters more difficult, the pandemic that began in 2020 has cut a path of devastation across Canada and around the world, threatening everyone's health and causing millions of workers to lose their jobs. Indeed, COVID-19 – a severe respiratory disease – has shown itself to be an illness of inequality, exploiting the most vulnerable: the elderly, workers in low-wage jobs, racialized workers, and temporary foreign workers. The pandemic has also ushered in the most serious economic crisis since the Great Depression of the 1930s. For as countries have reacted with strict containment and lockdown policies to help suppress the virus, economic activity has contracted sharply and employers have laid off workers in droves.[1]

Just as striking has been the one-sidedness of much government reaction to these twin crises of health and unemployment. In the early months of the pandemic, public officials in Canada and elsewhere took emergency measures to ensure health and economic survival. They provided income support and job retention schemes for millions of workers, passed a host of instruments to allow businesses to stay afloat, and supplied billions to financial actors in order to keep credit markets liquid.[2] As the pandemic has evolved, it has become clear that despite such stimulus, a quick rebound is anything but guaranteed, and the outlook for a broad and sustainable recovery seems bleak.

Canadians face a future of mass unemployment and recession because, even as vaccines have been developed and mass inoculation campaigns rolled out in record time, recovery is expected to take several years. One problem has been the continual emergence of new variants of COVID-19, with new waves of infection and hospitalization as a result. A second is that the effectiveness of vaccines declines over time, necessitating new or repeated vaccination – a huge concern amid the global surge of cases and variants. A third problem is that governments throughout the pandemic have routinely lifted restrictions too early, only to reimpose them within weeks or months. This has left many harmful and long-lasting health and economic repercussions as populations are exposed not only to a deadly virus but also to rising government and household debt, the underfunding of social programs, declining job quality, and worsening income security.[3]

If that were not enough, the climate crisis remains just as pressing, alongside global threats to the natural world and wildlife. With the onset of the pandemic, concentrations of greenhouse gases in the atmosphere dropped as workplace lockdowns and travel bans took effect. But this encouraging trend proved temporary, and rapidly rising CO_2 emissions have roared back to the forefront of global crises. The consequences – increasing temperatures and climate-related disasters such as wildfires, droughts, and floods – are far beyond anything we have experienced before. Scientists continue to raise warnings that current agricultural, mining, and industrial practices could lead to the mass extinction of life on Earth as economic **globalization** chronically undermines the planet's life-sustaining ecosystems.[4]

This piling on of global challenges – viral disease, long-term economic shocks, inadequate labour laws and social protection, and threats to the natural world – has made trends in Canada far more cause for worry than for optimism. Indeed, the challenges are particularly fraught with **risk** for any of the millions in **precarious employment** or left otherwise vulnerable: such individuals are far more likely to be infected and to die from the virus than is a worker with what many in Canada generally think of as a good job with decent working conditions, employment security, and income. So too the response of Canadian officials to the COVID-19 pandemic has been highly uneven, providing business and financial markets with seemingly unlimited funds while millions have been thrown into unemployment. At the same time, Canada has remained saddled with one of the highest rates of unemployment among advanced industrial economies.[5]

In all these ways, the pandemic has laid bare Canadian economic and political inequalities, exposing ever-widening gaps between the very rich and the rest of the population. It has also exposed the short-sightedness of public officials and the inadequacy of numerous labour and social policies – shortcomings that have left many workers and families vulnerable to economic shocks and perhaps more virulent viruses well into the future.

So, even as vaccines and treatments roll out, researchers and international agencies the world over are suggesting that the pandemic needs to function as a turning point for citizens and government alike – a critical moment when states commit themselves to urgent action to ensure a sustainable future that serves all people.[6] Unfortunately, there may be only a small window of opportunity to create a more just economy in the wake of the pandemic. So taking advantage of this chance will require a great deal of effort from workers, unions, and citizens alike. Above all, it will mean people coming together to strengthen Canada's democratic power, so that it better serves our economy and our society.

These core themes – inequality, politics, power, and achieving a better future for workers by winning equitable and sustainable solutions – are at the heart of this book.

WHY ARE LABOUR LAWS AND PUBLIC POLICY IMPORTANT?

Research indicates that the path to understanding accelerating economic and political inequality and the inadequacy of government responses lies in considering how each country has shaped its labour laws, employment policies, and social policies. International comparisons are telling.

Denmark has a more egalitarian and supportive social democratic approach to meeting the needs of its citizens. Known as *flexicurity*, this set of policies was born out of struggles between labour and business groups over the better part of the twentieth century, with each seeking to carve out the kind of society they wanted.[7] Only after years of conflict were citizens, organized business interests, and government able to compromise over three defining ideals that all Danes today believe they have the right to enjoy: employment protection for good jobs through strong labour laws that regulate wages and hours; income security for all workers through well-funded **unemployment insurance** and old age, sickness, and disability programs; and government-provided training or public jobs for all workers to ensure they can actively participate in the labour market – that is, find good jobs if they were laid off.

Labour laws such as these have helped ensure that most Danes are now paid reasonably well. In addition, union strength and labour laws covering much of the workforce meant that employers and unions were able to quickly negotiate a comprehensive wage subsidy policy when the pandemic struck. During the downturn, the Danish government covered 75 percent of the salaries of all employees, whether unionized or not, just as they had done ten years earlier in the financial crisis of 2009–10.[8]

Canada's history has been very different. Neither unions nor social democratic parties (such as the New Democratic Party) have been as powerful or as politically influential as those in Denmark.[9] Consequently, business and the very wealthy have long had the upper hand, and there has long been strong support for a more free market approach whose chief priorities are business growth and profits.

Such historical differences have created contemporary distinctions in how governments tackle the challenges posed by globalization, massive technological change, or new crises like the global COVID-19 pandemic. Notably, governments differ in their responses to conflict between the power of private business in politics and in workplaces, on the one hand, and citizens' demands for greater equality and adequate health, safety, and social protections, on the other. Here there is much to learn from the great variation in democracies across countries.

Some countries, like Denmark, opt for a protective and progressive approach that takes the well-being of its citizens and labour markets more seriously while curbing the power of business.[10] By contrast, in countries such as Canada and the United States, where affluence often buys influence, governments have tended to double down on efforts to meet business priorities through corporate tax cuts, public service reductions, and deregulation of labour standards, thereby reinforcing growing disparities between the rich and the majority of citizens.

This divergence between corporate power and public power – between business and people – sheds light on why excessive business power often leads to greater inequality and a weaker economy. It also underscores the need to rebalance public power so that democracies can pass better labour laws and employment policies – and thereby provide people with the resources and opportunities to work with dignity and live up to their potential.

More than ever, citizens have at their disposal realistic ideas about how to shape a better future. Yet if they are to seize this opportunity, a first step is to create or rebuild strong labour organizations and political coalitions to challenge excessive business control of major investments and business influence on public authorities.

Canadian Labour Policy and Politics explores these issues and explains how our labour laws and employment-related public polices generate their effects, and why these laws and policies have evolved to the disadvantage of people on the job. Focusing on tensions between capitalism and democracy, it spells out how and why Canada's legal and public policy mechanisms – in theory operating to protect workers and uphold their right to a decent standard of living – often leave workers in low-wage, precarious jobs with little economic or social security while providing business with a low-cost flexible workforce.

This book develops several key themes:

- how federal and provincial government policies designed to promote economic competitiveness and lower business costs – an approach often referred to as **neoliberalism** – have undermined labour laws and employment policies across Canada
- how growing business influence on public policy makers has weakened employment protections, muted **worker voice**, and reduced job quality through **labour market deregulation**
- the primary effects of these new policy directions, including inequality, low-wage work, and bad jobs, which affect all workers but typically are most harmful to youth, women, recent immigrants, and racialized minorities
- policy alternatives grounded in a more inclusive, progressive world view, and the reasons why these are necessary to create a broadly shared prosperity.

WHAT HAS GONE WRONG?

Part 1 provides the context for much of what has gone wrong for workers in Canada, beginning with the twin forces of growing corporate power and rapidly increasing economic and political inequality. These trends have recast government policy choices – above all, structuring markets in ways that have allowed corporations and finance to soar while doing little to help workers left trying to survive in low-wage, part-time, and temporary employment.

From this starting point, the chief cause of many of Canada's recent unequal transformations has been the adoption of neoliberal policies by government officials acting under pressure from organized business interests to improve corporate growth and profitability.[11]

Neoliberalism

Neoliberalism is an economic philosophy and accompanying set of policy principles that emerged in the 1940s through the work of economists such as Friedrich Hayek and Milton Friedman. It assumes that competition for economic wealth is humanity's defining characteristic, and that when citizens act freely as market consumers or business owners the well-being of society is lifted for all. Competing in the market, it claims, sorts us into a natural hierarchy of economic winners and losers. Any attempt to moderate economic competition and its consequences tends to disrupt the discovery of this allegedly natural order.

These ideas were first embraced by business-friendly politicians in the late 1970s and early '80s, such as Prime Minister Margaret Thatcher in the United Kingdom (1979–90) and President Ronald Reagan in the United States (1981–89), and by subsequent governments including that of Prime Minister Brian Mulroney in Canada (1984–93). To implement this philosophy, they cut taxes, privatized and outsourced public services to private for-profit companies, retrenched social programs, and restricted trade union rights. As a result, governments in countries such as Canada and the United States did much less to redress imbalances of income and resources than they had in previous decades, and much more to assist business by carrying out aggressive tax cuts, cutting public services, and deregulating labour markets in order to help boost corporate profitability.

As business owners and those with economic power wielded growing political influence, public policy was rewritten in their favour. Policy actions were introduced so that government power would return to advancing older, so-called liberal economic principles that emphasized business and competition, and advocated that Canadians should trust the market to provide wages, essential services, and investments in basic infrastructure.[12] And with the wider adoption of neoliberal models over the past few decades, policies governing the private and public sectors alike have prioritized the interests of private business and investors while neglecting many of the growing costs for average Canadians. Those costs can be calculated in terms of stagnating wages, rising precarious employment, and lack of access to essential public services like universal childcare.

Nevertheless, it's important to note that although these developments have done much to colour contemporary politics and policy making, large differences exist in the degree to which public officials are committed to such business-first policies. In Finland, Norway, and Denmark, for example, where neoliberal policies have not been as widely utilized, income inequality remains far lower than in Canada and the United States. In the Nordic countries, higher percentages of workers are covered by collective agreements; trade unions are stronger not only in the workplace but also within the political system; and greater proportions of citizens, community groups, and unions effectively pressure political parties and governments to uphold social programs that benefit society as a whole.

These developments are explained in greater detail in Part 1 of this text, which provides international comparisons while assessing the driving forces behind neoliberal politics and policies in Canada. By looking at how Canada compares with the United States, Sweden, and Denmark, these opening chapters demonstrate how and why Canada's workers, unions, labour laws, and employment policies fit into broader longer-term political and economic developments.

Chapter 1 examines the problems caused by the COVID-19 pandemic and evaluates Canadian attempts to protect the health and well-being of citizens on and off the job in comparison to those of other countries. It discusses how ill-prepared Canadian political and economic systems were to deal with the virus, revealing a common source for these difficulties: politics and policies favouring the interests of corporations and the wealthy over those of the wider populace. The chapter concludes by proposing progressive policy alternatives, starting with those that would help Canada achieve a clean energy economy. These key themes – inequality as the product of a flawed economic system, politics that have been captured by economic elites and their allies, and the need for inclusive policies that protect the planet – are echoed throughout the book.

Chapter 2 focuses on how governments in Canada and elsewhere have systematically supported business interests by promoting financial liberalization, as well as free trade and investment policies, in recent decades. With business using its formidable resources to shift the political terrain, elected officials have pursued long-term policy strategies that facilitate business growth and profit while redirecting the financial rewards to major shareholders and senior executives. This chain of business developments and business-first policies has brought increased layoffs, temp work, and short-term contracts – a **fissuring** of employment that has left more and more workers vulnerable to wages, few or no benefits, and little job security.[13]

Such connections between public policy and business, financial deregulation and labour cost cutting, and free trade and economic globalization are the first piece of the puzzle, explaining why income growth is being redistributed to the benefit of a few at the cost of the wider Canadian workforce. They also help account for the insistence of Canada's corporate and financial executives on prioritizing their own oversized pay packages while often refusing to provide personal protective equipment, implement social distancing, or offer paid sick leave as the pandemic took hold. Indeed, in many flourishing enterprises, workers who complained about or refused unsafe work found themselves threatened or even fired.[14]

Deregulation

A second reason why neoliberal policies have fuelled inequality in Canada is that they have prompted provincial officials to deregulate labour markets by watering down and failing to enforce labour laws and employment regulations and standards. This has allowed employers much greater discretion to lower wages and to impose harsher working conditions as they see fit.[15]

Neoliberal policies often target collective employment relations such as laws governing union certification, strikes, and **collective bargaining**, which are thought to impede the freedom of markets and limit the ability of firms to set contracts between managers and individual workers at market prices (see chapters 3 and 4).[16] From a neoliberal perspective, regulating employment relations – through labour legislation, collective bargaining, a **minimum wage**, or mandated paid sick and parental leave – promotes inflationary wage levels and creates overly rigid labour markets that limit the incentive to hire more workers.

The logical extreme of this business-oriented view is to see the role of labour law and employment policies as simply to support market forces and create incentives for people to work harder for whatever wages they can get. Politicians and state officials who adopt this standpoint – as so often happens in Canada and the United States – consequently often seek to expose workers to competitive market forces by dismantling or undermining the collective protections of labour laws and collective agreements. Such goals are similarly served by weakening or eliminating pro-labour programs, such as unemployment insurance, and other hard-won labour rights and employment standards, or by freezing the minimum wage for many years so that it no longer provides basic income security.

Consider the number of Canadians in low-paying jobs. Although the definition differs considerably across countries, one widely used measure of low pay is that it is less than two-thirds of the median hourly wage or less than two-thirds of the median annual earnings of all full-time workers. Using this definition, Canada has the third-highest level of low-wage work among rich industrial countries, with 22 percent of full-time workers in low-wage employment in 2015 – behind only that of Ireland and the United States.[17]

Even more telling is the proportion of workers in part-time, temporary, and solo or bogus self-employment, who now make up over 40 percent of the total Canadian labour market. Such non-standard employment is rapidly redefining what is considered a normal job, as more and more workers are stuck with low wages, little job or income security, and few long-term prospects. In 2015, roughly 7 million Canadians in such non-standard employment averaged just $15,000 in annual earnings, less than a third of what the average full-time/full-year worker earned.

It is these precarious workers who have been most exposed to job and income losses during the COVID-19 pandemic. And while many were helped by CERB and its successor programs, some still found themselves and their families going hungry as they struggled to pay rent or mortgages, bills, and other costs in the wake of layoffs and long-term unemployment.[18]

THE POLITICS OF LABOUR POLICY

Part 2 of the text examines the impact of neoliberalism and deregulation in greater detail, analyzing why so many workers have been left without adequate protection or representation. Arguably, more democratic politics should help to improve wages and working conditions. Because citizens have the right to vote and protest and express their opinions, logic suggests that Canadian government policies reflect citizens' voices and address their concerns with better wages and social programs.

However, firms and financial interests can have seemingly unlimited access to governments and far greater influence than citizens do in shaping policy. By contrast, the policy needs and preferences of workers and other Canadians are increasingly ignored. Consequently, more and more people are becoming exasperated with their politicians and governments. At the same time, issues of race, religion, and immigration divide Canadians, leaving some with neither time nor energy to pay much attention to politics, and others finding no reason to trust that their governments will enact many policies most voters prefer. Making matters more difficult is that workers who were once well organized by unions and civic associations have seen these atrophy and their leaders turn in a dozen different political directions.

These skewed social and political developments raise troubling questions about changes in the relationship between capitalism and democracy in Canada in recent decades. Are Canadian governments becoming more attuned to the interests of business and the wealthy than to the majority of their electorate? To what extent is economic inequality linked to increasing bias in political voice, representation, and public policy making? Has the transformation of democratic politics influenced our labour laws and employment regulations, and coloured how elected officials have responded to the COVID-19 pandemic?

Part 2 assesses the impact of these political shifts on several crucial policy areas: industrial relations and collective bargaining, provincial and federal employment standards, union certification procedures, health and safety, temporary worker policies, and income transfer and service programs. In each of these areas, the text evaluates the following:

- how laws and public policies are designed to work
- how well they are implemented and enforced
- how they fit into overall policy directions
- who benefits and who pays as a result of these policies
- the political dynamics generating these policies.

Part 2 begins with a survey of major political shifts across Canada's provinces. These are crucially important to understand as provincial labour laws and regulations cover some 90 percent of the national workforce (see Chapter 5). While noting provincial variations, the text examines how powerful business interests and the affluent have reshaped the terrain of public policy making in their favour.

Most notably, organized business interests have used their economic and political power to exert disproportionate pressure on core areas of public policy-making with the goal of creating a more deregulated and flexible labour market. In turn, provincial and federal governments have implemented policy and regulatory reforms to roll back labour rights. Or just as often officials have sought to avoid wider political controversy by simply blocking improvements or weakening the enforcement of employment rules. When these strategies have proved insufficient, many governments have introduced new policies (or updates to existing policies) that fall outside of standard labour laws and regulations, such as temporary foreign worker programs.

Subsequent chapters examine how this government opposition to collective labour regulation has harmed workers, altering labour laws in ways that tip the balance toward employer concerns with so-called economic efficiency and away from equity and worker voice. Chapter 6 examines such shifts in the **federally regulated private sector**: the roughly 10 percent of the labour force engaged in sectors such as banking, railways, aviation, telecommunications, pipelines, and roads that cross provincial and international boundaries. Whereas federal jurisdiction has historically often been seen as a more model employer – with labour legislation and employment standards that frequently surpass those in most provinces – the shift to neoliberal models of public management and labour market deregulation has also facilitated the growth of precarious employment in the federally regulated private sector.

Chapter 7 explores how crucial areas of labour law – like union certification and union organization in new workplaces and sectors – have either been recast or more often allowed to atrophy, creating additional hurdles for workers who want to unionize their workplaces. These moves have meant that labour law reform has failed to keep up with the changing face of work, making labour laws less effective and less relevant. Even though the workforce has grown by nearly 40 percent over the past twenty-five years, to more than 18 million, fewer and fewer workers are able to organize unions in their workplaces and to garner the potential benefits of collective agreements.

Other essential areas of labour legislation – such as workers' health and safety – have seen no significant improvement, with thousands of workers across Canada suffering critical injuries, even death, both on and off the job. (Chapter 8). New legislation has also encouraged non-standard employment and low-wage work, most notably through the legalization of temporary employment on a nationwide scale. For example, temporary foreign worker programs have given employers in an ever-growing number of sectors – from agriculture, child and elder care, and restaurants to construction and high-tech – the right to apply for and employ thousands of temporary migrant workers. This often includes employers having the effective power to deport them (see Chapter 9).

Nor have Canada's social programs kept pace with issues of low-wage work and income security (Chapter 10). In fact, rather than protect workers against turbulent labour markets, Canadian governments have focused more on debt reduction and to cutting or freezing social programs. In addition, governments have cut benefit rates, tightened rules of eligibility for programs, or quickly repealed universal programs once introduced, such as CERB. Such program overhauls – and reversals – have contributed to ever greater fear and insecurity among workers, especially for those in low-paid, insecure jobs, and particularly for women and others with greater care responsibilities for children and elders at home. Canada now ranks near the bottom among advanced industrial economies in social spending.

Taken together, these developments suggest that federal and provincial governments have reshaped how our labour markets work fashioning a much more market-driven order by privileging employer goals across a range of laws, policies, and regulations. In doing so,

public officials have significantly weakened collective employment relations to the detriment of large numbers of working Canadians, their families, and communities. It is this systematic deregulation of the labour market that has put many workers across the country at higher risk of unemployment, stress, infection, and in some cases death.

POLICY BARRIERS ACROSS THE LABOUR MARKET

Part 3 examines how neoliberalism and de-regulation have reshaped specific parts of the public- and private-sector labour markets, both before and during the pandemic. The chapters look at industries from private services and manufacturing to public health care and long-term care for the elderly, and illustrate how government policies that promote **labour market flexibility** often contribute to a wider deterioration in the quality of work. As these chapters demonstrate, the costs fall disproportionately on more vulnerable workers: women, young people, and people of colour.

Across the Canadian labour market, changes to economic and labour policies that are supposed to boost economic growth, enable firms to be more efficient, and make their workforces more flexible are instead creating bad jobs: those providing insecure and unstable employment, low wages, few or no benefits such as paid sick leave and pensions, too few work hours with no worker agency over schedules, and/or limited long-term prospects for improvement.[19]

Numerous workers in bad jobs – who typically have no union protection – deal with a host of other problems as well. For example, those doing on-call work lack job security and basic labour protections.[20] Uber drivers and Foodora couriers generally have no right to a minimum wage or vacation pay because they are falsely deemed to be self-employed. Others who work through temporary employment agencies in manufacturing or security services similarly have no right to basic employment standards such as sick leave or family leave. All workers in such jobs are in precarious positions, and this has left an ever-larger proportion of the workforce unable to achieve an adequate standard of living or to improve their work conditions.

As Part 3 emphasizes, bad jobs don't exist because of natural market processes, nor does low pay reflect lack of skill, talent, or productivity.[21] Rather, this dysfunction is rooted in government support for employer interests (in the form of a cheaper and more flexible workforce) at the expense of government protections for workers.[22] For with the declining strength of unions and their political allies, even workers who previously enjoyed good jobs frequently now feel that they have to put up with worsening work conditions as a new reality.[23] To a large degree, it is this failure of governments in Canada to uphold or improve basic rules protecting jobs and wages that accounts for the rising number of bad jobs – and for the widening income and wealth gap across the labour market.

In the private service sector, which generates almost two out of every three jobs in Canada, firms have cut costs by making positions part time and temporary, and adopting flexible work arrangements that shift the risk of too few hours and little job security onto workers (Chapter 11). This has exposed workers in the sector – especially in cleaning, care, retail stores, and restaurants – to non-standard, precarious work.

In private-sector manufacturing, the consequences of deregulation can be found in a marked shift in government behaviour. Not merely removing themselves from regulating how the market operates as Free Trade agreements are ostensibly supposed to do, Canadian

governments have actively intervened. They have devised new rules that more exclusively serve business interests, either by legislating new and trade investment policies or by waiving competition policies for multinationals to expand their operations. Similarly, governments have allowed firms to hire more and more workers on a notionally self-employed or temporary basis (see Chapter 12). Such public policies have benefited American and other foreign automakers significantly. But they have also put Canadian autoworkers in direct competition with global supply chains located in Mexico and China, where wages and labour standards are far lower. And rather than support displaced workers with effective job-creation programs or investments in retraining for a clean energy economy (as Denmark has done), Canadian officials have largely looked the other way as workers are forced into unemployment or lower-paying jobs.

In the **public** sector, similar policy changes have undermined good jobs and labour protections. For example, **care work** in hospitals, long-term care facilities, and social service agencies used to provide many better jobs with secure employment. Recent government austerity drives have cut budgets and shifted public services in the sector to private firms and for-profit providers, pushing numerous frontline care workers into worse jobs with lower wages (Chapter 13). In hospitals and health care services, too, **new public management** models emphasize flexible work scheduling, variable work hours, and compressed work weeks. These translate into higher caseloads, more patients, and an ever-increasing number of job responsibilities – typically with less time to do the added work and with far less support from employers (Chapter 14).

Employer discrimination and other policy obstacles continue to harm **First Nations** workers and their families (Chapter 15). As members

POLICIES FOR HEALTH AND SAFETY

- comprehensive nationwide vaccination, infection testing, and contact tracing
- personal protective equipment in all workplaces
- paid leave for all sick and quarantined workers
- support for workers with additional family care needs through income transfers and services
- mandatory health and safety training for all workers and supervisors
- more preventative inspections and health and safety enforcement campaigns in workplaces
- protections from employer reprisals for workers who refuse unsafe work or make complaints about workplace conditions
- increased public funding for injured workers and their rehabilitation
- increased penalties for firms that repeatedly violate health and safety regulations

POLICIES FOR SOCIAL PROTECTION

- universal, high calibre public childcare
- significant expansion of appropriate social housing
- fully publicly funded postsecondary education, adult education, and retraining programs
- vigorous public job creation and retention schemes
- accessible and supportive employment insurance for all workers
- a permanent universal basic income

POLICIES FOR THE LABOUR MARKET

Workplace Regulation
- stronger laws to allow workers to form unions and negotiate collective agreements
- limits on employers' right to interfere with attempts to unionize
- **compulsory arbitration** to help workers and employers achieve collective agreements
- new regulations to allow unions to form collective agreements across entire sectors covering wages, working conditions, and benefits
- amendments to labour laws that exclude temporary foreign workers or exempt employers from paying minimum wages or abiding by employment standards

Minimum Wages
- minimum wages tied to a **living wage** that ensures a decent, dignified standard of living
- independent commissions that regularly adjust minimum wages

Employment Standards
- legislation to provide medical and dental benefits to all, including part-time and temporary workers
- legislated paid sick leave, paid maternity leave, and paid emergency and family leave for all workers
- government publicity campaigns to ensure broad awareness of basic employment rights and obligations
- effective government enforcement of labour standards, and competent inspections of all workplaces and individual complaints
- adequate, timely penalties to deter employers from breaking labour laws and regulations

POLICIES FOR ENVIRONMENTAL SUSTAINABILITY

- realistic carbon budgets and an adequate carbon tax on fossil fuels to meet **greenhouse gas (GHG) emissions** targets
- GHG emissions reduction of 75 percent by 2030 and net-zero emissions by 2050
- deployment of clean and renewable energy systems nationwide
- a public environmental agency to reorganize economic sectors for sustainability
- measures to ensure worker rights and unionized jobs in the transition to a renewable energy economy
- public retraining for all workers, especially those displaced from fossil fuel sectors, so they can produce, build, install, and maintain renewable energy infrastructure and retrofit buildings for improved energy efficiency
- new investments in natural infrastructure to restore forests and wildlands, reclaim mines and oil sites, and improve biodiversity
- ambitious, rapid expansion of affordable/ free public transportation

of sovereign nations with land claims that are central to the exercise of that sovereignty, Indigenous people often find their work lives fundamentally shaped by Canadian government policy, or absence of policy. This can result in insufficient resources for job training and education, and a lack of effective anti-discrimination and anti-harassment measures. Moreover, a current emphasis on casinos as a means of economic development in some Indigenous communities has created many low-wage, non-union, precarious jobs.

In almost every case of deregulation – and policy failure – studied in this book, workers have been left relatively poorer and less economically secure. The numbers of those who struggle have expanded beyond blue-collar production workers and communities built around factories. They also include families feeling the effects of underfunded social safety nets, and millions who rely on an inadequate minimum wage and little more to make ends meet. These groups are casualties of labour market deregulation policies intended to free labour markets of institutional rigidities.

BUILDING A BETTER FUTURE

Part 4 concludes by examining the opportunities and hurdles that workers, their families, and communities now face in their efforts to attain better employment, a more sustainable environment, a clean energy economy, and a more democratic political system. Since the start of the pandemic, environmental organizations, trade unions, international policy agencies, and others have called for initiatives that **build back better**.[24] Faced with health, environmental, and economic crises, people the world over have begun to realize that a return to business as usual will not be enough to restore sufficient good jobs, nor will the status quo be anything but environmentally destructive.

Indeed, COVID-19 has shown that there is no healthy economy without a healthy society and sustainable environment, and that true prosperity is not simply about individual wealth. Rather, it is about how we as citizens live, work, learn, and play in ways that are sustainable and meet everyone's basic needs and human rights.[25]

If a recovery plan is to help all Canadians, its design must ensure collective prosperity and environmental sustainability. The pandemic has demonstrated that when a crisis is urgent enough, governments can take dramatic action to help people – and do so much more quickly than anyone could have anticipated. But while some governments have seized the opportunity to make big investments in health and environmental sustainability, others have not. Canada falls into the second group.

As a start, a recovery plan should provide workers with comprehensive testing and tracing systems, protective equipment, and paid sick days and quarantine facilities, governments must also build stronger public services. These include effective labour and public health inspectorates, integrated health information networks on virus infection rates, and policies that protect families and communities. Just as important for a more caring society is the expansion of public long-term care, public home care, and publicly funded assisted living for seniors. These policies are the first way that Canada and other societies can build back better.[26]

An equally essential part of building a better future entails ambitious plans to enact inclusive labour laws and employment policies to link democratic citizenship from our workplaces to our local, provincial, and federal governments.[27] This deepening of democracy involves policies that can turn bad jobs into good ones by legislating and enforcing better labour laws, including significant participation and decision-making by workers in relation to workplace issues that affect them, by enacting higher minimum wages adjusted to a living wage, or by improving health and safety regulation. Implementing reforms such as these will not only ensure a shared and collective prosperity. It will also provide workers with the individual and collective voices to gain greater security and opportunity in their work and family lives.[28]

Finally, new policies are essential to extending more democratic control over our shared future. The climate emergency is clear: a **Green New Deal** is needed, one that commits government to developing clean energy infrastructure while phasing out coal, oil, and gas, and to planning alternative jobs and livelihoods for a **just transition**.[29] As the problems of global warming multiply, it is vital to launch a policy agenda now that tackles the political and economic interests tied to fossil fuels and at the same time develops a **zero-carbon economy**. Just as essential are new initiatives that protect the natural world and ensure greater biodiversity to, among many other benefits, help reduce the likelihood of to prevent the outbreak of future infectious diseases.

Yet as this text points out, the main difficulty isn't any shortage of progressive policy options or evidence that more worker-friendly, environmentally responsible, and democratic policies would benefit societies such as Canada. Nor have many Canadians, especially young people, environmentalists, and unionists, been politically inactive in their support for such policies. The fundamental problem lies in the power of corporations, the influence of employer organizations, and the ubiquity of corporate media. These forces are able to limit democratic voices and shape public expectations as to which public labour policy reforms can be regarded as politically realistic.

Developing solutions will certainly be a challenge for workers and citizens, but as the past century has demonstrated, significant hurdles are not insurmountable. During the Great

Depression and in the wake of the Second World War, citizens mobilized and agitated for democratic reforms, and unions launched massive strikes. This marshalling of countervailing power allowed people to win huge reforms that regulated business and oversaw an expanding economy that distributed income widely in the postwar period.[30]

Today brings signs of a reinvigorated politics as more citizens and more workers are increasingly concerned to tackle the COVID-19 pandemic as well as the climate crisis. Increasingly, workers are building new alliances and seeking collective agreements and public policies that alter the rules of markets dominated by fossil fuel interests (see Chapter 16). It's not uncommon for media reports to suggest that many workers are opposed to fighting **climate change** because of its costs and potential job loss, or that Canada's oil and gas sector is too economically important to allow even discussion about phasing out fossil fuel infrastructure. But the truth is that many labour unions in Canada and elsewhere are increasingly giving urgent priority to raising climate issues among the general public and in the workplace.

There are also signs of more innovative **union organizing**, as well as renewed efforts to bring unionized and non-unionized workers together (Chapter 17). Consider, for example, recent campaigns to organize GoodLife fitness instructors, bike couriers and delivery drivers, and fast-food workers who are challenging their employers with strikes and protests to demand better wages and working conditions. Just as notable, through new worker-centred organizing to raise the minimum wage for all workers – such as the Fight for $15 and Fairness movement (now named "Justice for Workers: Decent Work for All" in Ontario) and the Agriculture Workers Alliance – coalitions of unions and non-union workers have built networks to extend solidarity.

These are encouraging trends that suggest a more vital and powerful labour politics is possible, with unions and citizens once again working on issues beyond wages and working conditions, and building more effective citizen power through direct action.[31] Such progressive politics has been central to the widening and deepening of democracy in the past, and its current re-emergence within Canada, the United States, and other countries again suggests that citizens can find a wider common good despite the fragmentation of their work and community lives. The pandemic too provides new opportunities for unions and citizens alike to unite to improve public policy for the better.

Yet, as the final chapter reminds us, there are no easy solutions. Activists and unions face daily challenges in gaining and retaining the resources they need to keep a foothold in politics long enough to make politicians listen. So too free markets and further investment are not only undermining economic sustainability, they are also fundamentally skewing the debates over how to address our problems with inequality and the climate crisis. To take on these challenges, citizens will require a re-energized and motivated democratic politics. That will take new union organizing and ambitious political mobilizing. It will necessitate unions, progressives, and environmentalists building broad coalitions. It also must involve mass protests and progressive organizations across Canada taking elections seriously. But it will be how we respond – and act collectively in taking on these challenges – that will help determine the kind of Canada – and world – we can collectively build for each other.

For people the world over, this is an epoch-defining moment. The COVID-19 pandemic has made us reflect on what is most important and what we most value in our societies. Many are finding renewed optimism and new inspiration in the idea that a better future does seem possible now. But if governments are to embrace more egalitarian, inclusive, democratic, and sustainable public policies, this will only be the result of citizens developing plans, working hard, and using their political imaginations to build public power. Only with these bold steps forward can a more just, prosperous, and democratic Canada become a reality.

NOTES

1   OECD, *Building Back Better: A Sustainable Resilient Recovery after COVID-19*, OECD Policy Responses to Coronavirus (COVID-19), June 5, 2020, https://www.oecd-ilibrary.org; IMF, *World Economic Outlook Update, June 2020* (New York: International Monetary Fund, 2020).

2   See OECD, *OECD Employment Outlook 2020: Worker Security and the COVID-19 Crisis* (Paris: OECD Publishing, 2020), https://doi.org/10.1787/1686c758-en. Liquidity refers to the availability of private credit. In other words, in a liquid credit market, it's easier for banks, the financial sector, and corporations to borrow money.

3   OECD, *OECD Economic Outlook*, issue 1 (June 10, 2020), https://doi.org/10.1787/0d1d1e2e-en.

4   IEA, *Sustainable Recovery: World Energy Outlook Special Report*, June (Paris: International Energy Agency, 2020), https://www.iea.org/reports/sustainable-recovery; Secretariat of the Convention on Biological Diversity, *Global Biodiversity Outlook 5* (Montreal: Secretariat of the Convention on Biological Diversity 2020), https://www.cbd.int/gbo/gbo5/publication/gbo-5-en.pdf.

5   IMF, *World Economic Outlook Update,* June 2020.

6   International Labour Organization, *A Policy Framework for Tackling the Economic and Social Impact of the COVID-19 Crisis*, Policy brief, May 2020, https://labordoc.ilo.org/discovery/delivery/41ILO_INST:41ILO_V2/1270849990002676; Esmé Berkhout, Nick Galasso, Max Lawson, Pablo Andrés Rivero Morales, Anjela Taneja, and Diego Alejo Vázquez Pimentel, *The Inequality Virus: Bringing Together a World Torn Apart by Coronavirus through a Fair, Just, and Sustainable Economy* (Oxford: Oxfam International, 2021); Rhiana Gunn-Wright, Kristina Karlsson, Kitty Richards, Bracken Hendricks, and David Arkush, *A Green Recovery: The Case for Climate-Forward Stimulus Policies in America's COVID-19 Recession Response* (New York: Roosevelt Institute, 2020).

7   Kathleen Thelen, *Varieties of Liberalization and the New Politics of Social Solidarity* (New York: Cambridge University Press, 2014).

8   Peter Goodman, "The Nordic Way to Economic Rescue," *New York Times*, March 28, 2020.

9   Barry Eidlin, *Labor and the Class Idea in the United States and Canada* (New York: Cambridge University Press, 2018); Bryan D. Palmer, *Working-Class Experience: Rethinking the History of Canadian Labour, 1800–1991* (Toronto: McClelland and Stewart, 1992).

10   Jérôme Gautié and John Schmitt, eds., *Low-Wage Work in the Wealthy World* (New York: Russell Sage Foundation, 2010).

11   David Harvey, *A Brief History of Neoliberalism* (New York: Oxford University Press, 2006); Thomas Piketty, *Capital in the Twenty-First Century* (Cambridge, MA: Harvard University Press, 2014); Joseph E. Stiglitz, *The Price of Inequality: How Today's Divided Society Endangers Our Future* (New York: W.W. Norton and Company, 2013).

12   Lars Osberg, *The Age of Increasing Inequality: The Astonishing Rise of Canada's 1%* (Toronto: James Lorimer and Company, 2018).

13   David Weil, *The Fissured Workplace: Why Work Became So Bad for So Many and What Can Be Done to Improve It* (Cambridge, MA: Harvard University Press, 2014).

14 Robert Reich, "America's Corporate Elite Must Place the Health of Their Workers before Profit," *The Guardian*, May 17, 2020.

15 Colin Crouch, "The Neo-Liberal Turn and the Implications for Labour," in *The Oxford Handbook of Employment Relations: Comparative Employment Relations*, ed. Adrian Wilkinson, Geoffrey Wood, and Richard Deeg (New York: Oxford University Press, 2014).

16 Lucio Baccaro and Chris Howell, *European Industrial Relations: Trajectories of Neoliberal Transformation* (New York: Cambridge University Press, 2017); Jake Rosenfeld, *What Unions No Longer Do* (Cambridge, MA: Harvard University Press, 2014).

17 OECD, *In It Together: Why Less Inequality Benefits All* (Paris: OECD Publishing, 2015), https://dx.doi.org/10.1787/9789264235120-en.

18 Statistics Canada, *Food Insecurity during the COVID-19 Pandemic, May 2020*, June 24, 2020, Cat. no. 45280001 (Ottawa: Statistics Canada, 2020), https://www150.statcan.gc.ca/n1/en/catalogue/45280001202000100039.

19 International Labour Organization, *World Employment and Social Outlook: Trends 2019* (Geneva: International Labour Office, 2019), https://www.ilo.org/wcmsp5/groups/public/−dgreports/−dcomm/−publ/documents/publication/wcms_670542.pdf; David Howell and Arne L. Kalleberg, "Declining Job Quality in the United States: Explanations and Evidence," *RSF: The Russell Sage Foundation Journal of the Social Sciences* 5, no. 4 (2019): 1–53.

20 Chris Warhurst, Françoise Carré, Patricia Findlay, and Chris Tilly, *Are Bad Jobs Inevitable? Trends, Determinants and Responses to Job Quality in the Twenty-First Century* (New York: Macmillan International Higher Education, 2012).

21 Arne Kalleberg, *Precarious Lives: Job Insecurity and Well-Being in Rich Democracies* (Cambridge: Polity Press, 2018); Françoise Carré and Chris Tilly, *Where Bad Jobs Are Better: Retail Jobs across Countries and Companies* (New York: Russell Sage Foundation, 2017).

22 Annette Bernhardt, Heather Boushey, Laura Dresser, and Chris Tilly, eds., *The Gloves-off Economy: Problems and Possibilities at the Bottom of America's Labor Market* (Ithaca, NY: Cornell University Press, 2008); Joseph E. Stiglitz, *Rewriting the Rules of the American Economy: An Agenda for Growth and Shared Prosperity* (New York: W.W. Norton and Company, 2015).

23 Jim Silver, *About Canada: Poverty* (Halifax: Fernwood Publishing, 2014).

24 BlueGreen Alliance, *Manufacturing Agenda: A National Blueprint for Clean Technology Manufacturing Leadership and Industrial Transformation* (Washington: BlueGreen Alliance, 2020), https://www.bluegreenalliance.org/wp-content/uploads/2020/06/2020_BGA_Manufacturing_Agenda-vFINAL.pdf; Canadian Centre for Policy Alternatives, *Alternative Federal Budget Recovery Plan* (Ottawa: Canadian Centre for Policy Alternatives, 2020); OECD, *Building Back Better*.

25 International Labour Organization, *World Employment and Social Outlook 2018: Greening with Jobs:* (Geneva: International Labour Office, 2018), https://www.ilo.org/wcmsp5/groups/public/−dgreports/−dcomm/−publ/documents/publication/wcms_628654.pdf; Jeremy Brecher, *Climate Solidarity: Workers vs. Warming* (West Cornwall, CT: Labor Network for Sustainability and Stone Soup Books, 2017).

26 Canadian Centre for Policy Alternatives, The Canadian Women's Foundation, and Ontario Nonprofit Network, *Recovery through Equality: Developing an Inclusive Action Plan for Women in the Economy* (Ottawa: Canadian Centre for Policy Alternatives, 2020); Canadian Centre for Policy Alternatives, *Alternative Federal Budget Recovery Plan* (Ottawa: Canadian Centre for Policy Alternatives, 2020).

27 Jim Stanford and Daniel Poon, *Speaking Up, Being Heard, Making Change: The Theory and Practice of Worker Voice in Canada Today* (Vancouver: Centre for Future Work, 2021).

28 Rafael Gomez and Juan Gomez, *Workplace Democracy for the 21st Century* (Ottawa: Broadbent Institute, 2016); Kalleberg, *Precarious Lives*; Guy Standing, *A Precariat Charter: From Denizens to Citizens* (New York: Bloomsbury Academy, 2014).

29 International Labour Organization, *World Employment and Social Outlook 2018.*

30 Jacob Hacker and Paul Pierson, *American Amnesia: How the War on Government Led Us to Forget What Made America Prosper* (New York: Simon and Schuster, 2016); Donald Sassoon, *One Hundred Years of Socialism* (London: I.B. Tauris and Company, 1996).

31 Stephanie Luce, *Labor Movements: Global Perspectives* (Cambridge: Polity Press, 2014).

Part 1

WHAT HAS GONE WRONG?

1 Finding Better Ways Out of the COVID-19 Pandemic

John Peters

> "It can feel as if a whole way of being is passing from us. But that presents an opportunity too – as individuals, as a society – to cast off what isn't working. We can take a hard look at dated systems – that have for too long fostered social inequality and environmental damage – and make an honest commitment to fixing them. We can look at others, and at ourselves, and choose to be kinder. We can find better ways."
>
> – Esi Edugyan, author of *Washington Black* and Giller Prize winner

CHAPTER SUMMARY

The coronavirus pandemic has not only been the worst health crisis in the past 100 years. It has also triggered one of the most severe economic downturns since the Great Depression of the 1930s. This chapter reviews how governments in Canada have responded to these twin crises and assesses their actions in terms of whether they have supported workers, kept people safe, and provided a just and sustainable recovery plan.

In a comparative analysis, this chapter argues that Canada's approach has been inadequate, oriented more to preserving the wealth of an elite few - and the health and well-being of well-paid and well-protected knowledge workers - than to making jobs in essential sectors safer or better paid. It concludes that Canadians deserve much more, starting with a far more comprehensive and equitable approach focused on care and people, as well as a recovery plan that facilitates the just transition to a **low-carbon economy**.

KEY THEMES

This chapter will help you develop an understanding of:

- the destructive toll of the COVID-19 pandemic
- how Canada's policy response compares to that of other countries, such as the United States, Denmark, and Finland
- the political economy that contextualizes the shortcomings of Canadian economic, labour, and social policies
- the crucial components of a recovery plan that will enable Canada to make the transition to a just and sustainable future.

THE IMAGES ARE STARTLING and disturbing. Hospital hallways full of people lying on stretchers and hooked to oxygen masks, others in beds and attached to ventilators. Nurses swathed in layers of protective gear, taking virus swabs from people as they wait in long lines of cars. Rising homelessness is evident on city streets around the country. Stress is etched on the faces of laid-off workers in the restaurant, hotel, travel, and tourism industries as they worry about how they'll cope with rent, kids, and lockdowns now that they are unemployed.

Along with the images are equally alarming discussions about the impacts of the COVID-19 pandemic. Commentators have referred to the crisis as a monster, comparing it to an "asteroid hitting our social systems" and bringing a "tsunami" of problems.[1] For in addition to the human toll levied by the disease, the pandemic has ushered in the biggest global crisis of our time and brutally exposed the inability – or unwillingness – of countries to meet the needs of people and the planet.

This chapter first examines the range of problems caused by the pandemic itself and then assesses shortcomings in Canada's efforts to tackle important issues like pandemic planning and climate change. These problems are tightly linked facets of a skewed political and economic system that is oriented toward large corporations and extreme wealth at the expense of smaller-scale enterprise and workers, and one that puts our society at ever greater risk in its pursuit of unsustainable growth and profit.

Despite this gloomy assessment, the chapter concludes on a positive note by observing that there are now several opportunities to find better ways – that is, to develop solutions that provide more equitable and sustainable outcomes for a majority of Canadians. But to develop these solutions and recover from the pandemic will require rectifying how politics and policy making currently work in Canada.

Protecting people's health and well-being in the workplace and the wider community (such as by allowing more workers to have a say through independent unions and meaningful participation in statutory health and safety committees) must go hand in hand with renewed efforts to counter injustice and inequality in society. Similarly, tackling climate change, decarbonizing the economy, and escalating the use of clean energy will be essential in getting Canada and the world out of its current economic slump. Only by adopting a multi-pronged approach to recovery will it be possible for Canadian governments to manage the pandemic and create a sustainable economy that will work for all.

THE TOLL OF COVID-19

Since the first cases of COVID-19 appeared in December 2019, the virus has cut a destructive path across countries, and all indicators suggest it will not stop any time soon. In fact, the sooner we recognize that this is now an endemic disease – a virus that is constantly present – the more quickly we can create long-term plans that allow a safe reopening of shuttered businesses. Since the 1990s, similar viral zoonotic diseases – Ebola, SARS, MERS, and Rift Valley fever – have killed millions annually, as a steady stream of new pathogens have leapt from animals to humans with the globalization of large-scale factory farming of animals and the unrelenting deforestation of tropical environments.[2] COVID-19 may be the most contagious of these recent viruses, but common to all new zoonotic viruses is their rapid spread and mutation.[3]

The speed with which they emerge is aggravated by global travel. Over the course of 2020, there were more than 85 million confirmed COVID-19 cases and more than 1.8 million deaths. By mid-2021, more than 4 million cases were being identified weekly and the death toll had risen to 4.1 million. By 2022, estimates of the direct and indirect impacts of the COVID-19 virus on the world's population had reached nearly 15 million global deaths (WHO 2022). Indeed, with more contagious variants spreading around the world, the second year of the pandemic was far more deadly than the first, and the third deadlier still. The rapid rise of such a highly transmissible and deadly virus revealed the devastating cost of failing to adequately prepare for or respond to an epidemic.[4]

In 2021, the development of several effective vaccines was certainly a cause for hope in wealthy countries, as health officials thought that inoculation and wider immunity might break the typical pattern of flu and zoonotic epidemics. These discoveries were the result of decades of previous research as well as billions of dollars that governments provided to support clinical trials and the retrofitting of factories through 2020. By early 2021, five vaccines had been authorized for use in large-scale inoculation campaigns in leading industrial countries, and by 2022 approximately 66 percent of the world's population had received at least one dose of a COVID-19 vaccine (Our World in Data, Coronavirus [COVID-19] Vaccinations).

However, such optimism came with reservations, as scientists warned that the virus and its multiplying variants were likely to cause significant illness for years to come.[5] New COVID-19 variants – such as Delta, Omicron, and their subvariants – evolved more quickly than countries were able to inoculate their populations, and vaccine effectiveness appeared to wane over time. In addition, because of an intellectual property rights regime that places the right of pharmaceutical companies to profit by restricting access to lifesaving treatments ahead of the human right not to die from a new disease, vaccines have been in short supply for the more than 3 billion people in the developing world, and in some cases, wholly unavailable.

Thus, even as countries lifted restrictions and reopened their economies in mid-2021, a fourth wave of infection and hospitalizations quickly took hold, and then a smaller fifth wave in early 2022, forcing governments to either reverse course or to begin to live with the consequences of the virus. And with variants continuing to win the race against vaccination, and new infections of the unvaccinated or only partially vaccinated rising, it appears that the virus will become endemic.[6] This would mirror the pattern of previous pandemics, such as the 1918–20 influenza epidemic, which wrought serious health consequences for several years – with knock-on effects for global development and economic recovery.[7]

Such knock-on effects can be seen clearly in the major – and often tragic – economic impacts of the pandemic.[8] Throughout 2020 and 2021, even as stock markets soared and billionaire wealth rose rapidly, real economic output plummeted and unemployment swelled across countries. Early in the first wave and then with more resolve in the winter wave of 2021, governments reacted with a range of emergency measures to protect people's health, support the economy, and provide benefits to the many newly jobless. Most notably, around the world, public officials enacted lockdowns and stay-at-home measures that were repeated over the course of 2020 and 2021 to stave off overwhelming rates of infections and fatalities.

Initially, in both North America and Western Europe, it was believed that after a couple of months of such restrictions and accompanying rescue packages, economies would simply start up where they had left off, ushering in what was termed a V-shaped recovery. Indeed, in mid-2020, government officials in Canada, the United States, and Western Europe were so optimistic that they lifted several national travel restrictions and hundreds of thousands of vacationers took to travelling with few, if any, tests or quarantine.[9]

But by late 2020, with a devastating second wave of infection, cities and states reimposed tough restrictions. Then winter forced people indoors in the northern hemisphere, and the virus took hold in countries with high levels of poverty. By late 2021, a third wave of transmission deepened the global health crisis and led to tightened economic lockdowns, with new Delta variants proving more virulent and contagious in many parts of the world, and quickly accounting for the majority of new cases and deaths. By early 2022, a fourth wave, driven by the Omicron variant, was causing governments to keep in place – or reimpose – restrictions and lockdowns.

Worldwide, such lockdowns and health, travel, and social restrictions shuttered entire industries – airlines, tourism, hotels, and restaurants – and closed basic public services such as schools, universities, and daycares. The result was an unemployment crisis so severe that 94 percent of the world's workers were living in countries with workplace closures by the end of 2020 – closures that were equivalent to 255 million full-time employees being laid off.[10] With its many job retention and social support programs, Western Europe experienced far fewer mass layoffs and much less unemployment, but by June 2020 the official unemployment rate in Canada and the United States had risen to more than 13 and 14 percent, respectively – the highest levels in decades and the highest among advanced industrial economies – before declining to 9.4 percent in Canada in December 2020 and 8 percent by mid-2021.[11]

However, the unemployment rate is only a rough measure of the devastating economic impact of the pandemic. In both Canada and the United States, millions simply stopped looking for work and thus were not counted in official statistics. In Canada, a better estimate of how many were out of work or working only occasionally is found in the number of people who were receiving newly rolled-out emergency response benefits.[12] By early July 2020, more than 8 million Canadians were reliant on various support programs. Put another way, 42 percent of the labour force was either laid off, on temporary layoff, or scraping together a couple of hundred dollars a week while drawing emergency benefits. Six months later, more than 6.5 million still relied on government income programs, and only two-thirds of the jobs lost in March and April had returned. Those in low-wage jobs – especially women and younger workers – were the least likely to be back at work. Only numbers from the Great Depression of the 1930s are in any way comparable to the scale and scope of the economic shock caused by the pandemic (see Chapter 3).[13]

Given such problems, it was clear that the recovery from the pandemic would continue to be difficult and drawn out, with feeble economic and employment growth moving in tandem with waves of infection and hospitalization.[14]

A DISEASE OF INEQUALITY

Also becoming clear by the end of 2021 was that COVID-19 was a disease of inequality.[15] While initially spread by business people and tourists travelling between major international cities such as New York, London, and Toronto, the virus quickly exploited those most vulnerable: the elderly, personal support workers in long-term care homes, essential retail workers in precarious low-wage jobs, temporary foreign agriculture workers and their families. In Canada, as elsewhere, those who were older and had weakened immune systems were the most likely to die, not always from the virus itself but also from lack of care in long-term care homes and reduced access to hospitals (see Chapters 13 and 14). It is perhaps no surprise, then, that of the 26,000 deaths initially attributed to COVID-19 in the country in 2020, more than 90 percent were among those aged sixty and above, and a majority of the victims were residing in woefully underfunded, understaffed, and often privately run long-term care facilities.[16]

Such deaths were largely due to the lack of a national standard for elder care, which left residents of the two largest provinces exposed to the vagaries of mostly privately run long-term care homes. Without staff to help them eat and drink, some seniors were left to die from malnutrition and dehydration.[17] While COVID-19 may be listed on their death certificates, it is more accurate to characterize these deaths as the product of neglect and indifference.

The next hardest hit group was the most economically vulnerable.[18] The virus spread quickly in the poorest and highest-density neighbourhoods in Canada, often where immigrants and visible minorities live in cramped apartments or multigenerational homes. In these communities, racialized workers did not have the ability to work remotely or savings that would permit them to refuse unsafe work.[19] So, while the laptop class and professional workers generally stayed home and ordered their goods and services online, employees in low-wage jobs returned to their workplaces in order to keep the online and care-giving economy running, doing frontline jobs in health and long-term care, as well as in industries deemed essential such as food processing, food retail, distribution, and goods transport. These workers not only faced elevated levels of risk, but they often had no basic protective equipment. Already disadvantaged workers thus suffered the most from the pandemic.

Equally at risk were temporary migrant farm workers, who were deemed essential and exempted not only from stay-at-home orders and quarantine regulations but also from any form of union representation or basic labour and safety protections. By mid-2020, over 600 migrant farm workers in Canada had tested positive for the virus and the number of full-scale outbreaks was climbing.[20] Two migrant workers died and hundreds complained about appalling living conditions, overcrowded bunkhouses, lack of testing and protective equipment, and the refusal of federal and provincial officials to either inspect or enforce the limited employer guidelines for health, safety, and working conditions.[21] Thus, in the absence of worker organizations or collective bargaining rights, and with limited government oversight, many so-called essential migrant farmworkers were left to cope on their own or rely on the benevolence of their employers. Some of those took adequate precautions, but far too many did not.

So too other vulnerable workers in Canada were the first to be laid off, or paradoxically, the first who were made to work harder. This was the finding of a University of Toronto study that revealed a double liability of low-wage work during the economic shutdown: while on average workers in every income range experienced a large reduction in hours, the only workers to experience significant *increases* in hours were those in the lowest earning range.[22] In other words, low-wage workers were more likely to be laid off in sectors like travel and hospitality, but those who were deemed essential, such as Amazon warehouse workers, saw their hours increase along with their risk of exposure to the virus.

In these ways, the pandemic exposed the many failings of Canada's low unionization rate, weakly enforced employment laws, threadbare elder care system, and insufficient social programs. It laid bare the inequalities of the country's labour, social, health, and education systems – in a crisis that similarly hit low-wage workers and communities living in poverty around the world.[23]

ON DIFFERENT PLANETS

Official responses to the tsunami of problems caused by the pandemic have differed significantly. Many countries made unprecedented efforts to reduce workers' exposure to COVID-19. Some introduced measures to contain and mitigate the virus while also safeguarding the public and workers, and planning for a sustainable, equitable economic recovery. Others employed a focused strategy that targeted aggressive contact tracing, quick testing, and protection for the most vulnerable – seniors and those in care homes – while keeping schools open and allowing the rest of society to operate as normally as possible. Still others did none of the above.[24]

Canada, as always, was somewhere in the middle. It took steps to contain the virus, provide income supports for laid-off workers, and do the bare minimum to safeguard the public. But it was also among a few advanced industrial economies to offer little in the way of public supports for employed workers and made no moves toward a sustainable **green economy** recovery.

Put in a broad comparative perspective, the most notable distinction in policy approaches was between a zero-tolerance mobilization to stop the viral spread and measures to simply slow the process so that infections would not exceed what the health care system could handle.[25] Some countries implemented a whole range of policies addressing the virus, from containment measures and innovative health responses to a suite of emergency economic and labour market policies (Table 1.1). Others played down the threat posed by the virus and resisted implementing basic safety measures.

In Taiwan, Vietnam, and Hong Kong, for example, sweeping controls on travel were implemented along with efficient track-trace-and-isolate systems, widespread mask wearing, and quarantines of those infected. Much of this

occurred well before the World Health Organization (WHO) declared a global pandemic. New Zealand and Australia also immediately closed their borders and required hotel quarantine for all national arrivals, complemented by testing. These measures – along with strict economic lockdowns during periodic outbreaks – were crucial in keeping the virus at bay. Consequently, these countries were able to reopen far more quickly, with far less economic damage and with almost no loss of human life.

By contrast, the United States was the most egregious example of a rich country where public officials either scorned the science on the coronavirus or downplayed its virulence, treating the disease like a common flu and aiming merely to limit the speed of its spread. With few if any restrictions on travel and only a limited number of states initially enacting rules for face coverings and workplace closures, these catastrophic decisions put millions of people at risk. With only 4 percent of the global population, the United States quickly recorded over 22 percent of all COVID-19-related deaths and cases worldwide – approximately 1 million deaths and counting as of spring 2022 – the most of any country.

For many months, President Donald Trump (2017–21) refused to acknowledge the threat, maintaining that the virus would go away with the heat of the summer, or perhaps that scientists would discover a way to inject powerful light or disinfectants into the body to sterilize the infection.[26] But despite these far-fetched claims, infections and deaths exploded in the United States over the course of 2020 and 2021, with one punishing surge followed by another. Making matters worse, a number of state governors initially followed the president's advice and quickly proclaimed the virus over. As they reopened their states, some even moved to ban cities from enacting basic health measures like face masks, business closures, and social

TABLE 1.1 **Policy measures in response to COVID-19**

Elimination, containment, and mitigation policy	Health policy	Economic policy	Labour market policy
Restrictions on international travel Border closures	Testing	Income supports and benefits	Wage supports Job retention schemes
School closures Workplace closures	Contact tracing	Debt relief for individuals Debt relief for businesses	Paid sick leave
Cancellation of public events	Mandated facial coverings	Rent deferrals Eviction bans	Income support for quarantined workers
Restrictions on gathering size	Vaccine investment	Fiscal stimulus	Support for telework
Closures of public transport Restrictions on public transport	Public information	Direct loans and grants to businesses	New occupational health and safety regulations and monitoring
Stay-at-home measures	Emergency health investments	Accommodative monetary policies	Support for family care
Restrictions on individual movement	Vaccination campaigns	Investment in green energy and green economy	Ban on worker dismissals for economic reasons
–	–	International support for vaccination	Health guidelines for protective equipment

Sources: Data from International Monetary Fund, Policy Tracker, "Policy Responses to COVID-19," https://www.imf.org/en/Topics/imf-and-covid19/Policy-Responses-to-COVID-19; Thomas Hale, Noam Angrist, Rafael Goldszmidt et al., "A Global Panel Database of Pandemic Policies (Oxford COVID-19 Government Response Tracker)," *Nature Human Behaviour* (2021), https://doi.org/10.1038/s41562-021-01079-8.

distancing.[27] For the world's superpower, these patterns of official negligence and half-hearted measures were deadly. Only once President Joe Biden took office in January 2021 did the United States finally act aggressively and implement a national strategy to coordinate mass vaccine production and distribution – though with the lower vaccination rates and widespread mistrust of medical professionals fuelled by right-wing media, the United States continue to experience record numbers of hospitalizations and deaths.

Certainly, Canada was not among the negligent and science-denying countries – a list that includes the United States, Brazil, and, initially, the United Kingdom. But with the world's thirty-ninth-largest population, Canada ranked thirty-second in cumulative cases and twenty-sixth in total deaths in early 2022.[28] So, even with the relatively rapid roll-out of vaccination programs, it was not among the countries now regarded as coronavirus success stories.

Indeed, Canada appears to be on a different planet from some other countries in terms of its pandemic response (Figure 1.1). In the first two years of the pandemic, Finland and Norway, for example, which implemented a range of elimination, health, and labour measures to keep the virus under control, had experienced only a couple of thousand deaths; New Zealand, with

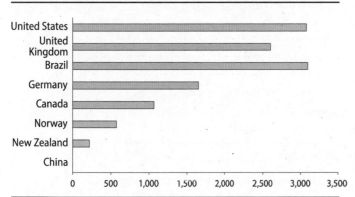

FIGURE 1.1 Coronavirus death rates per 1 million population

Source: Worldometer COVID-19 Data, "Reported Cases and Deaths by Country or Territory," May 22, 2022, https://www.worldometers.info/coronavirus/#countries.

its elimination strategy, only fifty-six. Even when population size is taken into account, and after many Nordic countries had relaxed their restrictions in early 2022, Norwegians were two times less likely to die from COVID-19 than Canadians, New Zealanders five times less likely.[29] Meanwhile, China – with the world's largest population and where the virus originally broke out – experienced among the fewest deaths in the world. What explains such remarkable differences?

Part of the answer, at least with regard to China, may reside in the accuracy of data and reporting. But another explanation for Canada's poor record was its limited and half-hearted efforts to contain and mitigate the spread of the virus at the outset. Unlike comparable countries (Finland and New Zealand have similarly sized, export-oriented economies), where travel was immediately restricted as well as subject to testing and quarantine, travellers continued to flood into Canada through mid-March 2020 with no screening or quarantine requirements – despite what was supposed to be an official ban on non-essential travel. Even with border restrictions, few if any rules or quarantine procedures were applied to the more than 5 million

so-called essential travellers who arrived over the rest of 2020.[30]

Indeed, it was not until February 2021, eleven months after the first outbreak, that Canadian officials finally put in place mandatory testing and quarantine measures for travellers entering the country – though still with little to no enforcement.[31] Only in the Atlantic provinces did premiers enact restrictions on all travellers. But as these provinces accounted for only 6 percent of the total population, their success at keeping infections minimal in the region had little wider impact. The lack of a coordinated national effort meant that Canadians were routinely heavily exposed to potentially infected travellers and workers, as were the residents of all countries that failed to implement functional border controls and testing procedures.[32]

Many places with previous experience of zoonotic viruses, like Taiwan, Hong Kong, South Korea, and Vietnam, were much better prepared to adopt emergency health measures. Their governments had already fought avian flu, MERS, and SARS, and with the discovery of COVID-19, officials immediately began extensive testing and tracing, quarantining the ill (often in separate, publicly provided accommodations), and made masks ubiquitous.[33] Such policies were crucial to these countries' successful early efforts to contain and eliminate the virus.

In Finland and Denmark – both of which have long had the highest tax rates and most comprehensive and well-funded social programs of the advanced industrial countries – testing and contact tracing were well developed within the health system before the pandemic, and officials were able to swing into action straight away. By the end of 2020, for example, Denmark had conducted five times more testing per capita than had been done in Canada, and in this way provided managers, workers, and parents alike with the knowledge that they and their children were safe at work, school, or daycare.

Finland developed a contact tracing app that was downloaded by more than 90 percent of its population. So, even though Denmark and Finland were among the first countries to largely reopen their economies in early 2020, comprehensive testing and tracing kept infections under control throughout much of the year.[34]

By contrast, the Canadian provinces never ramped up their testing and tracing. Instead, politicians had on-again/off-again relationships with health care experts, and in light of minimal coordination from the federal government, largely charted their own course through lockdowns, re-openings, and public health measures. Further, provincial governments competed with one another for necessary medical supplies and protective equipment and developed their own highly divergent mix of policy measures for "essential" industries, indoor restrictions, masks, and travel orders.[35] The federal government developed a national contract-tracing app, but with no public information, little support, and no active adoption by provincial public health authorities, it proved of little use.

The end result was that federal and provincial policy responses were introduced sporadically, with little forethought and coordination.[36] Strikingly, even when the federal government provided funding to undertake contact testing and tracing, some provincial governments left millions unspent.[37] Journalist André Picard called this approach "cautious incrementalism." But a better characterization might be "negligent incrementalism," given the toll in terms of cases, deaths, and public confusion across the country.

A HARD LOOK AT DATED SYSTEMS

Certainly, at first glance, the economic responses of Canada and the United States suggest fundamentally contrasting power structures and fundamentally divergent levels of political responsiveness. In Canada, Prime Minister Justin Trudeau donned a mask, limited border travel, and urged people to stay home during provincially ordered lockdowns. The federal government followed this up with never-before-seen measures such as the Canada Emergency Response Benefit (CERB) for individuals and a wage subsidy program for employers to use instead of laying off their workers.[38] By contrast in the United States, cases broke records throughout 2020–21, with hospitals and medical staff constantly overwhelmed. Officials in many highly populated states balked at introducing policies such as mask wearing, social distancing, or stay-at-home measures.[39]

But focusing on these differences hides more than it reveals. An objective look at the economic policies both national governments implemented – and at the systematic reorientation of power and economic policy by capital and corporate elites for their own benefit – exposes how the crisis largely bolstered the ability of the largest and most monopolistic business interests to amass wealth. For in both Canada and the United States, the story of politics in recent decades has been one of the rich getting richer, and of big business in key sectors like technology and fossil fuel energy using connections and influence to win ever-greater gains.[40] The current crisis has only accentuated these trends.

These parallel histories of inequality can be seen in any number of areas, but most clearly in the economic policy responses of the two countries (see Table 1.1). As in previous crises, the Canadian and US governments accumulated billions of dollars in debt in order to keep their economies afloat. As before, they offered tax breaks, direct bailouts, and special exemptions to large corporations but only the most modest supports to small, independently owned local enterprises. As before, the two central banks bought up billions of dollars of debt from corporations, private-sector banks, and financial traders to keep the financial system from collapsing. And as before, only the very wealthy in both countries have benefited from record-low interest rates and targeted pro-business policies.[41]

In March 2020, financial markets came close to collapse, as trillion-dollar economies lurched to a halt in the wake of government-ordered lockdowns.[42] But central banks around the world stepped in to flatten the curve of financial panic, quickly buying up debt from banks, money funds, and major corporations – a policy known as **quantitative easing**. These actions were led by the US Federal Reserve, which offered up US$2.3 trillion in credit purchases. The Bank of Canada was also charged with immediately providing $200 billion to shore up financial markets and corporations alike, a figure raised to $600 billion by the end of 2020. And to ensure that banks and financial markets would be able to address any credit shortfalls in lending, these central banks both introduced repurchase agreement (repo) operations, a form of short-term borrowing whereby investors could borrow government securities and sell them back the next day at a slightly higher price. The purpose was to funnel large amounts of cash into money markets.[43]

The results? In Canada, stock markets and corporations quickly recovered their losses and then made record profits. By December 2020, with the central bank purchasing more than $159 billion in private-sector debt and securities, the Toronto Stock Exchange had staged one of its biggest rallies ever, having surged more than 42 percent since its COVID-19 low in March. By March 2021, the stock market index was at an all-time high, more than 10 percent above its previous five-year average.

Corporate bond markets also went into overdrive, as companies sold off debt to the central bank and drove up corporate wealth through speculation.[44] Corporate executives quickly took advantage of record-low interest rates and liquid capital markets to raise funds to buy up company stock, pay out shareholder dividends, and give even more generous compensation to their chief executives.[45] And big business and big banks took advantage of near zero-cost loans to buy billions in stocks, real estate, other companies, and financial assets cheaply, furthering their own profits.[46]

Consequently, as millions took to the streets in the United States, Canada, and around the world to protest racial injustice and growing inequality throughout 2020, the very richest saw their profits soar.[47] Canada's major banks reported billions in profits and paid out commensurate dividends to their shareholders. The wealthiest twenty billionaires in the country amassed more than $28 billion in just a few months. Following astronomical gains in their company valuations, CEOs such as Tobias Lütke of Shopify, now Canada's largest publicly traded company, and Chip Wilson of Lululemon Athletica now have billions in stock options that they can exercise.[48] The profits of Loblaws supermarket chain, as another example, also jumped 21 percent for the first quarter of 2020, meaning its top executives could expect exceptional compensation similar to that in 2019, when they split $57 million in stock options and bonuses.[49]

In these ways, government support for large corporate and financial interests and the wealthy during the pandemic only accelerated the trends of recent decades. From 2001 to 2015, the number of Canadians whose net worth was at least US$50 million nearly quadrupled, from 803 to 2,840. The number of billionaires doubled.[50] And the incomes of the top 1 percent of earners tripled to nearly $800,000 per year. By contrast, by the end of the period 40 percent of Canada's working population, those in **non-standard employment**, saw their annual income stuck at $15,500 per year.

THE SHORTCOMINGS OF CANADA'S RESCUE PACKAGE

The pandemic also uncovered the many problems of Canada's labour laws and safety nets: the fourth pillar of government response to the pandemic (see Table 1.1). Federal and provincial efforts to improve protections for workers and the elderly were certainly welcome, but systemic weaknesses quickly became all too apparent. By way of comparison, while the federal government provided more than $150 billion directly to businesses and another $169 billion in financial liquidity, workers who were unemployed or on part-time furlough received $111 billion, less than one-third of total government spending on the virus over 2020.[51]

Such striking levels of business support – as well as income programs for the unemployed and partially employed – were common to all the countries that attempted to mitigate the virus rather than effectively eliminate it at the start. In contrast, because of their efforts at containing the virus, Denmark and Finland had to spend only a fraction of what Canada, the United States, and the United Kingdom did in their efforts to cope with the virus and to prop up their economies with recurrent lockdowns (Figure 1.2).

To its credit, the federal government quickly brought in two new income support programs – the Canada Emergency Response Benefit and the Canada Emergency Wage Subsidy (CEWS) – the first new income supports in more than fifty years.[52] Modelled on similar programs already in place in Western European countries such as Spain and Denmark, the spending has worked – to a degree. For many low-wage workers laid off in restaurants, retail stores, and the gig economy, the $2,000 per month benefit was actually a good deal more than they typically received in wages in consecutive months of a year. And in terms of the overall economy, the

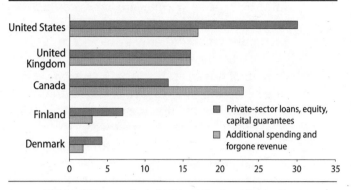

FIGURE 1.2 **Government spending in response to the pandemic, 2020 (% of GDP)**

Sources: IMF, *World Economic Outlook Update, 2020*; David MacDonald, *Picking up the Tab: A Complete Accounting of Federal and Provincial COVID-19 Measures in 2020* (Ottawa: Canadian Centre for Policy Alternatives, 2021).

program largely replaced the income that had disappeared from the labour market because of mass layoffs.[53] It also helped workers who had fallen ill or had to quarantine.

But by September 2020, the federal government had officially ended the CERB program and replaced it with a labyrinth of new unemployment policies, leaving significant numbers worse off and excluding hundreds of thousands from benefits.[54] Further updates in fall 2021 continued to restrict accessibility, benefits, and the length of claims, all of which worsened the unemployment protection and sick leave supports for precarious workers and the self-employed.

Similarly, the crisis underscored weaknesses in the Canadian social protection system. With regard to childcare and family policies, Canada and the United States are notorious outliers among advanced industrial economies. Neither has universal childcare programs (though by March 2022, all provinces had carved out their own provincial plans to obtain national funding in an effort to begin developing better childcare programs in the coming years); neither provides adequate family benefits. The limited childcare available is very expensive. Outside Quebec (which has over half of the country's childcare spaces), parents are left to cobble together a patchwork of programs, tax credits, and family support to provide childcare.

But with the onset of the pandemic, neither the federal nor most provincial governments – the exceptions being Quebec and British Columbia – were willing to help with school or daycare. Schools and daycares were closed in most provinces for the bulk of 2020 (BC being an exception again), passing the costs of the pandemic on to working families, who were forced to cover childcare, schooling, and employment. Unsurprisingly, women were hit hardest. Many either lost or were forced to step back from their jobs because of family responsibilities.[55] In early 2021, the federal government promised more funding in the run-up to establishing a better family policy. But with several provinces facing deficits and no promise of long-term federal investment, childcare centres across Canada remained closed while others had revenue shortfalls that threatened their long-term operation.

The ripple effects of inadequate social protection were enormous. Without accessible childcare, mothers had to quit their jobs and stay at home to take on unpaid work. This not only cost the economy billions but also risked leaving women permanently disadvantaged in the labour market. Just as important, without secure public funding, public childcare centres were not able to address long-term health- and safety-related costs. These policy failures mean that women, workers, and the wider community have not received fair and reliable support either during the pandemic or in terms of a long-term recovery plan.

Without serious attempts to deal with COVID-19 long term or meet the challenges of other zoonotic viruses by addressing gaps in labour law and the safety net, and transforming our energy systems and infrastructure, Canada's corporate elites continue to put workers and their families at risk.

THE OPPORTUNITY TO BUILD BACK BETTER

Given how little is still known about the long-term effectiveness and impacts of COVID-19 vaccines, and the power of emerging coronavirus variants, research strongly suggests that vaccination is only one part of any recovery plan. Yet there are still no clear guidelines across Canadian provinces or federally on the criteria for imposing or lifting lockdowns or other restrictions. This is significant because both locking down and lifting restrictions come with drawbacks for the medium- to long-term health of the population. Easing measures too soon leaves people exposed to new variants and infection; keeping them in place too long causes unemployment and social isolation.[56] Nor does any province have a comprehensive system of testing, tracing, isolating, and providing support to deal with future variants or new viruses. Few federal government resources are designated for care homes. And there are no economic recovery policies to ensure jobs return in sectors hardest hit by COVID-19 lockdowns and to help the country make the transition to a sustainable, zero-carbon future.

Despite this muddled picture, the expert advice about reopening and recovery is actually straightforward. So long as people face significant risks of infection and illness, many will not be willing to go to work, enter a restaurant, or attend a concert.[57] And without a recovery plan that tackles climate change and environmental degradation, people around the world face an increasingly bleak future of existential threats: climate-related extreme weather events, biodiversity loss, deforestation, and the acidification of oceans.[58]

As numerous health experts have pointed out, COVID-19 is now endemic. Like seasonal flu, we can expect more waves of infection in the coming months and years as the virus continues to mutate. To deal with this, a nationwide vaccination campaign is a first step alongside a comprehensive system of testing, tracing, isolating, and supporting those infected is thus crucial to keep the virus in check and workers safe.[59] Data must be shared, and individuals and their families supported if they contract the virus. For any recovery plan to work effectively, governments must make a commitment to improve **public health** where it matters – at the workplace – and subsequently take steps to ensure health and safety in all sectors of the economy so people can work safely and enjoy the freedoms they once had.

In addition, some of the most essential elements of a safe and sustainable recovery package are the introduction of universal daycare and the reopening of schools.[60] Children need schools and daycare to learn, exercise, and socialize with their friends. Parents need educators and childcare workers to help them raise their children and to enable them to go to work. Certainly, there are risks. But as countries like Norway, Denmark, Finland, and even much-maligned Sweden (which famously eschewed mandated lockdowns) have shown, students can return to school with few problems and very low risk to teachers. To do so, basic public health measures are essential to help control community transmissions of the virus.

In Canada, the federal government did provide new funds for provincial governments to reopen schools and childcare spaces in mid-2020. But because schools and childcare facilities were minimally funded to begin with – and provinces did nothing – no school or childcare system had the money to hire more teachers and childcare workers, build and expand spaces, or implement routines to limit numbers of students in classrooms.[61] An inclusive recovery for women and families will require governments to step up with the funding necessary for teachers and daycare providers to build the systems of learning and care needed for the future. The new Early Learning and Child Care plan and accompanying provincial agreements (signed in 2021 and 2022) provide a start, with reductions in fees for more parents. But without real investments in new spaces and public provision, many parents across Canada will still be left without adequate services.

Permanently legislating paid sick leave and preventing sickness must also be a priority in a viable and inclusive recovery. The core function of a paid sick leave program is to protect workers' jobs, health, and incomes during illness. That's essential during a pandemic as it allows infected workers to self-isolate without concern for their incomes. In this fashion, paid sick leave not only protects workers and their families but also helps contain the virus and preserves jobs by creating an orderly context for addressing outbreaks.

The federal government did begin discussions with the provinces on ten paid sick leave days per year but was unable to get provincial premiers to pass the legislation. Consequently, the federal government finally moved in late 2020 to introduce the Canada Recovery Sickness Benefit.[62] This was a step in the right direction, but the program was temporary, the eligibility criteria were restrictive, and the benefit was available only to workers who had a COVID-19-related illness (see Chapter 5). In a pandemic, this is the minimum. To ensure that workers can stay safe at work and not feel pressure to go to work while sick, governments must legislate paid sick leave policies for all workers, regardless of contract, citizenship, or residency status.

Finally, migrant workers need to be protected (Chapter 9). In the public mind, doctors, firefighters, and police have always been considered essential workers. But as the pandemic revealed, the workers picking our food, working in food-processing plants, keeping transportation systems running are equally essential – and they deserve to be treated as such. All migrant workers should be granted **permanent residency** status so that their migration status isn't tied to a specific employer, allowing them to leave unsafe or exploitive work.[63] A sustainable recovery must include protecting workers on farms, and must end exemptions of migrant and agricultural work from regular labour laws and regulations. Most important, agricultural workers should be granted the same rights as all other workers. This includes guaranteeing the right to unionize, to earn real hourly minimum wages without penalties or deductions, and to have access to protective equipment as required. Equally critical are regular COVID-19 testing and penalties for employers who fail to provide safe conditions and adequate housing, both of which are necessary for social distancing. Measures such as these are the first steps to making sure that migrant workers can work safely and live with a modicum of dignity.

Over 2020 and 2021, as governments and researchers began to consider how to address the pandemic and the climate crisis, calls to build back better became ubiquitous. For example, Canadian private-sector union Unifor and the international **Organisation for Economic Co-operation and Development (OECD)** have put out the demand that governments do a good deal more than return to business as usual to tackle the triple emergencies of the climate crisis, skyrocketing inequality, and mass unemployment.[64] These and other organizations argue that recovery policies must reduce the likelihood of future shocks while improving worker well-being.

In this regard, a more comprehensive assessment of Canadian federal and provincial policy would suggest that public officials put most of their effort into rescue packages. But much else was missing, and it is clear that Canada will require a far better – and far more inclusive – set of long-term strategies to build back better. The serious risks in returning to previous, unsustainable patterns are simply too high to ignore. Measures to rebuild health, well-being, and work are the initial steps of such a people-centred recovery. Equally important is a plan to create a greener and fairer economy.

ACHIEVING A SUSTAINABLE GREEN RECOVERY

One of the most striking aspects of the pandemic has been its effects on the environment. The International Energy Agency estimates that daily greenhouse gas emissions fell by a quarter in the first few months of lockdown, and had declined 6 percent by the end of 2020 compared to 2019 – the largest drop in seventy years.[65] This brief respite from smog and pollution provided a glimpse of what a future with fewer emissions could look like.

As international environmental agencies cautioned, however, there was little reason for optimism. Governments and financial institutions continued to shy away from prioritizing climate and instead provided billions of dollars to the fossil fuel sector.[66] Rather, despite the fact that the last three decades have been the warmest on record, and the past five years the hottest yet, oil and gas consumption and emissions are forecast to rise unabated, particularly so in Canada.[67] Few countries are doing enough to shift to cleaner energy systems, and even fewer are making the emissions reductions necessary to reach the Paris Agreement target of net zero by 2050.[68]

The estimated costs of and damages from failing to keep global temperatures within reasonable limits are astronomical. According to one recent report, the world is looking at losses of $800 trillion by 2100 if global warming is kept to 2 degrees Celsius or so.[69] The consequences for agriculture, food supplies, and oceans, and the resulting increase in climate-related disasters, are expected to cost trillions more. In 2021, Western Canada experienced record-breaking heatwaves and drought, causing hundreds of wildfires of extraordinary intensity. A longer fire season compounded the catastrophe and strained resources.

Such interrelated shocks of economic crisis, the pandemic, and climate change-induced ecological damage pose major challenges to economies worldwide. Policy experts and scientists nonetheless believe that we can deal with such shocks - if governments actually make climate plans that create good jobs in sustainable industries.[70] In this regard, a first step is to develop an appropriate recovery program that would build renewable energy sources such as wind, solar, and geothermal, manufacture more electric vehicles, and expand high-speed rail and public transportation systems. This would not only put the energy sector on a sustainable path, but it would also create millions of new jobs in manufacturing.[71]

A sustainable recovery blueprint would also set out realistic carbon budgets and transition targets, and invest in energy efficiency and building retrofits, allowing everyone from businesses, homeowners, and factories to schools, hospitals, and universities to upgrade and modernize.[72] A just recovery plan could then also improve climate resilience by restoring forests and wetlands and investing in training and programs to turn out skilled workers who can address climate change. Such comprehensive measures provide a base from which greenhouse gas emissions can be dramatically reduced, energy costs lowered, and economic growth immediately boosted. Only in these ways can governments effectively cut fossil fuel pollution and move toward a zero-emission economy.

International research is also finding that renewal efforts must deal with the factors that make future pandemics more likely, rather than simply counter the symptoms of the COVID-19 pandemic. A second step to recovery is to address agrifood production and large-scale factory farming - key drivers of the vast expansion of infectious diseases. Seventy-five percent of all new human infectious diseases originate from zoonotic viruses, those that jump from animals to people, primarily as a result of the proximity of massive industrialized pork and poultry facilities to both major urban metropoles and nearby woodlands where viruses from wildlife hosts jump to livestock and humans.[73] The phasing out of such unsustainable food production practices - and the redevelopment of more sustainable agriculture based on local plant-focused farms and small-scale livestock farming - is crucial to building a more resilient and safer environment. An added benefit is the fact that by supporting sustainable agriculture, economies can generate better jobs and create healthier communities.[74]

Eradicating the coronavirus and constructing a clean and sustainable economy in these ways will undoubtedly be costly. But developed countries have the ample resources and flourishing financial and corporate sectors necessary to make that future a reality. Estimates suggest some $73-140 trillion from advanced industrial economies over the next couple of decades would be sufficient, or 2-4 percent of their annual gross domestic product (GDP). This is a considerable sum, but it represents only a fraction of the human and economic cost associated with climate change, zoonotic disease, and unemployment. And research suggests that such spending could easily be financed if governments committed themselves to taxing companies and the wealthy, cracking down on tax havens, and enacting international taxation frameworks that prohibit companies from shifting profits to lower-tax jurisdictions.[75]

So too a **green recovery** plan offers multiple opportunities for workers from all backgrounds to get the jobs and training they need, while building up communities regardless of their current economic circumstances. As international research has shown, a sustainable, zero-carbon world is essential to addressing our economic problems. Not only can it help us tackle inequality and injustice, projects that cut greenhouse gas emissions have been shown to deliver far higher returns for government spending than conventional stimulus packages do – and they provide immediate economic relief.[76] Now, as governments plan to invest trillions of dollars in reviving their economies over the next few years, researchers are demonstrating there is no better way to spend those dollars than on low-carbon energy systems and infrastructure that also deliver jobs.

Canada's governments have a once-in-a-lifetime opportunity to shape a better future. The natural inclination is to take the easy way out. But as Canadian and international organizations have noted, the time to build back better has arrived.

WE CAN FIND BETTER WAYS

Can Canadians look at others and at ourselves and choose to be not only kinder but smarter? Can we, as celebrated contemporary writer Esi Edugyan asked at the beginning of this chapter, find "better ways"?

The answer is yes – but with caveats.

First, while governments nearly everywhere have tried to contain the virus and provide support to those who have suffered job loss or ill health, the differences in performance have been stark – especially between North America,

Europe, and Southeast Asia. Relative to other global regions, Canada's federal and provincial governments have done the bare minimum. In contrast, Denmark, Finland, and Norway implemented recovery plans that prioritized vaccination, testing, tracing, isolation, and support to keep the virus in check. Other countries also invested in their education and care systems, hiring more teachers, opening new spaces, and taking extra health precautions to allow parents to send their children to school and go to work without worry. Several European economies – as well the United States – are now laying out detailed policy packages for achieving their climate targets, generating new green jobs, and building a clean energy, fossil fuel-free economy. But Canada's governments so far have not.

Second, the power of business and big finance continues to present a major barrier to progressive change – most particularly in the United States, but in Canada too. Corporations and financial actors have gained enormous sway over workers, and have turned to federal and provincial governments to reinforce this power time and again. However, what the pandemic has taught us is that such a laissez-faire, business-first approach holds innumerable problems. A genuine recovery plan must curb the influence of business and the wealthy.

Third, regardless of nationality or income, all citizens around the world have the same rights to good health and clean air, an adequate standard of living, and a liveable planet. If Canada and the rest of the global community are to live up to this basic principle, only a more caring and egalitarian form of politics offers a way forward. Such a political necessity has become even more important with the likelihood that pandemic risks and climate change will plague us for years to come.

There are no guarantees that these lessons will be learned. We could just as easily reinstate pro-growth agendas that benefit only corporations and the wealthy few. But make no mistake: this is a time of enormous importance, offering both crisis and opportunity for Canadians. Citizens, unions, and workers will have to work hard to build the public power necessary to chart a better course forward. But this journey must start from an awareness of our national failures in addressing the pandemic, the lack of jobs, and inadequate labour and social protection, or developing an official transition strategy away from fossil fuels. We must then seize the opportunity to draft blueprints and get to work at building the transformative policy mechanisms that will change our society – and our world – for the better.

ADDITIONAL RESOURCES

Berkhout, Esmé, Nick Galasso, Max Lawson, Pablo Andrés Rivero Morales, Anjela Taneja, and Diego Alejo Vázquez Pimentel, *The Inequality Virus: Bringing Together a World Torn Apart by Coronavirus through a Fair, Just, and Sustainable Economy* Oxford: Oxfam International, 2021.

Davis, Mike. *The Monster Enters: COVID-19, Avian Flu, and the Plagues of Capitalism.* New York: OR Books, 2020.

International Labour Organization. "COVID-19 and the World of Work." https://www.ilo.org/global/topics/coronavirus/lang-en/index.htm.

–. *World Employment and Social Outlook 2018: Greening with Jobs.* Geneva: International Labour Office, 2018. https://www.ilo.org/wcmsp5/groups/public/–dgreports/–dcomm/–publ/documents/publication/wcms_628654.pdf.

Organisation for Economic Co-operation and Development. "Tackling Coronavirus (COVID-19)." https://www.oecd.org/coronavirus/en.

NOTES

1 Mike Davis, *The Monster Enters: COVID-19, Avian Flu, and the Plagues of Capitalism* (New York: OR Books, 2020); Jacob Hacker, "Average Workers Can't Bear Any More Risk," *The Atlantic*, May 31, 2020.

2 United Nations Environment Programme, *Preventing the Next Pandemic: Zoonotic Diseases and How to Break the Chain of Transmission* (Nairobi: United Nations Environment Programme and International Livestock Research Institute, 2020).

3 Davis, *The Monster Enters.*

4 Donald McNeil, "The Pandemic's Big Mystery: How Deadly Is the Coronavirus?" *New York Times*, July 4, 2020.

5 Megan Scudellari, "How the Pandemic Might Play Out in 2021 and Beyond," *Nature*, August 5, 2020.

6 Nicky Phillips, "The Coronavirus Is Here to Stay – Here's What That Means," *Nature*, February 16, 2021; Ingrid Torjesen, "COVID-19 Will Become Endemic with Decreased Potency over Time, Scientists Believe," *British Medical Journal* 372 (2021), https://doi.org/10.1136/bmj.n494.

7 OECD, *Strengthening the Recovery: The Need for Speed*, OECD Economic Outlook Interim Report, March (Paris: OECD Publishing, 2021), https://doi.org/10.1787/34bfd999-en.

8 OECD, *Employment Outlook 2020: Worker Security and the COVID-19 Crisis* (Paris: OECD Publishing, 2020), https://doi.org/10.1787/1686c758-en.

9 International Civil Aviation Organization, *2020 Passenger Totals Drop 60 Percent* (New York: United Nations, 2021).

10 International Labour Organization, "ILO Monitor: COVID-19 and the World of Work. 5th edition," Briefing note, June 30, 2020 https://www.ilo.org/global/topics/coronavirus/impacts-and-responses/WCMS_749399/lang-en/index.htm.

11 OECD, *Employment Outlook 2020*.

12 David Macdonald, "Transitioning from CERB to EI Could Leave Millions Worse Off," *The Monitor*, Canadian Centre for Policy Alternatives, September 15, 2020, https://monitormag.ca.

13 Ibid.; Committee for the Coordination of Statistical Activities (CCSA), *How COVID-19 Is Changing the World: A Statistical Perspective* (New York: UNCTAD, 2020), https://data.unicef.org/resources/how-COVID-19-is-changing-the-world-a-statistical-perspective.

14 International Labour Organization, *Global Wage Report 2020–21: Wages and Minimum Wages in the Time of COVID-19* (Geneva: International Labour Office, 2020), https://www.ilo.org/wcmsp5/groups/public/–dgreports/–dcomm/–publ/documents/publication/wcms_762534.pdf.

15 Esmé Berkhout, Nick Galasso, Max Lawson, Pablo Andrés Rivero Morales, Anjela Taneja, and Diego Alejo Vázquez Pimentel, *The Inequality Virus: Bringing Together a World Torn Apart by Coronavirus through a Fair, Just, and Sustainable Economy* (Oxford: Oxfam International, 2021); International Labour Organization, "ILO Monitor: COVID-19 and the World of Work. 7th edition," Briefing note, January 25, 2021, https://www.ilo.org/global/topics/coronavirus/impacts-and-responses/WCMS_767028/lang–en/index.htm.

16 Paul Webster, "COVID-19 Highlights Canada's Care Home Crisis," *The Lancet* 397, no. 10270 (2021), https://doi.org/10.1016/S0140-6736(21)00083-0.

17 Berkhout et al., *The Inequality Virus*.

18 Jennifer Yang, Rachel Mendleson, and Andrew Bailey, "Toronto's COVID-19 Divide: The City's Northwest Corner Has Been 'Failed by the System,'" *Toronto Star*, June 28, 2020, thestar.com.

19 Migrant Workers Alliance, *Unheeded Warnings: COVID-19 and Migrant Workers in Canada*, June 2020, https://migrantworkersalliance.org/wp-content/uploads/2020/06/Unheeded-Warnings-COVID19-and-Migrant-Workers.pdf.

20 Kathryn Blaze Baum and Tavia Grant, "Essential but Expendable: How Canada Failed Migrant Farm Workers," *Globe and Mail*, June 8, 2020, theglobeandmail.com.

21 Kourtney Koebel and Dionne Pohler, "Labor Markets in Crisis: The Double Liability of Low-Wage Work during COVID-19," *Industrial Relations: A Journal of Economy and Society* 59, no. 4 (February 2021): 503–31.

22 Ontario's Long-Term Care COVID-19 Commission, *Final Report*, April 30, 2021 (Toronto: Queen's Printer for Ontario, 2021), http://www.ltccommission-commissionsld.ca/report/pdf/20210623_LTCC_AODA_EN.pdf

23 OECD, *Employment Outlook 2020*.

24 Thomas Hale, Noam Angrist, Rafael Goldszmidt et al., "A Global Panel Database of Pandemic Policies (Oxford COVID-19 Government Response Tracker)," *Nature Human Behaviour* 5 (2021): 529–38; OECD, *Employment Outlook 2020*.

25 Jay Patel and Devi Sridhar, "We Should Learn from the Asia-Pacific Responses to COVID-19," *The Lancet Regional Health Western Pacific* 5, no. 100062 (December 2020), https://doi.org/10.1016/j.lanwpc.2020.100062.

26 Bess Levin, "Trump Claims Coronavirus Will 'Miraculously' Go Away by April," *Vanity Fair*, February 11, 2020; Poppy Noor, "'Please Don't Inject Bleach': Trump's Wild Coronavirus Claims Prompt Disbelief," *The Guardian*, April 24, 2020.

27 David A. Graham, "Governors Are Passing the Buck on Coronavirus Back to Mayors," *The Atlantic*, June 18, 2020.

28 Andre Picard, "100 Days into the Pandemic, We've Moved from Anxiety to Complacency, without Much Reason to Do So," *Globe and Mail*, June 19, 2020, theglobeandmail.com.

29 John Hopkins University and Medicine, Coronavirus Resource Center, Mortality Analyses, "Cases and Mortality by Country," May 8, 2022. https://coronavirus.jhu.edu/data/mortality.

30 Sophia Harris, "Majority of Travellers Entering Canada during COVID-19 Given OK to Not Quarantine," *CBC News*, November 18, 2020, www.cbc.ca.

31 Kelley Lee and Anne-Marie Nicol, "Why Canada Doesn't Know How Many COVID-19 Cases Are Linked to Travel," *The Conversation*, February 1, 2021, theconversation.com; Louis du Plessis, John T. McCrone, Alexander E. Zarebski et al., "Establishment and Lineage Dynamics of the SARS-CoV-2 Epidemic in the UK," *Science* 371, no. 6530 (February 2021): 708–12.

32 Smriti Mallapaty, "What the Data Say about Border Controls and COVID Spread," *Nature* 589 (January 14, 2021): 185; Francesco Parino, Lorenzo Zino, Maurizio Porfiri, and Alessandro Rizzo, "Modeling and Predicting the Effect of Social Distancing and Travel Restrictions on COVID-19 Spreading," *Journal of the Royal Society Interface* 18 (2021), https://doi.org/10.1098/rsif.2020.0875.

33 Donald McNeil, "The Virus Can Be Stopped, but Only with Harsh Steps, Experts Say," *New York Times*, March 22, 2020.

34 Daniel Ornston, "The Nordic Model Encourages Inclusion, Using the Welfare State to Promote Solidarity," *Policy Options*, June 26, 2020, https://policyoptions.irpp.org.

35 Robyn Doolittle, Michelle Carbert, and Daniel Leblanc, "Canada's Lost Months: When COVID-19's First Wave Hit, Government and Health Officials Were Scattered and Slow to Act," *Globe and Mail*, June 25, 2020, theglobeandmail.com.

36 Emily Cameron-Blake, Helen Tatlow, Thomas Hale et al., "Variation in Canadian Provincial and Territorial Responses to COVID-19," Blavatnik School of Government Working Paper, March 15, 2021, https://www.bsg.ox.ac.uk/sites/default/files/2021-03/BSG-WP-2021-039.pdf; Picard, "100 Days."

37 David Macdonald, *Picking up the Tab: A Complete Accounting of Federal and Provincial COVID-19 Measures in 2020* (Ottawa: Canadian Centre for Policy Alternatives, 2021).

38 David Parkinson, "Why Canada's Emergency Benefits Are the Right Tool for the Economic Downturn," *Globe and Mail*, May 13, 2020, theglobeandmail.com; Chris Roberts, "Liberals' COVID-19 Support Measures Reveal Crisis in Canada's Low-Wage Job Market," *The Bullet*, April 16, 2020.

39 Farah Stockman, Mitch Smith, and Guilia McDonnell Nieto del Rio, "Daily Death Toll Rises in Some States," *New York Times*, July 10, 2020; Lauren Weatherby, "U.S. Virus Cases Climb toward a Third Peak," *New York Times*, October 15, 2020.

40 Jacob Hacker and Paul Pierson, *Let Them Eat Tweets: How the Right Rules in an Age of Extreme Inequality* (New York: Liveright Publishing, 2020).

41 IMF, *Global Financial Stability Update June 2020* (New York: International Monetary Fund, 2020); International Labour Organization, "ILO Monitor: COVID-19 and the World of Work. 7th edition."

42 Adam Tooze, "How Coronavirus Almost Brought Down the Global Financial System," *The Guardian*, April 14, 2020.

43 Jeffery Cheng, Tyler Powell, and David Wessel, "What's the Fed Doing in Response to the COVID-19 Crisis? What More Could It Do?" Brookings Institute, January 25, 2021; Bank of Canada, *Quarterly Financial Report – Third Quarter 2020* (Ottawa: Bank of Canada, 2020).

44 Mark Rendell, "Canadian Bond Market Slows after Hitting Record High in April and May," *Globe and Mail*, July 9, 2020, theglobeandmail.com.

45 Nick Baker, "In the Worst of Times, the Billionaire Elite Plunder Working-Class America," *Counterpunch*, September 3, 2020.

46 Ibid.; Larry Elliot, "The Only V-shaped Recovery after Coronavirus Will Be in the Stock Markets," *The Guardian*, August 18, 2020.

47 Alex Hemingway and Michal Rozworski, "Canadian Billionaires' Wealth Skyrocketing amid the Pandemic," *Policy Note* (September 2020).

48 Hemingway and Rozworski, "Canadian Billionaires' Wealth."

49 David Macdonald, *The Golden Cushion: CEO Compensation in Canada* (Ottawa: Canadian Centre for Policy Alternatives, 2021).

50 Credit Suisse, *Global Wealth Handbook 2015* (London: Credit Suisse, 2015).

51 Macdonald, *Picking up the Tab.*

52 David Macdonald, "What's at Stake in the Move from CERB to EI?" *The Monitor*, Canadian Centre for Policy Alternatives, August 10, 2020, https://monitormag.ca.

53 Parkinson, "Why Canada's Emergency Benefits."

54 Macdonald, "Transitioning from CERB to EI."

55 Yue Qian and Sylvia Fuller, "COVID-19 and the Gender Employment Gap among Parents of Young Children," *Canadian Public Policy* 46, no. S2 (August 2020): S89–S101.

56 Statistics Canada, "Provisional Death Counts and Excess Mortality, January to December 2020," March 2021, https://www150.statcan.gc.ca/n1/daily-quotidien/210310/dq210310c-eng.htm.

57 International Labour Organization, "ILO Monitor: COVID-19 and the World of Work. 5th edition," Briefing note, June 30, 2020, https://www.ilo.org/global/topics/coronavirus/impacts-and-responses/WCMS_749399/lang–en/index.htm; OECD, *OECD Employment Outlook 2020.*

58 Cameron Hepburn, Brian O'Callaghan, Nicholas Stern, Joseph Stiglitz, and Dimitri Zenghelis, "Will COVID-19 Fiscal Recovery Packages Accelerate or Retard Progress on Climate Change?" *Oxford Review of Economic Policy* 36, supplement 1 (May 2020): s359–s381.

59 The Royal Society and British Academy, *COVID-19 Vaccine Deployment: Behaviour, Ethics, Misinformation, and Policy Strategies*, October 21, 2020, https://royalsociety.org/-/media/policy/projects/set-c/set-c-vaccine-deployment.pdf; Donald G. McNeil, "A Dose of Optimism, as the Pandemic Rages On," *New York Times*, October 12, 2020.

60 Canadian Centre for Policy Alternatives, *Alternative Federal Budget Recovery Plan* (Ottawa: Canadian Centre for Policy Alternatives, 2020).

61 Kristin Rushowy, "Opening Ontario Schools Safely amid COVID Could Require up to $3.2 Billion Funding for Staff, Cleaning Supplies, Say Liberals, Staff Union," *Toronto Star*, July 27, 2020, thestar.com.

62 David Fairey and Kaitlyn Matulewicz, "The New Federal Paid Sick Leave Program Is Not Enough," *The Tyee*, July 21, 2020, https://thetyee.ca; Kaitlyn Matulewicz and David Fairey, "New Federal Sickness Benefit Falls Short," *The Province*, September 28, 2020.

63 Migrant Workers Alliance, *Unheeded Warnings.*

64 OECD, *Building Back Better: A Sustainable Resilient Recovery after COVID-19*, OECD Policy Responses to Coronavirus (COVID-19), June 5, 2020, https://www.oecd-ilibrary.org.

65 IEA, *The Impact of the COVID-19 Crisis on Clean Energy Progress* (Paris: International Energy Agency, 2021), https://www.iea.org/articles/the-impact-of-the-covid-19-crisis-on-clean-energy-progress.

66 Energy Policy Tracker, "G20 Analysis," https://www.energypolicytracker.org/region/g20. Rainforest Action Network, *Banking on Climate Chaos: Fossil Fuel Finance Report 2021*, https://www.ran.org/bankingonclimatechaos2021.

67 David Carrington, "Climate Emergency: 2019 Was Second Hottest on Record," *The Guardian*, January 15, 2020; Angela V. Carter and Truzaar Dordi, *Correcting Canada's "One Eye Shut" Climate Policy* (Victoria, BC: Cascade Institute, 2021); David Hughes, *Canada's Energy Sector: Status, Evolution, Revenue, Employment, Production Forecasts, Emissions and Implications for Emissions Reduction* (Vancouver: Canadian Centre for Policy Alternatives, 2021).

68 IEA, *Sustainable Recovery: World Energy Outlook Special Report*, June (Paris: International Energy Agency, 2020), https://www.iea.org/reports/sustainable-recovery.

69 Andrew P. Dobson, Stuart L. Pimm, Lee Hannah et al., "Ecology and Economics for Pandemic Prevention," *Science* 369, no. 6502 (2020): 379–81, https://doi.org/10.1126/science.abc3189.

70 IEA, *Sustainable Recovery*; International Labour Organization, *World Employment and Social Outlook 2018: Greening with Jobs* (Geneva:

International Labor Office, 2018), https://www.ilo.org/wcmsp5/groups/public/—dgreports/—dcomm/—publ/documents/publication/wcms_628654.pdf; Robert Pollin, "Green Economics and Decent Work: A Viable Unified Framework," *Development and Change* 51, no. 2 (2019): 711–26.

71 Hepburn et al., "Will COVID-19 Fiscal Recovery Packages Accelerate."

72 Jeremy Brecher, *Climate Solidarity: Workers vs. Warming* (West Cornwall: Labor Network for Sustainability and Stone Soup Books, 2017), https://labor4sustainability.org/wp-content/uploads/2017/06/Climate-Solidarity.pdf.

73 United Nations Environment Programme, *Preventing the Next Pandemic.*

74 International Labour Organization, *World Employment and Social Outlook 2018.*

75 Mark Jacobson, "Impacts of Green New Deal Energy Plans on Grid Stability, Costs, Jobs, Health, and Climate in 143 Countries," *One Earth* 1 (December 2019): 449–63; Emmanuel Saez and Gabriel Zucman, *The Triumph of Injustice: How the Rich Dodge Taxes and How to Make Them Pay* (New York: W.W. Norton and Company, 2019).

76 International Labour Organization, *World Employment and Social Outlook 2018*; Blue-Green Alliance, *Manufacturing Agenda: A National Blueprint for Clean Technology Manufacturing Leadership and Industrial Transformation* (Washington: BlueGreen Alliance, 2020), https://www.bluegreenalliance.org/wp-content/uploads/2020/06/2020_BGA_Manufacturing_Agenda-vFINAL.pdf; Rhiana Gunn-Wright, Kristina Karlsson, Kitty Richards, Bracken Hendricks, and David Arkush, *A Green Recovery: The Case for Climate-Forward Policies in America's COVID-19 Response* (New York: Roosevelt Institute, 2020); Hepburn et al., 2020.

2 Globalization and the Rise of Bad Jobs

Stephanie Luce

CHAPTER SUMMARY

This chapter provides an introduction to globalization and explains how and why globalization has spurred the growth of bad jobs with low wages, little security, and no benefits. Over the past few decades, national and global economies have changed significantly. Because of trade liberalization and financial deregulation, firms have expanded enormously and spread their production activities worldwide.

At the same time, with the growing importance of financial systems to economies, large transnational corporations have transformed their traditional orientation in favour of strategies based on the maximization of shareholder value and profits. This financialization of firms – alongside their construction of global operations – has led managers to adopt a range of measures to cut labour costs, including reducing workforces, increasing labour market flexibility, and expanding non-standard employment, all in the effort to boost returns to shareholders.

The COVID-19 pandemic and accompanying recession in 2020–21 exacerbated these trends, hitting vulnerable populations and countries more harshly and exposing and heightening existing inequalities in national and international labour markets.[1]

KEY THEMES

This chapter will help you develop an understanding of:

- globalization and the forces behind it
- financialization and its effects on firms and employment
- employer responses and labour market flexibility
- the growth of bad jobs
- a future for good jobs in the wake of the COVID-19 pandemic.

IT HAS BEEN OVER ten years since the global economic crisis of 2008–9, but the job market has not recovered, particularly for young people. Young people have always had higher unemployment rates than older workers, but compared to previous decades it now takes longer for a young worker to find stable employment. And it is more likely that young workers will be underemployed. College graduates will fare better than those without degrees, but even holding a postsecondary degree is no guarantee of stable work. The global pandemic and economic slowdown of 2020 has only exacerbated these problems.

Millennials are now the largest generation in Canada, comprising 27 percent of the population. They are also the most educated, but studies show they have been and will be slower to launch than earlier generations due to lower incomes, fewer assets, and a weak labour market.[2]

Why is this? Could it be that globalization is responsible for the fate of young workers? What is globalization, what are the forces behind it, and what is the relationship between globalization and jobs?

NEOLIBERAL SHIFTS

People talk about globalization as if it were something new, somehow created in the last few decades with the growth of computers and cell phones. In fact, the economy has been heavily globalized in the past. For example, international investments in developing countries were higher in relation to the global economy during the late nineteenth and early twentieth centuries than they are today, according to economics analyst Doug Henwood.[3] Canada and the United States, in fact, experienced globalization even earlier as Indigenous land that was colonized by European powers, bringing flows of people and investment.

In the aftermath of the First World War, many nations tightened their borders to immigrants and to trade. Following the Second World War, countries opened their borders somewhat but in a regulated fashion. In the early 1970s, a variety of factors led to a massive recession in most Western countries. Economic growth stalled while unemployment and inflation rose. Governments and corporations responded with what has become known as neoliberalism and corporate restructuring. The crisis created an opening for politicians to begin enacting policies designed to improve conditions for investors, such as deregulating industries, implementing tax cuts for the wealthy and corporations, and privatizing industry.

The move to neoliberal policy was pushed by President Ronald Reagan in the United States and Prime Minister Margaret Thatcher in the United Kingdom. In Canada in the early 1980s, Bank of Canada governor Gerald Bouey decided to address inflation by tightening the money supply and driving up interest rates. This led to an interest rate shock (similar to one in the United States) that was intended to protect banks and the financial sector. It did so at the expense of workers and the rest of the economy, laying the foundation for neoliberalism in that it was a deliberate decision to prioritize the needs of finance. A few years later, Brian Mulroney was elected prime minister and began implementing some neoliberal policies, albeit not nearly so aggressively as in the United States and United Kingdom. Throughout the 1980s, 1990s, and 2000s, both Conservative and Liberal politicians pushed neoliberal reforms.

The adoption of transnational free trade agreements is a case in point. One of the early examples was the 1989 Canada–United States Free Trade Agreement (which in 1994 became the basis of the North American Free Trade Agreement, adding in Mexico, and was then substituted by the United States–Mexico–Canada Agreement in 2020). Most economists support free trade, but these trade agreements were not just about reducing tariffs in order to increase trade in goods and services; indeed, average tariffs had already been reduced considerably. Rather, the trade agreements passed under neoliberal leaders have prioritized loosening restrictions on flows of international investment. This makes it easier for Western companies to move jobs and money across borders, for investors to expand options for new possibly high-return investments, and for investors to move money around the globe to reduce (or evade) taxes.

The agreements have also encompassed lowering so-called non-tariff barriers to trade, among them environmental protections, labour laws, and licensing restrictions, such as against genetically modified seeds. Politicians have weakened or voided many of these protections in the name of free trade. Neoliberal trade agreements are based on the idea that governments should reduce restrictions and regulations on investors and corporations (while at times increasing restrictions on people, such as through tighter immigration laws). Even where voters and politicians have pushed back against free trade agreements, for the most part corporations still have relatively free rein to move investments and jobs around the world.

FINANCIALIZATION

A key piece of neoliberal reform was deregulation of financial markets. As with other neoliberal reforms, this was done in order to make it easier for investors to move money and expand opportunities for investment. Financial markets had been regulated in order to protect against some of the risky behaviours that had led to recessions in the past, and to control potential conflicts of interest.

Financial deregulation included measures such as removing restrictions that prevented banks from setting their own loan interest rates, allowing banks to merge, and permitting commercial banks to use deposits to make stock purchases. Investors and banks had more latitude to make risky investments, and some analysts have blamed this for the Asian financial crisis of 1997–98 and the global economic crisis of 2008.

But deregulation is only a part of a larger trend of **financialization** that has taken place over the past forty years. Since the early 1980s, the share of profits coming from the financial sector has vastly outpaced those from the sale of goods and services.[4] This trend has several key impacts.

Financialization creates pressure on corporations to focus heavily on short-term stock market performance in order to appease investors. Instead of balancing a variety of goals and objectives, corporate managers place the utmost importance on maximizing shareholder value, often by tapping into new sources of market capital to boost company liquidity, profits, and dividends. In other words, managers are putting less money into long-term assets that would build the firm, and more money into short-term financial instruments and a greater payout on corporate dividends.[5]

As Figure 2.1 shows, Canadian non-financial companies (NFCs) have come to rely on an extraordinary amount of financial assets, even more than those in the United States and the United Kingdom. In all three countries, over the course of the 1990s and 2000s, NFCs turned to an ever-wider assortment of market-based financial products for operation and profitability, primarily by using their debt to fund purchases of financial assets. They increased their holdings of short-term paper (fixed-income securities that mature within a short time, such as some bonds and certificates), advances (funding provided on the basis of a future commitment or payment), and money market assets (short-term investment instruments that can easily be converted to cash). The general trend for non-financial companies (NFCs) across the Organisation for Economic Co-operation and Development (OECD) was an increase in financial assets of some 70 percent of GDP between 1990 and 2010. In Canada, it is clear that NFCs quickly took to using an array of financial assets to boost returns, with corporations increasing the financial assets on their revenue balance sheets from 91 percent of GDP in 1990 to more than 160 percent of GDP in 2010.

Stock prices rise and fall based on many factors, some of which are not necessarily good for the long-term health of the firm or other stakeholders. For example, stock prices tend to rise when a company announces mass layoffs or plans to move production offshore. This gives perverse incentives to corporate managers looking for short-term gains in shareholder value. Studies found greater short-termism among US and UK managers in the 1990s and early 2000s than in other industrialized countries, but the practice has since spread widely.[6]

CEOs and top managers are often paid based on their short-term profit performance as well, including direct payment in stock options. This creates additional incentive to make short-term decisions based on increasing stock prices rather than making long-term investments in the company or in the workforce. It can take a lot of time and resources to develop innovative products, or to train workers on new technologies or processes. Managers cannot afford to invest in long-term growth in the way they could in the past.

Politicians have also adapted. Individual investors and corporations have greater ability to move their money and more leverage to demand favourable policies from governments. Corporations play cities, states, and countries

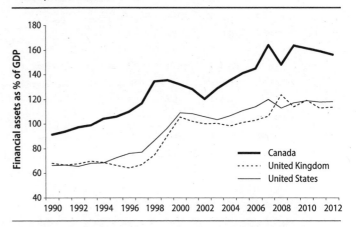

FIGURE 2.1 Canadian non-financial corporations, financial assets, 1990–2012

Source: Data from OECD Statistics, "National Accounts – Financial Accounts – Financial Balance Sheets – Non-Consolidated (Annual)," https://stats.oecd.org/Index.aspx?QueryId=37241.

against one another, threatening to move away and take jobs with them if politicians don't lower corporate tax rates or provide generous subsidies. City managers have responded by creating favourable business climates. In 2018, for example, Amazon announced it would build a new corporate headquarters and invited US and Canadian cities to compete against one another. In the end, 238 cities submitted bids to the corporation, promising a host of benefits from low taxes to access to public land.

Corporate tax rates have fallen in most major countries. For example, in just ten years, from 2008 to 2018, Canada reduced rates from 31.4 to 26 percent. That may not sound like a lot, but a company like Tim Hortons made US$3.15 billion in revenue in 2017. In broad terms, the lower tax rate would mean a savings of US$154 million a year, though the actual tax bill a corporation pays depends on a variety of factors, including exemptions and deductions, so this is just a hypothetical example. Canadian corporations also operate within a system of generous depreciation rules, exemptions, deductions, and credits (sometimes termed *loopholes*). These special provisions have further lowered their tax bills and effective tax rate – the share of their profits they actually pay in taxes – to 15.5 percent.[7] In addition, as governments like Canada's sign tax treaties with tax havens around the world, corporations have opened new subsidiaries and shifted their profits to lower tax jurisdictions.

Consequently, the Conference Board of Canada estimates that the country has an annual tax avoidance gap – the difference between what the Canada Revenue Agency should be collecting and what business is actually paying – of roughly C$20–40 billion.[8] Such corporate tax shortfalls mean shrinking budgets and reduced government services. Public-sector jobs and wages are cut. This impact is summed up in an op-ed from the *Globe and Mail*, about teacher unions: "Wherever you live in Canada, whatever party your provincial government happens to belong to, strife in the schools is about to become a way of life. The public-sector pie is shrinking, and everybody on the public payroll will have to take a hit."[9]

Financialization has also led to corporate restructuring overall. Firms look to redirect their capital into the most lucrative aspects of the work. More money goes into financial activities and less into productive activities, such as producing goods and services. What does this look like?

CORPORATE RESTRUCTURING

Corporations began to restructure in a serious way in the 1980s in the United States and the United Kingdom as they struggled to rebuild their profits after the prolonged economic slowdown of the 1970s. This involved several key trends.

First, firms in many industries have pursued large-scale consolidation, which has given them oversized economic and political power.[10]

BOX 2.1 APPLE AND THE NEW CORPORATE FINANCIAL LOGICS

For decades, Apple was the face of innovative technology as Steve Jobs built it from scratch into a multi-billion-dollar international company. But after he died in 2011, the company reduced its investment in research and development. Apple has introduced very few exciting new products in almost ten years. Instead, new CEO Tim Cook has shifted the company's focus to a new way to profit: manipulating money. How does that work?

In 2013, for example, Apple Inc. borrowed $17 billion. It didn't need the money, as it had $145 billion in its account. But with the borrowed funds it could repurchase its own stocks, driving the price up and providing healthy dividends to stockholders. (Cook himself is one of the largest shareholders.) As business columnist Rana Foroohar writes, Apple "now spends a large amount of its time and effort thinking about how to make more money via financial engineering rather than by the old-fashioned kind."[11]

Another form of financial engineering is moving money around the globe in an effort to avoid paying taxes. The result? Apple spends less effort on innovating, redistributes more of its income into stockholder dividends, and fails to pay its fair share of taxes to support public goods.

Through mergers and acquisitions, a small number of large transnational firms have come to control sectors ranging from grocery stores, hotels, and restaurants to telecommunications, energy, airlines, and entertainment. The situation is most extreme in the United States. According to the *Economist*, two-thirds of all industries have become more concentrated since the 1990s. But the problem is not unique to American companies. In 2018, portfolio manager Martin Pelletier wrote about Canada in a *Financial Times* op-ed, "We have become a nation of oligopolies giving up competition for so-called stability."[12] Industry consolidation means that a few large firms have inordinate power over setting prices, wages, and product choices.

Industry consolidation varies by sector and country, but transnational corporations and their affiliates have grown in many parts of the world. For example, in the United States, the top four firms control more than 90 percent of market share in industries including wireless telecommunications, soft drink production, major household appliance manufacturing, and food services. On a global scale, the top five firms control the majority of markets such as footwear, health care services, movies and entertainment, internet and direct marketing services, tobacco, and semiconductor equipment.[13] While transnational corporations have existed for centuries, their numbers have exploded in recent years. In 1995, there were approximately 39,000 multinational enterprises. By 2010, there were about 104,000. Their foreign affiliates grew from 251,000 to 892,000 in the same period.[14]

And in Canada, a small number of international corporations with global operations and connections dominate the major economic sectors. In the oil and gas sector, for example, Shell, BP, Chevron, and ExxonMobil dominate investment and exports. In the auto sector, Toyota, Honda, and the American Big Three –

Ford, General Motors, and Stellantis (formerly Chrysler) – all have extensive operations tied to exporting autos and auto parts to the United States. While in the world-leading Canadian mining sector, it is foreign giants Glencore, Rio Tinto, Vale, and BHP that run the largest operations and account for the majority of exports.

Second, firms have cut back to their core functions and contracted out the less-profitable components, such as janitorial, landscaping, customer service, and even accounting and legal work. They have even cut their core workforce to minimum levels and hired temporary workers or independent contractors to fill in when needed. Harvard economist David Weil calls this process **fissuring**, because it leads to divisions between groups of workers in the same enterprise. While they may all work in the same building, these employees now work for many different employers.[15]

Third, alongside outsourcing, corporations have offshored: they move parts of the work once done in house or locally to other regions or countries. This can allow a corporation to get the work done more cheaply if it goes where wages are lower and regulations are weaker. It also enables a corporation to drive down prices by forcing subcontractors to compete against one another to win a contract. More than 80 percent of manufacturing firms operating in Canada use outsourcing or offshoring in their activities, and this is especially prevalent in the auto and chemical industries.[16]

Fourth, offshoring has helped firms to develop what are known as global supply chains: networks of firms across multiple countries that convert raw goods to finished products. This is not a new concept, but economic restructuring, neoliberal deregulation, complex accounting practices, and new trade and investment agreements have made it easier and more desirable for firms to expand these chains.

THE COVID-19 CRISIS

Financialization and corporate restructuring have created an unstable, unequal global economy. Some signs that the economy was in trouble were emerging by January 2020, as the World Bank predicted the weakest economic growth since 2009.[17] Analysts worried about weak manufacturing performance, trade uncertainty, and the likelihood of a global debt crisis. Within a matter of weeks, the impact of COVID-19 was felt in China and throughout global supply chains. Within months, the global economy was experiencing the worst slowdown since the Great Depression.

The pandemic, combined with a structurally weak foundation, has led to economic disaster. By the summer of 2020, real global GDP had dropped 5.2 percent from the previous year. The advanced economies experienced a 7 percent drop. Canada fared better but still saw unprecedented decline (Chapter 1).[18]

Governments around the world have stepped in with aid packages to assist those hurt by the slowdown and to buoy their economies (see Chapter 1). The packages vary greatly in terms of aid for workers, but almost all have funnelled huge bailouts to large corporations in the form of subsidies, loans, tax deferrals, export guarantees, and more. Many countries, and especially the United States, gave a disproportionate share of the support to banks and corporations. Canada directed more than $320 billion to business and financial institutions.[19] Indeed, corporations such as Corus Entertainment and Bell Canada received tens of millions of dollars in public money to pay their labour force even as they gave their executives millions in bonuses and paid millions more to their wealthy shareholders.[20]

This influx of government funding has contributed to investor confidence, keeping stock markets high despite the dramatic drop in GDP.

CEOs are also using stock buyback strategies to increase the value of their shares, distorting the market even further. This in turn has benefited the wealthy who own most of those stocks. Just as with the last recession, the rich are getting richer through this crisis. The five wealthiest Canadian billionaires increased their combined wealth by 9 percent in the first two months of the lockdown, and by another 3 billion in the next two months.[21]

Some wealthy people and firms are getting richer through government assistance and stock market manipulations. Some are profiting directly from the pandemic – such as tech firms and online platforms, delivery services, and some medical fields.

LABOUR MARKET FLEXIBILITY

What has this meant for workers? All of these trends – the policy shift toward neoliberalism, financialization, corporate restructuring, and responses to the pandemic – have had major impacts on jobs and wages.

A key plank of neoliberal reform is labour market flexibility. The idea is to make it as easy as possible for employers to maximize profit. One constraint on profit is wages, so neoliberal governments have sought to keep wages low, such as by refusing to raise statutory minimum wages. Policy makers have also made it easier for employers to hire and fire workers, with the idea that companies need to respond quickly to a global market. State agencies have been defunded and are consequently slower to investigate and prosecute employers that violate labour and employment laws. Many countries have weakened their labour laws to reduce the costs of hiring and firing, lowering or eliminating mandatory severance pay and payment for unjust dismissals, introducing temporary contracts, and reducing unemployment insurance eligibility and payment.

Flexibility also includes strategies to shift the risk of employment from employers and governments onto workers: converting full-time jobs to part time; eliminating job security; increasing the use of temporary, seasonal, and limited-term contract work; implementing just-in-time scheduling; and subcontracting work.

Fissured firms can reduce their wage bill and cut back on benefits. In some industries, companies have hired more workers as on-call, which means they can be brought on with almost no notice. If customer flow is slow – for example, if a restaurant patio has to close because of rain – employers are not even obligated to pay their staff. They can send workers home early or not bring them in at all, even if those workers had made the commitment to be at work that day.

With a union contract, labour is a fixed cost: employers are committed to hiring a given number of people for a given number of hours at a set wage through the life of a contract. Without unions – or contracts – employers can convert this fixed cost to a variable cost, adjusting the number of workers, hours worked, or even the wage paid by the hour or day, according to consumer demand.

By converting labour from a fixed to a variable cost, employers demonstrate to shareholders that they are more easily able to adapt to the vagaries of the market. Firms can reduce labour costs when orders slow down and increase labour supply when demand increases. By weakening or eliminating contracts and commitments to provide benefits, firms increase managerial control and their own ability to plan.

BAD JOBS

What is a bad job? Certain aspects of work are subjective: whether you like your co-workers, or think the job is a good fit for your personality. Others – pay rates, access to benefits, and job

---

BOX 2.2   THE REALITY OF FLEXIBILITY

Oneika works for a multinational retailer while also going to school. She remarks, "The scheduling issue is good and bad. It's good because you can have a flexible schedule to accommodate classes, but it is also bad because I think the managers hold it against you if you say you cannot work certain days."[22]

Retail workers were among the first to experience the reality of flexibility. Often they need flexible hours to study or take care of children, but employers expect workers to remain available and on call. They must call in the night before or morning of the shift to see if there is work for them. If not, no work and no income.

Because the pay is so low, many workers struggle to get more shifts but can't, sometimes because of the seasonal nature of the work but also because employers don't want full-time employees. Ashley, who also works for a multinational retailer, explains: "Sometimes I'll pick up shifts when people call out, thinking that [the company will] give me more shifts in the future. But they don't and I ask myself, 'Why in the world am I making myself available for you all these days?'"

---

security – are more objective. Sociologist Arne Kalleberg notes that good jobs also include opportunities for pay increases and advancement, along with some control and autonomy over their work. And by most accounts, the ratio of bad jobs to good jobs has changed dramatically in many countries over the past few decades. There is also an increasing gap between the good and bad, making it less likely that young people who enter the market with a bad job will be able to work their way up a career ladder into a good job. This isn't due to bad luck or an economic downturn but to the trends mentioned above: neoliberal policy, corporate restructuring, globalization, and weaker labour unions.

Some analysts note the rise of the service sector as a factor in this shift, but a manufacturing job isn't necessarily a good one. Today, fissured workplaces mean that manufacturing firms may hire low-wage temporary agency workers to work on the line beside full-time high-wage workers. In 2018, the average wage for manufacturing workers in Canada was $22.86 per hour, much lower than the average wage of $26.82 for all workers. At $22.86, a full-time worker would receive gross pay of just under $46,000 per year. The Living Wage for Families Campaign estimates basic living costs for various family sizes and types across the country, and the average manufacturing wage is not much higher than the basic living wage needed in many parts of the country.[23] Part-time manufacturing workers earn much less: on average, just $16.30 per hour in 2018.

It isn't just a problem in manufacturing. Despite increased productivity and higher education levels, Canadian workers overall have seen hardly any increase in average wages since the 1970s. Even the public sector, which is traditionally a source of good jobs, has seen a shift toward flexible and temporary work. A 2018 study compared temporary and permanent public-sector employees in Canada. It found a persistent gap in job quality in terms of employment security, access to leave benefits, and income trajectories. The public sector appears to rely more heavily on temporary workers as a share of total employees than does the **private sector**.[24]

Good jobs still exist in Canada, as they do in the United States and other countries. But they are harder to come by, and a greater share of the new jobs created are bad jobs. For example, the twenty occupations that will have the greatest new job growth in the United States over the next ten years will account for about 5 million new jobs, or approximately 42 percent of all new jobs created. But only six of these occupations pays a median annual wage high enough for a worker to support a family. The other fourteen all have median annual wages below $40,000 per year. Where are the job openings? Food preparation workers, restaurant servers, personal care aides, home health aides, janitors and cleaners, cooks, labourers, nursing aides, landscapers, and customer service representatives. Even some of the occupations in the medical field that require training, such as medical assistant and medical secretary, have median annual wages of US$32,480 and US$34,610, respectively. High-wage jobs still exist, but they are fewer and harder to get.[25]

A growing share of jobs have not only stagnant wage levels but are also what some analysts call precarious, or contingent. Definitions vary, but most agree that precarious employment is characterized by variable hours, irregular schedules, little or no job security, and few or no benefits such as pensions. The Law Commission of Ontario reported in 2013 that one of every five jobs in the province is precarious.[26] The **International Labour Organization (ILO)** has been tracking the growth of **non-standard employment**, which includes temporary employment, part-time work, temporary agency work, and disguised employment relationships (involving **employee misclassification** as independent contractor or self-employed contractor). The ILO reports that non-standard employment relationships are on the rise in industrialized and developing countries around the world, and across a range of occupations and industries.[27]

WORKING IN A PANDEMIC

The concept of a bad job has taken on a new dimension in the pandemic. Workers have suffered in multiple ways. Some frontline workers, such as doctors and nurses, normally have good jobs in terms of pay and benefits, but they have had to risk their lives to treat COVID-19 patients, often without adequate personal protective equipment. Others on the frontline were already in irregular or precarious jobs, such as food workers (in meat-packing plants, in the fields, or in grocery stores) and delivery workers.

In other sectors, workers suffered mass layoffs or furloughs. This hit some low-wage sectors particularly hard, such as hotels, restaurants, entertainment, and in-person retail. Canada lost almost 2 million jobs in April 2020, and official unemployment jumped from under 6 percent in February to over 14 percent in April. Labour market economists found that job losses were particularly acute among disadvantaged workers and suggested that COVID-19 could be deepening existing inequalities.[28]

As previous recessions have demonstrated, without regulation or oversight corporations take advantage of a crisis to restructure in ways that shift costs and risks onto workers. This time, increased fissuring of the workplace can be expected. Large employers will have even greater power in a slack labour market, enhancing the division between owners and workers. Amazon offers a prime example. Owner Jeff Bezos saw his personal wealth grow by $48 billion in the first few months of the pandemic, while hundreds of thousands of Amazon workers risked their personal safety in warehouses and out making deliveries. When warehouse workers struck in New York, Amazon fired one of the organizers.[29]

Some governments have contributed to the problem. In a survey conducted by the International Trade Union Confederation of 121 trade union representatives from 95 countries, respondents from half of the countries surveyed reported that their governments had embedded labour and human rights restrictions in their pandemic measures.[30]

THE PROSPECTS FOR YOUNG WORKERS

Neoliberalism, corporate restructuring, and a turn to labour market flexibility have been particularly hard on young workers. The ILO estimates that about 40 percent of young workers worldwide are currently unemployed and looking for work, or working in jobs that pay poverty wages. That is over 71 million young people without jobs, and another 145 million who have jobs but still live in poverty. Some young people with low-wage jobs are in school, but a large number are what the ILO calls NEETs: Not in Employment, Education, or Training. On a global scale, one in five people aged fifteen to twenty-four is classified by the ILO as being in the NEET category.[31]

Conditions for young people are most serious in South Asia and North Africa, but even in wealthy countries young people are suffering high rates of unemployment and underemployment. Youth unemployment rates in Canada tend to move in the same direction as rates for adults, though they are always higher. In the 1970s, however, young people were most commonly either full-time students or full-time workers. Today, young people are not only more likely than older workers to be unemployed but also more likely to be working part time. This includes youth who attend school part time, and work part time to pay for it. Tuition is still much lower in Canada than in the United States, but it has been rising steadily. Average tuition fees for undergraduate education rose by approximately 85 percent 1995–2018, adjusted for inflation.[32]

There has also been an increase in young people who would prefer to work full time but can find only part-time work. In 2017, almost half of all young workers in Canada said they worked part time, and of those, almost one in five would prefer full-time work.[33] And when young people do find work, the average quality of the job is likely to be poor. According to a survey conducted by the *Globe and Mail*, "Almost one-quarter of the generation of young adults born between 1981 and 2000 are working temporary or contract jobs, nearly double the rate for the entire job market. Almost one-third are not working in their field of education, 21 per cent are working more than one job, and close to half are looking for a new job."[34] Even when official unemployment rates have dropped, young people report having trouble finding work in their field, or finding jobs that provide full-time hours or pay a living wage.[35]

The pandemic has made this worse. An ILO global survey found that young people are experiencing "systematic, deep and dispropor-tionate" impacts in terms of employment, education, and mental well-being. The effect is most severe for young women and youth in lower-income countries.[36]

FROM BAD JOBS TO GOOD JOBS

These trends suggest a grim future for young workers, and indeed for a large section of the labour force in many countries. But many of the jobs once considered good jobs didn't start out that way. For example, most manufacturing work began as low wage, insecure, and dangerous. Only with legislation and unionization were manufacturing jobs converted from bad to good.

When workers form unions in their workplace and negotiate contracts with their employer, they tend to improve the pay and quality of the job. Canadian unionized workers earn $5.28 more per hour than their non-unionized counterparts. The wage premium is even higher

---

BOX 2.3   EATING OR PAYING TUITION?

The University of Alberta in Edmonton has a campus food bank. It was established in 1991 to provide food and toiletries to students, staff, and alumni. Food bank staff report that a growing number of students are using the food bank for necessities, particularly at the beginning of the term when they are waiting for paycheques or loan payments to come in.

Former student David Fischer noted, "You know it comes down sometimes to that point where you're making the decision between paying the tuition and eating."[37]

BOX 2.4   THE JOB MARKET FOR YOUNG WORKERS

John graduated with a bachelor's degree in psychology in 2016 but couldn't find work in his field. He began applying for full-time work in the year before graduation, but despite sending over 200 resumes, he heard back from only a few employers and had only one interview. He didn't get the job. Instead, he continued to work in the retail shop where he had been as a student, and to live with his parents because he could not afford rent.

John volunteers doing counselling at a local hospital to build his resume and make connections. It's rewarding work but has not resulted in job leads. He says his parents don't understand and think he should be able to find work by walking into hospitals and asking to speak to the manager.

for women and young workers. Union members are far more likely to have pensions, extended health insurance, and dental coverage, for example.[38] Unions can also bargain for stable work schedules, premium pay for on-call work, and minimum guaranteed work hours. And unions provide job security that most workers do not have. Indeed, workers with union protection have fared better under COVID-19 than their non-union counterparts, as they are more likely to have access to paid sick leave, more channels to demand safety equipment, and greater job security.[39] Trade unions have fought to win agreements with employers and governments to protect workers.[40]

Unfortunately, due in part to poor leadership and organizing – and in part to weak labour laws and a strong and coordinated employer attack – unions have been losing membership in many countries, and numerous commenta-tors believe this is a key reason for the shift from good jobs to bad. The International Monetary Fund also sees the decline of unions as part of the explanation for the massive growth in inequality. Unions can provide benefits for individual workers, but they also stabilize macro-economies.

COVID-19 may create openings for workers to win better conditions, as the extent of the crisis has emphasized the key role that essential workers play in running our economies and keeping us safe. Already, governments appear to have learned from the 2008 crisis that austerity or small measures will not suffice. But the pandemic has also enabled certain billionaires and corporations to profit from people's desperate situations and from generous stimulus packages. Whether the pandemic leads to a transformative moment will be a matter of tremendous political struggle.

ADDITIONAL RESOURCES

Forhoohar, Rana. *Makers and Takers. The Rise and Fall of American Business.* New York: Crown Publishing, 2016.

Harvey, David. *A Brief History of Neoliberalism.* New York: Oxford University Press, 2006.

Luce, Stephanie. *Labor Movements: Global Perspectives.* Cambridge: Polity Press, 2014.

Steger, Manfred, and Ravi K. Roy. *Neoliberalism: A Very Short Introduction.* New York: Oxford University Press, 2010.

NOTES

1 Esmé Berkhout, Nick Galasso, Max Lawson, Pablo Andrés Rivero Morales, Anjela Taneja, and Diego Alejo Vázquez Pimentel, *The Inequality Virus: Brining Together a World Torn Apart by Coronavirus through a Fair, Just, and Sustainable Economy* (Oxford: Oxfam International, 2021).

2 Andrew Heisz and Elizabeth Richards, *Economic Well-Being across Generations of Young Canadians: Are Millennials Better or Worse Off?* Statistics Canada, April 18, 2009, Cat. no. 11-626-X № 092 (Ottawa: Statistics Canada, 2009), https://www150.statcan.gc.ca/n1/pub/11-626-x/11-626-x2019006-eng.htm.

3 Doug Henwood, "Beyond Globophobia," *The Nation*, November 13, 2003.

4 Greta Krippner, "The Financialization of the US Economy," *Socio-Economic Review* 3, no. 2 (2005): 173–208.

5 Jim Stanford, *Having Their Cake and Eating It Too: Business Profits, Taxes and Investment in Canada: 1961 through 2010* (Ottawa: Canadian Centre for Policy Alternatives, 2011).

6 Dominic Barton, Jonathan Bailey, and Joshua Zoffer, *Rising to the Challenge of Short-Termism* (Boston: FCLT Global, 2015), https://www.fcltglobal.org/wp-content/uploads/fclt-global-rising-to-the-challenge.pdf.

7   Michael Devereux, Katarzyna Bilicka, S. Lepove, and Giorgi Maffini, *G20 Corporation Tax Ranking* (Oxford: Oxford University Centre for Business Taxation, 2012).

8   Conference Board of Canada, *Canadian Tax Avoidance: Examining the Potential Tax Gap* (Toronto: Conference Board of Canada, 2017).

9   Margaret Wente, "Teachers Unions Are Obsolete," *Globe and Mail*, January 12, 2013, theglobeandmail.com.

10 Barry C. Lynn, "America's Monopolies Are Holding Back the Economy," *The Atlantic*, February 22, 2017, www.theatlantic.com.

11 Rana Foroohar, *Makers and Takers: The Rise and Fall of American Business* (New York: Crown Publishing, 2016), 46.

12 Martin Pelletier, "Why Canada's History of Industry Consolidation Is Good for Investors, but Bad for Consumers," *Financial Post*, July 16, 2018, financialpost.com.

13 Andrea Alegria, Agata Kaczanowska, and Lauren Setar, "Highly Concentrated: Companies That Dominate Their Industries," *IBISWorld*, February 2012, http://www.themarketworks.org/sites/default/files/uploads/charts/Highly-Concentrated-Industries.pdf; Capital Group, n.d., https://www.capitalgroup.com/europe/capitalideas/article/global-consolidation-5-charts.html.

14 Malgorzota Jaworek and Martin Kuzel, "Transnational Corporations in the World Economy: Formation, Development and Present Position," *Copernican Journal of Finance and Accounting* 4, no. 1 (2015): 55–70.

15 David Weil, *The Fissured Workplace: Why Work Became So Bad for So Many and What Can Be Done to Improve It* (Cambridge, MA: Harvard University Press, 2014).

16 Innovation, Science and Economic Development Canada, *Survey of Innovation and Business Strategy (SIBS)* (Ottawa: Science and Economic Development Canada, 2009).

17 World Bank Group, *Global Economic Prospects: Slow Growth, Policy Challenges* (Washington, DC: International Bank for Reconstruction and Development/The World Bank, 2020).

18 Ibid.

19 David Macdonald, *Picking Up the Tab: A Complete Accounting of Federal and Provincial COVID-19 Measures in 2020* (Ottawa: Canadian Centre for Policy Alternatives, 2021).

20 Patrick Brethour, Tom Cardoso, Vanmala Subramaniam, and David Milstead, "Wage Subsidies Were Meant to Preserve Jobs. In Many Cases, the $110.6-Billion Response Padded Bottom Lines," *Globe and Mail*, May 8, 2021, updated May 11, 2021, theglobeandmail.com.

21 Gabriella Sobodker, "COVID-19, the GAFAM and the Top 5 Canadian billionaires," TaxCOOP tax brief, https://taxcoop.org/wp-content/uploads/2020/07/GAFAM_EN.pdf.

22 Stephanie Luce, Sasha Hammad, and Darrah Sipe, *Short-Shifted* (New York: Murphy Institute and the Retail Action Project, 2014), https://stephanieluce.net/reports.

23 Employment and Social Development Canada, "Opportunity for All: Canada's First Poverty Reduction Strategy," (n.d), https://milescorak.com/2018/08/21/canadas-official-poverty-line-what-is-it-how-could-it-be-better; Amy Minsky, "Average Hourly Wages in Canada Have Barely Budged in 40 Years," *Global News*, June 15, 2017, globalnews.ca; Living Wage for Families BC, "What Is a Living Wage?" www.livingwageforfamilies.ca/what_is_living_wage.

24 Natasha Stecy-Hildebrandt, Sylvia Fuller, and Alisyn Burns, "'Bad' Jobs in a 'Good' Sector: Examining the Employment Outcomes of Temporary Work in the Canadian Public Sector," *Work, Employment and Society* 33, no. 4 (2018): 560–79.

25 Bureau of Labor Statistics, Occupational Employment Statistics, "Occupations with the Most Job Growth, 2016–2026," https://www.bls.gov/careeroutlook/2017/article/occupational-projections-charts.htm.

26 Law Commission of Ontario, *Vulnerable Workers and Precarious Work* (Toronto: Law Commission of Ontario, 2013).

27 International Labour Organization, *Non-Standard Employment around the World*

(Geneva: International Labour Office, 2016), www.ilo.org/wcmsp5/groups/public/@dgreports/@dcomm/@publ/documents/publication/wcms_534326.pdf.

28 Louis-Philippe Beland, Abel Brodeur, Derek Mikola, and Taylor Wright, "Here's How the Coronavirus Is Affecting Canada's Labour Market," *The Conversation*, May 13, 2020, theconversation.com.

29 Hiatt Woods, "How Billionaires Got $637 Billion Richer during the Coronavirus Pandemic," *Business Insider*, August 3, 2020, www.business insider.com; Annie Palmer, "Amazon Fires Three Employees Who Were Outspoken Critics of Its Labor Practices," *CNBC*, April 14, 2020, www.cnbc.com.

30 ITUC, "ITUC Global COVID-19 Survey," June 2020, https://www.ituc-csi.org/IMG/pdf/200701_ituc_COVID-19_globalsurveyreport_en.pdf.

31 International Labour Organization, *Global Employment Trends for Youth 2017: Paths to a Better Working Future*, 20 November (Geneva: International Labour Office, 2017), https://www.ilo.org/wcmsp5/groups/public/—dgreports/—dcomm/—publ/documents/publication/wcms_598669.pdf.

32 Royal Bank of Canada, *The Cost of Credentials: The Shifting Burden of Post-Secondary Tuition in Canada*, June 2018, http://www.rbc.com/economics/economic-reports/pdf/other-reports/Tuition June2018.pdf.

33 Martha Patterson, *Who Works Part-time and Why?* November 6, 2018, Cat. no. 71-222-X (Ottawa: Statistics Canada, 2018), https://www150.statcan.gc.ca/n1/pub/71-222-x/71-222-x2018002-eng.pdf; Statistics Canada, "Canadian Youth and Full-Time Work: A Slower Transition," *Canadian Megatrends*, May 17, 2018, https://www150.statcan.gc.ca/n1/pub/11-630-x/11-630-x2017004-eng.htm.

34 Rob Carrick, "'I Can't Even Get a Job Waitressing': Gen Y on Its Work Woes," *Globe and Mail*, November 12, 2017, theglobeandmail.com.

35 Eddy S. Ng, Sean T. Lyons, and Linda Sweitzer, "Millennials in Canada: Young Workers in a Challenging Labour Market," in *The Palgrave Handbook of Age Diversity and Work*, ed. J. Parry and J McCarthy (London: Palgrave Macmillan, 2017); Don Pittis, "Despite Low Unemployment, Young People Say Finding a Job Is as Difficult as Ever," *CBC News*, February 9, 2018, www.cbc.ca.

36 International Labour Organization, *Youth and COVID-19: Impacts on Jobs, Education, Rights and Mental Well-Being*, Survey report, August 11, 2020 (Geneva: International Labour Office, 2020), https://www.ilo.org/global/publications/lang—en/index.htm.

37 Slav Kornik, "Growing Number of University Students Relying on Food Banks," *Global News*, August 23, 2014, globalnews.ca.

38 Canadian Labour Congress, "Why Unions?" https://canadianlabour.ca/uncategorized/chapter-6-union/#why.

39 Celine McNicholas, Lynn Rhinehart, Margaret Poydock, Heidi Shierholz, and Daniel Perez, *Why Unions Are Good for Workers – Especially in a Crisis Like COVID-19*, August 25, 2020 (Washington, DC: Economic Policy Institute, 2020), https://files.epi.org/pdf/204014.pdf.

40 European Trade Union Confederation, "Trade Unions and Coronavirus," https://www.etuc.org/en/trade-unions-and-coronavirus.

3 An International Perspective on Low-Wage Work

Bryan Evans and Carlo Fanelli

CHAPTER SUMMARY

For increasing numbers of workers in Canada, low-wage work isn't just a temporary gig – it's a long-term reality. The country has one of the highest rates of low-wage work among advanced industrial economies globally. In some other economies – especially the Nordic countries of Denmark, Finland, Norway, and Sweden – low-wage work is rare and most jobs are secure. There, government regulations provide far more support to workers and their families, both on the job and between jobs. Government supports include not only better laws but also job training, generous unemployment insurance, and other benefits including pensions.

The COVID-19 pandemic that swept the world in 2020 prompted unprecedented state intervention, first to close down large parts of the economy and then to provide recently unemployed workers with the financial means to survive the closures. But pandemic-driven health and safety lockdowns alongside widespread layoffs starkly revealed the depths of social and economic inequality in Canadian society. Most notable was the profound impact on low-wage workers, who bore the brunt of workplace closures and exposure to risk.

This chapter explains why Canada and other advanced industrial countries differ in terms of their political and policy response to the expansion of low-wage work. It examines how key policies and institutions shape working conditions, how we work, how much we get paid, how secure our jobs are, and how and why incomes vary across countries. These policies include those which expand collective bargaining and thus increase union density, public social expenditure, and the minimum wage. This chapter demonstrates that what government policies do – or don't do – has a huge impact on the kinds of jobs that people have. If Canadians are to improve their jobs and wages, they will have to win new rules that ensure better job security, wages, and opportunity.

KEY THEMES

This chapter will help you develop an understanding of:

- how minimum wages across Canada fail to provide a living wage
- how labour market institutions and public services support better jobs and wages
- how the Canadian labour market compares with that in other advanced industrial countries
- key problems in Canada's labour market and social policies.

MORE AND MORE, low-wage, dead-end jobs are the only jobs available. These are the bad jobs that people may be able to get by on but not get ahead on. Better-paid, more-secure jobs with decent opportunities for advancement – the good jobs that used to offer access to a middle-class standard of living – have become scarce. And basics such as decent housing, higher education and training, transportation, and healthy food are becoming more unaffordable for many. In Canada – as well as in the United Kingdom and Germany – about 20 percent of the full-time workforce lives on low wages from jobs that pay less than two-thirds the national median hourly wage (Figure 3.1). An even higher proportion of Americans suffer low wages. Yet most workers in countries such as Finland, Sweden, and Denmark have much better pay.

What accounts for the increasing precariousness that workers face? Why do more and more workers have to live with low pay and without any say about their working conditions? With few employment protections and with little or no job security?

One reason for these growing problems is that low-wage work has become normalized because of government policy. Some politicians and government officials argue that workers are akin to commodities that employers buy and workers sell, similar to the buying and selling of oranges, copper, cotton, or cars. As employers, firms look to buy the most cost-effective labour available. As employees, workers sell their labour power: their physical, mental, and other capacities to work as goods on the labour market. In turn, the market, based mainly on demand and supply of types of labour, determines wages and other working conditions.

Following such logic, government officials have increasingly adopted the idea that workers, and labour markets more generally, should be only lightly regulated if they are to function effectively – which is to say, labour markets should

FIGURE 3.1 **Low-wage work by country, 2017**

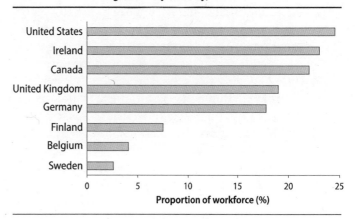

Source: Data from OECD Statistics, "Labour – Earnings – Incidence of Low Pay," https://stats.oecd.org.

be lower cost and more profitable for business. Labour protections such as minimum wages and workers' right to join unions and to bargain collectively are to varying degrees seen as obstacles to competitive labour markets. In this view, employers should have the flexibility to decide wages and working conditions, and the right to hire and fire workers as needed.

While free market approaches to labour markets declined after the Second World War, as unions and more labour-oriented politics grew more powerful, this orientation has become increasingly common once again in Canada and in other countries. This is particularly so since the 1980s, when various dominant political parties and governments began to turn toward neoliberal policies with the goal of enacting a wave of institutional and legal changes that were supposed to loosen the constraints on the economy and free it to grow – but instead worsened jobs and concentrated wealth at the top.

Second, the double-digit inflation of the late 1970s and early '80s threatened both business profits and living standards, which consequently led governments in Canada, the

United States, and the United Kingdom to abandon their commitment to full employment and policies that protected workers. Instead, governments began to emphasize competitiveness and, in that respect, the need for lower labour costs across the workforce.[1] In other words, the inflation crisis in these years was an opportunity for public officials to re-assert capitalist class power by eroding labour rights and social entitlements.

Third, and increasingly, government policy turned to a program of enhanced trade and investment liberalization, labour market deregulation, and **privatization** – selling off of public services and publicly owned industries to private enterprises and multinational corporations. The new policy goal was controlling inflation and boosting economic growth.[2] High unemployment, previously public enemy number one, came to be a tool in fighting inflation. After all, unemployed workers don't consume as much, and those still working moderate their demands for fear that they too will become unemployed. Consequently, the focus of governments began to narrow, concentrating on how to change the rules of labour markets to better suit business and finance. And over the course of the 1990s and 2000s, that meant deregulating labour markets to make them more flexible and cost competitive.

A fourth reason for the growth of low-wage work in recent years lies in workplace developments. In the context of stagnant economic growth through the 1980s and '90s, employers focused on increasing the pace and intensity of work and lowering their labour costs. One of the ways they sought to reshape their workplaces was through flexible employment arrangements that increased the prevalence of shift work and part-time, casual, or seasonal contracts.[3] Part-time and temporary workers were beneficial to firms as they could be paid less, with consequently lower employer obligations to fund benefits like unemployment insurance or a pension plan.

These changes in employment relations had the intended effect. The Organisation for Economic Co-operation and Development (OECD) found that **union density** declined from an average of 20 percent to 17 percent between 1995 and 2010. Over the same period, union density in Canada declined from 28 to 26 percent, in the United Kingdom from 30 to 25 percent, and in the United States from 13 to 11 percent.[4]

A final reason for why low-wage work has become so widespread is the global financial crisis of 2008–9, which exacerbated the trends just described. The share of jobs categorized as low wage rose across the European Union (EU) from 16.7 percent in 2006 to 17.2 percent in 2014. Within the Eurozone (comprising countries using the euro as their shared currency), the rise was from 14.3 to 15.7 percent over the same period. Since the OECD uses a narrow definition of low-wage work that excludes part-time workers, its statistics are a less reliable indicator of low-wage trends, but it nevertheless reports a marked increase in low-wage work for full-time workers in countries including the United States, Canada, the Netherlands, Spain, Germany, and Denmark.[5] Thus, rather than strengthening the labour market and improving wages and working conditions, the combined impact of the policy choices of governments over the past few decades has been to worsen jobs and put the price of a good life out of reach.

LOW-WAGE WORK IN COMPARATIVE PERSPECTIVE

Perhaps most interesting is the way in which particular rules and policies of different countries either amplify or moderate the worst effects of low-wage work and labour market inequality. The degree to which workers are shielded from employer demands for flexibility and broader economic upheavals depends on pre-existing social and economic policies, labour laws, and employment regulations that generate significant protective lock-in or insulation effects.[6] The characterization as "lock-in" captures how historically rooted labour protections can endure. For example, countries that have inclusive labour market institutions and regulatory mechanisms extend the gains won by unionized workers to non-unionized workers and therefore have far lower levels of low-wage work and much greater income equality. Denmark and Sweden are examples. Good minimum wages, employment protection legislation, the enforcement of national labour laws, and benefit systems for the jobless and low-income households also help to ensure that workers find better jobs with better wages and benefits.

So too do good public services and public programs that provide security for workers and their families. Some of the most serious risks people experience – especially relating to health, employment, and income – can be reduced if there is a comprehensive system of public social programs and benefits. And where governments have assumed responsibility for the provision of an expansive set of public goods paid for through a robust system of relatively high taxation, citizens have access to everything from health care to basic and higher education, vocational skill formation, and public transportation. These policies have done much to protect the welfare of workers and the broader population.

Yet countries approach the rules governing labour markets and social policies very differently. The Nordic countries have a history of cooperation and coordination between business, government, and unions, and often a reasonably wide consensus (though this does waver at times) that economic growth, shared prosperity, and good jobs go hand in hand. Labour standards are high, and extensive labour laws and rules ensure that the majority of workers are covered by collective agreements, and that social programs and benefits are generous. Indeed, one of the more distinctive features of these countries is that wages are often negotiated at the sector level – all auto production, all health care, and all retail, for example – with all employers and all workers represented at one bargaining table.[7]

By contrast, governments and business in Canada, the United States, and the United Kingdom have a much less generous perspective on labour market rules and social policies. In these countries, sometimes referred to as *liberal market* economies, public officials are more likely to follow the desire of big business not to be constrained by unions and collective agreements, and businesses generally do not have to abide by employment standards like overtime pay or generous minimum wages.

In these countries, employers attempt to keep their workforces flexible, there are very few unionized workers and unionized workplaces, and managers can hire and fire workers as they see fit. Unsurprisingly, social policy in liberal market economies is understood by business as a burden that undermines their competitiveness as it raises the overall cost of labour.[8] As a result, liberal market economies like that of Canada generally have lower levels of social spending, more meagre benefit programs, and the lowest rates of trade union density.

CANADA AND LOW-WAGE WORK

Canada is often presented as a high-tax, generous welfare state with good public services. But when its political economic makeup is evaluated against that of various European countries, it becomes clear this is not an accurate description (Chapter 4). Certainly, Canada is more socially progressive than the United States. Its public health care system, for example, provides every citizen with access to critical health care services. By contrast, in the United States, 28.5 million people have no health coverage at all, and many more have inadequate private coverage. Similarly, only 27 percent of the unemployed in the United States receive benefits, compared to nearly 40 percent in Canada.

A comparison of collective **bargaining coverage** in Canada and Western European economies nonetheless reveals large differences, with clear implications for the extent of low-wage work. Figure 3.2 shows the relationship between collective bargaining coverage and low-wage work: as the proportion of workers covered by collective agreements rises, the proportion of low-wage work decreases, whereas low-wage work increases as the proportion of collective bargaining coverage declines. In Canada and the United States, where wages are largely set by employers, workers are more than three times more likely to be in low-wage work than in countries such as Finland, Sweden, and

Belgium, where collective bargaining coverage is extended to more than 85 percent of the workforce. Put in this comparative light, the general absence of union representation and protection for the vast majority of the Canadian labour force has very serious consequences, making workers especially vulnerable to low pay.

Similarly, comparing social expenditures in Canada and the United States to those in Western Europe makes it obvious that more generous social policies are also crucial to improving jobs and wages. Figure 3.3 demonstrates that when higher proportions of a country's gross domestic product is directed to public social expenditures – like health care, childcare, employment insurance, housing, and family support – fewer workers are in low-wage employment. This is because more generous and supportive social policies typically force employers to compete with social benefits by paying better wages. And in countries where more of the workforce is unionized, unions have very effectively pressured governments to increase and maintain social policy expenditures. Again, in this comparative perspective, Canada is very similar to the United States, with among the lowest commitments to public social services (less than 20 percent of GDP), and one of the highest levels of low-wage work.

Figure 3.2 situates Canada among a cluster of countries where the incidence of low-wage work also corresponds to comparatively low trade union density. The declining density of trade union membership, particularly so in the private sector, speaks to the need for union campaigns to reverse this in conjunction with public policies to facilitate trade union organizing.

Figure 3.3, which compares the incidence of low-wage work with the proportion of state expenditure on social programs, shows us that Canada, in comparative terms, again fares poorly. The casual observation is that the liberal market economies (Canada, United States, UK,

FIGURE 3.2 **Low-wage work and collective bargaining coverage 2017**

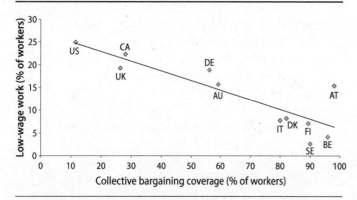

Note: AT = Austria, AU = Australia, BE = Belgium, CA = Canada, DE = Germany, DK = Denmark, FI = Finland, IT = Italy, SE = Sweden, UK = United Kingdom, US = United States.

Sources: OECD Statistics. "Decile Ratios of Gross Earnings: Incidence of Low Pay" and "Collective Bargaining Coverage," *Labour Force Statistics.* https://stats.oecd.org/. Accessed on May 9, 2022; Mason and Salverda 2010.

Ireland) spend less on social programs and have higher incidences of low-wage work than countries such as Germany, Austria, Denmark, Belgium, Sweden, Italy, and Finland. Since 1945, the latter countries have applied a policy of economic coordination between the state, capital, and labour, which we may loosely characterize as social democratic.

LOW-WAGE WORK AND THE PANDEMIC

Through the COVID-19 pandemic, Canadian political leaders turned to the phrase "We're all in this together" to give expression to the need for national solidarity in the face of a crisis that was unprecedented since the end of the Second World War. The lived experience of the pandemic presented a more fragmented picture, revealing a sharp distinction in how low-wage workers, primarily women and racialized minorities, were affected by the social and economic disruption created by the virus. Economic polarization over the past forty years has given rise to a variety of morbid symptoms in socio-economic and political terms, but the government response to the pandemic flew in the face of neoliberal dogma.

First, unemployment increased rapidly and dramatically – especially in the service sector – as Canadian governments ordered the complete closing of large parts of the economy. In May 2020, two months into workplace closures, the official unemployment rate had risen to 13.7 percent. The significance of this number requires some historical perspective, as it marked the highest level of unemployment in the entire post-1945 period. Even the very deep recessions of the early 1980s and '90s brought high-water marks of 13.1 percent unemployment in 1982 and 12.1 percent in 1992. Following the global financial crisis of 2008, the number of unemployed in Canada crested at 7.4 percent in 2009 before gradually declining.[9] One must reach back to

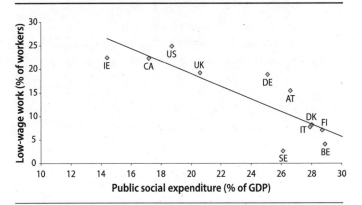

FIGURE 3.3 **Low-wage work and social expenditure, 2017**

Note: AT = Austria, BE = Belgium, CA = Canada, DE = Germany, DK = Denmark, FI = Finland, IE = Ireland, IT = Italy, SE = Sweden, UK = United Kingdom, US = United States.
Source: OECD Statistics. "Social Expenditure Aggregated Data," *Social Expenditure Database*. https://stats.oecd.org/Index.aspx?DataSetCode=SOCX_AGG. Accessed on May 9th, 2022.

the Great Depression to find higher unemployment: a historic and unbroken high of 19.3 percent in 1934.[10]

From a global perspective, unemployment levels have also spiked. European economies experienced the most significant contraction in history, with close to 60 million jobs lost by mid-2020 on top of pay cuts and reductions in hours worked.[11] At the same time, the United Nations warned that some 1.5 billion workers in the informal economy of the Global South were at risk of job loss – nearly half of the global workforce.[12]

In Canada, the overall pandemic unemployment rate masked the extent to which low-wage workers bore a disproportionate economic burden. Among workers earning $16 per hour or less prior to the closures, more than 50 percent either lost their jobs or lost a majority of their working hours as working time was cut back in response to the restrictions.[13] The COVID-19 recession also came to be termed the *she-cession*, given the comparatively large number of women affected. By July 2020, female participation rates in the labour force had dropped to their lowest level in thirty years.[14] As schools, food and beverage, retail, and hospitality sectors closed, jobs held disproportionately by women made up 62 percent of the total number lost through February and March.[15] By the end of April 2020, the mid-point of the first wave of lockdowns, 5.3 million women had lost their jobs – 61 percent of all workers who lost employment due to the lockdowns.[16] The gendered challenges of combining working from home with childcare and other responsibilities was widely noted.

A variety of additional metrics underline the degree to which Canadian precarious workers were adversely affected through the pandemic. Employment levels for temporary workers dropped 30.7 percent, compared to 16.1 percent for those with permanent status. Non-union workers employment fell by 21.2 percent against 10.2 percent for union members.[17]

Recovery from the pandemic is expected to do little to address the expansion of precarious employment. As one analyst noted, "If existing trends hold, then the post-pandemic recovery will involve massive numbers of Canadian workers being thrust into increasingly precarious working conditions."[18]

THE PROBLEMS OF CANADA'S MINIMUM WAGE

Low-wage labour in Canada and the United States is complicated by the legal authority of both national and provincial or state governments to set a minimum wage. Some US cities also possess the power to set local minimum wages that apply to their own employees, external contractors, and/or all workplaces within a given jurisdiction. By contrast, although some Canadian municipalities can set minimum wages for their own employees or subcontractors, they cannot do so city wide. The Canadian labour movement is somewhat stronger than

that in the United States in terms of union density and social democratic political representation – in the form of the New Democratic Party (NDP) – but an inadequate minimum wage system has combined with highly restrictive union certification procedures and laws that allow firms to evade employment standards legislation. That makes it much more likely that workers will be stuck in low-wage "McJobs" with few prospects for career advancement or income security.

As of January 1, 2019, the highest minimum wage in Canada was in Alberta ($15) and the lowest in Saskatchewan ($11.06).[19] At the same date, five US states had no minimum wage: Alabama, Mississippi, Louisiana, South Carolina, and Tennessee. The lowest minimum wages were $5.15 per hour in Georgia and Wyoming, while the highest were in Massachusetts at $12 per hour (scheduled to move to $15 per hour on January 1, 2023), and Washington at $12 per hour.[20] The federal US minimum wage is $7.25. Despite state-level approval of pittance wages, in the United States the higher of either the state or federal minimum applies, which means that the actual enforceable wage in no- and low-minimum-wage states is $7.25. Forty-one local governments in the United States have adopted a city minimum wage rate above the state rate.[21]

As in the United States, minimum wages in Canada can be described as a political moving target that is negotiated in multiple and often conflicting ways across the political landscape. Fluctuations across the country are marked by a pattern of rise and fall: the average minimum rose substantially in constant dollars from 1965 to 1976, fell in the late 1970s and first half of the '80s, levelled off in the late '80s, gradually recovered in the first part of the '90s, and then flattened between 1997 and 1999 before falling slightly in 2000 and 2001.[22]

One way to think about provincial minimum wages and whether they do in fact provide the minimum someone could live off is to look at the proportion of workers who earn minimum wage in any given province. From 1997 to 2014, the number of Ontario workers earning the minimum wage grew by nearly 400 percent, and by the end of that period, 695,000 workers in the province held a minimum wage job.[23] Moving beyond the statutory minimum wage, a 2018 study by the Alberta government using $15 per hour or less as a low-wage cut-off found that more than 20 percent of all Canadian workers were in fact low waged. From the highest proportion of low-wage workers to the lowest by province, the study found the following rates of low-wage work:

- Nova Scotia, 30 percent
- New Brunswick, 28.2 percent
- Prince Edward Island, 27.7 percent
- Newfoundland and Labrador, 25.4 percent
- Manitoba, 23.4 percent
- Ontario, 22.2 percent
- Quebec, 20.6 percent
- British Columbia, 19.5 percent
- Saskatchewan, 18.5 percent
- Alberta, 13.5 percent.[24]

At 8.6 percent, Ontario had the highest proportion of workers earning the statutory minimum wage out of the ten provinces as of 2017. In other Canadian provinces, the figures were as follows:

- Prince Edward Island, 7.8 percent
- Nova Scotia, 7.8 percent
- Newfoundland and Labrador: 7.3 percent
- New Brunswick, 7.2 percent
- Alberta, 6.4 percent
- Quebec, 6.2 percent
- Manitoba, 6.0 percent
- British Columbia, 4.8 percent
- Saskatchewan, 2.8 percent.[25]

A Statistics Canada study in early 2018 found that the proportion of minimum-wage workers had risen from 6 percent in early 2017 to 10 percent of all employees.[26] What's more, close to one in three minimum-wage workers today has a postsecondary degree, up from one in four twenty years earlier. To put it differently, despite ongoing investments in postsecondary education, the proportion of minimum- and low-wage workers continues to rise year after year as the share of middle-income earners erodes and income inequality increases.

MINIMUM VERSUS LIVING WAGES

The central critique of the minimum wage is that it has proven to be an ineffective policy instrument to address low-wage work because provincial governments (which, for the most part, set the minimum) have been unable for political reasons to adjust the rate upward to reflect income adequacy. The result is that the minimum wage in every province and at the federal level is far from meeting the real needs of low-wage workers, and many remain stuck in working poverty. Demands for living wages have emerged in response.

A living wage, unlike the minimum wage, takes into account such factors as quality of life and well-being. In short, it is both economically and socially beneficial. A living wage is calculated by taking into account the actual costs of housing, transportation, and raising children in a specific location. For example, in Toronto, the living wage for 2018 was at $21.75 per hour, substantially higher than the $14 per hour general minimum wage at the same time.[27]

In assessing the adequacy of a given minimum wage level, the 2006 Federal Labour Standards Review recommended considering it in relation to basic poverty levels or standards of living.[28] Previous research in the United States found that raising minimum wages to a level approximating a living wage resulted in both higher individual incomes and more hours worked.[29] The most extensive gains went to entry-level workers, whose average wages and personal savings rose. But workers experienced other improvements, such as quality-of-life factors like time spent with family and improved health.[30] When the minimum wage was increased to a living wage in Boston, New Haven, and Hartford, the proportion of workers living in severe poverty dropped from 34 percent to 13 percent between 1998 and 2001, while the number of families considered poor also decreased from 41 percent to 28 percent.[31]

Those opposed to raising minimum wages to a level of income adequacy argue that statutory increases will result in job losses and reduced hours of work, will benefit only younger

---

BOX 3.1   DID A MINIMUM WAGE HIKE KILL JOBS IN ONTARIO?

In late 2017, the Liberal government of Kathleen Wynne passed Bill 148, the Fair Workplaces, Better Jobs Act, 2017. Among various changes to employment standards, the bill included provisions requiring employers to pay part-time, casual, and temporary employees at the same rate as full-time employees doing the same job, and to pay workers three hours' wages for shifts cancelled with less than forty-eight hours' notice. The bill also stipulated that all workers would be eligible for ten days of emergency leave, two of which must be paid. Perhaps the biggest news, however, was that the minimum wage would increase to $14 per hour on January 1, 2018, and to $15 per hour by 2019.

In the lead-up to the passage of the legislation, the business community had warned that it would lead to catastrophic job losses. A paper commissioned by the Ontario Chamber of Commerce claimed that 185,000 jobs would disappear in the first two years, while a TD Bank analysis predicted a loss of up to 90,000 jobs. Restaurants Canada and the Fraser Institute labelled Bill 148 a "job killer," contending that it would reduce employment opportunities and lead to layoffs. Even the Financial Accountability Office of Ontario predicted some 50,000 job losses.

Fast-forward a year and what actually happened? Ontario added 78,000 new jobs, bringing the unemployment rate down to its lowest in nearly twenty years. Some employers, such as Tim Hortons franchise owners, did retaliate by cutting shifts, breaks, and even jobs. They were met with a significant public backlash and threats to boycott the very profitable company. (Even parent company Restaurant Brands International lashed out at "rogue" franchises.) Despite this open class war, jobs grew across the labour market as a whole, in particular full-time work, while total hours worked in the food and accommodation services industry actually increased year over year.

In the end, the dire predictions of the big business lobby turned out to be a misleading attack against living wages. This did not stop the incoming Conservative government of Doug Ford from repealing the planned minimum wage increase to $15. Bill 47 froze the minimum wage at $14 until at least 2022 and eliminated paid sick days, equal-pay-for-equal-work provisions, and rules that made it easier to join a union.

What might these political swings say about the strengths and limitations of protective labour legislation? Is more needed to defend and extend workers' rights?

---

workers dependent on their parents, and will do little to alleviate working poverty. Whether assessed internationally, domestically, or in localized contexts, however, there is little evidence to support such claims. Close to 40 percent of minimum-wage workers are adults over the age of twenty-five and thus well into their working lives.[32] Numerous studies have shown that higher minimum wages boost demand, improve productivity by raising workplace morale, and lower business costs related to employee turnover, training, and absenteeism.[33]

Implementing living wages may also have positive effects beyond employees directly affected, as other workers may receive wage boosts along with lower-paid workers. This upward pressure on wages can often enhance labour's bargaining power and help redistribute wages to low- and median-wage workers across the labour market. The fight for living wages has also deepened and extended labour–community coalitions, strengthening networks of resistance in a coordinated push for progressive political reforms across cities and communities. Finally, living wage campaigns have also raised awareness about the persistence of low-wage work and precarious employment more generally, extending these conversations to the growing gap between rich and poor.

There is little evidence to support the often-heard assertion that firms respond to higher wages by reducing the number of employees, cutting hours, reducing training, or shifting to part-time work. On the contrary, minimum wage increases have been found to combat working poverty, particularly for vulnerable workers. And employers paying living wages have found that they lead to increased employee skills development and performance, higher job satisfaction, improved staff retention, and long-term reputational benefits.[34]

COMBATTING LOW-WAGE WORK, STRENGTHENING BARGAINING POWER

The International Labour Organization (ILO) marked its centenary in 2019. Now with 187 members, the United Nations agency sets international labour standards and advocates for enhanced work opportunities and social protections. Central to the ILO's 100-year history has been an emphasis on improving jobs through collective bargaining – that is, by institutionalizing labour laws that allow independent unions to negotiate with employers over their conditions of employment, wages, working time, and methods of dealing with conflicts in the workplace. The ILO has thus sought to uphold collective agreements, which are signed by both parties and outline the rights and responsibilities of both employees and employers. In this way, collective agreements typically go above and beyond basic employment standards legislation and statutory minimum wages.

Collective bargaining has generally been the foundation of the postwar class compromise. The postwar class compromise refers to the period following the end of the Second World War when most liberal democratic capitalist states adopted a range of reforms to institutionalize trade union rights, worker protections such as workplace health and safety standards, and minimum employment standards governing hours of work, paid vacations, sick leave, and much more. It also saw the expansion of public services including health care, education, and social services.[35] It emerged as a public policy tool to stop the downward spiral of wage competition, institutionalize methods for resolving conflicts, and empower workers, giving them some control over their working conditions. In effect, collective agreements extend the rule of law to the workplace.[36] And in doing so, compensation in unionized workplaces is far more equitable, with higher wages for lower-paid workers and less of a wage gap for women, younger workers, and racialized groups. Unionized workers are also more likely to have full-time, permanent positions and to work longer for their employers. Finally, unionized environments tend to be safer, with increased support services and lower rates of critical injuries, mobility impairments, lost time due to injury claims.

As researcher Susan Hayter and scholar Jelle Visser have argued, in the postwar period, "It was considered desirable that the norms and rules negotiated between organized employers and the union(s) be made generally applicable."[37] In other words, that these negotiated standards be made applicable to all workers and workplaces whether or not they were unionized. In the wake of neoliberalism, that is no longer the case. Precarious and low-wage work is increasingly generalized, as are anti-labour legislation and drastic expenditure reductions to public services. The results have been a continued decline in **real wages** and the erosion of the total labour share of wages.[38]

Better and more egalitarian policies to address this erosion would include enhancements to statutory minimum wages, employment protection legislation, the removal of barriers to unionization, legal restrictions on the use of temporary workers, and equal pay rules that are spread more evenly across the labour market. Further measures that would strengthen working-class economic security are extending unemployment insurance, providing income protection during parental leave, augmenting child and elder care benefits, and ensuring access to affordable housing and free public transit, to name just a few.[39]

Because low-wage work does not appear to be a self-correcting problem, we need to challenge the notional common sense of neoliberalism and confront the wider capitalist context that leaves workers dependent on the priorities of business.[40] If history is any indication, the only force capable of securing a radical redistribution of wealth and power is the same force that secured the postwar class compromise: large-scale mobilization and millions of people demanding change.

RENEWING THE GOLDEN AGE?

The thirty years from 1945 to 1975 are considered by many to have marked a **golden age of capitalism**, and with it a better **social democracy** and a more comprehensive welfare state. Starting roughly with the elections of Margaret Thatcher and Ronald Reagan, that has been followed by four decades of neoliberal restructuring. Perhaps we can label this period the terrible age of neoliberalism, but the point is that the neoliberal era has now run a decade longer than the so-called golden age of class compromise.

The expansion of low-wage work is directly attributable to this change. Upholding the same principles and policies that got us into this mess will not reverse its course. Any substantive reform agenda will have to begin with raising wages from the bottom up.

COVID-19 has been one spur toward such a reform agenda, teaching us a great deal about precarious work and the inequality that is embedded in the occupational structures and the organization of work. In early 2021, the ILO noted that the pandemic had brought the most severe crisis for the world of work since the 1930s.[41] Consequently, the agency has called for a human-centred recovery led by good jobs and focused on improved employment income, workers' rights, and broader social dialogue to promote a transition to a more inclusive, resilient, and sustainable world of work.

So-called unrealistic proposals – like the demand for a living wage – are today the only ones that stand a chance of making a realistic difference. Like their American counterparts,

Canadian workers face labour laws that fail to protect workers and employment regulations that provide little job security and little in terms of sick days or paid parental leave. At the same time, they lack access to good childcare, a secure and accessible employment insurance system, and adequate pension plans. These are political and policy choices – not simple determinants of economic competitiveness.

Better labour laws, better social policies, and better minimum wage policies would all improve jobs and workers' incomes. As the mobilizations of recent years pushing for a $15 minimum wage and better labour laws in both the United States and Canada have shown, despite the small gains such campaigns have achieved we are still a long way from fully realizing these reforms. Instead, the problems of low-wage work, inadequate labour, and poor social policies persist. What replaces them will depend to a large degree on whether trade union and citizen mobilization succeeds or fails in fundamentally shifting public opinion and government policy.

ADDITIONAL RESOURCES

Bernhardt, Annette, Heather Boushey, Laura Dresser, and Chris Tilly, eds. *The Gloves-off Economy: Problems and Possibilities at the Bottom of America's Labor Market.* Ithaca, NY: Cornell University Press, 2008.

Gautié, Jérôme, and John Schmitt, eds. *Low-Wage Work in the Wealthy World.* New York: Russell Sage Foundation, 2010.

Kalleberg, Arne. *Precarious Lives: Job Insecurity and Well-Being in Rich Democracies.* Cambridge: Polity Press, 2018.

John Schmitt. *Low-Wage Lessons.* Washington, DC: Center for Economic and Policy Research, 2012. https://cepr.net/report/low-wage-lessons.

NOTES

1   Jamie Peck, *Constructions of Neoliberal Reason* (London: Oxford University Press, 2010).

2   Susan Braedley and Meg Luxton, eds., *Neoliberalism and Everyday Life* (Montreal and Kingston: McGill-Queen's University Press, 2010).

3   Greg Albo and Carlo Fanelli, "Austerity against Democracy: An Authoritarian Phase of Neoliberalism?" *Teoria Politica: An International Journal of Theory and Politics* (2014): 65–88; Bryan Evans and Carlo Fanelli, eds., *The Public Sector in an Age of Austerity: Perspectives from Canada's Provinces and Territories* (Montreal and Kingston: McGill-Queen's University Press, 2018).

4   OECD Statistics, "Trade Union Density in OECD Countries," 2018, https://stats.oecd.org/Index.aspx?DataSetCode=TUD.

5   Bryan Evans, Carlo Fanelli, and Tom MacDowell, eds., *Rising Up: The Fight for Living Wage Work in Canada* (Vancouver: UBC Press, 2021), 253.

6   James Mahoney, "Path Dependence in Historical Sociology," *Theory and Society* 29, no. 4 (2000): 507–48; James Mahoney and Kathleen Thelen, "A Theory of Gradual Institutional Change," in *Explaining Institutional Change: Ambiguity, Agency, and Power*, ed., James Mahoney and Kathleen Thelen, (Cambridge: Cambridge University Press, 2010), 1–37.; S.E. Page, "Path Dependence," *Quarterly Journal of Political Science* 1, no. 1 (2006): 87–115; Paul Pierson, "The Limits of Design: Explaining Institutional Origins and Change," *Governance* 13, no. 4 (2000): 475–99; T. Rixen and L.A. Viola, "Putting Path Dependency in Its Place: Towards a Taxonomy of Institutional Change," *Journal of Theoretical Politics* 27, no. 2 (2015): 301–23.

7   Torben Iversen and David Soskice, "Politics for Markets," *Journal of European Social Policy* 25, no. 1 (2015): 76–93.

8   Peter Hall and David Soskice, eds., *Varieties of Capitalism: The Institutional Foundations of Comparative Advantage* (Oxford: Oxford University Press, 2001).

9   Statistics Canada, "Labour Force Survey, June 2017," July 7, 2017, Chart 3: Unemployment rates in Canada and the United States, 1976 to 2016, https://www150.statcan.gc.ca/n1/daily-quotidien/170707/cg-a003-eng.htm.

10 David Macdonald, "Canada's Job Losses Reach Great Depression Levels: Here's How We Move Forward," *The Monitor*, Canadian Centre for Policy Alternatives, June 5, 2020, https://monitormag.ca; Geoff Mason and Wiemer Salverda, "Low Pay, Working Conditions, and Living Standards," in *Low Wage Work in the Wealthy World*, ed. Jerome Gautie and John Schmitt (New York: Russell sage Foundation, 2010).

11 Marine Strauss, "McKinsey Predicts Near Doubling of Unemployment in Europe," *Reuters*, April 19, 2020, www.reuters.com; Etienne Schnerider and Felix Syrovatka, "This Eurozone Crisis Will Be Even Worse Than Last Time," *Jacobin*, April 23, 2020, www.jacobinmag.com; Moritza Kraemer, "The Eurozone Is at Risk of a Debt Crisis Worse Than the Last One," *Financial Times*, April 9, 2020, ft.com.

12 United Nations, "Nearly Half of Global Workforce at Risk as Job Losses Increase Due to COVID-19: UN Labour Agency," *UN News*, April 28, 2020, news.un.org.

13 Matt Lundy, "Eight Charts That Explain Canada's Job Devastation – and the Long Road to Recovery," *Globe and Mail*, May 14, 2020, theglobeandmail.com.

14 Tara Deschamps, "Women's Participation in Labour Force Reaches Lowest Level in Three Decades Due to COVID-19: RBC," *CBC News*, July 16, 2020, www.cbc.ca.

15 Erica Alini, "Welcome to the 'She-Session': Why This Recession Is Different," *Global News*, May 9, 2020, globalnews.ca.

16 David Macdonald, "Gender Impact of Canada's Income Supports," *The Monitor*, Canadian Centre for Policy Alternatives, April 27, 2020, https://monitormag.ca.

17 Jim Stanford, *Ten Ways the COVID-19 Pandemic Must Change Work for Good*, Canadian Centre for Policy Alternatives, Report, June 3, 2020, https://www.policyalternatives.ca/publications/reports/10-ways-COVID-19-must-change-work.

18 Bruce Kecskes, "The Coming Precarity: Employment in Canada after the Crisis," *The Bullet*, May 15, 2020, https://socialistproject.ca.

19 Retail Council of Canada, "Minimum Wage by Province," October 2018, https://www.retailcouncil.org/resources/quick-facts/minimum-wage-by-province.

20 National Conference of State Legislatures, "State Minimum Wages," 2019, http://www.ncsl.org/research/labor-and-employment/state-minimum-wage-chart.aspx#Table.

21 Economic Policy Institute, "Minimum Wage Tracker," 2019, https://www.epi.org/minimum-wage-tracker.

22 Ken Battle, *Restoring Minimum Wages in Canada* (Ottawa: Caledon Institute of Social Policy, 2011).

23 Trish Hennessy, "Ontario's Precariat," *Hennessy's Index* (June 2015), Canadian Centre for Policy Alternatives, www.policyalternatives.ca/index.

24 Government of Alberta, "Alberta Minimum Wage Profile April 2017–March 2018," www.work.alberta.ca.

25 Statistics Canada, "Labour Force Survey, December 2018," January 4, 2019, https://www150.statcan.gc.ca/n1/daily-quotidien/190104/dq190104a-eng.htm?HPA=1&fbclid=IwAR0q48rD6uZDYeGMhcsVa7g1hYp9kNgLEdAIRmHUpTxcX3qdXWpkrficOxA.

26 Rene Morissette and Dominique Dionne-Simard, *Recent Changes in the Composition of Minimum Wage Workers*, June 13, 2018, Cat. no. 75-006-X (Ottawa: Statistics Canada, 2018), https://www150.statcan.gc.ca/n1/pub/75-006-x/2018001/article/54974-eng.pdf.

27 Aaron Broverman, "Minimum Wage vs. Living Wage: How Ontario's Cities Stack Up," *TVO*,

November 13, 2015, https://www.tvo.org; Living Wage Employers, "Ontario Living Wage Network," 2018, http://www.ontariolivingwage.ca/living_wage_by_region.

28 Kevin B. Kerr, *Federal Minimum Wages and Low-Income Workers in Canada* (Ottawa: Canadian Electronic Library, 2013).

29 E. Jardim, Mark C. Long, Robert Plotnick, Emma van Inwegen, Jacob Vigdor, and Hilary Wething, "Minimum Wage Increases and Individual Employment Trajectories," NBER Working Paper no. 25182 (2018); Barry Ritholtz, "Labor Market Is Doing Fine with Higher Minimum Wages," *Bloomberg*, January 24, 2019, www.bloomberg.com; Statistics Canada, "Labour Force Survey, December 2018."

30 Michael Reich, Peter Hall, and Ken Jacobs, "Living Wage Policies at the San Francisco Airport: Impacts on Workers and Businesses," *Industrial Relations* 44, no. 1 (2004): 106–38; Deborah M. Figart, *Living Wage Movements: Global Perspectives* (London: Routledge, 2004); Oren M. Levin-Waldman, *The Political Economy of the Living Wage: A Study of Four Cities* (Armonk, NY: M.E. Sharpe, 2005).

31 Mark Brenner and Stephanie Luce, *Living Wage Laws in Practice: The Boston, New Haven and Hartford Experiences* (Amherst, MA: University of Massachusetts, Political Economy Research Institute, 2005).

32 Diane Galarneau and Eric Fecteau, *The Ups and Downs of Minimum Wage*, Cat. no. CS75-006/1-2014-6E-PDF (Ottawa: Statistics Canada, 2014).

33 Evans, Fanelli, and MacDowell, eds., *Rising Up.*

34 Ibid.

35 John Peters, "Neoliberal Convergence in North America and Western Europe: Fiscal Austerity, Privatization, and Public Sector Reform," *Review of International Political Economy* 19, no. 2 (2012): 208–23.

36 David J. Doorey, *The Law of Work: Industrial Relations and Collective Bargaining* (Toronto: Emond Publishing, 2017).

37 Susan Hayter and Jelle Visser, eds., *Collective Agreements: Extending Labour Protection* (Geneva: International Labour Organization, 2018).

38 John Peters, "Labour Market Deregulation and the Decline of Labour Power in North America and Western Europe," *Policy and Society* 27 (2008): 83–98.

39 Brian Nolan, ed., *Inequality and Inclusive Growth in Rich Countries: Shared Challenges and Contrasting Fortunes* (London: Oxford University Press, 2018).

40 John Schmitt, *Low Wage Lessons* (Washington, DC: Center for Economic and Policy Research, 2012), https://cepr.net/report/low-wage-lessons.

41 International Labour Organization, "ILO Monitor: COVID-19 and the World of Work. 7th edition," Briefing note, January 25, 2021, https://www.ilo.org/global/topics/coronavirus/impacts-and-responses/WCMS_767028/lang-en/index.htm.

4 Globalization, Work, and Labour Market Deregulation

John Peters

CHAPTER SUMMARY

Since the onset of the pandemic in 2020, countless working Canadians have been left unprotected and unsafe at work, and millions have been caught in a cycle of low-paid temporary jobs. This chapter argues that workers face such risks in large part because of business-friendly neoliberal polices that have deregulated labour markets in order to lower labour costs for employers.

The chapter begins by discussing the origins of labour law and employment policies, and then examines some causes of the political shift to neoliberalism. It subsequently details the process – embodied differently in different countries – of deregulating labour markets as an outgrowth of the concept that labour laws and related labour and social policies interfere with employers' ability to maximize efficiency and profitability.

The chapter ends with the observation that after forty years, the trend toward deregulation may be ending, as the pandemic has forced governments to implement policies contrary to market supremacy and low-cost labour. At the same time, in the face of economic, climate, and health crises, workers are searching for new solutions, spearheaded by efforts to build back better and to end racial inequality. Such actions may signal new approaches to tackling the problems we face.

KEY THEMES

This chapter will help you develop an understanding of:

- why progressive labour laws and employment policies developed in the twentieth century
- why and how Canada's **labour regime** differs from that of Nordic countries
- the role of business in pushing for major changes to public policy, labour law, and social protection in order to increase workforce flexibility, bring down the cost of labour, and reduce the number of permanent employees
- how neoliberalism has shifted government priorities for the labour market away from equality and toward efficiency and deregulation
- how COVID-19 may spur progressive labour law and public policy change.

OVER THE COURSE OF 2020–22, the COVID-19 pandemic exacerbated inequalities and revealed widespread work insecurity. Nurses and long-term care workers across Canada lacked protective gear and fallen ill. Temporary foreign farm workers were forced to go to work sick, and workers in Alberta processing plants died because of the lack of testing. Transport workers were fired for refusing unsafe work and protesting against the lack of safety procedures. All the while, the ranks of the unemployed swelled by the millions, and workers deemed essential by governments across the country had to put their lives and those of their families in danger for lack of basic protection at work (Chapter 1).

Such developments have only accentuated long-term trends of work insecurity and inadequate health and legal protections for workers not only in Canada but also in other advanced industrial economies.[1] Over the 2010s, more than 40 percent of the Canadian workforce was in low-wage and precarious employment. In the United States, low-wage insecure employment grew to such an extent that more than 45 percent of workers and their families lacked the money to cover rent, food, emergencies, and accidents.[2] In Western Europe, more than 40 percent of young workers are stuck in a cycle of bad jobs, temporary employment, and limited prospects.[3]

We like to think such things cannot happen in a democracy, a system that is supposed to provide not only the right to vote but also the right to be heard by government and to get help when we are in trouble. Democracy, after all, encompasses the right of citizens to form associations that are formally recognized, such as trade unions to give workers a voice in their workplaces and to provide safety on the job. Just as often, we think of democracy as a system in which governments do right by their citizens, ensuring that they are looked after through major crises.

But as the past two centuries have shown, and recent events have again brought to the fore, democracy has always faced two fundamental challenges: the divide between the rich and everyone else, and the ability of ordinary citizens to act collectively to make sure that governments pursue the common good.[4] Too often, democratic political systems have given officials a mandate to act as they please between elections, with little reference to the concerns of citizens, unions, or social organizations. Just as frequently, governments have worked with only the concerns of business top of mind, fearing the consequences of policies that could cause a withdrawal of capital. And this massive imbalance in power has been especially noticeable whenever workers have pushed for better labour laws, social policies, and health and safety protections to guarantee basic fairness and security in their everyday lives – while businesses have attempted to protect their profits and control of resources and workplaces.[5]

Ever since the American (1774–87) and French (1789–99) revolutions, men and women have fought for the right to form associations of like-minded workers, to have some say in what they are paid, to withhold their labour, and to have limits placed on the length of their workday. Only in the aftermath of the Second World War (1939–45) did citizens gain the power to pressure elites into political concessions, and democracies around the world – including Canada – finally took steps to recognize workers' rights and enact policies such as universal health care and public pensions.[6]

Over the past few decades, however, political power has turned again. Now, not only do workers often lack the clout to turn down unsafe work, but employers have the capacity to ignore workers' safety concerns. Trade unions are losing both members and the political muscle to keep laws, institutions, and policies in place that uphold their essential economic and social rights. And even though this turn against economic rights and workers' organizations has occurred unevenly, the general trend – especially in Canada and the United States – has been the weakening, erosion, or non-enforcement of labour laws and employment policies.[7]

Why are labour laws, unions, and employment policies at the heart of the fight for democracy? And why are they under pressure again? This chapter examines each of these questions. First, it investigates the history of workplace rights and policies, along with their implications for democracy and labour market regulation. Second, it compares workplace rights and policies in Canada with those in other countries. Third, the chapter explores how business pressure has led to a neoliberal model of labour market deregulation. Finally, it identifies a possible silver lining of the pandemic: it may actually set the stage for new laws and policies that would improve work and democracy in twenty-first-century Canada.

DEMOCRACY, WORK, AND EMPLOYMENT REGULATION

Democracy is relatively new. A little over 200 years ago, no government was accountable to its people, fair and competitive elections didn't exist, and only aristocrats and the wealthy had the freedom to express their opinions.[8] By the 1920s, some twenty-five countries had developed popular political participation, and adult men, at least, had gained the right to vote and make their voices heard. By 2000, seventy-eight countries had liberal democratic institutions, including Canada, the United States, and all the countries of Western Europe.

The history of more developed – and more progressive – democracies is even more recent. Only since the 1950s have advanced industrial economies recognized workers' right to bargain over wages and working conditions, the importance of a minimum wage, and the rights of all citizens to protection against accident and old age, better health services, and family support. Indeed, only since the 1970s have majorities in the labour force been covered by a wide range of public services and insurance programs. Put another way, it has only been in the past three or four generations that major improvements to the quality of democratic life, as well work and family life, have occurred.[9]

Why has democracy in any version been such a recent development? Part of the explanation is that for centuries, land owners, aristocrats, and militaries ruled the world, and did much to ensure their power over property, people, and commerce continued. The American and French revolutions were the first to begin challenging this old order, and they ushered in a century of rebellion and political change the world over.[10] But even though the idea that the people should be consulted and that governments should be held accountable began to take hold more widely, one thing did not change: people with property had the right to manage their land and businesses as they liked, and did everything in their power to keep their workers from having a say over what they earned and how much they should work.

Workers and families soon challenged this state of affairs using their new ideas of democracy, protest, and political parties. But well into the early 1900s, workers in Canada as well as the United States were routinely charged with "criminal conspiracies" against business if they formed labour unions or walked off the job for better wages.[11] More seriously, striking workers could come face to face with military or police might. If they stayed out on strike, they risked losing their jobs permanently because employers – with public official support – were legally allowed to hire replacements and to blacklist worker activists so that no business would hire them. Democracy between the 1800s and early twentieth century was very much a battle between the will of ordinary workers and those with money, power, and influence.

Two major developments changed the status quo – and changed the nature of politics and what we think of as democracy today. One was the First World War (1914–18) and Second World War (1939–45). These terrible wars of the early twentieth century were not only the deadliest conflicts in history; they also created economies with vast new manufacturing and industrial bases, as well as states with enormous taxing and planning power. In the process they changed the way in which states and citizens interacted, creating nations whose public officials relied on binding consultations with citizens, and governments subsequently had the responsibility to ensure the well-being of all citizens: rich and poor, men and women.[12]

The second set of transformative factors was the emergence of political parties representing socialism, labourism, and social democracy. These new parties represented labour movements and supported the ideal of democracy that worked on behalf of the people.[13] Driven by the broad mobilization of worker communities and through the efforts of Industrial Workers of the World organizers, between 1875 and 1920 unions and labour movements around the world forged political parties to pursue the social well-being of workers and the betterment of society: voting rights, improved water and sewer systems, and legislation that restricted daily working hours and child labour.

For decades, these labour and political organizations faced significant hurdles, and only a very few gained access to government prior to the 1930s. By the 1950s and well into the 1970s, however, political parties of the left were regularly in government in most advanced industrial economies in Western Europe and, backed by trade unions, stayed in power well into the 1990s. The exceptions were Canada and the United States, where labour-associated parties were able to win office only infrequently at the municipal and state or provincial level, never nationally. Canada at least had a designated labour party. The Co-operative Commonwealth Federation (CCF), which was succeeded by the New Democratic Party in 1961, pushed Conservative and Liberal governments of the day toward outcomes with greater social justice.[14]

Adherents of labour-related political parties believed that all people were entitled to a decent life, whether they worked as cleaners or teachers or nurses or on the assembly line. And they believed that all citizens had the right to be involved in managing or having a say in their governments and in the making of public policy. For that vision to be realized, such parties needed to win political power. Only through political channels could they safeguard democracy from inequality and ensure that citizens received adequate medical care, family support, and income security when older or unemployed.[15]

As a result of these two major developments, workers, unions, and associated political parties won important gains in the aftermath of the Second World War. Over the following decades, labour-backed governments – or, as in Canada, governments under pressure from labour parties and trade unions – began to make real efforts to limit the power of big business and the wealthy, while redistributing wealth so that all could benefit. Governments introduced a host of new labour laws, as regulators attempted to maintain full employment while recognizing basic labour rights and improving workplace conditions.[16] For example, governments brought in minimum wages, legislation to encourage the formation of collective agreements, and a range of regulations on layoffs and benefits, all with the goal of limiting the power of employers and significantly improving the wages and jobs of workers.[17]

Social policy too became more than the simple alleviation of extreme poverty. Under pressure from unions, social movements, and political coalitions, governments slowly introduced formal and informal rights entitling citizens to enjoy services not provided by the market, such as health care and pensions.[18]

New economic policies supported this expansion of social programs. Named after British economist John Maynard Keynes, these policies have become known as Keynesian demand management. They are based on his idea that modern capitalism had to be actively regulated by government if countries were to prevent economic crises like the Great Depression of the 1930s, and that governments could use taxation alongside spending on economic infrastructure and public services to spur economic growth and create new jobs.

Moreover, Keynes and other progressive economists and public administrators argued, social policies could serve a dual economic and social justice purpose: on the one hand, they could provide the income and spending the economy needed to function and grow steadily despite market downturns; on the other, they could protect workers and their families against unemployment and accidents, or against difficulties associated with raising a family or growing old and unable to work. Businesses also saw the advantage of such reforms, which encouraged them to invest and foster their prosperity despite the loss of some political power.

THE CANADIAN LABOUR REGIME IN COMPARATIVE PERSPECTIVE

From 1945 until the late 1970s, Canada, the United States, and Western Europe all developed a labour regime consisting of labour rights and accompanying laws and institutions, social security programs, and income security transfers (Table 4.1). Seeking ways to meet workers' demands for a say in their wages and working conditions and at the same time lower industrial conflict and facilitate economic growth, states passed legislation in support of collective labour rights.[19]

Under pressure from unions and progressive political parties, governments established comprehensive and universal programs of unemployment insurance, public pensions, and family allowances that transferred income to those who were unemployed, elderly, or had children. And to guarantee some income security in the face of risks such as gender discrimination or accidents or employers unwilling to sign up to collective agreements, government introduced universal statutory laws and better occupational health and safety policies. Then, by the 1960s, in response to the demands of

TABLE 4.1 **Advanced industrial democracies and the postwar labour regime**

Labour rights	Social security	Income security
Right to associate	Unemployment insurance	Occupational health and safety
Right to collective bargaining	Old age pensions	Minimum wage
Right to organize new workplaces	Family allowances	Pay equity
Right to strike	Child care*	–
Right to union security	Vocational training	–
Right to co-determination*	–	–
Workers' right to sit on corporate board*	–	–

* In Western Europe only

workers in the growing public sector, such as health care and postal services, governments extended collective bargaining rights to their public workforces.[20]

Despite the shared commitment of North American and Western European governments to recognize citizens' rights to better work and make certain that all benefited from greater economic growth, countries differed significantly in how far they went in granting workers greater power, as well as in how much effort they would put into redistributing income and offering social services more equitably. In Sweden, the extension of collective bargaining across entire industries and sectors provided unions with the opportunity to organize rapidly to represent workers, and by the mid-1960s, union density (the proportion of workers in a national labour market who are union members and covered by collective agreements) exceeded 75 percent. In Denmark and Belgium, with similar laws to Sweden, union coverage in the 1960s was even higher at 80 percent.

By contrast, in Canada business remained largely hostile to unions and labour law reform. As a result, labour legislation developed in a rather restricted way, with unions able to organize only on a workplace basis (see Chapter 5). This meant they had to work hard at winning the right to represent workers in every work-site, no matter how small or large (see Chapter 7). And labour laws did little to rein in employers who were opposed to unions. Modelled on American labour legislation, institutional hurdles in Canada made it far more difficult than in Europe for workers to organize new workplaces and to extend the benefits of collective agreements more widely. By 1965, union density was only 29 percent in Canada and 25 percent in the United States.[21] Governments in Canada and the United States were similarly reluctant to extend social and income security measures, and by the early 1970s were spending only two-thirds

or less of what countries Sweden and Belgium were on health and social security programs.

Why the divergence? Explanations differ, but as various recent studies have argued, the biggest factors were institutional and political.[22] North American labour movements were highly fragmented. Unions in Canada were more effective than their American union brothers and sisters in winning labour law reforms and better social policies. In the United States, governments and business were even more resolute in opposing unions and progressive labour legislation. Yet in Canada, unions were split between American and Canadian allegiances, by politics, and across the French-English divide.[23] This limited their ability to have a consistent approach to dealing with governments or business, and curbed their strength in garnering the attention of governments and officials.

Given the important role of provincial governments and federalism in establishing labour law and employment policy, that weakness was significant. It also meant that Canadian unions could never develop uniform support for a political party on the left. Unlike Western Europe, Canada never elected a federal social democratic government, and only sporadically elected New Democratic governments at the provincial level.[24]

By contrast, labour movements won major public policy victories in Nordic countries such as Sweden, Denmark, and Norway, where they functioned as an economic and political force.[25] In these countries, unions not only had a role to play in formulating economic and social policy at the top levels of government; they were also integral in helping social democratic parties win office. Unions were seldom fragmented by political beliefs, and instead worked to administer unemployment insurance funds and training for workers across their labour markets. And by the mid-1970s, workers and their unions in Sweden won co-determination, allowing them to elect worker representatives to the boards of directors of large firms.

In these ways and others, European workers became core actors in the political economies of their respective countries, with a major role in redirecting their democracies to prioritize equality and social well-being. Such progress has had significant long-term consequences for social spending, union density, and equality.[26]

NEOLIBERALISM, GLOBALIZATION, AND THE NEW BUSINESS DEMANDS

As the past four decades have shown, neither equality nor democracy are permanent achievements. They must be constantly fought for and defended, won and lost. And in recent years, it has become clear that in Canada – as in much of the world – we are becoming far less equal.[27]

The start of the 1980s brought a transition away from the broad-based postwar support for labour regimes and full employment to a new politics of neoliberalism that prioritized business interests, profits, and the expansion of multinational corporations and global finance. The clearest markers of this shift were the elections of Ronald Reagan (1981–89) in the United States and Margaret Thatcher (1979–90) in the United Kingdom. These two politicians shared a belief in the power of supposedly self-regulating free markets to create better economic outcomes, and in the concept that the actions of government were themselves the problem in society.[28] In Canada, the election of Brian Mulroney (1984–93) federally, the rise of Conservative premiers in the Western provinces, and a Conservative government under Mike Harris (1995–2002) in Ontario signalled a similar shift.

Supported by a change in direction among international economic institutions such as the International Monetary Fund (IMF) and the World Bank, these governments helped reset much of the global economic and political agenda. The new political common sense contended that business regulation and support for workers and citizens were at the root of poor economic growth and unemployment in the late 1970s and early '80s. Following this premise, and under heavy pressure from business and neoliberal elites, political parties began implementing policies, regulations, and institutions that put business concerns first.[29] In Canada, federal and provincial governments started to overturn Keynesian priorities and convert neoliberal ideas into concrete policies

TABLE 4.2 **Comparing policy priorities**

	Keynesian (1945–79)	Neoliberal (1980–present)
Attitude toward government	Necessary for market regulation and development of social goods	Inefficient for market growth Reforms required to stimulate business, trade, and investment
Economic goals	Full employment Regulation of finance Expansion of public expenditure	Low inflation Free trade and deregulated finance Low corporate taxation
Attitudes toward social policy	Essential for citizens and equality Social programs reduce social risk, improve income distribution, and ensure steady economic growth	Impediment to economic growth Social program generosity should be reduced Reforms needed to promote employment and individual responsibility Citizens to pay fees for public services

and programs that allowed business to grow globally and lower all their costs, from taxes to labour and tariffs (Table 4.2).[30] In terms of social policy and income security, neoliberal frameworks meant governments were shifting away from programs and services that provided for collective well-being in favour of making society "fit" for competition and weaning citizens off government support.[31]

What accounts for such a wholesale shift in politics and policy? One can point to the serious economic problems of the late 1970s and early '80s – soaring price inflation, low growth, and spiking unemployment, a combination referred to at the time as *stagflation* – in marked contrast to the high economic growth and low unemployment of the postwar years. So too rising public debt was seen as a burden on productive sectors of the economy, and tax cuts and the retrenchment of public services were considered necessary for growth.[32] But equally notable was the expansion of business power.[33]

As inflation rose, business profits declined through the 1970s and into the 1980s. At the same time, workers went on strike in unprecedented numbers for wages that kept pace with inflation, and business worried about unsustainable labour costs. The result was a major counteroffensive. Corporate elites poured vast new resources into politics – not just to lobby on particular bills but also to shape the political climate. Business massively increased its political giving, expanding the capacity of business-oriented political parties to gain power and make the case for economic policies that best helped markets and firms. To top it off, business money cultivated a cadre of lawyers, accountants, and consultants who were committed to advancing a deregulatory and tax-cutting agenda.

Of equal significance was the decline of private-sector unions and organized labour.[34] With widespread globalization and corporate

restructuring, Canadian workers lost manufacturing jobs and the economy was deindustrialized. Neither Canada nor the United States had particularly strong labour movements, and even from these low starting points unions in the private sector experienced a rapid decline. In Canada, the figure went from 26 percent in 1980 to 14 percent by 2016, and once powerful and politically active private-sector unions lost hundreds of thousands of members.

The near disappearance of organized labour in the private sector has left a majority of workers with little opportunity for advancement, and with fewer resources to push for better wages or more progressive government policies. Consequently, unions in Canada struggled to defend existing institutions and policies, and workers were largely marginalized from participation in the political process. It is this decline of organized labour – the core equalizing institution in pluralistic societies – that provides an equally important explanation for why Canadian governments turned their policy making away from labour and toward capital.[35]

The upshot of such a business-led transformation of government was profound.[36] Over the past few decades, the goals of democracy have been slowly reversed as governments become increasingly fixated on making their societies more competitive. Powerful multinational corporations, businesses, and employer organizations have pushed for governments to cut taxes, reform key aspects of the postwar labour regime, and turn a blind eye to employers who compete on the basis of low-wage and precarious employment contracts.

LABOUR MARKET DEREGULATION

Though the issue is subject to much debate, scholars note that there is a great deal of evidence suggesting a long-term convergence in labour and employment policies across countries over the past few decades.[37] According to critical observers, this convergence has been due to rightward ideological shifts that emphasize private property, individual freedom, and market competition. More market-oriented observers suggest that the impetus has come from economic pressures that make "pure equity" policies harder to sustain in the absence of an efficiency rationale for business profitability.[38] Others argue that business the world over faces greater competition and consequently requires lower labour costs, along with economic policies that promote offshoring and technological changes that reduce the need for high-cost labour.[39]

Regardless of the cause, since the 1980s – as governments signed trade deals, eliminated capital controls, deregulated financial markets, and privatized state enterprises – public officials were undoubtedly left with fewer and fewer macroeconomic policy tools with which to adjust to economic conditions, support workers, and create a more equitable distribution of income.

Subsequent policy prescriptions for labour market deregulation and notional economic competitiveness were then rooted in an ideological stance that was both pro-business and anti-union.[40] Following standard neoclassical economic theories that claim any interference in markets produces less than optimal outcomes, governments attempted to make labour and social policies conform more closely to market and business priorities.[41] Just as frequently, officials simply let **non-standard employment** and labour insecurity grow, fearing that any countermeasures will not be good for business. These developments have meant that deregulation – the unwinding, erosion, and limited enforcement of laws, policies, and regulations governing labour markets – is now the dominant labour market policy paradigm around the world. The economic success of countries, it is now claimed, depends on the willingness of policy makers to expose labour to wider market forces.

What have these shifts meant for the postwar regime of robust labour rights and social

TABLE 4.3 **Role of government in labour markets**

Policy area	Keynesian (1945–79)	Neoliberal (1980–present)
Labour rights and wages	Legislate new labour laws Set wages collectively Stabilize income and macro-economy	End wage rigidity Restrict labour laws and labour rights Improve firm profitability Lower inflation Freeze minimum wages
Employment protection	Expand employment protection Regulate working hours Increase incentives for firms to hire full-time workers	Limit employment protection Permit flexible working hours Recognize and expand temporary labour contracts
Income and social security	Expand income and social security programs Improve collective well-being Manage economic downturns	Limit and reduce income and social security programs Increase incentives for workers to re-enter job market Limit accessibility to unemployment benefits

Sources: Colin Crouch, "The Neo-Liberal Turn and the Implications for Labour," in *The Oxford Handbook of Employment Relations: Comparative Employment Relations,* ed. Adrian Wilkinson, Geoffrey Wood, and Richard Deeg (New York: Oxford University Press, 2014), 589–614; Guy Standing, Beyond the new paternalism: Basic security as equality. (New York: Verso, 2002).

and income security policies? Often a great deal.[42] For example, under the neoliberal paradigm, unions and collective bargaining institutions are seen by employers as artificially raising the price of labour and creating workplace rigidities that inhibit them from responding to consumer demand and competitive market pressures (Table 4.3). To correct this, governments have routinely attempted to dismantle or overhaul collective bargaining institutions. Similarly, employment protection laws such as those mandating overtime and severance payouts, and employer social costs like unemployment insurance (typically retitled "employment insurance") or pensions, are said to inhibit firms from maximizing efficiency by prohibiting rapid adjustments to their labour forces with changing market conditions. Government-enacted reforms therefore provide employers with greater leeway to bargain individually with workers, or to allow employers to opt out of collective agreements altogether and to hire and fire workers as needed.[43]

Major shifts in labour policy that favour business can likewise be seen in regulations that used to provide support for good jobs and full-time employment. Now, official priorities give employers more freedom in the types of employment contracts available to them, with options to hire workers on a part-time, temporary, or self-employed basis. In Canada, this has been achieved by weakening employment standards and creating more temporary foreign worker contracts.

Finally, governments have gone along with business-friendly economic theories that transfer responsibility for income security and job loss back to individuals. Rather than maintaining a safety net that provides social and income security if workers are laid off, have an accident at work, or retire, governments have instead adopted employment models that emphasize individual responsibility and activation:

implementing policies that press individuals to re-enter the labour market regardless of the problems they face (see Chapters 9 and 12).[44] As a result, unemployment benefits and income security programs have been reduced, benefit duration cut, and access restricted to income supports – all in order to increase incentives, or activate individuals so that labour markets will function more smoothly for business.

What are the broader consequences of such labour market reforms? Opinions differ, but some suggest such changes – as well as the failure to introduce more positive and countervailing reforms – have tilted the balance of power firmly away from workers and strongly toward employers who have the interest and capacity to influence policy.[45] These policy changes have sharpened the division between economic winners and losers and are at the root of poorer-quality jobs and the rise of low-wage work.[46]

A CHANCE TO RESHAPE LABOUR MARKETS AND SOCIETY?

Throughout 2020–21, each day often brought news of innovative policy developments that would have been seen as impossible even a year earlier. Unlike the global financial crisis of 2008, Canada and other countries reacted quickly to the economic slowdown and enacted an unprecedented set of fiscal and social policies (Chapter 1). In Canada and the United States, new unemployment insurance benefits – with more adequate minimums – were extended to millions of workers suddenly thrown out of work. Across Western Europe, governments established or extended job retention schemes that allowed companies to cut hours of work, or even halt work entirely, while keeping workers officially employed and in receipt of benefits.[47] Some governments funded rent moratoriums that prevented landlords from collecting rent and banks from collecting mortgage payments.

Others strengthened or extended paid sick leave programs. Even temporary, self-employed, and part-time workers and students – routinely excluded from income-support programs in the past – were provided with financial support as they were among the hardest hit by employer layoffs. Such progressive interventions only a year earlier were regularly disparaged by government officials as "economy wrecking."

Strikingly, these developments echo earlier periods of history when crises ushered in change for the better.[48] The Great Depression and the Second World War led to the mass mobilization of workers pushing for dramatic new policies like unemployment insurance, universal health care, and family support. So too flu epidemics led governments to develop national health care services. At such moments of great crisis, what is broken in a society is revealed, and citizens unite to win major reforms and political progress. Similarly, it appears there is no going back to normal following the current pandemic. Citizens are now mobilizing to demand that governments take action to avert disaster from viral threats and climate change, and to fix our societies and economies.

If the scope of progressive changes related to COVID-19 has been impressive, however, it is important to keep in mind both the immediate business response and the long-term trends. By the fall of 2020, the United States had terminated its supplementary benefits, and in the spring of 2021, new benefits passed by the Joe Biden administration provided only short-term income support. In Canada, the federal government wound down its pioneering Canada Emergency Response Benefit (CERB) in the fall of 2020 and replaced it with a suite of programs that left millions of recipients worse off, and another half million with no federal income supports at all.[49] The ending of the program came after intense lobbying by business associations that claimed CERB was a disincentive for workers to return to their jobs as the benefit was higher than the minimum wage.[50] Similarly, business associations across the country lobbied provincial officials not to introduce paid sick days, arguing the additional costs would only hurt their businesses and in the long term lead to more layoffs. Thus, precarious workers were often forced to go to work regardless of how they or their family members were feeling (chapters 1 and 5).[51]

Such developments mirror longer trends. The financial crisis of 2008–10 and the recession of the early 1990s, for example, brought pro-business government intervention aimed at maintaining the primacy of big business and financial markets.[52] Indeed, the last four decades of economic history have generally been a story of governments taking advantage of crises to systematically weaken public services, hamstring regulatory bodies, lower taxes for the wealthy, and incrementally undermine union power and labour laws. Although the COVID-19 crisis may pose a threat to neoliberal policy solutions, and the temporary introduction of policies may help workers and the broader society, it is just as clear that business and governments alike have long been able to rapidly adapt to crises while upholding the principles of market primacy and business profitability.

RESTORING EQUALITY

Can these trends be reversed? Could more balanced and egalitarian policies be adopted? And will health, climate, and employment crises force governments and businesses to address these complex issues with longer-term thinking and comprehensive solutions that involve good social protections, sustainability, and equality?

As the Organisation for Economic Co-operation and Development (OECD) and the IMF have recently reminded the world, the sooner major reforms are enacted, the better off everyone will be.[53] Both of these international organizations have recognized the unfairness of the class divide between professionals able to work in the comfort and safety of their homes during the pandemic and those who are either employed in low-paid precarious work or now unemployed and facing an uncertain future. But so too both organizations point out that unless workers are protected and the unemployed provided with stable incomes, some people will be forced back to work earlier than is safe, while others will face eviction and long-term job loss. Such trends pose long-term economic problems – problems that can only be solved if governments carry forward the momentum for progressive change and deliver the sustainable policy improvements necessary for healthy and secure workplaces.

Another silver lining of the recent crisis is its exposure of the fallacy that governments cannot act for fear of upsetting markets and growth. Canadians – and workers the world over – now understand that when pushed, governments can in fact do extraordinary things to protect them, and business will have to go along.

Finally, another cause for optimism lies in union activity. Unions have been pushing for new rights and powers for workers. In Canada, they have begun to campaign for paid sick leave for all workers, better health and safety monitoring and compliance, and short-term work benefits. The leading private-sector union, Unifor, has launched a policy to overhaul labour laws and industrial policy as a clean energy economy is developed. So too the United Steelworkers have worked tirelessly across North America to promote comprehensive policies for jobs, training, and industry in their efforts to achieve a sustainable economy and a Green New Deal. And activists everywhere are protesting against racism and police brutality, and calling for the redirection of law enforcement funding into education, parks, health care, and training and childcare programs.

The problem is not a lack of progressive policy options or evidence that worker-friendly and democratic policies bring broad benefits. Rather, the major problems lie in politics – and above all the power of corporate monopolies and finance to influence democracy and public policy. For even though the pandemic has allowed more people than ever to connect the dots between problems and solutions, organized labour is finding it increasingly difficult to provide an effective counterweight to the efforts of large corporate actors to thwart worker-friendly legislation – a problem made acute during the pandemic as layoffs caused trade unions to suffer large membership losses.

Countering these problems in both the short term and the future will be a challenge. But as the history of the past century has shown, these hurdles are not insurmountable. What is required is political action and mobilized citizens – broad social and political movements that can pressure governments to enact policies to protect workers from the consequences of precarious work and the global pandemic.

ADDITIONAL RESOURCES

Crouch, Colin. *Post-Democracy*. Cambridge: Polity Press, 2006.

Eidlin, Barry. *Labor and the Class Idea in the United States and Canada*. New York: Cambridge University Press, 2018.

Luce, Stephanie. *Labor Movements: Global Perspectives*. Cambridge: Polity Press, 2014.

Western, Bruce. *Between Class and Market: Postwar Unionization in the Capitalist Democracies*. Princeton, NJ: Princeton University Press, 1997.

NOTES

1 Arne L. Kalleberg, *Precarious Lives: Job Insecurity and Well-Being in Rich Democracies* (Cambridge: Polity Press, 2018).

2 David R. Howell and Arne L. Kalleberg, "Declining Job Quality in the United States: Explanations and Evidence," *RSF: The Russell Sage Foundation Journal of the Social Sciences* 5, no. 4 (2019): 1–53.

3 Patrick Emmenegger, Silja Häusermann, Bruno Palier, and Martin Seeleib-Kaiser, "How We Grow Unequal," in *The Age of Dualization: The Changing Face of Inequality in Deindustrializing Societies*, ed. Patrick Emmenegger, Silja Häusermann, Bruno Palier, and Martin Seeleib-Kaiser (New York: Oxford University Press, 2012), 3–26.

4 Jacob Hacker and Paul Pierson, *Let Them Eat Tweets: How the Right Rules in an Age of Extreme Inequality* (New York: Liveright Publishing, 2020).

5 Eric Hobsbawm, *Workers: Worlds of Labour* (New York: Pantheon Books, 1987).

6 Bruce Western, *Between Class and Market: Postwar Unionization in the Capitalist Democracies* (Princeton, NJ: Princeton University Press, 1997).

7 Kalleberg, *Precarious Lives.*

8 David S. Potter, David Goldblatt, Margaret Kiloh, and Paul Lewis, *Democratization*, vol. 2 (Cambridge: Polity Press, 1997).

9 Christopher Pierson, *Beyond the Welfare State? The New Political Economy of Welfare* (Pittsburgh: Penn State Press, 1998); Goran Therborn, *European Modernity and Beyond: The Trajectory of European Societies, 1945–2000* (Thousands Oaks, CA: Sage, 1995).

10 Eric Hobsbawm, *Age of Revolution: 1789–1848* (London: Hachette, 2010).

11 Craig Heron, *The Canadian Labour Movement: A Short History* (Toronto: James Lorimer and Company, 2012); Judy Fudge and Eric Tucker, *Labour before the Law: The Regulation of Workers' Collective Action in Canada, 1900–1948* (Toronto: University of Toronto Press, 2004).

12 Eric J Hobsbawm, *Age of Extremes: 1914–1991* (London: Little Brown and Company, 1995).

13 Bhaskar Sunkara, *The Socialist Manifesto: The Case for Radical Politics in an Era of Extreme Inequality* (London: Hachette 2019).

14 Donald Sassoon, *One Hundred Years of Socialism* (London: I.B. Tauris and Company, 2010).

15 Sunkara, *The Socialist Manifesto.*

16 Harry Arthurs, "National Traditions in Labor Law Scholarship: The Canadian Case," *Comparative Labour Law and Policy Journal* 23, no. 3 (2002): 645–78; Judy Fudge, "The New Discourse of Labour Rights: From Social to Fundamental Rights," *Comparative Labour Law and Policy Journal* 29, no. 1 (2007): 29–66.

17 Western, *Between Class and Market.*

18 Pierson, *Beyond the Welfare State.*

19 Western, *Between Class and Market.*

20 Christoph Hermann and Jörg Flecker, eds., *Privatization of Public Services. Impacts for Employment, Working Conditions, and Service Quality in Europe* (New York: Routledge, 2012).

21 Barry Eidlin, *Labor and the Class Idea in the United States and Canada* (New York: Cambridge University Press, 2018).

22 Ibid.; Patrick Emmenger, *The Power to Dismiss: Trade Unions and the Regulation of Job Security in Western Europe* (New York: Oxford University Press, 2014); Kathleen Thelen, *Varieties of*

Liberalisation and the New Politics of Social Solidarity (New York: Cambridge University Press, 2014).

23 Heron, *The Canadian Labour Movement;* Bryan D. Palmer, *Working-Class Experience: Rethinking the History of Canadian Labour, 1800-1991* (Toronto: McClelland and Stewart, 1992).

24 Western, *Between Class and Market.*

25 Gerasimos Moschonas, *In the Name of Social Democracy: The Great Transformation: 1945 to the Present* (New York: Verso 2002).

26 Evelyne Huber and John D. Stephens, *Development and Crisis of the Welfare State: Parties and Policies in Global Markets* (Chicago: University of Chicago Press, 2001).

27 Facundo Alvaredo, Lucas Chancel, Thomas Piketty, Emmanuel Saez, and Gabriel Zucman, *World Inequality Report 2018* (Cambridge, MA: Belknap Press of Harvard University Press, 2018).

28 Manfred Steger and Ravi K. Roy, *Neoliberalism: A Very Short Introduction* (New York: Oxford University Press, 2010).

29 David Harvey, *A Brief History of Neoliberalism* (New York: Oxford University Press, 2006).

30 Stephen Clarkson, *Uncle Sam and Us: Globalization, Neoconservatism, and the Canadian State* (Toronto: University of Toronto Press, 2002); Bryan Evans and Charles W. Smith, eds., *Transforming Provincial Politics: The Political Economy of Canada's Provinces and Territories in the Neoliberal Era* (Toronto: University of Toronto Press, 2015).

31 Bob Jessop, *The State: Past, Present, Future* (Cambridge: Polity Press, 2016).

32 Andrew Glyn, *Capitalism Unleashed: Finance Globalization and Welfare* (New York: Oxford University Press, 2006).

33 Colin Crouch, *Post-Democracy* (Cambridge: Polity Press, 2006); Jacob Hacker and Paul Pierson, *Winner-Take-All Politics: How Washington Made the Rich Richer - And Turned Its Back on the Middle Class* (New York: Simon and Schuster, 2010).

34 Jake Rosenfeld, *What Unions No Longer Do* (Cambridge, MA: Harvard University Press, 2014); David Camfield, *Canadian Labour in Crisis: Reinventing the Workers' Movement* (Halifax: Fernwood Publishing, 2011).

35 John Peters, *Jobs with Inequality: Financialization, Post-Democracy, and Labour Market Deregulation in Canada* (Toronto: University of Toronto Press, 2022).

36 Crouch, *Post-Democracy*; Alice Martin and Annie Quick, *Unions Renewed: Building Power in an Age of Finance* (Medford: Polity Press, 2020); Jane McAlevey, *A Collective Bargain: Unions, Organizing, and the Fight for Democracy* (New York: HarperCollins Publishers, 2020).

37 Rafael Gomez and Morley Gunderson, "The Integration of Labour Markets in North America," in *Capacity for Choice: Canada in a New North America*, ed. G. Hoberg (Toronto: University of Toronto Press, 2002), 104-28; Lucio Baccaro and Chris Howell, *European Industrial Relations: Trajectories of Neoliberal Transformation* (New York: Cambridge University Press, 2017).

38 Gomez and Gunderson, "The Integration of Labour Markets."

39 Harvey, *A Brief History of Neoliberalism.*

40 Rebecca Gumbrell-McCormick and Richard Hyman, *Trade Unions in Western Europe* (New York: Oxford University Press, 2013).

41 Colin Crouch, "The Neo-Liberal Turn and the Implications for Labour," in *The Oxford Handbook of Employment Relations: Comparative Employment Relations*, ed. Adrian Wilkinson, Geoffrey Wood, and Richard Deeg (New York: Oxford University Press, 2014), 589-614.

42 Lucio Baccaro and Sabina Avdagic, "The Future of Employment Relations in Advanced Capitalism: Inexorable Decline?" in *The Oxford Handbook of Employment Relations*, ed. Wilkinson, Wood, and Deeg, 701-25.

43 Baccaro and Howell, *European Industrial Relations.*

44 Amilcar Moreira and Ivar Lodemel, "Governing Activation in the 21st Century," in *Activation or Workfare? Governance and the Neoliberal Convergence*, ed. Amilcar Moreira and Ivar Lodemel (New York: Oxford University Press, 2014), 289–326.

45 Lane Kenworthy, *Jobs with Equality* (New York: Oxford University Press, 2008); Hacker and Pierson, *Winner-Take-All Politics*.

46 Guy Standing, *The Corruption of Capitalism: Why Rentiers Thrive and Work Does Not Pay* (London: Biteback Publishing, 2016).

47 IMF, *World Economic Outlook Update, June 2020: A Crisis Like No Other, An Uncertain Recovery* (New York: International Monetary Fund, 2020), https://www.imf.org/en/Publications/WEO/Issues/2020/06/24/WEOUpdateJune2020; OECD, *OECD Employment Outlook: Worker Security and the COVID-19 Crisis* (Paris: OECD Publishing, 2020), https://doi.org/10.1787/1686c758-en.

48 Jacob Hacker and Paul Pierson, *American Amnesia: How the War on Government Led Us to Forget What Made America Prosper* (New York: Simon and Schuster, 2017).

49 David Macdonald, "Transitioning from CERB to EI Could Leave Millions Worse Off," *The Monitor*, Canadian Centre for Policy Alternatives, September 15, 2020, https://monitormag.ca.

50 Canadian Federation of Independent Business, "Getting Canadians Back to Work Will Require Significant Changes to Wage Subsidy and CERB Programs," June 10, 2020; Business Council of Canada, "Letter to Finance Minister Morneau Outlining Measures to Boost Public Confidence and Help Set the Stage for a Lasting Economic Recovery," June 23, 2020; Pedro Antunes, "Extend Wage Subsidy Program, Not Individual Response Benefits," *Globe and Mail*, July 9, 2020, theglobeandmail.com.

51 Amanpreet Brar, Carolina Jimenez, and Gaibrie Stephen, "No Paid Sick Days, Unvaccinated Workers, the Rise in COVID-19 Variants: Perfect Conditions for a Deadly Storm," *Toronto Star*, March 31, 2021, thestar.com; Alex McKeen and Celiana Gallardo, "'It's Like You're Forced to Go to Work': Three Ontario Workers on What It's Like to Not Have Paid Sick Days," *Toronto Star*, April 28, 2021, thestar.com.

52 Colin Crouch, *The Strange Non-Death of Neo-Liberalism* (Cambridge: Polity Press, 2011).

53 OECD, *OECD Employment Outlook 2020*.

Part 2

THE POLITICS OF LABOUR POLICY

5 Provincial Governments and the Politics of Deregulation

John Peters

CHAPTER SUMMARY

Over the past few decades, it has been common for Canadian provincial governments to implement changes that deregulate labour markets and weaken worker voice: that is, to undermine labour law protections, ignore new and growing problems in workplaces and labour markets, and encourage employment flexibility that allows companies to focus on profits rather than on better jobs and wages for their workforce.

To understand why and how provincial officials have pursued such policies, it's necessary to examine key factors in the contemporary political system that are associated with post-democracy: the influence of business, the declining sway of unions and citizens, and the strategies that allow conservative, business-friendly parties to divide citizens and distract them from economic policies that do not help them. Post-democratic politics is essential to explaining what is behind provincial labour policy reforms in recent decades, and why governments have been so successful at ignoring citizens' interests and workplace concerns.

KEY THEMES

This chapter will help you develop an understanding of:

- the rise of income inequality in Canada
- how a political shift toward post-democracy has allowed elected representatives to entrench labour market laws and policies that disadvantage workers and citizens
- how growing business power to influence governments is shaping public policies that foster low-wage, insecure, non-unionized jobs
- how provincial governments have deregulated labour markets and employment relations in three different ways: legislative and policy reform, policy drift, and layering-in
- how governments have used the pandemic to reinforce labour market deregulation.

OVER THE PAST COUPLE of decades, income inequality has increased rapidly across the Canadian labour market, in large part due to the growth of low-wage, **non-standard** employment at the expense of secure, well-paying jobs. Some provincial governments have promoted this development by reforming provincial labour laws and employment policies to conform more closely to business priorities, others by passively allowing labour markets to drift toward low wages and non-standard jobs, or others still by layering-in new employment policies and regulations that are not covered by labour legislation.

Why and how have they done so? Democracy, we think, is supposed to create harmony between what citizens want and what governments do, as politicians respond to popular majorities. But as inequality grows and governments double down on deregulation, the citizen-government relationship seems characterized by dissonance instead.

Post-democracy explains these seemingly contradictory developments. Provincial political systems increasingly orbit the most right-wing elements of the business lobby. At the same time, organized labour and the public have lost the resources they need to exercise democratic citizenship. Canadian political culture today is marred by growing public distrust of government and feelings of powerlessness related to widening social and economic inequality. These changes to democratic politics help to explain why governments have embraced business priorities and not only failed to pass legislation to counter rising inequality but also deregulated labour markets by rolling back, watering down, or contravening progressive labour laws and employment policies.

THE CHALLENGE OF INEQUALITY

The impacts of rising income inequality on liberal democratic countries such as Canada can be seen in many different ways.[1] The distribution of income influences everything from educational attainment and life expectancy to rates of drug addiction and crime, levels of social trust, and health. The greater income inequality is, the worse it is for people's everyday lives – not just for the poorest but at *every* income level.[2] Societies with more equal distribution of income tend to experience more stable economic growth and investment, as well as much higher levels of overall prosperity. Conversely, income and wealth inequality disfigure democracies by giving the wealthy the means to influence governments while undermining the democratic participation of citizens and the policies that share prosperity.

Nowhere can the problems of inequality be seen more clearly than in the experience of visible minorities in Canada both on and off the job during the pandemic. Across the country, racialized workers have been far more likely than their white counterparts to contract the coronavirus, roughly twice as likely to feel the effects of layoffs, and more likely to encounter health and safety failings on the job.[3] The case of Cargill High River meat-processing plant in Alberta is typical; because of a work-while-sick culture, more than 1,000 immigrant and racialized workers contracted COVID-19.

The problems of inequality can also be seen in government reaction to the outbreak by funnelling billions of dollars into financial markets and corporations rather than jobs (Chapter 1). Both the federal and provincial governments enabled unprecedented corporate borrowing while allowing companies to lay off millions of workers. As stock prices soared, workers in entire industries were unemployed almost overnight, with little regard for their skills or performance.[4] It is clear from such developments that while Canadians all faced the same storm, not all in were in the same boat – or any boat.

Over the past thirty years, Canadian governments have done little to counter rising inequality. Not since the 1930s has top income inequality (and the income disparities between the richest 1 percent of income earners and the bottom 90 percent of workers) been greater than today.[5] Canada is at an extreme among advanced industrial countries in terms of top income shares, lagging behind only the United States.[6]

Figure 5.1 demonstrates the scale of this disparity. In 2014, average household income before taxes and government transfers (such as pensions and welfare payments) was $62,350. But this figure hides massive differences in income distribution. For the 6.7 million families who make up the bottom half of Canadian income earners, earnings averaged just $18,100, a third of the average family income. Those at the top – and especially at the very top – made huge income gains. Whereas in 1992 the richest 1 percent had incomes twenty-six times larger than the average household in the bottom 50 percent, by 2014 the figure was forty-six times greater.

This soaring gap between the rich and everyone else is partly explained by recent public policy changes to finance, banking, housing, and real estate that have benefited an elite few. But the growth of low-wage, non-standard jobs is a significant contributor as well.[7] Two of every five Canadian workers work in non-standard employment and earn less than one-third of the average full-time worker's annual pay: that is, less than $15,000 per year (Figure 5.2). Among advanced economies, Canada stands out as having one of the greatest wage and income disparities for those in non-standard work.[8]

THE POLITICS OF INEQUALITY

Theoretically, such developments should not occur. If inequality increases and jobs and working conditions worsen, citizens in a democracy

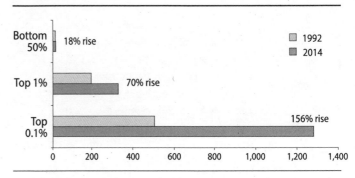

FIGURE 5.1 **Average Canadian real household incomes ($000), 1992 and 2014**

Source: Data from Statistics Canada, "Market and After-Tax Incomes of Economic Families T1 Family File Tax Data."

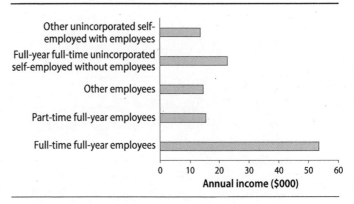

FIGURE 5.2 **Annual earnings in standard and non-standard employment, 2015**

Source: Data from Statistics Canada, Canadian Income Survey, "Percentage of Workers with Low Annual Earnings and Low Hourly Wages, by Industry, Canada, 2012–2015."

could be expected to respond by demanding and winning reforms.[9] In turn, politicians are supposed to listen and then make policies in ways that help the majority. The reality is different.

Some citizen groups have indeed tried to improve the economic system. For example, the Fight for $15 movement to raise the minimum wage in the United States and Canada has grown significantly, and even won some

BOX 5.1 INDICATORS OF INEQUALITY

For years, discussions of income inequality typically focused on the Gini coefficient. However, as a single number defining inequality from 0 to 100, the Gini provides only a very general sense of how full-time workers and their families are faring, what taxes and transfers are doing to reduce inequality, and how one country compares to another. As recent scholarship has pointed out, analysis that relies only on Gini coefficients gives little indication of how unequal a country has become or how rapidly inequality has risen.[10]

A more nuanced analysis looks at what is happening among the richest – those in the top 1 percent of income earners – and among the millions in low-wage work. Assessing income distribution in this way is a more informative and practical approach to understanding the growing gap between the rich and the working poor.[11]

Researchers therefore use tax data to track income trends. In Canada, the top 1 percent comprises about 250,000 households, and their tax information reveals a striking picture of soaring incomes. At the other end of the spectrum, data specific to the lowest 10, 20, 30, or 40 percent of the labour force can be used to track low-wage work trends. Using the wage and tax data of both full-time employees and those in various kinds of non-standard employment gives researchers a better handle on the widening divide between those in good jobs and those in bad ones, and typically in low-wage work.[12]

There is no standardized definition of low-wage work across countries, but the Organisation for Economic Co-operation and Development (OECD) defines low pay as less than two-thirds of median hourly earnings for full-time workers.

notable victories in recent years (see Chapter 16). However, most governments across North America have not responded favourably. Newly elected Conservative governments in Ontario and Alberta in the past few years have immediately passed "open for business" legislation that cut or froze minimum wages, removed paid sick days, and loosened legislation for employers to pay workers less.[13] More broadly, provincial governments have done nothing to strengthen labour laws or social protections during the pandemic, and in general officials have ignored union calls to enact paid sick days and refused to make it mandatory for employers to provide personal protective equipment.

Researchers have attempted to make sense of these puzzling and often counterintuitive developments by reference to the concepts of *post-democracy* and *winner-takes-all politics*.[14]

According to these theories, capitalism and democracy are often in profound conflict with each other. Business wants policies that will improve profitability and growth, while workers and citizens want policies that will support good jobs and incomes and create equal, secure societies. As business interests have gained the resources to actively corrode the workings of democracy, however, workers and citizens have either lost the resources to succeed at interest-group politics or been politically marginalized because of widening inequality and growing public cynicism. To make matters more difficult, conservative parties often mix business-first economic priorities with right-wing cultural appeals that divide citizens on the basis of race, nationalism, or immigration.[15]

As a consequence, firms now have unparalleled access to public officials and play a central role in carving out business-friendly public policy. As citizens grow more divided and distracted, business and elites have shifted government policies and political resources increasingly in their own favour. Although elections can lead to minor policy changes benefiting labour for a time, the story of democracy has become about government catering to those with money; the priorities and preferences of everyone else come a distant second – if they are considered at all.[16]

When crafting such policies and regulations, public officials often highlight racial, ethnic, and racial divisions and play on outrage to emphasize social conflicts. In turn, governments and political parties justify business-led priorities as being in the broader public interest because they help provincial and national economies to compete against the economies of other provinces and countries. Provincial officials also tend to oppose new or existing national programs and policies as being too costly or unnecessary, and blame unions or poverty activists as outside influences. In reality, ministries regularly deliver flexible, minimally regulated labour markets with readily available low-cost and low-wage labour, while drastically undermining the working and living conditions of many in the workforce.[17]

In the Canadian context, four notable trends have accompanied post-democracy: growing business influence on politics and public opinion; the corresponding turn of political parties toward business owners and the wealthy, reinforced by declining citizen political participation; the waning ability of unions and organized labour to protect worker-oriented labour and social policies; and government adoption of various policy models to benefit business interests at the cost of better jobs and a more egalitarian distribution of income.

These post-democratic developments can be most clearly seen at the provincial level, because Canada has one of the most decentralized federal systems in the world and provincial governments are responsible for a significant share of tax, transfer, and public service programs.[18] Provincial governments also oversee the majority of labour and employment policies. In general, provincial officials have direct jurisdiction over nine out of ten Canadian workers through labour laws that govern collective bargaining for unionized workplaces. In addition, through their legislative powers provincial governments set out labour regulations such as minimum wages, basic employment standards, health and safety requirements, and pay equity rules for non-unionized, private-sector employees. Because of this leading provincial role, it is not surprising that business organizations have much success in shaping the labour policy priorities of provincial officials.

BUSINESS PRIORITIES AND LOBBYING

Over the past few decades, business organizations – from large to small – have increased their involvement in political and policy issues.[19] In part, this agenda has focused on expanding managerial control over workers and lowering labour costs. As more firms in Canada compete in American and global markets, managers have become increasingly concerned with keeping domestic wages below those of international competitors.[20] In the service and hospitality sectors (hotels, retail, and food services), branding and advertising costs have skyrocketed, leading employers to look for savings – often by fissuring their employment relations using subcontracting, franchising, and self-employed agency workers to reduce labour costs.[21] At the same time, the growth of global firms and operations with financial obligations in sectors across the labour market has prompted employers to vigorously oppose all proposals that would improve labour laws or employment standards and potentially raise wage and benefit costs.

Added to this, small businesses across Canada have similarly opposed higher minimum wages and employment standards. Agricultural producers – under pressure from corporate retailers to supply cheaper produce – frequently try to cut their labour costs by importing cheap, easily controlled temporary foreign workers from low-wage countries in the Global South.

Looked at more generally, such employer opposition to higher labour standards is rooted in attempts to eliminate the union-based industrial relations system that workers organized in Canada after the Second World War. To achieve this, the business lobby has put enormous new efforts into provincial politics, not just to influence specific bills but also to reshape the political culture. Across the country, the number of lobbyists has grown. For example, 914 business lobbyists were registered in Ontario in 2000, and 150 firms directly lobbied the government. By 2010, over 1,900 business lobbyists held more than 5,900 meetings with government officials, including more than 1,300 meetings with the premier and other senior officials.[22]

The Canadian Chamber of Commerce (CCC) has also expanded and now represents over 420 chambers across the country and more than 192,000 businesses. The CCC campaigns in all provinces to reduce corporate taxes, cut government social spending, increase policy supports for business competitiveness, and restrict minimum wage increases.[23] Likewise, Restaurants Canada (formerly the Canadian Restaurant and Foodservices Association) has offices in all provincial capitals in order to lobby officials and oppose increases to the minimum wage, stop improvements in union certification procedures, and hold up employer pension contribution increases.

Further advancing business interests, major firms and employer associations have established public coalitions and launched campaigns to oppose labour legislative reforms and shape public opposition. In 1992 in Ontario, for example, employer organizations including the Canadian Manufacturers Association, as well as agricultural and small business associations, joined the All Business Coalition and the More Jobs Coalition to campaign against a short-lived labour reform bill put forward by the New Democratic Party (NDP) government. In 2015–17, the Keep Ontario Working coalition, led by the Ontario Chamber of Commerce and backed by hotel, restaurant, and small business associations, campaigned vigorously against proposed legislation to increase the minimum wage, provide sick days for part-time and temporary workers, and institute new notice rules for shift work. The anti-union Openshop Contractors Association has also established business coalitions in British Columbia, Saskatchewan, and Ontario to eliminate union certification procedures and protections. Such business coalitions are also common in the agricultural sector, as producers try to block collective bargaining reforms.

Then there is the "war" of ideas, where corporations have provided research institutes with large grants to conduct research and advocacy on the benefits of tax competitiveness, free trade, and labour market deregulation.[24] Free market corporate think tanks such as the multimillion-dollar Fraser Institute and the C.D. Howe Institute flood the media with research reports, opinion editorials, and news releases touting the benefits of tax cuts and weaker labour laws and employment policies. They assert that their national media coverage is three times that of pro-labour think tanks.[25]

Finally, over the past three decades, Canadian businesses have also poured vast resources into influencing elections and promoting business-friendly politicians and parties. At a time when election campaign costs are rising dramatically, right-wing political parties and politicians have been relying ever more heavily on these corporate donors.[26] There are few provincial constraints on party financing, especially in non-election years and leadership and nomination races. In the oil- and gas-rich provinces of Alberta, Saskatchewan, and Newfoundland and Labrador, for example, there are no limits to political contributions, and pro-business parties enjoy enormous fundraising advantages over pro-labour parties. This is used to full advantage during elections: in these three provinces, business-aligned parties take in more than half of all political donations. Their main donors are businesses and business executives.

The results have been that over the past twenty years, right-wing parties have outspent all competing parties combined by at least a two to one margin. In Ontario and British Columbia, business donations to the dominant Liberal and (in Ontario) Conservative parties are now typically fifteen times the sums that unions provide to the New Democratic Party. This surge in corporate political resources has done much to shift the balance of power in favour of business interests in Canada's provincial legislatures.

THE DECLINING POLITICAL POWER OF ORGANIZED LABOUR

In stark contrast, the political power of organized labour has declined in step with the rise of business political power. In the past, the success of unions in winning labour law reforms contributed significantly to greater social equality, particularly income equality, by increasing wages especially for the lowest-paid workers and strengthening the social wage through policies such as public education, health care, and unemployment insurance.[27] Social scientists have shown that organized labour has had enormous impact on the advancement of labour law and social programs across countries.[28] And labour unions with large memberships and close ties

to progressive political parties have often won better labour legislation and more generous social programs. From this perspective, democracy works far better when unions and economic rights are strong.

But even though unions have launched attempts to renew their strength, the Canadian labour movement as a whole has lost ground in step with labour movements around the world (see Chapter 16).[29] Overall union density is falling, particularly in the private sector. In the 1970s, close to a third of all private-sector employees belonged to unions, and the dominant trend was steadily rising wages not only for unionized workers but also for non-unionized workers who benefited indirectly as their employers increased their wages and benefits to keep up with these gains. Today, private-sector union density has fallen to 14 percent (the lowest since the 1920s), unions rarely strike, and many unions and workers have little experience of mass struggle and solidarity.

To add to these difficulties, union membership losses have reduced membership dues, depleting union financial and staff resources. Lacking the money, unions have been unable to mount the sophisticated lobbying and public relations campaigns that are commonplace to business. Consequently, private-sector unions in particular lack the resources to lobby governments, conduct public research, and defend workers against the efforts of business lobbies.

The relationship between organized labour and the NDP, and between labour and the Parti Québécois (PQ) in Quebec, has also begun to fray. During the heyday of union expansion in the 1960s through to the early 1980s, unions in Western Canada and Quebec helped form provincial governments.[30] These NDP and PQ governments consulted unions on key policies, and to varying degrees tried to counterbalance business influence on public policy by passing worker-friendly labour laws and social policies.

Some governments also set up public corporations to provide a range of public benefits, from resource development to public transportation.

Union relationships with the NDP and the PQ have weakened considerably in recent years, however, in large measure because of increasingly sharp disagreements over policy and legislation. In the 1990s, with the election of four NDP and PQ governments across the country during a major economic downturn, unions expected government policies to provide greater job protection, more jobs, better pay and benefits for public-sector workers, and improvements to public services. In the context of business attacks and weakening economic conditions, these left-of-centre provincial governments turned instead to deficit reduction and public-sector labour reforms. This led unions to split into pro- and anti-government factions, undermining worker support for these centre-left political parties and eroding organized labour's political strength.[31]

Financial and institutional links between unions and their once supportive political allies were also weakened over the 2000s, as unions split over the best political strategy to pursue and which political parties to support.[32] The Canadian Auto Workers, now recast as Unifor, shifted away from supporting the NDP in favour of so-called strategic voting, backing specific candidates – whether Liberal, Green, or Bloc or Parti Québécois – who it deemed had the best chance of winning individual ridings. As a result, the parties of the left have largely distanced themselves from unions and the world of work, leaving them with little in terms of distinctive political principles.

This trajectory has, in turn, fundamentally fragmented the political interests and power of the labour movement. For with the ongoing de-unionization of the private sector and diminished union political advocacy, fewer unions are committing substantial resources to party politics. That means fewer workers actively involved in get-out-the-vote drives and other election activities, and fewer unionized workers talking with friends, family members, and neighbours about better policy alternatives. On many issues, both union and non-union workers have been left without any clear political party champion. This deterioration in union–political party relations has strengthened post-democracy in Canada, accelerating public policy shifts away from reducing income inequality and toward promoting the interests of employers and the corporate sector.

CITIZENS OF POST-DEMOCRACY

Why are workers in bad jobs with stagnant incomes – and citizens more generally – not working together to push for better labour laws and employment policies? Part of the answer is the political fragmentation of the labour movement, which has led to a strange situation in which the majority of people typically act against their own economic best interests. At the same time, many better-off citizens are motivated by concerns about growth and the opportunity to buy homes, or see their identities in terms of us versus them – where *them* includes the poor and immigrants. Among those with high incomes, a focus on protecting and building wealth is often connected to beliefs about individual competition, playing by the rules, and proper respect for social betters.[33] Each of these developments means that there is ever greater political polarization among citizens, each heading in a different direction.

Worsening this divide is rising income inequality, which has numerous and widespread negative impacts on citizens' political involvement, weakening everything from everyday civic participation and social cohesion to the degree of compassion people feel for others and their sense of common interest with other citizens and community members.[34] Most critically, income inequality erodes trust in governments to do the right thing, whereas when fewer people live in poverty and equality is higher, more people tend to vote, contributing in turn to stronger support for public services and social programs.[35]

In Canada, the corrosive impact of inequality is especially evident in non-union workplaces and more flexible workplaces, where workers in non-standard employment are often anxious and marginalized, with little time and even fewer resources to participate in politics. Consequently, in province after province, as low-wage work and income inequality have risen, overall voter turnout has declined, even while citizens with high incomes turn out in great numbers.[36] The consequences for democracy and public policy are immense. Without strong political participation by low-income citizens, parties and politicians turn to the minority who do vote: the affluent, professionals, and small business owners.[37]

At the same time, the political priorities of many middle-class Canadians focus on taxes (and tax cuts), and policies that support home ownership or provide a boutique set of tax credits for sports, tuition, and investments.[38] Often those who are professional, educated, and in well-paying jobs vote for the pro-business parties. And while many support policies to improve public health care and public school systems, others oppose increased welfare transfers to the poor. Among this better-off voting public, typically two-thirds or more vote for centre and centre-right parties such as the Liberals and Conservatives, or for business-oriented provincial parties such as the Saskatchewan Party or the Coalition Avenir Québec.[39] These voting preferences help to explain why provincial governments are so unresponsive to the policy needs of the poor and workers in non-standard employment, and why

provincial officials largely oppose the policy priorities of organized labour.[40]

Adding to these trends in post-democracy is the growing power of the wealthy and their influence on policy making. Political parties in Canada have always been business oriented by virtue of their funding sources, business participation, and party personnel. But the soaring wealth of the very rich has tilted politics further in this direction because at the top, the political voices of the affluent and highly educated have grown louder and more frequent.[41]

Most comparative studies find that very high-income individuals prefer less wealth redistribution and lower taxes, especially in the form of cuts to taxes on dividends and capital gains. They also favour free trade and deregulation and tend not to support universal social programs financed by taxes.[42] And unlike poorer Canadians, they can back up their positions with serious money, contributing substantially to provincial electoral campaigns. This too has led to a major shift in democratic politics – with political parties moving emphatically away from mobilizing a broad public and toward targeting their efforts at securing affluent contributors while courting extreme, nationalist, anti-immigrant, or pro-gun single-issue activists.

POST-DEMOCRACY AND LABOUR MARKET DEREGULATION

The trend of political accommodation of business interests, alongside the influence of small business owners and a shrinking middle class, has led to a range of policies – corporate tax cuts, trade liberalization, and financial deregulation – to support markets and firms in their efforts to remain competitive (see Chapter 6). In turning their attention to business priorities, some provincial governments have focused on direct **labour market reform**. Others have refused to update labour policies and procedures:

a case of policy drift. And still others have taken the approach of layering-in new policies, such as permitting greater inflow of temporary foreign workers or welfare-to-work schemes that forcethoserequestingsocialassistancetotakelow-paying, low-skill, often precarious jobs.

Provincial officials have used these strategies to keep citizens in the dark about their policy priorities for deregulation, and to gradually divide the workforce by marginalizing some workers or targeting others for special entitlements. In these ways, governments can introduce unpopular labour laws and employment policies and then sustain support for them. Similar patterns can be seen in provincial government responses to the COVID-19 outbreak.

Reform

In enacting major reforms of their labour markets, governments in British Columbia, Alberta, and Saskatchewan in the early 1980s were the first movers. In these provinces, Social Credit and Conservative governments intervened directly to restructure the labour market and shrink the public sector.[43] By changing labour legislation, they made it harder for unions to organize and harder for non-unionized workers to get ahead by freezing minimum wages, justifying such policies with the argument that they were bolstering the freedom of employers to control wages and hire and fire workers.

Right-wing provincial governments also launched major labour policy changes during the 1990s and 2000s to reverse pro-labour legislation enacted by previous NDP governments. In the mid-1990s in Ontario, for example, the Conservative government repealed laws that barred companies from hiring replacement workers (or scabs) during strikes, rescinded collective bargaining rights for agricultural workers, and made it easier for employers to interfere with union organizing.[44] In 2007, the

---

BOX 5.2 POLICY REFORM IN SASKATCHEWAN

With the election of Premier Brad Wall (2007–18) and the right-of-centre Saskatchewan Party, the province immediately embarked on major labour law and public policy reforms. These included terminating members of the provincial labour board who were seen as too sympathetic to labour and rewriting labour laws.

With respect to the private sector, the 2007 Trade Union Amendment Act overhauled union certification procedures, replacing a simple card-check system with a vote and granting managers the right to "communicate" to employees during organizing drives. These and other changes made the province one of the most difficult in which to organize new workplaces, most notably in the construction sector. In 2014, the Saskatchewan

Employment Act loosened restrictions on employer use of overtime and scheduling while indexing it to inflation in such a way that the minimum wage remains among the lowest in the country.

In the public sector, the government enacted the Public Service Essential Services Act, giving itself the power to restrict collective bargaining rights for public-sector workers whose services were deemed essential. In 2012, the Saskatchewan Federation of Labour launched a Charter challenge against the laws at the Supreme Court, which ultimately ruled that the legislation was not permissible in its existing form. It was a minor setback for a government that had otherwise succeeded in gutting labour and bargaining rights.

Saskatchewan Party government curtailed the right to strike for public-sector workers, and made it harder for workers to join or form a union, while allowing construction firms to set up non-union affiliates to circumvent their unionized workforces.[45] In Ontario in 2018, the Conservative government rolled back numerous Liberal policies that had provided minimum wage increases, legislated paid emergency leave for non-unionized workers, and set out new scheduling rights for workers in non-standard employment. The Conservatives also reduced the power of the Ontario Labour Relations Board and made union organizing more difficult. In making all such reforms, provincial government emphasis was on promoting business interests while weakening the role of unions and undermining policies that provided greater security for workers on the job.

Drift

Another way in which public officials have deregulated labour markets is through drift: inaction or blocking policy updates in the face of major deteriorations to workplace trends and income stability.[46] Because government officials often prefer to avoid direct political fights when they enact unpopular policy reforms, it can be easier to use indirect measures to weaken labour laws and employment standards. For example, provincial governments often reduce employers' costs by delaying increases to the minimum wage. In Ontario, the real minimum wage (the value of the wage once inflation is accounted for) was $9.93 an hour in 1975. In 2010, the real minimum wage was still only $10.25 an hour. The minimum wage has thus effectively been frozen for over thirty years.[47]

Governments also provide employers with a free hand to pay workers substandard wages, contrary to normal legal requirements, by reducing the number of workplace inspectors and workplace inspections.[48] Fines are also minimal and are seldom levied on small businesses with few employees.

Another drift pattern is the lack of regulation of temporary work agencies that provide larger enterprises with services such as cleaning, security, and clerical work. These temp agencies officially employ some three-quarters of a million workers in Canada. When provincial officials undertake inspections, they frequently find that agencies fail to pay temp workers overtime, public holiday pay, or vacation pay. The bigger firms that hire these workers meanwhile evade responsibility for workplace protection, compensation premiums, or payroll taxes such as deductions that contribute to Canada's Employment Insurance program.[49]

A final regular drift tactic is the enactment of back-to-work legislation in order to freeze the wages and benefits of public-sector workers. Despite collective agreements that ostensibly give these workers the right to bargain collectively and the right to strike, provincial governments routinely introduce legislation to limit public-sector pay and lower public-sector labour costs.[50] Back-to-work legislation has been employed in every province in Canada multiple times in order for governments to impose settlements. Most notably in Quebec in the 1980s, and again in the early 2000s, Liberal governments enacted back-to-work legislation to impose wage and job cuts and to freeze wages. Since 2007, when the Supreme Court ruled that all workers have a constitutional right to bargain collectively, governments have used this tactic less often, although they still do so when strikes are prolonged and bargaining negotiations are notionally at an impasse.

In these and other ways, provincial governments have achieved greater labour market flexibility for employers. Rather than resort to across-the-board deregulation, officials have simply failed to update labour policies, frozen collective agreements, and left numerous workers

BOX 5.3 POLICY DRIFT IN ONTARIO

The Conservative government of Mike Harris in Ontario (1995–2002) claimed that the province's slow growth was the consequence of its industrial relations and employment regulations, and actively attempted to reduce the scope of unions while reforming employment standards to improve labour market flexibility. When the Liberal government of Dalton McGuinty came to power (2003–13), more labour-friendly legislation was introduced and improvements were made to the minimum wage and employment standards, but in some contexts these reforms did little more than chip away at the edges of previous policy, and in others the government bowed to pressure and killed legislation aimed at improving wage and workplace protection.

For example, the Liberal government blocked numerous attempts to update legislation regarding strikes and to bar companies from using replacement workers. It also refused to prevent businesses in cleaning, food, janitorial, and security from re-incorporating under a different name to rid themselves of collective agreements and unionized workforces. Similarly, rather than increase workplace inspections to address employment standards violations, the Ministry of Labour cut back staff and only rarely investigated workplaces or enforced labour regulations.

Finally, despite numerous studies, advocacy campaigns, and a legal challenge, the government failed to improve the labour rights of or workplace conditions for foreign agricultural workers. In these ways, policy drift over the 2000s increasingly pushed Ontario workers into low-wage jobs, non-standard employment contracts, and non-unionized positions.

outside of normal employment relationships through temp agency work and fixed-term contracts. It is not what governments have done but what they have not done that helps account for worsening pay and working conditions.

Layering-In

Finally, provincial governments have allowed employers to avoid employment standards by hiring workers under the federal government's Temporary Foreign Worker Program (TFWP). This policy layering-in introduces employment contract revisions that fall outside provincial labour laws and enables employers to hire temporary foreign workers in a wide range of sectors and occupations.[51]

Canada has long had temporary foreign worker programs for agriculture workers and live-in family caregivers (Chapter 9). Beginning in the 1990s, these programs were expanded to provide larger low-wage, flexible workforces in industries such as construction, food services, cleaning, and meat packing.[52] This legalized precarity ensured that migrant workers made few demands on social programs such as pensions and health care, had very little or no access to unionization and normal employment protections, and had to return to their home countries when their work permits expired.

Over the past twenty years, agriculture, fast food, and construction employers have increasingly relied on temporary foreign workers in low-skill programs, while employers in information technology, finance, and hospitals have lobbied successfully for special immigration work permit systems to recruit skilled workers through the federal Global Skills Strategy (GSS) program. In both cases, immigration rules have been rewritten to accommodate growing demand for low-cost labour that bypasses provincial labour laws, effectively layering-in classes of workers recruited specifically to maximize profits in target industries.

The continuous revision and expansion of the seasonal agricultural workers program and live-in caregiver program is a case in point (see chapters 7 and 8). Now each province and territory except Quebec has a Provincial Nominee Program (PCP) that establishes its own set of rules and policies within the federal TFWP. Temporary foreign workers can be recruited into a range of economic sectors and in a variety of streams, from high-wage (skilled trades and information technology) to low-wage (agriculture, restaurants, clerical, and sales) and to global talent (business, finance, and consultancy). This has resulted in the expansion of temporary foreign worker annual permits from approximately 106,000 in 1985 to more than 389,000 in 2018. But despite the growing importance of temporary foreign workers throughout the economy, many not only lack proper protection but have no access to core labour rights and basic social services.

COVID-19 AND DEREGULATION

At first glance, a number of federal initiatives appear to run counter to these long-term trends of deregulation and business priorities. In the first stages of the crisis, the federal government launched social policies aimed at supporting workers and their families due to layoffs and containment policies (Chapter 1). But unlike countries such as Denmark or Germany, where comprehensive unemployment insurance and job retention schemes have long been in place, the Canadian federal government insisted that the programs were only temporary measures to deal with the problems of the pandemic.[53]

Further, the programs were enacted by a minority government, meaning that it had to rely on the support of other political parties in parliament: the New Democratic Party and Bloc Québécois.[54] But under business lobbying, the emergency relief benefit was quickly replaced by a complex employment insurance system that left hundreds of thousands with no income support.[55]

At the provincial level, long-term deregulatory trends have continued unabated. The Alberta government, for example, introduced multiple pieces of legislation over 2020-21 to open the province for business again and to lower employer costs.[56] One bill introduced everything from a lower minimum wage for young workers to a way for employers to side-step overtime pay by providing time off in lieu. A second bill rewrote labour law and collective bargaining to the heavy advantage of employers. A third reversed previous improvements to health and safety legislation, leaving workers with few opportunities to refuse unsafe work and few prospects of adequate support should they be hurt on the job. A host of other measures overturned collective bargaining for much of the province's public sector. All these reforms favour employers and undermine worker voice and bargaining power.

So too the struggle to introduce paid sick leave during the pandemic is a clear illustration of drift and the tendency of provincial governments to ignore the major problems facing workers in the crisis. Responding to growing numbers of workers who fell ill in long-term care facilities and hospitals, officials in a number of provinces moved to introduce official job-protected leave for reasons relating to COVID-19 – but balked at requiring employers to pay for it.[57] Indeed, just eighteen months earlier in Ontario, the newly elected Conservative government repealed paid sick day legislation, citing its costs for employers.

Only six months after the onset of the coronavirus outbreak, in September 2020, did the federal government finally legislate the Canada Recovery Sickness Benefit (CRSB) for people sick or forced to self-isolate due to COVID-19.[58]

The one-week waiting period for eligibility, and the fact that the program only covered COVID-19-related illness, severely limited its scope and long-term effectiveness.

A final set of problems has emerged with federal and provincial layering-in of essential worker legislation. The new law designates whole sectors of the economy essential, effectively allowing companies to operate in fields from condominium construction to agriculture and empowering employers to keep workers on the job. Existing health and safety legislation contains rudimentary health and safety guidelines to uphold workplace safety. But this effectively means employers are under little obligation to ensure a safe work environment during the pandemic. Similarly, nothing has been done to ensure that workers have the right to refuse unsafe work. Some employers have done better than others in honouring sick leave edicts and supporting workers in avoiding infection. But more workers have been put at risk.

Consequently, on farms and in food-processing plants, hundreds of workers have been exposed to the virus as employers ramp up production (Chapter 8). In long-term care, frontline staff have been offered public expressions of appreciation but not basic personal protective equipment or wages and sick leave provisions that would ensure economic security and good health.[59] Transport and delivery services, which have ballooned with the spike in e-commerce, have rapidly expanded their workforces and increased employee workloads, often without concern for basic safety precautions or worker access to sick days.[60]

Such developments suggest that governments and employers alike continue to be more committed to short-term costs and employer power than to long-term prosperity and the voices and interests of workers in a safe and secure world.

WINNING THE TUG OF WAR

Wages, income support, basic health and safety, job security, social protection: all these and more are determined by the everyday tug of war between business and workers. And with the help of governments (most notably provincial ones), employers have been winning time and again. As a result, citizens are losing their ability to organize countervailing power that would influence public policy making. More and more often, governments are systematically weakening the policy and institutional achievements that workers struggled to achieve in the mid-twentieth century.

COVID-19 has forced the federal government to introduce much-needed legislation to support workers during the crisis. But even this has proven temporary, and many workers are still being left out. At the provincial level, the situation appears bleaker. Whether through legislation governing how a new union can or cannot be organized, or through minimum wages and employment standards that inadequately support workers and their families, provincial governments continue to provide employers with opportunities to restructure, outsource, and de-certify their unionized workforces as well as new opportunities to lower costs, speed up production, and enforce greater worker compliance and management control. With respect to the large and growing non-unionized private-sector labour market, provincial governments are increasingly enabling employers to exercise power in the workplace as well as in public policy making.

Such political dynamics help to explain why provincial governments have been deregulating labour markets. They also help us to understand *how* they have done so, with approaches ranging from reform to drift and layering-in. Compelling policy makers to move in a more progressive direction focused on good jobs, equality, and expanding democracy in the workplace and society will mean hauling the tug of war between business and workers back to the side of people and democracy. Public power has always been built by people themselves standing up and acting for their own betterment.

However, to confront post-democracy will require not only good unions and more organizing (Chapter 17) but also a revitalized labour movement, strong community-based organizations, and a political party willing to fight for a better future (Chapter 18).

ADDITIONAL RESOURCES

Bernhardt, Annette, Heather Boushey, Laura Dresser, and Chris Tilly, eds. *The Gloves-off Economy: Problems and Possibilities at the Bottom of America's Labor Market.* Ithaca, NY: Cornell University Press, 2008.

Gomez, Rafael, and Juan Gomez. "Workplace Democracy for the 21st Century: Towards a New Agenda for Employee Voice and Representation in Canada." Broadbent Institute Discussion Paper, 2016. https://www.broadbentinstitute.ca/workplace_democracy.

McBride, Stephen. *Working? Employment Policy in Canada.* Oakville, ON: Rock's Mills Press, 2017.

Stanford, Jim, and Daniel Poon. *Speaking Up, Being Heard, Making Change: The Theory and Practice of Worker Voice in Canada Today.* Vancouver: Centre for Future Work, 2021.

Workers' Action Centre. *Still Working on the Edge: Building Decent Jobs from the Ground Up.* Toronto: Workers' Action Centre, 2015.

NOTES

1 Anthony B. Atkinson, *Inequality – What Can Be Done?* (Cambridge, MA: Harvard University Press, 2015); Joseph Stiglitz, *The Price of Inequality: How Today's Divided Society Endangers Our Future* (New York: W.W. Norton and Company, 2013).

2 Richard Wilkinson and Kate Pickett, *The Spirit Level: Why Greater Equality Makes Societies Stronger* (New York: Bloomsbury Press, 2010).

3 Cherise Seucharan and Dakshana Bascaramuty, "83% of COVID-19 Cases in Toronto among Racialized People from May–July, Data Suggest," *Globe and Mail,* July 30, 2020, theglobeandmail.com; Feng Hou, Kristyn Frank, and Christophe Schimmle, "Economic Impact of COVID-19 among Visible Minority Groups," *StatCan COVID-19* (Ottawa: Statistics Canada, 2020).

4 David Macdonald, *COVID-19 and the Canadian Workforce* (Ottawa: Canadian Centre for Policy Alternatives, 2020).

5 Lars Osberg, *The Age of Increasing Inequality: The Astonishing Rise of Canada's 1%* (Toronto: James Lorimer and Company, 2018); OECD, *In It Together: Why Less Inequality Benefits All* (Paris: OECD Publishing, 2015), https://dx.doi.org/10.1787/9789264235120-en.

6 Facundo Alvaredo, Lucas Chancel, Thomas Piketty, Emmanuel Saez, and Gabriel Zucman, *World Inequality Report 2018* (Cambridge, MA: Belknap Press of Harvard University Press, 2018).

7 Eoin Flaherty, "Top Incomes under Finance-Driven Capitalism, 1990–2010: Power Resources and Regulatory Orders," *Socio-Economic Review* 13, 3 (2015): 417–47; Thomas Piketty, *Capital in the Twenty-First Century* (Cambridge, MA: Harvard University Press, 2014).

8 OECD, *In It Together.*

9 Pablo Beramendi, Silja Hausermann, Herbert Kitschelt, and Hanspeter Kriesi, "Introduction: The Politics of Advanced Capitalism," in *The Politics of Advanced Capitalism,* ed. Pablo Beramendi, Silja Hausermann, Herbert Kitschelt, and Hanspeter Kriesi (New York: Cambridge University Press, 2015), 1–66.

10 Joseph E. Stiglitz, Amartya Sen, and Jean-Paul Fitoussi, *Report by the Commission on the*

Measurement of Economic Performance and Social Progress (2009), https://www.economie.gouv.fr/files/finances/presse/dossiers_de_presse/090914mesure_perf_eco_progres_social/synthese_ang.pdf.

11 Atkinson, *Inequality*.

12 OECD, *In It Together*.

13 Bob Barnetson, "Kenney's War on Workers: Contracts Broken, Wages Cut and Unions Undermined," *Alberta Views*, January 1, 2020, albertaviews.ca; Chloe Rockarts and Gerard Di Trolio, "Ford Takes on Bill 148: But There is Resistance," *The Bullet*, October 26, 2018, https://socialistproject.ca.

14 Colin Crouch, *Post-Democracy* (Cambridge: Polity Press, 2006); Jacob Hacker and Paul Pierson, *Winner-Take-All Politics: How Washington Made the Rich Richer – And Turned Its Back on the Middle Class* (New York: Simon and Schuster, 2010).

15 Jacob Hacker and Paul Pierson, *Let Them Eat Tweets: How the Right Rules in an Age of Extreme Inequality* (New York: Liveright Publishing, 2020); Cas Mudde, *The Far Right Today* (Cambridge: Polity Press, 2019).

16 Colin Crouch, "The Global Firm: The Problem of the Giant Firm in Democratic Capitalism," in *The Oxford Handbook of Business and Government*, ed. Graham Wilson, Wyn Grant, and David Coen (New York: Oxford University Press, 2010), 148–72; Jacob Hacker and Paul Pierson, "Winner-Take-All Politics: Public Policy, Political Organization, and the Precipitous Rise of Top Incomes in the United States," *Policy and Society* 38, no. 2 (2010): 152–204.

17 Lucio Baccaro and Chris Howell, *European Industrial Relations: Trajectories of Neoliberal Transformation* (New York: Cambridge University Press, 2017).

18 OECD, *Government at a Glance 2013* (Paris: OECD Publishing, 2013), https://doi.org/10.1787/gov_glance-2013-en.

19 John Peters, *Jobs with Inequality: Financialization, Post-Democracy, and Labour Market Deregulation in Canada* (Toronto: University of Toronto Press, 2022).

20 Jim Stanford, "The Geography of Auto Globalization and the Politics of Auto Bailouts," *Cambridge Journal of Regions, Economy and Society* 3 (2010): 383–405.

21 David Weil, *The Fissured Workplace: Why Work Became So Bad for so Many and What Can Be Done to Improve It* (Cambridge, MA: Harvard University Press, 2014).

22 Office of the Integrity Commissioner of Ontario, *Office of the Integrity Commissioner of Ontario Annual Report 2010–2011* (Toronto: Publications Ontario, 2011).

23 Jamie Brownlee, *Ruling Canada: Corporate Cohesion and Democracy* (Halifax: Fernwood Publishing, 2005).

24 Jamie Brownlee, *Ruling Canada: Corporate Cohesion and Democracy* (Halifax: Fernwood Publishing, 2005).

25 Donald Gutstein, *Not a Conspiracy Theory: How Business Propaganda Hijacks Democracy* (Toronto: Key Porter Books, 2010).

26 Peters, *Jobs with Inequality*.

27 Barry Eidlin, *Labor and the Class Idea in the United States and Canada* (New York: Cambridge University Press, 2018); Bruce Western, *Between Class and Market: Postwar Unionization in the Capitalist Democracies* (Princeton, NJ: Princeton University Press, 1997).

28 Evelyne Huber and John D. Stephens, *Development and Crisis of the Welfare State: Parties and Policies in Global Markets* (Chicago: University of Chicago Press, 2001).

29 Jake Rosenfeld, *What Unions No Longer Do* (Cambridge, MA: Harvard University Press, 2014).

30 Desmond Morton, *The New Democrats 1961–1986: The Politics of Change* (Toronto: Copp Clark Pitman, 1986); Jacques Rouillard, *Le syndicalisme Québécois: Deux siecles d'histoire* (Montreal: Boreal, 2004).

31 Bryan Evans and Ingo Schmidt, eds., *Social Democracy after the Cold War* (Edmonton: Athabasca University Press, 2012).

32 Gerasimos Moschonas, *In the Name of Social Democracy: The Great Transformation: 1945 to the Present* (New York: Verso, 2002).

33 Linda McQuaig and Neil Brooks, *Billionaires' Ball: Gluttony and Hubris in an Age of Epic Inequality* (Boston: Beacon Press, 2012).

34 Robert Andersen, Brian Burgoon, and Herman van de Werfhorst, "Inequality, Legitimacy, and the Political System," in *Changing Inequalities in Rich Countries: Analytical and Comparative Perspectives*, ed. Wiemar Salverda, Brian Nolan, Daniele Checchi et al. (New York: Oxford University Press, 2014); Robert Erikson, "Income Inequality and Policy Responsiveness," *Annual Review of Political Science* 18 (2015): 11–29; Peter Mair, *Ruling the Void: The Hollowing of Western Democracy* (New York: Verso, 2013).

35 David Brady, *Rich Democracies, Poor People: How Politics Explain Poverty* (New York: Oxford University Press, 2009).

36 Vincent Mahler, "Exploring the Subnational Dimension of Income Inequality: An Analysis of the Relationhip between Inequality and Electoral Turnout in the Developed Countries," *International Studies Quarterly* 46, no.1 (2002): 117–42; Vincent Mahler, "Electoral Turnout and Income Redistribution by the State: A Cross-National Analysis of the Developed Democracies," *European Journal of Political Research* 47, no. 2 (2008): 161–83.

37 Hacker and Pierson, *Winner-Take-All Politics*.

38 Alan R. Walks, "The City-Suburban Cleavage in Canadian Federal Politics," *Canadian Journal of Political Science* 38, no. 2 (2005): 383–413.

39 Jared Wesley, ed., *Big Worlds: Politics and Elections in the Canadian Provinces and Territories* (Toronto: University of Toronto Press, 2016).

40 Greg Albo and Bryan M. Evans, eds., *Divided Province: Ontario Politics in the Age of Neoliberalism* (Montreal and Kingston: McGill-Queen's University Press, 2019); Andrew MacLeod, *A Better Place on Earth: The Search for Fairness in Super Unequal British Columbia* (Madeira Park, BC: Harbour Publishing, 2015).

41 Linda McQuaig and Neil Brooks, *The Trouble with Billionaires: Why Too Much Money at the Top Is Bad for Everyone* (Toronto: Penguin Canada, 2010).

42 Benjamin Page, Larry Bartels, and Jason Seawright, "Democracy and the Policy Preferences of Wealthy Americans," *Perspectives on Politics* 11, no. 1 (2013): 51–73; Anthony Kevins, Alexander Horn, Carsten Jensen, and Kees Van Kersbergen, "Yardsticks of Inequality: Preferences for Redistribution in Advanced Democracies," *Journal of European Social Policy* 28, no. 4 (2018): 402–18.

43 Leo Panitch and Donald Swartz, *From Consent to Coercion: The Assault on Trade Union Freedoms,* 3rd ed. (Aurora, ON: Garamond Press, 2003).

44 Charles Smith, "Class, Power, and Neoliberal Employment Policy," in *Divided Province*, ed. Albo and Evans, 275–306.

45 Charles Smith and Andrew Stevens, "The Architecture of Modern Anti-Unionism in Canada: Class Struggle and the Erosion of Workers' Collective Freedoms," *Capital & Class* 43, no. 3 (2018): 459–81.

46 Jacob Hacker, *The Great Risk Shift: The Assault on American Jobs, Families, Health Care, and Retirement and How You Can Fight Back* (Oxford: Oxford University Press, 2006).

47 Ken Battle, *Restoring Minimum Wages in Canada* (Ottawa: Caledon Institute of Social Policy, 2011).

48 Andrea Noack, Leah Vosko, and John Grundy, "Measuring Employment Standards Violations, Evasion, and Erosion – Using a Telephone Survey," *Relations Industrielle/Industrial Relations* 71, no. 1 (2015): 86–109.

49 Judy Fudge and Kendra Strauss, eds., *Temporary Work, Agencies, and Unfree Labour: Insecurity in the New World of Work* (New York: Routledge, 2014); Sara Mojtehedzadeh, "Ontario's Temp Agencies, Then and Now," *Toronto Star*, May 10, 2015, thestar.com; Law Commission of Ontario, *Vulnerable Workers and Precarious Work* (Toronto: Law Commission of Ontario, 2012).

50   Panitch and Swartz, *From Consent to Coercion.*

51   Eric Tucker, "Farm Worker Exceptionalism: Past, Present, and the Post-Fraser Future," in *Constitutional Labour Rights in Canada: Farm Workers and the Fraser Case*, ed. Fay Faraday, Judy Fudge, and Eric Tucker (Toronto: Irwin Law, 2012), 24–46.

52   Leigh Binford, *Tomorrow We're All Going to the Harvest: Temporary Foreign Worker Programs and Neoliberal Political Economy* (Austin: University of Texas Press, 2013).

53   Canada, Department of Finance, *Economic and Fiscal Snapshot 2020*, Cat. no. F2-277/2020E-PDF (Ottawa: Department of Finance, 2020), www.canada.ca/en/department-finance.html.

54   Sean Kirkpatrick, "Extend CERB and Provide Paid Sick Leave If You Want Our Votes, Singh Tells Trudeau," *Globe and Mail*, September 23, 2020, theglobeandmail.com.

55   David Macdonald, "Canadian Workforce Unevenly Protected from COVID-19," *The Monitor*, Canadian Centre for Policy Alternatives, March 16, 2020, https://monitormag.ca.

56   Barnetson, "Kenney's War on Workers."

57   David Doorey, "COVID-19 and Labour Law: Canada," *Italian Labour Law Journal* 13, no. 1S (2020); David Fairey, "Legislated Paid Sick Leave Long Overdue," *Policynote*, May 4, 2020, policynote.ca.

58   Kaitlyn Matulewicz and David Fairey, "New Federal Sickness Benefit Falls Short," *Policy Note, October 1, 2020.*

59   Tamara Daly, Ivy Lynn Bourgeault, and Katie Aubrecht, "Long-Term Care Is Essential but Essentially Under-Recognized," *Policy Options*, May 14, 2020, policyoptions.irpp.org; David McKie, "Long-Term Care Homes Were in Crisis Well before Politicians Woke Up to the Problem," *Canada's National Observer*, April 29, 2020, www.nationalobserver.com.

60   PressProgress, "Amazon Rolls Back Unpaid Leave as Workers Told of 'Additional' COVID-19 Case at Ontario Warehouse," Media release, May 9, 2020, https://pressprogress.ca/amazon-rolls-back-unpaid-leave-as-workers-told-of-additional-COVID-19-case-at-ontario-warehouse.

6 Precarious Employment in the Federally Regulated Private Sector

Leah Vosko, Andrea M. Noack, Adam King, and Rebecca Hii

CHAPTER SUMMARY

This chapter is concerned with employment in Canada's federally regulated private sector (FRPS). This sector, which covers industries like road, rail, and air transport, banking, and telecommunications, has historically been more worker friendly in terms of collective bargaining and some labour standards than its provincial counterparts. Nonetheless, precarious employment still exists in the federally regulated private sector.

The chapter first provides a brief history of the division of federal and provincial governmental powers and the consequences for labour legislation. It then compares employment in the FRPS to both the public and the provincially regulated private sectors across the country. By way of conclusion, the chapter considers various policy changes that could limit precarious employment among federally regulated workers across Canada, particularly in light of the COVID-19 pandemic.

KEY THEMES

This chapter will help you develop an understanding of:

- how the federally regulated private sector (FRPS) differs from the provincially regulated private sector (PRPS)
- how industry characteristics are related to precarious employment in the FRPS
- how different regulatory regimes in federal and provincial jurisdictions influence conditions of work and employment
- policy alternatives to address precarious employment and extend the better employment conditions in the FRPS to other Canadian workers.

AS A FEDERATION, Canada has federal, provincial, and territorial jurisdictions, and the Constitution divides the power to enact and enforce laws between provincial and territorial legislatures and the federal parliament. In most instances, provinces are responsible for setting and enforcing laws and policies governing labour relations and labour standards. Labour relations encompass the right to organize unions and to collective bargaining. Labour or employment standards set out minimum wages and make provisions for working time, vacations and leaves, and termination or severance of employment. In several key industries, however, the federal government is responsible for these domains.

In the FRPS, historically, collective bargaining and especially labour standards laws have in some regards been more worker friendly than those established in several provinces. In terms of job security and working conditions, some FRPS employment is akin to public-sector employment. The industrial composition and regulatory environment of the FRPS make the standard employment relationship – full-time permanent employment in which the worker has one employer, works on the employer's premises, and has access to statutory entitlements and social benefits – more common than it is in the provincially regulated private sector (PRPS). That said, precarious employment still exists in the FRPS.[1]

Because early federal governments designated some industries as vital to national interest, federal legislation has often set a relatively high bar for labour relations and standards. In 1944, the Order in Council P.C. 1003 established workers' rights to form unions and bargain collectively. Two decades later, in 1965, various pieces of legislation relating to industrial relations, occupational health and safety, and labour standards were brought together and updated as the Canada Labour Code. Part III of the Code set some minimum labour standards at levels higher than those prevailing in the provinces, meaning that federal jurisdiction has set policy precedents even though labour falls generally within provincial jurisdiction.

Precarious employment has the potential to erode the relatively better working conditions in the FRPS. Since the early 2000s, the changing nature of employment in Canada has prompted the federal government to initiate several task forces to review collective bargaining and labour standards laws and policies, especially those falling under the Canada Labour Code, and to make recommendations for reform. In 2004–06, a commission on fairness at work undertook an extensive review of the Code, yet its policy suggestions went largely unimplemented. In 2017, the Liberal government constituted a group of academic experts and subsequently convened a tripartite panel on modern federal labour standards that made recommendations on how to improve labour standards in the FRPS. The government then began to implement some of them, albeit incrementally.

Comparing employment in the FRPS to both the public and the provincially regulated private sectors across the country reveals the areas in which the FRPS continues to provide greater protections than its provincially regulated counterparts, and the issues that undermine those relatively better conditions. Neoliberal trends such as the drive for so-called labour flexibility and increased competition have made inroads into the FRPS. Firm dynamics such as vertical disintegration, whereby businesses focus on their core competencies and rely increasingly on supply chains (i.e., labour supplied by smaller contractors or even individuals) for more peripheral activities, are a central driver of precariousness in employment. In particular, they are linked to workplace fissuring on the one hand and independent contracting on the other hand.[2] Taken together, these dynamics are limiting the reach of collective bargaining and weakening labour standards in the FRPS. Moreover, the COVID-19 pandemic has exacerbated these trends by increasing economic pressure on firms and workers in some federally regulated industries.

THE FEDERAL JURISDICTION

As a federation, Canada divides the powers to pass laws and regulations between the provincial and federal governments. This division of powers dates from the inception of the Dominion of Canada with the British North America (BNA) Act in 1867 and is enumerated in sections 91 and 92 of the contemporary Constitution of Canada.[3] But the division is not always tidy.

The reach of federal power over property and civil rights, including labour relations and employment standards (which are usually provincial matters), has been a recurring question throughout Canadian history. The BNA Act made explicit federal power over property and civil rights in sectors of national importance. If the federal government was going to be responsible for the development of a nationwide postal service, for example, by extension it needed the ability to legislate on the terms of employment in the relevant workplaces. Moreover, federal jurisdiction over labour relations and standards in specific sectors, such as transportation that crosses provincial boundaries, applies to those employed in both public and private industry. Accordingly, not all employment relations were or are matters of provincial concern.

It's important to remember that Canada's jurisdictional division of responsibilities was devised at a time when the majority of the population worked in subsistence agriculture, and the reach of government - particularly in the realms of economy and labour - was fairly limited. As industrialization took hold in the early twentieth century and greater numbers of

Canadians entered the labour market and worked for wages, limitations on federal power impeded progressive policy implementation. Early federal attempts to regulate hours of work and legislate on minimum wages were struck down by the courts as unconstitutional, and the unevenness of employment standards between provinces became a concern.[4] As Barbara Cameron notes, however, the federal government could legislate measures only for industries over which its responsibility had been specifically assigned.[5]

The jurisdictional division was altered somewhat over the period spanning the Great Depression and Second World War. Responding to pressure from the labour movement and other social activists, the federal Conservative government introduced a series of reforms sometimes referred to as part of Canada's New Deal in 1935. These pieces of legislation combined to introduce unemployment insurance and a new minimum wage, legislate hours of work, and provide for rest periods in certain industries. The subsequent Liberal government of William Lyon Mackenzie King contested the constitutionality of the reforms, however, and was ultimately successful in repealing them on the grounds that the provinces had jurisdiction over minimum employment standards.[6]

Despite the failure of these initial reforms, the economic hardships of the Great Depression motivated a reconsideration of the nature of federal legislative power over matters of national economic interest. Eventually, constitutional amendments were needed to institute a national program of unemployment insurance and an old age pension. As well, in response to the rising number of strikes calling for union recognition, the Privy Council intervened in 1944 with Order 1003, guaranteeing the right of workers to form unions and providing mechanisms to compel employers to bargain with newly certified unions.[7]

In the realms of labour relations and standards, the federal jurisdiction slowly began to draft model legislation providing workers with more protection than its provincial counterparts. Prior to 1968 and the enactment of the Canada Labour Code, separate pieces of legislation addressed not only labour relations but also different labour standards pertaining to hours of work and wages, and, in some cases, different standards were applied to different industries. Some of those differential standards remain today, such as hours of work in the transportation sector.

Part I of the Code came to form a single piece of legislation that sets out the scope and substance of labour relations applicable to workers seeking to form and maintain unions (that is, to pursue certification and negotiation and maintain collective agreements) and to their employers, as well as to currently unionized workers and their employers. Part II of the Code governs occupational health and safety standards in the federal jurisdiction. Finally, Part III establishes minimum labour standards for employees in the federally regulated private sector. Newly enacted, Part IV of the Code now sets out Administrative Monetary Penalties (AMPs), which are additional fees that can be imposed on employers found to have contravened certain labour standards.

By introducing social minimums that often exceeded provincial employment standards, the federal government exerted pressure on provincial governments, some of which had vociferously resisted the introduction of minimum standards altogether. The Ontario Department of Labour, for example, claimed that Part III set the bar too high – that is, higher than the province intended in its own Employment Standards Act.[8] On some items, standards contained in the Code exceeded those established through collective bargaining, a state of affairs that encouraged unionized workers to both push for more in their collective agreements and to pressure provincial governments for further improvements in employment standards. Nonetheless, the legacy of industrial disparities continues and is increasingly visible in pockets of precarious employment within particular industries, especially those in which vertical disintegration and independent contracting are pronounced.

WHO ARE FEDERAL JURISDICTION EMPLOYEES?

Contemporaneously, federal jurisdiction over employment is defined based on the industries in which people work. Industries that typically span or cross provincial boundaries tend to fall under federal jurisdiction, as do industries that are conceptualized as being in the national interest. Road, air, rail, and maritime transportation, banking and telecommunications, postal services and pipelines, grain storage and milling, the construction of tunnels, bridges and canals, uranium ore mining, and Indigenous government activities on First Nations reserves are all under federal jurisdiction. The exact scope of the federal jurisdiction nevertheless remains poorly defined. In some cases, the courts have decided the matter, and the result is a patchwork of jurisprudence about the limits of the federal jurisdiction. These challenges are particularly pronounced in the context of Indigenous activities.

We use data from the Statistics Canada Labour Force Survey (LFS) to develop a profile of the people employed in federally regulated industries.[9] Because of unclear jurisdictional boundaries, as well as the way industries are classified in the LFS, it's not possible to identify every employee who works in a federally regulated industry or to exclude all those who don't. Not all employees engaged in Indigenous government activities on First Nations reserves are identifiable in the data, for example, nor are employees engaged in uranium ore mining or building tunnels, bridges, and canals. As well, this analysis includes only formal employees, unless otherwise noted.

In 2018, more than a million people were employed in the federally regulated private sector (FRPS). When they are not unionized or covered by a collective agreement, these workers' labour standards are established by Part III of the Canada Labour Code. For unionized workers, they are covered by Part I, along with the relevant collective agreement negotiated between the union and the employer. Workers in the FRPS are distinct from public-sector employees who work for the federal government. The latter are largely unionized, and their terms of employment are regulated through the Federal Public Sector Labour Relations and Employment Act and the Public Service Employment Act.

Employees in the federally regulated private sector are most commonly found in Ontario (36 percent), Quebec (21 percent), and Alberta (19 percent).[10] British Columbia accounts for another 12 percent, while all other provinces have a much smaller proportion of employees in the jurisdiction (Figure 6.1). This distribution reflects that of employees across Canada more generally, although Alberta has a slightly higher proportion of FRPS employees relative to their share of overall employment,

FIGURE 6.1 **Distribution of FRPS employees by province, 2018**

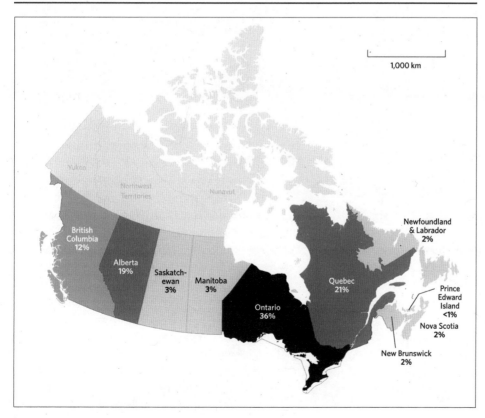

Source: Data from Statistics Canada, Labour Force Survey, 2018.

TABLE 6.1 **Sociodemographic characteristics of employees, 2018**

		Employees (%)			
		Public sector	FRPS	PRPS	Canada total
Share of Canadian employees		24	7	70	100
Gender	Male	37	62	55	51
	Female	63	38	46	49
Age group	15–24	7	8	19	16
	25–54	72	73	63	66
	55+	21	19	18	19
Immigration status	Born in Canada	81	71	74	76
	Settled immigrant (>10 years)	14	21	17	16
	Recent immigrant (<10 years)	4	8	9	8
Immigration status by gender	Immigrant men (recent/settled)	7	17	14	12
	Immigrant women (recent/settled)	11	12	13	12
	Canadian-born men	29	45	41	39
	Canadian-born women	52	26	33	37
Education	No high school diploma	2	6	11	9
	High school diploma	14	25	30	26
	College/trade certificate/diploma	36	37	36	36
	University degree	48	33	24	30

Note: Totals do not add to 100 percent because of rounding.
Source: Data from Statistics Canada, Labour Force Survey, 2018.

whereas Ontario and Quebec have a slightly lower proportion.

Not surprisingly, some federally regulated industries are more prominent in specific provinces and territories. For instance, oil and gas and pipeline employees are concentrated in Alberta, whereas maritime transportation workers are concentrated in the Atlantic provinces and British Columbia. Bank employees are more likely to be located in Ontario and Quebec, while employees in milling, rail transportation, and road transportation are more likely to be located in Manitoba or Saskatchewan (although the Atlantic provinces and Quebec also have high shares of road transportation employees). Employees in air transportation, postal services, and telecom services tend to be spread more evenly across the country, although British Columbia has a slightly higher share of air transportation workers, Ontario has a slightly higher share of postal workers, and Alberta has a slightly lower share of telecom workers.

The demographic profile of employees in the FRPS reflects its industrial contours (Table 6.1). Although women constitute fully 49 percent of employees in Canada, they make up just

38 percent of employees in the FRPS and the majority in just one federally regulated industry. Employees in federally regulated industries are also older, on average, than employees in provincially regulated industries or the labour force more generally. Only 8 percent of FRPS employees are under twenty-five, compared to 16 percent of employees overall. Although industries under federal jurisdiction employ about the same proportion of recent immigrants as those outside of it, immigrants who have been in Canada for more than ten years are over-represented in the FRPS, a phenomenon that is particularly pronounced among immigrant men. As well, employees in the FRPS tend to have higher levels of education than employees in the PRPS, and those with university degrees are over-represented – a phenomenon that is particularly evident in the banking industry.

PRECARIOUS EMPLOYMENT IN THE FEDERALLY REGULATED PRIVATE SECTOR

Precarious employment encompasses forms of paid work characterized by labour market insecurities, such as a low degree of certainty around continuing employment, low income, a lack of control over the labour process, and limited access to regulatory protection. It is shaped by the relationship between employment status (paid or self-employment), form of employment (temporary or permanent, part time or full time), social context (geography, occupation, and industry), and workers' social location (or the interaction between social relations, such as gender and race, and legal and political categories, such as citizenship).[11]

Although precarious and non-standard forms of employment are not synonymous, there is a relationship between them because, historically, labour laws and policies have taken the standard employment relationship to be the norm. For this reason, forms of employment differing from this model have come to be linked with greater precariousness. Employees in federally regulated industries are more likely to be employed full time than employees in either provincially regulated industries or employees in the public sector. They are also more likely to be in permanent jobs. Within the FRPS, 91 percent of employees are full time (compared to 82 percent of employees overall), and 93 percent are permanent (compared to 87 percent of employees overall). When these two job characteristics are combined, fully 86 percent of FRPS employees are in full-time, permanent positions, substantially more than the 74 percent of employees in the public and private sectors combined.

The notion of a standard employment relationship was established as a norm for male citizens in the post–Second World War period, fuelled in part by social programs designed to reintegrate returning servicemen. The masculine character of many federally regulated industries has probably helped to ensure that full-time permanent employment has remained more prominent in the FRPS than in other sectors. Indeed, in the FRPS, fully 38 percent of employees are Canadian-born men who are working in full-time permanent jobs, an employment situation that is reminiscent of an older economic order. In contrast, employees with that demographic profile constitute just 29 percent of the PRPS and 23 percent of the public sector.

Still, larger economic trends such as industrial restructuring have had some influence on employment in the FRPS. Increased national and global competition and deregulation have contributed to processes such as vertical disintegration, typified by the tendency of lead businesses to avoid having employees through contracting out, franchising, and the use of extended supply chains, akin to what David Weil characterizes as fissuring.[12] Independent contracting, particularly of the sort where the self-employed person does not employ others, is a driving force in the erosion of the terms and conditions of work and employment that characterize the FRPS. Fully 92 percent of workers in federally regulated industries are employees, compared to only 85 percent of workers in other industries. Only 6 percent of workers in federally regulated industries are in solo or bogus self-employment, and just 2 percent are self-employed with employees. Despite these low proportions, independent contracting and other forms of precarious employment exert a downward competitive pressure on wages and standards, particularly if they are concentrated in specific industries. For example, solo self-employed workers in the FRPS are most often in road transportation (independent truckers) or postal services (independent couriers), where we see the largest share of workers facing employment precarity. The remaining industries under federal jurisdiction have low levels of self-employment.

Despite the low proportion of self-employment and the high proportion of employees in full-time permanent positions, some employees in federally regulated industries experience other dimensions of labour market insecurity, such as a lack of union representation, low wages, short job tenure, and small firm sizes. Figure 6.2 shows how many FRPS, PRPS, and public-sector employees are in precarious employment as a proportion of the employees in each sector, and specifically how they compare on each of these four dimensions.

Firm size is a good indicator of employees' access to regulatory protection. Previous research demonstrates that employment standards are less strongly enforced among workers in small firms, partly because it is difficult for labour inspectorates to spread their often scarce resources across workplaces, and because larger firms tend to be more financially and administratively able to abide by the regulations set out in labour standards legislation.[13] In terms of firm size, the FRPS tends to more closely resemble the public sector than the PRPS. Because of its industrial composition, the FRPS is composed disproportionately of large firms: in 2018, large firms of 100 or more employees employed 82 percent of workers in the jurisdiction. The small firms with twenty or fewer employees in the FRPS are overwhelmingly clustered in road transportation, and particularly freight trucking.

Job tenure serves as a useful indicator of precarity in terms of both continuing employment and protection from job turnover (Figure 6.2). Access to certain job protections, such as severance pay and vacation time – as well as protections against wrongful dismissal in the case of the FRPS – are linked to length of employment in a single job. In this analysis, employees who have held their position for less than a year are considered to have short job tenure. By this measure, the FRPS again more closely resembles the public sector than the PRPS. Only 16 percent of employees in the FRPS have short job tenure, compared to 24 percent of employees in the PRPS and 12 percent of employees in the public sector. Within

FIGURE 6.2 **Dimensions of precarious employment, 2018**

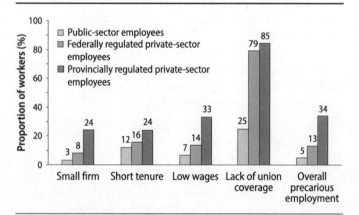

Source: Data from Statistics Canada, Labour Force Survey, 2018.

the federally regulated private sector, the pro-portion of short-tenure employees is highest within the road transportation industry, and again, particularly in freight trucking.

Low hourly wages function as an indicator of low income. As noted in Chapter 5, the Organisation for Economic Co-operation and Development (OECD), defines low wages as those less than two-thirds of the median annual wage for full-time employees. The LFS doesn't provide that information, but applying the same calculation to the median hourly wage in each province provides a cutoff ranging from $20.50 in Prince Edward Island to $28.85 in Alberta for 2018. Low-wage work is notably less common in the FRPS than in its provincial counterpart, though it is still higher than in the public sector: 14 percent of employees in the FRPS earn low wages, double the share of low-wage public-sector employees but substantially less than the 33 percent in the PRPS. Within the FRPS, low-wage workers are over-represented in air transportation, road transportation, and postal services.

Low-income employees are more likely to rely on standards governing minimum wages. Before December 29, 2021, there was no specific minimum wage for workers in the FRPS. Between 1996 and this latter date, the Canada Labour Code pegged the federal minimum wage to the prevailing minimum in the province or territory in which the worker was employed. As part of a package of labour standards reforms, the Liberal government reintroduced a federal minimum wage, starting at $15 per hour and set to be annually inflation-adjusted each April based on the national Consumer Price Index.

Unlike some provincial employment standards, the Canada Labour Code does not permit specific youth or student minimum wage rates. Consequently, all young employees must be paid the regular minimum wage. About 4 percent of employees in the federally regulated private sector report hourly wages at or below the general minimum wage in their province, slightly higher than in the public sector (2 percent) but substantially lower than in the provincially regulated private sector (12 percent).

Finally, **union coverage** is one indicator of employees' workplace protections and degree of control over the labour process. Employees who are not unionized or covered by a collective agreement must rely on minimum labour standards laws, and they may have fewer mechanisms to assert their voices in the workplace. In contrast to firm size, job tenure, and low wages as indicators of precarity – dimensions that reflect the historical role of the FRPS as a model employer – when it comes to union coverage, FRPS employment much more closely resembles that in the PRPS than in the public sector. Some 79 percent of employees lack union coverage, compared to 85 percent in the PRPS and only 25 percent of employees in the public sector. Across federally regulated industries, the coverage is also quite uneven, with very low levels in banking, pipelines and oil and gas, and road transportation but higher levels in the air, rail, and maritime transportation industries (Table 6.2).

Overall, employment in the federally regulated private sector is more similar to employment in the public sector on three dimensions of precariousness: small firm size, short job tenure and low wages (Table 6.2). These results reflect the historical positioning of the federal jurisdiction as a "model employer." In contrast, when it comes to union coverage, the federally regulated private sector is more closely aligned with the provincially regulated private sector.

Given the need to understand precarious employment as a multi-dimensional and multi-faceted phenomenon, we combine these four indicators to create a composite measure of precariousness, which deems jobs to be precarious if they are characterized either by at least three of these four indicators or by the presence

TABLE 6.2 **Indicators of precariousness in FRPS industries, 2018 (%)**

Industry	Proportion of FRPS employees	Precarious job	Small firm	Short tenure	Low wage	Lack of union coverage
Road transportation	23	22	25	23	18	87
Postal services	4	18	7	13	19	68
Air transportation	10	14	6	14	25	49
Telecommunications	14	11	5	12	12	67
Banking	33	11	2	13	12	93
Rail and maritime transportation	5	7	4	15	8	39
Pipelines, oil and gas, milling	12	5	5	16	5	87
Total	100	13	8	16	14	79

Source: Data from Statistics Canada, Labour Force Survey, 2018.
Note: Some industries are combined in this table in order to meet the confidentiality requirements for Statistics Canada data.

of low wages and another one of the remaining indicators. We prioritize low wages given the growing body of research demonstrating the correlation between low-wage employment and high levels of insecurity.[14]

This composite measure of precariousness illustrates how employees in the FRPS are positioned overall relative to the public sector and the PRPS. While 34 percent of employees under provincial jurisdiction are working in precarious jobs, the figure is only 13 percent in the FRPS. Although it is clear that employment in a federally regulated industry is less likely to be precarious than employment in an industry under provincial jurisdiction, the share of precarious employment in the FRPS is still more than double that in the public sector, where it is just 5 percent. The low share of precarious public-sector employment is likely to reflect the higher rate of unionization, which is typically associated with improved working conditions.

The relatively low level of precarious employment in the FRPS generally obscures substantial variations among industries. For instance, 22 percent of employees in road transportation are in precarious jobs as a result of the comparatively high proportion of small

firms and lack of union coverage in this industry, along with relatively high numbers of short tenure and low-wage employees. Similarly, 18 percent of employees in the private postal service industry are in precarious jobs, primarily because of the low union coverage and low wages in this industry.

Notably, these two federally regulated industries, which have the highest levels of precarious employment, are also those with the highest levels of self-employment and solo self-employment. In contrast, some federally regulated industries – such as pipelines, oil and gas and grain milling, and rail and maritime transportation – have relatively low levels of precarious employment, primarily because of comparatively strong wages and the scarcity of small firms.

THE IMPACT OF COVID-19 ON THE FRPS

As in many sectors and industries, the COVID-19 pandemic exposed problematic work and employment practices in the FRPS, but the impact has not affected all industries equally.

Labour Force Survey data for 2019 and 2020 shows that five industries experienced the greatest proportional decline in people employed and at work between April–June 2019 and April–June 2020: accommodation and food services; other services, such as repair/maintenance and personal care services; information and cultural industries; retail trade; and transportation and warehousing. Two of the five include employees who are part of the FRPS. Telecommunications employees are part of the information and cultural industry. But most notably, many FRPS employees are in the transportation and warehousing industry, since much of this work crosses provincial borders. Employees working in road, air, rail, and maritime transportation and in postal services are all part of this industrial grouping.

Within the transportation industry, the effects of the pandemic on employment and working conditions have also been uneven. Air transportation employees have been strongly affected by restrictions and public health concerns that reduced demand for domestic and international air travel. These employees experienced layoffs, job losses, and reduced hours. Air Canada laid off 50–60 percent of its workforce in summer 2020, and other major carriers followed suit. Even though federal labour regulations provide employees with protections in situations of mass termination or layoffs, airlines applied to be exempted from these rules. Although some (such as WestJet) later withdrew their exemption requests, Air Canada pursued the matter, ultimately receiving temporary layoff extensions allowing it to avoid paying substantial termination pay to employees out of work between April and December 2020. Rail transportation workers also experienced layoffs as a result of reduced demand.

Workers in the road transportation industry were affected differently, as many were considered to be essential and allowed to cross international borders without quarantining in order to maintain supply chains. During the pandemic, these employees experienced increased health and safety risks because they were required to travel to areas with coronavirus outbreaks and had to work longer shifts in order to compensate for supply chain disruptions. These intense working conditions were compounded by closures of businesses and rest stops that serve truck drivers, making it difficult to find a place to take a break on the road.

Employment in other FRPS industries, such as banking, was much less affected by the pandemic. Rather predictably, FRPS industries with the highest levels of precarious employment were also those that were most strongly affected. Although the full effect of the pandemic on the Canadian economy and labour force are still unknown, it has become clear that in general, workers who were already disadvantaged in the labour force have become even further disadvantaged in the face of challenging economic conditions.

PROTECTING AND EXTENDING FRPS WORKING CONDITIONS

The better protections and working conditions found in the FRPS relative to the PRPS arose and persist in part because of the industries within this jurisdiction. A relatively large segment of employment within the sector tends to look like the normative standard employment relationship: full-time permanent paid employment in large firms and historically male-dominated industries characterized by decent pay and other benefits.

Given the well-documented spread of precarious employment in Canada as a whole, it's important to understand why the federal jurisdiction continues to provide relatively greater security, and to consider how those superior conditions of work and employment might be preserved, improved upon, and extended to workers in the PRPS across the country. The answer lies in policy developments and alternatives to limit or reverse precarious employment and extend the better working conditions found in the FRPS to workers in its ambit who currently lack them.

First, preserving and strengthening the quality of FRPS employment requires addressing issues related to the scope of the Canada Labour Code. At base, a worker must be classified as an employee to gain access to the full range of rights and protections provided for under the Code. That roughly 116,000 workers in federally regulated industries report they are self-employed – and thus are not covered by all of the Code's provisions – is therefore troubling.

Placing the onus more firmly on employers to prove that a worker is not an employee could limit or reverse the growth of independent contracting and self-employment, particularly in the road transportation industry. The model first enshrined in January 2020 in California Assembly Bill (AB5) deems any person who supplies labour services for monetary compensation to be an employee unless the employer meets criteria established through a three-part legal test to determine the worker's employment status. The "ABC test" stipulates that any worker classified as self-employed must be free from employer control or direction, be performing work outside of the business entity's usual operations, and be engaged in an independently established trade, occupation, or business.[15]

In 2018, the federal Liberal government, as part of its Budget Implementation Act, or Bill C-86, introduced amendments to Part III of the Canada Labour Code in order to curb employers' resort to employee misclassification (as "independent contractors," etc.) as a means of evading labour standards legislation and the costs associated with worker protection. Although Bill C-86 introduces an amendment that makes it the employer's responsibility to prove a worker is properly classified, the criteria are weaker than those proposed by the ABC test.

Addressing precarious employment in the federal jurisdiction also requires policies to mitigate the negative consequences of workplace fissuring, extended supply chains, and other forms of vertical disintegration – namely, the growth of small firms in some industries. Because precarious employment is so often associated with complex ownership structures and extended supply chains, the federal government and its provincial counterparts need to change how labour standards legislation attributes employment-related responsibility in, for example, cases of wages owed. Just as businesses often employ contract or limited-term workers as a cost-saving strategy, they frequently utilize distancing strategies, such as using temp agency workers or solo self-employed contractors, in order to avoid legal responsibility for employees.

The various entities responsible for these workers must be made joint and severally liable for adhering to the laws that govern workers' rights. Bill C-86 attempted to address employer responsibility through additional amendments to Part III of the Canada Labour Code. For example, since the adoption of these amendments, during the inspection of a temporary help agency, an investigator may enter the premises of the business that hired the labour contractor in order to collect records and/or carry out other duties related to the investigation. Nevertheless, they cannot hold related entities jointly liable for adhering to all labour standards.

Relatedly, Bill C-86 also extended the concept of equal pay for equal work to part-time, temporary agency and contract workers performing the same kind of work with the same skill, effort, or responsibility as permanent employees. Although this provision is a positive step for workers in non-traditional employment, it doesn't prevent employers from limiting or withholding other rights and entitlements on the basis of form of employment, such as extended health benefits or pension plans.[16]

Extending equality provisions beyond pay could go some distance toward improving the material security of workers without full-time permanent positions. Because they would reduce business savings from subcontracting or other distancing strategies, such measures could act as a disincentive to using temp agency workers and other labour contractors, and thus curb competition that takes place at workers' expense.

The pandemic also made clear the importance of access to sick leave for all workers, including those in the federal sector. In October 2020, the federal government temporarily instituted two paid leaves for employees in the FRPS: a two-week job-protected leave for those who contracted COVID-19 or had to isolate because of a potential exposure, and a twenty-six-week job-protected caregiving leave for those with dependent children or family members whose schools or facilities had closed. Although these leaves stayed in place until May 2022, eligibility criteria were progressively tightened and, consequently, uptake dropped off. Additionally, the federal government, quite belatedly, introduced legislation to grant federally regulated employees ten days of paid sick leave in December 2021, though delayed their coming into force for another year.[17]

Lastly, the FRPS has a relatively low rate of collective bargaining agreement coverage. Despite being better compensated and more secure than workers in the PRPS, only 21 percent of FRPS employees are unionized or covered by a collective agreement. Although this coverage is higher than that of employees in the PRPS (15 percent), it falls considerably short of union density in the public sector (75 percent). Because of the **union advantage** – the higher pay and better conditions that accrue to unionized employees – increasing union density would help to raise conditions at the bottom of the income distribution scale and improve pay for those in forms of employment identified with precariousness.

Additionally, because unions are the primary mechanism for facilitating employees' collective voice in the workplace, they also allow employees to counterbalance employers when major changes are made to the labour process or to work rules, as happened in many workplaces during the pandemic. Unionized employees were better able than their non-unionized counterparts to ensure safe working conditions, particularly for essential workers who had to continue their jobs as the coronavirus spread.

Barriers to unionization, such as workplace fissuring and other variegated ownership structures, necessitate changes to the laws governing unionization to allow greater access to collective bargaining. Simply put, it is more difficult for workers to form or join unions when they are spread across workplaces or businesses, when they are engaged by temporary employment agencies, or when their employment is otherwise insecure. As others have argued, in certain domains, such as transport, it is time for unions and workers' advocates to pursue a model of industrial relations centred on the sector rather than the firm, as well as to secure successor rights (legal provisions which allow a union to continue to represent employees in a bargaining unit and also allow for the continuation of collective agreements when a cohesive business or function is sold, transferred, or otherwise divested). In industries that we have identified as the sites of precariousness (e.g., road transportation), subcontracted workers, and workers in small firms could benefit from provisions for models of industry-level collective bargaining (oft called "sectoral bargaining") that allow for improved conditions of work and employment to be generalized across a given industry.[18]

BUILDING ON HISTORICAL ADVANTAGE

In several ways, the federally regulated private sector continues to be characterized by employment conditions that are better than those in the provincially regulated private sector. Larger firms, a lower proportion of workers in precarious employment, and slightly higher union coverage indicate that FRPS employees have relatively better working conditions than their provincial counterparts. As well, the superior working conditions in the FRPS are shaped in part by social minimums set out in the Canada Labour Code that are somewhat better than those in the PRPS. Nonetheless, precarious employment is more prominent in some industries in the FRPS than in others, with an accompanying erosion of labour standards.

In many respects, the FRPS remains a more worker-friendly jurisdiction than the PRPS, not only in terms of the lower precarious employment but also with respect to who is most affected. Indeed, FRPS employees who belong to historically disadvantaged social groups, such as women, recent immigrants, and young people, experience far less precarious employment than those in provincially regulated industries. These comparatively better conditions of employment can also be interpreted as a holdover flowing from its relatively high proportions of men, older workers, and full-time permanent jobs, and owing to the history of industries and occupations deemed to be in the national interest.

At times, the FRPS has functioned as a model for provincially regulated private-sector employment across the country, particularly in the realms of industrial relations and labour standards. To ensure that the precarious employment characteristics of the PRPS don't spread into FRPS – and that workers are better protected when extraordinary circumstances such as the pandemic arise – new policies must address the changing nature of employment and workplaces, and workers and unions need to exert pressure to make that happen.

ACKNOWLEDGMENTS

The analyses presented in this chapter were conducted at the University of Toronto Research Data Centre, which is part of the Canadian Research Data Centre Network (CRDCN). The services and activities provided by the University of Toronto RDC are made possible by the financial or in-kind support of the SSHRC, the CIHR, the CFI, Statistics Canada, and the University of Toronto. The views expressed in this paper do not necessarily represent those of the CRDCN or its partners.

We thank Heather Steel for her input on this chapter as well as editors John Peters and Don Wells.

ADDITIONAL RESOURCES

Vosko, Leah F. *Precarious Employment: Understanding Labour Market Insecurity in Canada.* Montreal and Kingston: McGill-Queen's University Press, 2006.

Weil, David. *The Fissured Workplace: Why Work Became So Bad for So Many and What Can Be Done to Improve It.* Cambridge, MA: Harvard University Press, 2014.

NOTES

1   Leah F. Vosko, *Managing the Margins: Gender, Citizenship, and the International Regulation of Precarious Employment* (Oxford: Oxford University Press, 2010). Leah F. Vosko, *Temporary Work: The Gendered Rise of a Precarious Employment Relationship* (Toronto: University of Toronto Press, 2000).

2   David Weil, *The Fissured Workplace: Why Work Became So Bad for So Many People and What Can Be Done to Improve it* (Cambridge, MA: Harvard University Press, 2014).

3   Peter W. Hogg, *Constitutional Law of Canada* (Toronto: Carswell, 2009).

4   Mark P. Thomas, "Setting the Minimum: Ontario's Employment Standards in the Postwar Years, 1944–1968," *Labour/Le Travail* 54 (Fall 2004): 49–82.

5   Barbara Cameron, "Social Reproduction and Canadian Federalism," in *Social Reproduction: Feminist Political Economy Challenges Neo-Liberalism*, ed. Kate Bezanson and Meg Luxton (Montreal and Kingston: McGill-Queen's University Press, 2006), 45–74.

6   Ibid.

7   Stephen McBride, "Coercion and Consent: The Recurring Corporatist Temptation in Canadian Labour Relations," in *Labour Gain, Labour Pains: Fifty Years of PC 1003*, eds. Cy Gonick, Paul Phillips, and Jesse Vorst (Winnipeg and Halifax: Society for Social Studies and Fernwood Publishing, 1995), 79–96.

8   Thomas, "Setting the Minimum."

9   Canada's Labour Force Survey collects information about the employment and self-employment activities of Canadians on a monthly basis: https://www.statcan.gc.ca/en/survey/list. It provides the government with information about the major labour market trends, such as shifts in employment across industrial sectors, hours worked, labour force participation, and unemployment rates. Data are weighted to reflect the Canadian population. Statistics Canada, *Guide to the Labour Force Survey* (Ottawa: Minister of Industry, 2016). The following discussion is based on LFS data from 2018.

10 For 2018, Statistics Canada released Labour Force Survey data only for people living in the ten provinces, not the territories.

11 Leah F. Vosko, "Precarious Employment: Towards an Improved Understanding of Labour Market Insecurity," in *Precarious Employment: Understanding Labour Market Insecurity in Canada*, ed. Leah F. Vosko (Montreal and Kingston: McGill-Queen's University Press, 2006), 3–39.

12 Weil, *The Fissured Workplace.*

13 Vosko, *Precarious Employment*; Andrea M. Noack and Leah F. Vosko, *Precarious Jobs in Ontario: Mapping Dimensions of Labour Market Insecurity by Workers' Social Location and Context* (Toronto: Law Commission of Ontario, 2012).

14 See, for example, contributions to Eileen Applebaum, Annette Bernhardt, and R.J. Murnane, eds., *Low-Wage America: How Employers Are Reshaping Opportunity in the Workplace* (New York: Russell Sage Foundation, 2003).

15 Notably, after concerted lobbying by ride-sharing and other app-based companies, in November 2020 California electors endorsed Proposition 22, which allows app-based ride-share and delivery drivers to be classified as independent contractors.

16 Applebaum, Bernhardt, and Murnane, eds., *Low-Wage America.*

17 Eric Tucker, Leah F. Vosko, and Sarah Marsden, "What We Owe Workers as a Matter of Common Humanity: Sickness and Caregiving Leaves and Pay in the Age of Pandemics," November 2020, https://digitalcommons.osgoode.yorku.ca/scholarly_works/2810.

18 Sue Cobble and Leah F. Vosko, "Historical Perspectives on Representing Workers in 'Non-Standard' Employment," in *Nonstandard Work: The Nature and Challenges of Changing Employment Relations*, ed. Françoise J. Carré, Marianne A. Ferber, Lonnie Golden, and Stephen A. Herzenberg (Champagne, IL: Industrial Relations Research Association, 2000), 291–312.

7 Why It's Hard to Organize a Union and Negotiate a Decent Contract

Rafael Gomez and Jennifer Harmer

CHAPTER SUMMARY

Labour law is supposed to balance three some-times conflicting objectives: the economic efficiency demanded by employers, the desire of workers to have some say in their wages and job conditions, and a wider societal need for equality. Compared to labour law in countries such as Germany and Austria, however, Canadian laws emphasize employer interests and efficiency at the expense of workplace voice and broad-based union representation.

This chapter examines the role of labour law and public policy in Canada and its impact on unions, workplaces, and the rise of bad jobs. It examines how labour law limits union certification, in particular by making unions organize individual workplaces rather than industries or sectors. The chapter addresses legal and regulatory problems that unions face in negotiating a first contract, and then details the aggressive union-avoidance strategies of private-sector employers and the inability or unwillingness of labour boards to adequately address employer violations of labour law.

The chapter concludes by describing some alternative labour laws and policies to increase worker voice, improve equality in the labour market, and maintain or even improve economic efficiency. Readers are encouraged to critically assess the alternatives proposed to address union decline in order to make their own determination about which path would be best for Canada's workers to follow.

KEY THEMES

This chapter will help you develop an understanding of:

- labour law and its impact on jobs, the workplace, and equality
- barriers to organizing a union and securing a first contract
- how current Canadian labour laws and legislation prioritize employer interests
- opportunities to rethink and revise the worker representation system.

COMMONLY, WE THINK about our jobs and work in exclusively economic terms: work as a commodity (something that can be exchanged, replaced, or outsourced) or a factor of production (no different from machinery or land). But thinking about everyday work in these ways ignores that labour is supplied by human beings. The essential human quality of labour has been brought into relief during the COVID-19 pandemic. Around the world, jobs that were once thought of as low skilled and unimportant to a twenty-first-century economy – retail clerks, cleaners, personal support workers – were transformed into essential services almost overnight, on par with medical practitioners and emergency first responders.

The reality, of course, is that these jobs were *always* essential from a broad socio-economic perspective, but under the narrowest economic lens of marginal value, the low wages and societal status these professions commanded meant they were invisible to most or unimportant to those in power.

The global pandemic exposed the fact that as workers, we do not simply exist alongside capital in the production process, like a machine or a computer. We are also in a *relationship* with capital – with business owners and employers who are in a position of power. These relationships are not purely economic. They are also social and political, and are shaped by governments, laws, and democratic institutions. And the decisions we make – about how to protect our jobs, about the role we have in determining our wages and working conditions, and about what kind of economy our society wants – govern how we work, how we are paid, what work benefits we receive, and the kind of life we can expect in particular jobs.

These processes are evident in employment relationships and the labour laws established to balance economic efficiency, equity, and voice at work.[1] In many countries, strong trade unions act as a powerful mechanism to assist with this balancing act, and labour laws and public policies play a key role in supporting or hindering the establishment of unions. Countries with accommodating labour laws that allow strong, independent trade unions to operate without interference or encumbrance often have the highest levels of economic development and equality, as well as the most developed kinds of political freedom.

But labour laws, and with them access to trade unions, differ widely across countries. In Canada, worker access to trade unions is limited by the nature of laws and institutions we have inherited from our neighbour south of the border. Provincial and federal labour law is fashioned after the US **Wagner** Act model of collective bargaining, which allows for union representation in individual workplaces but makes it difficult for workers to join a union or to organize one for the first time in a non-union setting. Wagner-style labour law also gives employers much leeway in opposing the establishment of unions and collective bargaining in the workplace.

In this respect, a trend has emerged in Canada that is troubling for organized and unorganized labour alike: the gradual decline of **union density** and collective bargaining coverage in the private sector. The non-union workplace is now common in the private sector, and millions of workers have never experienced union membership. Because strong unions are associated with greater job security and better benefits and wages for their members – and because collective bargaining also prompts non-union employers to standardize management practices, and increase wages and working conditions to match those of their unionized counterparts – union decline has coincided with a rise in non-standard, precarious work, or bad jobs. Canada's current labour laws have contributed to this problem in large measure by placing limits on worker voice and instead prioritizing a rather narrow conception of managerial efficiency, which equates maximal employer discretion with better economic outcomes.

UNIONIZATION OVER TIME AND ACROSS COUNTRIES

Part of the reason for declining unionization in Canada lies in the changing nature of work. Growth in **non-standard employment** has made it difficult for unions to organize under the existing Wagner-style model for several reasons.

First, because single worksites need to be organized one at a time, with the majority support of workers in each establishment, established trade union organizers typically offer their support only to workplaces that are large enough that they are likely to win an organizing drive. These tend to be places where standard well-paying jobs already prevail, such as public-sector organizations. Second, non-standard jobs are often performed by young people, new-

comers to Canada, and racialized workers. For these workers, getting decent work and trade union representation is usually difficult in the face of employer opposition. Finally, public policy in the form of labour laws plays a key role in workers' ability to form and join a union. The politics that informs labour laws differs substantially across the country and around the globe, creating significant variations in types of collective representation and union density and coverage.

As seen in Figure 7.1, union density (the proportion of workers who are members of trade unions) and collective bargaining coverage (the proportion of workers covered by collective agreements) appear high in Canada when compared to our nearest neighbour and most similar economic counterpart, the United States, but relatively low when compared to Western European countries.[2] Almost all member countries of the Organisation for Economic Co-operation and Development (OECD) have experienced a decline in union density since the 1980s. In fact, in countries such as the Netherlands and Germany, one can see the wide variation between bargaining coverage (which has remained above the OECD average) and density (which is much lower than in Canada).[3] Since unions rely on membership dues to fund their activities, the trend toward lower density – having actual dues-paying members – emphasizes that unions are under threat, even in countries like Germany that support collective bargaining through sectoral approaches and industry-wide agreements that apply to all workers regardless of whether they are members.

Disparate rates of unionization also illustrate the varied nature of historical struggles for fundamental workplace rights. The politicization of employment protections means that worker wins and losses in the political arena have a profound impact on real workplace protections and access to unions. As seen in Figure

FIGURE 7.1 Union density and coverage in selected OECD countries, 2018

Source: OECD Statistics, "Employment and Labour Market Statistics."

7.1, one in three Canadian workers today is covered by a collective agreement – almost 5 million individuals.[4] While this is indeed impressive, Figure 7.2 shows that most union representation is in the public sector, covering those who work for any level of government, a government service or agency, a Crown corporation, or a government-funded establishment such as a hospital, school or university, or utility. Public-sector unionization, representing close to 80 percent of all employees, is strong and stable in Canada. Union membership in the private sector, covering those who work as employees of a private firm or business, has meanwhile fallen from a high of 30 percent in the early 1980s to 20 percent in the mid-1990s and been stagnant since. This at the same time that the size of the non-unionized private-sector workforce has increased.[5]

The fall of private-sector unionism is the most obvious immediate cause of union decline in Canada. It is underpinned by the emergence of forces such as globalization, the shift from manufacturing to services, and advances in human resource management (e.g., management-led efforts to offer workers voice and non-union grievance procedures), all of which have challenged the primacy of unionism in the private sector. The effect of the decline extends beyond individual workers to encompass rising income inequality in Canadian society as a whole, which has been pernicious and well documented by labour economists.[6] But it extends further still, as industrial relations scholarship has emphasized the link between falling private-sector unionization and declining civic participation and increasingly polarized, populist politics.[7]

THE ROLE OF LAW IN LABOUR POWER

While many factors have led to varying levels of unionization around the globe and between the

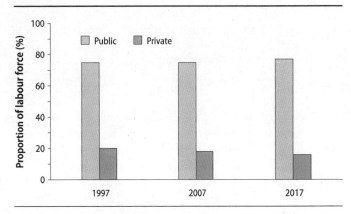

FIGURE 7.2 **Public- vs private-sector union density in Canada, 1997–2017**

Source: Statistics Canada, Table 14-10-0132-01: Union status by industry, https://doi.org/10.25318/1410013201-eng.

Canadian private and public sectors specifically, two factors are especially significant: the historical development of labour law in the particular country and the direct-action power struggles between workers and employers over labour rights.

Historically, governments in Canada ultimately acted and unions gained legislative protection only after unrest and battles between workers and employers – sometimes many years after. When legislation stalled, union activism re-emerged, culminating in the Winnipeg General Strike of 1919, a key event that demonstrated both the frustration and the power of organized labour. It also displayed the aggressive efforts of employers (abetted by government) to stop union organizing.

By the 1930s, industrial unions in Canada and the United States had succeeded in organizing many workers, regardless of the obstacles or the skill or trade in question.[8] Reflective of this new broad-based industrial union movement, the National Labor Relations Act (the Wagner Act) was passed in the United States in 1935 and deemed constitutional after a 1937

Supreme Court case. A similar framework was adopted in Canada (Order in Council P.C. 1003) in 1941.[9] This framework, which is still used today, focuses on workplace collective bargaining as a means to bring workers and employers together and channel conflicting interests through collective bargaining and its myriad institutions.[10]

Though Canada lagged behind the United States in the adoption of these reforms, subsequent decisions made the labour environment more favourable north of the border. For example, the Wagner Act was significantly weakened in the United States by the Labor Management Relations Act of 1947 (the Taft-Hartley Act). Among other provisions, the new act prohibited the *closed shop* (an arrangement that makes union membership a condition of employment), allowed states to prohibit the *agency shop* or *dues check-off* (requiring employees who are covered by a collective agreement to pay fees to a union to cover the costs of its bargaining on their behalf), narrowed the definition of *unfair labour practices*, and introduced specified *unfair union practices*.

Following the adoption of the Taft-Hartley Act, a number of states enacted so-called right-to-work laws, which banned both closed and agency shops. The Wagner Act was further amended in 1959 by the Labor–Management Reporting and Disclosure Act (Landrum-Griffin Act), which banned secondary boycotts and limited the right to picket. More recently, in the 2018 *Janus v American Federation of State, County, and Municipal Employees* case, the US Supreme Court invalidated agency shop provisions for all public-sector employees. Essentially, this means that public-sector unions can no longer require non-member employees to pay for union activities from which they benefit.

By way of contrast in Canada, union dues must be paid by all workers in a unionized workplace, as a result of a Supreme Court decision from 1946 known as the **Rand Formula**. Beginning in the 1960s, collective bargaining and agency shop rights were extended to all workers in the Canadian public sector, whereas in the United States this happened on a more limited basis.[11] In Canada, after enabling legislation was passed both federally and provincially allowing public-sector workers the right to strike (something rarely permitted in the United States), the public-sector union rate took off and has not abated since.

A key factor in the success or failure of unionism is the role played by financial and human resources in enabling unions to represent their current members and expand their reach. Here again, Canadian trade unions had an advantage over their US counterparts due to the Rand Formula. The formula dates back to an arbitration decision by Justice Ivan Rand of the Supreme Court of Canada in 1946 that ended a United Auto Workers strike at a Ford plant in Windsor, Ontario. At the heart of the decision was recognition of the union as the bargaining agent for *all* workers at the plant. Justice Rand decided that union dues should be paid by all those who benefited from the union contract, not just the signed members of the union. Rand saw agency shop provisions as fostering labour peace and a harmonious labour relations climate. This feature is a crucial component of successful unionism in Canada, avoiding the *free-rider problem* (getting union benefits without paying for them) and securing financial resources for the labour movement.[12] In the United States, however, over half of state governments now prohibit workers and management from automatically deducting dues payments from the paycheques of workers represented by the union, thereby hampering the financial viability of trade union operations.

Public policy, in particular legislation, is therefore central to the process of organizing unions and negotiating collective agreements.

In this regard, one of the distinguishing features of Canadian labour law is the multiple jurisdictions that constitute the legislative landscape. As a federation, legislative coverage in Canada is decentralized, which results in a number of frameworks across the nation. Workers in neighbouring jurisdictions may find themselves with different working conditions and entitlements, and a complicated system of laws dictates the rules governing union formation and worker representation.[13] The decentralized nature of union organization also means that workplaces are generally organized on a workplace-by-workplace basis. This creates a very costly environment for unions to gain members. There are exceptions by industry and differences across provinces in this regard. The construction industry, for example, has a form of sectoral bargaining in several jurisdictions, including Ontario, the largest.[14] Nevertheless, the existence of multiple jurisdictions makes sectoral bargaining and the extension of bargaining coverage to non-union workers almost impossible.

Another key feature of Canadian labour law is the application of the **Charter of Rights and Freedoms**. Although the Charter recognizes freedom of association, freedom of peaceful assembly, and freedom of thought, these rights have some notable limitations. Some of the most significant Charter challenges relating to union representation have identified the limits of freedom of association. Laws that are widely deemed to be reasonable in a free and democratic society may be an exception to the Charter, such as the right for minority opinions and the individual civil liberties of minority groups to be protected from some majority rules practiced inside unions (e.g., the use of union funds to support causes that are opposed on religious or moral grounds by individual union members). Further, provincial legislatures may invoke the notwithstanding provision despite a perceived infringement on

---

BOX 7.1 THE WAGNER ACT

The Wagner Act, officially the National Labor Relations Act of 1935, is the most important piece of labour legislation enacted in the United States in the twentieth century. Its main purpose was to establish the legal right of most workers to organize or join labour unions and to bargain collectively with their employers. Agricultural and domestic workers were notably exempted. The Wagner Act gets its name from the person who sponsored the bill, Democratic senator Robert F. Wagner of New York.

The Act guaranteed the right of workers to organize and outlined the legal framework for union and management relations. In addition to protecting workers, the Act protected employers from unlawful strike activity and provided a framework for collective bargaining. Designed during the Great Depression of the 1930s – a time when workers and owners often clashed violently over whether workers could elect unions to represent their interests at the workplace – the Act stabilized labour relations.

The Wagner Act also created the National Labor Relations Board (NLRB), which oversees union–management relations. The NLRB designates the legal structure for forming and decertifying unions and conducting elections. The Board investigates charges by workers, union representatives, and employers that their rights under the Wagner Act have been violated.

Charter-specific rights.[15] These caveats can create barriers to access to unions and to bargaining alongside coworkers even if these activities broadly have Charter protection.

Industrial relations scholars have long embraced the notion that better labour market outcomes emerge when there is balance of efficiency, equity, and voice (EEV), in the employment relationship. Constitutional provisions relating to equity and voice reinforce the notion of labour rights as a human right, whereas government policies that drive business interests (such as initiatives to reduce red tape) prioritize property rights and efficiency.

Although in Canada struggles to embed mechanisms that facilitate worker voice in workplaces are ongoing, many highly prosperous countries in Europe, including Germany and Sweden, have enshrined systems of worker voice in the private sector without a seeming cost to efficiency. While more worker voice could lead to conflict over policy and legislation, the evidence suggests that the benefits (such as increased communication and involvement at work) often outweigh the potential costs (such as limits to limits on employers' freedom of decision-making and increased time spent bargaining and negotiating).

HURDLES TO ORGANIZING A UNION

Unions provide benefits to workers in the form of increased wages and benefits, improved job security, and protection from potentially arbitrary or inconsistent management decision making.[16] They also benefit the workforce as a whole and the general public, since unions advocate for social and public policy reforms that affect individuals who are not members and reduce social and economic inequality generally.[17] In addition to promoting equity, they encourage worker voice and even productive efficiency. A union provides an opportunity for employees to voice their ideas to management and have a hand in workplace decision making. Further, collective bargaining systems facilitate communication between management and workers, and can disseminate useful shop-floor knowledge that improves production and service delivery.[18]

Not surprisingly, research shows that many non-union workers would prefer to have collective bargaining and that a majority of existing members are in favour of keeping their unions. This challenges the widespread belief that declining union membership is due to a lack of worker interest. Nevertheless, even workers who want unionization face costs in the form of employer hostility and legislative barriers.[19]

Among the factors that undermine successful workplace organizing, the greatest impediment is how unionization is politically and legally structured in Canada. In every jurisdiction in the country, each non-union workplace has to be organized individually even if the parent company is the same. If workers want to organize Tim Hortons, for example, the majority of workers in each establishment has to vote in favour of unionization in order to begin collective bargaining. For individuals with no experience establishing unions (which is to say, most workers), forming one in a non-union workplace is a significant challenge.[20]

The default in Canada is a non-union/no-voice status in each and every workplace. This means that all private-sector workplaces are, by design, unorganized, non-unionized environments until either an employer voluntarily recognizes a staff or employee association, a union forms from within, or a successful external organizing drive from a national or international union takes hold.[21] Otherwise, there is essentially no formal collective representation at work.

Each step outlined in the certification process is prescribed in labour relations legislation and subject to change with the election of a new government and the introduction of new laws. Labour relations legislation includes the required level of support for certification, and this often fluctuates with the government in power. Therefore, all these policies and procedures are malleable within the jurisdiction and government of the day.

Canadian labour laws often challenge the concept of labour rights as human rights because they don't guarantee voice and freedom of association at work. Rather, as currently constructed, the laws simply permit workers to organize for access to these indelible rights. Further, even though laws exist to protect workers and the organizing process, this does not mean they are always followed, an issue known as the *compliance problem*. For example, it is against the law for an employer to punish, demote, or fire an employee for union-related activity, but they frequently do. This is why enforcement of labour laws is essential to ensure workers and unions are protected and their Charter rights are not violated.

Another major challenge to collective representation is employer resistance, often driven by fear of a domino effect at other locations. This highlights an underlying problem with the Wagner Act model in that it requires every workplace – even for a vast retail chain or corporate entity that operates numerous identical locations – to go through an independent organizing process. The costly process is fraught with risk of failure, which may not be sustainable for a relatively small group of workers who have limited ability to withhold their labour on a broader (sectoral) scale.

These accumulated barriers have led to falling union certification drives and win rates in the private sector. Figure 7.3 shows approved certification and decertification applications in Ontario as an example. Decertification involves an election in which a majority of employees

BOX 7.2 THE WALMART SAGA

The United Food and Commercial Workers (UFCW) International Union attempted to organize a Walmart store in Jonquière, Quebec. The workers were successful, but Walmart has an avowedly anti-union stance. The company is headquartered in Arkansas, a state with a union density rate of less than 5 percent.

As proven in court, the company's executives instructed the local management to bargain in bad faith with the union, thereby thwarting an otherwise successful organizing drive. The fight for unionization, subsequent failure to obtain a first contract, and then closure of the store – followed by years of litigation culminating with a Supreme Court decision that vindicated the workers' struggle but failed to restore their jobs – has been well documented in labour circles. While the attempt by workers to assert their labour rights at Walmart was honourable, the cost to themselves and to the UFCW was high.

One of the lessons learned from this case, and others like it, is that retail workers in Canada – many of whom are part time, young, and working for minimum wage – find the process of unionization extremely difficult. The tortuous steps required (local union organizing, card checks, majority voting procedures, etc.) date back to various federal and provincial labour relations acts that were created in the late 1940s. At the time, a stable employment relationship and permanent job were embedded in the assumptions that guided those drafting postwar labour laws. They do not reflect the reality of many service-sector jobs and workplaces today.

The rules governing union certification, though intended to offer protection to workers, today present barriers to unionization in Canada and have subsequently led to a unionization rate of 11 percent for wholesale and retail workers, and 5.6 percent for workers in the accommodation and food services nationwide in 2018.

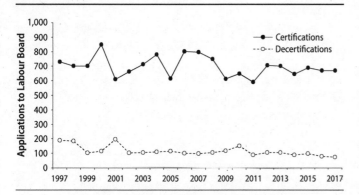

Source: Data from Ontario Labour Relations Board, Applications for Union Certification and Decertification, OLRB annual reports 2000–18, https://cirhr.library.utoronto.ca/digital-collections/ontario-labour-relations-board-annual-reports.

indicate that they no longer wish to be represented by a union. While the figure reflects a bumpy but progressive fall in certification attempts since the late 1990s, decertification attempts have been low and steady, as is the case in most jurisdictions using a Wagner Act approach.

STEPS IN GAINING UNION REPRESENTATION

A close investigation of the steps required to organize and certify a union reveals some stumbling blocks to workers gaining voice. Once those are understood it is possible to identify potentially important options for Canadian workers.

Certifying a Union

Imagine that a majority of workers want collective representation at their workplace. Most of the time in Canada, the journey to union representation will be long and drawn out. Typically, workers must first sign membership cards (the card check), which demonstrates their desire to join the union. A substantial portion of employ-

ees (typically 40–50 percent, though this varies by jurisdiction) must sign cards for the process to move to the next step. The employer, perhaps sensing that a vote for unionization is likely, might decide at this stage to bargain voluntarily with its employees.[22] If this tactic proves unsuccessful, the union will apply for certification to the **labour relations board**.

Next, an election is planned at the workplace. Eligible workers submit secret ballots during the certification election, which is run by the labour relations board in the given jurisdiction. This mandatory election determines if a majority of employees want to join the union.[23] Mandatory voting, as opposed to a simple card check or automatic certification based on indicators of employee support, is another major barrier. Union organizing is much more likely to succeed via card check-only systems than via voting systems, and several provincial governments have recently made legislative changes that appear to make unionization more difficult, particularly with respect to moves toward secret-ballot elections for certification.[24]

Even after a successful election, the question of who is eligible to join the union is fundamental. In Canada, only employees are eligible to be union members, but determining employee status can be complicated.[25] In particular, new technologies that enable platform work have blurred the line between employee and independent contractor. Further, workers labelled as *associates*, *partners*, or *managers* are often excluded from organizing drives even if their job titles belie their actual level and role in the organization. The rationale for excluding these workers is that trade unions should operate free from employer or management involvement. A conflict of interest could occur if a manager were in the same bargaining unit as an employee when disciplinary issues arise. In some jurisdictions, however, managers may unionize in separate bargaining units.[26]

While some consider the organizing steps to be necessary for due process, many union advocates believe they are in fact costly hurdles that slow or impede access to collective representation. Certainly there is no evidence to suggest that these bureaucratic obstacles help workers organize unions.

Negotiating a First Contract

Once certification is granted, unions often face a second hurdle in negotiating a first contract. Under law, employers and employees must **bargain in good faith** and do so exclusively with each other. The union also has the **duty of fair representation**, meaning that it has to act fairly on behalf of all individuals represented (even those who voted against organizing and wish to remain non-members).[27] Thus, negotiating the first contract is an important milestone for a new union and employer. It is a recognition of employee intention to have the union act as its negotiator. It legitimizes the union and establishes the formalized employment relationship enshrining the goal that labour and capital come together to resolve differences and find common ground.

Negotiating a first contract is often a very difficult and arduous process. In Ontario, for example, the success rate of unions negotiating first contracts without third-party involvement is only 38 percent. In the United States the rate is even lower at 20 percent. Both these figures are low because first agreements are often more difficult to bargain than other contracts.[28] It's essential that the parties develop at least a minimal level of trust in the relationship. They must also learn to bargain in good faith. If a contract isn't reached or one of the parties walks away from negotiations, a third party may be brought in to help establish an agreement. In this regard, several jurisdictions in Canada provide for compulsory first contract arbitration. This could be in the form of automatic access to arbitration, provision of arbitration at the discretion of the labour board, or even imposition of the first contract. British Columbia's model provides for intensive mediation for first contracts and access to contract arbitration as a

---

BOX 7.3 THE UNIONIZATION OF WESTJET

Despite being in business since the mid-1990s, and being in an industry with high rates of unionization, it wasn't until 2018 that WestJet Airlines became the subject of a union drive. The Canadian Union of Public Employees (CUPE) filed an application with the Canada Industrial Relations Board to represent 3,000 cabin crew members after a clear majority signed cards supporting the union drive.[29] The top issues for the cabin crew were scheduling, long work days, compensation that defined flying time purely as hours in the air, and how they felt treated by management. The next step was for the flight attendants to elect an executive and create a bargaining committee to negotiate the first contract, which occurred in late 2018.

The campaign to unionize the flight attendants came not long after the Air Line Pilots Association was certified to represent WestJet pilots. The employer and union agreed to binding arbitration after negotiations failed to reach a contract, and the arbitrator identified the terms for the first collective agreement.[30] The pilots voted in favour of the agreement, which increased wages, tightened job security, and improved working conditions.

Prior to unions forming at WestJet, the company had a system of internal workplace committees in which workers met with management and discussed issues of mutual interest. The WestJet system of non-union representation lasted for nearly twenty years and was a precursor to collective representation. One could argue that it prevented unionization from arising earlier, but it can equally be said that it laid the foundation for the successful union certification drive that ensued.

way to address failures by both parties and/or any employer transgression. Compulsory first contract arbitration is therefore a mechanism to avoid strikes and lockouts.[31] Finally, once a collective agreement has been negotiated, it needs to be ratified by a vote of members.

Once an agreement is in place, employees are no longer allowed to strike until such time as that contract expires. Further, there may be opportunities for raids from other unions to take over representation of the bargaining unit if members are not happy with the negotiation process of their union. A raid occurs when enough members feel that they would be better off with another union representing their interests. Union members and/or another union that catches wind of the disgruntlement initiates the raid.

Unfair Labour Practices and Employer Resistance

A final legal barrier to unionization is that the law allows employers and governments alike to oppose the formation of new unions.[32] Probably because unions shift the balance of power toward employees, and because they may increase labour costs for employers, business owners often oppose the establishment of unions in their individual workplaces. Employer efforts to keep unions out and retain full control over wages and working conditions can occur before, during, and even well after a successful union drive. Canada's labour law system is highly decentralized, and the private sector is largely bereft of union presence, so firms have a strong incentive to remain union free at the workplace.

Before an organizing drive, employers may take action to reduce the likelihood of a union forming. While this is permissible, promises and threats are not allowed because they influence an individual's free choice and thus fall under **unfair labour practices (ULPs)**, a category

of actions that labour boards are entrusted with preventing and punishing. Employers nonetheless often commit ULPs in attempts to quash union drives. While unions can also engage in ULPs, the vast majority are committed by the employer. Examples include threats to close a worksite where workers intend to unionize or to fire union organizers. Some of the more common anti-union ULPs used in the United States are prohibited in Canada. In the United States, for example, employers can hold captive audience meetings of workers. At such meetings, where worker attendance is required and union views are expressly kept out, management might make its anti-union position known and voice threats about workplace closure if workers form a union.[33]

Employers also frequently enlist the help of outside consultants and lawyers to implement union avoidance tactics.[34] Among the most effective anti-union strategies are training managers to deal with the unionization campaign and limiting union communication with potential members. Employers might also prohibit union organizers from soliciting potential members on private property. Under Canadian law, an employer may also forbid individuals acting on behalf of the union from soliciting support during work hours at the worksite.[35]

In some circumstances, differing legitimate freedoms may conflict, such as the employer's freedom of expression and the employees' freedom to organize a union without coercion. Jurisdictions within Canada have identified similar language around ULPs, and labour boards have remedies for these practices, which may even include certifying the union with less than the required level of employee support when employer intimidation is overt.[36] Such measures are intended to protect the integrity of the collective bargaining process, but, as is painfully obvious, the process can be cumbersome for workers only interested in having a modicum of representative voice at work.[37] Finally, after a union has been established, employers might encourage support (subtly enough to evade a ULP) for decertification.[38]

LABOUR POLICIES AND STRATEGIES FOR INCREASING WORKER VOICE

No major reforms to labour law have been made in the United States since the late 1950s. The main impact of this policy atrophy is a deep decline in unionism. Moreover, as described above, the cumbersome process involved in certifying a union is at the root of the problem in the private sector. In the face of private-sector union density decline and of the considerable barriers to unionization embedded in the Canadian system of labour relations, what are the options for increasing worker voice? Two alternative policy approaches would probably yield greater returns: improving existing laws, and democratizing workplaces.

Improving Existing Laws

While the Canadian context provides opportunities for employee voice beyond unionism, such as voluntarily recognized employee associations and workplace committees, unionism is still the predominant vehicle for employee voice.[39] Collective bargaining and union representation can address many current problems faced by workers, but labour law must be reformed to make it easier for workers to organize and certify. Amending the existing Wagner Act model to improve worker say in decision making at non-union worksites is a plausible option. Reforms such as automatic card certification and elimination or reduction of secret ballot voting would increase the number of workers with access to collective bargaining and positively influence union density.[40]

Introducing reforms to the existing Wagner Act model to improve worker say in decision making at non-union worksites is an option that would meet some of the significant demand for collective voice mechanisms among non-union employees.[41] While the Canadian context provides opportunities for employee voice beyond unionism, such as voluntarily recognized employee associations and workplace committees, unionism is still the predominant vehicle for employee voice.[42] Collective bargaining and union representation can address many current problems faced by workers, but labour law must be reformed to make it easier for workers to organize and certify. Amendments such as automatic card certification and elimination or reduction of secret ballot voting would increase the number of workers with access to collective bargaining and positively influence union density.[43]

One has to ask, however, how effective this option would be. How well would adjustments to existing laws empower workers and unions to keep up with the changing nature of work? Probably not as much as proponents of these legal changes would like to admit. This is why a tweak or even an expansion of the Wagner Act model would be insufficient.

Democratizing Workplaces

This second option is decidedly more ambitious. It involves rethinking the framework and institutions that shape the world of work. This begins with a national conversation about what the fundamental rights of individuals working in this country should be. Are there irremovable protections or opportunities that should be guaranteed to all, regardless of their job or jurisdiction? If so, a constitutional amendment may be necessary, or a modernization of legislation, to guarantee more expansive and fundamental worker rights.

One practical option may be to enable multi-establishment and regional bargaining units. This approach could involve centralized, industry-level bargaining that pools small organizations and small groups of otherwise unorganized workers. In nineteen countries worldwide, bargaining is almost always done at the industry or national level while still allowing for regional and workplace-specific amendments and exclusions.[44] Whether collective bargaining takes place at the national, sectoral, or workplace level is the single most important predictor of bargaining coverage.[45]

Why not provide a more just balance of employer and employee interests in every workplace? The fact that labour is increasingly dissociated from a single worksite, and is instead more often being managed through platforms like Uber and TaskRabbit, necessitates a bolder response. Flexible work, irregular hours, and working from home (accelerated by the COVID-19 pandemic) have all grown tremendously, making workers more difficult to unionize. The recent trend toward platform work, in which workers communicate with customers directly through an electronic medium, means that there is no oxygen-breathing management, just an algorithm masquerading as a labour intermediary.

Reforms in this space would have to be far reaching and focus on how current policies and procedures apply to the reality of work today. New laws in this context should centre on support for the creation of professional employee associations or craft-style unions that would negotiate with the platform owners over better terms and conditions of work and a higher percentage of payments. A more radical system of promoting worker-owned cooperatives in the platform economy would be better still. Cooperative enterprises are owned and run by the employees, and some argue that although this model is technically a non-union option, it can provide workers with a far higher degree of representation and workplace voice than traditional forms of collective bargaining.[46]

Unions should also reconsider whom they serve and how they operate. They need to extend the benefits of unionism to a broader set of workers who are not dues-paying members and might never be organized for the purpose of collective bargaining. Unions could reflect on how to reach the unemployed, underemployed, and those who have been marginalized by the new economy – groups encompassing typically under-represented demographics such as young people, new Canadians, and racialized workers. This approach is sometimes labelled **social unionism**, and it is experiencing a surge in jurisdictions across Canada and particularly in Quebec, where it has been a dominant model for some time.[47] Social unionism occurs when unions join struggles for social justice, advocating for those with little or no political voice and helping to provide progressive political alternatives to growing populist movements of the far right (see Chapter 18).

Unions could also innovate by embracing communication technology to connect with workers abroad and push for improved international standards of work. Globally oriented unionism would move away from nationalist approaches to organizing and worker advocacy and toward one that crosses borders, just as capital crosses borders to generate revenue and expand markets.[48]

Some labour scholars advocate for systemic legislative reforms, such as stronger human rights laws, layoff provisions, minimum wages, and protections against elimination of jobs. This approach would necessitate reshaping labour-management institutions to normalize a universal form of collective bargaining. To achieve these goals, unions would have to push for more participatory forms of representation, such as German-style works councils functioning at the local level to represent workers while complementing national labour negotiations. Laws that provide representation for workers on company boards would also be needed.

These reforms would provide workers with a more active position inside organizations without recourse to a costly and low-probability organizing drive. More fundamentally and importantly, this heterodox approach would also enable workers to have more say in the decision making that profoundly affects their lives at work and beyond. In some industrial relations systems – in Germany, Denmark, Norway, Sweden, and Finland, for example – unions and workers are considered social partners, and unions therefore cover far larger numbers of workers than they do in Canada or the United States.[49]

A VOICE FOR THE FUTURE

Labour laws and collective bargaining are central to improving the lives of workers, their ability to secure good jobs, and the functioning of workplaces. Trade unions are an essential part of achieving a balance between labour and capital in the economy broadly, along with a more equitable mix of equity, efficiency, and voice at work.

Overcoming the barriers to unions and collective bargaining and finding opportunities to improve worker voice can yield rewards for individuals and society. As the world of work changes, it is important to challenge the notion that only full-time, permanent employees in a single workplace can join unions. All workers should be able to realize their labour rights as human rights and be guaranteed a minimum floor of voice and representation that includes access to due process, collective bargaining, and input into decision making.

A more meaningful goal is the elimination of bad jobs, such that all workers achieve a high standard of living and decent work regardless of job title or employment status. The collective realization under lockdowns that essential work is often low paid and undervalued has reinforced the need for this endeavour. Industrial relations scholars tend to view the world through the lens of work, and that has been no different during the pandemic. When provincial governments announced lockdown measures and elected leaders admonished us all to "stay the blazes home," (i.e., Stephen McNeil, premier of Nova Scotia, speaking at a news conference on April 3, 2020) the thoughts of those who study work immediately turned to those who were working harder and risking more as a result.

Indeed, many workers have shouldered the brunt of the public health response to COVID-19 since the first lockdown: the personal support workers (PSWs) in nursing homes, the retail workers in supermarkets and big box stores, and the warehouse employees working in online fulfillment centres. Each time a provincial government official announced a lockdown order, risk was shifted from one group of citizens to another. Online orders were fulfilled by workers who could not shelter in place but instead had to work alongside hundreds of others in windowless warehouses dotting the fringes of the country's major urban centres. Largely non-unionized box store workers faced added risks through contact with thousands of shoppers.

The shocking thing was that no one – not even progressive media outlets – drew attention to these work- and health-related problems when lockdown measures were debated. The plight of overworked and burned-out Amazon warehouse employees was occasionally spotlighted in one section of the newspaper while an editorial in another castigated anyone who questioned the inherent inequality embedded in lockdowns or indeed their efficacy in reducing COVID-19 transmission.

Nor did elected officials address the problems associated with continually expanding the list of essential care workers who were required to go to job sites while stay-at-home orders were in place (Chapter 13). The health risks faced by PSWs were by far the worst. Lockdowns shut down the reserve army of family and volunteers that once made the sector viable. At the same time, the situation made the understaffing, poor pay, and terrible working conditions in this sector depressingly apparent. And with each successive lockdown, this often invisible army of care workers faced ever rising rates of infection.

Unions are the only bulwark against abuse and lack of recognition for frontline staff. The lack of union penetration in Walmart box stores and Amazon warehouses, for example, allowed far too many abuses and unsafe working conditions to persist for far longer than if these workplaces had been unionized.[50]

The current legislative framework for unions was late in coming to Canada, and employer efforts to repeal, undermine, or simply ignore these rules have become more aggressive and wide ranging. Workers and unions constantly attempt to defend and extend social protections and to increase existing collective rights (equity and voice), while capital and managers constantly seek to reduce regulatory burdens and to advance policies to foster business success (efficiency). How different jurisdictions resolve this tension is central in determining who is ultimately unionized.

Tension over efficiency, equity, and voice remains at the heart of workplace political struggles. The state of unions and the parameters within which they bargain in Canada are not fixed, and there are opportunities for more comprehensive worker representation. Twenty-first-century labour market realities require a new, more effective vision to support workers' representative voice.

ADDITIONAL RESOURCES

Canadian Labour Congress. https://canadianlabour.ca. Information about unions and their most important issues.

Canadian Law of Work Forum. http://lawofwork.ca. Research and discussion on some of the latest issues in the world of work.

Hicks Morley. *Setting up Shop in Canada? What U.S. Employers Need to Know about Canadian Labour Law.* Part 2. September 12, 2018. https://www.youtube.com/watch?time_continue=246&v=YMqWTqLkG8E&feature=emb_logo. Video discussing some of the key differences between Canadian and US labour law. It highlights issues such as the Rand Formula and the responsibilities of the employer during union drives and negotiations.

Industrial Relations and Human Resources Library. https://guides.library.utoronto.ca/CIRHRLibrary Guide. A University of Toronto portal to online and print resources on the key issues for workers and unions.

International Labour Organization. "Statistics and Databases." https://www.ilo.org/global/statistics-and-databases/lang-en/index.htm. Data and tables on various topics of work including employment, wages, and unionization across the globe.

Organisation for Economic Co-operation and Development. "The Future of Work." http://www.oecd.org/employment/future-of-work. Information on the changing nature of work across the globe in terms of collective bargaining, regulatory matters, and recommendations to help workers make the transition.

NOTES

1 John Budd, *Employment with a Human Face* (Ithaca, NY: Cornell University Press, 2004).
2 OECD Statistics, "Trade Union Density in OECD Countries," April 27, 2018, https://stats.oecd.org/Index.aspx?DataSetCode=TUD.
3 Ibid.

4   Statistics Canada, Table 14-10-0065-01: Employee wages by job permanency and union coverage, monthly, unadjusted for seasonality, https://doi.org/10.25318/1410006501-eng.

5   Rafael Gomez, *Employee Voice and Representation in the New World of Work: Issues and Options for Ontario* (Toronto: Queen's Printer, 2016).

6   David Card, Thomas Lemieux, and Craig Riddell, "Unions and Wage Inequality," *Journal of Labor Research* 25, no. 4 (Winter 2004): 519–59.

7   Rafael Gomez and Juan Gomez, "Workplace Democracy for the 21st Century: Towards a New Agenda for Employee Voice and Representation in Canada," Broadbent Institute Discussion Paper, 2016, https://www.broadbentinstitute.ca/workplace_democracy.

8   Robert Hebdon and Travor C. Brown, *Industrial Relations in Canada* (Toronto: Nelson Education, 2016).

9   David J. Doorey, *The Law of Work: Industrial Relations and Collective Bargaining* (Toronto: Emond Publishing, 2017).

10 Hebdon and Brown, *Industrial Relations.*

11 Ibid.

12 Daphne Gottlieb Taras and Allen Ponak, "Mandatory Agency Shop Laws as an Explanation of Canada–US Union Density Divergence," *Journal of Labor Research* 22, no. 3 (2001): 514–68.

13 Doorey, *The Law of Work.*

14 Wesley B. Rayner, Mike Rayner, James G. Knight, and Brian MacDonald, eds., *Canadian Collective Bargaining Law: Principles and Practice* (Toronto: LexisNexis Canada, 2017).

15 See Fiona A.E. McQuarrie, *Industrial Relations in Canada*, 4th ed. (Toronto: John Wiley and Sons Canada, 2015); Rayner et al., *Canadian Collective.*

16 Statistics Canada, Table 14-10-0065-01; Dwayne Benjamin, Morley Gunderson, Thomas Lemieux, and Craig Riddell, *Labour Market Economics* (Toronto: McGraw-Hill Ryerson, 2017).

17 Barry Eidlin, *Labor and the Class Idea in the United States and Canada* (Cambridge: Cambridge University Press, 2018).

18 Benjamin et al., *Labour Market.*

19 Eidlin, *Labor and the Class Idea.*

20 Gomez, *Employee Voice.*

21 Ibid.

22 John W. Budd, *Labor Relations: Striking a Balance* (New York: McGraw-Hill Education, 2018).

23 Ibid.

24 Benjamin et al., *Labour Market.*

25 McQuarrie, *Industrial Relations.*

26 Rayner et al., *Canadian Collective.*

27 Ibid.

28 Joel Cutcher-Gershenfeld, Thomas A. Kochan, and John Calhoun Wells, "How Do Labor and Management View Collective Bargaining," *Monthly Labor Review* 121 (Spring 1998): 30; C. Michael Mitchell and John C. Murray, *The Changing Workplaces Review - Final Report: An Agenda for Workplace Rights*, May (Toronto: Ontario Ministry of Labour, 2017), https://files.ontario.ca/books/mol_changing_workplace_report_eng_2_0.pdf.

29 Ross Marowits, "WestJet Loses Another Unionization Battle as CUPE to Represent Flight Attendant," *CityNews*, August 1, 2018, toronto.citynews.ca.

30 See Kyle Bakx, "Majority of WestJet Flight Attendants Sign Union Cards, Says CUPE," *CBC News*, July 9, 2018, www.cbc.ca; Canadian Free Press, "Arbitrator Sets Contract Terms for WestJet Pilots after Lengthy Negotiations," *CTV News*, December 21, 2018, www.ctvnews.ca.

31 Mitchell and Murray, *Changing Workplaces*; Rayner et al., *Canadian Collective.*

32 Doorey, *The Law of Work.*

33 Rayner et al., *Canadian Collective*; Budd, *Labor Relations*; McQuarrie, *Industrial Relations.*

34 Budd, *Labor Relations.*

35 McQuarrie, *Industrial Relations.*

36 Ibid.

37 Rayner et al., *Canadian Collective.*

38 Budd, *Labor Relations.*

39 Michele Campoleiti, Rafael Gomez, and Morley Gunderson. "Say What? Employee Voice in Can-

ada," in *What Workers Say: Employee Voice in the Anglo-American Workplace*, ed. Peter B. Freeman, Peter Boxall, and Peter Haynes (Ithaca, NY: Cornell University Press, 2007), 49–71.

40 John Godard, *Industrial Relations, the Economy, and Society* (Concord: Captus Press, 2017).

41 Michele Campoleiti, Rafael Gomez, and Morley Gunderson. "What Accounts for the Representation Gap? Decomposing Canada–US Differences in the Desire for Collective Voice," *Journal of Industrial Relations* 53, no. 4 (2011): 425.

42 Michele Campoleiti, Rafael Gomez, and Morley Gunderson. "Say What? Employee Voice in Canada," in *What Workers Say: Employee Voice in the Anglo-American Workplace*, ed. Peter B. Freeman, Peter Boxall, and Peter Haynes (Ithaca, NY: Cornell University Press, 2007), 49–71.

43 John Godard, *Industrial Relations, the Economy, and Society* (Concord: Captus Press, 2017).

44 Ibid.

45 Jelle Visser, Susan Hayter, and Rosina Gammarano, "Trends in Collective Bargaining Coverage: Stability, Erosion or Decline?" International Labour Organization, *Labour Relations and Collective Bargaining*, Issue brief no. 1 (November 1, 2017).

46 Gomez, *Employee Voice.*

47 Hebdon and Brown, *Industrial Relations.*

48 Ibid.

49 Godard, *Industrial Relations.*

50 Tavia Grant, "Business Is Booming at Amazon Canada, but Workers Say the Pandemic Is Adding to Safety Concerns," *Globe and Mail*, January 10, 2021, theglobeandmail.com.

8 The Politics of Health and Safety at Work

Andrew King

CHAPTER SUMMARY

This chapter explores relationships between work, politics, and the health of workers in Canada. It begins with a discussion about the extent of work-related injury and illness, and how official information minimizes and distorts the **hazards** that workers experience. The chapter outlines the evolution of **occupational health and safety (OHS)** from the industrial revolution to the present, and describes the creation and role of the health and safety movement.

This chapter explains the responsibilities of employers, workers, unions, and governments in protecting workers' health and safety in the workplace, examining how neoliberal policies have undermined worker protections. It explores four key challenges to health and safety practice: the myth of worker carelessness, the limits of enforcement, inadequate protection from employer reprisals, and the increasing prevalence of workplace violence. Finally, the chapter reflects on how workers' experience of the COVID-19 pandemic has been made worse by these same neoliberal policies.

KEY THEMES

This chapter will help you develop an understanding of:

- why work is hazardous to health
- how politics and power influence the implementation and effectiveness of OHS policy
- the development of OHS laws
- the importance of worker participation and representation in efforts to improve health and safety
- the challenges to workers' health presented by neoliberal policies and the pandemic.

WORK TAKES A HUGE toll on workers' lives. From the earliest days of mechanization – when workers' bodies could literally be chewed up and spewed out and their families left in poverty – the risks have only proliferated. Increasing technological sophistication in industrial processes throughout the twentieth century has led to more frequent and more varied injuries. Toxic chemical exposure caused cancer. The repetitive motions of work on conveyors has created musculo-skeletal injuries to almost all the body's joints, and sometimes fatalities.

These historical risks are compounded today by technological advances that increase workers' cognitive responsibilities on the job while reducing their control over the work to be done. In a predominantly services-based economy, stress and workplace violence have become major concerns. Preventative strategies to improve occupational health and safety (OHS) still reflect much of the industrial past and have not caught up with changes in workplaces. Neoliberal policies of deregulation and limited enforcement of workers' rights have exacerbated these limitations and undermined effective worker representation in health and safety. As a result, thousands die from workplace-related injuries and illnesses in Canada every year that are not counted in official statistics, and hundreds of thousands more are injured or made ill by their work (Figure 8.1).

The COVID-19 pandemic has shone a spotlight on the health and safety problems that workers face both on and off the job. Health care workers, home care workers, and migrant workers were among the hardest hit, and their experiences have shown the important relationships between workers' rights and worker health. For example, in Ontario, the elimination of mandatory paid sick days for workers just months before the pandemic began and the government's subsequent refusal to reimplement them during the pandemic worsened outbreaks in workplaces where workers had no union protection.[1]

Getting accurate numbers of workers killed, injured, or made sick by work is difficult. Even during the heart of the COVID-19 crisis, when concern about rising numbers of cases was increasing rapidly, public health and government officials were reluctant to record and publish the number of workplace outbreaks, citing concerns about company confidentiality.[2] The high number of deaths in long-term care, for example, was linked to the reluctance of private for-profit providers to reveal the serious risks of illness faced by their underpaid workforce.[3] Further, official statistics in Canada continue to count only a small proportion of work-related deaths, a fraction of work-related injuries, and an even tinier proportion of occupational diseases. And the federal government routinely underestimates the prevalence of work-related injuries and illnesses. Indeed, the official number of workplace fatalities in Canada may be less than a tenth of the actual number due to a very narrow definition of what constitutes a work-related death.[4]

FIGURE 8.1 **Workplace fatalities and work-related deaths in Canada, 2016**

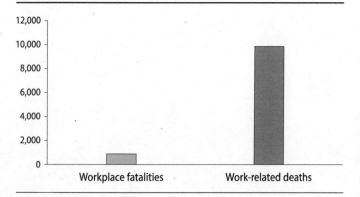

Source: Steven Bittle, Ashley Chen, and Jasmine Hebert, "Work-Related Deaths in Canada," *Labour|Le Travail* Vol. 82 (Fall 2018), 159–87; Association of Workers' Compensation Boards of Canada "2016 Fatalities in Canada."

Why does this matter? When public officials and employers systematically underestimate cases of illness or death, they also minimize the related problems. Corporations, business leaders, and politicians often speak of how safe and healthy work is today, and they point to declining numbers of workplace injuries. But they consequently demand fewer inspections, fewer investigations, and the elimination of penalties. Such strategies do much to put off attempts by workers to improve their working conditions.

Official statistics for Ontario, for example, show a decline in total reported work-related injuries, as reflected by overall claims (both lost time and no lost time) (Figure 8.2). Other provinces exhibit a similar decline. At the same time, however, the number of critical injuries per year, including fatalities, has not changed very much at all (Figure 8.3). In general, one would expect total injuries and critical injuries to follow the same trajectory. Critical or serious injuries are much more likely to be reported accurately, however, so it is more likely that there has been no real decline in overall accidents either. The actual trend of work-related injuries is hidden because workers are discouraged from reporting them.

So too the International Labour Organization (ILO) estimates that work-related diseases kill nearly 3 million workers annually.[5] Work-related cancers account for 29 percent of these deaths, and work-related circulatory illnesses such as cardiovascular disease and stroke account for another 35 percent. These deaths are often caused by exposure to hazardous chemicals and carcinogens like asbestos in the workplace. The long latency of these occupational diseases (manifesting themselves years after exposure) does not make them any less deadly. It is estimated that some 11,000 workers in Canada die annually from work-related illnesses, but only a small proportion turns up in official statistics.[6]

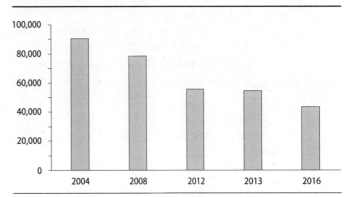

FIGURE 8.2 **Allowed lost-time claims in relation to covered workforce, Ontario, 2004–16**

Source: updated from 2015 Prism Economics and Analysis for the Ontario Ministry of Labour, Training, and Skills Development, Prevention Branch, *Market Metrics and Service Research Report.*

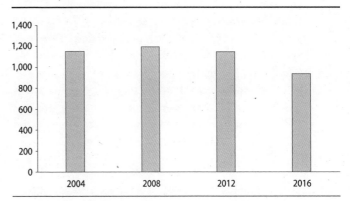

FIGURE 8.3 **Critical injuries reported to the Ontario Ministry of Labour, 2004–16**

Source: updated from 2015 Prism Economics and Analysis for the Ontario Ministry of Labour, Training, and Skills Development, Prevention Branch, *Market Metrics and Service Research Report.*

Just as important, occupational stress has surpassed other causes of injury and illness at work – but again, its impact goes largely uncounted. While it has long been recognized that stress contributes to the frequency and seriousness of physical injuries, Conservative government officials have questioned the damage it does to mental health, leading compensation boards to ignore the problem for years.

Consequently, victims have been left uncompensated despite well-documented increases in mental illness among workers. Only after years of litigation – and after courts and tribunals in British Columbia and Ontario declared denial of compensation for chronic stress contrary to the Charter of Rights and Freedoms – were changes made and claims accepted.[7] Why did workers have to wait so long?

Workplace violence is also widespread and seldom counted in official statistics. Ranging from unwanted and persistent harassment to discrimination, and from physical threats to acts of violence against workers in the course of doing their jobs, workplace violence is frequently experienced by female workers in private and public workplaces alike. In the public sector, unions have campaigned for years to improve precautions. But two decades of consistent cuts to the public sector have left behind highly stressed workers having to deal with patients and clients increasingly angry with declining service.

Consequently, despite what official statistics report, for growing numbers of workers – and for all those precarious workers with uncertain hours of work, places of work, and few if any protections – the workplace is a major cause of ill health and injury.[8] Work is becoming less safe and workplaces less healthy.

INTERNATIONAL COMPARISONS

It's not easy to compare worker health and safety in different countries, as different definitions and factors shape what is reported. The ILO maintains a database called ILOSTAT to log worker injury and death statistics reported from countries worldwide. While the numbers are conservative, they at least provide estimates of accidents and injuries that are reasonably consistent with each other.

Comparatively, Canada ranks with several other industrialized countries when it comes to work-related deaths due to accident or injury. The United States has the worst annual rate, at 3.7 fatalities per 100,000 workers, compared to two per 100,000 in Canada. It should be noted that Canada's statistics include deaths due to occupational diseases, which account for more than 50 percent of the annual total and are not counted in many other countries. When the Canadian figure is limited to fatal injuries only and compared to countries like Sweden, Finland, and Denmark, whose figures do not include deaths due to occupational disease, the rates are similar. Canada also shares with these countries laws that require worker participation in occupational health and safety decision making (Figure 8.4).

OCCUPATIONAL HEALTH AND SAFETY, AND THE INJURED WORKERS' MOVEMENT

In the past, unionized factory work that provided long-term job security and good wages and benefits were considered to be good jobs. However, this type of work was often repetitive, laborious, and wore out even the strongest over time.

FIGURE 8.4 **Comparative annual work-related fatality rates, 2010–15**

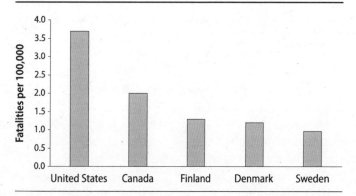

Source: Data from International Labour Organization, ILOSTAT, "Statistics on Safety and Health at Work," Occupational fatalities per 100,000, https://ilostat.ilo.org/topics/safety-and-health-at-work.

Empirical studies reveal that when workers have more control over the risks and hazards they face at work and have good social support, their work environment becomes safer and healthier.

But the bad jobs that have emerged with neoliberalism are the opposite. Neoliberal changes to labour laws and regulations have promoted employer interests, weakened unions, and put individual workers at a disadvantage. More and more, bad jobs have taken away control, security, and support, and workers have been left at greater risk of injury, illness, death, or **psychosocial hazards**. Such hazards have emerged as a result of the increased demands of and reduced control over their jobs that workers experience as a consequence of deregulation and technology. Temporary workers paid low wages and provided no benefits are at higher risk of ill health because they lack basic rights, including representation and voice in the workplace. How well workers' rights are recognized and upheld across a country significantly shapes how well workers are actually protected by health and safety laws and policies (see Chapter 3). This is an important context to consider when looking at how occupational health and safety works in Canada, how it is enforced, and who is at risk.

The rights of workers, including OHS and workers' compensation, are the responsibilities of individual provinces and territories as a result of Canada's highly decentralized political system. The federal government has direct responsibility for only about a tenth of the workforce: those employed in the federal sector (see Chapter 6). Only a few important joint OHS federal-provincial laws exist, such as that governing the hazardous chemicals information system. Nonetheless, although OHS protection varies across jurisdictions, provincial, territorial, and federal OHS protections are generally similar. The Ontario experience is the focus here.

Since the industrial revolution began in Canada in the nineteenth century, occupational health and safety has often been a life-and-death struggle between employers and workers – between those who create the conditions for work and those who carry out the work. In most respects, laws have favoured the authority of employers. Thousands of workers suffered serious injuries, including dismemberment and death, in the early years of industrialization. By the late 1800s, however, Canadian workers had mobilized through their unions and communities to build public support against this injustice.[9] Using public protest and high-profile, publicly reported litigation, they gained support from researchers, health care practitioners, journalists, lawyers, communities, and politicians to improve working conditions and secure compensation for families of workers who were killed and injured.

The **health and safety movement**, which was born out of these struggles, is a network of workers and their unions and supporters. By the early twentieth century, the movement had pushed governments to provide compensation for injury and death on the job, and to pass the first health and safety laws giving inspectors the power to inspect workplaces and to enforce minimum OHS standards.[10] Beginning with Ontario in 1914, territorial and provincial governments established publicly owned corporations called workers' compensation boards (WCBs) to oversee the collection of financial premiums from employers to pay for compensation to injured workers and families of killed workers.

During and after the Second World War, workers organized unions in steel, automotive, rubber, electrical, and other key manufacturing industries. Faced with increasing exposure to toxic chemicals and other hazardous working conditions, unionized workers collectively confronted their employers. With the support of community activists, lawyers, and doctors, they exposed the extensive damage suffered by workers, their families, and their communities, and the resulting poverty of injured workers.

Militancy was especially prevalent in the economically crucial mining industry. The United Steelworkers (USW) union defeated the International Union of Mine, Mill and Smelter Workers (IUMMSW), also known as Mine Mill, for dominance of the mining sector and turned its attention to health and safety. Steelworker union locals across Canada became militant, and one of the best-known health and safety strikes occurred in the 1970s in the uranium mines of Elliot Lake, in northern Ontario. That action triggered a royal commission into health and safety known as the Ham Commission.[11] In truth, worker activism in mines and mills and industrial workplaces all over Canada were garnering ever-broadening social support.

Political pressures from workers and their allies, supported by the New Democratic Party, led to the comprehensive health and safety legislation that we have today. Workers gained the right to know the **hazards** they face at work, the right to participate in decisions about their health and safety either through a representative or directly in discussions with their employer, and the right to refuse unsafe work. Laws were implemented to prohibit employers from disciplining workers who raised OHS concerns or sought to have health and safety acts enforced. Workers also won the right to contact a government inspector if their employer did not respond appropriately.

These developments were part of a series of social and legislative reforms in Canada that began after the Second World War and reached their height in the 1970s and '80s before the shift in favour of neoliberalism and away from social justice that began in the 1990s. During the 1970s, an independent injured workers'

movement emerged to address the injustice and poverty that many permanently disabled workers were experiencing. Particularly strong in Quebec, Ontario, and British Columbia, this movement was able to win improvements in decision making, fairness, return to work, and benefits for permanently disabled workers.

Most notably, workers made a crucial trade-off regarding their legal rights: they gained the right to compensation for work injuries regardless of fault, but in turn employers were granted immunity from individual legal suits for causing injuries. Overseeing the trade-off were revamped workers' compensation boards, with directors appointed by governments. WCBs have different names – Workplace Safety and Insurance Board in Ontario and WorkSafeBC in British Columbia, for example – but they carry out the same functions. The WCBs fund training and research and facilitate injured workers' return to work. In Ontario, for example, WCBs have come to fund employer safety associations, worker occupational health clinics, and an occupational health and safety training centre for workers. Similar progress occurred in other provinces and other parts of the developed world at the same time.

The hallmark of health and safety legislation in Canada is the Internal Responsibility System (IRS), a system of self-regulation by employers with worker input and government oversight. Territorial, provincial, and federal governments establish the rules and regulations for workplaces within their jurisdictions. Governments appoint inspectors (in some jurisdictions called prevention officers) who inspect workplaces and investigate health and safety incidents. Inspectors have the power to order health and safety improvements, to stop work, and to lay charges. Charges under health and safety laws can be laid against employers for any infraction but are used primarily when workers are killed or injured.

In the 1990s, however, some provincial governments began to cut back benefits for injured workers, stigmatizing them as lazy and over-compensated. The injured workers' movement played a key role in resisting these policies, forming organizations such as the provincial Ontario Network of Injured Workers Groups (ONIWG) and the national Canadian Injured Workers Alliance (CIWA). Over the years, the injured workers' movement has worked in collaboration with independent researchers and with the labour movement. An important means of communication for the movement is the Injured Workers Online website.

Unions have also actively advocated for improved health and safety. In 2004, Canada's *Criminal Code* was amended to allow the prosecution of corporate employers for manslaughter and/or criminal negligence when a worker is killed. To date there have been few prosecutions, however, and the USW is leading a campaign entitled Stop the Killing! to pressure governments to apply the law more effectively.

KEY CHALLENGES TO HEALTH AND SAFETY

Work shouldn't hurt or make us sick. In school and at home, we are expected to take care of each other and to be respectful and fair. Why is the experience at work often so very different? Typically, at work we are expected to do what we are told and often to put up with conditions that may be unsafe. Managers may regard raising a concern as insubordination and threaten discipline, sometimes even firing the worker who sounds the alarm.

In school and at home, the people in charge are usually concerned about our welfare and well-being. At work, the people in charge are concerned primarily with higher profit and lower costs. As current debates about minimum wages and living wages demonstrate, even the wealthiest corporations campaign to keep wages low and workers insecure in order to control and exploit the people they employ. This perspective reinforces an attitude toward safety and health that emphasizes individual fault, devalues workers' experiences, and undermines government enforcement.

Since the 1980s, neoliberal political attacks on state regulation of employment relations, along with a focus on competitive economic globalization, have had predominantly negative effects on occupational health and safety regulations and workers' compensation in Canada (see chapters 4 and 5). Free market corporate ideologies have weakened government enforcement by limiting the numbers and activities of workplace inspectors. They have also promoted policies that emphasize the individual responsibility of workers and leave health and safety mainly to an employer's initiative. The consequences have been evident during the pandemic, as vulnerable workers – migrant agricultural workers, personal service workers in long-term care, and temporary workers – are put at higher risk for COVID-19.

Public politics and private employer power combine to influence how we think about health and safety at work in Canada. The following are four key issues that illustrate this point.

The Myth of Worker Carelessness

A common approach to health and safety at work, especially by employers and managers, is to blame the worker when things go wrong. Safety posters and campaigns highlight the consequences of careless worker behaviour, for example, but there is no evidence this is effective in reducing accidents. Instead, such an approach often discourages workers from reporting their concerns.

Nevertheless, behaviour-based safety has a substantial following, especially among management health and safety consultants. In effect, it shifts responsibility and blame onto

BOX 8.1 BEHAVIOUR-BASED SAFETY

Martha was relieved when she finally got her first full-time job after several discouraging weeks of looking. The company assembled food orders for customers, and she was responsible for finding the products and putting the orders together.

Every morning, her manager produced a sheet with all the workers' names on it and a comment beside each name. All the comments were negative, some were quite harsh, and they were often unfair. Typically the complaint was that the worker was being too slow. Other comments were about workers having bad posture and not being careful enough when working.

When Martha fell after tripping on a tray, she twisted her ankle and broke a wheel on the cart she used to assemble orders. She reported the incident to management as required and was told she should get a tensor bandage and get back to work.

The next day her ankle was still very sore and she walked with a limp. When she returned to work, a comment written beside her name on the sheet indicated that she had been careless and had caused damage to company property. It went on to say that she was lucky she did not have to make a workers' compensation claim. By the end of the day, depressed and still limping, she left work without making a claim.

Two days later, her ankle still throbbing with pain, she was called into the boss's office and lectured about what he described as her "stupid carelessness." Martha had had enough.

"That was not my fault," she declared. "You know, my understanding is that the supervisor should not have put the tray there." She felt proud that she was able to stand up for herself.

workers, even though management organization of work profoundly restricts the ability of most workers to control their activities.[12]

Are workers usually to blame? Certainly people make mistakes, but workers in particular kinds of workplaces with similarly poor conditions are much more likely to be hurt or injured or to fall ill because of their jobs. The widespread belief that workers are to blame for accidents and illness on the job is based on a fallacy of single causes. That is, while a worker's actions may have triggered or responded to an immediate hazard, the worker is usually in the situation not by choice but because of job requirements imposed by management.

For example, for a long time it was commonly thought that young workers just entering the workforce usually had the highest risk of injury because they tended not to treat their jobs seriously enough. Research shows, however, that the increased risk new workers often experience is frequently stronger among workers who are twenty-five and older and in their first month on the job than among workers fifteen to twenty-four years old.[13]

Other research has demonstrated that the risk of ill health and injury is often highest among those in low-wage and more precarious jobs. Contract workers and gig workers generally have little or no support at work. Those with the least control over their work are often at the bottom of the workplace hierarchy. They more frequently experience the highest risks and more frequently suffer injury or illness as a result.[14] The employment insecurity associated with this kind of employment is also related to higher and more chronic workplace stress, which adds another dimension to workers' vulnerability.[15]

The Limits of Enforcement
While conservative governments today frequently emphasize voluntary compliance,

BOX 8.2 A FACE OF WORKPLACE DISCRIMINATION

Abe was happy when he got a job as a dishwasher/bus boy at Walter's Restaurant and Pizzeria. The place was well known in the neighbourhood for its traditional food and large portions. The owner, Walter, promised him regular hours and an opportunity to earn more as he learned the ropes.

He started that weekend. The kitchen was dirty, with stuff scattered everywhere. Walter warned him that the dish dryer was very hot and that he had to be careful around the electrical outlets. Otherwise he was pointed to the dirty dishes in the sink and told to make sure that he kept up with cleaning them.

Abe focused on his work. As his shifts went by, he got to know his coworkers. They gave him advice when he had questions and helped him out from time to time. Two asked him to join them when they went out after work.

It was different when Walter was around. Workers were quieter than usual, keeping their heads down to avoid being seen. From time to time, Walter would talk up to individual workers, often escalating his conversation to shouting that they had failed to clean a table or that their service was too slow. Walter's language was abusive and demeaning. Abe did not like to witness this and would quickly head back into the kitchen.

One day, Abe came in before his evening shift. As he often did, he asked the cook to prepare him something for dinner. When he came back to the kitchen to get the food, the owner was visibly angry. "Did you do this? Did you do this?" the owner yelled at Abe, brandishing a dish in one hand. Before Abe could reply, the owner rushed toward him, threw the plate on the floor, and shoved him into the kitchen wall, yelling at him, "Get out, get out!"

Abe went home, very upset. When he told his friends, they all told him that the owner couldn't do that. When Abe returned to the restaurant to confront the owner, he was told by his supervisor that he wasn't wanted anymore. The owner refused to talk to him.

whereby employers voluntarily improve health and safety, it is widely recognized that OHS laws have to be enforced by governments. If they are not, some employers will take advantage in order to reduce costs, and as they do so, other employers follow to increase their profits and to compete. Enforcement is necessary to prevent this vicious domino effect.

There are two general approaches to enforcement by workplace inspection. The first, proactive inspection, uses data from compensation claims and accident reports to identify critical areas and then targets particular economic sectors and employers accordingly. The second, reactive inspection, responds to OHS complaints, usually from workers. Reactive inspections have tended to predominate, although proactive inspections often have broader enforcement impacts on employer behaviour.[16]

Inspectors respond when workers formally refuse what they deem to be unsafe work. In Canada, if a worker is not satisfied with the response of the employer to this work refusal, she or he has the right to request that a government inspector be contacted. Often employers see inspection as interference with their ability to manage work as they see fit. In this context, many workers are reluctant to take this next step as it can lead to being demoted or, more likely, fired.[17] Yet if the worker doesn't ask for an inspector to respond to his or her work refusal, the inspector cannot protect the worker. It's a real dilemma. Workers represented by unions usually have greater protection, as collective bargaining agreements set out grievance and arbitration processes to resolve disputes. Unions can help workers make complaints through workplace health and safety committees. Most important, union contracts provide the possibility of reinstatement when employers want to fire workers for making health and safety complaints.

Enforcement entails both general statements of prohibitions and individualized penalties. Researchers have found strong evidence of positive health and safety effects from inspections with penalties but little evidence of positive effects from inspections with only general statements and no penalties.[18] Employers who refuse to comply with an inspector's order, or who violate rules set out in OHS legislation and regulations, can be prosecuted and fined. In some cases, the manager in charge can be sent to jail. However, prosecutions are seldom conducted except when workers are killed.

The courts in Canada have ruled repeatedly that OHS legislation is designed to promote public health and safety. As a consequence, the law is to be generously interpreted in a manner that is in keeping with its public welfare objectives, and narrow or technical interpretations that interfere with or frustrate those objectives are to be avoided.[19] In the end, however, whether or not OHS laws are enforced depends mainly on political decisions by governments.

Inadequate Protection from Reprisals

Workers who have safety and health concerns often fear that voicing those issues will be interpreted as challenging their employer and will bring reprisal. A second worry is that management will not listen to their concerns. In one Canadian study, teenaged workers were unwilling to speak up as they feared being fired or ignored because of their lack of work experience

and status, and believed that ultimately their actions would not make a positive difference.[20] In some cases, workers even fear that their workplace will close in response to their complaint. And for increasing numbers of workers, the built-in insecurity of their employment relationship makes them hesitate to express concerns. Recent work-related deaths at Fiera Foods, a large bakery in Toronto, for example, were all classified as deaths of temporary workers even though they had worked at the company for long periods – in one case for more than five years. Thus, employers' power can seriously inhibit workers' ability to exercise their rights to voice legitimate safety concerns.

Health and safety laws clearly forbid an employer from punishing a worker who raises a health and safety concern or refuses to do unsafe work. However, there is no penalty for the employer. In Ontario, no employer has ever been prosecuted or fined for firing a worker for raising a health and safety concern despite the thousands of claims that have been made over the past forty years or more. Workers who are fired or disciplined may make a claim for lost wages to a government tribunal or through arbitration if they are represented by a union. Between April 2006 and March 2017, over 1,200 formal claims were made to the government tribunal, and that number doesn't include complaints that were handled as grievances via a union process.

The importance of voicing OHS concerns cannot be overemphasized. Many unions and worker health and safety training centres provide training to encourage workers by teaching them the procedures for making complaints and the strategies for addressing them. The Ministry of Labour, Training, and Skills Development provides a confidential call-in number for complaints, and inspectors still respond in person to formal complaints. High schools provide basic information to students, and employers are required by law to provide all employees with information on how to complain.

Workers who insist that their employers address health and safety concerns are often motivated by commitment to social justice and labour rights, with a strong belief in fairness that their unions, families, and communities have instilled in them. Their persistence in getting their concerns addressed is often a reaction to feeling that they have been wronged. They believe it is important to take the next step and call the government OHS inspector to come in and enforce the law.[21]

The Prevalence of Workplace Violence
Another major OHS hazard for workers today is occupational or workplace violence, and its concomitant impact on mental health. Many workers suffer harassment and violence, but women, racialized workers, and workers with disabilities suffer disproportionately. Sexist, racist, homophobic, and ablest behaviour at work is hurtful and creates risks of further injury. Numerous high-profile media stories have reported shocking incidents of harassment in workplaces ranging from police forces to entertainment and media firms.

An international review conducted for the International Labour Organization analyzed the full range of occupational violence: physical, psychological (including harassment, bullying, and verbal abuse), and sexual violence (including sexual harassment and assault); discriminatory harassment; and criminal, intimate partner, and technology-based violence (including cyberbullying).[22] According to the report, workers in health care are at particularly high risk of occupational violence. Patients and clients whose capacity may be impaired are often known to strike out. Similarly, teachers have to deal with being targets of student violence while also trying to defuse violence between students.

As the ILO report points out, psychosocial hazards (stress created by the organization of work, such as excessive hours or workloads) are often associated with problems of bullying and harassment. Job strain (high work demands combined with limited control over work), job insecurity, and poor psychosocial safety (working in fear of negative consequences) promote workplace bullying. Other forms of workplace aggression, including incivility, are also often precursors to occupational violence.[23]

The ILO report analyzes various government policies to reduce occupational violence. In Canada, the most well known is a voluntary standard established by the Canadian Standards Association in 2013. Known as the National Standard of Canada for Psychological Health and Safety in the Workplace, the guidelines describe processes that employers should have in place to protect workers from harassment and violence at work. However, many Canadian employers who need to adopt this standard are not doing so.[24] Similarly, some Canadian laws require employers to assess the risks of violence at work and to consult worker health and safety representatives before creating their OHS policies. Yet while many Canadian employers have put policies in place to assist victims and discipline perpetrators, few have addressed the psychosocial hazards that are fuelling an epidemic of workplace violence.[25]

In the past, occupational health and safety was regarded primarily in terms of the contract between employers and workers, but increasingly it is seen as a human right. In that context, many argue, health and safety should also be under the broader protection of human rights.[26] A major challenge is that employers and governments often view such hazards as matters of labour relations that are largely unconnected to health and safety. The impact on workers suffering mental illness or injury because of workplace violence and stress can nonetheless be as profound as a serious injury due to falling. Too often, employers fail to address this issue.

COVID-19 AND WORKER HEALTH AND SAFETY

Over 2020–21, Canadians found themselves in the midst of a pandemic that closed borders, shuttered workplaces, and put workers at risk, especially those workers considered essential. But government intervention was neither direct nor conclusive. The Ontario government, for example, declared a state of emergency on March 17, 2020, but then released a long list of so-called essential services that were entitled to remain open. That permitted some 35 percent of businesses to continue to function. Ontario workplaces were also subject to an ever-varying set of rules for locking down and reopening, often with different regional rules on social distancing, face masks, and permissible group sizes. Schools were allowed to open at the end of August, but just a month later closures were enacted when the numbers of cases climbed with a second wave.

This patchwork approach can also be seen within three groups of workers identified as high risk: health care emergency responders, personal service workers in long-term care, and temporary foreign workers. In Quebec and Ontario, where the majority of fatalities from COVID-19 occurred in long-term care facilities, personal service workers were highly exposed. In Alberta, the Cargill High River meat-packing plant became a COVID-19 hotspot in March 2020, as did similar plants in Quebec and Ontario and in other parts of the globe. Migrant workers in the Windsor area of Ontario were also seriously affected in June and July 2020, as the virus went through the workforce on crowded farms. But even though these workers were characterized as heroes essentially for doing their jobs, they often worked without

adequate pay or protection. Despite federal and provincial commitments to increase health inspections and improve housing with the outbreak of the pandemic, migrant workers continued to fall ill and several died. They lacked health care access and information, continued to live in cramped and inadequate housing, and were forced to work under threat of termination and deportation.[27]

It was also difficult to track what was happening. As reported by the *Toronto Star*, public health units – to which all cases of COVID-19 were to be reported – at first neither tracked workplace outbreaks nor released any information because of supposed concerns about confidentiality, and began to do so only after public outcry.[28] What is known is that health care and education unions took the government to court to protect their members. Also clear was that neither the federal nor provincial governments wanted to involve unions in the process.

The pattern of systematically ignoring the voices of workers was a replay of the government response to Severe Acute Respiratory Syndrome (SARS) in 2003. The city of Toronto was hit hard by SARS, but throughout this first zoonotic outbreak, government officials and employers often refused to confer with health care workers and their unions. Instead, joint health and safety committees and worker representatives were ignored. Workers in health care were often inadequately protected, and two nurses and one doctor died and hundreds of others fell ill.

An independent commission was set up to examine what had gone so wrong in the response to SARS. In the resulting report, Justice Archie Campbell lambasted government and management for their failure to involve worker representatives. The report recommended that a precautionary approach be taken as a guiding principle throughout Ontario's public health and worker safety systems. When there was reasonable evidence of an impending threat to worker health, authorities should not wait for proof that workers were sick or being killed before taking steps to avert the threat. Rather, the existence of a hazard should trigger action to protect workers – and worker representatives should be involved.[29]

Fast-forward to 2020, and Canada generally and Ontario specifically were still ill-prepared for a viral outbreak and still unwilling to confer with workers or unions. In the two years prior to the COVID-19 outbreak, Ontario's Conservative government failed to adopt the precautionary principle. In fact, in 2019 it reversed legislation that provided workers with a minimum number of paid sick days. Similarly, in the months before the pandemic, the government enacted cutbacks in public health, education, and community legal assistance.

When the pandemic hit, it was déjà vu. An independent review conducted for the Canadian Federation of Nurses Unions by a former senior advisor to the Ontario SARS Commission concluded that the Ontario government and public health authorities had largely ignored and marginalized worker representatives. Even joint agreements on health and safety negotiated in good faith with governments were sidestepped, and only a significant increase in work refusals by health care workers led to government action.[30] Teachers had similar frustrations in their dealings with government and public health officials, as their concerns regarding back-to-school recommendations went unheeded. Teacher unions filed a complaint with the Ontario Labour Relations Board in August 2020 regarding health and safety but the case was dismissed on a technicality, leaving it up to individuals to make individual complaints.[31]

As the president of the Institute for Work and Health (IWH), a government-funded OHS research centre, wrote, "We can conservatively estimate that a non-trivial 20 per cent of

COVID-19 infections among working-age adults in Ontario can be attributed to workplace transmission."[32] It is therefore unsurprising that surveys by management consultants identified a reluctance on the part of workers to return to work. In one survey, six out of ten workers said they would not go to work if it was not safe. In another, workers said they were relying on their employer to make sure the workplace was safe.[33]

As of early 2022, there is growing activism among workers who having carried us through the pandemic and are demanding better wages and better conditions. It is clear that the pandemic has reignited workers' concern with their health and safety at work. New networks have emerged to provide research and information in support of worker health. The next phase of knowledge activism about health and safety appears set to begin.

MAKING DEMANDS ON POWER

As American slavery abolitionist and social reformer Frederick Douglass emphasized over 150 years ago, "Power concedes nothing without a demand." That has certainly been true of the improvements in occupational health and safety that Canadian workers have achieved. Major breakthroughs have led to changes in OHS laws and practices, and to greater participation from workers and unions in making work safer. Leading up to these advances were lengthy periods of worker activism supported by unions, community organizations, and other social organizations.

Since the 1990s, neoliberal government policies have weakened worker rights and led to increased exploitation and ill health. Physical and chemical hazards remain in many workplaces, and they are exacerbated by deregulation. Making matters more difficult, psychosocial hazards are almost unregulated.

At the heart of these issues is the degree of control workers have – or do not have – over the work they do. When workers' rights are weakened, so is their ability to protect themselves, and this has been especially true during the onslaught of COVID-19. But the pandemic has also opened up new opportunities to discuss how to improve worker health and safety, and to involve workers in the process. Moving forward, there is no shortage of potential for health and safety activism, and no shortage of areas in need of reform.

ADDITIONAL RESOURCES

Canadian Centre for Occupational Health and Safety. www.ccohs.ca.

European Trade Union Institute. "Occupational Health and Safety and Working Conditions." www.etui.org/Topics/Health-Safety-working-conditions.

Injured Workers Online. www.injuredworkersonline.org.

Lewchuk, Wayne, and Marlea Clarke. *Working without Commitments: The Health Effects of Precarious Employment.* Montreal and Kingston: McGill-Queen's Press, 2011.

Nichols, Theo, and David E. Walters, eds. *Safety or Profit? International Studies in Governance, Change and the Work Environment.* New York: Routledge, 2014.

Occupational Health Clinics for Ontario Workers. www.ohcow.on.ca.

Premji, Stephanie, ed. *Sick and Tired: Health and Safety Inequalities.* Halifax: Fernwood Publishing, 2018.

Quinlan, Michael. *Ten Pathways to Death and Disaster: Learning from Fatal Incidents in Mines and Other High Hazard Workplaces.* Sydney: Federation Press, 2014.

Workers Health and Safety Centre. www.whsc.on.ca

NOTES

1   Ryan Patrick Jones, "Federal Sickness Benefit Falls Short of Paid Sick Leave Protections, Advocates Say," *CBC News*, January 14, 2021, www.cbc.ca.

2   Sara Mojtehedzadeh and Jennifer Yang, "More Than 180 Workers at This Toronto Bakery Got COVID-19 – but the Public Wasn't Informed. Why Aren't We Being Told about Workplace Outbreaks?" *Toronto Star*, August 10, 2020, thestar.com.

3   Richard Warnica, "The Problem with Profits," *Toronto Star*, January 26, 2021, thestar.com.

4   Steven Bittle, Ashley Chen, and Jasmine Hébert, "Work-Related Deaths in Canada," *Labour/Le Travail*, 82 (2018): 159–87.

5   Jukka Takala, Päivi Hämäläinen, Kaija Leena Saarela et al., "Global Estimates of the Burden of Injury and Illness at Work in 2012," *Journal of Occupational and Environmental Hygiene* 11, no. 5 (2014): 326–37.

6   Päivi Hämäläinen, Jukka Takala, and Kaija Leena Saarela, "Global Estimates of Fatal Work-Related Diseases," *American Journal of Industrial Medicine* 50, no. 1 (2007): 28–41.

7   The only exceptions before 2012 were Quebec and Saskatchewan. Court and tribunal decisions in British Columbia and Ontario have declared that denial of compensation to victims of workplace stress is contrary to the Charter of Rights and Freedoms.

8   Wayne Lewchuk and Marlea Clarke, *Working without Commitments: The Health Effects of Precarious Employment* (Montreal and Kingston: McGill-Queen's University Press, 2011).

9   Michael Piva, "The Workmen's Compensation Movement in Ontario," *Ontario History* 67, no. 1 (1975): 39; R.C.B. Risk, "This Nuisance of Litigation: The Origins of Workers' Compensation in Ontario," in *Essays in the History of Canadian Law*, ed. David H. Flaherty (Toronto: University of Toronto Press, 1983), 418–92.

10 Eric Tucker, *Administering Danger in the Workplace: The Law and Politics of Occupational Health and Safety Regulation in Ontario, 1850–1914* (Toronto: University of Toronto Press, 1990).

11 Ontario, *Report of the Royal Commission on the Health and Safety of Workers in Mines* (Toronto: Ministry of the Attorney General, 1976), https://archive.org/details/reportofroyworkmine00onta.

12 James Frederick and Nancy Lessin, "Blame the Worker: The Rise of Behavioral-Based Safety Programs," *Multinational Monitor* 21, no. 11 (2000): 10; Andrew Hopkins, "What Are We to Make of Safe Behaviour Programs?" *Safety Science* 44, no. 7 (2006): 583–97.

13 F. Curtis Breslin and Peter Smith, "Trial by Fire: A Multivariate Examination of the Relation between Job Tenure and Work Injuries," *Occupational and Environmental Medicine* 63, no. 1 (2006): 27–32.

14 These important findings were part of one of the largest and longest worker health studies, called the Whitehall Studies. For more information on this and other important studies visit www.unhealthywork.org, the website of the Center for Social Epidemiology.

15 Wayne Lewchuk, Marlea Clarke, and Alice De Wolff, "Precarious Employment and the Internal Responsibility System: Some Canadian Experiences," in *Workplace Health and Safety: International Perspectives on Worker Representation*, eds David Walters and Theo Nichols (London: Palgrave Macmillan, 2009), 109–33.

16 Leah F. Vosko, Eric Tucker, Mary Gellatly, and Mark. P. Thomas, "New Approaches to Enforcement and Compliance with Labour Regulatory Standards: The Case of Ontario, Canada," *Comparative Research in Law & Political Economy*, Research Paper no. 3½011, https://digitalcommons.osgoode.yorku.ca/clpe/69.

17 Andrew King and Wayne Lewchuk, "Occupation Health and Safety: A Failure to Protect the Right of Workers to Participate in Enforcement," *Relations industrielles/Industrial Relations* 77, no. 1 (2022): 1–24.

18 Emile Tompa, Christina Kalcevich, Michael Foley et al., "A Systematic Literature Review of the Effectiveness of Occupational Health and Safety Regulatory Enforcement," *American Journal of Industrial Medicine* 59, no. 11 (2016): 919–33.

19 *Ministry of Labour v City of Hamilton*, 58 O.R. (3d) 37.

20 Sean Tucker, Nik Chmiel, Nick Turner, M. Sandy Hershcovis, and Chris B. Stride, "Perceived Organizational Support for Safety and Employee Safety Voice: The Mediating Role of Coworker Support for Safety," *Journal of Occupational Health Psychology* 13, no. 4 (2008): 319–30; Jennifer J. Kish-Gephartet, James R. Detert, Linda Klebe Treviño, and Amy C. Edmondson, "Silenced by Fear: The Nature, Sources, and Consequences of Fear at Work," *Research in Organizational Behavior* 29 (2009): 163–93; Sean Tucker and Nick Turner, "Waiting for Safety: Responses by Young Canadian Workers to Unsafe Work," *Journal of Safety Research* 45 (2013): 103–10.

21 King and Lewchuck, "Occupation Health and Safety."

22 Katherine Lippel, "Conceptualising Violence through a Gender Lens: Regulation and Strategies for Prevention and Redress," *University of Oxford Human Rights Hub Journal* 1 (2018): 142.

23 Ibid., 155.

24 Diane Kunyk, Morgan Craig-Broadwith, Heather Morris, Ruth Diaz, Emiline Reisdorfer, and JianLi Wang, "Employers' Perceptions and Attitudes toward the Canadian National Standard on Psychological Health and Safety in the Workplace: A Qualitative Study," *International Journal of Law and Psychiatry* 44 (2016): 41–47.

25 Andrew King, Teresa Symanski, and John Oudyk, "Practical Steps for Preventing Stress Hazards at Work," *OOHNA Journal* (Fall/Winter 2018): 18.

26 Leslie I. Boden, "Reexamining Workers' Compensation: A Human Rights Perspective," *American Journal of Industrial Medicine* 55, no. 6 (2012): 483–86.

27 Migrant Workers Alliance, *Unheeded Warnings: COVID-19 and Migrant Workers in Canada*, June 2020, https://migrantworkersalliance.org/wp -content/uploads/2020/06/Unheeded-Warnings -COVID19-and-Migrant-Workers.pdf.

28 Mojtehedzadeh and Yang, "More Than 180 Workers."

29 Archie G. Campbell, *Spring of Fear: The Sars Commission Final Report* (Toronto: SARS Commission, 2006), http://www.archives.gov. on.ca/en/e_records/sars/report/index.html.

30 Mario Possamai, *A Time of Fear: How Canada Failed Our Health Care Workers and Mismanaged COVID-19* (Ottawa: Canadian Federation of Nurses Unions, 2020).

31 Elementary Teachers Federation of Ontario, "OLRB Dismissal of Unions' Case Leaves Ontario's Flawed Back-to-School Plans without Legal Scrutiny," Media release, https://ett.ca.

32 Cam Mustard, "What Research Can Do: Estimating the Role of Workplaces in COVID-19 Transmissions," *Institute for Work and Health*, August 25, 2020, www.iwh.on.ca.

33 Sarah Dobson, "6 in 10 Workers Won't Go Back to Work If It's Not Safe: Survey," *Canadian HR Reporter*, August 6, 2020, www.hrreporter. com; Ilya Banares, "More Than Half of Canada's Workers Fear Returning to the Office," *Bloomberg News*, August 6, 2020, www. bnnbloomberg.ca.

9 Treating Temporary Migrant Workers as Disposable People

Philip Kelly, Janet McLaughlin, and Don Wells

CHAPTER SUMMARY

The Canadian economy has become increasingly reliant on temporary migrant workers. While many permanent immigrants to Canada have opportunities to build careers and establish families, certain categories of migrant workers are systematically relegated to a precarious second-tier labour market that blocks or delays pathways to citizenship.

This chapter analyzes the working and living conditions of caregivers.[1] It provides a **whole worker approach** that focuses holistically on these workers not simply as employees but also as members of families and communities.[2] The federal government requires workers who come to Canada under these programs to leave their families behind in their countries of origin, creating transnational families whose members are separated for long periods.

The chapter explains temporary migrant worker programs for agriculture workers and caregivers, and their contributions to the growth of low-wage precarious employment. The chapter also discusses key examples of political activism by migrant workers and their allies – unions and advocacy organizations – in promoting public policy changes to improve their living and working conditions as well as the well-being of their transnational families.

KEY THEMES

This chapter will help you understand:

- the growth and extent of the temporary migrant workforce in Canada
- why temporary migrant workers regularly experience low wages and poor working conditions
- the roles of federal and provincial governments in expanding the Canadian temporary migrant workforce while limiting labour rights
- key health and social impacts of temporary migrant worker programs on workers and their families
- political activism and policy reforms to improve the wages, working conditions, and economic security of migrant workers and their families, including rights to permanent residency and Canadian citizenship.

EVERY YEAR, TENS OF thousands of migrant workers come to Canada from other countries to work temporarily, serving us coffee at Tim Hortons, taking care of our children and our sick and elderly, growing and harvesting our fruit and vegetables, building our houses, cleaning our hotel rooms, and doing all sorts of other jobs that benefit their employers and many others.

Although temporary foreign workers (TFWs) migrate from many countries and are employed in diverse occupations, they have in common a precarious relationship to employment and their right to stay in Canada. TFWs also have fewer rights than workers who are Canadian citizens or have permanent residency, which provides most of the rights of citizens, along with the right to apply for citizenship. Even after years working here, many TFWs who are categorized as low skill or low wage (especially those in seasonal agriculture) have little chance of gaining permanent residency and citizenship.[3]

Employers typically have extraordinary power over these employees. Because they lack numerous labour rights, and government enforcement of the labour rights and standards they do have is often inadequate, these workers' living and working conditions are often poor.[4] They typically experience highly variable work hours and pay, are exposed to occupational health and safety risks, and lack access to health care and workers' compensation.[5] When they are sick or injured, their employers may send them back to their home countries before their contracts have expired.[6] They have no seniority rights that provide more job security for those who have worked longer for their employers. Their employers decide whether to renew their contracts. They are, essentially, disposable workers.

From 1980 to 2014, some 1.3 million TFWs came to Canada. Between 2007 and 2014, the annual number of TFWs exceeded the number of economic immigrants who were given permanent residence status (Figure 9.1). While TFW numbers have declined somewhat recently, they remain a significant part of the Canadian labour market. In 2017, over 113,000 such positions existed in the Temporary Foreign Worker Program (TFWP).

FIGURE 9.1 **Immigrant arrivals by immigration category, 2000–17**

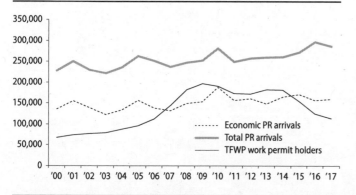

Source: Data from Immigration, Refugees and Citizenship Canada (IRCC), Facts and Figures, 2017, https://open.canada.ca. Tables: "Canada: Permanent Residents by Category" and "Temporary Foreign Worker Program work permit holders with valid permit(s) in calendar year by program."

FIGURE 9.2 **TFWP permit holders by category and year of permit activation, 2006–20**

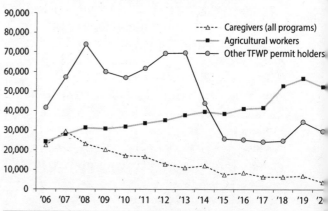

Source: Data from Immigration, Refugees and Citizenship Canada (IRCC), Facts and Figures, 2017, and other tables, https://open.canada.ca.

Young and healthy, Bonifacio Eugenio-Romero flew from Mexico in 2020 to work on a pepper farm in Ontario. He was one of thousands of people employed each year under the Seasonal Agricultural Worker Program (SAWP). Like most SAWP workers – all of whom come from poor countries – Bonifacio felt compelled to come. He needed to support his family.

Due to the pandemic, the federal government had barred most travellers from crossing the Canadian border but made an exception for these migrant agricultural workers. Because he grew and harvested our food, Bonifacio was categorized as an "essential worker." Agricultural work is often dangerous, and because of COVID-19 these dangers had multiplied. For workers like Bonifacio, it is difficult if not impossible to maintain social distancing at work or in the often unsanitary, crowded bunkhouses where they sleep. Many migrant farm workers report that their employers do not provide them with personal protective equipment, health and safety training, or access to testing and health care supports.

In 2020, almost 9 percent of the approximately 20,000 migrant farm workers who came to Ontario tested positive. While on the farm, Bonifacio contracted the virus.[7] He self-isolated in a hotel room, but his symptoms worsened and he called emegency services in distress. Half an hour later, he died. Just thirty-one years old, Bonifacio was one of three young Mexican agricultural workers who died of COVID-19 in the province that year. His widow was left scrambling to pay for his repatriation to Mexico and his funeral expenses. She had lost her breadwinner and the love of her life.[8]

Things could have been very different if Bonifacio had been able to get health care earlier. If his working and living conditions in Canada had been as safe from the pandemic as they could have been. If our governments had not made him disposable.

The TFWP has multiple components, with separate streams for workers who make high or low wages, and specialized programs for agriculture and caregiving, which are the focus of this chapter. Figure 9.2 shows the number of work permits that were signed or became effective annually from 2006 to 2020. New permits in the caregiver categories have declined from a peak in 2007 due to program changes, but the agricultural stream has grown significantly. Prospective employers apply annually to the federal government for permission to hire TFWs. If these employers certify that Canadian workers are unavailable for such jobs, the TFWP provides temporary work permits for non-Canadians.

WHO GAINS AND WHO LOSES FROM THE TFWP

The overarching goal of TFWP policies has been to meet employers' demands for low-cost, flexible, just-in-time workers. Both Liberal and Conservative federal governments have viewed these policies as a win-win-win for Canadian employers, consumers, and TFWs themselves. The programs are strongly influenced by the insistence of agricultural employers and their organizations that temporary migrant workers are essential for profitability. The Canadian Agricultural Human Resource Council (CAHRC) contends that there is a growing gap between the number of agricultural workers required and the number available under prevailing wages and working conditions, and it expects the shortfall to reach 114,000 workers by 2025. According to the Council, the problem led to $1.5 billion in lost sales in 2014.[9]

The SAWP is also held to benefit Canadian consumers, who gain from more affordable, secure, high-quality, locally grown food. Additionally, the program creates related jobs in agricultural equipment, food processing, grocery stores, transportation, and other food industry sectors linked to agricultural production.

Similar arguments are made in favour of employing TFW caregivers, who provide dedicated, more affordable in-home childcare and care for seniors and other family members, enabling Canadians to balance employment and care obligations. Temporary migrant workers in care work, most of whom are women, help make it possible for Canadians (also disproportionately women) with primary responsibility for the care of their own children and other relatives to take paying jobs. As well as providing a more equitable gender balance in the workforce, this offers employers a larger pool of employees from which to recruit.

It is often suggested that even though temporary migrant workers have fewer rights and suffer worse working conditions than other workers in Canada, they should be grateful to have jobs that generally pay more than such jobs in their home countries. Some also argue that employing TFWs in bottom-rung jobs rejected by Canadian workers creates jobs and strengthens the economy because it helps employers who might otherwise shut down to compete more profitably.

On the other hand, there are those who complain that TFWs take jobs from Canadians who should have priority in hiring. Some also argue that employment of migrant workers at low wages and with poor working conditions reduces incentives for employers to raise wages and improve working conditions for other workers in Canada.[10] According to these critics, employers should increase wages and benefits to attract Canadian workers instead of hiring precarious, low-paid workers from abroad.

Related to this view is the contention that governments should adopt stronger, more effective agricultural and industrial policies. Examples include policies such as cheaper, more easily available credit to invest in agriculture, more highly subsidized crop insurance, more tax breaks, stronger price supports for agricultural commodities, more research and development assistance (including for organic production), more skills-training programs, and land access for those who want to become farmers, including younger workers, Indigenous people, and communities and cooperatives.

With respect to migrant caregivers employed through the TFWP, a frequent criticism is that governments should provide publicly funded or subsidized childcare facilities so that low-wage in-home childcare is not necessary. Such views help to inform competing policy directions for temporary migrant workers in Canada.

RACIAL AND GENDERED DISCRIMINATION

Relying on racialized workers to fill labour shortages is not new in Canada. Such workers were often hired on a temporary basis, in part reflecting a dominant view before the 1960s among Canadian settlers of European origin that Asians and Black people were unassimilable. White American and Western European immigrants, by contrast, were more readily afforded high occupational status.[11] Historically, recruitment of TFWs, especially in economic sectors where their work was considered lower skilled, has often been based on ethnic, racial, and gender discrimination. In the late nineteenth and early twentieth centuries, Canadian employers in mining, forestry, fruit farming, railway construction, and other sectors hired cheap unskilled labour from Asia and Southern and Eastern Europe. More recently, employers have tended to prefer Caribbean and Filipina women for domestic work and Caribbean and Mexican men for agricultural work.[12] A small number of women have also participated in agricultural work in recent years, and the range of countries has expanded to include such nations as Guatemala, Thailand, and Indonesia.

Systemic state discrimination based on racial and ethnic differences to distinguish between those considered worthy of permanent settlement and those deemed valuable only for temporary labour stretches back to Canada's initial nation building and beyond. Canada was founded on the violent displacement of **Indigenous peoples** by white settlers who deemed them racially inferior. After Confederation in 1867, racialized workers were allowed to migrate to Canada only temporarily to do dirty, dangerous, and demeaning jobs: "the jobs that Canadians won't do," according to a Canadian mining executive in 1903.[13] Despite their important contributions to the economy, those who performed these jobs were generally considered unworthy of immigration or citizenship rights. As Ricardo Trumper and Lloyd Wong note, *foreigner* was a "racialized label of nonwhiteness that connoted highly controlled mobility, while *white* implied a settler's capability."[14] Racialized workers have typically held jobs that were lower paid and less desirable than those of their settler counterparts, who were deemed to be white and thus ascribed a higher status in racialized social, cultural, economic, and political hierarchies.

UNFREEDOM AND THE SEASONAL AGRICULTURAL WORKER PROGRAM

Agricultural workers are a hugely important part of the TFWP (Figure 9.2). Each year around 50,000 arrive under the program's agricultural category. Most come from Mexico, Jamaica, and other Caribbean countries under the SAWP.[15] The federal government allows SAWP workers to stay in Canada for a maximum of eight months to dig, cultivate, fertilize, spray herbicides, weed, pick, pack, and transport fruits, vegetables, tobacco, and other agricultural products. Working for the most part on farms and in greenhouses, and often living in isolated bunkhouses when they are not working, they are invisible to the rest of society much of the time.

Although the labour laws governing these workers are under provincial jurisdiction, and employer organizations authorized by the Canadian government manage the day-to-day operations of the SAWP, it is a national program under federal government jurisdiction. With few exceptions, the government forbids SAWP workers Canadian citizenship and does not allow them to bring their spouses or children when they come to work in Canada.

According to legal scholar Fay Faraday, SAWP workers are confined to a "zone of exceptionality" that excludes them from rights other workers have in Canada.[16] In Ontario, this separate legal status lies at the centre of a magnified imbalance of power in their employment relationships that makes it much more difficult for SAWP workers to voice their needs or organize to improve their working and living conditions. As a report to the provincial minister of labour concluded, racialized restrictions on their immigration and work permits, substandard housing conditions, and the lack of collective bargaining rights in Ontario constitute "unfree labour," while former minister of immigration Jason Kenney has said that SAWP workers suffer "quasi-indentured status."[17]

This unfreedom is embodied in work contracts that are negotiated by Canadian employers, the Canadian government, and the governments of the countries that send SAWP workers. No worker representatives are permitted to participate in these negotiations.[18] Under the contracts, "tied" work permits require each SAWP worker to work only for the specific employer named in the permit. A 2018 federal government report notes a power imbalance embodied in the permits that "favours the employer and can result in a migrant worker enduring misconduct, abuse or other forms of employer retribution."[19] Changing employers is difficult and rare.[20] The federal government gives employers the right to "name" (recall) workers they allow to be rehired on a new permit. SAWP employers are also given the right to fire these workers, with no appeals or grievance process, which normally results in repatriation to their home countries. By pitting workers and governments from different sending countries against each other in competition for SAWP jobs, Canada gives employers even more power.

Agricultural work often exposes workers to toxins, dangerous machinery, extended periods of work in harsh weather, and other risks related to the way their jobs are organized, such as prolonged bending and lifting and workdays sometimes eighteen or more hours long. Consequently, provincial occupational health and safety rights to which SAWP workers are entitled are especially important, but OHS regulations are often inadequate and unenforced.[21]

There is often a big difference between workers' formal or paper rights and the rights they have the power to exercise in practice (Chapter 7). Many SAWP workers are afraid that if they were to insist on their formal health and safety rights, or rights related to their working and living conditions, their employers would fire them or not name them to be hired back the following year. Similarly, although SAWP workers have the formal right to unionize in most provinces (except Ontario, where over half the workers are employed), employers' power often inhibits them from doing so.

Despite the massive power imbalance in this and other areas, some migrant workers have been trying to improve their working conditions through direct resistance on the job. Their actions became particularly apparent during COVID-19 outbreaks, when some groups of migrant farm workers collectively walked off their jobs, demanding job improvements and health protections.[22] Others have held marches and protests, including meetings to light "candles of resistance," calling for immigration rights.

Canadian governments have also negotiated neoliberal international trade and investment policies that have worsened economic conditions for many workers in Mexico (home to about half of SAWP workers) and other SAWP-sending countries. The 1994 North American Free Trade Agreement (NAFTA) that Ottawa negotiated with the United States and Mexico, for example, forced Mexican corn, dairy, and other farmers to compete against large-scale, highly mechanized, and massively subsidized US agribusinesses. This "squeezed farmers out of production and into poverty," forcing them to "sell off their lands and migrate."[23] Within a few years of NAFTA being signed, almost 5 million Mexican farming families had lost their land.

This and other neoliberal policies through which the Mexican government has reduced public spending on public education, health care, welfare, and other social policies have deepened rural poverty, putting more pressure on Mexicans to apply to the SAWP.[24] These policies contribute to a system of mutually reinforcing employer and state power that creates conditions under which thousands of SAWP workers are pushed to leave their families to come to Canada and submit to hard, exhausting, and often dangerous work.

SACRIFICING TRANSNATIONAL FAMILIES

The requirement that SAWP workers, almost all of whom are fathers, leave their spouses and children behind constitutes a contradictory double sacrifice: a sacrifice *for* their families and *by* their families.[25] A SAWP father explains: "So much misery. Such poverty. I had to leave everything behind to try to be better. I say, 'How is it possible that I have my children and I haven't seen them grow up?' ... I tell [my children] about how the sacrifice ... being away and far, is only in order to help them ... It affected me emotionally."[26]

SAWP workers often report that their family members suffer depression, anxiety, and other psychological damage from being separated. Many children come to regard their fathers as strangers, and some report feeling abandoned by fathers who left to work in Canada. "Because [my children] didn't see me, they became like very sad, depressed," one SAWP father observed. His five-year-old son is being treated for depression.[27]

In their fathers' absence, many children rebel against their mothers' authority. Their school attendance and grades decline, and some turn to drugs and petty crime.[28] A Mexican school principal speaking about the daughters of SAWP workers reported that for some, the main problem, "when girls are about twelve years old, is pregnancy."[29] And the workload for women whose husbands have left for Canada often increases substantially as they work on farms and manage the family finances.[30] One overworked wife at home in Mexico reported that she had miscarried because she was forced to lift heavy things.[31] Feelings of anger, resentment, and distrust can increase for both children and parents under the burden of these long-distance relationships. Sometimes they cause families to break up.

DEBATING POLICY REFORMS

Unions, community supporters, faith organizations, worker health clinics, and migrant justice groups are pressuring governments to improve working and living conditions and labour rights under the SAWP.[32] For example, Justice for Migrant Workers (J4MW), a non-profit organization of students, labour activists, and others, advocates particularly for agricultural workers, using media publicity, caravans of migrant worker protesters, and political lobbying for workers injured on the job, forcibly deported by employers, or abused.[33] Another prominent support group, the Migrant Workers Alliance for Change, brings unions together with advocacy groups and individuals across the country to demand fundamental labour rights, access to social services, and a path to citizenship for migrant workers and migrant students.

The main union supporting temporary agricultural workers is the United Food and Commercial Workers union. The UFCW has organized Agriculture Workers Alliance support centres to help workers with complaints related to pay, hours of work, housing, employer abuse, health, workers' compensation, income taxes, and other issues. The UFCW also lobbies governments to gain parental, pension, unemployment, and other benefits for these workers. Other organizations, such as local community groups, support SAWP workers through health clinics, health and safety workshops and know-your-rights training, community dinners, religious services, entertainment events, bicycle repairs, and research and advocacy for better public policies.

With some exceptions, agricultural employers and their political allies oppose policy changes to improve labour rights and conditions for migrant workers.[34] Since agricultural work is not only physically hard but also requires long hours in bad weather, especially when crops are being harvested, most employers give high priority to flexible work hours. They often assert that improved labour standards would increase their costs and damage their economic viability. As well, farmers often face high prices for financial credit and for production inputs, such as fertilizers and pesticides, but low prices for their products. Prices tend to be set in international markets, and international competitors frequently employ workers with even lower labour standards. Many American agricultural producers, for example, employ undocumented migrant workers who toil for even lower wages and under worse conditions than those in Canada.

In addition, food retailers usually have the upper hand in negotiating with food suppliers. Dominated by a few powerful corporations, such as Loblaw, Sobeys, Walmart, and Metro, they are linked to financial stakeholders focused on maximizing profits.[35] In this context, some SAWP employers fear that increased labour costs could make them less competitive.[36] Some small family-owned farms operate within the SAWP, but these are particularly vulnerable to large-scale agribusiness competition and becoming far less common as farm operations consolidate. Indeed, half the SAWP employers surveyed by the Canadian Agricultural Human Resource Council (CAHRC) in 2017 reported gross agricultural revenues exceeding $1 million, and over a quarter had revenues exceeding $2 million. At the same time, as few as 94,000 people own half of Canada's farmland.[37] According to research by the Conference Board of Canada, partly as a result of increasing mechanization, the agricultural sector has had the "strongest labour productivity gains of any major sector over the past twenty years."[38]

There is little evidence that unionization and collective bargaining rights threaten most agricultural employers' economic viability. As noted, many of these farms are large, profitable agribusinesses. An Ontario government Task Force on Agricultural Labour Relations concluded that collective bargaining rights in other provinces didn't have a significantly negative impact on farm economics.[39] And according to the UFCW, which organized SAWP workers in British Columbia, Manitoba, and Quebec and negotiated collective agreements including higher wages, workplace protections, grievance procedures, seniority hiring rights, and health and safety training and committees, these employers have not experienced job losses or bankruptcies.[40] Moreover, in addition to helping to reverse the race to the bottom in agricultural working conditions across much of Canada, improving SAWP workers' rights may in fact improve farms' productivity, public image, and business models.[41]

Higher wages are particularly important for these workers. Their remittances are essential to family survival and the main reason they participate in the SAWP. However, the money they send home is usually not enough to raise their families out of poverty.[42] SAWP workers' take-home wages could be increased by reducing the amount employers deduct from their wages for travel and housing costs. Other policy proposals include ensuring that SAWP workers have access to the benefits they pay for via mandatory contributions to Employment Insurance, and providing them with portable health insurance that includes coverage after they return home.

Another important proposal is to replace their tied, single-employer work permits with sector-wide work permits that would enable workers to change jobs within the agricultural sector and reduce their extreme dependence on one employer.[43] Seniority rights could help workers with longer employment to reduce their vulnerability to employer favouritism and improve their job security. Also being proposed is providing workers who have been fired with a fair appeals/grievance process. SAWP workers could also receive health care and other support services, including mandatory health and safety training, in their own languages. In addition, workers and their families could have some choice in deciding the duration of their contracts. This would help them to balance their income needs against the toll of prolonged separations. As well, female SAWP workers could have greater support during pregnancy, including rights to safe work, prenatal care, and protection from premature employment terminations due to pregnancy. Most fundamental, SAWP workers could have the right to choose permanent residency and family reunification in Canada.[44] As the global climate crisis increases consumer demand for Canadian agricultural commodities, employers will need skilled, experienced, permanent agricultural workers.

GENDER, RACE, AND THE POLITICS OF THE CAREGIVER PROGRAM

Another longstanding TFW program is the Caregiver Program (CP), which has had various names and forms over its history. This federal government program has also created a racialized labour zone of exceptionality, in this case mainly for female migrant workers providing care for children, the elderly, and those with high medical needs. Under traditional patriarchal divisions of labour, most care work in the home has been assigned to women. Over the last half century, however, increasing rates of female labour force participation have contributed to growing shortages of home care labour. Growing demand for care workers is also driven by a rapidly aging population. In the absence of adequate public childcare and eldercare policies, families have had to turn to private in-home care solutions. Quebec, where high-quality publicly subsidized childcare is available, is a partial exception (and this model is gradually being rolled out in other provinces, with federal government support, between 2021 and 2027).

Prior to the 1950s, most women migrating to Canada to work as nannies were from Europe and were entitled to apply for permanent residency when they arrived. By the mid-twentieth century, however, women from the Caribbean started to fill vacancies for care work under the federal West Indian Domestic Scheme, and the labour pool of domestic workers shifted from largely white to predominantly women of colour.[45] By the early 1980s, another federal government scheme, the Foreign Domestic Movement, required migrant care workers to be employed for two years in Canada before being eligible to apply for permanent residency. Initially the scheme largely recruited Caribbean women.

By the time it became the Live-In Caregiver Program (LCP) in 1993, women from the Philippines had begun to dominate the scheme. Between 1993 and 2015, four of every five arrivals under the LCP (almost 100,000 women in total over that period) were Filipinas.[46] In part this reflects the Philippine government's labour export policy of training and marketing its workers for jobs in other countries.[47] As a result, the Philippine economy in general, and many households specifically, have become dependent on migrant workers' remittances. In 2018, some US$1 billion of these remittances came from Canada.[48] Thus, both Canadian and Philippine government policies have fostered the creation of a separate gendered and racialized segment of the Canadian labour market.

In contrast to programs in other countries, Canadian care worker migration programs include a pathway to permanent residency. While in this respect Canada's policy is more benign, LCP applicants have had to fulfill strict conditions, including working only for the employer specified in their work permits, thereby making it difficult for them to change jobs. Until 2014, when the Canadian government changed this stipulation, they were also required to live in that employer's house, a space dominated by their employer, making them a captive labour force. This live-in requirement has been associated with cases of workers being physically, sexually, and emotionally abused.

The vulnerabilities of caregivers were strikingly revealed during the COVID-19 pandemic. Shelter-at-home policies meant that caregivers living in their employers' homes had no respite from their workplaces. Others who were living elsewhere were in some cases suddenly terminated, losing both their source of income and potentially their right to apply for permanent residency.[49] Meanwhile, the high COVID-19 infection rate in the Filipino community reflects how many former caregivers are channelled into jobs in health care and social assistance that involved exposure to the virus in vulnerable settings such as long-term care homes.[50]

After twenty-four months of service, caregivers may apply for an open work permit, which allows them to work for any qualified Canadian employer. Eventually they may apply for permanent residency. In 2019, the federal government also started granting open work permits to workers with tied permits who are being abused or are at risk of being abused. Before becoming permanent residents, caregivers have only limited access to social services, educational programs, and union rights. Long processing times to approve their permanent residency applications have added more years of family separation.

With removal of the live-in requirement but implementation of more restrictive conditions on gaining permanent residency, the LCP changed significantly in 2014. The federal government created two channels of immigration: caring for people with high medical needs, and caring for children. Both require high education

levels, work experience, and English or French proficiency. For both channels, Ottawa imposed quotas restricting the number of workers who could be granted permanent residency.

In 2019, the caregiver program was again revised with the creation of two five-year pilot programs: the Home Child Care Provider Pilot and the Home Support Worker Pilot. In these programs, caregivers won the right to bring their family members with them when they first come to Canada. Spouses and dependent children may also work and study in Canada. Caregivers will no longer be tied to a specific employer. These new programs have been criticized, however, for excluding some caregivers who are already working in Canada. Furthermore, as Figure 9.2 shows, the number of workers arriving as caregivers has declined dramatically in recent years. Just as this pathway to immigration is becoming more humane, it is being made available to fewer people.

CAREGIVER ACTIVIST POLITICS

Activists have played a crucial role in critiquing careworker programs and promoting policy improvements. In the 1970s and '80s, the Toronto feminist group INTERCEDE, for example, brought together domestic workers from the Philippines, the United Kingdom, and the Caribbean to campaign for the right to permanent residency under the slogan "Good enough to work, good enough to stay." Partly due to their campaigning, a pathway to immigration was incorporated into the Foreign Domestic Movement in 1981.

As the LCP became dominated by women from the Philippines, activist organizations emerged in the Filipino community, such as the Caregivers Action Centre and the Philippine Women Centre.[51] In some cases, they have called for women to be given permanent residency on arrival in Canada (under the slogan

"Landed Status Now!"). In other cases, the call has been "Scrap the LCP!" on the grounds that it is a racist and imperialist exploitation of women of colour. To an extent, both calls have been answered. The latest version of the program grants provisional permanent residency on arrival and allows family members to accompany caregivers. As noted, however, the program is now open to far fewer migrants.

Transnational activist groups have also created links between Canada and the Philippines. GABRIELA and Migrante, for example, are Philippines-based women's and migrants' rights organizations, respectively, with branches across Canada. Such organizations stress that living in the home of an employer leaves workers vulnerable to verbal, physical, and sexual abuse, lack of privacy, and unregulated working hours, including significant unpaid overtime. Also, because caregivers spend at least two years as temporary foreign workers and are tied to a specific employer, they cannot obtain their rights without fear of deportation (just like migrant agricultural workers). This prevalent climate of fear, in which employers have extraordinary power, is a key reason why activists have argued for permanent residency on arrival. And since caregivers cannot get access to settlement or education services before becoming permanent residents, they often remain stuck in domestic work even after achieving immigrant status, rather than being able to pursue the careers for which they were educated.[52]

As is the case for workers under the SAWP, the caregiver program often harms families. Many caregivers leave their own children behind in the Philippines to look after other people's children in Canada. Despite the contention of the minister of immigration, refugees, and citizenship in 2018 that family reunification is "a central pillar of Canada's immigration program," it usually takes years before family members are reunited as permanent residents.[53]

Research indicates that long separations can make family relationships difficult to revive, and the children of caregivers who arrive in their teenaged years may struggle in the Canadian school system. The troubles experienced by caregivers can therefore have knock-on effects for the next generation.[54]

THE FUTURE FOR THE WHOLE WORKER

Employment of temporary foreign workers in Canada raises fundamental dilemmas. Does the demand for low-cost agricultural produce to feed a largely urban society justify the employment conditions imposed on foreign workers, and enforced separation from their families? Do the needs of Canadian families for childcare and eldercare outweigh the needs of caregivers and their families? And if the needs of agricultural producers and working families are important, can they be addressed through public policies other than by importing low-cost, temporary, precarious labour?

This chapter has explored the consequences of policy choices that have made Canada dependent on marginalized foreign workers in large segments of its labour force. TFW programs have a long history of creating distinctively racialized and gendered pockets of marginality. This chapter has focused, in particular, on whole workers in order to evaluate these programs based not just on the labour involved but also on the wider lives of workers as parents, spouses, and community members.[55]

While political demands for low-cost, flexible labour are an enduring feature of the Canadian economic system, hopeful examples can be found of activism promoting pro-worker policies and campaigning for migrants' and workers' rights. Caregiver programs, in particular, have seen significant policy improvements because of activism by care workers and their allies. The struggle continues.

BOX 9.2 A CAREGIVER AND HER FAMILY

Like many caregivers, Melona Banico was well educated and had a professional career in the Philippines, where she worked for eight years as a schoolteacher. When an aunt in Toronto offered her employment under the Live-In Caregiver Program (LCP), Melona took the opportunity. Like others, she saw it as a pathway to financial security and an education for her children, even if it meant leaving them in the Philippines to be raised by her parents.

In 2009, after two years of LCP employment, Melona borrowed money to hire a lawyer and apply for permanent residency. The application took years to make its way through the Canadian immigration system. Meanwhile, Melona continued working in multiple low-paid jobs and sending money home.

After almost ten years, her children were able to join her, arriving at Pearson International Airport on a cold winter's night in 2016. By then, her daughters, Judelyn and Jeah Mae, were twenty-six and fourteen, and her son, Jade, was twenty-four. Judelyn's son, Clyde, was ten. Judelyn's husband stayed behind in the Philippines, as did Jade's girlfriend and one-year-old daughter. Thus, the reunification created new separations and long-distance relationships.

The documentary *My First 150 Days* (by Diana Dai, 2017) documents the family's first six months in Canada as they settle into their new home. While they recognize how hard Melona worked to provide for them over the years, the reunification is fraught. They have left behind a comfortable lifestyle supported by their mother's remittances, as well as the grandparents who cared for them. In Toronto, they have to adjust to a new culture, an absence of friends, a cramped apartment, and little income. Jade and Judelyn urgently need to earn money to support their mother and their partners back in the Philippines. Without financial resources for education or retraining, they have to settle for fast food and cleaning jobs.

The story of the Banico family highlights the human costs of migrant work. While Canadian families benefit from low-cost childcare or eldercare, caregivers themselves are painfully separated from their own families. Marriages sometimes fail and children become estranged from their parents. When reunification does happen, often years later, relationships must be rebuilt and the mother's marginalized employment is often reproduced in the poor and restricted job options her children face.

The dream of a good life in Canada works out for some, but not for others.

ADDITIONAL RESOURCES

Caregivers Action Centre. www.caregiversactioncentre.org.

Dai, Diana. *My First 150 Days.* Documentary film, 2017. www.tvo.org/video/documentaries/my-first-150-days.

Justicia for Migrant Workers. www.justicia4migrantworkers.org.

Migrant Rights Network. www.migrantrights.ca.

Migrant Workers Alliance for Change. www.migrantworkersalliance.org.

Migrant Worker Health Project. www.migrantworker.ca.

Migrante Canada. www.migrante.ca.

NOTES

1 The terms *temporary foreign worker* and *temporary migrant worker* are used interchangeably in this chapter. The Temporary Foreign Worker Program (TFWP) is one of several ways in which temporary residents may work in Canada. More

workers obtain permits under the International Mobility Program, but these tend to be for highly skilled occupations, employment after graduation from a Canadian institution, or through international agreements. International students may also obtain work permits while they are studying. The TFWP is of primary interest in this chapter because the permits issued under the program tend to be for jobs that employers claim Canadians are unwilling to do. Data from Immigration, Refugees and Citizenship Canada (IRCC), "Facts and Figures 2017: Immigration Overview – Permanent Residents," https://open.canada.ca/data/en/dataset/082f05ba-e333-4132-ba42-72828d95200b. See also Elana Prokopenko and Feng Hou, *How Temporary Were Canada's Temporary Foreign Workers?* (Ottawa: Social Analysis and Modelling Division, Statistics Canada, 2018).

    The analysis in this chapter is based in part on the following sources: 74 interviews with SAWP workers, their spouses and children, and their children's school teachers; 128 questionnaires with Filipino students in five high schools in Ontario's Halton Catholic District School Board; and 215 questionnaires with their parents and guardians. The authors are grateful to those interviewed and to all who helped with interviews, transcription, and analysis. Special thanks to André Lyn, Aaraón Diaz Mendiburo, Jennilee Austria, Biljana Vasilevska, Josephine Eric, Carmen Condo, the late Stan Raper, Ron Estaban, and Caren Menchavez. The authors also thank the students, parents, teachers, principals, and staff of the Halton Catholic District School Board for help with the Caregiver Program component of the research.

2 Jane McAlevey argues that "whole workers organizing" enables workers to confront their subordination and promote their interests both in their family and community lives and inside the workplace. See *No Shortcuts: Organizing for Power in the New Guilded Age* (New York: Oxford University Press, 2016) and *Raising Expectations (and Raising Hell)* (New York: Verso Press 2012).

3 Judy Fudge and Fiona MacPhail, "The Temporary Foreign Worker Program in Canada: Low-Skilled Workers as an Extreme Form of Flexible Labour," *Comparative Labour Law and Policy Journal* 31, no. 5 (2009): 6–45. Job skills are often conceptually complex and difficult to measure. Such formal designations often reflect differences in wages rather than in skills.

4 Eric Tucker, Sarah Marsden, and Leah Vosko, *Federal Enforcement of Migrant Workers' Labour Rights in Canada: A Research Report* (Toronto: Osgoode Hall Law School of York University, 2020). Despite official government requirements that employers provide "adequate, suitable and affordable housing" to SAWP workers, there is much evidence of employer non-compliance and government failure to do inspections and to interview workers during inspections. See Dan Levin, "Foreign Farmworkers in Canada Fear Deportation If They Complain," *New York Times*, August 13, 2017. Responding to criticism, Ottawa introduced new housing inspection requirements in 2018. Advocates are concerned these still do not go far enough.

5 Janet McLaughlin, Jenna Hennebry, and Ted Haines, "Paper versus Practice: Occupational Health and Safety Protections and Realities for Temporary Foreign Agricultural Workers in Ontario," *Pistes: Interdisciplinary Journal of Work and Health* 16, no. 2 (2014): 2–17.

6 Aaron Orkin, Morgan Lay, Janet McLaughlin, Michael Schwandt, and Donald Cole, "Medical Repatriation of Migrant Farm Workers in Ontario: A Descriptive Analysis," *Canadian Medical Association Journal* 2, no. 3 (2014): E192–E198.

7 Kieran Leavitt, "Outgoing Medical Officer of Health Criticizes Ottawa for Treatment of Migrant Workers and Asks for Airport Vaccinations," *Toronto Star*, March 25, 2021, thestar.com.

8 Laura Clementson, "'He Was a Good and Caring Person,' Says Wife of Migrant Worker Who Died

of COVID-19 on Ontario Farm," *CBC News*, June 19, 2020, www.cbc.ca.

9 Canadian Agricultural Human Resource Council, *A Review of Canada's Seasonal Agricultural Worker Program, 2017*, https://cahrc-ccrha.ca/sites/default/files/Emerging-Issues-Research/A%20Review%20of%20Canada%27s%20SAWP-Final.pdf.

10 Canada, House of Commons, *Temporary Foreign Worker Program: Report of the Standing Committee on Human Resources, Skills and Social Development and the Status of Persons with Disabilities*, 42nd Parl., 1st Sess., 2016: 18, https://www.ourcommons.ca/Content/Committee/421/HUMA/Reports/RP8374415/humarp04/humarp04-e.pdf.

11 Donald Avery, *Reluctant Host: Canada's Response to Immigrant Workers 1896–1994* (Toronto: McClelland and Stewart, 1995), 8.

12 Patricia Daenzer, "An Affair between Nations: International Relations and the Movement of Household Service Workers," in *Not One of the Family: Foreign Domestic Workers in Canada*, ed. Abigail Bakan and Daiva Stasiulis (Toronto: University of Toronto Press, 1997), 81–118; Vic Satzewich, *Racism and the Incorporation of Foreign Labour: Farm Labour Migration in Canada since 1945* (New York: Routledge, 1991).

13 Avery, *Reluctant Host*, 7.

14 Ricardo Trumper and Lloyd L. Wong, "Canada's Guest Workers: Racialized, Gendered, and Flexible," in *Race and Racism in the 21st Century Canada: Continuity, Complexity and Change*, ed. Sean P. Hier and B. Singh Bolaria (Peterborough, ON: Broadview Press, 2007), 151–70.

15 The primary agriculture stream has three other components in addition to the SAWP: the agricultural stream; primary agriculture – low wage; and primary agriculture – high wage. About three-quarters of the TFWs in the agriculture stream come under the SAWP. Employment and Social Development Canada, *Temporary Foreign Worker Program – Overview*, May 3, 2018, https://www.cfa-fca.ca/wp-content/uploads/2018/06/ESDC_TFWPUpdate_PrimaryAgriculture Overview.pdf.

16 Fay Faraday, *Canada's Choice: Decent Work or Entrenched Exploitation of Canada's Migrant Workers?* (Toronto: Metcalf Foundation, 2016), 30.

17 Michael Lynk, *Review of the Employee Occupational Exclusions under the Ontario Labour Relations Act, 1995* (Toronto: Ontario Ministry of Labour, 2015), 37–38; Daniel Tencer, "Temporary Foreign Workers Subject to 'Quasi-Indentured Status,' Jason Kenney Says," *Huffington Post Canada*, September 20, 2014, www.huffington-post.ca.

18 Fay Faraday, *Made in Canada: How the Law Constructs Migrant Workers' Insecurity*, Summary report (Toronto: Metcalf Foundation, 2012), 15.

19 Immigration, Refugees and Citizenship Canada, *2018 Annual Report to Parliament on Immigration*, Cat. no. Ci1E-PDF (Ottawa: Immigration, Refugees and Citizenship Canada), https://www.canada.ca/content/dam/ircc/migration/ircc/english/pdf/pub/annual-report-2018.pdf.

20 In 2019, Ottawa announced that SAWP workers and other TFWs have the right to apply for open work permits to escape abusive employers. To be granted an open permit, however, the worker must prove the abuse, and it can be difficult to transfer to a new employer having done so.

21 McLaughlin, Hennebry, and Haines, "Paper versus Practice."

22 Syed Hussan, "Fighting on All Fronts," *The Monitor*, Canadian Centre for Policy Alternatives, March 30, 2021, 18, https://monitormag.ca/articles/fighting-on-all-fronts.

23 United Nations Conference on Trade and Development, *Mexico's Agricultural Development: Perspectives and Outlook* (Geneva: United Nations, 2014), xvi.

24 On land loss, see Greg Grandin, *The End of the Myth: From the Frontier to the Border Wall in the Mind of America* (New York: Metropolitan Books, 2019), 243. Millions of Mexicans have also migrated to the United States since NAFTA

was signed, with Canada the second top destination. See Gerardo Otero, "Neoliberal Globalization, NAFTA and Migration: Mexico's Loss of Food and Labor Sovereignty," *Journal of Poverty* 15, no.4 (2011): 384–402.

25 Only about 3 percent of SAWP workers are women, most of whom are mothers. Janet McLaughlin, Don Wells, Aaraón Diaz Mendiburo, André Lyn, and Biljana Vasilevska, "'Temporary Workers,' Temporary Fathers: Transnational Family Impacts of Canada's Seasonal Agricultural Worker Program," *Relations Industrielles/ Industrial Relations* 72, no. 4 (Autumn 2017): 682–709; Aaraón Diaz Mendiburo, André Lyn, Janet McLaughlin, Biljana Vasilevska, and Don Wells, "Sacrificing the Family for the Family: Impacts of Repeated Separations on Temporary Foreign Workers in Canada," in *Precarious Employment: Causes, Consequences and Remedies*, ed. Stephanie Procyk, Wayne Lewchuk, and John Shields (Winnipeg: Fernwood Publishing, 2017), 44–56.

26 This and subsequent quotations from Mexican SAWP workers are translations of Spanish interview transcriptions. Dr. Aaraón Diaz Mendiburo conducted the interviews with SAWP workers and their families in their villages in Guanajuato State, Mexico, in 2012. Research based on the interviews was published in McLaughlin et al., "Temporary Workers" and in Diaz Mendiburo et al., "Sacrificing the Family."

27 McLaughlin et al., "Temporary Workers," 691–92.

28 Leigh Binford, *Tomorrow We're All Going to the Harvest: Temporary Foreign Worker Programs and Neoliberal Political Economy* (Austin: University of Texas Press, 2006), 11; Adriana Rosales-Mendoza and Linamar Campos-Flores, "Family Separation and Emotional Bonds: Women of Chiapas and Yucatan, Mexico, Facing Male Migration to Quebec, Canada," *International Journal of Care and Caring* 3, no. 2 (2019): 285–86.

29 McLaughlin et al., "Temporary Workers," 694.

30 Jenna Hennebry, "Transnational Precarity: Women's Migration Work and Mexican Seasonal Agricultural Migration," *International Journal of Sociology* 44, no. 3 (2014): 42–59.

31 McLaughlin et al., "Temporary Workers," 694.

32 Leah Vosko, *Disrupting Deportability: Transnational Workers Organize* (Ithaca, NY: Cornell University Press, 2019).

33 For more information, visit http://justicia4 migrantworkers.org.

34 For discussion of policy proposals to improve labour rights and working conditions for SAWP workers, see McLaughlin et al., "Temporary Workers," 695–700. An important exception to the position of the agricultural industry in general is Canada's National Farmers Union, a major organization that promotes the economic and social betterment of farmers. The NFU has called for improvement in the working and living conditions of migrant (and Canadian-born) workers, including a shift from "tied" to "open" work permits. See, for example, National Farmers Union, "NFU endorses MoVE Campaign for Migrant Workers' Rights," Media release, March 31, 2016, https://www.nfu.ca/nfu-endorses-move -campaign-for-migrant-workers-rights.

35 A United Nations special rapporteur highlighted links between Canada's concentrated agricultural sector and the creation of agricultural TFWs as a "marginalized category" to compensate for the failure to create working conditions that are more attractive to Canadian workers. See Olivier De Schutter, *Report of the Special Rapporteur on the Right to Food* (New York: Human Rights Council, 2012). See also Kerry Preibisch, "Managed Migration and Changing Workplace Regimes in Canadian Agriculture," in *(Mis)managing Migration: Guestworkers' Experiences with North American Labor Markets*, ed. David Griffith (Santa Fe, NM: School for Advanced Research Press, 2014), 86; and Janet McLaughlin, "Strengthening the Backbone: Local Food, Foreign Labour and Social Justice," in *Nourishing Communities: From Fractured*

Food Systems to Transformative Pathways, ed. Irena Knezevic, Alison Blay-Palmer, Charles Levkoe, Phil Mount, and Erin Nelson (New York: Springer Publishing, 2017), 23–40. On financial stakeholders in the food supply chain, see Miriam Stichele, "How Financialization Influences the Dynamics of the Food Supply Chain," *Canadian Food Studies* 2, no. 2 (2015): 258–66.

36 Michael Burt and Robert Meyer-Robinson, *Sowing the Seeds of Growth: Temporary Foreign Workers in Agriculture* (Ottawa: Conference Board of Canada, 2016).

37 Canadian Agricultural Human Resource Council, *A Review of Canada's Seasonal Agricultural Worker Program*, December 2017, https://cahrc-ccrha.ca/sites/default/files/Emerging-Issues-Research/A%20Review%20of%20Canada%27s%20SAWP-Final.pdf, 8; Darrin Qualman, Annette Desmarais, Andre Magnan, and Mengistu Wendimu, *Concentration Matters: Farmland Inequality on the Prairies* (Ottawa: Canadian Centre for Policy Alternatives, 2020), 15.

38 Michael Burt and Robert Meyer-Robinson, *Sowing the Seeds of Growth*, 3.

39 Task Force on Agricultural Labour Relations, *Report to the Minister of Labour*, First Report, June 1992 (Toronto: Ontario Ministry of Labour, 1992), 3.

40 Mark Thomas, "Producing and Contesting 'Unfree Labour' through the Seasonal Agricultural Worker Program," in *Unfree Labour? Struggles of Migrant and Immigrant Workers in Canada*, ed. Aziz Choudry and Adrian Smith (Oakland, CA: PM Press, 2016), 21–36; Stan Raper, UFCW National Representative, communication to Don Wells, May 4, 2017.

41 McLaughlin, "Strengthening the Backbone," 25.

42 Don Wells, Janet McLaughlin, André Lyn, and Aaraón Diaz Mendiburo, "Sustaining Precarious Transnational Families: The Significance of Remittances from Canada's Seasonal Agricultural Worker Program," *Just Labour: Canadian Journal of Work and Society* 22 (Autumn 2014): 1.

43 Migrant worker advocates have informed the Canadian government that too few approved jobs are available to make it possible for most TFWs to change employers. There is also fear that SAWP employers may blacklist workers who try to change employers, refusing to hire those on lists of workers deemed undesirable. See Migrant Workers Alliance for Change, *Temporary Foreign Workers Program in Canada: Migrant Worker Priorities 2019*, May 18, 2019, https://migrantworkersalliance.org/wp-content/uploads/2019/06/Final_-Migrant-Worker-Policy-Priorities-May-2019.pdf.

44 Anelyse Weiler and Janet McLaughlin, "Listening to Migrant Workers: Should Canada's Seasonal Agricultural Worker Program be Abolished?" *Dialectical Anthropology* 43 (2019): 381–88.

45 Audrey Macklin, "On the Inside Looking In: Foreign Domestic Workers in Canada," in *Maid in the Market: Women's Paid Domestic Labour*, ed. Wenona Giles and Sedef Arat-Koc (Halifax: Fernwood Publishing, 1994), 16.

46 Philip Kelly and Conely de Leon, "Rescripting Care Work: Collaborative Cultural Production and Caregiver Advocacy in Toronto," in *Precarious Employment: Causes, Consequences and Remedies*, ed. Stephanie Procyk, Wayne Lewchuk, and John Shields (Winnipeg: Fernwood Publishing, 2017), 91–108.

47 Geraldina Polanco, "Culturally Tailored Workers for Specialised Destinations: Producing Filipino Migrant Subjects for Export," *Identities: Global Studies in Culture and Power* 24, no. 1 (2017): 62–81; Robyn Rodriguez, *Migrants for Export: How the Philippine State Brokers Labor to the World* (Minneapolis: University of Minnesota Press, 2010).

48 Bangko Sentral ng Pilipinas, "Overseas Filipinos' Cash Remittances: Online Statistical Database" September 9, 2019, https://www.bsp.gov.ph/SitePages/Statistics/External.aspx?TabId=8.

49 Ethel Tungohan, "Filipino Healthcare Workers during COVID-19 and the Importance of

Race-Based Analysis," Broadbent Institute, News and Blogs, May 1, 2020, https://www.broadbent institute.ca/filipino_healthcare_workers_during_ covid19_and_the_importance_of_race_based_ analysis.

50 Statistics Canada, "The Weekly Review, August 4 to August 7, 2020," https://www150.statcan. gc.ca/n1/daily-quotidien/200807/dq200807a -eng.htm.

51 Ethel Tungohan, "The Transformative and Radical Feminism of Grassroots Migrant Women's Movement(s) in Canada," *Canadian Journal of Political Science* 50, no. 2 (2017): 479-94.

52 Rupa Banerjee, Philip Kelly, Ethel Tungohan et al., "From 'Migrant' to 'Citizen': Labor Market Integration of Former Live-In Caregivers in Canada," *ILR Review* 71, no. 4 (February 2018): 908-36.

53 Immigration, Refugees and Citizenship Canada, *2018 Annual Report.*

54 Geraldine Pratt, *Families Apart: Migrant Mothers and the Conflicts of Labor and Love* (Minneapolis: University of Minnesota Press, 2012); Jennilee Austria, Philip Kelly, and Don Wells, "Precarious Students and Families in Halton, Ontario: Linking Citizenship, Employment and Filipino Student Success," in *Precarious Employment: Causes, Consequences and Remedies*, ed. Stephanie Procyk, Wayne Lewchuk, and John Shields (Winnipeg: Fernwood Publishing, 2017), 57-73; Philip Kelly, *Understanding Intergenerational Social Mobility: Filipino Youth in Canada*, IRPP Study no. 45 (Montreal: Institute for Research on Public Policy, 2014); Austria, Kelly, and Wells, "Precarious Students and Families."

55 McAlevey, *No Shortcuts.*

10   Poverty, Jobs, and Social Policy

Jim Silver

CHAPTER SUMMARY

Poverty is directly related to the kinds of jobs we have or don't have. It is also related to the social wage and whether governments provide public programs, income transfers, and services to workers and their families. The COVID-19 pandemic has revealed the relatively threadbare condition of Canada's social wage and how close to poverty – one or two paycheques away – many Canadians actually are.

This chapter examines why poverty is so high in Canada, and how the rise of precarious employment has added to the numbers of the working poor. It also investigates the concept of complex poverty, which has severely damaging long-term effects that cause poor health, lower educational outcomes, and the erosion of democracy.

The chapter concludes by noting that poverty is not inevitable. Governments can dramatically reduce the incidence and severity of poverty and low-wage precarious employment by funding social benefits such as pensions and health and unemployment insurance. But will they? To force action, citizens will have to mobilize and demand that poverty be solved through the implementation of progressive social policies.

KEY THEMES

This chapter will help you develop an understanding of:

- what poverty is and who is poor
- relationships between precarious labour and poverty
- the role of social policy and the social wage in reducing poverty and improving jobs
- policy alternatives to provide income and social security.

MOST PEOPLE ARE POOR because they don't have a job, or because they have one that is poorly paid or part time or irregular. Certain types of families are more likely than others to be poor, but again, this is largely because of their relationship to the paid labour force. A lone-parent family with a child or children under school age, for example, is more likely to be poor than a two-parent family, because childcare responsibilities are likely to keep the single parent from full-time paid employment.

More than two decades ago, Canada's precarious labour market was identified as the primary cause of persistent poverty.[1] People were working but were still poor. In 2008, approximately two-thirds of poor families in Canada had at least one family member in the paid labour force.[2] Families are especially vulnerable to poverty when the sole income earner is self-employed or working part time or in a temporary job. And members of racialized groups, especially women, are over-represented in part-time low-wage employment.

From 1976 to 2012, the number of self-employed Canadians more than doubled to 2.7 million, as corporations reduced their workforce and government employees were laid off. Similarly, the proportion of jobs that are part time grew steadily from one in twenty in the 1950s to one in five by the early to mid-1990s, where it has stayed. Part-time workers typically earn lower hourly wages than full-time workers, and are less likely to be unionized and to have benefits: pensions, medical/dental, paid sick leave, and so forth. The importance – and the current inadequacy – of paid sick leave has been clearly revealed by the pandemic.

Workers in non-standard or precarious jobs – bad jobs – constitute a growing proportion of the Canadian labour force (chapters 3 and 5). In 2011 in the Greater Toronto–Hamilton labour market, for example, only half of those employed had permanent full-time employment with benefits. By 2016, for the first time fewer than half of all jobs in Canada were full-time and full-year jobs.[3]

Poverty is also about governments, and government social policies and programs. In countries where governments adequately fund a range of benefits, such as pensions and health and unemployment insurance, the proportion of the population that is poor – the incidence of poverty – may be low. This is the case in Sweden and other Nordic countries (Chapter 3). These government-provided benefits can be thought of as a social wage that supplements individual wages. When governments reduce the social wage and rely more on the market, as in the United States, the incidence of poverty is likely to be higher.

In this era of government austerity, neoliberal governments have *deliberately* attempted to reduce the social wage because doing so helps to increase profits and, the argument goes, to make the economy more competitive (chapters 4 and 5). It also punishes those who are poor and in bad jobs, and increases the number of working poor – those working but at wages so low they are still poor – by undercutting the social supports and income transfers necessary for secure work and higher standards of living. The COVID-19 pandemic has made this reality fully transparent. At the same time, it has made very clear how important to our collective economic and social well-being are the day-to-day jobs done by truck drivers, grocery clerks, health care aides, and others.

Thus, the significant reduction or elimination of poverty would require a much higher level of government investment in the social wage than is currently the case in Canada.

WHERE IS THE POVERTY LINE?

We often measure poverty in quantitative terms, by reference to a poverty line. If a family's or individual's income is below the figure established by the poverty line, it is considered poor. Using this measure can yield insight into the temporal and spatial incidence of poverty. That is, are poverty rates going up or down over time, and are they higher in some countries than in others, and in some regions of a country than in others? A quantitative analysis can also reveal what kinds of people are most likely to be poor. These characteristics are important to know if we are to make sense of poverty.

Nevertheless, there are limits to what quantitative data can tell us. In particular, a focus on the numbers too often implies that poverty is *only* about a shortage of money. Much of Canada's poverty is complex poverty, however, meaning that it involves a range of interacting problems beyond low income.[4]

There is endless debate about what the poverty line is, or where it is. Several versions are used in Canada, including the after-tax low-income cut-off (AT LICO), the after-tax low-income measure (AT LIM), and the market basket measure (MBM). The federal government announced in 2018 that the MBM now determines the official poverty line. But all poverty measures are at least in part arbitrary and relative.

POVERTY TRENDS IN CANADA

Figure 10.1 shows the trend line for poverty, as measured by the AT LICO, for the forty years from 1976 to 2016, and reveals several important features. Poverty rises during economic downturns. The incidence of poverty rose following the recessions in the early 1980s, early 1990s, and 2007-8. It peaked in 1996 following a recession at the beginning of the decade and the huge cuts in federal government social program spending in the mid-1990s. Poverty will have risen again in 2020 and 2021 as the result of massive pandemic-related job loss, a picture that will become fully clear only once Statistics Canada data becomes available.

BOX 10.1 MEASURES OF POVERTY

The after-tax low-income cut-off (AT LICO) considers a family to be low income when it spends 20 percent more of its after-tax income on food, clothing, and shelter than the average family does. Adjustments are made to accommodate seven family sizes and five ranges of community population, resulting in thirty-five LICOs. The AT LICO often produces a lower incidence of poverty than other measures because it uses a base year of 1992 to measure the costs of food, clothing, and shelter. It needs to be re-based to more accurately reflect today's costs.[5]

The after-tax low-income measure (AT LIM) establishes poverty at 50 percent of the median income, adjusted for family size. The median income is the point at which half the population has lower incomes, and the other half higher incomes, so this measure establishes poverty at half of this median figure.

The market basket measure (MBM) calculates actual expenditures on shelter, food, clothing, transport, and other basic needs to produce a "modest, basic standard of living."[6] Adjustments are made for family size and costs in different locations. A family of a particular size in a particular community experiences low income or poverty if its actual income cannot purchase this basket of essentials. This measure depends, of course, on just what is and is not included in the basket.

Except during the 2007–8 recession, the incidence of poverty was in decline from its 1996 peak until the pandemic. This is partly attributable to falling unemployment over that period, a reflection of the strong connection between poverty and people's relationship to the paid labour force.

The pre-pandemic decline was also due to the introduction in 1997 of the Canada Child Tax Benefit and the National Child Benefit Supplement, which were combined in 2016 into the Canada Child Benefit (CCB). The CCB pays up to $6,496 per month per child under six, and up to $5,481 per month per child aged six to seventeen, although most recipients don't receive these maximum amounts. Almost two-thirds of recipients are single parents.[7] These tax-free payments, scaled to parents' income, have lifted many families with children out of poverty, although there are still approximately 1.2 million children – one in every six children in Canada – living in poor families.

Moreover, if measured by AT LIM, poverty has continued to rise in recent years. This can probably be attributed to the growing gap between the rich and everyone else in Canada. Because it is set at 50 percent of median income, the AT LIM reflects income inequality as well as poverty.

But even measured by the AT LICO, the absolute numbers of those who are poor is remarkably high: approximately 2.8 million people in 2016 (Figure 10.1). Canada continues to have a higher poverty rate than many other countries – higher, for example, than Poland, Portugal, and Italy – ranking twenty-fifth out of thirty-five primarily richer developed economies, according to data for 2015 produced by the Organisation for Economic Co-operation and Development (OECD).[8]

Further, the poverty gap is large. It represents the difference between a poor family's income and the LICO. If the LICO were $10,000

FIGURE 10.1 **AT LICO poverty, 1976–2016**

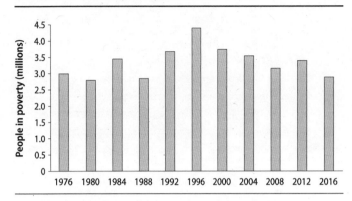

Sources: Data from Statistics Canada, Survey of Consumer Finances, Survey of Labour and Income Dynamics, and Canadian Income Survey.

and a family's income were $7,000, for example, the poverty gap would be $3,000, or 30 percent. The gap has been at or greater than this level for years. This means that, on average, those whose incomes are below the AT LICO are well below that poverty line.

Therefore, the fact that the incidence of poverty has been in relative decline in recent years as measured by AT LICO provides small comfort to those concerned with social justice. More than that, the COVID-19 pandemic and the loss of jobs that has followed have once again driven up the poverty rate in Canada.

PEOPLE AT RISK OF POVERTY

Although poverty and employment status are closely connected, socio-demographic factors also have significant and overlapping roles in determining who is poor. Different family configurations – single-parent, two-parent, living alone – carry different levels of risk, as do such characteristics as gender, age, (dis)ability, and ethnicity.

Family Dimensions
Particular family types are more likely than others to be poor (Figure 10.2). Single unattached

FIGURE 10.2 Low-income rates by family type, 2016

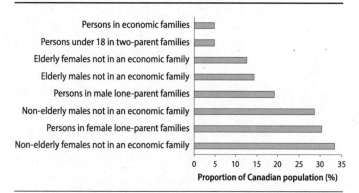

Source: Statistics Canada, Low-Income Survey.

individuals and single parents are especially vulnerable to poverty. Approximately 30 percent of single-parent families are poor, largely because of the challenge of finding a decently paid job with the flexibility for the worker to care for their children. Two-parent families are much less likely to be poor, generally because if two people are working for wages they are more likely to have the income to pay their bills.

Women, Seniors, People with Disabilities

Women have long been more likely than men to be poor. Women are more likely to be earning the minimum wage and to be working part time. Even when working full time, women earn on average only 74 percent of what men earn.[9] In 2022 Equal Pay Day – the day until which the average woman has to work to earn what the average man earned the previous year – is April 12. Women on average have to work 15.5 months to earn what the average man earned over the previous 12 months. The annual *Global Gender Gap Report*, which measures gender income disparity, ranked Canada thirty-fifth globally in 2016, down from twentieth in 2012.[10]

Almost one in four Canadians with disabilities had incomes below the AT LIM in 2014. Again, this is related to employment. Seventy-nine percent of Canadians aged twenty-five to sixty-four without a disability were employed in 2014, compared to 49 percent of those in the same age range with a disability.[11]

Seniors form another disadvantaged group and are experiencing growing poverty. Measured by the AT LIM, poverty among seniors rose from about 4 percent in 1995 to 11 percent in 2013.[12] Again, women are especially affected, with almost one in three single women seniors below the AT LIM in 2013. This is largely because of the declining value of Canadian government pensions, including Old Age Security, the Guaranteed Income Supplement, and the Canada Pension Plan, as well as a reduction in both the number who have employee pensions and the quality of those pensions. This is a good example of the importance of government social spending in lifting people out of poverty – or not.

Youth and Children

Young people also have a higher incidence of poverty, largely because of low wages and bad jobs – that is, jobs that are part time, contract, non-union, and with few or no benefits and little or no security. In 2012, record numbers of Canadians between fifteen and twenty-four were working part time, and about 70 percent of them wanted full-time work.[13] A 2017 survey of millennials (those born between 1981 and 1996) in Hamilton found that nine in ten preferred full-time permanent employment but fewer than half had such employment.[14] A record number of young people have *never* held a job. In 2017–18, 15 percent of Canadians aged twenty-five to twenty-nine, 376,000 people, were neither working nor in education.[15] These problems are being accentuated by the pandemic.

Largely due to precarious employment and inadequate social policies, the incidence of child poverty in Canada is also exceptionally high, even though it had, at least pre-pandemic, declined since its peak in 1996. The Conference

Board of Canada ranked Canada an abysmal fifteenth out of seventeen industrialized countries for child poverty.[16]

In the Greater Toronto Area in 2012, one in ten children of European ancestry lived in poverty, compared to one in five children in East Asian families, more than one in three children in Arab and West Asian families, and one in two children of African families.[17] Just under half of all children who arrived in Canada between 2011 and 2016 lived in poverty in 2017.[18]

The term *child poverty*, however, is misleading. Most poor children are poor because their families are poor and lack good jobs with good wages. And growing up in a poor family can cause lasting damage. For example, delayed vocabulary development occurs four times more frequently among children from low-income families; and about one in six teens from poor families is neither working nor in school, compared to only one in twenty-five from middle- or higher-income families. The result is *poverty of opportunity*: children who grow up in poor families are, on average, less likely to do well in life than are children in non-poor families.[19]

This has long been the case. In 1975, the National Council of Welfare made much the same argument:

> To be born poor is to face a lesser likelihood that you will finish high school, lesser still that you will attend university. To be born poor is to face a greater likelihood that you will be judged a delinquent in adolescence and, if so, a greater likelihood that you will be sent to a correctional institution. To be born poor is to have the deck stacked against you at birth, to find life an uphill struggle ever after.[20]

Racialized and Indigenous Poverty

Members of most racialized groups – defined for the purposes of this study as those who are non-Caucasian or non-white, excluding Indigenous people – have a much greater chance of being poor. In 1996, the incidence of poverty for racialized groups was double the Canadian population overall. By 2006, it was triple, and by 2016, racialized families were four times as likely to be poor.[21] This is partly because racialized Canadians are more likely to be employed in low-paid service jobs in the private sector. These are the kind that students are also more likely to have – restaurant and retail store jobs, for example – and are the types most adversely affected by the pandemic. Racialized women earn, on average, about half of what non-racialized men earn – reflecting what Sheila Block and Grace-Edward Galabuzi call the "colour-coded nature of work" in Canada.[22] Not surprisingly, members of racialized groups have been hit particularly hard by the COVID-19 pandemic.

For Indigenous people, the situation is even worse. In 2006, their median income was 30 percent lower than the rest of Canadians. That gap had narrowed since 1996 but at a rate that would take sixty-three years to close.[23] Indigenous children are especially likely to be poor. While 17 percent of all Canadian children live in families that are poor, as measured by the LIM, the rate for First Nations children is 50 percent. In Manitoba and Saskatchewan – both with large Indigenous populations – the rate of poverty for First Nations children in 2006 was 62 and 64 percent, respectively.[24]

Directly related to poverty and its origins in colonial history, Indigenous workers and their families often face difficult employment prospects.[25] In Manitoba, for example, the unemployment rate for Indigenous people is double that of the population as a whole, and while many Indigenous people are employed, a particularly high proportion work in precarious service-sector jobs.[26]

If Indigenous, racialized, and young Canadians are considered together and their situation extrapolated into the future, the prospects are alarming. Indigenous people constitute the country's youngest and fastest-growing demographic; the proportion of Canadians who are racialized is expected to double to a third by 2031; and Indigenous and racialized Canadians, especially their children, experience very high rates of poverty. So if current trends of low-wage work and limited job prospects continue, poverty will grow for these groups, as will the number of young Canadians who are poor.

Reflections of Poverty

Housing prices are making matters worse. The average price of housing has grown far faster than incomes, and again, the pandemic has exacerbated the problem. Across much of the country, particularly in large cities, home ownership is priced beyond the reach of low-income Canadians.

The same is the case with university tuition, which in most provinces has risen far faster than real wages. Provincial governments, in total, are reducing their share of university costs – from 77 percent in 1992 to 55 percent in 2012 – meaning that students pay an ever-growing proportion. From 1993-94 to 2015-16, the average cost of tuition and other student fees doubled when adjusted for inflation.[27] Thus, when students graduate they are likely to be squeezed by paying for student loans and expensive housing, while in many cases struggling with precarious jobs that pay little and have few long-term prospects.

Food bank usage reflects the same concerns. In March 2019, Canadians made just over a million visits to food banks across the country – more than the population of cities such as Hamilton and Winnipeg, and more than twice the combined population of Regina and Saskatoon. That year, almost one in every two people using food banks lived in a single-person household, one in three was a child or youth – although children and youth constituted just a fifth of the population – and those on disability and pension were also a significant proportion of users.[28] As rich as Canada is, food banks are no longer considered unusual. And as Food Banks Canada explains it, "The key factor at the root of the need for food banks is low income," the result of eroded social assistance programs and low-paying jobs.[29] One in six food bank users is employed, because the proportion of workers in poorly paid, precarious jobs continues to grow.

Unless action is taken, this problem will worsen. Food Banks Canada reported in 2020 that in the wake of the pandemic, the food bank system was unable to accommodate "a tidal wave of new clients while maintaining its level of support for long-term need created by decades of social policy neglect."[30]

COMPLEX POVERTY

Poverty is complex – it has numerous and interconnected causes and effects on citizens' everyday work and family lives. It is not simply a question of lacking the income to buy basics like food, clothing, or housing. Poverty also means that people face particularly adverse effects on their health and education. The reason why some groups of people are healthier than others has less to do with biomedical factors or lifestyle – such things as smoking, being overweight, or not getting enough exercise – than with what researchers call *social* determinants.[31] Living conditions – quality of housing, employment status, and especially poverty – are particularly important in shaping health outcomes. The pandemic has revealed this with startling clarity. Those who are poor are much more likely to suffer poor health and to do poorly in school. In such ways, poverty becomes chronic and intergenerational, which makes it especially complex.

Other effects of poverty include the loss of self-confidence and erosion of self-esteem, and in some cases even a sense of hopelessness about the future.[32] This too contributes to the reproduction of poverty and makes it difficult to counter.

THE PROBLEM OF INEQUALITY

Income inequality also produces adverse consequences, and has grown dramatically. This trend was evident before the pandemic, and inequality has worsened significantly since. Indeed, Oxfam International has called COVID-19 the "inequality virus."[33] In recent decades, the real incomes of working Canadians have stagnated, while the incomes of the rich have skyrocketed. In 1998, the 100 highest-paid chief executive officers in Canada earned 106 times the average Canadian worker. In 2019, that ratio was a remarkable 202 times. Each CEO in this top group received an average of $10.8 million annually, earning as much by 11:17 am on the first working day of the year – that is, in *less than half a day* – as the average Canadian full-time employee earned in the *entire year*.[34] In January 2018, Canada's highest minimum wage was $13.60 per hour; the average hourly wage of the 100 highest-paid CEOs was just under $2,500.[35]

BOX 10.2 TEMPORARY VERSUS COMPLEX POVERTY

Kemal is a university student. He shares an apartment with a friend, works part time for minimum wage, and visits his parents – his mother is a medical doctor and his father an accountant – for occasional meals at their suburban home. He does well in school and hopes to be an architect like his uncle.

Janine lives with her mother, who has addiction issues and is on social assistance. Their poorly maintained, bedbug-infested inner-city apartment is in a rough neighbourhood. Her father is rarely around. He has health issues and often lives in a rooming house. Neither parent has ever held a paid job for any length of time, nor have any of Janine's siblings. Two brothers are street gang members; one is in prison. Few of her friends have graduated from high school, and none has attended university. Janine, who was good at school, has completed Grade 12 but can't find a job. She thinks racism is a factor. Things are not good at home and she is thinking of moving out and applying for social assistance.

Both Janine and Kemal are poor as calculated by standard poverty measurements, but Janine and her family are experiencing complex poverty. Not only are they almost always short of money but also their housing is awful, their health is problematic, they have low levels of education and limited work experience, and violence is a factor in their lives, as is racism. They are, and feel, socially excluded from the mainstream and their self-confidence is low. Sometimes Janine's parents believe there's no hope for a better future.

Although he is currently short of money, Kemal is much more likely to have a healthy, happy, and fulfilling life than Janine, because hers is made complex by multiple interacting problems. These problems create a web or trap from which it is hard to escape. It already is a trap for her parents and two brothers. Although Janine is intelligent, her fate may be the same as theirs, reproducing the family's poverty.

This dramatic increase in the gap between the rich and the rest of us is important because the literature on the social determinants of health shows definitively that a wide range of social ills – poor educational outcomes, poor health, lower life expectancy, and a higher incidence of crime, for example – are strongly associated not just with poverty but also with income inequality. Income inequality is also strongly associated with reduced capacity for democratic participation by the poor, and it concentrates economic and political power among elites.[36]

INVESTMENT IN THE SOCIAL WAGE

To reduce poverty and income inequality, and to protect people from the many adverse consequences of low-wage work, governments must invest in social programs – what policy experts refer to as the social wage. Yet in recent decades, prior to the pandemic, social programs have been eroded. The pandemic – and the federal government's response in the form of the Canada Emergency Response Benefit (CERB) and its successor, the Canada Recovery Benefit (CRB) – has made it clear that a strong social wage is essential for our collective well-being (Chapter 1). But what will happen once the pandemic ends?

It's important to recognize that the level and quality of the social wage is a product of struggles engaged in over decades by many, including and perhaps especially the labour movement and social democratic political parties. In the face of enormous opposition from the corporate sector, they have had to fight for such gains as medicare and the Canada Pension Plan. When the postwar economic boom came to an end in the late 1960s and early '70s, the corporate sector seized the advantage, aggressively promoting neoliberal ideas such as cutting government spending,

reducing taxes on corporations and the wealthy, and restricting access to social assistance. The welfare state has been badly damaged as a result. It is working people and the poor who have paid the price of a reduced social wage.

Improvements to the social wage will happen only if and when working people organize effectively and resolutely to ensure they do. This is especially important in the wake of the pandemic, because the corporate community will push aggressively for big cuts in government spending, and the social wage will be targeted.

Federal social program spending as a share of gross domestic product (GDP) before the pandemic peaked in 1982 at almost 21 percent, then declined sharply to about 12 percent in 1999–2000 and 2000–1, the lowest level as a share of the Canadian economy since 1950–51. In 2016–17, it was back to just over 15 percent of GDP but still well below the level of 1982.[37] As of 2016, Canada ranked a low twenty-second out of thirty-eight OECD nations on social spending as a percentage of GDP.[38]

The erosion of social spending is directly related not only to the struggles of working people but also to dramatic changes in the economy. The social policy initiatives of the 1960s and early '70s – medicare, the Canada Assistance Plan, the Canada Pension Plan, the addition of the Guaranteed Income Supplement to Old Age Security, and reforms to Canada's Employment Insurance, for example – were funded out of the proceeds of the thirty-year economic boom following the end of the Second World War. Sustained economic growth and relatively low unemployment generated the government revenue to pay for the new social programs that working people had organized to demand. With the end of the postwar boom in the 1970s, this fiscal dividend disappeared and the corporate sector fought back.

The welfare state erected during the post-war boom had removed much of the fear of unemployment and poverty that made people anxious to work, whatever wages and conditions were on offer. If profitability were to be fully restored, many employers and governments believed that the relative security created by the welfare state had to be eroded. Thus, governments cut social spending to weaken workers' bargaining power and drive up profits. This has often been justified by claiming that the economy needs a more flexible labour force so that companies can respond quickly to the rapid pace of economic change. But flexibility generally means making jobs more precarious.

The pre-pandemic decline in social spending was facilitated by cuts in taxes for higher-income Canadians and corporations, leaving governments with less money for social programs. The federal corporate tax rate was almost 50 percent in the early 1980s but had dropped to 26.7 percent by 2016.[39] Federal taxes on high-income earners have also declined: in 1948, the top marginal income tax rate – the rate paid on earnings in an individual's highest tax bracket – was 80 percent. By 2009, that figure was 43 percent.[40] To put the consequences in perspective, from 2000 to 2005, the federal government lost over $100 billion in personal and corporate tax cuts.[41] This is money not available for spending on social programs.

A recent study found that while individual Canadians and corporations paid roughly equal shares of the total tax in 1952, by 2015-16, individual Canadians paid 3.5 times as much total tax as did corporations. This is partly a result of declining corporate tax rates but also because of tax avoidance as corporations use every legal loophole, most of them unavailable to ordinary workers, to reduce their taxes. In 2017, for example, Canada's five big banks, which already benefit from lower taxes than banks in any other G7 country, avoided $5.5 billion in taxes.[42]

These huge sums represent money *not* being invested in solving poverty. On the contrary, massive reductions in federal government revenues contribute to further cuts to the social wage, and this has been especially the case since the mid-1990s.

Provincial governments have also been cutting social expenditures. In Ontario, the Progressive Conservative government cut welfare rates by 21.6 percent in 1995, the largest single cut in the province's history. Social assistance payments are lower today than twenty years ago.[43] And in 2014, the poverty gap for different types of Ontario families receiving social assistance ranged from 33 percent to 59 percent. In other words, being on social assistance kept recipients *far* below the poverty line.[44] Across Canada, before the pandemic, provincial social assistance benefits were so low that 70 percent of recipients were food insecure, meaning that they lacked access to sufficient amounts of affordable and nutritious food.[45] The significant rise in food prices in 2022 will have added to food insecurity.

Canada's Employment Insurance (EI) program was also eroded in the pre-pandemic years. This crucial program was effectively privatized in 1989-90 as Ottawa terminated its contributions and left the financing completely in the hands of employees and employers. Stricter qualifying requirements and lower benefits followed in the early- to mid-1990s.[46] The proportion of unemployed Canadians receiving benefits has plummeted, from 74 percent in 1990 to less than 40 percent before the pandemic.[47] Since the 1990s, the EI account has accumulated surpluses, yet rather than use these to improve coverage, federal governments have used them to reduce taxes and balance budgets.

When unemployment benefits and social benefits are weak, the risk of job loss undermines workers' willingness to fight for higher wages. The fear and insecurity created by higher unemployment and reduced social benefits are therefore seen by those who benefit from higher profits as a good thing.

The effects of cutting social programs are also deeply gendered. When public-sector jobs are cut, it disproportionately affects women, for two reasons. First, women hold a disproportionate number of the public-sector jobs through which social services are delivered, and these jobs are unionized and relatively well paid. Second, cuts to social services that assist in raising families – childcare, social housing, for example – disproportionately affect women. The purpose of such cuts is "to individualize and re-privatize the responsibility for caring, socially reproductive labour," and when such supports to families are cut, the burden falls most heavily on women.[48]

A GENUINE ANTI-POVERTY STRATEGY

Are there alternatives? Yes, but those now on offer are weak. In 2018, the federal government announced its long-awaited national anti-poverty strategy, Opportunity for All. The strategy calls for reducing the national poverty rate by 20 percent by 2020 and 50 percent by 2030 but includes no new policies and, most importantly, no new money. It would be realistic, at least at this stage, to view this more as a public relations exercise than a real attempt to solve poverty.

BOX 10.3 POVERTY IS TOO EXPENSIVE

Although Janine's family bears the financial and emotional brunt of complex poverty, society also pays a financial price. Her brother is in a federal prison, which according to the Canadian non-profit John Howard Society costs about $115,000 annually per inmate. Her father frequently uses emergency health services, and police are often called to respond to the issues he faces. Homeless people impose high costs on health and police services – estimated by the Homeless Hub at $50,000 per year – and although Janine's father is rarely completely homeless, he is usually close.

Janine's mother receives social assistance. The minimum monthly payment in Manitoba, where she lives, is $677, or $8,124 per year, which is far below the poverty line. She has twice been to rehab to deal with addiction. On one occasion, when her mother was unable to care for them, Janine and her two brothers were taken into the custody of Child and Family Services. Janine may well end up on social assistance and experience related problems. The circumstances facing her, her parents, and her imprisoned brother – four people – cost society in excess of $170,000 per year, without counting the costs of addiction treatment and children taken into care.

If each of them had a decently paid full-time job, those costs would probably be reduced to zero, or close to zero, and each would be paying income taxes on their earnings. Instead of society paying to respond to the consequences of their complex poverty, they would be adding to the revenue available to governments to pay for improved health, education, and other public goods.

Feed Ontario, formerly the Ontario Association of Food Banks, estimates that the cost of poverty in Ontario alone in 2019 was between $27 billion and $33 billion per year, taking into account lost tax revenues and increased costs to the health and justice systems.[49]

Poverty, and especially complex poverty, makes no financial sense. It's too expensive.

A recently hotly debated response to poverty is to establish a guaranteed annual income (GAI), or basic income (BI), defined as "a stipend paid to families or individuals without the many conditions and rules that govern existing income-assistance programs."[50] Unusually, the idea is supported by some on the political left and some on the right. Some on the left argue that the current social assistance system has been so battered and diminished over the past forty years, and that artificial intelligence will so undermine the availability of paid employment over the next thirty years, that a basic income will become a necessity. As evidence of what a basic income could achieve they point to the success of CERB in saving Canadians who lost their jobs during the pandemic from destitution.

A basic income experiment conducted in Dauphin, Manitoba, in the 1970s worked well. In particular, there was a significant reduction in hospitalizations, especially for mental health reasons. Also, there was almost no adverse impact on employment. The only employment effect was that the BI made it possible for some young people, boys especially, to complete high school when they might otherwise have been forced to work, and for some mothers to stay at home longer with their babies.[51]

Most of those on the political right, by contrast, see the BI as a means of gutting social services even further than has already been the case.[52] The corporate-funded Fraser Institute, for example, argues that a BI system would have to replace all existing income supports, or at least a large portion of them, with a single program.[53] The BI would thus be paid for by eliminating government-funded social programs. Further, the new program would be pegged at a level low enough to push recipients into low-paid precarious jobs. Such a system would accentuate the neoliberalism and austerity of recent decades, and at the same time significantly weaken public-sector unions.

A better option, some progressives argue, would be to boost the social wage by making adequate investments in the publicly funded services that people need: a national childcare program; a national pharmacare and dental care program; an adequately funded social housing strategy; and a Green New Deal that allows us to make the transition from a carbon-based to a green economy, creating countless thousands of well-paid jobs.[54] This position is confirmed in a major report prepared for the government of British Columbia. It concluded that a basic income would not be the best way to deal with poverty, and that other policies would be more effective.[55] This comes back to the necessity of social investment by governments to defeat poverty, whether via an adequate basic income or more collective forms of the social wage.

Under the influence of neoliberal ideology, however, governments have chosen to dramatically reduce their role in providing support to those most adversely affected by global economic change. The result has been a widening gap between the rich and the rest of us, and the persistence of unacceptably large numbers of Canadians living in poverty, including a rapidly growing proportion of those who are employed.

It doesn't have to be this way. These are government choices. Poverty can be solved. But for governments to act to reduce poverty by increasing social investments, Canadians will have to mobilize to demand that this be done.

ADDITIONAL RESOURCES

Galabuzi, Grace-Edward. *Canada's Economic Apartheid: The Social Exclusion of Racialized Groups in
the New Century.* Toronto: Canadian Scholars'
Press, 2006.

Silver, Jim. *About Canada: Poverty.* Halifax: Fernwood
Publishing, 2014.

–. *Solving Poverty: Innovative Strategies from Winnipeg's Inner City.* Halifax: Fernwood Publishing,
2016.

NOTES

1   Ken Battle, *Precarious Labour Market Fuels
    Rising Poverty* (Ottawa: Caledon Institute, 1996).

2   Canada, *The National Child Benefit Progress
    Report, 2008* (Ottawa: Public Works and Govern-
    ment Services, 2012), https://www.canada.ca/
    content/dam/esdc-edsc/documents/programs/
    child-benefit/papers/progress-report-2008/ncb
    -pam-2008.pdf.

3   Martin and Lewchuk, *The Generation Effect.*

4   Jim Silver, *Solving Poverty: Innovative Strategies
    from Winnipeg's Inner City* (Halifax: Fernwood
    Publishing, 2016).

5   Jim Silver, *About Canada: Poverty* (Halifax: Fern-
    wood Publishing, 2014).

6   Statistics Canada, *Market Basket Measure (2008
    Base)* (Ottawa: Statistics Canada, 2010); Michael
    Hatfield, Wendy Pyper, Burton Gustajtis, *First
    Comprehensive Review of the Market Basket
    Measure of Low Income: Final Report* (Ottawa,
    Human Resources and Skills Development
    Canada, 2010).

7   Canada, *Strengthening the Canada Child Benefit*
    (Ottawa: Department of Finance, 2018).

8   OECD, Social Spending Indicator, 2018.

9   Canadian Women's Foundation, "Fact Sheet:
    Women and Poverty in Canada," 2018, https://
    canadianwomen.org/wp-content/uploads/2018/
    09/Fact-Sheet-WOMEN-POVERTY-September
    -2018.pdf.

10 World Economic Forum, *The Global Gender Gap
    Report 2016*, October 26, 2016 (Geneva: World
    Economic Forum, 2016), https://www.weforum.
    org/reports/the-global-gender-gap-report-2016;
    Canadian Centre for Policy Alternatives, "Shadow
    Report Finds Canada 'Missing in Action' on
    Women's Rights," *The Monitor*, December 2014.

11 Katherine Wall, *Low Income among Persons
    with a Disability in Canada* (Ottawa: Statistics
    Canada, 2017).

12 Robert Shillington, *An Analysis of the Economic
    Circumstances of Canadian Seniors* (Ottawa:
    Broadbent Institute, 2016).

13 Benjamin Tal, *Dimensions of Youth Unemploy-
    ment in Canada* (Toronto: CIBC World Markets,
    2013).

14 Joseph C. Martin and Wayne Lewchuk, *The
    Generation Effect: Millennials, Employment
    Precarity and the 21st Century Workplace –
    Executive Summary* (Hamilton, ON: McMaster
    University and PEPSO, 2018).

15 David Parkinson, "Public Daycare Could
    Boost Productivity, Statscan Finds," *Globe and
    Mail Report on Business*, October 11, 2018,
    theglobeandmail.com/business/rob-magazine.

16 Conference Board of Canada, *How Canada Per-
    forms: Child Poverty* (Ottawa: Conference Board
    of Canada, 2018), https://www.conferenceboard.
    ca/hcp/Details/society/child-poverty.aspx.

17 Ontario Common Front, *Falling Behind:
    Ontario's Backslide into Widening Inequality,
    Growing Poverty and Cuts to Social Programs*
    (Toronto: OCF, 2012).

18 Michael Polanyi, Beth Wilson, Jessica Mustachi,
    Manolli Ekra, and michael kerr, *Unequal City:
    The Hidden Divide among Toronto's Children
    and Youth – 2017 Toronto Child and Family
    Poverty Report Card* (Toronto: Children's Aid
    Society of Toronto, Social Planning Toronto,
    Family Service Toronto, Ontario Council of
    Agencies Serving Immigrants, and Colour of
    Poverty – Colour of Change, 2017).

19 David Ross and Paul Roberts, *Income and Child
    Well-Being: A New Perspective on the Poverty
    Debate* (Ottawa: Canadian Council on Social
    Development, 1999).

20 National Council of Welfare, *Poor Kids: A Report by the National Council of Welfare on Children in Poverty in Canada* (Ottawa: National Council of Welfare, 1975).

21 Sheila Block and Grace-Edward Galabuzi, *Canada's Colour Coded Labour Market: The Gap for Racialized Workers* (Ottawa and Toronto: Canadian Centre for Policy Alternatives and the Wellesley Institute, 2011); Homeless Hub, "Homelessness 101," http://homelesshub.ca/about-homelessness/homelessness-101.

22 Block and Galabuzi, *Canada's Colour Coded Labour Market.*

23 Daniel Wilson and David Macdonald, *The Income Gap between Aboriginal Peoples and the Rest of Canada* (Ottawa: Canadian Centre for Policy Alternatives, 2010).

24 David Macdonald and Daniel Wilson, *Poverty or Prosperity: Indigenous Children in Canada* (Ottawa: Canadian Centre for Policy Alternatives, 2013).

25 Truth and Reconciliation Commission, *Honouring the Truth, Reconciling for the Future: Summary of the Final Report of the Truth and Reconciliation Commission of Canada* (Winnipeg: Truth and Reconciliation Commission of Canada, 2015).

26 Lynne Fernandez and Jim Silver, *Indigenous Workers and Unions: The Case of Winnipeg's CUPE 500* (Winnipeg: Canadian Centre for Policy Alternatives-Manitoba, 2018).

27 Erica Shaker and David Macdonald, *What's the Difference? Taking Stock of Provincial Tuition Fee Policies* (Ottawa: Canadian Centre for Policy Alternatives, 2015).

28 Food Banks Canada, *Hungercount 2019 Report* (Mississauga, ON: Food Banks Canada, 2019).

29 Food Banks Canada, *Hungercount: A Comprehensive Report on Hunger and Food Bank Use in Canada, and Recommendations for Change* (Mississauga, ON: Food Banks Canada, 2012).

30 Food Banks Canada, *A Snapshot of Food Banks in Canada and the COVID-19 Crisis: Key Findings* (Mississauga, ON: Food Banks Canada, 2020).

31 Richard Wilkinson and Kate Pickett, *The Spirit Level: Why Greater Equality Makes Societies Stronger* (New York: Bloomsbury Press, 2010); Dennis Raphael, "Making Sense of the Social Determinants of Health Scene in Canada," in *The Social Determinants of Health in Manitoba*, 2nd ed., eds. Lynne Fernandez, Shauna MacKinnon, and Jim Silver (Winnipeg: Canadian Centre for Policy Alternatives, 2015), 114–33.

32 Jim Silver, *Solving Poverty.*

33 Esmé Berkhout, Nick Galasso, Max Lawson, Pablo Andrés Rivero Morales, Anjela Taneja, and Diego Alejo Vázquez Pimentel, *The Inequality Virus: Brining Together a World Torn Apart by Coronavirus through a Fair, Just, and Sustainable Economy* (Oxford: Oxfam International, 2021).

34 David Macdonald, *The Golden Cushion: CEO Compensation in Canada* (Ottawa: Canadian Centre for Policy Alternatives, 2021).

35 David Macdonald, *Climbing Up and Kicking Down: Executive Pay in Canada* (Ottawa: Canadian Centre for Policy Alternatives, 2018).

36 Wilkinson and Pickett, *The Spirit Level.*

37 Department of Finance Canada, *Fiscal Reference Tables*, September 2017 (Ottawa: Department of Finance, 2017), https://www.canada.ca/content/dam/fin/migration/frt-trf/2017/frt-trf-17-eng.pdf.

38 OECD, Social Spending Indicator. https://stats.oecd.org/.

39 Marco Chown Oved, Toby Heaps, and Michael Yow, "The High Cost of Low Corporate Taxes," *Toronto Star*, December 14, 2017, thestar.com.

40 Armine Yalnizyan, *The Rise of Canada's Richest 1 Percent* (Ottawa: Canadian Centre for Policy Alternatives, 2010).

41 Ibid.

42 Oved, Heaps, and Yow, "The High Cost of Low Corporate Taxes."

43 Homeless Hub, "Homelessness 101."

44 Kaylie Tiessen, *Ontario's Social Assistance Poverty Gap* (Ottawa: Canadian Centre for Policy Alternatives, 2016).

45 Nick Falvo, "Ten Things to Know about Canada's Newly-Unveiled National Housing Strategy," *The Monitor,* Canadian Centre for Policy Alternatives, December 18, 2017, https://monitormag.ca.

46 Jane Pulkingham and Gordon Ternowetsky, "Neoliberalism and Retrenchment: Employment, Universality, Safety Net Provisions and a Collapsing Canadian Welfare State," in *Citizens or Consumers? Social Policy in a Market Society,* ed. Dave Broad and Wayne Antony (Halifax: Fernwood Publishing, 1999).

47 Angela MacEwan, "How to Make Employment Insurance More Accessible," *Globe and Mail,* February 17, 2015, theglobeandmail.com.

48 Adrie Naylor, "Economic Crisis and Austerity: The Stranglehold on Canada's Families," *New Socialist,* April 4, 2012, https://newsocialist.org.

49 Celia R. Lee and Alexa Briggs, *The Cost of Poverty in Ontario: Ten Years Later* (Toronto: Feed Ontario, 2019).

50 Evelyn Forget, "Why a Canadian Basic Income Is Inevitable," *Globe and Mail Report on Business,* October 9, 2018, theglobeandmail.com/business/rob-magazine.

51 Evelyn Forget, *Basic Income for Canadians: The Key to a Healthier, Happier, More Secure Life for All* (Toronto: Lorimer, 2018).

52 Charles Murray, "A Guaranteed Income for Every American," *Wall Street Journal,* June 3, 2016, www.wsj.com.

53 Charles Lammam and Hugh MacIntyre, "Be Cautious about Ontario's Basic Income Plan," *The Fraser Institute Blog,* October 31, 2016, www.fraserinstitute.org.

54 Armine Yalnizyan, *Redistribution through a Basic Income: Are We Better off When We Have More Income, or Need Less of It?* (Ottawa: Canadian Centre for Policy Alternatives, 2017); John Clarke, "Basic Income: Progressive Dreams Meet Neoliberal Realities," *The Bullet,* January 2, 2017, https://socialistproject.ca.

55 David A. Green, Jonathan Rhys Kesselman, and Lindsay M. Tedds, *Covering All the Basics: Reforms for a More Just Society,* Final Report of the British Columbia Expert Panel on Basic Income (Victoria, BC: Government of British Columbia, 2020), 35.

Part 3

POLICY BARRIERS AND OPPORTUNITIES ACROSS THE LABOUR MARKET

11 The Low-Wage Service Economy and the Populist Moment

Mark Thomas and Steve Tufts

CHAPTER SUMMARY

This chapter explores the growth of service-sector employment, and with it the widespread incidence of bad jobs. It begins by mapping the growth of the service sector in Canada, looking at occupational and sectoral growth, as well as divisions and differences within the service sector itself.

This chapter then investigates the rise of precarious, low-wage jobs in the sector. It examines regulatory responses to precarious employment conditions by provincial and municipal governments, as well as collective bargaining strategies to address precarity through service-sector unions.

The chapter concludes by examining how service-sector workers use different kinds of organizing strategies to improve their working lives and transform bad jobs into good ones. Coalition- and campaign-based strategies such as the Fight for $15 and Fairness – now known as Justice for Workers! – show promise, but they also face numerous political obstacles. In considering the prospects for improving work and working conditions in the service sector, the chapter considers the impact of the COVID-19 pandemic and the significance of the current populist moment in Canada.

KEY THEMES

This chapter will help you develop an understanding of:

- work in the private service sector and the reasons for its growth
- why jobs in the service sector are often considered bad jobs
- the impact of the COVID-19 pandemic on jobs in the service sector
- how to transform bad service-sector jobs into good ones
- political hurdles that workers and unions face in trying to achieve progressive policy reforms.

THE SERVICE ECONOMY and postindustrial employment have grown exponentially in recent decades. What are the consequences? For some, service-sector jobs promise a transition to a knowledge-based world of self-fulfilling good jobs.[1] Others are more skeptical, arguing that the rise of precarious, fragmented, low-wage service work is only leading to greater polarization and labour conflict, as workers in bad jobs demand better wages, more control over their working time, and greater job security.[2]

In any consideration of the prospects for improving work and working conditions in the service sector, the populist moment in Canada is significant. In contemporary times, **populism** has been a prominent political force since the 2008 financial crisis.[3] While populism is often understood as a phenomenon of right-wing politics, and can be seen through political leaders such as Donald Trump in the United States and Doug Ford in Canada, it also has presence in left-wing movements and politicians, including in the Occupy Wall Street movement that arose in 2011.[4] The growth of precarious service-sector

jobs is implicated in this populist moment. To illustrate these dynamics, this chapter draws from recent experiences in Ontario, whereby the working conditions of precariously employed service workers were made more precarious by the actions of a right-wing populist government, while at the same time organizing among precarious workers, including those in the service sector, built on elements of left-wing populism to push for better working conditions.

A SNAPSHOT OF THE CANADIAN SERVICE SECTOR

A shift toward employment in the service sector can be seen throughout Canada for well over a century.[5] Over the first half of the twentieth century, agriculture and resource extraction lost their dominance, while the manufacturing and service sectors grew. By 1946, employment in agriculture and resource industries accounted for 30 percent of the Canadian labour force, while manufacturing accounted for another 25 percent and the service sector for about 40 percent, with the remainder in construction.[6] In the postwar period, agricultural employment continued to decline and growth in manufacturing employment stagnated. Service-sector employment, however, has grown to such an extent that four out of every five people in Canada aged fifteen and over is employed in service-producing industries.[7]

In 2018, 28.9 percent of workers in services-producing industries were unionized, which is the approximate unionization rate for all sectors of the economy. Service-sector unionization is uneven, however, as the overall rate is skewed by services dominated by government employment – education, health care, and public administration – all of which have rates of unionization much higher than the national average. By contrast, unionization in service industries characterized by private ownership

FIGURE 11.1 **Unionization rate (%) by industry, 2018**

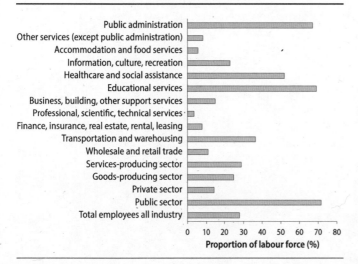

Source: Data from Statistics Canada, Table 14-1000132-01: Union status by industry, https://doi.org/10.25318/1410013201-eng.

is typically well below 11 percent (Figure 11.1). For example, only 5.6 percent of employees in accommodation and food services, a sector employing over 1 million workers, are unionized. Not surprisingly, these are the industries where bad jobs are most prevalent and where workers have been most vulnerable to COVID-19.

Economic explanations for the rise of service-sector employment often point to the particular features of service productivity (e.g., the inability to automate many services) and the growing penetration of capitalism into our everyday lives (e.g., purchasing takeout food versus unpaid cooking in the home). Indeed, the growth of the gig economy, or platform economy, has allowed private services to enter homes with online food delivery, commercial ridesharing, and even the rental of homes themselves.

Service-sector employment and growth have, however, been uneven. The gendered and racialized segmentation of the labour market is also deeply inscribed in the postindustrial workforce. Some service jobs are lucrative, while others are characterized by low wages and increasing precarity.[8] Further, regions, cities, and neighbourhoods are integrated into the global service economy to different extents.

BOX 11.1 THE RISE OF A NEW SERVANT CLASS?

Ridesharing (Uber, Lyft), home rentals (Airbnb), and food-service delivery (Foodora, SkipTheDishes) are used by millions of people each day. In many ways, these private-sector consumer services are simply part of a deeper trend of integrating formal exchange into home-based tasks that are central to the reproduction of a capitalist economy. For some time, researchers have noted that such tasks are increasingly accomplished by paying for services or even employing workers in the home (nannies, cleaners).

In much of the Global South, employing servants to cook and clean in middle- and upper-class homes remains a common practice, reflecting economic inequality. Sri Lankan writer Indi Samarajiva makes the somewhat wry suggestion that the gig economy more widely is really a matter of "white people discovering servants," as people use services whenever they need them.

Gig workers are geographically fragmented, working alone with few opportunities for interaction. In many cases, they are considered independent contractors rather than employees. But despite such misclassification, they are beginning to fight for better working conditions. Uber drivers in Toronto recently joined the United Food and Commercial Workers to seek better compensation and benefits. Similarly, the Canadian Union of Postal Workers launched #FoodstersUnited campaigns to organize bicycle and car delivery workers at Foodora. Recently, the Ontario Labour Relations Board (OLRB) recognized that workers employed by Foodora are not independent contractors and do have the right to unionize.

These campaigns to address growing inequality in the service economy face contradictions, external pressures, and employer opposition. During the COVID-19 outbreak, food delivery services expanded as they were the only option for restaurants to stay in business and for consumers to continue dining "out." At the same time, Foodora announced in April 2020 that it was pulling out of the Canadian market as Foodora Canada declared bankruptcy. While the company claimed it was absorbing losses in a competitive market, the pullout may have been related to the OLRB decision.[9]

The growth of women's paid labour has co-existed with the rise of both private- and public-sector services. Both male and female employment has been stagnant in goods-producing industries, but men are employed at higher rates in those sectors. At the same time, women dominate public service sectors such as health care, social services, and education, and lead employment in private services such as finance, real estate, and accommodation and food services. Male workers continue to dominate distributive services such as transportation and warehousing.[10]

The gendered division of labour is only one dimension of a segmented labour market. Immigrant and racialized workers are also over-represented in specific sectors of the service economy. These divisions typify what might be termed a creeping economic apartheid in Canada.[11] Again, at the national scale, immigrant workers are under-represented in resource extraction industries but do have a presence in manufacturing. In services, immigrants are slightly over-represented in transportation and warehousing, accommodation and food services, and professional and administrative support services, but they are vastly under-represented in arts and entertainment, education, and public administration.[12]

Similarly, workers self-identifying as *visible minority* (a much-criticized Statistics Canada category for racialized people) are under-represented in education and public administration, but are over-represented in largely private-sector services such as finance and real estate, and accommodation and food services.[13] Indigenous workers make up approximately 4 percent of the workforce and are over-represented in resource extraction and administration, largely due to their participation in resource development and public services in northern communities.[14] They confront significant barriers to entering the labour market.

The labour market is also segmented by age. Workers aged fifteen to twenty-four are concentrated largely in retail and food services, sectors that are well known for providing entry-level jobs and that have historically been dependent on the youth labour market – sometimes called the *secondary labour market*.[15]

Overall, women, immigrants, racialized workers, and young workers tend to be over-represented in sectors of the economy characterized by low unionization, lower rates of full-time work, and lower median and average annual incomes. Admittedly, these are only broad indicators of precarity, but marginalized groups do tend to work in sectors that have lower wages and benefits than others.

There are competing explanations for labour market segmentation in services and other sectors.[16] Human capital theorists argue that employers require skills and credentials that are simply unevenly distributed, with some groups having more human capital (e.g., education and training) than others. Human capital theory is challenged by structural approaches that identify forms of racial and gender discrimination as major determinants of unequal labour market outcomes.[17] Gary Becker argues that a "taste for discrimination" by employers leads to both inequality and poor economic performance. Racist and sexist hiring practices, for example, create mechanisms that misrepresent the human capital of workers and contribute to segmented markets.[18] Recruitment practices that rely on established social networks and systemic barriers, such as the devaluation of an immigrant's foreign credentials and training or demands for domestic experience, create employment inequality.

These practices result in dual or split labour markets whereby a group of core workers (white, domestically trained and credentialled older workers) constitutes the labour supply employers tend to prefer for certain sectors, such as education and public administration, at the expense of peripheral workers (workers of colour, foreign-trained, young workers) who are restricted from access to higher-income service jobs.[19] Pierre Bourdieu explains how labour market segmentation is reproduced because specific cultural capital, status, and knowledge of practices (such as how to portray confidence in a job interview) can be converted into more opportunities in the labour market for dominant groups.[20]

Patterns of labour market segmentation are also evident at different geographic scales, even if the forms of segmentation change. For example, Toronto has a thriving regional economy, with significant employment in good service jobs. Capital and labour continue to concentrate in the Greater Toronto Area, where immigrants are now the majority of the workforce. Labour market segmentation is nevertheless still evident. Immigrants are under-represented in management, education, and public administration, for example, and over-represented in manufacturing, transportation, and warehousing. Racialized workers are similarly distributed in low-wage service industries, forming a large part of the accommodation and food services sector. Indigenous workers form less than 1 percent of the labour market but are over-represented in lower-wage services and public administration.

In smaller urban centres, patterns of labour market segmentation are different. Smaller communities often have a lower percentage of immigrants and racialized workers than metropolitan centres. Yet women, young, racialized, and immigrant workers are still over-represented in sectors such as accommodation and food services. Smaller regional centres also employ a lower percentage of the labour force in finance, real estate, professional, and technical services but relatively more workers in health care, social services, and public adminis-

tration. Why this difference at the subregional scale? Toronto, a global city with huge concentrations of capital and labour, employs hundreds of thousands of workers to manage financial flows and global production. Cities in northern Ontario, however, are more dependent on the public service sector as a source of stable employment.[21]

Labour market segmentation in paid service work has a damaging effect. It is about the exclusion and marginalization of specific groups, and indeed entire communities, from services that historically provide higher wages and benefits and greater employment security.

Almost expectedly, the impact of COVID-19 has had an unequal impact on a fragmented service labour market. Some have characterized the impact as a *she-cession*, given that the over-representation of women in sectors such as health care, retail, and hospitality meant women experienced higher job losses and were burdened with additional childcare responsibilities as schools closed.[22]

LOW-WAGE SERVICE-SECTOR EMPLOYMENT

Integral to the growth of the service sector has been the rise of forms of non-standard and precarious employment: part-time jobs, temporary jobs, and **solo or bogus self-employment**. Notable growth in non-standard employment began in the 1970s and continued through the 1990s and 2000s.[23] Its rise has been driven largely by practices that aim to make business operations, scheduling, and wages more flexible from the perspective of the employer.[24] This is particularly so in businesses in the private service sector.

Precarious employment is defined in relation to factors that include lack of job security, low wages, low control over the labour process, and low regulatory protection.[25] While not all non-standard employment is precarious, and not all precarious employment occurs through non-standard jobs, job security and wages for part-time and temporary jobs are typically lower than comparable full-time permanent jobs, with fewer (if any) health and pension benefits, and fewer opportunities for upward mobility. These kinds of jobs are typically less likely to be unionized. Thus, working conditions such as wages, vacation pay, and hours of work are more likely to be regulated through minimum employment standards legislation, which typically provides lower standards than do collective bargaining agreements.[26]

Though precarity is a general trend, forms of non-standard work associated with precariousness are more prevalent in the service sector. While full-time employment continues to be the norm in both goods- and services-producing sectors, both part-time and temporary employment are more prevalent in the service sector (Figure 11.2). Additionally, while conditions of precariousness are more often associated with non-standard employment, full-time jobs may themselves be precarious, for example through low wages.[27]

FIGURE 11.2 **Form of employment by sector, 2016**

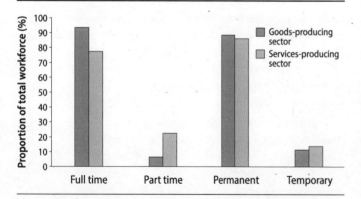

Source: Data from Statistics Canada, Table 14-10-002301: Labour force characteristics by industry, annual, https://doi.org/10.25318/1410002301-eng; and Table 14-10-007201: Job permanency (permanent and temporary) by industry, annual, https://doi.org/10.25318/1410007201-eng.

As the service sector is highly diverse, it is necessary to look within the sector itself to get a clearer picture of the occupations most likely to have bad jobs. Part-time employment is most prevalent in accommodation and food services (42 percent), which are also the occupations with the lowest levels of pay and unionization. Part-time employment is also high in information, culture, and recreation occupations (28 percent), as well as in wholesale and retail trade (28 percent). Part-time work contributes to flexibility by allowing employers to vary hours of work in line with changing business conditions. For workers, this typically means scheduling uncertainty and limited access to things like Canada's Employment Insurance program, pensions, and sick days.

The service economy is characterized by a mix of full- or part-time and permanent or temporary arrangements: temporary full-time work, permanent part-time work, and so forth. Temporary employment is particularly prevalent in information, culture, and recreation occupations (24 percent), and is also comparatively high in business, building, and other support services (22 percent), as well as in accommodation and food services (18 percent). The shift to temporary work has been a key driver of precarity, resulting in part from employers' intentions to be able to increase or decrease their workforces on short notice, rather than the desire of workers to hold short-term jobs. The trend is contributing to fissured workplaces, in which jobs are broken up and outsourced to temporary help agencies, franchisees, subcontractors, and other firms. As a result, an increasing proportion of individual workers are treated not as employees but as independent contractors who lack the regulatory protections associated with employee status.[28]

Low pay is often a key indicator of precarity (Figure 11.3). Average hourly wages in services-producing sectors ($25.24) are lower than those in goods-producing sectors ($27.61), and specific service industries are particularly low paid. Accommodation and food services, for example, have an average hourly wage of $14.38, well below that for both the goods- and services-producing sectors. Low hourly wages are also prevalent in business, building, and other support services ($18.96), as well as in wholesale and retail trade ($19.65). Given the gendered and racialized divisions of labour that characterize precarious work in the service economy, the prevalence of low wages in these occupations contributes to wider patterns of gendered and racialized inequalities in employment income.

As is true of work in the service sector generally, forms of non-standard and precarious employment are deeply gendered and racialized. Women are twice as likely to work part time as men, in part because they must balance paid work with unpaid household labour, and in part due to gender discrimination in the labour market.[29] Racialized women and men are disproportionately represented in low-income forms of employment, which, as demonstrated above, are more prevalent in particular service-sector occupations.[30]

Another dimension to service-sector precarity lies in the nature of service work itself, as its socially interactive nature introduces a particular form of control into the labour process.[31] More specifically, this occurs through the role of *emotional labour*, whereby interactive work involves a triangular relation between workers, managers, and customers. Not only are the *physical* actions of workers subject to traditional forms of managerial control, the *self-presentation* of the worker through the act of providing the service becomes part of the control structure of the workplace. Workers' looks, use of language, personalities, feelings, thoughts, and attitudes are all subject to formal and informal dynamics of control.

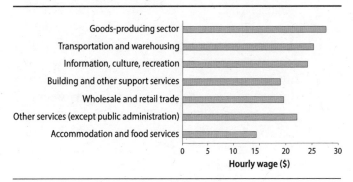

FIGURE 11.3 **Employee wages in the service sector, 2016**

Source: Data from Statistics Canada, Table 14-10-006401: Employee wages by industry, annual, https://doi.org/10.25318/1410006401-eng.

In the interactive service workplace, the customer jointly supervises workers along with management, such as by providing service feedback. Since lack of worker voice in conditions of employment is a key contributor to precariousness, this additional layer of customer-directed labour control intensifies the precarity of work in the service sector. These forms of control are not absolute, however, as the interactive nature of service work also presents workers with opportunities for multiple forms of everyday, informal resistance, such as absenteeism, slacking off, theft, and altering or personalizing uniforms.[32]

During the pandemic, issues affecting caring services – including the ability to exert control in the workplace and strike a balance between work and home life – have become even more acute. In some instances, workers have been able to shift to working remotely from home but are then confronted with issues such as childcare, eldercare, and isolation. Those who have been deemed essential and continued to attend their worksites, such as health care workers, face challenges of burnout and exposure to COVID-19. This has been especially evident in long-term eldercare facilities, which were devastated by the pandemic.

IMPROVING SERVICE WORKING CONDITIONS

Working conditions in the service economy are regulated through labour laws and unionization, but union coverage in private service sector occupations – and with it protection of workers' rights, wages, and working conditions – is very low. The United Food and Commercial Workers (UFCW) has attempted to organize workers in wholesale and retail trade, and UNITE-HERE has tried to do the same in accommodation and food services; however, such efforts have faced many challenges. The typically small size of workplaces, high rates of employee turnover, lack of union presence, and high degree of precariousness make workers in the sector more vulnerable to employer retribution. In larger workplaces that should be easier to unionize, employers are often aggressively anti-union, going to great lengths and expense to engage in union avoidance strategies.[33]

As control over scheduling is a major concern for workers in the sector, particularly in retail and food services, unions have sought to use collective bargaining to provide greater work hours certainty and stability. A notable breakthrough occurred in 2015 with a collective

---

BOX 11.2 AIRPORT CONTRACT FLIPPING

Airports employ workers in hundreds of occupations, ranging from pilots and airport administrators to food services and baggage handling. Competitive pressure on airports is fierce, and one way to control costs is through contract flipping for subcontracted airport workers. When a service provider, often a multinational firm, reaches the end of its contract, the airport contracts a new provider to perform the work at a lower cost. As a result, workers are forced to re-apply for the same job at the new firm. Their wages are reset at entry level, and they lose annual wage increases and accrued vacation time earned over years with the previous employer.

The cost to workers and communities is huge. Workers in precarious conditions due to contract flipping are often forced to work multiple part-time jobs. Some refuse to accept the reset and find low-wage employment elsewhere. Added turnover – as high as 160 percent annually in some areas – increases training costs and reduces productivity as newly hired workers find themselves training even newer hires, creating gaps in experience and knowledge of safe operating procedures.

Workers are pushing back against these conditions. The Toronto Airport Workers' Council (TAWC), an organization of unions representing airport workers, has not only fought against the practice for years but has also supported the Fight for $15 and Fairness movement and advocated for an airport minimum wage.

These efforts have paid off. The federal government opened discussions to close a loophole in the Canada Labour Code that allowed contract flipping and to guarantee workers protection for wage increases gained through years of service. Although the populist Progressive Conservative government of Ontario froze the minimum wage at $14 per hour when it was elected in 2018, many airport contracts have established $15 as the lowest wage level in collective agreements. Airport workers continue to organize to raise standards across this increasingly important service industry even in the midst of the pandemic, when air passenger traffic declined by as much as 95 percent in airports such as Pearson International.

---

agreement between the UFCW and Loblaws which established minimum hours guarantees and improved the predictability of scheduling.[34]

Another strategy that unions have pursued is organizing workers across an entire occupational group rather workplace by workplace. In the United States, the **Justice for Janitors** campaigns to organize office cleaning service workers through the Service Employees International Union (SEIU) have been a notable success.[35] In a recent Canadian example, a coalition of unions at Toronto Pearson International Airport has sought to improve standards for airport service workers, with some success.[36] Broader approaches are not widespread in the Canadian context, however, as Canadian labour laws generally support union organizing and collective bargaining at the level of each individual workplace, which prevents broader groups of workers from organizing and bargaining together through one large union.

As the vast majority of workers in the services-producing sector are not unionized, however, various efforts have focused on improving provincial employment standards legislation for basic workplace protections. Such legislation typically sets a very low floor and is poorly enforced. Thus, it has been frequently targeted for reform by workers' advocates and through campaigns organized by precariously employed workers.[37] Legislative reforms recently introduced in Ontario provide examples of regulatory protections that could improve conditions for workers in the low-wage service sector.

Growing public pressure to address precarious employment, including in the service sector, came from Ontario's province-wide Fight for $15 and Fairness campaign, which included elements of a left-wing **populist** attack on wealthy elites. In response to this pressure and following a major review of the provincial labour and employment legislation, the then Liberal government introduced the Fair Workplaces, Better Jobs Act, 2017, which came into effect on January 1, 2018.[38] This legislation included several reforms to the provincial Employment Standards Act (ESA): a minimum wage increase to $15 an hour; equal pay for casual, part-time, temporary, and seasonal employees doing substantially the same work as full-time/permanent employees; minimum compensation for scheduled work that is cancelled; and the introduction of two paid personal emergency leave days and the extension of this benefit to small workplaces.

Although not specific to the sector, these ESA reforms would have had significant implications for service-sector workers, given their low level of unionization. However, building on a right-wing populist platform that cast these protections, and particularly the increased minimum wage, as a threat to Ontario's economy, the Progressive Conservative government under Premier Doug Ford repealed key provisions of the legislation and froze the general minimum wage at $14. The government also suspended both the proactive workplace inspections program and the hiring of additional enforcement officers, and cancelled a planned review of ESA exemptions and special rules.[39]

Regulatory strategies to address precarious employment have also been developed at the municipal level. In the United States, municipal ordinances have made breakthroughs in improving workplace protections and even establishing new workplace rights for low-wage service workers. For example, in 2015, San Francisco introduced a bill of rights for retail workers. It includes: a requirement to pay two to four hours of wages for on-call shifts when workers are not called in or are sent home before their shift ends; two weeks' notice of work scheduling, with extra pay for scheduling changes; equal treatment of full- and part-time workers, including benefits, vacation time, and hourly wages; and part-time workers' right to have access to full-time employment before employers hire additional part-timers or temporary workers.[40] Under pressure from the Fight for $15 campaign, some municipalities have introduced $15 minimum wage ordinances, the most notable of these being Seattle in 2015.[41]

Low wage rates also became an issue during the COVID-19 outbreak. In some sectors "pandemic pay" was established in an effort to increase retention and reduce absenteeism. For example, some Ontario frontline health care workers received pay increases, and major grocery retailers in Canada raised hourly rates by $2 per hour.[42] In both cases, however, the increase was only temporary. Unsurprisingly, when employers reduced the rates to previous levels, they faced a public backlash.

COVID-19 AND THE SERVICE SECTOR

Since March 2020, there have been many reports about the consequences of COVID-19 for the working world. The International Labour Organization (ILO) reports an unprecedented loss of working hours resulting from both lost employment and reduced hours due to pandemic restrictions, though these impacts have varied significantly by region, sector, and occupation.[43] Globally, employment in accommodation and food services, as well as retail, was particularly affected, with a disproportionate impact on young workers, women, and low- and medium-skilled workers.

The impact on service-sector employment in Canada was severe though highly uneven, varying considerably by occupation. Some parts of the sector experienced complete work stoppages for extended periods due to provincial lockdowns. The pandemic particularly affected jobs in hospitality services, food and beverage services, and various personal care services. For example, employment in accommodation and food services declined sharply in the initial months of the pandemic and six months into the pandemic was still 20 percent below pre-pandemic levels.[44]

Depending on provincial regulations, some segments of the service sector were able to remain open under restrictions such as shorter hours of operation. This included businesses operating in retail sales of so-called non-essential goods. Businesses in this segment were also subjected to full closures during some periods, again depending on regulations. Other segments of the service sector remained in operation as essential services, food retail being the most notable example, placing enormous strain and risk on these workers, who were frequently engaged in direct interaction with the general public throughout the pandemic.

The pandemic also made itself felt on the service sector in relation to the racialized and gendered divisions of labour discussed previously. Racialized inequalities in the workplace became more pronounced, including higher unemployment rates due to the concentration of certain racialized groups in industries that were disproportionately affected by the shutdowns, including accommodation and food services.[45]

Women also experienced greater job losses during the pandemic than did men, in part due to over-representation in accommodation and food services.[46] Additionally, women were frequently in frontline essential interactive service work during the pandemic. More than half of women workers are employed in occupations that involve some form of care work, clerical duties, food service, cashier work, and/or cleaning, creating increased risks to their health and safety as a result of their work.[47]

Women who remained working but in jobs that could not be done from home, for example in retail businesses that were able to remain open, reported having to choose between going to work or staying home to assist children with remote learning. Consistent with a broader global trend noted by the ILO, whereby women workers were more likely than men to drop out of the labour force during the pandemic, women retail workers were also more likely than men to have left a job during the pandemic due to childcare-related responsibilities and the inflexible scheduling practices in retail.[48]

POPULISM ON THE RIGHT AND LEFT

What are the consequences of the rise of service employment and the failure of provincial and federal governments to regulate persistent precarity in segmented labour markets? Fundamentally, workers in the service economy are fragmented and angry. They are also important.

While the emerging new economy is based on knowledge and innovation, it also requires a large number of workers to service that economy, specifically the low-wage and often precarious workers cleaning offices and serving restaurant meals to so-called knowledge workers. And service workers who are themselves engaged in new forms of knowledge production, such as data processing or call centres, are increasingly disenchanted with their economic insecurity.[49] These service workers – both those who are employed and those who are underemployed – may be open to forms of populist politics.[50] Indeed, the decline of manufacturing and the accompanying shift to services in advanced capitalist economies has driven support for both right-wing populism, which often includes elements of white nationalism and white supremacy, and left-wing populism, with its general critique of the One Percent, or economic elite.

Segmented labour markets that limit groups to bad jobs are not the only source of worker discontent. Specific groups of workers experience economic displacement, but so do entire communities that are unable to tap into the wealth of the global service economy. For example, Doug Ford's success in the 2018 Ontario provincial election – particularly in communities outside the Greater Toronto Area (GTA) that are challenged by the loss of manufacturing jobs and the decline of rural and resource economies – can be characterized as a "revenge of forgotten places."[51] The geography of these communities prevents them from connecting to the global service economy as easily as workers in the GTA. Moreover, within the context of a way of life defined by dependence on the car and a focus on home ownership, many workers outside large cities resent politics driven strictly by investment in affordable housing and transit in urban centres.

The uneven impact of COVID-19 has led to a range of populist reactions by employers and workers who feel forgotten by governments responding to the crisis. Millions of workers received the Canada Emergency Response Benefit (CERB). Employer groups attacked the program as a disincentive for workers to take low-wage jobs during the crisis, while workers facing lower benefits once the program concluded wanted governments to either ease pandemic restrictions or bail out their particular sectors. For example, a Facebook group named "Aviation workers made redundant in Canada by the COVID-19 crisis" grew to over 11,000 members in just a few weeks.[52] The group continued to exert populist pressure on the federal government to ease travel and quarantine restrictions so that people could start flying again in large numbers. It further claims that the sector was neglected by federal and provincial governments throughout the pandemic. Hospitality workers equally devastated by restaurant closures and the collapse of tourism have made similar appeals to the government and in some cases left the sector completely, creating a labour shortage during the recovery.

Some discontented workers are attracted to

the promise of right-wing populism to reverse the economic insecurity brought on by globalization and deregulation. Canada has experienced rising xenophobic, anti-immigrant sentiment and a desire, expressed by many, to turn the clock back to support good jobs in resource industries such as oil and mining as gas prices increase at the expense of the environment. But other, more progressive forms of resistance emerging over the past decade also contain populist currents. These include struggles for immigrant rights in the workplace, teachers' strikes over extremely low salaries in some US states, and calls for a Green New Deal to create millions of high-quality jobs that will confront the climate crisis and lift the global economy out of a recession sparked by the pandemic. Movements such as the Fight for $15 and Fairness are contesting the conditions of service-sector employment while also challenging institutionalized racism in the labour market. In response to the pandemic, this movement shifted its campaign to focus on the need for more mandatory paid sick days to protect worker health and help stem the spread of the virus.

Labour market segmentation and precarious service employment are thus leading to intertwined demands for redistribution of wealth and income (e.g., higher wages), social recognition (e.g., anti-racism, anti-sexual harassment in workplaces, formal recognition of foreign credentials), and more just and sustainable communities.[53] Such responses contain elements of left-wing populism in demanding better wages for workers at one end of the spectrum, while highlighting the injustice of elites who make millions annually at the other end. Here is where service workers can build broader struggles that link the fight for just workplaces and better jobs with efforts to build more inclusive communities, countering the sway of right-wing populist politicians who promise much but deliver little to working people.

ADDITIONAL RESOURCES

Herod, Andrew. *Labor*. Cambridge: Polity Press, 2018.

Ladd, Deena, and Sonia Singh. "Critical Questions: Building Worker Power and a Vision of Organizing in Ontario." In *Unfree Labour? Struggles of Migrant and Immigrant Workers in Canada*, edited by Aziz Choudry and Adrian Smith, 123–39. Oakland, CA: PM Press, 2016.

Workers' Action Centre. *Still Working on the Edge: Building Decent Jobs from the Ground Up*. Toronto: Workers' Action Centre, 2015.

NOTES

1   Daniel Bell, *The Coming of Post-Industrial Society: A Venture in Social Forecasting* (New York: Basic Books, 1973); Michael Hardt and Antonio Negri, *Commonwealth* (Cambridge: Harvard University Press, 2009).

2   Guy Standing, *The Precariat: The New Dangerous Class* (London and New York: Bloomsbury Academic, 2011).

3   John Judis, *The Populist Explosion: How the Great Recession Transformed American and European Politics* (New York: Columbia Global Reports, 2016); Mark P. Thomas and Steven Tufts, "Austerity, Right Populism and the Crisis of Labour in Canada," *Antipode* 48, no. 1 (2016): 212–30.

4   Chantal Mouffe, *For a Left Populism* (London: Verso, 2017).

5   Harvey J. Krahn, Graham S. Lowe, and Karen D. Hughes, *Work, Industry and Canadian Society*, 5th ed. (Toronto: Nelson, 2007).

6   Statistics Canada, "Historical Statistics of Canada, Section D: The Labour Force," Table

D266-289: Civilian employment by industry (1948 SIC), both sexes and males, annual averages, 1946 to 1964," https://www150.statcan.gc.ca/n1/pub/11-516-x/sectiond/4057750-eng.htm.

7 Statistics Canada, Table 14-10-0023-01: Labour force characteristics by industry, annual (× 1,000), https://doi.org/10.25318/1410002301-eng.

8 Doug Henwood, *After the New Economy* (New York: The New Press, 2003); Steven Tufts, "The Geography of the Ontario Service Economy," in *Divided Province: Ontario Politics in the Age of Neoliberalism*, ed. Greg Albo, Robert MacDermid, and Charles Smith (University of Toronto Press, 2019), 77–102.

9 Indi Samarajiva, "The Gig Economy Is White People Discovering Servants." Medium, June 11, 2019, https://medium.com/@indica/the-gig-economy-is-white-people-discovering-servants-d0bd47b154a; Canadian Union of Postal Workers, *Applicant v Foodora Inc. d.b.a. Foodora, Responding Party*, Ontario Labour Relations Board Case no. 1346-19-R, February 25, 2020; Tara Deschamps, "Foodora to Shut Down in Canada on May 11 amid Profitability Challenges," *CTV News*, April 27, 2020, www.ctvnews.ca.

10 Statistics Canada, Data Tables, 2016 Census, March 28, 2018, 98-400 X2016371, https://www150.statcan.gc.ca/n1/en/catalogue/98-400-X2016371.

11 Grace-Edward Galabuzi, *Canada's Economic Apartheid: The Social Exclusion of Racialized Groups in the New Century* (Toronto: Canadian Scholars Press, 2006).

12 Statistics Canada, Data Tables, 98-400 X2016371.

13 Statistics Canada, Data Tables, 2016 Census, March 28, 2018, 98-400 X2016359, https://www150.statcan.gc.ca/n1/en/catalogue/98-400-X2016359.

14 Statistics Canada, Data Tables, 2016 Census, 98-400 X2016192, May 30, 2018, https://www150.statcan.gc.ca/n1/en/catalogue/98-400-X2016192.

15 Statistics Canada, Data Tables, 2016 Census, March 28, 2018, 98-400 X2016364, https://www150.statcan.gc.ca/n1/en/catalogue/98-400-X2016364.

16 See Jamie Peck, *Work-Place: The Social Regulation of Labor Markets* (New York and London: The Guilford Press, 1996).

17 Edna Bonacich, Sabrina Alimahomed, and Jake B. Wilson, "The Racialization of Global Labor," *American Behavioral Psychologist* 52, no. 3 (2008): 342–55; Mark Thomas, "Neoliberalism, Racialization, and the Regulation of Employment Standards," in *Neoliberalism and Everyday Life*, ed. Susan Braedley and Meg Luxton (Montreal and Kingston: McGill-Queen's University Press, 2010), 68–89.

18 Gary Becker, *The Economics of Discrimination* (Chicago: University of Chicago Press, 1957).

19 Edna Bonacich, "Advanced Capitalism and Black/White Race Relations in the United States: A Split Labor Market Interpretation," *American Sociological Review* 41, no. 1 (1976); Richard Edwards, *Contested Terrain: The Transformation of the Workplace in the Twentieth Century* (New York: Basic Books, 1979).

20 Pierre Bourdieu, *Distinction: A Social Critique of the Judgement of Taste* (London: Routledge, 1984).

21 Tufts, "The Geography."

22 Naomi Lightman and Ted McCoy, "Canada's She-Cession: COVID-19, Care Work and the Decline of the Service Sector," *Rabble.ca*, April 29, 2020; Leah Vosko, *Temporary Work: The Gendered Rise of a Precarious Employment Relationship* (Toronto: University of Toronto Press, 2000).

23 Andrew Jackson and Mark P. Thomas, *Work and Labour in Canada: Critical Issues*, 3rd ed. (Toronto: Canadian Scholars Press, 2017).

24 Poverty and Employment Precarity in Southern Ontario (PEPSO), *It's More Than Poverty: Employment Precarity and Household Well-Being* (Hamilton, ON: PEPSO, 2013), https://socialsciences.mcmaster.ca/pepso/documents/2013_itsmorethanpoverty_report.pdf; Standing, *The Precariat*.

25 Leah Vosko, ed., *Precarious Employment: Understanding Labour Market Insecurity in Canada* (Montreal and Kingston: McGill-Queen's University Press, 2006).

26 Jackson and Thomas, *Work and Labour in Canada.*

27 PEPSO, *It's More Than Poverty.*

28 David Weil, *The Fissured Workplace: Why Work Became So Bad for So Many and What Can Be Done to Improve It* (Cambridge, MA: Harvard University Press, 2014).

29 Jackson and Thomas, *Work and Labour in Canada.*

30 Sheila Block and Grace-Edward Galabuzi, *Persistent Inequality: Ontario's Colour-Coded Labour Market* (Ottawa: Canadian Centre for Policy Alternatives, 2018).

31 Linda McDowell, *Working Bodies: Interactive Service Employment and Workplace Identities* (Malden, MA: Wiley-Blackwell, 2009).

32 Robin D.G. Kelley, *Race Rebels: Culture, Politics, and the Black Working Class* (New York: The Free Press, 1996).

33 Stephanie Ross and Larry Savage, *Labour under Attack: Anti-Unionism in Canada* (Halifax: Fernwood Publishing, 2018).

34 Sara Mojtehedzadeh, "Loblaws Rings in Better Scheduling for Part-Time Workers," *Toronto Star*, August 22, 2015, thestar.com.

35 Lydia Savage, "Justice for Janitors: Scales of Organizing and Representing Workers," *Antipode* 38, no. 3 (2006): 645–66.

36 Sara Mojtehedzadeh. "Pearson Workers Fear Good Jobs in Peril over Contract-Flipping," *Toronto Star*, June 11, 2015, thestar.com; Mary Wiens, "Long Hours, Low Wages Linked to Rise in Accidents on Pearson Tarmac," *CBC News*, February 16, 2017, www.cbc.ca; Jordan House and Gray Paul, "The Toronto Airport Workers' Council: Renewing Workplace Organizing and Socialist Labor Education," *Labour Studies Journal* 44, no. 1 (2019): 8–31.

37 Mark P. Thomas, *Regulating Flexibility: The Political Economy of Employment Standards* (Montreal and Kingston: McGill-Queen's University Press, 2009).

38 C. Michael Mitchell and John C. Murray, *The Changing Workplaces Review – Final Report: An Agenda for Workplace Rights*, May (Toronto: Ontario Ministry of Labour, 2017), https://files.ontario.ca/books/mol_changing_workplace_report_eng_2_0.pdf.

39 Mark P. Thomas, "'For the People'? Regulating Employment Standards in an Era of Right-Wing Populism," *Studies in Political Economy* 101, no. 2 (2020): 135–54.

40 Stephanie Luce, "Time Is Political: The Fight to Control the Working Day Remains One of Our Most Important Labor Struggles," *Jacobin*, July 20, 2015, jacobinmag.com.

41 Jonathan Rosenblum, *Beyond $15: Immigrant Workers, Faith Activists, and the Revival of the Labor Movement* (Boston: Beacon Press, 2017).

42 Tavia Grant and Kathryn Blaze Baum, "Front-Line Workers Receiving Pay Increases from Big Companies," *Globe and Mail*, March 25, 2020, theglobeandmail.com.

43 International Labour Organization, "ILO Monitor: COVID-19 and the World of Work. 7th edition," Briefing note, January 25, 2021, https://www.ilo.org/global/topics/coronavirus/impacts-and-responses/WCMS_767028/lang–en/index.htm.

44 Statistics Canada, "Labour Force Survey, March 2020," *The Daily*, April 9, 2020, Cat. no. 11-001-X, https://www150.statcan.gc.ca/n1/daily-quotidien/200409/dq200409a-eng.htm?HPA=1; Statistics Canada, "Economic Impacts and Recovery Related to the Pandemic," October 20, 2020, modified March 4, 2021, Cat. no. 11-631-X, https://www150.statcan.gc.ca/n1/pub/11-631-x/2020004/s5-eng.htm.

45 Statistics Canada, "Economic Impacts."

46 Ibid.

47 Melissa Moyser, *Women and Paid Work*, Statistics Canada, Women in Canada: A Gender-based Statistical Report, March 8, 2017, Cat.

no. 89-503-X, https://www150.statcan.gc.ca/n1/pub/89-503-x/2015001/article/14694-eng.htm.

48 International Labour Organization, "ILO Monitor"; Sapna Maheshwari and Michael Corkery, "As School Begins, Mothers Working Retail Jobs Feel Burden," *New York Times*, September 21, 2020, www.nytimes.com.

49 Hardt and Negri, *Commonwealth*.

50 Standing, *The Precariat*.

51 Zack Taylor, "Ontario's 'Places That Don't Matter' Send a Message," *Inroads: The Canadian Journal of Opinion*, 2018, http://inroadsjournal.ca.

52 Aviation Workers Made Redundant in Canada by the COVID-19 Crisis, Facebook (Group Page), www.facebook.com/groups/3564215546923455.

53 Hardt and Negri, *Commonwealth*; Standing, *The Precariat*; André Gorz, *Farewell to the Working Class: An Essay on Post-Industrial Socialism* (London: Pluto Press, 1980).

12 The Decline of Good Manufacturing Jobs

John Holmes

CHAPTER SUMMARY

High-paying, stable manufacturing jobs, many of which were unionized and came with pensions and other benefits, provided prosperity for workers during Canada's golden age of capitalism. But both jobs and job quality have declined significantly in the manufacturing sector. Why? And what are the major implications for labour policy and politics?

This chapter examines how globalization, technology, and recent economic policy changes have affected jobs, wages, and working conditions in Canadian manufacturing. The chapter begins with an overview of changes in employment and output for the sector as a whole. In addition to documenting the growth and subsequent loss of good manufacturing jobs, it reviews some of the explanations advanced for the relative decline in manufacturing employment.

The text then turns to a more in-depth look at one particular manufacturing industry: the automotive industry, which includes both motor vehicle manufacturing and the manufacture of the myriad parts and components that go into a fully assembled car or light truck.

The chapter thus explores the impact of globalization on manufacturing employment and job quality, and how the restructuring of automobile production globally and across North America in particular has affected Canadian autoworker jobs. It concludes by explaining how economic slumps and technology-driven productivity increases have not only erased jobs but also diminished those that remain through lower wages, work intensification, and weakened union protection.

KEY THEMES

This chapter will help you develop an understanding of:

- the importance of manufacturing and the auto sector to the Canadian economy and labour market
- how globalization has restructured manufacturing
- the impacts of economic restructuring on workers, job quantity, and job quality
- recent changes to auto sector employment relations and unionized collective agreements.

MANUFACTURING REMAINS A vital component of Canada's economy. In 2018, it directly accounted for 10.5 percent of the country's entire GDP, employed about 1.73 million people – 9.3 percent of the Canadian workforce – and generated $354 billion in exports that represented 68 percent of total merchandise exports. Furthermore, manufacturing activity generates significant spinoff effects: manufacturers purchase goods and services produced in other sectors, and manufacturing workers' wages fuel consumer spending.[1]

Historically, manufacturing has provided secure full-time and well-paid jobs. In the decades immediately following the Second World War, young people in communities such as Windsor, Oshawa, and Hamilton could leave high school, even without earning a diploma, and secure a factory job with a wage sufficient to support a middle-class lifestyle. Many of these workers were members of the large and powerful industrial unions formed in the 1930s and '40s to represent unskilled and semi-skilled workers employed in large manufacturing facilities. By the early 1980s, close to 50 percent of Canadian manufacturing workers were covered by union agreements. As such, and in addition to good wages and some degree of job security, they enjoyed decent benefit packages that included extended health care and pensions.

Much has changed in the intervening years. Far fewer jobs are now available in manufacturing, and many young workers who previously might have found employment in the sector are now subject to the vagaries of precarious service-sector work. Older workers who have lost manufacturing jobs through plant closures or downsizing face a stark choice between lower-paid jobs in the service sector or prolonged unemployment. It's true that many remaining manufacturing jobs are still relatively good ones, especially when compared with jobs in personal services. The Canadian Manufacturing Coalition reports that over 95 percent of manufacturing jobs today are full time and pay 14 percent above the national average wage.[2]

Nevertheless, the steady decline in union density and increased competitive pressure to lower labour costs have diminished the quality of those jobs. Manufacturing real wages have stagnated, company pension plans have shifted financial risk onto workers, commonplace tiered wage and benefit structures disadvantage recently hired workers, and there is greater use of temporary workers who enjoy few employment protections.

The International Labour Organization (ILO) reports that the global economic impact of the COVID-19 pandemic has been far greater than the 2009 global financial crisis and forecasts that the recovery will be uneven and lead to greater inequality.[3] The impact on manufacturing employment in Canada was immediate. Between February and April 2020, over 300,000 manufacturing jobs, roughly one in six, were lost as workplaces closed down or curtailed production due to disrupted supply chains and health risks to workers.[4] Health risks were especially high where people worked in close proximity to each other on assembly (e.g., vehicle manufacturing) or disassembly (e.g., meat packing) production lines. As plants began to reopen, the recovery was uneven across the sector and there were still 82,500 fewer manufacturing jobs in August 2020 than in February.

Although dramatic, the impact of the pandemic should be viewed in the context of a half-century of declining *relative* importance of the Canadian manufacturing sector and, since the early 2000s, the *absolute* loss of good jobs. Between 2004 and 2010, plant closings and mass layoffs spelled the end of 586,500 Canadian manufacturing jobs, 268,500 of which were unionized. Although relatively well paid, many of the good jobs lost had been held by men with lower skills and at most a high school diploma.

Laid-off workers found it very difficult to get new jobs paying anywhere near their previous wages. The recession that accompanied the global financial crisis of 2008–9 hit the manufacturing sector especially hard, and even though the number of manufacturing jobs stabilized at around 1.72 million after 2009, it's unlikely that such job losses will ever be fully regained. Consequently, manufacturing jobs requiring a high school diploma or less are now much harder to find. With the increased use of technology on the shop floor, which is a trend that is likely to intensify in response to the pandemic's disruption, an increasing proportion of traditionally blue-collar production occupations now favour workers with at least some post-secondary education.

The automotive industry once generated thousands of intensely repetitive but highly productive and unionized jobs for manual workers in both the United States and Canada, with wages that were among the highest in manufacturing. It has long played an iconic and transformative role in the development of North American manufacturing, pioneering not only new methods and systems of manufacturing but also new forms of unionization, labour relations, and collective bargaining. The auto industry also draws inputs from a wide range of other manufacturing industries, such as steel, aluminum, plastics, glass, rubber, and, increasingly, electronics. Thus, booms and slumps in the auto industry cause significant ripple effects across the broader manufacturing sector.

Although it remains one of Canada's leading manufacturing industries in terms of **manufacturing value-added** and export volumes, the auto industry has suffered a decline in output and employment since achieving record levels of vehicle production in the late 1990s. Thus, it provides a good vehicle (pun intended!) for ana-lyzing the challenges that have beset manufacturing and the Canadian labour market over the past two decades.

TRENDS IN CANADIAN MANUFACTURING

Manufacturing activity is heavily concentrated in central Canada. In 2018, Ontario had 44.4 percent of manufacturing jobs nationwide and Quebec had 28.2 percent. These numbers were only modestly lower than in 1976, when the two provinces accounted for 78 percent of Canadian manufacturing jobs. In declining order of size, the manufacturing industries employing the largest number of workers in 2017 were food processing (227,027 workers), transportation equipment (195,661), fabricated metal products (152,561), machinery (130,404), plastics and rubber (98,011), and wood products (93,081).

Three related trends have shaped the evolution of Canadian manufacturing over the last half-century. First, as the service sector grew in importance, manufacturing contributed a steadily declining share of GDP. Second, not only did the proportion of the total workforce employed in manufacturing decline but also the absolute number of workers in manufacturing today is much lower than it was in 2000. Third, the introduction of new manufacturing technologies increased output per worker to such an extent that the overall level of manufacturing output rose even while the sector lost workers and its share of total GDP declined. This third trend was especially pronounced following the 2007–9 financial crisis, a period in which real value-added in manufacturing steadily increased while employment remained flat at best.

A recent US study observed that the story of manufacturing is bittersweet.[5] On the one hand, increased productivity has benefited consumers by producing a more varied and affordable range of manufactured products. On the other, productivity gains mean that fewer workers are required to produce the growing volume of manufactured goods.

DECLINING MANUFACTURING EMPLOYMENT

The longer-term trajectory of manufacturing employment in Canada and the United States is similar. Employment in this sector has progressively declined in relative importance as employment in the service sector has expanded. However, there are also some important differences.

In the United States, the absolute number of manufacturing jobs increased steadily after the Second World War, reaching a peak of 19.6 million in 1979 before beginning to fall. After briefly stabilizing during the 1990s economic expansion, manufacturing jobs declined after 2000 and fell sharply during the 2007–9 recession. By the end of 2017, there were 6.0 million fewer manufacturing jobs than in 1979.[6]

In Canada, the overall labour force almost doubled between 1976 and 2018, and jobs in service-producing industries increased from 6.28 million to 14.73 million over that period. In sharp contrast to the public and private service sectors, which saw their combined share of total jobs rise from 65.4 percent to 78.9 percent, the manufacturing sector share fell from 19.1 percent to 9.3 percent, cutting in half the sector's relative importance as a source of jobs. In absolute terms, the number of manufacturing jobs in Canada fell by 133,000 from 1976 to 2018, a decline of just over 7 percent. However, this relatively modest decline in comparison to the United States conceals a roller-coaster pattern within the period (Figure 12.1).

Significant loss of manufacturing jobs accompanied recessions in the early 1980s and

again in 1991–92, but employment rebounded both times. The rebound was especially strong following the 1991–92 recession, as Canada added over 500,000 manufacturing jobs between 1993 and 2002. Over that period, a lower-valued dollar improved the cost competitiveness of Canadian-based manufacturers, and, in contrast to the United States, the share of total employment taken by manufacturing jobs actually increased. As the value of Canadian currency steadily increased during the early 2000s, however, manufacturing employment began to fall again – and then the 2008–9 financial crisis struck.

In Newfoundland and Labrador, New Brunswick, Nova Scotia, Quebec, Ontario, and British Columbia, at least one in ten manufacturing jobs were lost between 2004 and 2008. Hardest hit was Ontario, which lost over 198,000 jobs, or 18 percent of its manufacturing workforce, in those four years.[7] More manufacturing jobs were lost between 2001 and 2009 than had been added

FIGURE 12.1 **Manufacturing employment and GDP, Canada, 1976–2018**

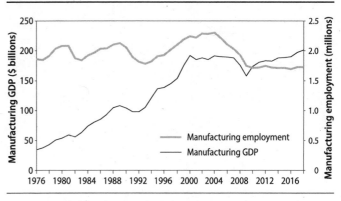

Sources: Data from Statistics Canada, Table 14-10-0023-01: Labour force characteristics by industry, annual, https://doi.org/10.25318/1410002301-eng; Table 36-10-0394-01: Gross domestic product (GDP) at basic price in current dollars, https://doi.org/10.25318/3610039401-eng; and Table 36-10-0401-01: Gross domestic product (GDP) at basic prices, by industry, https://doi.org/10.25318/3610040101-eng.

during the previous decade. Every industry suffered, but job losses were especially severe in paper, primary metal, wood products, and transportation equipment manufacturing, which all lost over 30 percent of jobs during this period. Some industries, notably computer and electronics, paper, and primary metal, continued to hemorrhage jobs after 2009, but others regained modest numbers of jobs (Figure 12.2).

Nonetheless, every manufacturing industry had fewer jobs in 2017 than in 2001 (Figure 12.2), and the total number of manufacturing jobs in 2017 was lower than in 1976 (Figure 12.1). Some of the hardest-hit industries – for example, paper, wood products, and primary metal – tend to be concentrated in a relatively small number of geographically isolated communities, where the loss of manufacturing and associated spin-off jobs has decimated local economies.

MANUFACTURING VALUE-ADDED, PRODUCTIVITY, AND WAGES

After peaking in 2000, the absolute number of manufacturing jobs began to fall even as the broader Canadian economy continued to add jobs. Despite workforce reductions, however, total manufacturing value-added grew due to a steady increase in labour productivity. By 2018, labour productivity in the manufacturing sector was more than 25 percent higher than for the economy as a whole.

These value-added gains were captured largely as higher profits by capital, rather than translating into higher real wages for workers. Falling rates of unionization and the recession of 2007–9 also depressed wages. Although the average wage for manufacturing workers continued to be higher than the national average, manufacturing wage growth stagnated after 2009.

A recent study found that manufacturing decline in Canada since 2000 has reduced both the full-time employment rate and the wages of male workers.[8] Between 2000 and 2015, the percentage of men employed full time in manufacturing fell by 5 percentage points, and by at least 10 percentage points in key Ontario manufacturing cities such as Windsor, Oshawa, and Kitchener-Cambridge-Waterloo. A 5-percentage-point decline in the share of the population employed in manufacturing in a given city led, on average, to a 6.9 percent decline in the real weekly wages of men living in the area. Men aged twenty-one to thirty-five with a high school diploma or less were affected the most, as their real wages fell at least 8.7 percent.[9] Interestingly, the study found no evidence of similar declines for women workers.

FIGURE 12.2 **Employment by manufacturing industry, Canada, 2001–9 and 2009–17**

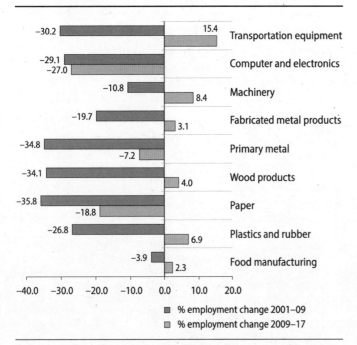

Source: Data from Statistics Canada, Table 14-10-0202-01: Employment by industry, annual, https://doi.org/10.25318/1410020201-eng.

In summary, although productivity and total value-added in manufacturing began growing again in the aftermath of the 2007–09 recession, Canada now has many fewer well-paid unionized manufacturing jobs than in 2000 and manufacturing wage growth has stagnated. With associated jobs also vanishing, the local economies of manufacturing-based communities have been dealt a serious blow.

EXPLAINING THE DECLINE IN MANUFACTURING JOBS

An American study emphasizes three broad trends that have shaped the evolution of manufacturing in recent decades and contributed to the decline in Western manufacturing economies: **automation**, networked forms of industrial organization, and globalization.[10]

Automation
Few sectors of the economy have been as affected by automation as manufacturing. From the very beginnings of industrial capitalism and the factory system in the second half of the eighteenth century, there has been a constant and inherently contradictory tendency to increase output and productivity by replacing production workers with ever more sophisticated machinery and technology. Mechanization and automation simultaneously create new jobs while eliminating existing ones.

In the first half of the twentieth century, for example, the introduction of the assembly line boosted factory productivity and output by simultaneously eliminating skilled jobs and creating new jobs for unskilled workers hired to perform repetitive, standardized tasks. In recent decades, computer-based production technologies, designed to automate routine tasks and dramatically increase manufacturing output with fewer workers, displaced many of those self-same unskilled assembly line workers.

Manufacturing based on robotics, computer-controlled machine tools, and lean manufacturing techniques require fewer workers on the factory floor. Estimates suggest as much as 88 percent of manufacturing job loss in the United States is attributable to technologically driven productivity growth.[11]

Increased investment in technology not only reduces employment but also requires workers with higher technical skill. Consequently, the current introduction of advanced manufacturing technologies such as 3D printing, advanced robotics, and machine learning is changing the structure of good manufacturing jobs in favour of workers with more education.[12] Even direct production jobs on the shop floor are shifting to workers with some postsecondary education, so that there are now far fewer good manufacturing jobs for workers with a high school diploma or less. Manufacturing still generates good jobs that pay well, but a smaller and more highly educated workforce now holds these jobs.

Networked Forms of Industrial Organization
Advanced information and communication technologies enable manufacturing firms to form complex coordinated networks that link them to other firms locally and across the globe. Manufacturers increasingly outsource services such as finance, accounting, advertising, legal, human resource management, logistics, and building services (cleaning, food services, etc.) to independent specialized service companies rather than providing such services in house.

One result of outsourcing is that jobs previously counted as residing in manufacturing establishments are now classified as jobs in the professional and business service sector. One study estimated that as much as 25 percent of the decline in US manufacturing employment between 1947 and 2002 was attributable to the reclassification of jobs due to outsourcing.[13]

Globalization

While it is by no means the only cause of North American manufacturing job loss, globalization is perhaps the most frequently cited cause, especially in right- and left-wing populist political discourse. Manufacturing is especially susceptible to work being moved offshore in search of lower-priced labour, unlike the personal service sector, where by definition the work must be performed locally.

International trade expanded after 1945, facilitated first by recurring rounds of tariff reductions under the **General Agreement on Tariffs and Trade (GATT)** and later by a proliferation of bilateral and multilateral free trade agreements. Trade liberalization, coupled with technological advances in logistics such as containerization for shipping goods, enabled North American and European manufacturers to develop integrated continent-wide and global production networks, and to relocate all or portions of their manufacturing operations offshore in order to reduce their labour costs. This caused the stock of manufacturing jobs in countries such as the United States, Canada, Germany, and the United Kingdom to shrink, as it rose in countries such as Mexico and Turkey (Figure 12.3).

The 1994 North American Free Trade Agreement (NAFTA), the eastward expansion of the European Union, and membership in the World Trade Organization for China in 2001 all facilitated the offshoring of manufacturing and the development of global supply chains.[14] NAFTA, for example, resulted in companies moving manufacturing jobs to Mexico from both the United States and Canada to capitalize on lower Mexican labour costs.

Manufacturing in Canada is especially vulnerable to the processes of economic globalization. Branch plants of foreign-owned transnational companies have always accounted for a large proportion of Canadian manufacturing capacity, and whereas such companies were once primarily US based, significant numbers of Asian and European global companies now also operate plants in Canada. Foreign companies dominate even sectors that once had high levels of Canadian ownership, such as steel. After 2000, and especially during the 2007–9 recession, the situation left the country vulnerable to closures or downsizing of manufacturing plants as companies struggled to restructure and rationalize production on a global scale.[15]

Across many countries, union density in the manufacturing sector also fell steadily between 1994 and 2018. In Canada, it fell by over one-third, and the decline in the United States was even steeper, now standing at less than 9 percent (Figure 12.4). Several factors account for this trend. Unionized plants have closed as companies relocate production, while management in newly opened plants in sectors such as the auto industry have fiercely resisted unionization. Outsourcing, subcontracting, networked production, and growing numbers of workers supplied through temporary employment agencies

FIGURE 12.3 **Location of manufacturing jobs, 1994–2018**

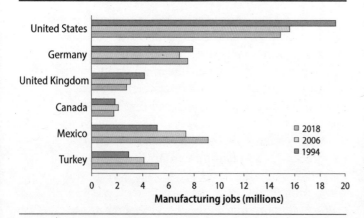

Sources: Data from U.S. Bureau of Labor Statistics; Federal Statistical Office of Germany (Destatis); UK Office for National Statistics; Statistics Canada; International Labour Organization; Organisation of Economic Co-operation and Development.

are fissuring both the workplace and labour market and weakening union density.[16]

In summary, various factors have combined to reduce the number of good manufacturing jobs in Canada and other advanced manufacturing economies, especially for workers with only modest levels of formal education. The 2009 financial crisis and accompanying recession caused an enormous loss of manufacturing jobs. In the wake of the recession, manufacturing output recovered much faster than employment due to gains in labour productivity as companies invested in increased automation.

Even if output were to increase dramatically, manufacturing firms are unlikely to add large numbers of jobs because advanced manufacturing technologies require far fewer direct production workers. With ongoing advances in artificial intelligence, manufacturing is expected to shed more jobs in the next decade, most of them in factory-floor production occupations currently filled by workers with a high school diploma or less.[17] In the wake of the COVID-19 pandemic, further worker displacement by automation is likely to address the vulnerability of manufacturing processes that require workers to be in close proximity.

THE CANADIAN AUTOMOTIVE INDUSTRY

Analyzing job loss and corporate restructuring in the automotive industry reveals much about the state of Canadian manufacturing as a whole. In 2018, the industry employed roughly 120,000 workers, split between vehicle manufacturing (44,000) and automotive parts manufacturing (76,000). It contributed $19 billion to GDP and generated $71 billion in exports, over 12 percent of Canada's export total.

Since 2000, the industry has experienced both an absolute loss of jobs and a diminution in the overall quality of remaining jobs. Interpreting the factors that have eroded good auto-

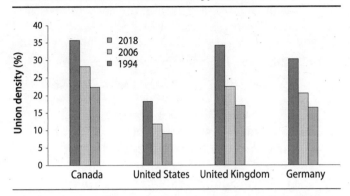

FIGURE 12.4 Unionized manufacturing jobs, 1994–2018

Source: Data from Statistics Canada; U.S. Bureau of Labor Statistics; UK Office for National Statistics. German union density from ILO Department of Statistics (ILOSTAT), manufacturing sector data not publicly available.

motive jobs requires understanding key aspects of the structure of the Canadian auto industry and of the North American automotive industrial relations system more broadly.

The Great Lakes Automotive Manufacturing Region

The Great Lakes Region (GLR), which is centred on Detroit and spans the Canada-US border, is the historic heartland of auto making in North America. Heavily concentrated in southern Ontario, Canadian automotive production is fully integrated with production across the GLR.[18] Prior to the onset of the COVID-19 pandemic, five global automakers – Toyota, Stellantis (formerly Fiat Chrysler Automobiles [FCA]), General Motors (GM), Honda, and Ford, referred to as original equipment manufacturers (OEMs) – built around 2 million vehicles annually in southern Ontario, close to 90 percent of which was exported for sale in the United States. Automotive parts suppliers, including large Canadian, Japanese, European, and American global suppliers, operate more than 700 manufacturing plants in Canada, most of them in Ontario. Around 60 percent of their product is exported, mainly to supply US assembly plants, and at the same time large volumes of imported US-made parts are used in the assembly of Canadian-built vehicles.

At the peak of employment in 2000, Michigan, Ohio, Indiana, and Ontario combined had 730,800 workers employed in automotive manufacturing. Heavily dependent on the Detroit Three, or D-3 (GM, Ford, and Chrysler), the GLR experienced a steady loss of automotive employment after 2000 as these American-based companies lost market share to Asian and European automakers. This culminated in the near collapse of the industry during the 2008-9 financial crisis. GM and what was then Chrysler underwent forced restructuring under bankruptcy protection, and widespread consolidation occurred within the supplier base.[19]

After the restructuring, auto employment in the GLR partially recovered. While it now must compete for new investment with more recently established and lower labour-cost vehicle manufacturing regions in the southern United States and Mexico, the GLR continues to dominate automotive production in North America.

The Automotive Industrial Relations System

A new and distinctive North American labour relations system, built on the concept of the industrial union, developed in the late 1930s. Previously dominant craft unions, which organized workers according to skilled occupation, were ill-suited to the task of organizing the burgeoning numbers of largely unskilled workers in mass production industries, such as automaking. The new industrial unions organized workers by workplace rather than by skill. Once organized, all unskilled and skilled production workers employed in a particular plant belonged to a legally defined local bargaining unit of the parent union.

The decentralized structure of industrial union locals might well have resulted in localized and fragmented collective bargaining. Instead a number of industries, but especially the auto industry, developed an institutionalized system of pattern and connective bargaining that linked national and local plant negotiations. This ensured uniformity in wages, benefits, and general contract provisions across plants within one company, and attempted to replicate wages and benefits across companies in the industry.[20]

In short order after its founding in 1935, the United Auto Workers (UAW) used the industrial union model to organize all US and Canadian workers employed by the D-3, as well as many workers in the independent automotive parts sector. Landmark 1948 GM–UAW collective agreements covered operations in both the United States and Canada and established a pattern that was to endure for the next thirty-five years. Labour contract bargaining was synchronized between the two countries, with the pattern set by contracts negotiated first in the United States.

The linking of wages to productivity growth was a key feature of the multi-year collective agreements. Industrial relations scholar Harry Katz and his colleagues observe that "from the late 1940s until the late 1970s, the application of wage rules and job control unionism produced steadily rising real compensation to auto workers and long-term growth in auto employment and production."[21] This enabled unskilled blue-collar American and Canadian autoworkers to attain the American dream: an affluent middle-class lifestyle.

This changed fundamentally after 1980 as Japanese and, later, Korean and European OEMs built non-union assembly and component plants in North America. The D-3 sought concessions from the UAW to address their deteriorating competitive position relative to the new foreign-owned plants. In the United States, the UAW had by 1990 agreed to so-called modern operating agreements that abandoned traditional annual base wage increases in favour of *contingent compensation* (lump sum payments and profit sharing). As a result, wages and employment practices began to vary between the D-3 and even between plants within the same company.[22]

Strategic differences between the Canadian wing of the UAW and the leadership in Detroit over concessions ultimately led Canadian autoworkers to leave the UAW and form their own national union – the **Canadian Auto Workers (CAW)** – in 1985.[23] The essentials of traditional connective and pattern bargaining endure in Canada to this day. Although no longer synchronized with the United States, automotive collective bargaining in Canada remains strongly influenced by UAW bargaining outcomes.

AUTOMOTIVE MANUFACTURING JOB LOSSES

The pattern of employment change in the Canadian auto industry over the past three decades mirrors the pattern for manufacturing as a whole: strong employment growth in the 1990s, peaking in 2000 and then followed by decline (Figure 12.5). The industry added 38,000 net jobs between 1992 and 2000, to reach 153,000, but then lost over 56,000 between 2000 and 2010. Despite modest recovery after 2010, there were over 33,000 fewer Canadian automotive jobs in 2018 than in 2000.

Plant closures in Ontario illustrate the ongoing impact of this trend on Canadian workers. In November 2018, GM announced that it would permanently close its Oshawa, Ontario, assembly plant by the end of the following year, shedding the remaining 2,600 hourly paid assembly jobs. An estimated 1,400 spinoff jobs at supplier plants linked to GM Oshawa would also be lost. The announcement stunned the community and the broader region.

GM had provided reliable full-time unionized jobs for several generations of workers. Although many of these jobs required intense, machine-paced, repetitive physical effort that took a heavy toll on autoworkers' bodies, they generated wages that were as much as 60 percent higher than the average Canadian manufacturing wage. Autoworkers' wages fuelled purchasing power to support businesses and jobs in the local service sector. Thus, the GM closure was likely to have a knock-on effect on local service-sector jobs. Widespread anger erupted in Oshawa following the announcement. Some workers engaged in **wildcat walkouts** and plant occupations. Some called for the plant to be taken into public ownership and transformed to produce green electric vehicles or other socially useful products.[24]

In July 2020, Ontario autoworkers were dealt another blow. FCA ended the third shift at its Windsor assembly plant, directly eliminating 1,500 assembly jobs as well as many spinoff jobs in the supplier sector. Combined, the GM and FCA decisions sent shock waves through an industry already shaken to its foundations during the 2008–09 financial crisis.

The onset of the global coronavirus pandemic has deepened job losses, exposing both the vulnerability of globalized automotive supply chains and the virus-related health risks associated with assembly line work. Production across the North American auto industry quickly shut down. Between February and May 2020, Canadian employment fell in vehicle and automotive parts manufacturing by 22.7 and 26.2 percent, respectively.[25] The industry slowly and haltingly began to reopen in late May, but workers' fears of contracting COVID-19 caused some plants to experience staffing shortages and work refusals. The value of shipments for the vehicle assembly industry in 2020 dropped by over 28 percent. A pandemic-related shortage of semiconductors caused fresh rounds of temporary plant shutdowns in 2021.

The absolute loss of jobs since 2000 resulted from the same general processes of automation,

FIGURE 12.5 **Automotive industry employment, Canada, 1991–2018**

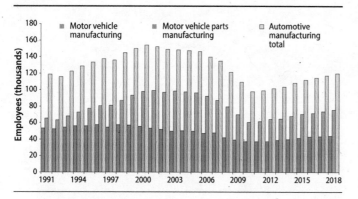

Sources: Data from Statistics Canada, Table 14-10-0243-01: Employment (SEPH), unadjusted for seasonal variation, by type of employee, https://doi.org/10.25318/1410024301-eng; and Table 14-10-0202-01, Employment (SEPH) by industry, annual, https://doi.org/10.25318/1410020201-eng.

outsourcing, and globalization that have affected the entire manufacturing sector, but each assumes a particular significance in the case of the auto industry. Building motor vehicles is an extremely complex manufacturing process given the literally thousands of individual parts that make up the finished product. From Henry Ford's introduction of assembly line production in the early twentieth century, through just-in-time and synchronous manufacturing, to today's investments in advanced manufacturing, the auto industry has been at the forefront in developing new manufacturing methods. As each development has led to ever-higher levels of automation and labour productivity, the impact on the quantity and/or quality of jobs has been profound.

The loss of automotive jobs also resulted, in part, from a progressive reduction of tariffs on imported automotive products and the pursuit of liberalized trade agreements by North American governments. The 1965 Auto Pact, which facilitated the integration of automotive production between Canada and the United States, contained safeguards to maintain specified lev-

els of automotive production in Canada. It was struck down by the World Trade Organization in 2001, and subsequent North American trade agreements contained no such safeguards.

NAFTA afforded automakers the opportunity to move some vehicle and parts production out of the United States and Canada to take advantage of much lower Mexican wages. Automotive investment in Mexico surged, and by 2018 Mexico accounted for more than 24 percent of all the vehicles built in North America – twice as many as Canada. Attracted by generous state-provided incentives, an increasing number of European, Japanese, and Korean OEMs and suppliers opened non-union plants in states across the southern United States, from South Carolina to Texas, again drawing automotive jobs away from the Great Lakes Region.

UNION CONCESSIONS AND DECLINING AUTOMOTIVE JOB QUALITY

The quality of remaining jobs has also diminished. In the early 2000s, the D-3 have faced mounting financial losses. Invoking the need to stay cost competitive with the growing foreign-owned non-union segment of the North American industry, these companies repeatedly demanded wage and benefit concessions from unions to reduce all-in labour costs.

The most pernicious and far-reaching concession was union acceptance of tiered wages and benefits, such that newly hired workers would receive lower wages and benefits than existing (so-called traditional) workers. Along with other wage concessions, this depressed real wages and eroded the wage premium enjoyed by autoworkers in comparison with the overall manufacturing sector (Figure 12.6). Wages in the Canadian automotive parts sector were 20 percent higher than the manufacturing average in the early 2000s but are now on a par. In assembly, they have fallen from 60 percent higher to less than 20 percent above the average across manufacturing.

Two factors undermined union bargaining power and weakened workers' ability to resist concessions. First, union density fell as unionized plants closed and unions failed to organize the growing number of North American manufacturing plants of foreign-owned automakers and suppliers. Second, the UAW and CAW faced the constant and very real threat that automakers would relocate production to Mexico if they resisted concessions. Consequently, union priority during collective bargaining shifted from wage and benefit improvements to securing company commitments for new investment and new product lines for plants threatened with closure.

The ascendency of financial capitalism and the financialization of the economy also had a decisive influence on automotive industry restructuring during this period (see Chapter 2). During the 1990s, the dictates of capital markets increasingly began to shape company strategies, forcing automotive firms to focus on shareholder value, a core doctrine of financialization.[26] After 2000, a growing number of large automotive suppliers in need of fresh capital to avoid impending bankruptcy were taken over and restructured by financial investors. The 2005–9 bankruptcy restructuring of Delphi, the giant former GM parts division, set the stage for ultra-concessionary bargaining across the automotive industry in the United States and Canada.[27] Led by Delphi's two largest shareholders, both financial hedge funds, the restructuring included a new agreement with the UAW establishing a wage of US$14 an hour for new hires (less than half the previous rate), and allowing Delphi to make all new hires either temporary or second-tier workers.

Continuing to lose market share, the D-3 pushed hard to extend Delphi-style concessions into the auto assembly sector and, over

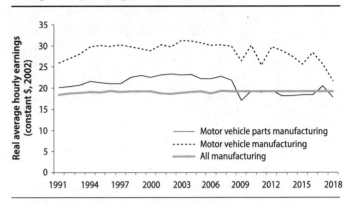

FIGURE 12.6 **Automotive versus all manufacturing real average hourly earnings, Canada, 1991–2018**

Sources: Data from Statistics Canada, Table 14-10-0247-01: Average hourly earnings for employees paid by the hour (SEPH), by industry, https://doi.org/10.25318/1410024701-eng; and Table 14-10-0205-01: Average hourly earnings for employees paid by the hour, by industry, monthly, unadjusted for seasonality, https://doi.org/10.25318/1410020501-eng.

successive rounds of bargaining, the UAW accepted permanent tiered wages and benefits for new hires. In 2007, the union agreed to reduce starting wage rates for newly hired non-core workers, who would also be excluded from the defined benefit pension plan and health benefits enjoyed by traditional workers. It was estimated that the concessions reduced the overall cost of a new hire to about one-third that of existing workers.

Earlier, the CAW had pragmatically granted local concessions on work rules and outsourcing to enable Canadian plants to compete for new product mandates. It was not until 2008, however, that the union agreed to contingent compensation in lieu of annual increases in base wage rates. While resisting a UAW-style permanent two-tier wage and benefit structure for new hires, the CAW agreed to a new hire grow-in system, under which new hires would start at 70 percent of base wages and attain 100 percent only after three years.

The increased influence of capital markets and the intrusion of the state into auto industry collective bargaining were both front and centre during the 2008–09 global financial crisis. On the point of financial collapse, GM and Chrysler were restructured under bankruptcy protection in the United States. The newly installed US administration under Barack Obama rejected GM's initial restructuring plan and urged automakers to make "every effort to achieve labor cost parity with the transplants."[28] In other words, GM was expected to bring its labour costs down to the level of non-union competitors such as Toyota. The UAW urged GM workers to ratify the concessionary agreement, in a message that reflected the extraordinary degree to which the state intervened in private collective bargaining: "The [U.S.] Treasury's Auto Task Force moved into GM headquarters in an effort to find deeper and quicker changes to GM's U.S. footprint ... Realizing that failure to meet the government requirements would surely mean the end of General Motors, your bargainers painstakingly put together modifications to the [2007] collective bargaining agreement to satisfy the Treasury Auto Task Force."[29] Such "modifications" resulted in extensive concessions, including permanent second-tier wages for all new hires.

Although GM and Chrysler did not file for bankruptcy protection in Canada, and the US Treasury Department orchestrated the bailouts in the United States, the Canadian federal and Ontario provincial governments contributed to the financial bailout packages and took equity holdings in both companies. Canadian governments provided roughly 20 percent of the US$100 billion total bailout package in return for commitments from GM and Chrysler to maintain their then current Canadian share of total North American production until at least 2016.[30] Following the Obama administration's lead, Canadian government financial aid to GM and Chrysler was conditional on the union accepting a range of concessions to bring labour costs closer to those at Toyota's Canadian plants.

Bargaining between the D-3 and the CAW in 2012 lengthened the grow-in period for new-hire wages and benefits from three to ten years and reduced the starting wage from 70 to 60 percent of the final job rate. A senior Unifor staffer later commented that in 2012, "The automakers insisted that unless we followed the UAW two-tier system, we would absolutely not secure any new investment ... The assessment of the union's leadership and bargaining committees was that this was no idle threat ... The union's strategy was to ensure our compensation remained broadly comparable to the UAW so that Canada stayed in the ballpark for investment."[31]

In the United States, the permanent two-tier structure was replaced in 2015 by a grow-in system under which newly hired workers transitioned to "traditional wages" within eight years, and in 2019, this was reduced to four years. The grow-in period for new hires in Canada was reduced from ten to eight years during 2020 contract bargaining – still twice as long as in the United States.

In sum, despite very significant increases in labour productivity over the last fifteen years, union concessions have dampened real wage growth for existing workers, reduced the wage premium autoworkers enjoyed over the manufacturing average, and ushered in lower, tiered wages and benefits to the disadvantage of recently hired workers. Unions did not make these concessions willingly. They made them in an effort to secure investment commitments from the D-3 to protect their members' jobs. But at best such commitments have proved to be good only for the life of a new collective agreement.

The industry has continued to shed jobs through plant closings, productivity gains, and outsourcing. The tiered wage structure has had a corrosive effect on solidarity and created serious frictions within the union membership. In many plants, union members working alongside each other perform identical work but receive different compensation. This is an affront to the long-cherished union principle of equal pay for equal work. When seeking ratification of recent collective agreements, the UAW and Unifor leaderships faced stiff challenges from the rank and file for their failure to eliminate tiered wages and benefits.

TRANSFORMATION AND TRANSITION

The ever-present drive to increase productivity by displacing workers through automation and international trade agreements that enable companies to move manufacturing offshore in search of lower-cost labour has eradicated many well-paid Canadian manufacturing jobs. Additionally, provincial labour laws have been recast in order to deregulate the labour market and create hurdles for workers seeking to unionize their workplaces, dampening wages and benefits for remaining manufacturing workers. By undermining the formerly prosperous blue-collar segment of the middle class, these manufacturing trends have contributed directly to growing labour inequality in Canada.

Recent events raise questions about the future of Canadian manufacturing jobs – but they also offer some grounds for optimism, especially regarding automotive jobs. The pandemic exposed the vulnerability of manufacturing to supply chain disruption and threats to workers' health and safety. However, as numerous companies pivoted to manufacturing face masks and shields, ventilators, and other emergency supplies, the pandemic also underscored that domestic manufacturing capacity matters. Firms rapidly converted plants to produce socially necessary goods, with crucial government-led industrial policy and support. The COVID-19 crisis also highlighted the importance of unions in providing workers with a collective voice to secure workplace safety measures and advocate for paid sick leave and improved pay for essential workers. The necessity for governments to implement temporary income support programs to help those who lost employment served to broaden calls for a guaranteed basic income.

The unpredictability of the Donald Trump administration with respect to trade issues – such as its imposition of stiff tariffs on steel and aluminum imports – created enormous uncertainty for manufacturers. Trump's promise to renegotiate NAFTA made companies reluctant to commit themselves to new investments in Canada and Mexico until after the process had been concluded. Although still favouring a Buy American policy, the successor administration of Joe Biden appears to recognize the global competitive advantage afforded the United States by maintaining an integrated North American economy. The phased implementation of complex and more stringent rules governing preferential automotive trade under the "new NAFTA" – officially known as the Canada-United States–Mexico Agreement (CUSMA) in Canada – will favour increased auto manufacturing in the United States and Canada at the expense of Mexico.[32]

As recent scientific reports and global climate activism underscore, the climate crisis means that business as usual is no longer an option. Canadians and citizens around the world must quickly find ways to transition their manufacturing, transportation, and energy systems to achieve a zero-carbon economy.[33] To achieve this transformation, new policies are required that support both workers and companies. These include everything from major supports for innovation research and development and retooling to retraining and skill upgrading for workers, and to consumer subsidies and deployment mandates for renewable energy.

After the Progressive Conservatives came to power in Ontario in 2018, Premier Doug Ford moved swiftly to scrap the provincial carbon pricing program, eliminate the consumer electric car incentive program, and roll back labour relations reforms. Although they improved manufacturing cost competitiveness and helped companies increase shareholder value, these actions impeded the process of transforming Ontario into a greener manufacturing economy and providing workers with good jobs.

Recent developments are more promising. In the United States, the Biden administration's focus on addressing the climate crisis and promoting electric vehicle development coincides with massive auto company investment in electric vehicle and battery development and production. In Canada, during the 2020–21 round of collective bargaining, Unifor secured commitments from GM, Ford, and FCA to begin building electric vehicles in several Ontario plants by 2025, with federal and provincial government support. While they represent a positive development overall, battery-powered electric vehicles require far fewer parts than conventional vehicles and the shift in production will bring significant job losses in plants currently producing internal combustion engines, transmissions, and fuel and exhaust systems.[34]

Major state-led infrastructure projects to address the transition offer opportunities for companies and unions alike to buy into clean energy industries. Workers fear job loss in any transition, and new training and workforce development programs are essential to ensure a just transition for workers displaced by the shift to a low-carbon economy. How Canadians, unions, and manufacturers address the twin defining issues of our times – the climate emergency and the pandemic – will shape the future of manufacturing work and the ability to create a more equitable and environmentally sustainable world.

ADDITIONAL RESOURCES

Gindin, Sam. *The Canadian Autoworkers Union: The Birth and Transformation of a Union.* Toronto: James Lorimer and Company, 1995.

Green Jobs Oshawa. *Triple Bottom Line Preliminary Feasibility Study of the GM Oshawa Facility: Possibilities for Sustainable Community Wealth.* September 13, 2019. https://www.greenjobsoshawa.ca/feasibility.html.

Moody, Kim. *On New Terrain: How Capital Is Reshaping the Battleground of Class War.* Chicago: Haymarket Books, 2017.

Rothstein, Jeffrey. *When Good Jobs Go Bad: Globalization, De-unionization, and Declining Job Quality in the North American Auto Industry.* New Brunswick, NJ: Rutgers University Press, 2016.

Rubin, Jeff. *Has Global Trade Liberalization Left Canadian Workers Behind?* CIGI Paper no. 163. Waterloo, ON: Centre for International Governance Innovation, 2018.

Yates, Charlotte, and John Holmes. *The Future of the Canadian Auto Industry.* Ottawa: Canadian Centre for Policy Alternatives, 2019. www.greenjobsoshawa.ca/feasibility.html.

NOTES

1   The Canadian Manufacturing Coalition (CMC) estimates that nearly three out of every ten dollars in wealth created in Canada can be traced back to the manufacturing sector and about 27 percent of all jobs across the country are tied to manufacturing. CMC, "Manufacturing in Canada," http://www.manufacturingourfuture.ca/english/manufacturing-in-canada/manufacturing-in-canada.html.

2   Ibid.

3   International Labour Organization, "ILO Monitor: COVID-19 and the World of Work. 7th edition," Briefing note, January 25, 2021, https://www.ilo.org/global/topics/coronavirus/impacts-and-responses/WCMS_767028/lang-en/index.htm.

4   Statistics Canada, Table 14-10-0355-02: Employment by industry, monthly, seasonally adjusted (x 1,000), https://doi.org/10.25318/1410035501-eng.

5   Anthony P. Carnevale, Ban Cheah, Neil Ridley, Jeff Strohl, and Kathryn Peltier Campbell, *The Way We Were: The Changing Geography of US Manufacturing from 1940 to 2016* (Washington, DC: Georgetown University Center on Education and the Workforce, 2019), https://cew.georgetown.edu/cew-reports/manufacturingstates.

6   Anthony P. Carnevale, Neil Ridley, Ban Cheah, Jeff Strohl, and Kathryn Peltier Campbell, *Upskilling and Downsizing in American Manufacturing* (Washington, DC: Georgetown University Center on Education and the Workforce, 2019), https://cew.georgetown.edu/cew-reports/manufacturing.

7   André Bernard, "Trends in Manufacturing Employment," *Perspectives on Labour and Income* 10, no. 2 (February 2009): 5, 10, https://www150.statcan.gc.ca/n1/pub/75-001-x/2009102/article/10788-eng.htm.

8   René Morissette, "The Impact of the Manufacturing Decline on Local Labour Markets in Canada," Statistics Canada, Analytical Studies Branch Research Paper Series, January 15, 2020, Cat. no. 11F0019M-Nº 440, https://www150.statcan.gc.ca/n1/pub/11f0019m/11f0019m2020003-eng.htm.

9   Ibid., 25.

10 Carnevale et al., *Upskilling and Downsizing*, 12.

11 Daron Acemoglu and Pascual Restrepo, "Robots and Jobs: Evidence from US Labor Markets," NBER Working Paper no. 23285, National Bureau of Economic Research, Cambridge, MA, March 2017, http://www.nber.org/papers/w23285; Michael J. Hicks and Srikant Devaraj, *The Myth and the Reality of Manufacturing in America* (Muncie, IN: Ball State University, 2017).

12 For an analysis of the changing composition of workers holding good jobs in the United States and the different educational pathways leading to such jobs, see Carnevale et al., *Upskilling and Downsizing*.

13 Giuseppe Berlingieri, "Outsourcing and the Shift from Manufacturing to Services," VOX CEPR Policy Portal, September 25, 2014, https://voxeu.org/article/outsourcing-and-shift-manufacturing-services.

14 David H. Autor, David Dorn, and Gordon H. Hanson, "The China Syndrome: Local Labour Market Effects of Import Competition in the United States," *American Economic Review* 103, no. 6 (October 2013): 2121–68. The authors estimate that nearly a quarter of the manufacturing employment decline in the United States between 1990 and 2007 resulted from increased competition with China. There is a certain irony in the fact that precisely the manufacturing workers whose jobs disappeared were the primary consumers of low-cost consumer goods produced offshore in countries such as China.

15 D. Michael Ray, Ian MacLachlan, Rodolphe Lamarche, "Economic Shock and Regional Resilience: Continuity and Change in Canada's Regional Employment Structure, 1987–2012," *Environment and Planning A: Economy and Space* 49, no. 4 (April 2017): 952–73.

16 See David Weil, *The Fissured Workplace: Why Work Became So Bad for So Many and What Can Be Done to Improve It* (Cambridge, MA: Harvard University Press, 2014).

17 McKinsey Global Institute, *The Future of Work in America: People and Places, Today and Tomorrow*, July 11, 2019, https://www.mckinsey.com/featured-insights/future-of-work/the-future-of-work-in-america-people-and-places-today-and-tomorrow.

18 Tod Rutherford and John Holmes, "Manufacturing Resiliency: Economic Restructuring and Automotive Manufacturing in the Great Lakes

Region," *Cambridge Journal of Regions, Economy and Society* 7, no. 3 (November 2014): 359–78.

19 Jim Stanford, "The Geography of Auto Globalization and the Politics of Auto Bailouts," *Cambridge Journal of Regions, Economy and Society* 3, no. 3 (November 2010): 383–405.

20 John Holmes, "Labour Relations and Human Resource Management in the Automotive Industry: North American Perspectives," in *The Global Automotive Industry*, ed. Paul Nieuwenhuis and Peter Wells (Chichester, UK: John Wiley and Sons, 2015), 118–38.

21 Harry Katz, John Paul MacDuffie, and Fritz Pil, "Autos: Continuity and Change in Collective Bargaining," in *Collective Bargaining in the Private Sector*, ed. Paul Clark, John Delaney, and Ann Frost (Champaign, IL: Industrial Relations Research Association, 2002), 55–90.

22 Larry Hunter and Harry Katz, "The Impact of Globalization on Human Resource Management and Employment Relations in the US Automobile and Banking Industries," *International Journal of Human Resource Management* 23, no. 10 (May 2012): 1983–98.

23 Sam Gindin, *The Canadian Auto Workers: The Birth and Transformation of a Union* (Toronto: James Lorimer and Company, 1995).

24 Russ Christianson, "Take the Plant, Save the Planet – The Case for Nationalization and Conversion of the Oshawa GM Plant," *The Bullet*, September 22, 2019, https://socialistproject.ca. During the pandemic, GM produced surgical facemasks in a small section of the Oshawa plant. During collective bargaining in late 2020, it was announced that Oshawa would reopen to assembly pickup trucks.

25 Statistics Canada, Table 14-10-0201-01: Employment by industry, monthly, unadjusted for seasonality, https://doi.org/10.25318/1410020101-eng.

26 Inge Lippert, Tony Huzzard, Ulrich Jürgens, and William Lazonick, *Corporate Governance, Employee Voice, and Work Organization: Sustaining High-Road Jobs in the Automotive Supply Industry* (New York: Oxford University Press, 2014), 24.

27 Gary Chaison, *The New Collective Bargaining* (Berlin: Springer Science and Business Media, 2012).

28 United States Government Accountability Office, *Summary of Government Efforts and Automakers' Restructuring to Date*, Report to Congressional Committees, GA-09-553, (Washington, DC: USGAO, 2009), 26.

29 United Auto Workers, *UAW General Motors Modifications to 2007 Agreement and Addendum to VEBA Agreement*, https://online.wsj.com/public/resources/documents/gmuaw.pdf.

30 Stanford, "The Geography of Auto Globalization," 399.

31 Bill Murnighan, "Unifor and Big Three Bargaining: A Response to Gindin's 'Different Ways of Making History,'" *The Bullet*, October 31, 2016, https://socialistproject.ca.

32 John Holmes, "New Trade Rules, Technological Disruption and COVID-19: Prospects for Ontario in the Cross-border Great Lakes Automotive Industry," *International Journal of Automotive Technology and Management* 22, no. 1 (March 2022): 106–27.

33 Naomi Klein, *On Fire – The Burning Case for a Green New Deal* (Toronto: Penguin Random House Canada, 2019).

34 United Auto Workers, *Taking the High Road: Strategies for a Fair EV Future* (Detroit, MI: UAW Research Department), https://uaw.org/wp-content/uploads/2019/07/190416-EV-White-Paper-REVISED-January-2020-Final.pdf.

13 Neoliberalism, Austerity, and the Crisis in Care Work

Donna Baines

CHAPTER SUMMARY

The COVID-19 pandemic has deepened a crisis in care work across Canada, particularly in long-term care for seniors. Care work in hospitals, long-term care, and social service agencies has long been provided by women and often under less-than-ideal conditions. But over the past decade, as governments have cut public funding for public services in the name of austerity, frontline workers in many care agencies and institutions have seen job quality decline and wages erode.

This chapter explores why and how public-sector job quality has declined, and with what consequences for care workers, especially women workers. The chapter reviews three eras of public policy and care, and then extends the analysis to the recent pandemic, providing examples of resistance to increasingly fragmented and polarized care.

The chapter concludes by pointing to a number of promising public-sector models that would improve not only the quality of public-sector jobs but also the delivery of services. The coming post-pandemic recession will make achieving any of these difficult, however, as they would necessitate decisive government action. Only the activism of unions, social movements, and citizens will ensure the improvements necessary to provide quality care for all Canadians.

KEY THEMES

This chapter will help you develop an understanding of:

- the nature of care services and work in the care sector, and why the work is gendered
- recent changes to public policy and how new public management, privatization, and contracting out have changed the delivery of care services and employment
- working conditions in the care sector
- current examples of care worker resistance and promising progressive policies and practices.

CARE IS PART OF everyone's life, regardless of wealth, race, gender, or ability. None of us would make it out of infancy without extensive care from parents and other caregivers. Childhood, ill health, injury, old age, and disability necessitate care, and it should be provided with dignity and respect. Most people also *provide* care at various points in their lives, as a sibling, parent, volunteer, or professional. Though the human need for care is universal, the ways in which societies respond to these needs vary considerably.[1]

Care work is generally viewed ideologically, as a natural activity of women, and few boundaries are placed on their presumed desire and capacity to provide it, regardless of pay or working conditions. This makes it difficult to improve wages and conditions. Indeed, even associating working conditions and pay with care is sometimes regarded as turning a warm, family-based, rewarding labour of love into a cold economic transaction.[2] In part, this is because care work is often located in the private realm – the private home, the private relationship, the private babysitter or private house cleaner – and within the intimate context of love, affection, relationship, dependence, and interdependence.[3]

Yet public policy is a pivotal aspect of **care provision** in any society. Sometimes governments step back completely, leaving people to find and pay for their own care. Other governments fund not-for-profit or for-profit private organizations to provide care service. And sometimes governments directly fund and provide care services. These various approaches to public policy, politics, and care fit into three eras: pre-welfare state/family; welfare state/shared risk; and neoliberalism, privatization, and re-individualized risk. The pandemic exposed numerous fault lines in society, principle among them the care of older people and those with COVID-19.

BOX 13.1 HOME VERSUS NURSING HOME

May has a job in the fast-food industry and lives at home with her parents. She helps to care for her elderly grandmother, who lives with them and whom she loves very much. May has never been in a nursing home. Although she believes she would be good at care work with older people, she is very uncomfortable with the idea of putting old people in institutions. Like many Canadians, she firmly believes that families – which usually means women – should provide loving, personal unpaid care for older people in their own homes.

May's friend recently got a job as a personal support worker at a nearby nursing home. She makes better wages than May does, and encourages May to apply to the nursing home for work. Eventually, May does and is successful.

She likes working with the residents and the other staff but finds her workload heavy. She feels so overburdened with technical tasks that she has little time to spend with the residents. May frequently finds that she must rush the residents through their days, just so she can get most of her work done. Some of the older people cannot be hurried and refuse to cooperate, or argue, cry, or both.

When this happens, May is miserable and falls behind in her tasks. She feels as though she is still working in fast food, just pushing orders through rather than using her compassion in a job where people's dignity and preferences should be respected.

In Canada, due to years of underfunding, nursing home care is available only for the very elderly (eighty and above) and the very frail. This means that most residents need a lot of care, and workers therefore have heavy workloads and often complex tasks to complete within excessively short timeframes. Underfunding also means that nursing homes hire the minimum number of higher-wage staff, such as nurses, and fill the gaps with lower-paid, lower-status care workers who may have little or no training but bear most of the heavy, hands-on care and emotional workload.

Feminist and critical theorist Nancy Fraser refers to a global care crisis in social reproduction and identifies the public policies precipitating this crisis.[4] Many people argue that we are returning to the pre-welfare state ideology of family care work, as governments back away from funding care of all kinds and private care remains available only to those who can afford it, leaving family members, most of them women, to meet the shortage.[5]

THE PRE-WELFARE STATE/FAMILY ERA

The pre-welfare state/family era dominated Canada from European contact in the fifteenth century to after the Second World War. Although Indigenous peoples had provided care for each other in various distinctive, extended kinship models, these systems of care were methodically dismantled in the post-contact period, alongside other pillars of Indigenous societies.[6] The dismantling was aimed at remaking Indigenous people into low-wage workers, particularly as domestic servants and agricultural workers. Nevertheless, forms of Indigenous care and culture were kept alive, often in secret, and are finding fertile ground in the resistance activities of Indigenous people today.

Among non-Indigenous populations, the pre-welfare state/family era of public policy and care was one in which richer people's care needs were met by unpaid family members, enslaved people, indentured servants, and domestic workers. In working families, most care came from unpaid family members, with women undertaking a double day of work in the home and workplace.[7] In both richer and poorer families, care work fell almost exclusively to women in their gendered roles as domestic servants, maids, nannies, governesses, mothers, sisters, aunts, and older female children. Adopting a stance known as *noblesse oblige*, the wealthy preferred to contribute to the common good by donating to charities and religious organizations rather than by paying taxes. During this period, labour and ethnic organizations joined together to create mutual aid and benevolent societies to support each other in the absence of government services and funding.

Until the late nineteenth century, hospitals and other care institutions were few in number, and those that existed were largely faith-based charities for the very poor. Not-for-profit and charitable service organizations provided community services including food banks, care for children, settlement services for immigrants, and programs for the indigent and elderly.[8] The need for care always outstripped these services, and they proved particularly inadequate when serious crises hit the economy, such as the Great Depression of the 1930s. Unemployment soared and, without government programs to support them, many people were forced to ride the railways in search of work or beg house to house for food and shelter.[9] Protests were widespread during this period and often put down ruthlessly by employers, police, and sometimes the military, as Canadians demanded support and social programs from governments, and state intervention to strengthen employment and working conditions in the ailing economy.

The Second World War put people back to work in the war effort and governments invested strongly in the economy.[10] The end of the war saw large numbers of Canadian soldiers with experience in armed struggle return to Canada, hoping for a better life. It also saw women, who had been employed in the war effort, pushed out of the paid workforce and back into the home to repopulate the country, provide unpaid care for families, and leave jobs vacant for returning soldiers.

THE WELFARE STATE AND PUBLICLY SHARED RISK

Canada was strongly influenced by the United Kingdom in the postwar period, when most citizens had no wish to return to another depression and knew that progressive government social and economic policies could successfully provide needed services, promote high levels of employment, and keep the economy buoyant.[11] The British Labour Party argued that governments should provide social programs to educate and keep the population healthy and to build a vibrant economy.[12] Rather than having families and individuals shoulder all the costs when they became ill, disabled, or unemployed, the costs should be shared across the entire population through taxes, of which the rich should pay proportionately more, with all citizens sharing the benefits of universal social programs. This was a sharp departure from the previous era in which individuals and families bore most of the risk and costs of care privately.

These ideas caught on quickly in Canada. Governments introduced universal services for all Canadians, such as medicare, and targeted programs for those who could establish need, such as social assistance and social care programs. The new public policies also provided employment opportunities for women, particularly in health care (nurses, dieticians, laundry workers, cleaners, medical social workers, physiotherapists, ward clerks), social services

(social workers, community workers, addiction counsellors, therapists), childcare (childcare workers, daycare cooks), long-term residential care for the elderly (nurses, therapists, personal support workers, nutritionists, recreation therapists, music therapists), services for people with disabilities (disability support workers, counsellors, respite workers, homecare workers), as well as the administration, office work, and policy jobs that grew up around these services.

Employment in public-sector care during this era tended to be full-time, permanent work with wages that were higher than in most other female-majority sectors of the economy, particularly after the late 1960s, when federal and provincial governments finally allowed public-sector workers to unionize. Although unions and feminist movements fought for improved wages and working conditions, women's generally lower wages continued throughout the welfare state era, replicating the gendered wage inequities of the past even as increasing numbers of women joined the labour force and the male breadwinner family model increasingly became a relic of the past.[13] Relative to men's pay, pay for most women in Canada had increased very little over the previous fifty years. In 1911, women earned 52.8 percent of what men earned; in 1971, they earned 58 percent.[14] By the 1960s, the fast-growing women's movement was joined by unions and community groups demanding that governments improve women's wages and provide high-quality universal childcare to enable women to join the labour force in even greater numbers while children benefited from safe and caring early childhood education.[15]

Pay equity is an important public policy that was introduced in the late 1970s. The policy compares the pay in job categories in which female workers predominate with the pay in comparable jobs in which male workers predominate. These evaluations are seen as fairer than simply comparing male and female wages in the same job category, because a category in which women predominated might have few or no men whose wages could be compared. Childcare work has long had almost no male workers, for example, and childcare workers are seriously underpaid. Pay equity thus provides significant benefits for many care workers.

In addition, individual comparisons between men and women in the same job fail to account for long-term, systemic gender discrimination in wages and conditions.[16] Thus, under pay equity evaluations, nurses and firefighters might be compared because the job characteristics are seen as requiring similar levels of skill, effort, and responsibility. In the 1980s, some provincial governments also passed legislation known as proactive pay equity, which required employers to examine their compensation practices and ensure that women and men received equal pay for work of equal value. It was not until 2018 that the federal government passed proactive pay equity. Even so, the wage gap remains significant. In 1996, women earned on average 66 percent of what men earned on average; by 2017, it was still only 69 percent.[17]

Pay equity and other policy initiatives such as employment equity, which requires employers to increase their representation of women (as well as racialized and Indigenous people and those with disabilities) were particularly important to care work jobs because they brought recognition to hiring discrimination, and to the importance of these care jobs and the skill and knowledge needed to perform them. They also finally started to ensure that care jobs were paid at more reasonable rates, though there is a long way to go in almost every form of care work.[18] Unfortunately, just as pay equity was ramping up in the 1980s and 1990s, the welfare state was ramping down. Many care work jobs, particularly those that had been professionalized (such as nursing and social work)

and better paid, were lost as federal and provincial governments began retreating from public programs providing social care.[19]

NEOLIBERALISM, PRIVATIZATION, AND RE-INDIVIDUALIZED RISK

One of the goals of the welfare state was that a well-educated, healthy population would participate in a broader range of economic and societal activity, leading to more democratic decision making and community development.[20] The welfare state saw a flowering of more representative labour organizations (unions and labour councils), community organizations (social planning councils, local community boards, public policy forums, and so forth), and more progressive social activism (feminist, peace, and anti-racism movements).

As the 1970s brought growing inflation and declining profitability, however, corporations, banks, and their political allies on the right began to attack welfare state policies, claiming that numerous social programs were an unaffordable luxury in the context of a rising national debt. They worked hard to elect more conservative federal and provincial governments that started cutting popular social programs and legislation that had supported union organizing, women's rights, community participation, and citizen empowerment.[21]

Known as neoliberalism, this third political era started in the 1980s and continues today. Neoliberalism is an approach to public policy that generally views private businesses and capitalist markets as efficient, effective, and ethical in promoting economic growth and profitability. Both an ideology and a policy orientation, neoliberalism is about transferring economic power from the state to corporations and banks. Among other things, it involves governments reducing environmental protection, wage protections, equity policies, and corporate taxes, and privatizing or defunding many government services and supports.[22] Further, neoliberal policy makers have tended to regard service users as the source of the social problems they face and to exhort them to take individual responsibility for social conditions over which they could not possibly have control, such as high unemployment, poor education and training systems, and increasingly overburdened and underfunded remaining health care and social supports.[23] Privatizing and defunding of government services have thus driven a growing crisis of care in Canada.

Under a process known as contracting out, instead of providing services themselves, governments invite non-profit and for-profit organizations to compete for government-funded contracts. The lowest bids are generally successful, which usually means that wages and working conditions are pushed down and work intensity, such as care caseloads, is driven up. As organizations shed their responsibilities to workers and communities, they often contract agencies to provide services such as cleaning, management, or meals. This use of for-profit services operating within the framework of non-profit or larger for-profit organizations produces fissured workplaces.[24]

Under government contracts, funded organizations are required to adopt a new public management (NPM) model. The intention is to ensure efficiency, effectiveness, and cost savings by measuring certain kinds of productivity outcomes.[25] Such outcome measures tend to break work into small, identifiable pieces, and standardize them so that they can be routinized and repeated easily by workers. This typically makes it possible for managers to speed up and intensify care work, and to replace higher-cost, higher-skill workers with lower-paid, lower-skill workers or even volunteers.[26] NPM processes also usually mean that employees spend more time measuring, recording, and documenting more aspects of their work, which tends to reduce their interaction with service users, such as those needing care. This often leads everyone involved in care relationships to feel alienated and frustrated.[27]

During the COVID-19 crisis, private chains of long-term care homes for seniors continued to pay high dividends to stockholders while residents and staff battled the virus. Evidence confirms that for-profit homes in Ontario and Quebec had older designs that contributed to the spread and severity of outbreaks and led to higher death rates.[28] The appalling toll gained widespread attention, and a 2020 Angus Reid poll found that two-thirds of Canadians wanted government to take over long-term care.[29] At the time of this writing, governments are yet to respond. Various economists and non-profit groups are now pushing government to step decisively back into deprivatizing long-term care, protecting vulnerable older people, and helping to rebuild the economy in the post-pandemic era.[30]

PRECARIOUS EMPLOYMENT IN THE CARE SECTOR

The nature of care is that it has to be provided when it is needed, rather than during prescribed time blocks.[31] For example, older people in nursing homes need their pain relieved when they feel it, rather than on scheduled medication rounds. Similarly, they need to be assisted to the toilet when required, not when schedules permit. Failing to ensure flexibility traps service users and workers in a pared-down, narrowly technical version of care in which human needs go unmet and workers feel pressured, ill treated, and demoralized.[32]

The open-ended, relationship-based, community-engaged practices that once characterized good-quality care are very difficult to turn into NPM measurement and standardized practices.[33] As a result, many practices based in social justice have quietly disappeared from workplaces, replaced with increasingly tightly scripted, easily measured work practices.[34] Workers have tried to retain practices such as relationship building, advocacy, and community development, but the system makes it very difficult. As one long-term child welfare worker noted, "My caseload is so huge that all I can do is assess, patch up, and rush on to the next family. It is like a hamster wheel we never get off and never really make anything or anyone better."[35] This neglect doesn't happen because workers are lazy or uncaring. It is instigated at the systemic level because society neither provides sufficient resources nor pays sufficient attention to care issues.

In health care and in long-term residential care for older people, government now requires the use of a tool known as the Resident Assessment Instrument, whereby data quantifying the care work must be collected daily and submitted to the government quarterly to justify funding and determine how much is received. This and other government reporting requirements have drastically increased documentation tasks among care workers. The result has been reduced time for the difficult-to-measure relational care that most workers, residents, and family members want.[36]

In a recent study of nursing home care in Ontario, many workers remarked that they were so rushed with body care tasks and documentation that they could do only the basics, or as one worker complained, "There's no time or space to do anything more; there's barely time to breathe." Care workers also said that staffing shortages compelled them to short-change residents, which they deeply regretted but had no ability to control. As one worker put it, "You just keep re-prioritizing as the day goes by and at the end of the day you know you haven't done 110 percent like you should when you look after people. They're not inanimate objects."[37]

BOX 13.2 CASH FOR CARE

Changes occur at May's nursing home. Cuts in government funding mean that her hours have been reduced and she is even more rushed and pressured during her shifts. Deeply concerned that the care the nursing home provides is inadequate, one of the families she works with offers to pay her wages in cash so that she can spend additional hours with their very ill family member. May has noticed that other workers provide these so-called extra hours of informal, under-the-table care. May wonders what happens to the families who cannot afford to pay for extra care.

As a result, family members sometimes hire private staff to supplement the overworked staff that the nursing home can barely afford due to government cutbacks. Sometimes referred to as *permanent austerity*, government policies of cutbacks, privatization, and constraint show no signs of abating in Canada.[38] In some provinces and areas of care, such as disability care in Ontario, governments have furthered privatization by adopting a cash-for-care model in which individuals or families are provided with direct payments in order to hire their own care workers.[39]

While the cash-for-care model may hold ideological appeal for people who view it as a competitive market mechanism providing more individual choice, it undermines the welfare state model of pooled risk and quality care, and further fissures workplaces. It also pressures individuals and families to stretch their payments as far as possible, often by paying personal support workers lower wages, hiring workers for shorter shifts, and providing more precarious job conditions (thereby increasing bad jobs).[40] In addition, these forms of privately funded care are less likely to attract highly skilled and credentialled people, and they make the care market even more precarious for workers as individuals and families compete in an underfunded context.[41] Workers in these situations often undertake short shifts on short notice with a variety of employers. They find themselves working alone, usually in people's homes, with little interaction with other workers and with access to their supervisors only via an app or digital platform. They must pay for their travel time between gigs and have few, if any, opportunities to improve their skills or move along a career path.

Gig work or on-demand platform work has been present for some time in the delivery and transportation services sector, through providers such as Deliveroo or Uber. Increasingly, it is moving into care work, with few policies to protect workers, service users, or communities and with strong incentives to undermine conditions and wages.[42] In essence, care work in the late neoliberal context increasingly resembles care work in the earliest pre-welfare state/family era of public policy and politics, in which governments provided little or no social care or social support programs, care workers had no policy protections, and those needing care had to exclusively rely on themselves, their families, or whomever they could afford to hire.

As noted earlier, public policy and a variety of political struggles created the Canadian welfare state following the Second World War, and along with it, well-educated skilled care workers who had the potential to gain better wages and conditions. Neoliberal politics has unravelled this model of delivery and equity, replacing it with care work that is standardized, more precarious, and of poorer and less reliable quality. As such, the environment of care is a deep source of tension and stress for those involved in providing or receiving such services. As in the past, the crisis is likely to be resolved only by political struggle to promote more progressive public policies.

ACHIEVING BETTER CARE AND BETTER CARE WORK

Policies to provide high-quality public care services are actually the result of political choices. They come from what governments choose – or choose not – to prioritize. Canadians are often told that we cannot afford better care, but countries with similar per capita gross domestic product spend a good deal more of their GDP than Canada does on care for the elderly and on other forms of care (see Chapter 14). And they produce far better outcomes, such as lower rates of violence, less use of psychotropic drugs, and higher-quality care.[43]

This suggests it is less the case that Canadian governments cannot afford better public care services but that they lack the political will. In Norway, Denmark, and Sweden, care workers and other citizens have fought hard through their unions, other social organizations, and political parties to implement more high-quality, comprehensive, and well-funded public care policies. As a result, governments in these countries currently spend two to three times more on long-term care services than do those in Canada (Figure 13.1).

FIGURE 13.1 **Public expenditure on long-term care as a share of GDP, 2015**

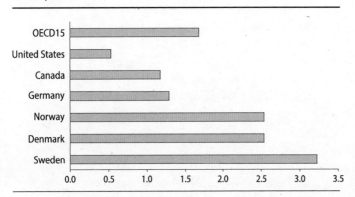

Source: OECD, Health at a Glance 2017: OECD Indicators (Paris, OECD Publishing, 2017), http://dx.doi.org/10.1787/health_glance-2017-en.

Similarly, while provincial governments have devoted a great deal of time to privatizing and supposedly modernizing long-term provision, they have done comparatively little to help seniors afford this care. Figure 13.2 shows the proportion of those over the age of sixty-five in several countries who receive long-term care and/or cash benefits or allowances to help pay for long-term care. The figures encompass services such as nursing and residential care homes, and care provided to the elderly in their own homes or in other community or institutional settings. Canada provides less than 20 percent of what Norway and Sweden offer elderly people in need of assistance, and about a third of what the typical advanced industrial economy does.

In Canada, care workers regularly and sometimes publicly undertake unpaid care work on the job. They work through their coffee and lunch breaks, stay late, come in on their days off, take work home with them, bring supplies from home when the workplace runs out, shop for service users, run errands, give service users manicures, do their makeup, and hair care, take service users to activities and on outings, fundraise for their employers, and much more.[44]

Although management depends on this unpaid work to extend their services – and thus unpaid care work is a form of exploitation – it can simultaneously be a form of resistance and empowerment for workers, service users, and communities.[45] Care workers often explain that they do unpaid work because their jobs have been stripped of aspects of care that convey warmth and connection, such as conversations, emotional support, or interactions. They frequently assign oppositional meanings to this unpaid work and blame the organization or society more widely for being uncaring.[46] Sometimes this analysis pulls care workers into activism and collective resistance both inside and outside the workplace.

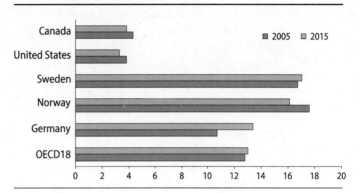

FIGURE 13.2 **Proportion of population sixty-five and older receiving long-term care, 2005 and 2015**

Source: Data from OECD, *Health at a Glance 2017: OECD Indicators* (Paris, OECD Publishing, 2017), http://dx.doi.org/10.1787/health_glance-2017-en.

Unions can offer a vehicle for such resistance. A number of care workers have commented that they became union activists in order to "have a voice" in the workplace and to recapture some of their autonomy, along with opportunities for greater fairness and a return to relationship-based care work they consider to have been lost under new public management systems and other neoliberal constraints.[47] This kind of activism is often framed as a moral project: something that advances fairness and rights and makes the world a better place.[48]

There are numerous examples of unions, workers, service users, their families, community members, and social action groups in Canada working together to prevent privatization or to bring services back in house, so that care facilities can provide higher-quality services themselves rather than outsourcing them to lower-quality, for-profit providers. Sometimes union activism has halted or even reversed the privatization of public care services. Union-led campaigns for legislation stipulating minimum hours of care per service user, particularly in long-term care, or bargaining this standard into collective agreements where legislation does not exist, are examples of how strategies for good care can be combined with strategies for better workloads and conditions.[49] These kinds of initiatives suggest a hopeful approach for those looking for more fairness and respect for all involved in care work relationships.

The COVID-19 crisis provides a new opportunity to fight for better care systems and to respect the work involved in caring. Continuing traditionally gendered expectations, care workers and other essential workers have been expected to be selfless during the pandemic – endlessly providing care work even when it has involved risking their health and even life. Recognizing that the low wages in the sector meant workers were moving between multiple precarious jobs, and that the situation brought risks of cross-contamination during the pandemic, some governments raised the wages of some care workers. This applied particularly to those working in long-term care with older people. Workers were also required to work at only one site in order to limit transmission of the virus.[50]

These measures were significant and represented recognition of the importance of these highly gendered jobs to the well-being of society. Increased pay and job security also acknowledged that these jobs cannot be done well and safely if they are fragmented, low paid, and precarious. However, rather than offering permanent recognition of the importance attached to care workers, in some jurisdictions, workers have already been told that wage top-ups are merely a temporary aspect of the pandemic response.

For the most part, the public has strongly supported government intervention during the pandemic, particularly in terms of health care funding, direct payments to unemployed and underemployed people, and economic stimulus. Yet many governments have signalled that funding cuts and austerity measures will be reintroduced after the pandemic. Economist Jim Stanford instead recommends increasing defi-cits in order to put money into the economy and pull the world out of what will otherwise be the worst depression of the last two centuries. He argues further that post-pandemic recovery requires a modern Marshall Plan, similar to the extensive government-funded program that rebuilt Western Europe after the Second World War.[51]

Broad social consensus will be needed if that is to happen. Care workers, people using care, average citizens, unions, and social movements will need to work together to build support for this kind of progressive and positive public policy agenda. There is reason for optimism, particularly if we can build on the social solidarity witnessed in voluntary self-quarantining and the nightly cheers and banging of pots and pans for essential workers. This kind of care-based, average citizen involvement – twinned with innovative and energetic social activism – can generate real alternatives to austerity and build a more socially just, inclusive, and environmentally sustainable society.

THE VALUE OF CARE

The highly gendered arena of care work contains a historical contradiction. It has been a site where women's work was valued, holding the potential for better wages and improved conditions. It is also site of poor pay and difficult conditions. While the welfare state pooled risk across large populations and increased the status and skill of care work, neoliberal policies have pushed care back into the private realm of informal work, temporary agencies, and the unpaid work of women in the home. This fragmented, privatized context and systemic undervaluing of care work contributed to the high death rate in long-term care facilities during the pandemic.

Unpaid care work is a form of resistance to a privatized, increasingly uncaring society. Care workers undertake unpaid care in order to provide some meaning to what they do in today's context of gig work and precarious employment, and to support service users and communities. Though these actions largely help individuals, the commitment to care for and about others simultaneously disrupts the neoliberal narrative of cynicism and individualism, and holds the potential to bring back equity-engaged public policy that can ensure high-quality care and rewarding care employment.

Care without pay, however, will not resolve the coming recession and ongoing urgent situation in care work. Solutions to this far-reaching crisis will require decisive government intervention in key care sectors such as long-term care in order to protect some of the most vulnerable people in society and ensure fair, high-quality employment. This will require the activism of unions and social movements – and strong support from the majority of us who provide and receive care across our lifetimes.

ADDITIONAL RESOURCES

Armstrong, Pat, and Hugh Armstrong. *About Canada: Health Care*, 2nd ed. Halifax: Fernwood Publishing, 2016.

Baines, Donna. "Moral Projects and Compromise Resistance: Resisting Uncaring in Nonprofit Care Work." *Studies in Political Economy* 97, no. 2 (2016): 124–42.

Baines, Donna, and Pat Armstrong. *Promising Practices in Long Term Care: Ideas Worth Sharing*. Ottawa: Canadian Centre for Policy Alternatives, 2015.

Daly, Tamara, and Pat Armstrong. "Liminal and Invisible Long-Term Care Labour: Precarity in the Face of Austerity." *Journal of Industrial Relations* 4, no. 58 (Winter 2016): 473–90.

Folbre, Nancy. "Measuring Care: Gender, Empowerment, and the Care Economy." *Journal of Human Development* 2, no. 7 (July 2006): 183–99.

NOTES

1   Mimi Abramovitz, *Regulating the Lives of Women: Social Welfare Policy from Colonial Times to the Present* (New York: Routledge, 2017).

2   Sharon Bolton and Gemma Wibberley, "Domiciliary Care: The Formal and Informal Labour Process," *Sociology* 48, no. 4 (October 2013): 1–16; Nancy Folbre, "Should Women Care Less? Intrinsic Motivation and Gender Inequality," *British Journal of Industrial Relations* 50, no. 3 (Fall 2012): 597–619.

3   Abramovitz, *Regulating the Lives of Women*, 198.

4   Nancy Fraser, "Captialism's Crisis of Care," *Dissent* 6, no. 4 (Spring 2016): 30–37.

5   Tamara Daly and Pat Armstrong, "Liminal and Invisible Long-Term Care Labour: Precarity in the Face of Austerity," *Journal of Industrial Relations* 4, no. 58 (Winter 2016): 473–90; Marjorie Cohen, "Neo-Liberal Crisis/Social Reproduction/ Gender Implications," *University of New Brunswick Legal Journal* 64, no. 1 (Spring 2013): 234; Folbre, "Should Women."

6   Donna Baines and Bonnie Freeman, "Work, Care, Resistance and Mothering: An Indigenous Perspective," in *A Life in Balance: Reopening the Family-Work Debate*, ed. Catherine Krull and Justine Sempruch (Vancouver: UBC Press, 2011), 67–80; Ron Bourgeault, *1492–1992: Five Centuries of Imperialism and Resistance* (Halifax: Brunswick Books, 1992).

7   Maureen Elgersman, *Unyielding Spirits: Black Women and Slavery in Early Canada and Jamaica* (London: Routledge, 2014); Abramovitz, *Regulating the Lives of Women*; Meg Luxton, *More Than a Labour of Love: Three Generations of Women's Work in the Home* (Toronto: Canadian Scholars' Press, 1980).

8   Pat Armstrong and Hugh Armstrong, *About Canada: Health Care*, 2nd ed. (Halifax:

Fernwood Publishing, 2016); Banakonda Kennedy-Kish, Raven Sinclair, Ben Carniol, and Donna Baines, *Case Critical: Social Services and Social Justice in Canada* (Toronto: Between the Lines, 2017).

9   Ernie Lightman and Naomi Lightman, *Social Policy in Canada* (Toronto: Oxford University Press, 2017); Kennedy-Kish et al., *Case Critical*.

10 Lightman and Lightman, *Social Policy*.

11 Ibid.

12 Jim Stanford, *Economics for Everyone: A Short Guide to the Economics of Capitalism* (London: Pluto Press, 2015).

13 Heike Trappe, Matthias Pollmann-Schult, and Christian Schmitt, "The Rise and Decline of the Male Breadwinner Model: Institutional Underpinnings and Future Expectations," *European Sociological Review* 31, no. 2 (September 2015): 230–42.

14 Mary Connelly, "Women in the Labour Force," *Canadian Encyclopedia*, 2006, https://www. thecanadianencyclopedia.ca/en/article/women -in-the-labour-force.

15 Lightman and Lightman, *Social Policy*; Luxton, *Labour of Love*; Stanford, *Economics for Everyone*.

16 Pat Armstrong and Mary Cornish, "Restructuring Pay Equity for a Restructured Work Force: Canadian Perspectives," *Gender, Work & Organization* 4, no. 2 (Summer 1997): 67–86; Susan Hart, "Unions and Pay Equity Bargaining in Canada," *Relations Industrielles/Industrial Relations* 57, no. 4 (Autumn 2002): 609–29.

17 Employment and Social Development Canada, "Government of Canada Introduces Historic Proactive Pay Equity Legislation," Media release, October 29, 2018, https://www.newswire.ca/ news-releases/government-of-canada-introduces -historic-proactivepay-equity-legislation -698938791.html.

18 Pat Armstrong, Hugh Armstrong, and Kristin Scott-Dixon, *Critical to Care: The Invisible Women in Health Services* (Toronto: University of Toronto Press, 2008).

19 Mary Cornish, "Closing the Global Gender Pay Gap: Securing Justice for Women's Work," *Comparative Labour Law & Policy Journal* 28 (March 2006): 219; Hart, "Unions and Pay Equity."

20 Kennedy-Kish et al., *Case Critical*; Stanford, *Economics for Everyone*.

21 Stanford, *Economics for* Everyone; Kennedy-Kish et al., *Case Critical*; Marjorie Cohen, "From the Welfare State to Vampire Capitalism" in *Women and the Canadian Welfare State: Challenges and Change*, ed. Pat Evans and Gerda Wekerle (Toronto: University of Toronto Press, 1997), 28–67; Lightman and Lightman, *Social Policy*.

22 Greg Albo and Bryan Evans, "From Rescue Strategies to Exit Strategies: The Struggle over Public Sector Austerity," *Social Register* 47, no. 1 (January 2010): 23–39; Stanford, *Economics for Everyone*.

23 Kennedy-Kish et al., *Case Critical*; Lightman and Lightman, *Social Policy*.

24 David Weil, "Understanding the Present and Future of Work in the Fissured Workplace Context," *RSF: The Russell Sage Foundation Journal of the Social Sciences* 5, no. 5 (2019): 147–65.

25 Tamara Daly, "Dancing the Two-Step in Ontario's Long-Term Care Sector: Deterrence Regulation = Consolidation," *Studies in Political Economy* 95, no. 2 (Spring, 2015): 29–58; Laura O'Neill, "Regulating Hospital Nurses and Social Workers: Propping up an Efficient, Lean Health Care System," *Studies in Political Economy* 95, no. 2 (Spring, 2015): 115–36.

26 Esther Munyisia, Ping Yu, and David Hailey, "How Nursing Staff Spend Their Time on Activities in a Nursing Home: An Observational Study," *Journal of Advanced Nursing* 67, no. 9 (April 2011): 1908–17.

27 Donna Baines, "Moral Projects and Compromise Resistance: Resisting Uncaring in Nonprofit Care Work," *Studies in Political Economy* 97, no. 2 (Spring 2016): 124–42.

28 Nathan Stall, Aaron Jones, Kevin Brown, Paula Rochon and Andrew Costa, "For-Profit Long-Term

Care Homes and the Risk of COVID-19 Outbreaks And Resident Deaths," *Canadian Medical Association Journal* 192, no. 33 (August 2020): E946–55, https://doi.org/10.1503/cmaj.201197.

29 Walter Chandler, "Majority of Canadians Want Nationalization of Long-Term Care Homes," *DH News,* May 26, 2020, dailyhive.com.

30 Jim Stanford, "We're Going to Need a Marshall Plan to Rebuild after COVID-19," *Policy Options,* April 2, 2020, policyoptions.irpp.org; Eric Sigurdson, "The Inequality Virus: Bringing Together a World Torn Apart by Coronavirus through a Fair, Just and Sustainable Economy," *Sigurdson Post,* February 2021.

31 Stephen Lopez, "Efficiency and the Fix Revisited: Informal Relations and Mock Routinization in a Nonprofit Nursing Home," *Qualitative Sociology* 30, no. 3 (Summer 2007): 225–47; O'Neill, "Regulating Hospital Nurses"; Karen Davies, "The Tensions between Process Time and Clock Time in Care-Work the Example of Day Nurseries," *Time and Society* 3, no. 3 (Summer 1994): 277–303.

32 Munyisia et al., "How Nursing Staff."

33 Baines, "Moral Projects"; O'Neill, "Regulating Hospital Nurses."

34 Kennedy-Kish et al., *Case Critical*; Lightman and Lightman, *Social Policy.*

35 Baines, "Moral Projects."

36 Daly, "Dancing the Two-Step"; O'Neill, "Regulating Hospital Nurses."

37 Donna Baines and Tamara Daly, "Borrowed Time and Solidarity: The Multi-Scalar Politics of Time and Gendered Care Work," *Social Politics: International Studies in Gender, State and Society* 28, no. 2 (Summer 2021): 392–93.

38 Paul Pierson, "Coping with Permanent Austerity: Welfare State Restructuring in Affluent Democracies," *Revue française de sociologie* 1 (April 2002): 369–406; Stephen McBride and Bryan Evans, *The Austerity State* (Toronto: University of Toronto Press, 2017).

39 Direct Funding Ontario, "History of Direct Funding," https://www.dfontario.ca/info/history.html.

40 Weil, "Understanding the Present"; Arne Kalleberg, *Good Jobs, Bad Jobs: The Rise of Polarized and Precarious Employment Systems in the United States, 1970s–2000s* (New York: Russell Sage Foundation, 2011).

41 Natasha Cortis, Fiona Macdonald, Bob Davidson, and Eleanor Bentham, *Reasonable, Necessary and Valued: Pricing Disability Services for Quality Support and Decent Jobs* (Sydney: University of New South Wales Social Policy Research Centre, 2017).

42 Gerald Friedman, "Workers without Employers: Shadow Corporations and the Rise of the Gig Economy," *Review of Keynesian Economics* 2, no. 2 (2014): 171–88; Neils Van Doorn, "Platform Labor: On the Gendered and Racialized Exploitation of Low-Income Service Work in the 'On-Demand' Economy," *Information, Communication & Society* 20, no. 6 (Summer 2017): 898–914.

43 Donna Baines and Pat Armstrong, *Promising Practices in Long Term Care: Ideas Worth Sharing* (Ottawa: Canadian Centre for Policy Alternatives, 2015); Albert Banerjee, Pat Armstrong, Tamara Daly, Hugh Armstrong, and Susan Braedley, "Careworkers Don't Have a Voice: Epistemological Violence in Residential Care for Older People," *Journal of Aging Studies* 33 (April 2015): 28–36.

44 Tamara Daly and Pat Armstrong, "Liminal and Invisible Long-Term Care Labour: Precarity in the Face of Austerity," *Journal of Industrial Relations* 4, no. 58 (September 2016): 473–90; Donna Baines, "Neoliberal Restructuring/Activism, Participation and Social Unionism in the Nonprofit Social Services," *Nonprofit and Voluntary Sector Quarterly* 39, no. 1 (February 2010): 10–28.

45 Baines, "Moral Projects."

46 Ibid.; Daly and Armstrong, "Liminal and Invisible."

47 Baines, "Neoliberal Restructuring."

48 Baines, "Moral Projects."

49 Canadian Union of Public Employees, "It's Time to Care: Ontario Seniors Need a Minimum 4-Hour Daily Care Standard to Be the Law,"

October 25, 2017, https://cupe.ca/its-time-care
-ontario-seniors-need-minimum-4-hour-daily
-care-standard-be-law.

50 Ashley Wadhwani, "'Pandemic Pay' to Give
Temporary Wage Top-Up to 250,000 B.C. Front-
Line Workers," *Victoria News*, May 2020, www.
vicnews.com; Richard Zussman, "B.C. Front-
Line Health Workers to Receive Pandemic
Pay Top-Up," *Global News*, May 19, 2020,
globalnews.ca.

51 Stanford, "We're Going to Need a Marshall
Plan."

14 Reforming or Eroding the Health Care Workforce?

Colleen Fuller

"The enjoyment of the highest attainable standard of health is one of the fundamental rights of every human being without distinction of race, religion, political belief, economic or social condition."

– Constitution of the World Health Organization, 1946

CHAPTER SUMMARY

This chapter provides an overview of the struggle for universal health care by Canadians, with a focus on the pivotal role unions played in achieving medicare. It describes the relationship between health care workers and the public, and the link between high-quality services and good working conditions for those who provide them.

The chapter looks at the importance of universal health care to workers and citizens, and how the struggle for a fully universal health care system is far from over. It examines the impacts of recent government initiatives to privatize and contract out services in health care, and how COVID-19 has shone a harsh spotlight on Canada's for-profit long-term care system. The conclusion notes the importance of union and community efforts to counter such efforts and to keep health care under broader public control.

KEY THEMES

This chapter will help you develop an understanding of:

- how the labour movement was involved in the development of universal health care in Canada
- the nature of the health care workforce and the importance of unionization
- the impacts of neoliberalism on health care budgets and employment relations
- contracting out in-home care
- the impacts of COVID-19 on Canada's health and long-term care systems.

UNIVERSAL HEALTH CARE is one of Canada's most cherished social programs. It is founded on the principle of social solidarity expressed in the trade union motto, "An injury to one is an injury to all," and of equality, as expressed by the Royal Commission on Health Services: "All must have access to needed health services through the same door."[1] It is also the product of many decades of collective struggle, beginning over a century ago, by people from all walks of life: workers and farmers, conservatives and progressives, young and old.

In 1963, the great American civil rights leader Martin Luther King Jr. said, "Of all the forms of inequality, injustice in health care is the most shocking and inhumane." Thus, the removal of barriers to health services is an important cornerstone of any democracy, establishing an assumption of equality between those who are in good health and those who aren't. Universal health care also acknowledges that we all need health care at different times of our lives, and that when such a need arises it should not condemn anyone to a life of poverty.

Our history is a record not only of how Canadians achieved medicare but also of how citizens and health care workers have joined together to ensure that health care is not just another market commodity. This struggle continues today with campaigns to expand universal health care to include essential programs such as home care, out-patient rehabilitation services like physiotherapy, and a national pharmacare plan to ensure Canadians have access to essential medicines without financial barriers.

WORKERS AND THE DEVELOPMENT OF HEALTH CARE

"We can't stand still. We can either go back or we can go forward. The choice we make today will decide the future of medicare in Canada."

The prescient words of **Tommy Douglas** still ring true. The Saskatchewan premier (1944-61) and first leader of the New Democratic Party (1961-71) is recognized as the founder of Canada's universal health care system. The government of his provincial Cooperative Commonwealth Federation, the precursor to the New Democratic Party (NDP), was the first in Canada to introduce a universal health care program. And Douglas helped lead the fight for national legislation through a multigenerational struggle that culminated in the landmark Medical Care Insurance Act of 1966. In combination with the 1957 Hospital and Diagnostic Services Act, it laid out a funding formula for the country's health care system, with costs shared between the federal and provincial governments.

Eighteen years later, Parliament took another important step toward a universal public health care system when it passed the **Canada Health Act**. The Act merged the two earlier laws and strengthened prohibitions on extra billing by doctors and hospital user fees. The 1984 Act, which has attained iconic status, reinforced the key tenet that all must have access to needed health services through the same door. The Act also enshrined five principles to govern the country's system of medicare: universality, public administration, comprehensiveness, portability, and accessibility.

Today health care as a human right is enshrined in the hearts and minds of Canadians. Prior to the twentieth century, however, health was considered a private affair that excluded involvement by the state. Access to a physician or a hospital was impossible for many poor and working-class families, who were instead forced to rely on charity or seek other arrangements. The first known health **prepayment scheme** (or insurance plan) in Canada was set up in 1665, when seventeen families in Montreal pooled their resources to pay the master surgeon at a local hospital to provide access to medical services if and when they were needed. Similar hospital-based prepayment schemes were scattered across the country by the late 1800s, providing free admission and free medicines, with reduced fees for physician care.[2]

But it was in the coal mines on Cape Breton Island that workers began to address the issue of access to health services in a more organized fashion. Families in Nova Scotia's mining communities experienced high levels of work-related injury and death, but most could not pay for physician or hospital care. In 1883, the Nova Scotia Provincial Workers' Association won Canada's first formal agreement with an employer to set up a system of compulsory "medical check-off."[3] The plan provided access to physician and hospital services for the 3,455 miners – 18 percent of them children – who worked in the Glace Bay collieries.[4]

The Nova Scotia system was later adopted in mining and logging communities in other parts of Canada with high rates of work-related injuries. Access to services was also in the interest of employers, who depended on a healthy workforce. But such workplace plans did not cover everyone, not even the families of miners and loggers, and thus many millions continued to face financial barriers to access. The impact became painfully clear at the end of Great Depression as Canada entered the Second World War. Poverty, unemployment, and limited access to health services for most of the population were reflected in a 44 percent rejection rate due to poor health among men called up to serve in the armed forces. A similar percentage of workers in manufacturing plants was in less than perfect health.[5]

In 1942, a House of Commons report provided a glimpse into the health of the population. The infant mortality rate in Canada was fifty-six deaths for every 1,000 live births in 1940, compared to thirty in New Zealand, where the public had universal access to health care.

Mortality rates among women, who had limited access to hospital care during childbirth, were "excessively high." Thousands of Canadians died in 1940 alone from communicable diseases such as influenza, tuberculosis, diphtheria, measles, and whooping cough. In each year between 1931 and 1941, an average of 15,000 Canadian children under the age of one died from preventable or controllable illnesses.[6]

Ten years later, the Canadian Sickness Survey provided another shocking picture of what injustice in health care meant for Canadians, their children, and their communities. The survey showed that low-income earners experienced twice as many disability days as higher-income earners. And despite their better overall health, Canadians at the higher end of the income scale spent nearly three times as much on health care as those at the lower end.[7]

As countries emerged from the Second World War, governments introduced a range of democratic reforms that included progressive social, health care, and welfare policies and recognized workers' rights to form unions (see Chapter 4). In 1946, the World Health Organization (WHO) enshrined health as a fundamental human right, and two years later, the United Nations embedded the principle in the Universal Declaration of Human Rights. By the end of the decade, many countries had responded to these principles by integrating universal health care into a broad social safety net that included education, child benefits, welfare, housing, and pensions, among other welfare state policies.

But Canada was a relative latecomer to the medicare table. It wasn't until 1957 that the federal government introduced universal public hospital insurance, ten years after Saskatchewan had done so. Then, in 1962, Saskatchewan pioneered another universal insurance program, this time covering community-based medical services for all residents in the province. A year earlier, Ottawa appointed the **Royal Commission** on Health Services (RCHS), or Hall Commission, to investigate the feasibility of a national insurance scheme covering medical services. The RCHS received presentations and submissions from hundreds of individuals and organizations. Among these were representatives of the trade union movement, who brought a high level of sophistication to debates about universal health care, reflecting the experiences of members across the country and in every part of the economy. In its brief to the Commission, the **Canadian Labour Congress (CLC)** described health care as "one of the major remaining gaps that needs to be filled in our social security system."[8]

The CLC rejected the concept of insurance as the basis for a new system, arguing that health care should be regarded as a public service.[9] It was joined by groups including farmers, women, public health advocates, and faith organizations in calling for a scheme that resembled Canada's public education system or Britain's National Health Service, which both funded and provided health care. The trade union movement and its allies urged that "broader objectives including preventive services, drugs, dental services and home care, as well as provision for the financial consequences of illness or injury" be included in a national health program.[10]

Despite the broad support for such a comprehensive health system, the Hall Commission recommended public health insurance, hoping that this option would not antagonize business interests or members of the Canadian Medical Association and its provincial counterparts. Doctors in Saskatchewan launched a strike when medicare was introduced in that province, and few governments were prepared to confront the medical profession. Today's system of public health insurance reflects the compromises governments made with opponents of so-called socialized medicine, in particular the medical associations.

Finally, in 1966, Ottawa passed the Medical Care Insurance Act establishing high national standards for medical services that provincial and territorial governments would have to meet in order to qualify for federal funds. In 1984, the federal government passed the Canada Health Act, ensuring that eligible Canadian residents have access to health services across the country. A key result of these policies has been a massive increase in the health care workforce.

WHAT CANADIANS HAVE AND DON'T HAVE

Before 1967, about half of Canadian workers, most of them unionized, were covered by employer-sponsored health insurance, known as extended or supplementary health benefits. The introduction of universal health care drastically reduced the role of both the insurance industry and employers as gatekeepers between illness and health care. Today the public health care system provides insurance, or protection, for Canadians when they need a doctor or have to go to a hospital. And most importantly, public health insurance plans cover all residents in the country who needs these services.

By contrast, working people in the United States continue to rely on their own personal resources or on an inadequate system of private health insurance coverage. Nearly half of all Americans are either uninsured or underinsured, and must pay out of pocket if they need health care. Even those with employer-sponsored health benefits rarely escape high premiums and out-of-pocket co-pays and deductibles – one reason why medical bills are the number one reason for personal bankruptcy in that country.[11] The lack of access by Americans to health care services during the COVID-19 pandemic resulted in an estimated 26 percent higher mortality rate than would have been the case with universal insurance, and much higher rates than other wealthy countries, including Canada and Norway.

The two systems also differ markedly in terms of flexibility. While public health insurance enables Canadians to choose their own physicians and hospitals, and gives them access to care regardless of where they work or travel across the country, Americans must navigate the insurance system to find hospitals and doctors that are in-network – that is, approved by their private insurer. If they are treated in an out-of-network hospital by an out-of-network physician, they will be billed for the services provided.[12]

Figure 14.1 demonstrates some of the stark differences between a publicly funded and provided health care system, like that in Canada and Norway, and the health care system in the United States, which is still run predominantly by private health insurers and private hospitals. The United States spends more than any other advanced industrial country in the world, taking up more than 17 percent of its gross domestic product in combined public and private health expenditures. Canada and Norway each spend 10–11 percent. The lack of universal health care in the US was put into stark relief during the first year of the COVID-19 pandemic when Americans, who represent 4 percent of the world's population, made up 15 percent of global mortality rates attributable to the virus.[13]

One of the biggest reasons for this difference is that the US health care system operates on market principles: private commercial insurers charge excessively high premiums, and private hospital corporations build profit margins into what they charge Americans for health services.[14] Another reason is that a public system – with a single public payer and largely not-for-profit provision of insured services – is simply more cost effective and does not require high profits to reward investors. Thus, both Norway and Canada maintain public health insurance systems that are more affordable and have far better health outcomes.

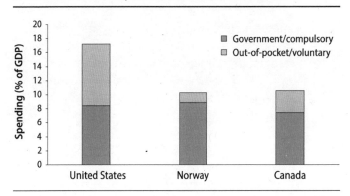

FIGURE 14.1 **Health expenditure as a share of GDP, 2016**

Source: Data from OECD, *Health at a Glance 2017: OECD Indicators* (Paris, OECD Publishing, 2017), http://dx.doi.org/10.1787/health_glance-2017-en.

As Figure 14.1 also shows, however, about 30 percent of Canada's total health expenditure is privately funded, through either commercial insurance or out-of-pocket payments. Individual Canadians spent about $37 billion, or almost $1,000 per person, in 2019, and the private insurance industry spent nearly $33 billion.[15] This is because services such as dental care, community-based physiotherapy and mental health counselling, prescription medicines, and long-term care have either never been included in the universal insurance system or have been privatized. Greg Marchildon, Ontario Research Chair in Health Policy and System Change, has estimated that only 42 percent of total health expenditures in Canada are covered by the principles of the Canada Health Act.

This reflects a deep flaw in the Canadian system, which has narrowed its focus to inpatient hospital and physician services while a broad array of necessary care to for-profit insurance companies and private providers that charge whatever the market will bear. In addition, Canada is the only developed country with a universal health care system that does not include universal coverage for prescription medicines obtained outside a hospital setting.[16] This leaves a wide-open field for private health insurers, 70 percent of whose benefit payouts are for drugs.[17] But the private insurance market isn't universal, and consequently such benefits are not available to all Canadians: higher-income earners, older men, and unionized workers are more likely to be covered than young women or any non-unionized employee working for a minimum wage.[18]

THE HEALTH CARE WORKFORCE

The introduction of universal health insurance in Canada triggered massive investments by all levels of government to ensure that both the physical and the human resources needed to provide services were in place. Between 1961 and 1971, the country's labour force grew by 33 percent overall, while jobs in the health sector increased by over 60 percent, three-quarters of them in hospitals.[19] Today, health care is one of the largest sectors of the economy, with a workforce of over 1.6 million, including 642,000 working in hospitals and 432,187 employed in long-term care and residential care facilities. The largest single profession in the sector is nursing, with almost 432,000 members, followed by allied health (including dieticians, occupational and respiratory therapists, social workers, speech pathologists, physiotherapists, and laboratory and radiation technologists) at about 188,000. There are nearly 87,000 physicians and about a million others in professions such as dental hygienists, midwives, and paramedics. Most other health-sector workers are employed in ancillary services, particularly in housekeeping, laundry, food services, and maintenance. This is a largely female and highly racialized section of the health care workforce.[20]

As the Canadian Labour Congress argued before the RCHS, high-quality health care depends on high-quality working conditions, including compensation.[22] Although health care employees are in different bargaining units, unions have helped build unity in a highly segmented and hierarchical workforce. Divided along professional and non-professional lines as well as sex and gender, race, ethnicity, and religion, union members have united around common issues ranging from bed closures to staffing. Unionization has also helped health care workers, many of whom are recent immigrants and women of colour, to build common ground with the public on the issue of quality within the health care system. These are often issues that also concern patients and the public, who rely on a well-functioning system to provide the services they need.

Unionization has also amplified the voices of a predominantly female and racialized workforce in public policy debates about the health care system.[23] Health care workers have shown how excessive workloads, understaffing, high staff turnover, low wages, lack of pay equity, poor occupational health and safety, contracting out, and privatization are issues of public interest. Health care unions often demonstrate how intimately connected their members' experiences in hospital-, community-, and home-based settings are to both the quality of care that patients experience and their ability to access services without financial and other barriers.

NEOLIBERALISM IN HEALTH CARE

Beginning in the late 1970s and early '80s, neoliberalism became the ideological flag of economists and politicians who promoted the policies of deregulation, privatization, and free trade as tools to empower corporations. In this vision of unfettered capitalism, citizens are transformed into individual consumers "who build and secure their lives via the market."[24]

Neoliberalism shifted Canada – and the world – away from the postwar era of welfare state development that embraced health care as both a fundamental human right and a crucial component of democracy, and toward policies that conceived of health care and many other public services as private commodities to be provided by business and to produce profits for investors (see Chapter 3).

This shift to a market-oriented health care system began very shortly after the introduction of the CHA in 1984, when the Progressive Conservatives led by Brian Mulroney (1984–93) formed the government and soon began to reduce social program spending and increase privatization. This proved to be a challenge in the health sector. Canadians not only consistently and overwhelmingly supported the sector, they also wanted to see ongoing public funding for a greater array of health and social services.[25] Nevertheless, Ottawa massively reduced cash transfers to the provinces for public health care, creating a cascade of provincial government funding cuts to hospitals and other non-physician health care providers.[26] These were followed by further cuts to public health care spending by the Liberal government in Ottawa under Jean Chrétien (1993–2003) in the mid-1990s.

These steep funding reductions triggered hospital and bed closures across the country, as well as layoffs and increased workloads for staff. A 1996 survey of major hospitals across Canada found that 85 percent had eliminated jobs during the previous two years, resulting in a 10 percent overall reduction of the hospital workforce.[27] The downsizing shifted care not only from in-patient to out-patient settings but also increasingly away from publicly funded, unionized institutions to for-profit, non-union companies: a process of privatization that included the contracting out or outsourcing of hospital services to global corporations.

Health care is very labour intensive, with wages and benefits constituting 60 percent of total hospital budgets.[28] Thus, it is not surprising that cost-cutting measures have focused on wages and benefits. According to many consultants, the core mission of the hospital sector is the provision of clinical care by doctors and nurses – core providers – who are aided by paramedical professionals such as laboratory technologists, social workers, physio- and occupational therapists, and pharmacists. So-called non-core functions, such as cleaning and food services, these consultants advise, could and should be outsourced to private companies in order to ostensibly reduce costs. This group has become the main target of cost cutting and outsourcing within the hospital system.

As a result, by 2009 three types of work within the support services category – laundry, housekeeping, and food services – accounted for 71 percent of the amount of money that hospitals spent on contracts with outsourcing companies.[29] Hospital employers said that these services were provided by workers whose wages and benefits were far in excess of those doing similar jobs in the private sector, particularly in industries such as hotels, restaurants, and janitorial services.[30] Supporters of outsourcing have argued, paradoxically, that hospital employees who provide non-core services are not essential to patient care, but when these same workers are employed by outsourcing vendors, they contribute to "the nutrition, cleanliness, and comfort of a patient" and increase the number of "successful healing outcomes."[31]

Although outsourcing was framed as a strategy to save the hospital system money, it targeted a vulnerable and racialized workforce composed mainly of lower-paid female workers. Much of the outsourcing of food and cleaning services in Canadian hospitals has gone to three large global corporations: Sodexo, based in France; Aramark, based in the United States; and Compass Group, based in the United Kingdom. Thus, public dollars now flow through hospitals to companies that often increase profits by paying lower wages, using part-time workers with fewer fringe benefits, and establishing broader – often worldwide – economies of scale.

For governments and health employers, convincing members of the public that privatization was in their interest was no easy task. Polls done in British Columbia in 2007, when the province was aggressively reducing the public-sector workforce, found over half of the respondents opposed the contracting out of hospital support services, expressing concerns about the impact on the quality of care.[32]

But despite such widespread concerns, the province introduced Bill 29, the Health and Social Services Delivery Improvement Act, in 2002. The bill was designed to weaken collective agreement provisions that restricted contracting out of services. It unilaterally cancelled union contracts affecting up to 28,000 workers in hospitals and long-term facilities, including 10,000 people who were fired outright, and paved the way for private firms to take over the management and delivery of food, laundry, cleaning, maintenance, clerical, and security services. These new employers were allowed to move workers to different hospitals within a single shift and to worksites hundreds of kilometres away for temporary assignments.[33]

Bill 29 also led to drastic wage cuts for those – most of them women – whose jobs were affected. Aramark, for example, paid staff $9.50 per hour for housekeeping services, compared to $18.32 for those doing the same job prior to Bill 29 – a cut of 48 percent. The legislation also eliminated pay equity provisions in collective agreements that had been won over three decades of struggle. Bill 29 took the province "from being a national leader in rates for health support services to one of the lowest in the country, significantly lower than the Canadian average," according to one study.[34]

Thus, Bill 29 represented one of the most notable cases of health care privatization in Canadian history. It was also one of the most significant cases of united opposition by unions and the public to health care legislation. Three unions – the Hospital Employees' Union (HEU), the BC Government and Service Employees' Union (BCGEU, now called the BC General Employees' Union), and the BC Nurses' Union (BCNU) – representing 100,000 health care workers launched a constitutional challenge against the law, which was widely condemned in Canada and internationally. The International Labour Organization (ILO) called on the provincial government to repeal the Act in order to comply with international labour standards.

The unions challenged the Act as a violation of Canada's Charter of Rights and Freedoms because it denied the right to freedom of association for unionized health care workers thereby eliminating their right to bargain collectively. The unions also cited the attack on equality rights because of the negative and disproportionate impact of the Act on female health care and community social services workers.[35] The BC Supreme Court nonetheless ruled that the provincial government had not violated Charter rights to freedom of association and equality rights.

In 2004, over 40,000 HEU members initiated an illegal strike to protect their union and their collective agreements with hospital and long-term care employers, and to protest the privatization of services in British Columbia. Another 30,000 public- and private-sector workers walked out in solidarity. Across the province, the public organized coalitions to support HEU and BCGEU members, and the provincial federation of labour began mobilizing its affiliated unions in anticipation of a general strike. Tens of thousands of people demonstrated in downtown Vancouver to demand that the Liberal government repeal the legislation and restore wages and collective bargaining rights, including protections against contracting out. The

HEU, the BCGEU, and the Health Employers Association of BC (HEABC) agreed to a settlement that mitigated some but not all of the provisions of the Act.

The unions subsequently appealed the earlier provincial court ruling to the Supreme Court of Canada, which, in a landmark decision, ruled that the Charter rights of union members in the BC health sector had indeed been violated. Under the ruling, the court extended the freedom of association provisions of the Charter to include the right to free collective bargaining, a ruling that had implications for union members across the country (see Chapter 17). In 2018, the New Democratic Party government in British Columbia repealed Bill 29. Harkening back to the labour movement's historical position that high-quality care is inextricably linked to high-quality working conditions, the HEU argued this was a "giant step towards restoring justice and fairness for health care workers and repairing the damage that's been done to health care delivery."[36]

The experience of BC hospital workers stands in harsh contrast to their counterparts in northern Europe. Canadian labour policies in the health sector are similar to those in Europe, where the right to organize and negotiate wages and working conditions is enshrined in law. In Nordic countries, however, the health sector is highly organized, and the labour model is characterized by social dialogue and high levels of cooperation between governments, employers, and unions.

In the Norwegian health sector, for example, the tripartite government-employer-union partnership model has produced effective strategies at both the workplace and legislative levels to address wage equality. In 2017, a survey of female health care workers found that 20 percent who worked part time were dissatisfied with their working hours. This led to a letter of intent in the hospital sector to increase full-time employment and the development of guidelines and recommendations to support implementation across the sector. Legislation was also introduced to create more full-time positions and improve conditions for part-time workers.[37] According to Norway's former minister of labour and social affairs, Anniken Hauglie, "Social dialogue is one of the fundamental principles and a tool for guaranteeing universal working rights."[38]

The level of unionization among health care workers in Norway and Canada is very similar, but in the United States, where health services are considered a market commodity, organizing drives have been far less successful. The United States has about 10 percent unionization across the economy, and in the health sector only about 7 percent of workers are union members.[39] This compares to rates of unionization in Canadian hospitals and residential and long-term care facilities of between 62 and 86 percent.[40] Nurses have the highest rate of unionization across the US economy, according to the Bureau of Labor Statistics, but at only 20.4 percent it falls well below Canada's estimated rate of 90 percent across the full range of the nursing profession. Yet studies have found that unionized nurses in the United States often outperformed their non-union counterparts in quality of care and productivity.[41]

CONTRACTING OUT IN-HOME CARE

Contracting out, or outsourcing, also occurs in the community sector, where regional and provincial authorities have contracted companies to provide home and residential care. Outsourcing escalated during the 1990s as many hospitals began implementing early patient discharge and delayed admissions policies – ostensibly designed to free needed hospital beds and ease wait times. But such strategies also shifted the burden and cost of care directly onto patients and their families. As patients shifted out of hospitals and into the community or the home, many of the services they needed moved beyond the reach of the Canada Health Act, which bans direct billing to patients for physician care and hospital services. This expanded opportunities for private insurance companies and private health care companies in the provision of home care (see Chapter 13).

In Manitoba, a comprehensive public home care system had been introduced in 1974, praised by public health and policy experts as one of the best long-term care systems in Canada and the United States.[42] This did not deter the provincial Progressive Conservative government from embarking on an aggressive campaign to contract out 25 percent of all home care service delivery. In April 1996, a for-profit company called We Care was contracted to provide home care and other community-based services, a move the government said would facilitate hospital discharges, thereby freeing up needed beds.[43] It quickly became apparent, however, that We Care nurses and other staff were paid much lower wages than those doing the same or similar work in the hospital sector. Issues related to increased workloads and temporary or part-time employment contracts undermined the quality of care provided. Eventually, 3,000 home care workers who were members of what was then known as the Manitoba Government Employees' Union (MGEU) went on a five-week strike.

Described as one of the most important strikes in the province's history, 3,000 personal care workers brought the government's plans to public attention, sparking widespread protest especially among elderly and disabled home care recipients and their families. Home care clients, seniors' organizations, and faith groups organized the Coalition to Save Home Care to combat the scheme, distributing Save Home Care signs to thousands of families. A poll commissioned by the MGEU found two-thirds of Manitobans opposed the privatization. The key issue that united patients, their families, and the unions representing home care employees was quality of care, including the continuity of relationships between clients and their carers. Families that were compelled to use private home care companies complained about a constant turnover in staff, with "a different person coming to the door all the time." Care providers complained that they "were always going to a different place" and "every week you have different clients."[44] The province was forced to abandon its contracting-out plans, and the strike ended when the government agreed to maintain the current workforce, reduce the percentage of contracted-out personal care work, and freeze plans to privatize home care in rural communities. Public health authorities were assigned responsibility for home care services and mandated to maintain them within the public system.

THE IMPACT OF COVID-19 ON PUBLIC HEALTH

In January 2020, the WHO declared COVID-19 "a public health emergency of international concern" as the disease swept around the globe, leaving very few countries untouched. At the time of the declaration, it was reported that there were only ninety-eight cases outside of China and that no one had died. But by early September, the number of reported cases per day increased worldwide and it was estimated that more than a million people had died. Six months later there were almost 127 million reported cases and 2.7 million deaths.[45]

It's fair to say that despite warnings of a possible global pandemic over many years, very few countries were prepared. COVID-19 highlighted the impact of decades of neoliberal austerity at both national and international levels. In Canada, holes in the social safety net combined with a weak public health infrastructure to undermine the capacity to respond. In 2015, the *Canadian Medical Association Journal* had criticized the federal government for measures that had "weakened the authority of the public health agency; muzzled scientists ... and eroded research support, while increasingly tying what remains to business interests rather than health benefits."[46] As the pandemic unfolded just a few years later, the country's most vulnerable populations – in particular, Indigenous people, communities of colour, poor, disabled, and elderly Canadians – were paying a very high price for these policies (Chapter 1).

The health care system is designed to provide hospital and medical services, but the broader goals of public health are "to keep people healthy and prevent injury, illness and premature death. It is a combination of programs, services and policies that protect and promote the health of all Canadians."[47] Like health care, responsibility for public health is shared by federal, provincial, and territorial governments. The Public Health Agency of Canada, created in 2004, collaborated with its provincial and territorial counterparts during the COVID-19 pandemic.[48] Both the health care and public health systems struggled to provide the country with powerful tools to test for, trace, and contain the spread of the disease.

The pandemic also highlighted deep inequities across race, class, immigration status, age, sex, and gender, as well as between urban and rural dwellers.[49] It pointed to the ongoing impact of colonization and the destruction of Indigenous communities that historically had embraced many tenets of public health, including that health is not just the absence of disease but a state of well-being.[50] During the pandemic, the lack of adequate housing and clean water in many First Nations, Inuit, and Métis commun-

ities, along with high poverty rates, increased vulnerability to the disease (Chapter 15). A year into the pandemic, reported cases of COVID-19 among Indigenous people in Canada were 187 percent higher than for non-Indigenous people, and the fatality rate among First Nations people living on reserves was 47 percent higher.[51]

By the time the coronavirus hit, Canada's system of caring for and supporting the elderly, another vulnerable group, had been the subject of years of research and concerted campaigning by families and health care workers for improvements in how services were provided and by whom.[52] But governments had not only largely failed to respond to these voices but also ignored a growing body of evidence showing that services provided by for-profit companies focused on delivering high returns on investment, not high-quality care.

Seniors over sixty-five years old have long been identified as the fastest growing demographic in Canada, and those over eighty-five constitute the majority of residents in long-term care (LTC).[53] Yet in the early 2000s, most provinces began to cut funding for LTC beds, reducing access to publicly funded, non-profit facilities (Chapter 13). At the same time, for-profit nursing homes were often overcrowded, understaffed, and poorly regulated. People who worked in the LTC sector were a highly racialized, underpaid workforce, often employed on a temporary and part-time basis, shifting from one job to the next in order to patch together a decent income. During the pandemic, there was no shortage of studies showing that for-profit nursing homes experienced higher rates of COVID-19 infections and related deaths among both staff and residents.

The first reported death in Canada due to COVID-19 occurred in a two-hundred-bed long-term care facility in North Vancouver, British Columbia, on March 8, 2020. Over the following two months, 20 of the 139 residents died from

COVID-19 and another 42 residents and 21 staff were infected.[54] The circumstances surrounding the first death and subsequent rapid transmission of the virus revealed weaknesses in the system of institutional elder care that experts and advocates had warned about in regard to both the prioritization of profit and the poor working conditions and low pay experienced by employees.

These experiences were not unique. A disproportionate share of infections and deaths occurred among both LTC residents and workers in other countries with similar economies, but Canada stood out. While its overall death rate due to the virus was below the average in the Organisation for Economic Co-operation and Development (OECD), LTC residents accounted for 81 percent of all reported COVID-19 deaths in the country, compared with an average of 42 percent in sixteen other OECD member states. At the same time, LTC workers accounted for 10 percent of Canada's total infections.[55]

These conditions produced a groundswell of activism during the pandemic. Building on the many years of campaigning, long-term care workers, health coalitions, unions, seniors' advocates, and academics were joined by growing numbers of physicians and health professionals demanding an end to understaffing, contracting out, and profit making in the sector. In British Columbia, this resulted in the seizure by health authorities of four facilities owned by the Retirement Concepts corporation.[56] It also sparked a national debate about public ownership, as Ontario families joined the provincial health coalition to demand increased recruitment and training of staff, improved working conditions, and a minimum of four hours of hands-on care per day for every resident.[57] Calls mounted for a strategy to eliminate the for-profit provision of services in the long-term care sector.

The pandemic brought into sharp relief the chasm between health care services funded and provided in a non-profit or public setting and those delivered by private investor-owned entities in residential long-term care. Canada's hospitals, almost all of which are non-profit and publicly funded, were directed by provincial health ministries on the steps needed to respond to COVID-19.[58] By contrast, the long-term care sector and other parts of the health care system were characterized by a predominance of private companies and a lack of public regulation. Staff were more likely to be non-union and underpaid. And, in for-profit facilities, there were higher rates of COVID-19 transmission.

The public health arena in numerous countries – like Canada – was seriously underprepared for the coronavirus pandemic. Some experts assessed Canada's performance in positive terms despite its slow initial response, which led to a shortage of supplies and seemingly contradictory public health recommendations.[59] But there are many lessons to be learned from the pandemic, including the importance of public funding, ownership, provision, and accountability for health care, and how important it is to link high-quality services with good working conditions in order to contain the spread of any disease and support the well-being of people more generally.

DEMOCRATIC RENEWAL OF THE HEALTH CARE SYSTEM

The rise of neoliberalism and privatization models has influenced the kind of health care system we have and labour relations in the sector. Because governments have supported private investors, shifted many services to corporations, and neglected to expand and update the public sector that delivers the majority of hospital and physician services, health care systems have been slowly transformed. Citizens and health care workers alike have felt the impact.

This is certainly true in the hospital sector, which has experienced decades of downsizing without a counterbalancing strategy to publicly fund and increase access to services delivered in community settings. Downsizing – promoted to save money and increase efficiency in the 1990s – became a code word for de-unionization, outsourcing, and privatization. But cost savings were found mainly by paying lower wages to a largely female and racialized workforce whose jobs shifted to large corporations or poorly funded non-profits. Unlike in Norway, where unions represent all health care workers regardless of where they work, health care workers in Canada frequently found themselves in non-union and privatized workplaces, where they experienced a significant decline in wages and working conditions, an increase in part-time and precarious employment, and a diminishment of their voices, which had been amplified by the unions that had represented them in the hospital sector.

Health care workers are not the only ones who felt the negative impacts of privatization. Health care services delivered outside the hospital or doctor's office are becoming increasingly inaccessible to a growing number of Canadians, particularly poor, low- and even middle-income earners, Indigenous people, racialized groups, the elderly, and people with physical and mental disabilities.

Yet many in Canada have been extraordinarily tenacious in defending a health care system that includes decent working conditions for those who work within it. An essential characteristic of these efforts has been ongoing solidarity between a health care workforce committed to providing high-quality care and a public committed to the principles at the foundation of medicare. As recent events have shown, workers and citizens have been able to move governments away from policies that focus mainly on business concerns.

In a post-pandemic world, the clash between those who support a stronger role for public ownership and delivery of health services and those who support free-market approaches has deepened. Countries with high levels of state intervention, such as Germany and South Korea, have outperformed countries that have leaned heavily on the free market, including the United States and the United Kingdom.[60] In Canada, the contrast is just as sharp between market-oriented, profit-driven service provision in the long-term care sector and the service-driven focus of publicly funded non-profit hospitals.

Such public policies are essential to a democratic renewal of Canada's health care system. But the preservation of universal medicare for generations to come will depend on the same factors that brought it into existence and which have been essential in keeping it in the face of neoliberal policies favouring for-profit delivery of public services: worker mobilization, citizen involvement, and political mobilization. As Tommy Douglas's words still remind us, there is no standing still. The choices we make will determine whether we can go forward in ways that meet the needs and expectations of all those who require access to health care services.

ADDITIONAL RESOURCES

Armstrong, Pat, and Hugh Armstrong. *About Canada: Health Care, 2nd Edition.* Halifax: Fernwood Publishing, 2016.

Blavatnik School of Government, University of Oxford. "COVID-19 Government Response Tracker." https://www.bsg.ox.ac.uk/research/research-projects/coronavirus-government-response-tracker.

Hacker, Jacob. *The Great Risk Shift: The Assault on American Jobs, Families, Health Care, and Retirement and How You Can Fight Back.* Oxford: Oxford University Press, 2006.

NOTES

1   Canada, Royal Commission on Health Services (RCHS), *Report of the Royal Commission on Health Services: 1965*, vol. 2 (Ottawa: Queen's Printer, 1965), 20.

2   Canada, Royal Commission on Health Services (RCHS), *Report of the Royal Commission on Health Services: 1964*, vol. 1 (Ottawa: Queen's Printer, 1964), 381–82.

3   Ibid.

4   Robert McIntosh, "The Boys in the Nova Scotian Coal Mines: 1873–1923," *Acadiensis* 16, no. 2 (Spring 1987): 35–50.

5   Malcolm G. Taylor, *Health Insurance and Canadian Public Policy: The Seven Decisions That Created the Canadian Health Insurance System* (Montreal and Kingston: McGill-Queen's University Press, 1978), 33.

6   Canada, House of Commons Special Committee on Social Security, *Report of the Advisory Committee on Health Insurance* (Ottawa: E. Cloutier, Printer to the King, 1942).

7   Canada, Department of National Health and Welfare and the Dominion Bureau of Statistics, *Illness and Health Care in Canada: Canadian Sickness Survey, 1950–51* (Ottawa: Dominion Bureau of Statistics, 1960). https://publications.gc.ca/collections/collection_2017/statcan/CS82-505-1954-eng.pdf. The term "disability days" referred to "days away from usual activity." See p. 5.

8   Canadian Labour Congress, "Submission to the Royal Commission on Health Services," Ottawa: May 1962.

9   Ibid., 8–10.

10 RCHS, *Report of the Royal Commission*, 1: 725.

11 David U. Himmelstein, Deborah Thorne, Elizabeth Warren, and Steffie Woolhandler, "Medical Bankruptcy in the United States, 2007: Results of a National Study," *American Journal of Medicine* 122, no. 8 (August 2009): 741–46.

12 Karan R. Chhabra, Kyle H. Sheetz, Ushapoorna Nuliyalu, Mihir S. Dekhne, Andrew M. Ryan, and Justin B. Dimick, "Out-of-Network Bills for Privately Insured Patients Undergoing Elective Surgery with In-Network Primary Surgeons and Facilities," *Journal of the American Medical Association* 323, no. 6 (June 2019): 538–47.

13 Travis Campbell, Alison P. Galvani, Gerald Friedman, Meagan C. Fitzpatrick, "Exacerbation of COVID-19 Mortality by the Fragmented United States Healthcare System: A Retrospective Observational Study," *Lancet Regional Health - Americas,* 12 (2022). https://www.sciencedirect.com/science/article/pii/S2667193X22000813

14 Jacob S. Hacker, *The Great Risk Shift: The Assault on American Jobs, Families, Health Care, and Retirement and How You Can Fight Back* (Oxford: Oxford University Press, 2006).

15 Canadian Institute for Health Information, *National Health Expenditure Trends, 1975 to 2019* (Ottawa: CIHI 2019); Gregory P. Marchildon, *Three Choices for the Future of Medicare* (Ottawa: Caledon Institute of Social Policy, 2004).

16 Steven G. Morgan and Katherine Boothe, "Universal Prescription Drug Coverage in Canada: Long-Promised Yet Undelivered," *Healthcare Management Forum* 29, no. 6 (2016): 247–54.

17 Lizann Reitmeier, *Report: Canadian Health Care Trend Survey*, Buck Consultants, July 23, 2019, https://buck.com/ca/2019-canadian-healthcare-trend-survey.

18 Mark Reesor and Brenda Martin, *Employer-Sponsored Health and Dental Plans – Who is Insured?* Ottawa: Applied Research Branch, Human Resources Development Canada,

Publication no. W-98-2E. March 1998; Statistics Canada, Labour Statistics Division, *Workplace and Employee Survey Compendium 2005*, Cat. no. 71-585-X (Ottawa: Statistics Canada, 2008), https://www150.statcan.gc.ca/n1/en/pub/71-585-x/71-585-x2008001-eng.pdf?st=zxmRo9VV.

19   Alice J. Baumgart, "Hospital Reform and Nursing Labor Market Trends in Canada," *Medical Care* 35, no. 10 (1997): 124–31.

20   Canadian Institute for Health Information, *Nursing in Canada, 2018: A Lens on Supply and Workforce* (Ottawa: CIHI, 2019), https://www.cihi.ca/sites/default/files/document/regulated-nurses-2018-report-en-web.pdf; CIHI, "Canada's Health Care Providers: Provincial Profiles, 2008–2017 – Data Tables," Spreadsheet, hcp-2017-data-tables-en-web; CIHI, *Physicians in Canada, 2017,* Summary report, February 2019, https://secure.cihi.ca/free_products/Physicians_in_Canada_2017.pdf. The figure for nurses includes registered nurses, nurse practitioners, licensed practical nurses, and registered psychiatric nurses.

21   Canadian Health Coalition, *Public Health Care: We've Got This!* http://www.healthcoalition.ca/wp-content/uploads/2019/06/Weve-got-this-Report-1.pdf.

22   Canadian Labour Congress, "Submission to the Royal Commission," 63–65.

23   Jennifer Jihye Chun, "Organizing across Divides: Union Challenges to Precarious Work in Vancouver's Privatized Health Care Sector," *Progress in Development Studies* 16, no. 2 (2016): 173–88.

24   Bryan Joseph Nelle, "Finding the Political: The Ethical Consumer and Neoliberalism" (PhD diss., UC Irvine, 2015), iv.

25   Matthew Mendelsohn, *Canadians' Thoughts on Their Health Care System: Preserving the Canadian Model through Innovation* (Montreal and Kingston: McGill-Queen's University Press, 2002).

26   Pran Manga, "Health Care in Canada: A Crisis of Affordability or Inefficiency?" *Canadian Business Economics* (Summer 1994): 56–70.

27   K.V. Rondeau and T.H. Wagar, *Workforce Reduction Practices in Canadian Hospitals* (Kingston, ON: Ontario Industrial Relations Centre, Queen's University, 1998).

28   Canadian Institute for Health Information, *Hospital Cost Drivers Technical Report – What Factors Have Determined Hospital Expenditure Trends in Canada?* (Ottawa: CIHI, 2012); Jo-Anne Marr, Richard Tam, Stephen Simms, Feria Bacchus, "An Integrated Outsourcing Solution at York Central Hospital," *Health Care Quarterly* 14, no. 1 (2011): 95–97.

29   Ibid.

30   Pamela Fayerman, "Hospitals Seek Wage Rollbacks," *Vancouver Sun*, March 11, 2004, vancouversun.com.

31   Jeremy G. Roberts, John G. Henderson, Larry A. Olive, and Daniel Obaka, "A Review of Outsourcing of Services in Health Care Organizations," *Journal of Outsourcing & Organizational Information Management* (June 2013): 1–10.

32   Pamela Fayerman, "HEU Insists BC Residents Opposed to Privatization," *Vancouver Sun*, March 20, 2003, vancouversun.com; Canadian Press, "Majority of Okanagan Residents Oppose Contracting Out of Hospital Services: Poll," *Kelowna Daily Courier*, June 6, 2007, www.kelownadailycourier.ca.

33   Hospital Employees Union, "Supreme Court Strikes Down Bill 29 Provisions in Landmark Ruling," Media release, June 8, 2007, https://www.heu.org/news-media/news-releases/supreme-court-strikes-down-bill-29-provisions-landmark-ruling.

34   Jane Stinson, Nancy Pollak, and Marcy Cohen, *The Pains of Privatization: How Contracting Out Hurts Health Support Workers, Their Families and Health Care* (Vancouver: Canadian Centre for Policy Alternatives, 2005).

35   Hospital Employees Union, "Key Information on Health Unions' Bill 29 Charter Challenge," Backgrounder, June 8, 2007, https://www.heu.org/sites/default/files/uploads/News%20Releases/Backgrounder%20Bill%2029%20key%20dates.pdf.

36 Hospital Employees Union, "Repeal of Discriminatory Health Labour Laws to Help Restore Fairness, Stability to Health Care, Says HEU," Media release, November 8, 2018, https://www.heu.org/news-media/news-releases/repeal-discriminatory-health-labour-laws-help-restore-fairness-stability.

37 Kristin Alsos, Kristine Nergaard, and Sissel C. Trygstad, *Getting and Staying Together: 100 Years of Social Dialogue and Tripartism in Norway*, June 2019 (Geneva: International Labour Office, 2019, https://www.ilo.org/wcmsp5/groups/public/—ed_dialogue/—dialogue/documents/publication/wcms_709868.pdf.

38 Anniken Hauglie, Minister of Labour and Social Affairs (Norway), "Tripartism and Social Dialogue in Norway," Statement to the 106th session of the International Labour Conference, Geneva, Switzerland, June 5–16, 2017, https://www.regjeringen.no/no/aktuelt/tripartism-part-of-the-same-future-experiences-from-the-norwegian-social-dialogue/id2555610.

39 US Department of Labor, Bureau of Labor Statistics, "Union Members – 2019," Media release, January 22, 2020, https://www.bls.gov/news.release/pdf/union2.pdf.

40 Pat Armstrong, Kate Laxer, and Hugh Armstrong, "The Conceptual Guide to the Health Care Module," *Gender and Work Database*, 2014, www.genderwork.ca/gwd/modules/health-care.

41 Arindrajit Dube, Ethan Kaplan, and Owen Thompson, "Nurse Unions and Patient Outcomes," *Industrial and Labor Relations Review* 69, no. 4 (2016): 803–33.

42 Frances Russell, "Home Care Is Healthy as Is," *Winnipeg Free Press*, March 1, 1996.

43 Jennifer Howard and Kay Willson, *Missing Links: The Effects of Health Care Privatization on Women in Manitoba and Saskatchewan* (Winnipeg: Centres of Excellence for Women's Health Program, Women's Health Bureau, Health Canada, 1999), http://www.womenandhealthcarereform.ca/publications/ml.pdf.

44 Colleen Fuller, "Home Care: What We Have and What We Need," Canadian Health Coalition, 2001, https://www.healthcoalition.ca/wp-content/uploads/2022/05/Fuller_HomeCare-What-we-need_2001.pdf.

45 World Health Organization, Diseases, Health topic: Coronavirus disease (COVID-19), "Timeline: WHO's COVID-19 Response," www.who.int/emergencies/diseases; and Health topic: Coronavirus disease (COVID-19), Situation updates: "WHO Coronavirus (COVID-19) Dashboard," www.who.int/health-topics.

46 Matthew B. Stanbrook, "Why the Federal Government Must Lead in Health Care," *Canadian Medical Association Journal*, Editorial, August 17, 2015, https://www.cmaj.ca/content/cmaj/early/2015/08/17/cmaj.150896.full.pdf

47 Chief Public Health Officer, *Report on the State of Public Health in Canada 2008: Addressing Health Inequalities* (Ottawa: Minister of Health, 2008), https://www.canada.ca/content/dam/phac-aspc/migration/phac-aspc/cphorsphc-respcacsp/2008/fr-rc/pdf/CPHO-Report-e.pdf.

48 Teresa Tam, "Fifteen Years Post-SARS: Key Milestones in Canada's Public Health Emergency Response" *Canada Communicable Disease Report* 44, no. 5 (2018): 98–101.

49 Aaron Wherry, "One Country, Two Pandemics: What COVID-19 Reveals about Inequality in Canada," *CBC News*, June 13, 2020, www.cbc.ca; Colleen Walsh, "COVID-19 Targets Communities of Color," *The Harvard Gazette*, April 14, 2020, https://news.harvard.edu/gazette; Aimée-Angélique Bouka and Yolande Bouka, "Canada's COVID-19 Blind Spots on Race, Immigration and Labour," *Policy Options*, May 19, 2020, policyoptions.irpp.org; Richard V. Reeves and Jonathan Rothwell, "Class and COVID: How the Less Affluent Face Double Risks," The Brookings Institution, March 27, 2020, www.brookings.edu; Jewel Gausman and Ana Langer, "Sex and Gender Disparities in the COVID-19 Pandemic," *Journal of Women's Health* 29, no. 4 (2020).

50 Lisa Richardson and Allison Crawford, "COVID-19 and the Decolonization of Indigenous Public Health," *Canadian Medical Association Journal* 192, no. 38 (2020): 2.

51   Indigenous Services Canada, "Coronavirus (COVID-19) and Indigenous Communities: Confirmed Cases of COVID-19," March 25, 2021, https://www.sac-isc.gc.ca/eng/1598625105013/1598625167707.

52   Pat Armstrong, Hugh Armstrong, Jacqueline Choiniere, Ruth Lowndes, and James Struthers, *Re-imagining Long-Term Residential Care in the COVID-19 Crisis* (Ottawa: Canadian Centre for Policy Alternatives, 2020).

53   Canadian Medical Association, *A Policy Framework to Guide a National Seniors Strategy for Canada*, August 2015, https://cma.ca/sites/default/files/pdf/News/policy-framework-to-guide-seniors_en.pdf.

54   Andrew Longhurst and Kendra Strauss, *Time to End Profit-Making in Seniors' Care* (Vancouver: Canadian Centre for Policy Alternatives, 2020); See also Jason Proctor, "'It Was Mayhem,' Families Caught in COVID 19 Outbreak at BC Care Home Say System Left Seniors at Risk," *CBC News*, March 26, 2020, www.cbc.ca.

55   Canadian Institute for Health Information, *Pandemic Experience in the Long-Term Care Sector: How Does Canada Compare with Other Countries?* (Ottawa: CIHI, 2020), https://www.cihi.ca/sites/default/files/document/COVID-19-rapid-response-long-term-care-snapshot-en.pdf.

56   Joanna Chui, "'Furious and Scared': Long before COVID-19, These Families Knew Canada's Long-Term-Care System Was Broken," *Toronto Star*, April 16, 2020, thestar.com.

57   Julie Ireton, "Families, Health Coalition Demand Action on Long-Term Care," *CBC News*, October 8, 2020, www.cbc.ca.

58   Allan S. Detsky and Isaac I. Bogoch, "COVID-19 in Canada: Experience and Response," *Journal of the American Medical Association* 324, no. 8 (2020): 743–44.

59   Ryan Flanagan, "Coronavirus Report Card: Experts Give Canada a B, U.S. an F," *CTV News*, July 25, 2020, www.ctvnews.ca.

60   Timothy I. Mellish, Natalie J. Luzmore, and Ahmed Ashfaque Shahbaz, "Why Were the UK and USA Unprepared for the COVID-19 Pandemic? The Systemic Weaknesses of Neoliberalism: A Comparison between the UK, USA, Germany and South Korea," *Journal of Global Faultlines* 7, no. 1 (2020): 9–45.

15 Racial Exclusion, Discrimination, and Low-Wage Work among First Nations

Yale Belanger

CHAPTER SUMMARY

This chapter provides a thematic overview of key issues facing First Nations workers, specifically, and more generally, Indigenous peoples: precarious employment and bad jobs, discrimination, and political exclusion. Employment is essential to personal development and identity, and central to generating the income to afford amenities such as housing. Steady work leads to social cohesion and creates a foundation on which to build a cycle of enhanced economic outcomes, improved education and skills, and sustainable, thriving communities. First Nations peoples in Canada, specifically, and Indigenous peoples generally, face complex barriers to employment that are associated with the ongoing manifestations of colonization, geography, and government policies.[1]

The chapter offers a brief history of First Nations wage labour activity that explains the constraints imposed by both government policies and social attitudes. In doing so, the analysis reveals the toll of labour exclusion on First Nations peoples, both individually and collectively, and for Canadian society, based on what experts studying these issues have determined, and offers several recommendations for change.

KEY THEMES

This chapter will help you develop an understanding of:

- First Nations worker challenges, from racism and discrimination to unemployment and underemployment
- long-standing precarious employment among Indigenous workers
- policy problems facing First Nations workers
- a range of policy responses to combat First Nations precarity, from education and skills training to enhanced discrimination and harassment policies for workplaces
- the impact of the COVID-19 pandemic on Indigenous employment and the shortcomings of the government response.

ALREADY VULNERABLE TO economic segregation and social isolation, Indigenous people in Canada confront disproportionate and persistent labour force exclusion.[2] Consequently, individual economic outcomes suffer, in turn impeding community economic sovereignty.[3] Seeking to reverse these trends, First Nations leaders – both independently and in partnership with government and industry – have pursued a four-decade strategy of substantial political and economic investment in workforce training, employment skills preparation, professional development, and skills upgrading.[4]

These ongoing efforts continue to be hindered by widespread employer discrimination and racism. When First Nations individuals do find work, they often find themselves in hostile environments. The geographic isolation of many First Nations communities forces members to travel hundreds of kilometres for work, while community leaders pursue local employment initiatives intended to balance local social, economic, and political priorities with regional and national ones. The pervasive threat of global economic downturn makes these efforts more difficult, as does the requirement to adhere to what is often seen as disruptive Indian Act legislation and restrictive Crown-Indigenous Relations and Northern Affairs Canada (CIRNAC) policies and guidelines.

First Nations employment in Canada – both within First Nations communities and in non-Indigenous towns and cities – is a complex phenomenon. Studies show that Indigenous workers across the country routinely find themselves in bad jobs with low wages, modest economic security, and limited hope for a better future. Those confronting these and like concerns frequently live insecure lives. They also have little ability to influence the wider rules, institutions, or decisions affecting them. With varying degrees of success, federal politicians and Indigenous leaders have confronted some of the forces that keep First Nations employment so precarious.

INDIGENOUS LABOUR TO THE 1980S

Indigenous peoples from the earliest moments of contact pursued economic relationships with the representatives of most of the major European powers entering North America. During this early contact period, Indigenous peoples had military and economic supremacy, creating the chance to institute equitable economic and political relations with the newcomers. This turned out to be a lost opportunity once growing immigrant populations started to overwhelm Turtle Island's populations in their unrelenting pursuit of the "free" North American lands European monarchs identified as *terra nullius* (uninhabited).

Soon a growing number of permanent settlements extended west into Indigenous-owned and occupied territories. Along a timescale matching the westward march of colonization, most Indigenous regional economies and trade networks would be overwhelmed as imported diseases decimated local populations – and First Nations found themselves increasingly excluded as economic partners. With their lands now occupied and economic traditions slowly changing or even disintegrating, many supplemented their traditional labours by working for settler merchants.[5]

The gradual shift toward wage labour emerged in the context of several developments. Local economic sufficiency was undermined by the decision of the British Crown following the Seven Years' War (1756–63) to discontinue what had been a long history of gift exchanges with its Indigenous allies, a move that obliterated one of several Indigenous economic pillars.[6] Treaties that had previously protected

Indigenous economic interests were increasingly being used to dispossess Indians of their lands, weakening the balance of political and economic power. Colonial officials exploited the situation, imposing governing institutions designed to facilitate the acquisition of coveted Indigenous lands now earmarked for settler growth and thus further undermining Indigenous economic development potential. Somewhat unexpectedly, in what remains a largely invisible trend in Canadian history, Indigenous wage labour emerged as integral to this early capitalism.[7]

Despite a willingness to work as labourers, First Nations were never able to convince colonial and later Canadian officials of their industrial preparedness. Consequently, by the time of Confederation in 1867, First Nations wage labour precarity, or precarious employment, was becoming the norm. The widely accepted belief in Indigenous–industrial incompatibility meant that hiring Indigenous people was rarely considered. Social attitudes such as these (including the increasingly common stereotype of the lazy Indian) were baked into policy, and bureaucratic ignorance soon developed regarding the prospective role of wage labour in revitalizing First Nations economies.

By the 1880s, First Nations peoples were effectively confined to their communities, where law, policy, and social convention constrained their economic pursuits, and their children were being sent to residential schools.[8] Strategies such as these wrote off First Nations communities as unworthy of long-term economic development and framed reserves and residential schools as sites where Indigenous individuals could acquire the skills they needed to guarantee a successful transition to life off reserve.

First Nations communities nonetheless struggled to remain autonomous and pursued their own economic improvement against the pull of urban migration and big business in industrialized cities. Farming, ranching, fishing, and hunting, and an enduring faith in the promise of local entrepreneurship underscored First Nations community development strategies.

Wages did not unfortunately develop into a substantial source of overall earnings for Indigenous individuals: just over 25 percent of income between 1899 and 1929.[9] Policy makers and non-Indigenous business owners seized upon the situation, considering that it was merely common sense to downplay First Nations demands for greater labour market access.[10] From the early twentieth century on, therefore, the absence of Indigenous employees was portrayed not as a consequence of unresponsive federal Indian policies or even as a problematic trend but as a product of failed First Nations economic strategies and an historically proven Indigenous inability to fully embrace the needs and potential of **industrial wage labour**.[11] Immigration policy also complicated matters over time by bringing non-Indigenous labourers to Canada who were frequently hired before Indigenous workers.[12]

Wage labour prospects continued to decline prior to the start of the Great Depression in 1929, after which they dropped off precipitously. Indigenous labour activity endured in regions that produced staples, but Indigenous workers were infrequently hired outside of the forestry, mining, farming, and ranching sectors. Widespread unemployment in the 1930s only heightened job competition, reinforcing societal stereotypes regarding the inability of First Nations people to adapt to industrial wage labour.[13]

Canadian policy makers chose instead to maintain the status quo, and by the 1940s, most First Nations economies were a mixture of agriculture and treaty-secured trapping and fishing. A handful of communities began to get access to modest funding from Indian Affairs Branch (IAB) to maintain reserve industries, but First Nations employment remained limited.[14] With

Indigenous people now fully integrated into the federal welfare system, precarious work in manufacturing and resource sectors in and nearby reserves was becoming normalized.

By the 1950s, First Nations individuals consequently started looking to the cities for educational opportunities and stable employment, making those who moved to improve their lives unwitting accomplices in the so-called Indian civilization project.[15] Social service delivery and employment initiatives both on and off reserve became convoluted in the process. Urban Indigenous peoples were frequently deemed ineligible for federal programs to aid with their urban transition, while status Indians living on reserve had greater access to a wider assortment of government programs, resulting in the exclusion of non-status Indians living off reserve.[16]

The slow pace of Indigenous urbanization unfortunately continued to limit employment prospects into the 1960s, when Indigenous people reportedly made less than one-fifth of the national per capita average income, and more than one-third of Indigenous households depended on welfare. Indigenous employment remained concentrated in primary, resource-based industries - forestry, fishing, trapping, guiding, food gathering, and handicrafts - where one in six jobs was deemed skilled employment. Ominously, technological change and amplified urbanization anticipated a decline in these numbers.[17]

Nor was the economic promise of the city realized. Declining urban industrial growth in the 1970s fostered additional "barriers of discrimination in employment, housing, and social life."[18] Relieved of their earlier optimism that city life would present more job opportunities, many urban Indigenous émigrés returned to their home reserves.

By the early 1980s, the Indigenous unemployment rate was roughly 2.2 times higher than that of the non-Indigenous population, rising to 2.5 times by 1991. Indigenous individuals over fifteen had an unemployment rate of 15.8 percent in 1981, compared with 7.2 percent for the mainstream population. An estimated 38 percent of registered Indians aged fifteen and over were employed, compared with 60 percent of the general population. Confronting substantial labour exclusion, 54 percent of Indigenous individuals refused to participate in the labour force (compared to 35 percent of the general population). Academics warned government officials of rampant unemployment and underemployment and growing welfare dependency.[19] Even those with steady work throughout the 1980s witnessed their income levels drop by 5 percent as non-Indigenous Canadian incomes rose by nearly 4.3 percent.

Substantial First Nations labour exclusion was by now a statistical reality, arguably institutionalized and certainly socially normalized, with available employment frequently precarious.

FIRST NATIONS LABOUR PRECARITY

By the 1980s, First Nations organizations such as the Assembly of First Nations (AFN) had started to challenge these devastating employment trends. At the same time, however, all workers in Canada were confronting the growth of non-standard forms of employment.[20] Classic Fordist employment had individuals occupying the same job for life, with predictable schedules, a moderately stable income, and access to social supports during times of unemployment. By the 1970s, however, organized labour had started to confront employment uncertainty, fluctuating incomes, diminished benefits, the deindustrialization and the decline of union representation, trends that grew considerably in the 1990s.[21]

Non-standard employment emerged: self-employment, part-time and temporary agency work, and fixed-term contracts. Labelled precarious employment, or labour precarity, jobs characterized by a lack of security have become pronounced trends in the last four decades.[22]

Labour precarity represented yet another barrier to Indigenous employment, alongside the Indian Act and the federal government's paternal and antiquated approach to First Nations development. Policy makers responded with what could best be described as political neglect or drift (Chapter 5), for they failed to provide First Nations and urban émigrés with the proper skills training beyond that supplied by the residential school system. Compounding these trends was municipal racism that employed overzealous oversight to discourage Indigenous urban residency.[23] First Nations leaders challenged these legislative and policy choices, as well as the federal government's inability (or refusal) to address prevailing social attitudes perpetuating Indigenous labour exclusion.

The lack of a coherent federal policy response, combined with restrictive Indian Act legislation and a collective social refusal to hire Indigenous people, saw precarity develop into an institutional force that continues to harm First Nations employment prospects. Intensifying this labour exclusion even more was the emergence of precarity as a larger socio-economic trend.

CONTEMPORARY FIRST NATIONS EMPLOYMENT

The annual contribution of Indigenous people to Canada's gross domestic product (GDP) is pegged at approximately $30 billion, signifying that their employment is fundamental to the country's ongoing successful development.[24] The National Aboriginal Economic Development Board likewise recently concluded that ending Indigenous labour exclusion would increase GDP by $27.7 billion.[25] Yet research consistently reveals that "the earnings disparity between Aboriginal and non-Aboriginal persons widens the more intensely one identifies as an Aboriginal person ... most significantly those who identify as First Nations."[26]

Table 15.1 presents statistical trends from 2010. That year, Indigenous people living off reserve earned roughly 12 percent less than their non-Indigenous counterparts, although there is also a significant disparity between the earnings of Indigenous women and Indigenous men. First Nations men and women made less than their Métis and Inuit counterparts, and First Nations people living on reserve made less than those living off reserve.

Statistics Canada data for 2007–17 (Table 15.2) shows that **Aboriginal people** had an un-

TABLE 15.1 **Full-time mean annual wages of First Nations people, 2010**

	Group	Mean annual wages ($)
Respondents living off reserve	Non-Indigenous males	66,944
	Non-Indigenous females	49,760
	All Indigenous identity males	58,051
	All Indigenous identity females	44,675
Indigenous identity of groups living off reserve	First Nations males	55,209
	First Nations females	43,284
	Métis males	60,166
	Métis females	45,015
	Inuit males	58,417
	Inuit females	54,706
Respondents living on reserve	Non-Indigenous males	58,764
	Non-Indigenous females	47,512
	Indigenous identity males	37,695
	Indigenous identity females	34,706

Source: Danielle Lamb, Margaret Yap, and Michael Turk, "Aboriginal/Non-Aboriginal Wage Gaps in Canada: Evidence from the 2011 National Household Survey," *Relations Industrielles/Industrial Relations* 73, no. 2 (2018): 225–413.

employment rate of 14.1 percent, almost double that of non-Aboriginal people (7.9 percent). First Nations unemployment was higher still, at 17.1 percent, and exceeded Métis unemployment by 5.7 percent. Overall, Aboriginal unemployment was 78.5 percent higher than that of non-Aboriginal people, and First Nations unemployment was 116.5 percent of non-Aboriginal unemployment. As seen in Table 15.1, First Nations are likewise earning less, and these two trends – higher unemployment and lower wages – remained relatively consistent from 2007 to 2017.

In conjunction with unemployment rates, labour participation and employment rates must also be considered, because people who have not been active workforce participants may not be classified as unemployed. Although they are not in the workforce, these individuals may be contributing to community development in unique ways, for not all Indigenous people in Canada aspire to capital accumulation. In the context of this discussion, however, and focus-ing on those who do seek improved labour market participation, ongoing labour exclusion offers the most likely explanation for lower participation rates and lower rates of employment: people may choose not to participate in the workforce if they believe that they will not be hired, based on personal experience or from witnessing ongoing racism and discrimination.

The data contained in Table 15.2 is suggestive. Once again, Indigenous employment rates are below non-Indigenous rates. That trend varied somewhat between 2007 and 2017, but the key themes remain consistent: a lack of good jobs, a lack of accessible education and training, and evident racial discrimination. Institutional and social forces often combine to obstruct First Nations employment, such as when reserve residents would like to work off reserve but lack access to education and training programs.

Reserves are plots of Crown lands located within traditional Indigenous territories that the Canadian government set aside for First

TABLE 15.2 Employment, Participation, and Unemployment Rates: First Nations, Métis, and Inuit, 2007–17 (%)

		2007	2010	2013	2017
First Nations	Unemployment Rate	12.5	17.1	13.5	13.5
	Participation Rate	62.4	58.3	60.9	62.0
	Employment Rate	54.6	48.3	52.6	53.6
Indigenous	Unemployment Rate	10.7	14.1	11.7	11.3
	Participation Rate	65.0	62.2	64.1	64.4
	Employment Rate	58.1	53.5	56.6	57.1
Métis	Unemployment Rate	9.2	11.4	10.1	9.1
	Participation Rate	67.3	66.2	67.3	67.1
	Employment Rate	61.2	58.7	60.5	61.0
Inuit	Unemployment Rate	0.0	0.0	0.0	0.0
	Participation Rate	71.0	64.6	69.6	60.5
	Employment Rate	65.1	54.9	64.0	51.5

Source: Statistics Canada, "Labour Force Survey."

Nations use and benefit, most of which were likewise intentionally located large distances from the closest non-Indigenous communities. Historically, the travel associated with leaving the reserve for work made securing off-reserve employment difficult – trends that remain conspicuous in the Prairie provinces and the provincial North. While still having to travel large distances to work by car, First Nations looking for work repeatedly find the residents of nearby towns and cities opposed to their presence. Where work can be found, it is frequently unsafe or occupies the realm of low-wage employment.

Despite these evident institutional and social pressures, and the slow progress being made as labourers, First Nations individuals want to participate in the labour economy. The First Nations participation rate rebounded in 2017 compared to 2007. All the same, the First Nations participation rate for 2017 lagged 2.2 percent behind the general Indigenous rate and 3.8 percent behind the non-Indigenous rate. Compared to unemployment rates, these are not statistically substantial differences and it is impossible to conclude definitively that these gaps are the result of racism and discrimination. It is nonetheless clear that First Nations have consistently weaker labour participation rates and higher unemployment rates than other Indigenous and non-Indigenous groups.

First Nations have three primary options to combat labour exclusion. First, reserve communities can enter into alternative land management options, leading to greater local control over development projects and thus employment.[27] Second, individuals can migrate to towns and cities, seeking improved economic and other development opportunities. Third, individuals may take off-reserve employment while continuing to live in a reserve community. The last option is a key point of discussion in an age when it has become common for expanding municipalities to envelop adjacent First Nations, thereby potentially mitigating the impact of geographic separation.[28]

Nevertheless, First Nations employment largely remains concentrated within reserve public administration, where social benefit payments are the primary source of regular income. Federal transfer payments – which finance everything from schools and social services to business start-ups and social assistance – remain the primary funding source for 54.1 percent of First Nations, compared to 25.6 percent of the non-Indigenous population.[29] This is a troubling trend, given proven First Nations desire to participate in the market economy and the resources that have been dedicated to federal programs and policy overhauls.[30] That First Nations peoples constitute a willing and increasingly educated workforce but remain unemployed while the federal government encourages immigration to fill national job vacancies is yet more evidence of persistent and arguably institutionalized labour exclusion.[31]

THE IMPACT OF PRECARIOUS EMPLOYMENT

Precarious Indigenous employment is the consequence of ineffectual federal and provincial programs and policies; it is characterized by low wages, wage and cultural discrimination, and a multitude of harmful stereotypes concerning Indigenous workers. These and similar forces have led to poor work experiences, lack of promotions, and job insecurity, perpetuating a cycle that affects both individuals and families, as parents under stress negatively influence their children.

The life circumstances of children from birth to age five are particularly predictive of later outcomes, from high school performance to poverty and employment non-participation. Also influencing these outcomes are living conditions, diet, and the regularized removal of children from communities for placement in child welfare and foster care systems (i.e., the Sixties Scoop and the Millennium Scoop).[32] Trends such as these contribute to long-term poverty because entrenched lifestyles are extremely difficult to change, making it less likely that Indigenous people will be able to break into the labour market.[33]

Perhaps the most important factor in ending labour exclusion is affordable housing. The World Health Organization (WHO) has long recognized that housing has a stabilizing socioeconomic role, and has consequently classified home ownership as a social determinant of health and well-being. Housing stability can improve personal and family mobility, thereby increasing personal employment opportunities and youth educational outcomes.[34] Home ownership opportunities and housing stability are likewise closely aligned with improved health outcomes.[35]

A systematic review of the impact of social determinants on the health and well-being of Indigenous people in Alberta found close links between unemployment and health inequity, elevated risk of cardiovascular diseases, mental health challenges, and unhealthy and high-risk lifestyles, including smoking, alcohol and substance abuse, unhealthy diet, physical inactivity, and domestic violence.[36] Directly related to household income, these and similar issues can cause greater labour mobility, which has consequences for personal identity and connection to location, social and family networks, the composition of the communities from which the population is drawn and to which the population is pulled, labour skills surpluses and shortages, and social needs related to health, education, and other government services.[37]

First Nations individuals must often take available work for the sake of making a wage. The odds of a First Nations person "getting a job that matches his or her skill set – regardless of level of education – is slightly better than the odds of securing employment in the first place."[38] First Nations employees therefore often work in stressful conditions, where they feel out of place or undervalued, and where job and financial insecurity is the standard. Poorer health outcomes develop as a result, aggravated by factors such as smoking, substance abuse, physical inactivity, and poor sleep. Greater work exhaustion can also develop in environments marked by a cultural conflict between the Canadian and First Nations ways of doing things.[39] One research study's participants noted that as employees, they had to allow their identity to be subsumed to better fit organizational needs.[40] Unfortunately, only a small percentage of First Nations people rise to management positions that would enable them to facilitate positive change, to challenge racism, or to improve our appreciation of what constitutes a representative workplace.[41]

Racism and discrimination play out in unique ways. Take the history of union efforts to exclude Indigenous workers to preserve non-Indigenous worker employment. As one study concluded, "After a history of exclusion from many unionized forms of employment, it is unsurprising that many Aboriginal workers view unions as a 'white man's tool' and look to their own governments to secure their employment."[42]

A contemporary non-union example from a small city in southern Alberta is also illuminating. In lieu of hiring from within the local urban Indigenous population (approximately 15 percent of the overall population), municipal leaders sought to employ individuals from what was described as an adjacent First Nations surplus labour pool. The growing urban Indigenous population was considered ill-prepared for the rigours of wage labour, due in part to evident social pathologies.[43] More tellingly, city leaders mused that the reserve unemployed were probably more adaptable and motivated to internalize the skills that make good employees. In other words, they would accept less desirable jobs to remain employed.

These examples reveal the ongoing consequences of socially embedded attitudes. On the one hand, given the kinds of exclusion and labour precarity they face, First Nations individuals often do not believe they will be appropriately protected even if they find work, making the prospect of ongoing participation in the workforce somewhat tenuous. On the other hand, employers remain wary of taking a risk on potential Indigenous employees deemed unreliable, or ill-suited to industrial work, or insufficiently educated to successfully pursue full-time employment.

IMPROVING FIRST NATIONS EMPLOYMENT

The many problems that First Nations workers and potential workers encounter are often interrelated, so addressing them requires a comprehensive set of solutions. Confronting systemic discrimination as individuals and as members of larger ethnocultural communities, First Nations people have lower employment, socioeconomic, and political outcomes. To address these complex forces, institutional and policy strategies that improve Indigenous employment outcomes are required across a range of actors, sectors, and levels of government.

Indigenous Organization Responses
Since its inception in 1982, Canada's largest First Nations political organization, the

---

BOX 15.1 FIRST NATIONS CASINOS AS EMPLOYERS

First Nations leaders seeking to boost local economies, encourage local entrepreneurship, and create an employment base, created a gaming industry that now generates close to $400 million in net revenue at seventeen for-profit casinos, two charity casinos, and video lottery terminals operating in British Columbia, Alberta, Saskatchewan, Manitoba, Ontario, and Nova Scotia.

Casino work remains an important aspect of Indigenous employment. Saskatchewan has made the greatest strides in this regard, with Indigenous employees making up 65 percent of the casino workforce in 2017, generating more than $51 million in wages and benefits. Measuring the impact of infrastructure and program investment is difficult, but wages have an immediate impact as they are quickly spent on products and services.

Casino employment has brought its own labour relations issues. The Federation of Sovereign

Indigenous Nations (FSIN) refused to recognize that provincial laws applied to casino workers, but the Saskatchewan Court of Appeal ruled that the province retained jurisdiction over unionized employees at First Nations casinos. The court further suggested that the FSIN was engaged in a union-busting scheme, even though most of the would-be union members were themselves First Nations members.[44]

The Ontario Labour Relations Board similarly determined that the Mississauga people of Scugog Island First Nation were not permitted to establish a distinct local labour code. Unhappy with the ruling, the chief and council sought a judicial review to decide whether the Mississauga had a legal right to "enact its own labour code to govern collective bargaining in relation to a commercial undertaking that operates on reserve land." The appeal failed.[45]

Assembly of First Nations (AFN), which represents status Indians and reserve populations, has fought for First Nations economic development and improved employment. Recent efforts include a set of resolutions affirming First Nations rights to improved economic and social conditions, addressing personal and systemic barriers to First Nations labour market opportunities, and supporting access and options to secure greater economic independence.[46]

The Native Women's Association of Canada (NWAC) offers its members and partner organizations business entrepreneurship and employment training, as well as financial literacy. The Congress of Aboriginal Peoples (CAP), which represents non-status Indians and urban Indigenous people, offers help with career planning, training, labour market information, resumé preparation, job searches, and interview techniques. It also provides funding for skills training; employer wage subsidies supporting work experience; and financial assistance, business training, and professional support to enable clients to develop a business plan or start a business. Finally, the Métis National Council (MNC) focuses on generating research and facilitating programs through the Rupertsland Institute: Metis Centre of Excellence, such as the Métis Scholar Awards and the Employment Counselling Diploma.

These representative organizations have the highest national political profiles, but hundreds more operate at local, municipal, provincial, and territorial political levels, reflecting an organizational infrastructure that is actively engaged in improving Indigenous employment outcomes. Take, for example, union advocacy. As previously noted, labour unions have a tenuous historical record when it comes to their Indigenous members' interests – even if they have the capacity to challenge contemporary impacts of labour exclusion. More recently, however, several labour unions have implemented

First Nations outreach programs, which also hold promise for Indigenous employee recruitment and job retention.[47]

Policy Responses

Because multi-level policy responses are required to address First Nations labour precarity, some analysts encourage overhauling federal and provincial policies and programs to ensure greater cultural representation. But as the late labour historian Rolf Knight noted in the 1970s, it was unclear how the Department of Indian Affairs administration actually affected Indigenous participation in wage labour.[48] His remark still resonates, and many First Nations leaders share his opinion. But they have also taken the time to suggest a range of changes – from federal and provincial governments guarantees of First Nations representation at the table when policy is developed to installing labour market intermediaries who would "facilitate, inform or regulate how workers are matched to firms, how work is accomplished and how conflicts are resolved."[49]

These strategies may necessitate legislating workplace diversity and oversight provisions, improving the cultural competence of non-Indigenous employees and management, and implementing hiring incentives. Additional steps may include investing more heavily in initiatives that focus on pathways into employment, such as Indigenous co-op and internship programs. Such measures would demand less federal and provincial intervention, thereby permitting First Nations business owners, organizations, and government programmers greater freedom to pursue their respective mandates.[50]

A key theme emerging from this dialogue is the importance of identifying workplace inequities as systemic barriers to improved Indigenous employment experiences. Guaranteeing the inclusion and protection of culture in the workplace is one important measure, in part by ensuring equity in terms of both promotions and representation in management. There is a corresponding need to ensure that anti-discrimination and anti-harassment policies are implemented effectively to prevent further marginalization of Indigenous people in the workplace.[51]

When considering off-reserve concerns, public policy scholars Phillip Lashley and Rose Olfert propose that Canada abolish its historical policy of promoting First Nations urbanization in favour of initiatives that promote greater access to off-reserve employment for reserve residents. Social policy expert Michael Mendelson has suggested modifying federal policies to better meet the needs of those living off-reserve.[52]

Educational Responses

Ironically and disturbingly, in an age of recon-ciliation that seeks to repair the damages wrought by Indian residential schools, education is still often touted as an avenue to employment suc-cess in simplistic terms.[53] More to the point, the most vocal proponents of education as the solution to Indigenous employment difficulties are the state and capital – despite Indigenous people's suspicion of their motives. Reconcilia-tion efforts are helping to slowly (re)build the trust that is a vital prerequisite before First Nations will accept the conclusions of academ-ics, politicians, and business leaders regarding the rehabilitative potential of education. But things are progressing slowly.

Proponents trumpet studies linking educa-tion with improved career options, lower un-employment rates, and higher incomes, and thus continue to advocate for increased invest-ments in Indigenous education and training as the means to boost secondary and postsecond-ary completion rates.[54] The assumption is that this will lead to higher education outcomes, in turn allowing First Nations people to move beyond precarious employment and in doing so reduce poverty and improve well-being.[55] Certainly, there is evidence for this approach, as shown by studies such as economist Eric Howe's examination of the value of the Métis Training to Employment (MTE) program in improving skills sets and contributing to the economy of Alberta. As the C.D. Howe Institute reported in 2016, however, greater investment is needed to improve graduation rates specific-ally at reserve schools, which currently jeopard-ize the ability of First Nations students to avoid poverty and lower employment outcomes.[56]

Behind the seemingly positive statistical trends lie troubling trends. For example, en-ticing young people to leave their communities means that many will not return due to a lack of employment (the very reason for leaving). That trajectory damages First Nations social capital while undermining local development potential. Those who do remain often become trapped in a cycle of hypermobility between reserves and nearby towns and cities, in a constant search for transitory, extra-community employment.

COVID-19 AND INDIGENOUS EMPLOYMENT

Starting in March 2020, the COVID-19 pandemic exacted a tremendous toll on the Canadian economy. Though the effects varied across eco-nomic sectors, sizable employment declines were commonplace, and First Nations workers were often the first to be laid off. In July of that year, Statistics Canada published an overview of these trends.[57] It's impossible to disentangle First Nations data from the overall Indigenous figures, but the effect on First Nations employ-ment and financial stability can be extrapolated from previous experience. One can conclude that pre-existing vulnerabilities, such as lower incomes and higher proportions living in poverty and experiencing food insecurity, led to more severe impacts among First Nations populations.

In the immediate post-pandemic period, 36 percent of Indigenous people versus 25 percent of non-Indigenous people experienced difficulty in meeting their financial obligations, which included keeping up with mortgage payments or paying for utilities and groceries. Some 65 percent of Indigenous people reported a strong or moderate financial impact compared with 56 percent of non-Indigenous people. Of Indigenous people reporting a strong or moderate financial impact, 44 percent applied for federal income support.

In response, the federal government developed several community-based programs to help alleviate economic concerns, with the following funding commitments:

- $34.3 million for territorial businesses
- $17.3 million in support for northern air carriers
- $15 million for the Northern Business Relief Fund
- up to $306.8 million in interest-free loans to small and medium-sized Indigenous businesses
- $270 million to supplement the On-Reserve Income Assistance Program to address increased program demands, assisting individuals and families to meet their essential living expenses
- $117 million in new funding to support community-owned Indigenous businesses
- $16 million in new funding to support Indigenous tourism.[58]

All things being equal, the pandemic demonstrated just how perilous labour precarity could be for First Nations workers, who now confront even greater health and labour market challenges. The influx of federal funding was welcomed, but none of it was distinctions based.

In lay terms, this means that the various pools of funding were made available through competition for numerous projects aimed at alleviating the impact of the pandemic in First Nations, Métis, and Inuit communities, and among off-reserve and non-status bands.

The September 2020 federal throne speech did little to allay fears that First Nations labour precarity was being ignored. While highlighting the need to restore pre-pandemic employment levels by incentivizing employers to bolster their hiring practices, by closing service gaps, and by improving housing – as well as trotting out a familiar refrain promoting the ongoing promise of reconciliation – the speech disregarded the specific issue of First Nations employment precarity.[59] Nor was consideration given to new labour laws or revamped economic policies to enhance First Nations employment and employee retention.

Rather than taking the opportunity to formally acknowledge the centrality of employment stability, and in turn promote the basic policy changes that would lead to First Nations income and labour security, Canada chose a path of non-progressive and insubstantial reforms.

BENEFITING US ALL

First Nations labour exclusion remains a substantial barrier to community development and individual self-sufficiency. Notably, First Nations people do not live exclusively in reserve communities, nor are reserves located in regions suited to industrial development. Institutionalized racism and discrimination hinder labour market participation for urban Indigenous individuals, a problem that cannot be resolved without aggressive government intervention and substantial changes in social attitudes.

Non-Indigenous Canadians remain convinced that First Nations economic inertia is caused by collective and individual failure to adapt to contemporary economic realities, all the while overlooking the influence of state-imposed rules and a history of economic discrimination that frequently overwhelms First Nations individuals and institutions.

These trends persist in the wake of mounting evidence substantiating how much improving First Nations employment participation would benefit Canada economically as a whole. But researchers and First Nations leaders exploring these and comparable issues have posited several reforms.[60] Certainly, employers and government officials have been slow to embrace this potential – even if four decades of incremental change show room for optimism.

ADDITIONAL RESOURCES

Anderson, Robert M., and Robert M. Bone, eds. *Natural Resources and Indigenous Peoples*, 3rd ed. (Don Mills, ON: Captus Press, 2016).

Brown, Keith G., Mary Beth Doucette, and Janice Esther Tulk, eds. *Indigenous Business in Canada: Principles and Practices*. (Sydney: Cape Breton University Press, 2017).

Fernandez, Lynne, and Jim Silver. *Indigenous Workers and Unions: The Case of Winnipeg's CUPE 500*. (Winnipeg: Canadian Centre for Policy Alternatives, 2018).

Lamb, Danielle, and Anil Verma. "Nonstandard Employment and Indigenous Earnings Inequality in Canada." *Journal of Industrial Relations* 63, no. 5 (2021): 661–83.

MacKinnon, Shauna. *Decolonizing Employment: Aboriginal Inclusion in Canada's Labour Market*. (Winnipeg: University of Manitoba Press, 2015).

Tough, Frank. "From the 'Original Affluent Society' to the 'Unjust Society.'" *Journal of Aboriginal Economic Development* 4, no. 2 (2005): 26–65.

NOTES

1 National Collaborating Centre for Aboriginal Health (NCCAH), *Employment as a Social Determinant of First Nations, Inuit, and Métis Health* (Prince George: University of Northern British Columbia, 2017).

2 See, for example, Arnold De Silvia, "Wage Discrimination against Natives," *Canadian Public Policy* 25, no. 1 (1999): 66–84; Krishna Pendakur and Ravi Pendakur, "Aboriginal Income Disparity in Canada," *Canadian Public Policy* 37, no. 1 (2011): 61–83. This chapter focuses on the experience of First Nations people but is applicable broadly to Indigenous groups in Canada. The term *Aboriginal* in this country indicates any one of the three legally defined culture groups (Métis, Inuit, and Indian) who self-identify as such. The term *First Nations* denotes reserve communities or bands, individuals who are members of First Nations, and those who self-identify as belonging to a First Nation. The term *Indian*, as used in legislation or policy, appears in discussions about such legislation or policy. The term *Indigenous* does not represent a legal category but is used to describe descendants of groups occupying a territory at the time when other groups of different cultures or ethnic origin arrived there, groups that have preserved almost intact the customs and traditions of their ancestors similar to those characterized as Indigenous, and those who have been placed under a state structure that incorporates national, social, and cultural characteristics distinct from their own.

3 Tony Fang and Morley Gunderson, "Vulnerable Groups in Canada and Labour Market Exclusion," *International Journal of Manpower* 36, no. 6 (2015): 824–47.

4 For a good overview of these developments, see Keith G. Brown, Mary Beth Doucette, and Janice Esther Tulk, eds., *Indigenous Business in Canada: Principles and Practices* (Sydney, NS: Cape

Breton University Press, 2017); and Robert M. Anderson and Robert M. Bone, eds., *Natural Resources and Indigenous Peoples*, 3rd ed. (Don Mills, ON: Captus Press, 2016).

5   See J.R. Miller, *Skyscrapers Hide the Heavens: A History of Indian-White Relations in Canada* (Toronto: University of Toronto Press, 1989); David R. Newhouse, "Modern Aboriginal Economies: Capitalism with a Red Face," *Journal of Aboriginal Economic Development* 1, no. 2 (2000): 55–64; Martha C. Knack and Alice Littlefield, "Native American Labor: Retrieving History, Rethinking Theory," in *Native Americans and Wage Labor: Ethnohistorical Perspectives*, ed. Alice Littlefield and Martha C. Knack (Norman: University of Oklahoma Press, 1996), 3–44.

6   Richard White, *The Middle Ground: Indians, Empires and Republics in the Great Lakes Region, 1650-1815* (Cambridge: Cambridge University Press, 1991). See also Rolf Knight, *Indians at Work: An Informal History of Native Labour in British Columbia, 1848-1930* (Vancouver: New Star Books, 1996); Frank Tough, *As Their Natural Resources Fail: Native Peoples and the Economic History of Northern Manitoba, 1870-1930* (Vancouver: UBC Press, 2011); John Lutz, "After the Fur Trade: The Aboriginal Labouring Class of British Columbia, 1849-90," *Journal of the Canadian Historical Association* 87 (1992): 69–94.

7   J.R. Miller, *Compact, Contract, Covenant: Aboriginal Treaty Making in Canada* (Toronto: University of Toronto Press, 2009); Arthur J. Ray, *Indians in the Fur Trade, 1660-1870* (Toronto: University of Toronto Press, 1974).

8   In an attempt to boost attendance, the Indian Act was amended in 1920, making it compulsory for status Indian children to attend residential schools.

9   Terry Wotherspoon and Vic Satzewich, *First Nations: Race, Class and Gender Relations* (Regina: University of Regina Press, 1993).

10 Robert F. Berkhofer, *The White Man's Indian: Images of the American Indian from Columbus to the Present* (New York: Vintage, 1979); Daniel Francis, *The Imaginary Indian: The Image of the Indian in Canadian Culture* (Vancouver: Arsenal Pulp Press, 2011).

11 Alvin M. Josephy, *Now That The Buffalo's Gone* (Norman: University of Oklahoma Press, 1984); Murray L. Wax, *Native Americans: Unity and Diversity* (Englewood Cliffs, NJ: Prentice-Hall, 1971).

12 See, for example, Keith Regular, *Neighbours and Networks: The Blood Tribe and the Southern Alberta Economy* (Calgary: University of Calgary Press, 2009).

13 Harold A. Innis, *Essays in Canadian Economic History* (Toronto: University of Toronto Press, 1957); and more generally, Harold A. Innis, *The Fur Trade in Canada: An Introduction to Canadian Economic History* (Toronto: University of Toronto Press, 1999). See also Robin Jarvis Brownlie, "'Living the Same as the White People': Mohawk and Anishinabe Women's Labour in Southern Ontario, 1920-1940," *Labour/Le Travail* 61 (Spring 2008): 41–68.

14 See generally Yale D. Belanger, "Labour Unions and First Nations Casinos: An Uneasy Relationship," in *First Nations Gaming in Canada*, ed. Yale D. Belanger (Winnipeg: University of Manitoba Press, 2011), 279-301. Responsibility for Indian affairs at Confederation was vested with Secretary of the State Responsible for Indian Affairs. In 1873, the responsibility was transferred to the Department of the Interior. The Department of Indian Affairs, a branch office of the Department of the Interior, was created in 1880. It operated until 1935, when it was dissolved as a cost-cutting measure. Responsibility for Indian affairs was transferred to the Department of Mines and Resources, where a sub-department was established, the Indian Affairs Branch (IAB). Responsibility was reassigned to the Department of Immigration and Citizenship in 1950, where it remained until an independent Department of Indian Affairs and Northern Development was established in 1966.

15 Noel Dyck, *"What Is the Indian Problem"*: *Tutelage and Resistance in Canadian Indian Administration* (St. John's: Institute of Social and Economic Research, 1991).

16 Sebastien Grammond, *Identity Captured by Law: Membership in Canada's Indigenous Peoples and Linguistic Minorities* (Montreal and Kingston: McGill-Queen's University Press, 2009).

17 Harry Hawthorn, *Survey of the Contemporary Indians of Canada*, vols. 1 and 2 (Ottawa: Department of Indian Affairs and Northern Development, Indian Affairs Branch, 1966).

18 J. Rick Ponting and Roger Gibbins, *Out of Irrelevance: A Socio-Political Introduction to Indian Affairs in Canada* (Toronto: Butterworths, 1980).

19 Andrew J. Siggner, "The Socio-Demographic Conditions of Registered Indians," in *Arduous Journey: Canadian Indians and Decolonization*, ed. J. Rick Ponting (Toronto: McClelland and Stewart, 1986), 57–83.

20 Leah F. Vosko, *Temporary Work: The Gendered Rise of a Precarious Employment Relationship* (Toronto: University of Toronto Press, 2000).

21 Greigory de Peuter, "The Contested Convergence of Precarity and Labour" (PhD diss., Simon Fraser University, 2010); Leah F. Vosko, Nancy Zukewich, and Cynthia Cranford, "Precarious Jobs: A New Typology of Employment," *Perspectives* 4, no. 10 (Winter 2003): 40–42.

22 Leah F. Vosko, ed., *Precarious Employment: Understanding Labour Market Insecurity in Canada* (Montreal and Kingston: McGill-Queen's University Press, 2006).

23 Jordan Stranger-Ross, "Municipal Colonialism in Vancouver: City Planning and the Conflict over Indian Reserves, 1928–1950s," *Canadian Historical Review* 89, no. 4 (2008): 541–80.

24 Toronto Dominion Bank, *The Long and Winding Road toward Aboriginal Economic Prosperity*, Special report, June 10, 2015, https://www.td.com/document/PDF/economics/special/AboriginalEconomicProsperity.pdf.

25 National Aboriginal Economic Development Board (NAEDB), *Reconciliation: Growing Canada's Economy by $27.7 Billion*, Background and Methods Paper, November 2016, http://naedb-cndea.com/reports/naedb_report_reconciliation_27_7_billion.pdf.

26 Danielle Lamb, "Earnings Inequality among Aboriginal Groups in Canada," *Journal of Labor Research* 34 (2013): 228.

27 For an example of alternative policy strategies see Courtney Jung, "The First Nations Land Management Act: Twenty Years of Reconciliation," *American Review of Canadian Studies* 49, no. 2 (2019): 247–61.

28 Phillip Lashley and M. Rose Olfert, "Off-Reserve Employment Options for On-Reserve First Nations in Canada," *Journal of Aboriginal Economic Development* 8, no. 2 (2013): 112–27.

29 Calvin Helin, *Dances with Dependency: Out of Poverty through Self-Reliance* (Woodlands Hills, CA: Ravencrest Publishing, 2006); National Aboriginal Economic Development Board, *The Aboriginal Economic Progress Report, 2015*, http://www.naedb-cndea.com/reports/NAEDB-progress-report-june-2015.pdf.

30 See, for example, Mark Milke, *Ever Higher: Government Spending on Canada's Aboriginals since 1947* (Vancouver: Fraser Institute, 2013).

31 Canada targeted 331,000 new permanent residents for 2019. This number was set to rise to 341,000 in 2020 and reach 350,000 by 2021.

32 The World Health Organization identifies social exclusion as one of the ten key social determinants of health. It occurs through structural and historical processes that produce social inequalities, leading to enduring health and economic disparities. See Grace-Edward Galabuzi, "Social Exclusion," in *Social Determinants of Health: Canadian Perspectives*, ed. Dennis Raphael, 3rd ed. (Toronto: Canadian Scholars Press, 2016), 388–418.

33 John Loxley, *Aboriginal, Northern and Community Economic Development* (Winnipeg: Arbeiter Ring Publishing, 2010).

34   Stefanie DeLuca and Elizabeth Dayton, "Switching Social Contexts: The Effects of Housing Mobility and School Choice Programs in Youth Outcomes," *Annual Review of Psychology* 35 (2009): 457–91.

35   Stephen Hwang, Esme Fuller-Thomson, J. David Hulchanski, and Toba Bryant, *Housing and Population Health: A Review of the Literature* (Ottawa: Canada Mortgage and Housing Corporation, 1999); Gary E. Evans, Nancy M. Wells, and Annie Moch, "Housing and Mental Health: A Review of the Evidence and a Methodological and Conceptual Critique," *Journal of Social Issues* 59, no. 3 (2003): 475–500.

36   Fariba Kolahdooz, Farouz Nader, Kyoung J. Yi, and Sangita Sharma, "Understanding the Social Determinants of Health among Indigenous Canadians: Priorities for Health Promotion Policies and Actions," *Global Health Action* 8 (2015): 1–16.

37   Christopher Adams, "Job Satisfaction and Aboriginal Labour Mobility among Non-Reserve Populations," *Journal of Aboriginal Economic Development* 7, no. 1 (2010): 56. See generally Mary Jane Norris and Stewart Clathworthy, "Aboriginal Mobility and Migration within Urban Canada: Outcomes, Factors and Implications," in *Not Strangers in These Parts: Urban Aboriginal Peoples*, ed. David Newhouse and Evelyn Peters (Ottawa: Policy Research Initiative, 2003), 51–78.

38   Coryse Ciceri and Katherine Scott, "The Determinants of Employment among Aboriginal Peoples," in *Aboriginal Policy Research: Moving Forward, Making a Difference*, ed. Jerry P. White, Susan Wingert, and Dan Beavon (Toronto: Thompson Educational Publishing, 2007), 21.

39   NCCAH, *Employment as a Social Determinant*; Aimy A. Racine, "Bicultural Identity Integration at Work: Effects of Identity Conflict on Role Conflict Perceptions and Exhaustion" (MA thesis, University of Waterloo, 2016).

40   Mark Julien, Karen Sommerville, and Jennifer Brant, "Indigenous Perspectives on Work-Life Enrichment and Conflict in Canada," *Equality, Diversity and Inclusion: An International Journal* 36, no. 2 (2017): 165–81.

41   Richard J. Klyne, "Employment Barriers and Aboriginal Working Life: Towards a Representative Workplace in Saskatchewan" (MA thesis, University of Regina, 2002).

42   Suzanne Mills and Tyler McCreary, "Social Unionism, Partnership and Conflict: Union Engagement with Aboriginal Peoples in Canada," in *Rethinking the Politics of Labour in Canada*, eds. Stephanie Ross and Larry Savage (Halifax: Fernwood Publishing, 2012), 128. See also, for example, Andrew Parnaby, "'The Best Men That Ever Worked the Lumber': Aboriginal Longshoremen on Burrard Inlet, BC, 1863–1939," *Canadian Historical Review* 87, no. 1 (2006): 53–78. For examples of mid-twentieth-century battles in which Indigenous leaders engaged, see Stuart Jamieson and Percy Gladstone, "Unionism in the Fishing Industry of British Columbia, Part I," *Canadian Journal of Economics and Political Science* 16, no. 1 (February 1950): 1–11; and Stuart Jamieson and Percy Gladstone, "Unionism in the Fishing Industry of British Columbia, Part II," *Canadian Journal of Economics and Political Science* 16, no. 2 (May 1950): 146–71.

43   See Yale D. Belanger and Katherine A. Dekruyf, "Neither Citizen nor Nation: Urban Aboriginal (In)Visibility and Co-Production in a Mid-Sized Southern Alberta City," *Canadian Journal of Native Studies* 37, no. 1 (2017): 1–28; Yale D. Belanger, Katherine A. Dekruyf, and Ryan Walker, "Calgary, Canada: Policy Co-Production and Indigenous Development in Urban Settings," in *Planning Innovations for Urban Sustainability: A Global Outlook*, ed. Sebastien Darchen and Glenn Dearle (New York: Routledge, 2018), 12–25.

44   See Belanger, "Labour Unions and First Nations Casinos."

45   See Yale D. Belanger, "First Nations Gaming in Canada: Gauging Its Past and Ongoing Development," *Journal of Law and Social Policy* 30 (2018): 175–84; Yale D. Belanger, "Indigenous Workers, Casino Development, and Union

Organizing," in *Boom, Bust, and Crisis: Labour, Corporate Power and Politics in Canada*, ed. John Peters (Halifax: Fernwood Publishing, 2012), 144–62; and Belanger, "Labour Unions and First Nations Casinos." The FSIN was formerly known as the Federation of Saskatchewan Indian Nations.

46 Assembly of First Nations, "Policy Sectors – Economic," https://www.afn.ca/policy-sectors/economic/#.

47 Lynne Fernandez and Jim Silver, *Indigenous Workers and Unions: The Case of Winnipeg's CUPE 500* (Winnipeg: Canadian Centre for Policy Alternatives, 2018); Suzanne Mills and Louise Clarke, "'We Will Go Side-by-Side with You': Labour Union Engagement with Aboriginal Peoples in Canada," *Geoforum* 40, no. 6 (2009): 991–1001. For a discussion of urban Indigenous infrastructure, see David Newhouse, "The Invisible Infrastructure: Urban Aboriginal Institutions and Organizations," in *Not Strangers in These Parts: Urban Aboriginal Peoples*, eds. David Newhouse and Evelyn Peters (Ottawa: Policy Research Initiative, 2003), 243–54.

48 Knight, *Indians at Work*.

49 Quoted in Shauna Mackinnon, "Making the Case for an Aboriginal Labour Market Intermediary: A Community-Based Solution to Improve Labour Market Outcomes for Aboriginal People in Manitoba," *Manitoba Law Journal* 37, no. 2 (2013): 281.

50 NCCAH, *Employment as a Social Determinant*.

51 Shauna Mackinnon, *Decolonizing Employment: Aboriginal Inclusion in Canada's Labour Market* (Winnipeg: University of Manitoba Press, 2015); Suzanne Mills and Tyler McCreary, "Culture and Power in the Workplace: Aboriginal Women's Perspectives on Practices to Increase Aboriginal Inclusion in Forest Processing Mills," *Journal of Aboriginal Economic Development* 5, no. 1 (2006): 40–50.

52 Lashley and Olfert, "Off-Reserve Employment Options," 112–27; Michael Mendelson, *Aboriginal People in Canada's Labour Market: Work and Unemployment, Today and Tomorrow* (Ottawa: Caledon Institute of Public Policy, 2004).

53 Truth and Reconciliation Commission, *Honouring the Truth, Reconciling for the Future: Summary of the Final Report of the Truth and Reconciliation Commission of Canada* (Winnipeg: Truth and Reconciliation Commission of Canada, 2015).

54 Evelyne Bougie, Karen Kelly-Scott and Paula Arriagada, "The Education and Employment Experiences of First Nations People Living Off Reserve, Inuit, and Métis: Selected Findings from the 2012 Aboriginal Peoples Survey," Statistics Canada articles and reports, November 25, 2013, 89-653-X2013001, https://www150.statcan.gc.ca/n1/en/catalogue/89-653-X2013001.

55 See, for example, Belayet Hossain and Laura Lamb, "The Impact of Human and Social Capital on Aboriginal Employment Income in Canada," *Economic Papers: A Journal of Applied Economics and Policy* 31, no. 4 (2012): 440–50.

56 Eric Howe, *Bridging the Aboriginal Education Gap in Alberta: The Provincial Benefit Exceeds a Quarter of a Trillion Dollars* (Edmonton: University of Alberta and the Rupertsland Institute Métis Centre of Excellence, 2012); Barry Anderson and John Richards, *Students in Jeopardy: Improving Results in Band-Operated Schools* (Toronto: C.D. Howe Institute, 2016).

57 Paula Arriagada, Kristyn Frank, Tara Hahmann, and Feng Hou, *Economic Impact of COVID-19 among Indigenous People*, July 14, 2020, Cat. no. 45280001 (Ottawa: Statistics Canada, 2020), https://www150.statcan.gc.ca/n1/en/pub/45-28-0001/2020001/article/00052-eng.pdf?st=TpiRVnY9.

58 Indigenous Services Canada, "Government of Canada Announced Funding for Indigenous Communities and Organizations to Support Community-Based Responses to COVID-19 (2020)," https://www.sac-isc.gc.ca/eng/1585189335380/1585189357198.

59 Governor General of Canada, "A Stronger and More Resilient Canada," Speech from the Throne – Canada – Periodicals, 23 September, 2020, https://www.canada.ca/en/privy-council/campaigns/speech-throne/2020/speech-from-the-throne.html.

60 See Howe, *Bridging the Aboriginal Education Gap*; NAEDB, *Reconciliation*.

Part 4

BUILDING A BETTER FUTURE

16 Labour and Climate Change

John Calvert

CHAPTER SUMMARY

In Canada, as everywhere, climate change poses enormous challenges for society, the economy, the labour market, and unions. This chapter focuses on the impact of climate change on work and examines how some Canadian unions are developing policies and collective bargaining strategies that support a shift to greener jobs and a low-carbon, climate-resilient economy. Such policies include training and education initiatives, construction of net-zero energy buildings, greening our transportation infrastructure, and plans for a just transition to protect workers' livelihoods as employment becomes more climate friendly.

This chapter concludes with an assessment of the cooperative efforts of the labour movement, environmental groups, and Indigenous organizations to push for better climate policies.

KEY THEMES

This chapter will help you develop an understanding of:

- the effects of human-created greenhouse gas (GHG) emissions and probably irreversible threats to civilization as global temperatures rise
- how climate change is affecting workers and workplaces in Canada
- the policies unions have developed to respond to global warming
- union efforts to influence Canadian and international public policy to incorporate principles of social justice and environmental sustainability
- the challenges of promoting just transition polices as an integral part of Canada's response to climate change.

THE SCIENCE IS CLEAR. There is an overwhelming consensus in the scientific community that climate change poses a fundamental threat to the future of our species and the ecology of the entire planet.[1] By the early 1970s, the scientific community began to recognize that greenhouse gases (GHGs), primarily carbon and nitrogen oxide emissions, caused the earth to absorb more heat, incrementally raising global temperatures. But it was National Aeronautics and Space Administration (NASA) scientist James Hansen's testimony to the US Senate in 1988 that triggered wider public recognition of the danger of global warming and the need for political action to address it.[2] That same year, the United Nations Environment Programme (UNEP) and the World Meteorological Organization convened the Intergovernmental Panel on Climate Change (IPCC) to bring together some of the world's best scientists to carry out in-depth research on its causes and no ways to reduce its anticipated adverse effects.

Since 1990, the IPCC has released six comprehensive reports documenting an accelerating increase in global temperatures.[3] These reports include input from thousands of preeminent scientists and are subject to a rigorous peer review process. This work has been supplemented by contributions from other scientific organizations that specialize in areas such as monitoring global atmospheric temperatures, measuring ocean acidification and water temperatures, assessing changes in sea level, calculating the retreat of glaciers and polar ice, measuring droughts, and documenting the increasing number and severity of extreme weather events, such as flooding, hurricanes, and tropical storms.[4]

The conclusion is in front of us: climate change is happening and is caused by human activity. If our species does not take tough measures to slow the volume of carbon and other greenhouse gases being emitted into the atmosphere, Earth may become largely uninhabitable for most species, including our own.[5] Figure 16.1 shows the increase in global temperatures since 1880. What is notable is the sharp rise over the past forty years and a steepening upward trajectory over the past decade.

The concentration of carbon and other greenhouse gases in the atmosphere is now higher than at any time in the past 800,000 years. Global temperatures have already risen by 1.1 degrees Celsius over pre-industrial benchmarks. The IPCC projects that in the worst case scenario, average temperatures could increase to between 3.3 and 5.7 degrees by 2100 without major efforts to mitigate this rise. At the 2015 United Nations Climate Change Conference in Paris, governments from around the world agreed that the increase must be kept below 2 degrees to avoid disastrous impacts – while establishing a preferred target of less than 1.5 degrees. But they have failed to meet these targets.

FIGURE 16.1 **Climate change and global temperatures, 1880–2020**

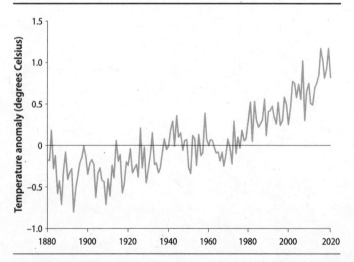

Source: National Aeronautics and Space Administration (NASA), GISS Surface Temperature Analysis, https://data.giss.nasa.gov/gistemp.

All regions of Earth will face massive disruption, but some will face particularly severe consequences more quickly. Higher average temperatures will trigger droughts, reduce food production, raise sea levels, and increase the intensity of storms. In some areas near the equator it will be simply too hot for farmers to work outdoors. Some densely populated areas of the world – including much of South and Southeast Asia, sub-Saharan Africa, Central America, and large areas of the Middle East and southern Europe – will become unlivable. This will trigger massive forced migrations triggering political, intercultural, and military conflicts. Rising sea levels will flood most coastal cities around the world. Hurricanes such as Sandy in New York and Harvey in Houston will become fiercer and more frequent, causing accelerating damage to agriculture, buildings, roads, power networks, and other critical societal infrastructure. In 2021, BC experienced an unprecedented heat wave with temperature rising to 49.6 degrees Celsius, followed later in the year by flooding that caused $9 billion in damage.

The Far North in Canada is already suffering a 2-degree increase, triggering permafrost melting and a retreat of Arctic Sea ice that is happening so quickly the Northwest Passage is already open without icebreakers.[6] These adverse effects will become increasingly widespread as global temperatures rise in the coming decades, leading to what scientists warn are likely to be irreversible *tipping points*, or climate feedback mechanisms.

There have been two broad kinds of responses to climate change. The first is **climate mitigation**, the goal of which is to limit the release of additional carbon and other GHGs into the atmosphere. This means reducing the use of coal, gas, oil, and other GHG-creating fossil fuels, and transitioning to renewable green energy such as solar, wind, geothermal, and hydro as quickly as possible. While the carbon already released will stay in the atmosphere for centuries, we can stop adding to it. Effective mitigation will require profound changes in our political, economic, and social priorities, including fundamental shifts in what and how we produce and consume. Not least, it will require transformations in how we work.

The second response to global warming is **climate adaptation**. As temperatures increase and weather events such as hurricanes, floods, and fires become more damaging, we will have to shelter ourselves. Among other things, this will mean protecting coastal communities from rising sea levels, implementing flood protection in low-lying cities, and strengthening the ability to deal with wildfires. It will also mean retrofitting infrastructure to deal with more extreme weather. And it will mean making new investments in health care to combat increases in infectious diseases.

There is a clear link between COVID-19, future pandemics, and climate change. As temperatures increase, opportunities emerge for pathogens to develop and spread, particularly among vulnerable populations. The rising temperature also shifts the range of insects and wildlife that host viruses and zoonotic diseases to new areas of the globe. Additionally, climate change has undermined the capacity of millions of people to respond to the pandemic due to weakened immune systems, a problem exacerbated by the unequal impacts of climate change within countries and globally. By undermining the resilience of populations, climate change has increased the ability of COVID-19 to spread among populations whose health it has compromised.

The federal government acknowledges the seriousness of the climate challenge. With the notable exception of the Stephen Harper government (2006–15) – which abandoned earlier climate commitments, withdrawing from the 1997 UN-sponsored **Kyoto Protocol** – Canada has at least officially been a strong supporter of international climate action. It participated in the 1992 United Nations Framework Convention on Climate Change that was ratified in Kyoto in 1997, supported the 2015 Paris Agreement, and followed this with commitments at the 2018 Conference of the Parties to the United Nations Framework Convention on Climate Change (COP 24) in Poland and the 2021 COP 26 in Glasgow.[7] The Canadian government also formulated domestic policies to implement internationally agreed climate targets, and in 2017 it released the "Pan-Canadian Framework on Clean Growth and Climate Change," which committed the country to a 30 percent reduction in GHG emissions by 2030 compared with 2005 levels.[8] In 2021, it increased this further to between 40 and 45 percent by 2030.

Nevertheless, there is an enormous gap between Canada's official policy goals and the mechanisms to implement them. Policies such as a modest carbon tax, stronger energy efficiency standards, subsidies for renewable energy, and support for provinces taking comparable actions fail to address the magnitude of the crisis.[9] Recent data indicates that Canada's emissions remained almost unchanged from 2000 to 2019 despite the various international commitments Ottawa has made. Figure 16.2 shows Canada's total release of carbon dioxide into the atmosphere in recent years measured in megatonnes (Mt). A megatonne is one million metric tons. The graph highlights the lack of real progress and reflects the failure of federal and provincial governments to implement effective policies.

GOVERNMENT CLIMATE POLICY

Environmentalists and scientists point to the contradictions inherent in federal policy. While committing to reducing GHGs, the federal government, along with several provinces, remains determined to support the continued expansion of fossil fuel production. It purchased the Kinder Morgan Trans Mountain bitumen oil pipeline for $4.5 billion and is spending another $17 billion – possibly much more - on its expansion to facilitate tar sands oil exports. And it continues to subsidize the industry through major tax breaks.

Meanwhile Alberta remains committed to increasing production of bitumen oil – the heaviest, dirtiest crude oil – investing $1.5 billion in TC Energy Corporation's Keystone XL Pipeline along with an additional $6 billion loan guarantee to the company.[10] In British Columbia, as part of a new $40 billion investment plan, transnational energy corporations are building gas pipelines and massive liquid natural gas (LNG) terminals on Indigenous lands to handle exports mainly to Asia.

These business-as-usual policies raise important questions about how serious governments in Canada are about achieving the country's agreed climate targets. What is clear is that Canada will have to do much, much more if it is to meet its international climate commitments.[11]

FIGURE 16.2 **Greenhouse gas emissions, 1990–2017**

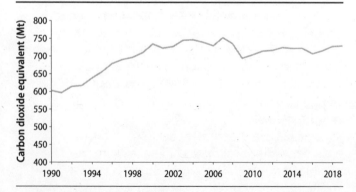

Source: Environment Canada, *National Inventory Report 1990–2019: Greenhouse Gas Sources and Sinks in Canada,* https://publications.gc.ca/site/eng/9.506002/publication.html.

While no country is perfect in the way it attempts to address climate change, Canada has a great deal to learn from how other governments have implemented polices to facilitate a just transition from carbon-intensive industries to greener forms of production. The United Nations Framework Convention on Climate Change (UNFCCC) has incorporated just transition as one of its core principles for restructuring the global economy. Its goal is to ensure that the transition to a low-carbon economy is handled fairly, and that workers and their communities don't bear an unreasonable burden in fulfilling society's efforts to address climate change. This means adopting a range of policy measures to provide workers with retraining, income support during the transition, and opportunities for new employment in low-carbon industries and services. The UNFCCC has carried out extensive research on the experience of its member countries with a view to identifying best practices and successful pathways to reducing the global carbon footprint.

In 2010, the European Union launched a program entitled Build Up Skills, whose purpose was to document existing workforce skills and develop a roadmap for the new competencies needed to implement the transition to a low-carbon economy. It provided financing to each of its member countries to carry out this analysis. The program identified areas of the future economy in which new or enhanced skills would be required, and outlined what countries needed to do to prepare their respective workforces. This has been followed by commitments by EU members to fill the training gaps. The initiative reflects an understanding that governments will have to plan the transition and put appropriate policies in place to ensure it succeeds.

Individual EU member countries have also undertaken just transition initiatives, as documented in a major study by Bela Galgóczi of the European Trade Union Institute.[12] Over the past two decades, for example, Germany has implemented a comprehensive plan to phase out heavy industry and coal production in the Ruhr Valley in extensive dialogue with workers, unions, companies, local governments, and affected communities.

The plan has provided alternative employment opportunities, training, and labour adjustment measures to facilitate an incremental, socially responsible shift to a low-carbon economy. The area has been transformed from dependence on traditional, energy-intensive manufacturing industries to a hub for advanced education, high-technology research, and low-carbon manufacturing and service enterprises. The development of a long-range just transition plan involving all stakeholders has been key to the region's green transformation, and the Ruhr provides an excellent example of what is possible.[13]

CLIMATE CHANGE AND THE ORGANIZATION OF WORK

As the UN Intergovernmental Panel on Climate Change stresses, both mitigation and adaptation will require substantial social and economic changes, particularly in production processes. Transforming what we produce, and how we produce and transport it, is key to lowering GHG emissions because production processes have huge carbon footprints.[14]

A central component is eliminating reliance on fossil fuels. This will be particularly challenging for Canada, given the primary role of coal, oil, and gas production in the economy and the amount of fuel used to transport people and goods within this vast country. But shifting to renewable energy sources will not be enough. We must implement sweeping energy conservation measures throughout the economy.

The consequences for workers will be significant, disrupting communities, regions, and entire provinces dependent on fossil fuel production and use. The transformation will mean adopting new technologies and developing new workforce skills. Energy production must refocus extremely quickly on wind, hydro, solar, and other renewables. Workplaces must become far more energy efficient, and incorporating the goal of net-zero energy use will compel many businesses to minimize and gradually eliminate the use of fossil fuels. Similarly, a dramatic reduction in the energy used to transport goods and people is required.

In sum, as the International Labour Organization (ILO) notes, the transformation to a low-carbon economy involves fundamental changes in what we produce and how we produce it.[15] Managing this will be Canada's great challenge throughout the twenty-first century, and the reorganization of work and workplaces is fundamental to reducing the national carbon footprint. Regardless of the kinds of work people perform, every workplace can contribute to that goal. All components of the economy – and all members of the workforce – will have to contribute if we are to succeed.

Not all workplaces or regions will be equally affected by climate change. Of course, the fossil fuel extraction sector, particularly in Alberta, Saskatchewan, British Columbia, and Newfoundland and Labrador, will see employment decline as the economy turns to renewable sources of energy. Nonetheless, many trades' skills are transferable to other kinds of construction work. Renovating the entire national building stock in the coming years to meet aggressive energy reduction targets will give a big boost to employment.

Jobs in manufacturing will continue to move away from resource-intensive processes to focus on more energy-efficient, technologically sophisticated modes of production. The shift from traditional car assembly to building electric vehicles is already underway, for example, and more investment will also flow to public transportation systems.

As the COVID-19 pandemic has demonstrated, working from home will become much more prevalent in a variety of industries and in parts of the public sector where face-to-face interaction is not essential or is needed only intermittently. This will have a significant impact on workplaces, reducing office space and commuting.

At the same time, there will be a growing need for employment in areas such as long-term care, home care, childcare, and other public services that require personal contact and cannot be readily replaced by technology. The extent to which jobs in these sectors have career paths and employment security will depend on the willingness of governments to treat them as services essential to a decent society. Equally important are the abilities of unions to negotiate such arrangements. Considering the pattern of neoliberal outsourcing that provincial and federal governments have adopted in recent years, there's no guarantee either of these will happen. Ensuring that the workers who provide these important services have decent employment conditions will be a significant component of a just transition.

Several key questions arise: How can Canadian workers have a meaningful voice in shaping the transformation? How can we enlist the extensive skills and intelligence of the people who produce goods and services to achieve our climate objectives? How can workers, with their multifaceted practical knowledge of production processes, make production greener?

This is where trade unions can play a crucial role.[16] Unions provide a formal structure through which workers can participate in implementing climate change initiatives. Because they are certified in law to represent workers, unions give employees a voice in shaping their terms and conditions of work. Thus they offer an institutional channel through which workers can contribute their valuable knowledge, skills, and expertise in greening their work and their workplaces.

Typically, employers decide what goods and services to produce and how to produce them, but unions believe it's necessary to expand the scope of collective bargaining to allow workers to participate in reorganizing the production process in order to lower the climate footprint of their workplaces. Many unions are working to lower the carbon emissions of the industries and workplaces in which their members are employed, and some have established policies to guide their members' climate activities at the workplace, including policies they believe employers and governments should adopt.[17]

Various unions have also pushed to include climate change provisions in their collective agreements. The research initiative Adapting Canadian Work and Workplaces to Climate Change (ACW) has an extensive database of contract provisions dealing with climate change for unions to draw on. Some agreements identify a specific initiative, such as implementing an energy audit of a particular workplace. More frequently, unions try to establish joint union–employer committees with a mandate to explore ways to reduce the climate footprint of the workplace. The success of these joint committees of course depends on the creativity and strength of the union and the willingness of the employer to implement their proposals.

At the same time, many in the labour movement want to ensure that making the transition to a low-carbon economy avoids causing enormous disruption to the lives and livelihoods of workers and the communities where they live.[18] Unions are helping to achieve Canada's climate change objectives in the following ways:

- promoting climate literacy among their members, both at the workplace and in the broader community
- negotiating climate change policies into collective agreements
- raising the profile of climate issues in the industries in which their members work, including identifying ways to lower the carbon footprints of production processes
- developing policies and programs that promote a just transition
- joining with environmental, First Nations, and social justice organizations to support climate policies locally, nationally, and internationally, including pressuring governments at all levels to take stronger action.

While many unions are evidently committed to addressing climate change, some have been reluctant to engage constructively with this issue. And some are deeply conflicted, trying to balance the desire of their membership to continue high-paying jobs in the resource sector with national commitments to cut reliance on fossil fuel production.

This tension is most apparent in the construction sector. Canada's Building Trades Unions (CBTU), a federation representing most unionized construction trades workers in the country, has been an advocate of new pipelines, liquid natural gas plants, oil sands facilities, and other fossil fuel projects as well as an expansion of nuclear energy. A significant part of some of its members' future incomes depends on energy production and related transportation infrastructure. While some skills can be transferred to renewable projects, others are dedicated to functions such as pipeline construction or heavy equipment operation in the tar sands.

In the absence of government policies to provide well-paid alternative employment,

BOX 16.1 UNIONS AND CLIMATE BARGAINING

The Canadian Union of Postal Workers (CUPW) represents rural and urban workers who process and deliver mail and parcels across Canada. Its employer, Canada Post, has 60,000 workers and operates the largest fleet of vehicles in the country. CUPW believes that shifting away from fossil fuels can significantly reduce the company's carbon footprint, arguing that as a Crown corporation Canada Post should take the lead in adopting electric vehicles. In support of its demand, CUPW has carried out extensive research on what other postal services have done internationally to adopt electric vehicles. CUPW has included this research in its package of climate change initiatives at the bargaining table.

The union has also identified how Canada Post can use its numerous rural post offices to incorporate electric vehicle charging stations in areas where distance and geography have created major gaps in access to charging outlets. While charging stations are proliferating in densely populated urban areas, rural communities have a significant shortage that Canada Post is uniquely able to fill. Incorporating charging stations would advance electrification of the company's own fleet operations while helping to facilitate the transition to electric vehicles in rural communities.

Including climate issues in bargaining gives unionized workers and employers the opportunity to discuss how they can work together to meet climate objectives. It stimulates discussion within the workplace – and within the union's membership – about the concrete ways in which members can advance climate goals, given their skills, knowledge, and detailed understanding of the work they do. Participation in **climate bargaining** can also play a role in membership education because details of the proposals are worked out, debated, and ratified at membership meetings.

some unions have questioned the urgency of reducing the country's carbon footprint if it threatens their members' jobs, a position that has been encouraged by their employers and provincial governments. In Alberta, the Conservative government has promoted pipeline construction, for example, and in British Columbia, the NDP government has promoted major investments in liquid natural gas processing plants. Unions have also been influenced by arguments that Canada should not be penalized for continuing to produce fossil fuels when other countries fail to curb theirs and when Canadian production is less environmentally damaging than foreign.

Some construction unions have also been at odds with environmentalists and First Nations, specifically over the Site C dam on the Peace River in British Columbia. Started by the previous provincial Liberal government and continued by the NDP, this massive project has been criticized for its damaging environmental impact in a region already heavily impacted by major dams. The current government and construction unions strongly support the project, believing that it will produce high-quality renewable hydroelectricity as well as high-paying jobs for their members. Other unions, particularly in the public sector, question the necessity of another dam given the environmental impact.

At the same time, construction unions also represent workers who will benefit from progressive environmental policies. Interestingly, the CBTU funded a major study in 2017 examining employment opportunities associated with greening the national economy. *Jobs for Tomorrow: Canada's Building Trades and Zero Emissions* estimated that by 2050, over a million construction jobs will be generated in new solar, wind, and geothermal energy projects if Canada is to meet its climate goals. Just under 2 million more will be created in the process of retrofitting commercial, industrial, and institutional building stock. And another 250,000 jobs will be needed to construct new public transit and high-speed rail systems.[19]

More recently, the CBTU has embarked on an initiative to promote climate literacy in the apprenticeship and training programs in the construction trades, reflecting an appreciation of the essential role of the skilled trades in addressing climate change. It also recognizes that we are moving toward a net-zero economy. The fact that the federation has promoted these climate initiatives underscores the complex and sometimes contradictory position on climate change that unions take when the various components of their membership are affected in quite different ways by climate policies.

Consequently, while the mainstream labour movement – as represented by the Canadian Labour Congress (CLC) – clearly supports tough policies to address the climate crisis and is determined to identify ways to move toward a zero-carbon economy, it still faces challenges in obtaining consensus on climate issues from unions. While the overall approach of the labour movement has been increasingly supportive of robust climate measures, the varying perspectives of its members reflect those of the broader Canadian public.

UNION EDUCATION PROGRAMS

The goal of climate literacy as an essential first step in motivating workers to act at the workplace and in the community is widely accepted by national union leadership and provincial and local union activists. Union climate education builds on a history of union training on collective bargaining, labour law, health and safety, communications, community advocacy, public policy, and other issues of concern to members. It reflects both growing awareness of the climate crisis among organized workers and the adoption of increasingly detailed union

climate policies. Much of this educational material encourages members to raise climate issues at the workplace and in the community, stressing the urgency of the issue and laying the foundation for climate change demands at the bargaining table. It also promotes links with numerous environmental groups across Canada.

Unions have also been working with the academic community to carry out research and advocacy on climate issues. Funded by the Social Science and Humanities Research Council, Adapting Canadian Work and Workplaces to Respond to Climate Change has brought together the Canadian Labour Congress, most major national unions, provincial federations of labour, and various labour councils with the academic community to build a solid research network for climate crisis initiatives. In cooperation with these labour organizations, ACW has built a database of collective agreement provisions on climate issues for the use of union locals in bargaining with their employers. It has also established a monthly newsletter summarizing climate change developments in Canada and internationally.

BUILDING SOCIAL JUSTICE INTO CLIMATE POLICIES

Unions represent workers producing fossil fuels and workers in a wide range of energy-intensive manufacturing industries, such as cement, steel, plastics, automobiles, and beverages. Many of these workers are concerned that they will lose their jobs as Canada shifts away from carbon-intensive energy production and manufacturing. Will they find new jobs with comparable wages and benefits? Or will they end up in precarious, low-wage jobs or unemployed?

Unions believe that all levels of governments must manage the transition and adopt policies to support workers in these sunset industries. Too often, governments have failed to provide adequate financial assistance, retraining, or other measures, leaving workers, their families, and in some cases whole communities to bear the brunt of plant closures and industry downsizing on their own and at enormous cost.

Recent government initiatives to green the economy show a similar lack of concern for workers. For example, British Columbia and Ontario have heavily subsidized the development of new hydro, wind, and solar electricity as part of extensively publicized climate change programs. But government policy has focused on awarding lucrative contracts to private power corporations while ignoring the contribution that existing publicly owned Crown corporations can make. Private firms are overwhelmingly non-union and offer wages, working conditions, and job security substantially inferior to publicly owned utilities, which could produce the same energy just as efficiently were it not for political bias in favour of private corporations.

Governments have also failed to ensure that private power companies receiving public contracts offer their jobs to First Nations and racialized workers, youth, and women, and to members of the communities where such projects are located.[22] Unions believe these and other recent examples of flawed policies underscore the need for a broader, more equitable, and fairer approach to transitioning to a low-carbon economy.

In 2018, the Canadian Labour Congress persuaded the federal government to establish the Just Transition Task Force for Canadian Coal Power Workers and Communities. This brought together provincial and federal officials, employers, environmentalists, finance specialists, and unions to develop strategies to move Canada out of coal-fired electricity generation.[23] The task force adopted a definition of just transition that reflects much of labour's perspective:

> A just transition is an approach to economic and environmental policy that aims to minimize the impact on workers and communities in the transition to a low-carbon economy. This approach includes involving workers and their communities in decisions that would affect their livelihoods, identifying and supporting economic opportunities for the future, and helping workers and communities to succeed and benefit from the transition.[24]

While the focus of the task force was a single industry, the CLC believes that it provides a model for a much wider approach. More recently, Canadian unions have endorsed the concept of a Green New Deal, an idea put forward by a coalition of union and climate activists in the United States to re-industrialize by investing in a comprehensive program to support green industries. The CLC sees many of its proposals as relevant to Canada.

The concept of a just transition is to ensure that climate policies integrate social, employment, and community components into a strategy to achieve a low-carbon economy. Unions argue that employers and governments must manage the transition to a low-carbon economy in a way that avoids victimizing workers and their communities.[25] In the words of former CLC president Hassan Yussuff, "Just Transition helps to put people at the heart of climate action, allowing us to be ambitious in meeting our climate commitments."[26] The concept is also key to garnering wide support for progressive climate policies. Since mitigating global warm-

ing will benefit everyone, all Canadians – and particularly the more affluent – should share in the costs, and if workers and their communities believe that they will be treated fairly, they are far more likely to support the transition.[27]

The COVID-19 pandemic has revealed the importance of incorporating public health strategies into a just transition as well. One of the most striking features of the pandemic has been its disproportionate effect on vulnerable workers. In key sectors of the economy, such as health care, food processing, grocery retailing, community social services, and public transit, workers performing essential services have suffered the greatest exposure to the virus.

The incidence of workers contracting COVID-19 in meat-processing plants, for example, has been shockingly high. Similarly, care aides and nurses in long-term care facilities have had a much higher rate of mortality than the general population. Workers in food stores, which have had to remain open even when governments locked down other areas of the economy, have also been particularly hard hit. This experience underlines the importance of measures such as adequate sick leave and safer working conditions to address health risks in economic recovery and transition plans (Chapter 1).

UNION PARTICIPATION IN INTERNATIONAL CLIMATE EFFORTS

Canadian unions have been active participants in global efforts to establish and monitor climate targets. Much of this work has been carried out in cooperation with environmental organizations and international union federations.

A key effort has been to encourage governments to adopt the "Solidarity and Just Transition: Silesia Declaration" formulated at the Conference of the Parties (COP) 24 climate forum in 2018.[28] The declaration was the result of an international union campaign to incorporate

BOX 16.3 CANADIAN UNION PARTICIPATION IN CLIMATE CONFERENCES

1992 United Nations Conference on Environment and Development (UNCED), also known as the Earth Summit, Rio de Janeiro, Brazil

1997 World Conference on Environmental Services, organized by International Conference on Emergency Medicine (ICEM)

1997 International Trade Union Confederation (ITUC) raises issue of just transition at the Kyoto Conference (COP 3), Japan

2002 World Summit on Sustainable Development, Johannesburg, South Africa

2006 Trade Union Assembly on Labour and the Environment, Nairobi, Kenya, organized with the International Labour Organization (ILO) and United Nations Environment Programme (UNEP)

2008 United Nations Climate Change Conference (COP 14), Poznań, Poland

2010 ITUC highlights just transition at United Nations Climate Change Conference (COP 16), Cancún, Mexico

2012 ITUC highlights just transition in final statement of the United Nations Conference on Environment and Development (UNCED), also known as the Earth Summit, Rio de Janeiro, Brazil

2013 ILO Conference on Just Transition and Green Jobs

2014 ITUC 3rd World Congress

2015 Paris Climate Conference (COP 21), France

2018 Katowice Climate Change Conference (COP 24), Poland

2019 Madrid Climate Change Conference (COP 25)

2021 Glasgow Climate Conference (COP 26)

just transition principles in United Nations climate policy recommendations. It emphasizes involving workers and communities in transition strategies, creating decent work, linking change to the seventeen UN Sustainable Development Goals, and encouraging developing countries, in particular, to adopt policies to create high-quality, climate-resilient jobs.

A GREEN NETWORK

The CLC has established extensive links with the Canadian and global environmental movement, jointly promoting climate change policies. Internationally, it works closely with the Climate Action Network, a group of 1,200 NGOs from around the world committed to promoting ambitious climate policies in their own countries and globally.

Along with environmental NGOs, social justice organizations, faith groups, and First Nations, the CLC has also formed the Green Economy Network (GEN), which published a founding set of principles based on working together to address climate issues. In a detailed position paper, the GEN noted Canada's lack of progress in meeting climate objectives and criticized the country's continuing promotion of fossil fuel production.[29]

The document identified three priorities for building a green economy: developing a renewable energy strategy, improving the energy efficiency of buildings, and expanding public transit. It argued for a carbon tax that would be increased over time to $200 per tonne. The strategy proposed that the federal government spend $46.5 billion over ten years on wind, solar, geothermal, and tidal renewable energy projects, financed by removing existing subsidies to the fossil fuel industry. This would create 58,000 new jobs while providing training and employment opportunities for First Nations and local communities.

In the building sector, the GEN proposed retrofitting 40 percent of Canadian homes by 2025 to achieve a 30 percent energy saving, and establishing more stringent building energy standards to achieve net-zero energy use. The proposed $50 billion in investment over the decade would generate 730,000 person-years of employment in construction and related supply industries. In the transportation sector, which accounted for 28 percent of Canada's GHG emissions in 2012, it proposed a $53 billion investment in public transit and an additional $26 billion for a high-speed rail network on the Montreal–Windsor and Edmonton–Calgary transportation corridors to generate an additional 136,000 person-years of employment.

In 2016, the coalition released another major plan advocating for the creation of a million green jobs over the next decade. The plan, promoted by David Suzuki, Canada's best-known environmental activist, outlined how these jobs could be funded and set out the steps to put this agenda into place.[30]

A DEMOCRATIC APPROACH TO THE CLIMATE EMERGENCY

Canadian trade union movement policies and leadership have signalled a strong commitment to major economic restructuring, based on the view that climate change is caused by human activity and that its effects will be devastating if tough measures are not taken quickly to mitigate and adapt to its effects.

Unions have taken significant steps in support of such measures, internally through membership education, at the workplace through collective bargaining, in the industries where their members are employed, and in the broader public policy arena. They promote the need for a just transition to ensure that the shift to a low-carbon economy is managed in a way that shares the burdens fairly.

This means fundamental changes to the work we do and the workplaces in which we do it. Workers possess enormous knowledge and skills about ways to lower the carbon footprint of their jobs, and they should be full partners in the process of change. This is a perfectly reasonable objective in a democratic society. As organizations that represent workers, unions have considerable capacity to facilitate this participatory and democratic process. The challenge for Canadian governments at all levels is to provide the appropriate policies and resources.

ADDITIONAL RESOURCES

Adapting Work and Workplaces to Respond to Climate Change, https://yorkspace.library.yorku.ca/xmlui/handle/10315/38593. The website contains a large collection of recent papers and studies on labour and climate change and is a significant resource for those interested in pursuing this issue in more depth.

Brecher, Jeremy. *Climate Solidarity: Workers vs. Warming*. West Cornwall, CT: Labor Network for Sustainability and Stone Soup Books, 2017.

Steering Committee of the Green Economy Network. "Making the Shift to a Green Economy: A Common Platform of the Green Economy Network," May 2011, https://digital.library.yorku.ca/yul-1121979/making-shift-green-economy-common-platform-green-economy-network.

McKibben, Bill. *Falter: Has the Human Game Begun to Play Itself Out?* New York: Henry Holt and Company, 2019.

Trade Unions for Energy Democracy. *Trade Unions and Just Transition: The Search for a Transformative Politics.* New York: City University of New York, 2018.

NOTES

1. Intergovernmental Panel on Climate Change (IPCC), AR6 *Synthesis Report: Climate Change. Contribution of Working Groups I, II and III to the Sixth Assessment Report of the Intergovernmental Panel on Climate Change* (Geneva: IPCC, 2022), https://www.ipcc.ch/report/sixth-assessment-report-cycle/ ; World Bank, *Turn Down the Heat: Confronting the New Climate Normal* (Washington, DC: Word Bank, 2014); National Aeronautics and Space Administration (NASA), Global Climate Change, Vital Signs of the Planet, Facts, "Climate Change: How Do We Know?" https://climate.nasa.gov/evidence; US Geological Service (USGS), FAQs, "Why Is Climate Change Happening and What Are the Causes?" https://www.usgs.gov/faqs/why-climate-change-happening-and-what-are-causes-1?qt-news_science_products=0#qt- ews_science_products.

2. US Senate Committee on Energy and Natural Resources, "Statement of James Hansen," Washington, DC, June 23, 1988, https://www.sealevel.info/1988_Hansen_Senate_Testimony.html.

3. Intergovernmental Panel on Climate Change (IPCC), Climate Change 2022: Mitigation of Climate Change (Geneva: World Meteorological Association, 2022), https://www.ipcc.ch/report/sixth-assessment-report-working-group-3/.

4. NASA, "Climate Change."

5. Rodney White, *Climate Change in Canada* (Oxford University Press, 2010).

6. Elizabeth Bush and Donald S. Lemmen, eds., *Canada's Changing Climate Report* (Ottawa: Minister of Environment and Climate Change, 2019). This study also contains a good explanation of climate science and links to numerous resources on various climate change issues. It is an ideal resource for students interested in finding out more about the issue, along with Rodney White's *Climate Change in Canada.*

7. United Nations Climate Change, Process and Meetings, The Kyoto Protocol, "What Is the Kyoto Protocol?" https://unfccc.int/kyoto_ protocol. On October 5, 2016, Canada ratified the Paris Agreement.

8. Canada, Environment and Natural Resources, "Canada's Priorities on Climate Change," modified January 27, 2020, https://www.canada.ca/en/environment-climate-change/services/climate-change/canada-priorities.html; and "Pan-Canadian Framework on Clean Growth and Climate Change," modified December 16, 2021, https://www.canada.ca/en/services/environment/weather/climatechange/pan-canadian-framework.html.

9. Green Economy Network, *Assessing the Federal Government's Actions on Climate Change* (Ottawa: Green Economy Network, 2017).

10. The decision by US president Joe Biden to cancel the project has left Alberta taxpayers on the hook for all the money Premier Jason Kenney foolishly invested in the project.

11. Climate Action Network, "Canadian Climate Accountability: A Letter to PM Trudeau and Minister McKenna from 33 CAN-Rac members, December 3, 2018," https://climateactionnetwork.ca/wp-content/uploads/2018/12/PanCanadian Accountability_FINAL.pdf.

12. Bela Galgóczi, "The Long and Winding Road from Black to Green: Decades of Structural Changes in the Ruhr Region," *International Journal of Labour Research* 6, no. 2 (2014): 217–40.

13. Bela Galgóczi, "Just Transitions Towards Environmentally Sustainable Economies and Societies for All. (Geneva: International Labour Office), 2018. https://www.ilo.org/global/topics/green-jobs/publications/WCMS_432859/lang–en/index.htm.

14. York University, Adapting Work and Workplaces to Climate Change (ACW), https://yorkspace.library.yorku.ca/xmlui/handle/10315/38593.

15. Olga Strietska-Ilina, Christine Hofmann, Mercedes Durán Haro, and Shinyoung Jeon, *Skills for Green Jobs: A Global View* (Geneva: International Labour Office, 2011), https://www.ilo.org/wcmsp5/groups/public/–dgreports/

—dcomm/—publ/documents/publication/wcms_159585.pdf.

16 Many workers are not organized, however, for reasons discussed in chapters 4 and 7. Consequently, they do not have comparable mechanisms to voice their collective views and concerns, and without an organization to represent them it is extremely difficult for them to participate in shaping workplace decisions.

17 Carla Lipsig-Mumme, Donald Lafleur and Geoff Bickerton, "Climate Change and Canadian Unions: The Dilemma for Labour, Work in a Warming World," Working Paper no. 2013–02, York University, Toronto, 2013 https://yorkspace.library.yorku.ca/xmlui/bitstream/handle/10315/39351/WP_2013-02_Lipsig-Mumme_Lafleur_Bickerton_Climate-Change-Canadian-Unions.pdf?sequence=1&isAllowed=y; Canadian Labour Congress, Unititled letter to Prime Minister Harper on climate change, Ottawa, November 17, 2015, https://canadianlabour.ca/news-news-archive-letter-former-prime-minister-harper-just-transition.

18 Trade Unions For Energy Democracy (TUED), "Trade Unions and Just Transition: The Search for a Transformative Politics," Working Paper no. 11, in cooperation with the Rosa Luxemburg Stiftung and Murphy Institute at CUNY, New York, April 2018, https://rosalux.nyc/wp-content/uploads/2021/09/tuedworkingpaper11_web.pdf.

19 Tyee Bridge and Richard Gilbert, *Jobs for Tomorrow: Canada's Building Trades and Net Zero Emissions*, July 2017, revised October 2017 (Vancouver: Columbia Institute, 2017), https://columbiainstitute.eco/wp-content/uploads/2017/09/Columbia-Jobs-for-Tomorrow-web-revised-Oct-26-2017-dft-1.pdf.

20 John Calvert and Corinne Tallon, "The Union as Climate Change Advocate: The BC Insulator's Campaign to 'Green' the Culture of the Building Industry in BC," Paper delivered to International Labour Process Conference, Berlin, April 2016, https://digital.library.yorku.ca.

21 Corinne Tallon and John Calvert, "Promoting Climate Literacy in British Columbia's Apprenticeship System: Evaluating One Union's Efforts to Overcome Attitudinal Barriers to Low Carbon Construction," Adapting Work and Workplaces to Climate Change, Working paper no. 201, Prepared for the International Labour Process Conference, Sheffield, UK, April 4–6, 2017.

22 John Calvert, *Liquid Gold: Energy Privatization in British Columbia* (Halifax: Fernwood Publishing, 2007).

23 Task Force on Just Transition for Canadian Coal Power Workers and Communities, *Final Report*, December 2018 (Gatineau: Environment and Climate Change Canada, 2019), https://www.canada.ca/en/environment-climate-change/services/climate-change/task-force-just-transition/final-report.html.

24 Environment and Climate Change Canada, Just Transition Task Force, "Backgrounder," modified February 18, 2018, https://www.canada.ca/en/environment-climate-change/news/2018/02/just_transition_taskforce.html.

25 UN Framework on Climate Change, "Just Transition of the Workforce and the Creation of Decent Work and Quality Jobs," Technical Paper, April 21, 2020, https://unfccc.int/sites/default/files/resource/Just%20transition_for%20posting.pdf.

26 Canadian Labour Congress, "Unions Call for Just Transition," April 22, 2019, https://canadianlabour.ca/canadas-unions-call-for-just-transition-and-ambitious-climate-action-this-earth-day/.

27 Hadrian Mertins-Kirkwood, *Making Decarbonization Work for Workers: Policies for a Just Transition to a Zero-Carbon Economy in Canada* (Ottawa: Adapting Work and Workplaces to Climate Change and Canadian Centre for Policy Alternatives, 2018); Hadrian Mertins-Kirkwood, Roadmap to a Canadian Just Transition Act. (Ottawa: Adapting Work and Workplaces to Climate Change and Canadian Centre for Policy Alternatives, 2021).

28 United Nations Climate Change Conference, "Solidarity and Just Transition: Silesia Declaration," COP24, Katowice, Poland, 2018.

29 Steering Committee of the Green Economy Network, "Making the Shift to a Green Economy: A Common Platform of the Green Economy Network," May 2011, https://digital.library.yorku.ca/yul-1121979/making-shift-green-economy-common-platform-green-economy-network.

30 The coalition members are as follows: Amalgamated Transit Union Canada, Canadian Federation of Students, Canadian Labour Congress, Canadian Union of Postal Workers, Canadian Youth Coalition, Climate Action Network, Columbia Institute, Council of Canadians, David Suzuki Foundation, Greenpeace, Kairos, International Union of Machinists and Aerospace Workers, National Union of Public and General Employees, Ontario Federation of Labour, Ontario Secondary School Teachers Federation, Pembina Institute, Polaris Institute, Public Service Alliance of Canada, Service Employees International Union, Sierra Club of Canada, Toronto and York Regional Labour Council, Unifor, and the United Steel Workers.

17 Organizing for Better Work

Don Wells

CHAPTER SUMMARY

Over the past twenty years or so, unions, workers, and their allies across Canada have been employing new tactics to improve work and public policy. This chapter introduces these efforts and explains their potential. It explores four kinds of organizing models challenging low-wage work and improving workers' rights and public services. It also explains key ideas and strategies behind these initiatives.

In examining these alt-labour (alternative labour) efforts, this chapter paints a picture of significant promise in Canada's new economic and social justice labour organizing – but it also stresses the need for more resources and political power if most Canadian workers are to achieve better work. The profound impact of the COVID-19 pandemic on work provides extraordinary openings to strengthen these and other initiatives to promote better jobs, full employment, and stronger worker voice inside and outside the workplace.

KEY THEMES

This chapter will help you develop an understanding of:

- recent efforts by unions to organize young workers, especially those with low-wage, precarious jobs
- recent social justice initiatives to help immigrant and migrant workers
- how unions and communities are working together in social justice coalitions to win better pay, working conditions, and social programs and services
- the hurdles low-wage, precarious workers face in winning better wages and working conditions.

ECONOMIC INEQUALITY AND precarious low-wage work are an increasing reality for workers across Canada. As chapters 3 and 4 discussed, in 2015 over a fifth of full-time Canadian workers held low-wage jobs, earning less than $14 an hour. Over a third of all workers earned less than $18,000 annually, meaning that they are categorized as working poor. Most are adults. Many have families. They are disproportionately women and racialized.[1]

These realities are especially striking because low-wage workers today are far better educated than previously. Two of every five have some college education or higher.[2] For many, the promise that education is a path to a good job has proved false. Further, tens of thousands of temporary foreign workers lack basic citizenship rights and union and employment protections. They are exceptionally vulnerable to low wages, workplace injuries, employer abuse, and substandard working and living conditions.

Despite growing public awareness of the high number of workers who are precariously employed in low-wage jobs, and despite public debate about needed policy improvements, most governments have done little. In Ontario in 2017 and Alberta in 2015, governments increased the minimum wage and introduced modest reforms to employment standards, including working hours. In 2019, however, these reforms were rolled back by incoming Conservative provincial governments. Ontario froze the minimum wage and cancelled future increases, while Alberta turned back overtime laws, permitted employers to pay young workers lower wages than the minimum for other workers, and made it more likely that workers would receive little or no increase in overtime pay rates.

Many, especially younger Canadians, are paying a high price. Across the country, government expenditures on postsecondary education and training have stagnated while tuition fees have risen.[3] Prioritizing business profitability and investment, many provincial governments have deregulated the labour market in many areas, including occupational health and safety protections.[4] At the same time, many employers have exerted pressure on unions to make wage and benefit concessions in contract bargaining and to weaken workplace rights.

In response, growing numbers of workers and unions have adopted unorthodox initiatives, including putting more resources into non-union, alternative forms of organizing, often to support young, racialized, and immigrant workers. Several unions are making strenuous efforts to compel employers and legislators to improve work and wages for low-wage precarious workers who are *not* union members. Often this goal leads labour activists to work with community organizations. In other cases, unions and workers cooperate, rediscover civil disobedience tactics, and sometimes risk assault and arrest to raise public awareness and support.

Behind these efforts is the hope that by launching creative, risky actions outside workplaces and in the streets, workers and their communities will gain the moral, cultural, and political momentum to challenge employers more effectively and provide political leadership in order to improve government labour policies.

Their actions emphasize social justice and social solidarity based on the need for *all* workers to be treated with dignity and to have equal labour rights.[5] Countering neoliberal claims that labour rights, better wages, and improved working conditions are job killers, unions and labour activists raise fundamental questions. How should we value work? Is work merely about producing goods and services efficiently in economic market terms? Or is it also about creating societies that serve human needs, provide opportunities for all of us to develop our human potentials, and uphold human rights?

Should society serve a privately owned and run economy, or should the economy serve society? And who should answer these questions?

Raising these kinds of fundamental questions has been central to **alt-labour** (alternative labour) activism, an approach to organizing that seeks social justice through collective action, often including mass protests and wildcat strikes that have not been officially approved by unions but are carried out by rank-and-file union members. Unions, activist groups, and workers are using alt-labour strategies to improve wages and working conditions for workers who are often not only *not* union members but have little prospect of becoming so in the near future. These include living wage and minimum wage campaigns, known as the Fight for $15 and Fairness (in Canada) and the Fight for $15 (in the US and other countries), that press employers and governments to raise the minimum wage to at least $15 an hour, among other improvements. The broader goals of Ontario's Fight for $15 and Fairness campaign, for example, include paid sick days, equal pay for equal work, personal leave, fairer work schedules, migrant worker rights, and reduction of barriers to joining unions.[6] Establishing non-profit worker centres to support young, racialized, and immigrant workers, is another example, as is conducting public campaigns to win legal rights and enforce existing labour laws.

Community unionism is a key form of alt-labour activism, bringing unions and community organizations and neighbourhood groups together to achieve common goals that are often not only "pro-worker" but also "pro-family" and "pro-community."[7] Labour–community coalitions move beyond narrow definitions of workers' interests to press for broader social gains, around issues such as better and more accessible education and training, health care, childcare and elder care, housing, and public transportation.

INNOVATIVE ORGANIZING STRATEGIES

Unions often face aggressive, well-funded employer opposition, especially when workers try to unionize and bargain their first collective agreements.[8] The legal process of certification, which enables employees to have a union they choose to be their bargaining agent with their employer, has become increasingly difficult.

It's also hard for most unions to extend collective agreements and protections to growing numbers of precarious workers. By outsourcing workers to subcontractors, and to franchisees such as Tim Hortons and McDonald's, companies create complicated employment networks of **fissured workplaces**. This occurs not only in fast food chains but also in cleaning and reception jobs in hotels such as Marriott and Hyatt, and with respect to so-called independent contractors such as Uber drivers and SkipTheDishes food delivery workers.[9]

These extraordinary challenges are a strong incentive to unions and workers to organize more effectively.[10] Increasingly, workers understand the limits of *individual* negotiations with managers and the need for stronger *collective* solutions to their employment problems.

Community Unionism
The Service Employees International Union (SEIU) is organizing groups such as janitors and health care workers across geographical areas and in specific communities by emphasizing common issues of workplace injustice. Known as the Justice for Janitors model of community unionism, this strategy is often effective if employees work in small or multiple workplaces.[11] Janitors, cleaners, and bike couriers often move among several buildings during their workdays, sometimes working several jobs for various employers. Thus many, especially young and immigrant workers, lack the time and job security for workplace actions, and union organizers

consequently find it difficult, time consuming, and counterproductive to use traditional methods of organizing each company one workplace at a time.

Sometimes unions focus on organizing in neighbourhoods and through faith, ethnic, and other immigrant cultural networks. Union organizers appeal to shared working-class values of greater economic fairness and workplace justice, highlighting the reality that workers in cleaning, agriculture, security, hotels, restaurants, recreation, logistics (transportation, storage, and distribution of goods, such as Amazon), retail, and other sectors typically have low, insecure wages and poor, intensified, and unsafe work conditions. They emphasize that these problems are not due to a few bad employers but are increasingly common, even in firms that are highly profitable.

In response to these problems, numerous unions are adopting variants of community unionism. Although tactics vary, labour organizers focus on involving community groups, personal networks, and rights organizations such as those opposing racism, sexism, and Islamophobia, and those promoting labour rights, immigration rights, and LGBTQ+ rights. This approach links workers' lives and personal values with their labour interests and values, giving priority to grassroots participation and decision making by workers and their communities. Workers themselves make connections between the needs of their communities and their own workplace goals. Underlying this model is a culture of broad social solidarity that helps to build worker capacities in a more inclusive and democratic political culture.

Community union initiatives sometimes launch well-publicized public protests and social events. Others educate workers and draw their support and participation through personal and community networks. They provide political coherence based on commitments to social justice and the moral imperative to do what is right for all workers, irrespective of ethnicity, race, gender, sexual orientation, citizenship status, or the nature of their employment contracts. This form of organizing can generate cultural political power through its potential to publicly shame employers and damage brand reputations, giving workers significant leverage at the bargaining table.

The model has been successful in major US cities. SEIU Justice for Janitors campaigns that combine rank-and-file workers, their personal networks, immigrants' rights groups, faith organizations, students, and community organizations to pressure employers have won collective agreements with better wages and working conditions for thousands of cleaners and janitors. In Vancouver, Toronto, and elsewhere in Canada, the SEIU has also won union protection and improved working conditions.[12] Through legal challenges and public campaigns, Justice for Janitors organizers have also targeted loopholes in labour laws that allow businesses to renege on union contractual obligations by flipping their employment contracts to non-union agencies and laying off workers (see Chapter 11).

Similar efforts have been made to organize fitness instructors and couriers – among the most precariously employed and lowest-paid workers in Canada. The new SEIU affiliate Workers United Canada Council, for example, has organized GoodLife Fitness instructors in Toronto: the first union certification of fitness instructors in Canada and the United States.[13] Traditionally, fitness instructors have had precarious self-employment contracts, thereby allowing employers such as GoodLife to avoid the costs of basic labour rights and protections such as minimum wages, pay equity, and parental leave and benefits, and denying these workers the right to join unions and to bargain collectively.

Workers United found a way to overcome this barrier. Communicating with GoodLife workers in Toronto and its suburbs through social media – a particularly suitable technique at a time when many more workers are in virtual workplaces, especially their homes – the union reached not only workers but also the wider public to draw attention to poor wages and working conditions. The GoodLife head office responded with an aggressive anti-union campaign to frighten workers and used legal challenges to block the union organizing effort. In response, workers launched an even wider social media campaign. Working with community organizations, they highlighted a key demand: paid sick days. They succeeded, and the campaign led to a model contract that Workers United is using to organize other fitness instructors.

The Canadian Union of Postal Workers (CUPW) has also been using a community organizing model. It has allied with rural communities and farmers' organizations to fight against post office closures and expand postal services in rural areas. CUPW has formed solidarity pacts with disability groups, retirees' organizations, and anti-poverty activists to help ensure that social assistance cheques are delivered during strikes. It created another solidarity pact with student and anti-poverty organizations to promote job creation and more accessible education, while opposing the use of scab labour during strikes.[14]

CUPW has also organized couriers and messengers in Montreal, Ottawa, Winnipeg, and other cities. With the expansion of courier business alongside the privatization of delivery services by Canada Post, thousands of delivery workers have been employed as independent contractors. As a result, they have low wages, no set hours, and few benefits and employment protections. To organize these workers, CUPW pressured courier firms to comply with basic employment standards and pay a minimum wage. Targeting key companies and then estab-

lishing worker community centres where couriers could meet, discuss problems, and rest, CUPW unionized couriers in several cities. In Toronto, courier companies are also using legal challenges to block union and worker efforts to unionize.

The United Food and Commercial Workers (UFCW) union has had several successes in organizing precarious workers. High-tech subcontracting company Uber, for example, claimed that its underpaid and overworked drivers were self-employed contractors. Although Ontario's labour law does not recognize them as employees, the UFCW welcomed Toronto Uber drivers as union members. They are campaigning for better wages and benefits, improved health and safety, and other gains. Retail workers have gained UFCW contracts as well, successfully organizing several Indigo stores. Using social media and celebrity advocacy to help organize their workplaces, these young, politically active workers are motivated especially by issues related to the COVID-19 pandemic. In Quebec, Ontario, and British Columbia, workers at cannabis dispensaries likewise campaigned electronically to organize their workplaces and gain UFCW contracts, including pandemic pay and personal protective equipment.

Community Chapters
In response to the rise of precarious non-union jobs, Unifor, Canada's largest private-sector union, created another model of community unionism called *community chapters*. The chapters link workers in Unifor local unions with non-union workers such as temp workers, freelancers, and other precarious workers, many of whom do not have the right to bargain collectively. Run by dues-paying members, these chapters provide non-union workers with access to health and dental plans, home and auto insurance, and other support, including training about labour rights, taxation, and other

issues. They also provide non-union workers with union advocacy to improve their rights and working conditions.

The Canadian Freelance Union (CFU) is one such chapter. CFU members include freelance writers, translators, video producers, photographers, and web designers, among others. Although the CFU is unable to bargain collective agreements, it provides members with advice about contracts and grievances, including how to fight widespread wage theft (not being paid for what they are rightfully owed), and how to get access to health and other benefits. Together, the CFU and Unifor assist freelancers on the job and press governments to improve wages and access to employment insurance benefits.

Another is the East Danforth Community Chapter in Toronto. Most of its members are women who have recently immigrated from Asian countries. Many are employed through temp agencies or do piecework (such as sewing clothing and other kinds of work paid for by the piece) in their homes. They belong to a South Asian women's community group that provides workplace training and leadership development, including help dealing with employment discrimination. Their community chapter works with Unifor local members to improve labour standards, including provincial minimum wages and occupational health and safety. A final example is the Unifor Unifaith Community Chapter of faith workers in the United Church of Canada, which advocates for these workers and their families, particularly regarding pension improvements.[15]

Community chapters are an example of a participatory approach to union advocacy in sectors and workplaces that have been especially difficult to organize. Workers, especially those who are low skilled, often face heavy odds against employers who retaliate by laying them off, cutting their hours, or replacing them. Despite the power imbalance between workers and employers, new union organizing models such as this are helping workers and their communities to win better wages and working conditions.

To succeed, these organizing efforts require time, money, and other resources that are in short supply in most unions. It can be difficult to build workers' confidence, especially with respect to fear that they may lose their jobs for trying to unionize. In addition, specialized and expensive research is often needed to understand relationships between particular companies and their contractors. Keeping organizing drives alive in the face of legal challenges by employers also typically requires huge financial resources. As seen in Chapter 7, unions can have great difficulty dealing with these resource problems. Among other strategic implications, these drives often don't bring in sufficient numbers of new workers to achieve the union density (proportion of unionized workers) to build the capacity to confront aggressive employers in the workplace and during contract bargaining.

Solidarity Unionism

Another approach that links workers' communities and workplaces is **solidarity unionism**. Using this strategy, workers organize their workplaces from the bottom up, often by forming workplace committees and by building cultures in which workers support each other on and off the job. They promote better work by defending one another against safety hazards, pay cuts, harsh supervision, and other issues. This frequently involves direct-action tactics that are often organized in part through social media: work slowdowns, sickouts (groups of workers protest by calling in sick), sit-downs or occupations (instead of picketing outside, workers sit down inside their workplaces and refuse to work), mass marches on bosses' offices, and so forth.

During the COVID-19 crisis, sanitation workers, bus drivers, warehouse workers, cooks, cashiers, food packers, drivers, health workers, educators, and others in hundreds of workplaces in the United States used such direct-action tactics. Among key goals were obtaining hazard pay, paid sick leave, and protection against infection, such as masks and gloves.[16] Often - for example during strikes against Whole Foods and Amazon - workers used social media to call on customers to boycott their stores. With the support of local farm workers' organizations, worker committees at fruit-packing companies coordinated strikes that prompted employers to sign agreements that they would provide protective equipment and implement other COVID-19 protections. Similarly, McDonald's workers in California walked out over unsafe working conditions after several workers contracted COVID-19. With support from their communities, they won safety improvements.[17]

One of the most successful internet-based organizing tools is Coworker.org. Its campaigns include winning health and safety protections for tens of thousands of Starbucks baristas, along with higher wages, improved work schedules, paid parental leave, and a dress code allowing workers to have visible tattoos. Coworker. org has also helped call centre workers gain protections against sexual harassment, and has been instrumental in thousands of workers winning increased workplace protections from the coronavirus. Starbucks workers have created a collective, Starbucks Partners, and have been coordinating their union organizing at Starbucks stores in the US and Canada in increasingly effective and public ways.

In July 2020, some twenty US unions joined other labour and political groups to organize the Strike for Black Lives. Calling for racial justice and the end of white supremacy inside and outside the workplace, as well as for protections from COVID-19 and other improvements, work-

ers in some twenty cities used direct action: strikes, mass marches, taking a knee, or walking off the job for eight minutes and forty-six seconds to commemorate George Floyd and others who have suffered racist police violence. This extraordinary effort enlarged the concept of a general strike into a vehicle for political action.[18] In Britain, the members-led United Voices of the World (UVW) trades union employs similar direct action and social media to gain living wages and other improvements, mainly for low-paid, racialized, immigrant, precarious workers in cleaning, security, hospitals, universities, and other sectors. Such tactics can help build workers' collective power to resist management.

Solidarity unionism is often built by a minority of workers in workplaces that have not been organized by a traditional union. In other cases, workers build solidarity unionism alongside traditional unions.[19] For example, at Canada's largest workplace, Pearson International Airport in Toronto, where approximately 40,000 people work, a group of employees created the Toronto Airport Workers' Council (TAWC), an organization based on principles of solidarity unionism that is open to all the airport's workers. The TAWC educates and organizes rank-and-file workers. It has successfully used direct action tactics, such as mass walkouts in unofficial "wildcat strikes," to stop the outsourcing of workers' jobs. Sometimes, as in the case of unionized airplane fuellers on strike at Porter Airlines in Toronto, solidarity unionism takes the form of strike support from other union and non-union labour groups.[20]

LIVING WAGE AND MINIMUM WAGE CAMPAIGNS

Hundreds of thousands of part- and full-time wage earners are living in poverty in Canada. These are the working poor. Unions and workers are undertaking public campaigns to raise the minimum wage, and even better to raise it to a living wage, as another innovative organizing strategy to address the issue. Unlike a minimum wage, which is a legal wage floor determined by governments, a living wage is determined by what workers need – based on their actual costs of living – to raise themselves and their families out of poverty and to participate meaningfully in the civic life of their communities.[21] A living wage is almost always higher than a minimum wage.

Living wage campaigns bring together the resources of unions, community and faith-based organizations, anti-poverty groups, progressive researchers, and others. The goal is to pressure governments, especially at municipal and provincial levels, to create a higher wage floor that is enforceable by statutory law.

Unions and community organizations are increasingly allying themselves in part because of declining capacity to meet their goals on their own, and because many workers and community members feel a desperate need to defend themselves against employer and government aggression. Their grassroots campaigns call for gains in pay and working conditions for millions of workers, especially those in low-wage, precarious work.[22]

Living wage campaigns began in the United States in the 1990s, and have since become especially widespread in Canada and parts of Europe.[23] In the United States, anti-poverty activists, religious leaders, and charitable organizations have been pushing municipal governments to adopt living wage ordinances for workers in their service departments and those working for municipal contractors and businesses. Over 140 American cities have passed living wage bylaws, with wage floors that are considerably higher than US federal and state minimum wages.

American unions have also partnered with community organizations to take on the low-wage policies of some wealthy corporations, including McDonald's, Walmart, and Amazon. Unions such as the SEIU have committed millions of dollars and hundreds of organizers to mobilize alongside community groups in pursuit of higher minimum wages. These campaigns also target US state legislatures to raise state minimum wages, which often do not meet the living wage, particularly in cities.

In addition to the idea that workers need higher wages to pay for their basic needs and those of their families, the argument is typically framed in terms of the glaring contrast between high corporate profits and executive salaries on the one hand and low wages on the other. Many low-wage workers have to go to foodbanks and other charities to survive. By focusing on these themes, launching workplace walkouts, and publicizing workers' personal stories, some campaigns have made dramatic gains. Numerous states have raised their minimum wages. Municipal governments, including San Francisco and Seattle, have passed minimum wage laws covering all workers in their respective cities. These are among the best minimum wages in the nation and serve as models for living wage campaigns elsewhere.[24]

In Canada, the living wage movement has been picking up momentum. Campaigns stress that provincial minimum wages don't keep pace with the cost of living. Workers, community activists, and unions across the country call for significant wage improvements through municipal living wage ordinances and provincial minimum wage increases.

In contrast to the United States, however, unions such as the SEIU and the UFCW have not committed such significant financial and organizational resources to mobilize precarious workers in Canada. Instead, unions more often work in coalitions with community organizations, and with the authoritative research organization the Canadian Centre for Policy

Alternatives, to enlighten municipal and provincial governments on the importance of raising minimum wages and enacting living wage policies. Several Canadian communities have living wage campaigns to encourage local businesses and municipal councils to adopt living wage policies.

In Ontario, the Workers' Action Centre and the Ontario Federation of Labour initiated a Fight for $15 and Fairness grassroots campaign that saw workers and their union and non-union allies across the province organize mass protests.[25] Supported by research from McMaster University and the United Way of Greater Toronto that highlighted growing labour precarity and its impact on workers and their families, they helped to build a strong labour–community movement that prevailed on the provincial government to review wage and employment standards.[26] The movement included universities and colleges, as unions such as UNITE HERE joined students, faculty, food service workers, and others in solidarity actions such as successful strikes promoting fairer wages and benefits.

The Ontario Liberal government passed the Fair Workplaces, Better Jobs Act in 2017, which introduced several key improvements. Among them were a higher minimum wage with annual increases; a requirement that employers pay part-time, temporary, and seasonal employees the same wage rate as regular workers; paid sick days; and increased vacation time and pregnancy leave.[27] In 2015 and 2018 respectively, advocacy groups in Alberta and British Columbia had similar success in encouraging New Democratic Party governments to introduce minimum wage increases in both provinces.

Campaigns for living wages and higher minimum wages have also had successes in Quebec. In 2016, anti-poverty and non-unionized worker groups united with major unions in the province to launch a key campaign called 5-10-15.

The main goals were to require employers to give workers five days' notice for work scheduling; ten paid days for sick or family-related leave; and a minimum hourly wage of $15. The Quebec government reformed minimum working standards in 2018, including a third vacation week for workers with at least three years of work seniority, additional paid leave days, and the prohibition of two-tier schemes to pay lower wages and pensions to newer workers.

Although these campaigns delivered important gains, subsequent Conservative election victories in Ontario and Alberta reversed most of them, underscoring the importance of continued engagement with the political party system as the electoral landscape shifts (Chapter 18). It also highlights the difficulties workers and citizens generally face when they try to maintain gains in labour law reforms (Chapter 7). Building stable labour policy improvements requires sustained union mobilization, in cooperation with the social justice movement and community organizers, to scale up from local organizing to provincial and national campaigns.

MIGRANT RIGHTS AND WORKER CENTRES

Annually over a 100,000 migrant workers come to Canada, joining tens of thousands more on temporary foreign worker contracts. Unlike immigrants, most have no rights to permanent residency and citizenship. In a context of limited government monitoring and enforcement, employer violations of these workers' rights are rampant. Access to citizenship rights is crucial because citizenship provides greater protection of labour rights. As a former federal immigration minister admitted, temporary foreign workers have "quasi-indentured status." Ontario's Ministry of Labour characterizes them as "unfree labour."[28]

Labour organizations including the Canadian Labour Congress promote stronger labour rights and standards for these workers. They also pressure provincial and federal governments to enforce labour laws, and employers to comply with their contractual obligations. Many community organizations also advocate for these workers and offer them legal services, health services, and other support, including solidarity and publicity in cases of forced deportation.

United Food and Commercial Workers has unionized temporary foreign agricultural workers in British Columbia, Manitoba, and Quebec and negotiated collective agreements that contain higher wages, grievance procedures, health and safety training, and other improvements. The UFCW has issued a legal challenge in Ontario to the provincial government's denial of these workers' rights to unionize and bargain collectively. The union has also provided Agriculture Workers Alliance support centres to help workers with problems related to pay, hours of work, housing, employer abuse, health, workers' compensation, income tax, and other issues. The UFCW also lobbies governments for additional rights for migrant farm workers, including parental, unemployment, and pension benefits.[29]

Other initiatives, such as the Workers' Action Centre (WAC) in Toronto, operate independently of the labour movement and focus less on union collective bargaining. Independent worker centres typically have few staff and limited financial resources. The WAC centres on workers organizing themselves in alliance with others, and links citizenship status, racial and gender discrimination, and low-paid, precarious work. Its members run the centre with high levels of democratic participation, developing collective leadership skills in workers' struggles. Broad-based labour campaigns include direct-action tactics such as demonstrations against wage theft. Other campaigns promote better wages and working conditions through reforms to the Ontario Employment Standards Act.[30]

Similarly, the Centre des travailleuses et travailleurs immigrants (Immigrant Workers Centre) in Montreal organizes immigrant workers using popular education that builds workers' skills and understanding of their rights while mobilizing around issues such as unpaid wages, employer abuse, and workplace injuries, and lobbying governments to increase the minimum wage. The centre also stresses policy issues such as strengthening migrant workers' eligibility for benefits under the Employment Insurance program.[31]

Founded by Filipino-Canadian activists, the centre works with several unions.[32] For example, recent campaigns to improve work mainly for temporary foreign agricultural and domestic workers led to an alliance with the Confédération des syndicats nationaux (CSN), the second-largest trade union federation in Quebec. In 2020, the Quebec government enacted rules to protect temporary foreign workers from the bad labour practices of personnel and recruitment agencies. The new rules include equal pay for equal work and shared responsibility of agencies and their employer clients to comply with wage regulations.[33]

Other community-labour groups have built national organizations with local chapters to push for better labour policies for temporary foreign workers. MIGRANTE-Canada organizes to promote improved labour standards and enforcement for migrants. Most of its efforts focus on domestic care workers from the Philippines, typically caregivers who arrive under the Temporary Foreign Worker Program (TFWP). The majority work and live in their employers' homes, which makes them especially vulnerable to psychological and sexual abuse by their employers. MIGRANTE defends these workers from exploitation, conducts worker education and research in collaboration with unions and universities, organizes advocacy campaigns in conjunction with faith and other community groups, and lobbies government agencies and politicians to support its policy goals.[34]

Another prominent example of this type of advocacy is Justice for Migrant Workers (J4MW), a non-profit organization that supports temporary foreign workers, particularly agricultural workers. Linking their organizing to intersecting class, race, and gender struggles, its volunteers use media publicity, caravans of migrant worker protesters, political lobbying, and write-in campaigns to promote labour policy reforms and to support workers who have been injured on the job, forcibly deported by employers, or abused in other ways.[35]

Another leading organization for migrant worker justice, KAIROS, is composed of Christian social activists who promote solidarity among temporary foreign workers, their host communities, and faith groups. Publicizing migrant workers' own stories of oppression in Canada, KAIROS advocates policy changes to strengthen the rights of migrant workers and their families.

The Migrant Rights Network, a cross-Canada alliance of migrant groups, works with climate action organizations and Indigenous rights groups as well as organized labour. It coordinates protests and conducts popular education about anti-racism and migrant justice. The largest migrant workers' rights organization in Canada, the Migrant Workers Alliance for Change, brings unions together with migrant worker advocacy groups and individuals to demand fundamental labour rights and access to social services and citizenship for temporary agricultural workers, caregivers, other temporary foreign workers, and migrant students.

These and other migrant worker rights organizations lobby federal and provincial governments to end damaging labour practices and conduct publicity campaigns to raise awareness of the inadequacies of government policies. They emphasize the need for better – and better-enforced – labour laws, and for pathways to permanent residency and citizenship rights. Achieving these goals also requires new international laws and institutions that secure workers' rights across borders.

LABOUR–COMMUNITY COALITIONS

Labour–community coalitions are another model of action to improve work and everyday lives. They promote social programs, such as universal health care and childcare and better public education. Public-sector unions, for example, have joined citizen groups in many countries to halt the dismantling of important public services, including health care. Labour–community coalitions have been founded to support citizens who lack essential public services such as childcare and decent social housing. Some coalitions campaign to stop government privatization of Crown corporations, utilities companies, and other public assets.[36] Others try to protect limited childcare spaces when provincial governments cut spending by privatizing the few available public childcare spaces.[37]

Particularly in the 1960s and '70s – an era of major labour discontent alongside peace, feminist, poverty, civil rights, gay, anti-racist, student, and other social movements – unions broadened their political values and goals. This development reflected the influence of active rank-and-file union members and the rising power of progressive politics, represented in the New Democratic Party and other political groups. The labour movement became stronger, more dynamic, and more relevant by integrating labour and other key social justice issues.

Since the **social movement politics** of those decades, however, most unions have been pushed into the defensive by governments that promote the core interests of corporations and the wealthy by lowering taxes on those groups while cutting public programs benefiting workers and poor people. These austerity policies have undermined the universality, accessibility, and quality of public services and in the process eliminated many stable, decently paid unionized jobs in the public service sector. It is in this context that unions, community groups, and individual citizens are uniting to restore public services that most Canadians need.[38]

Labour-community coalitions have had considerable success in opposing government policies that weaken the public health care system. Backed by the Canadian Union of Public Employees (CUPE), the union with the most members in the health care sector, these coalitions champion better, more accessible public health care across the country.

CUPE has paid particular attention to building provincial health coalitions in response to attempts by provincial governments to transfer funding to private medical companies and practices. In Ontario and Quebec, these coalitions have circulated public petitions countering neoliberal health care reforms and launched municipal plebiscites against hospital closures and privatizations.[39] Provincial coalitions also publicize the high costs of private hospitals, the lack of public accountability associated with privately provided services, and the damaging effect on patients when for-profit corporations cut the quality of their services to maximize financial gains for managers and shareholders. As Canadians learned tragically, COVID-19-related death rates were much higher and the quality of care lower in for-profit long-term care facilities, compared to publicly funded ones.[40]

Quebec's Coalition opposée à la tarification et à la privatisation des services publics (Coalition against Pricing and Privatization of Public Services), now Coalition Main rouge (Red Hand Coalition), has educated and mobilized citizens and unions against public-sector cuts.

Connecting some fifty retirees' associations, unions, and other diverse organizations, the coalition has opposed the Quebec government's neoliberal restructuring of public services.

The coalition has had significant momentum, especially during a massive student strike in 2012, the so-called Maple Spring, and again in 2015 against severe austerity measures by the Quebec Liberal government during negotiations for over half a million public-sector workers. Local unions created alliances with the public in defence of public services, particularly in the education sector. With parents and children, they organized demonstrations, including human chains surrounding public schools, under the slogan *Je protège mon école publique* (I protect my public school). Public-sector unions held strike days, including an illegal strike by college teachers. Ultimately, however, negotiations between the unions and the government did not substantially reverse the spending cuts.

Although these coalitions have been unable to halt privatization and government defunding of public services, in some cases they have helped secure union protections for workers whose jobs have been transferred to private companies. They have also brought sympathetic community members and organizations together. The resulting public pressure is making it harder for governments to transform the public health care system for private corporate benefit.[41]

Labour-community coalitions supporting universal childcare have had less success. Despite decades of activism, research, and professional advocacy, Canada is a childcare laggard, typically ranking among the lowest of rich countries in public spending on child and family care, as well as in the quality of childcare services.[42] Quebec is the only province to provide a relatively comprehensive public-private childcare system.[43] Indeed, most of the country's public childcare spaces are in Quebec. In other provinces, families have limited access to both public and private childcare spaces, and the latter are not required to conform to national standards. The high costs of childcare often force women in particular to forego employment (especially full time), training, and education in order to juggle excessive family demands. Consequently, women's movements, unions, and community organizations have been especially active in seeking progressive policy change in these areas.

In many European countries, childcare coalitions have influenced legislatures that have more balanced gender representation and prompted more sympathetic left-of-centre governments to deliver universal childcare and parental leave programs. In Ottawa and in provincial legislatures, these coalitions often face fierce opposition. Although childcare coalitions have won incremental policy improvements at the municipal and provincial levels, most families have to make do with a patchwork of childcare programs based primarily on insufficient tax credits, support from family members, and irregular, unregulated, private home childcare providers.[44]

In the early 2000s, under pressure from a national political advocacy campaign, Code Blue for Child Care, the federal Liberal government signed dominion-provincial agreements to phase in a national childcare program. On the election of a new federal Conservative government in 2006, however, the agreements were replaced by an annual income transfer that failed to cover the cost of one month of childcare.[45]

Now in 2022, more than seven years after first committing to a new childcare program, the federal Trudeau government has signed agreements with all ten provinces to provide $10-a-day childcare by 2026. The commitment was a hard-fought win by unions and activists. But families still worry whether they will finally see a truly universal and accessible childcare system.

ORGANIZING FOR PROGRESS

Especially over the past two decades, unions and workers have been turning to innovative organizing strategies. Minimum wage and living wage campaigns have been undertaken in response to the massive increase of low-wage, precarious jobs and burgeoning numbers of working poor. Worker centres are a growing focus, particularly of immigrant worker organizing. Grassroots social movements and labour-community coalitions have sprung up to counter government attempts to weaken labour rights, employment standards, and social programs. In all these efforts, unions, workers, and citizen activists have been finding new ways to cooperate effectively.

Will such actions lead to a more genuinely democratic Canada? Or will they fail to make a dent in economic and political inequality?

The modern history of Canada, the United States, and other major capitalist countries in the Global North suggests that fundamentally significant progressive political change requires strong labour movements, often combined with large-scale popular social movements. It was thanks to strong unions, massive numbers of workers, and widespread community solidarity that strikes built modern industrial unionism in Canada in steel, auto, electrical, rubber, mining, forestry, and other major sectors after the Second World War.

These momentous victories gave the labour movement a solid foundation and led to a post-war "golden age" that on the whole provided lower unemployment, greater job security, higher wages, improved health and safety, pensions, and other significant job improvements. Although the benefits were unevenly spread across industries and regions – and left out women workers in particular – they reflected an historically unprecedented shift in economic power, security, and income in favour of workers.

With growing economic power came growing political power for workers, farmers, and communities, a combination that was crucial to the achievement of a wide range of progressive public policies in the postwar era. These policies formed the core of Canada's welfare state, involving major improvements in public education, health care, social assistance, unemployment insurance, child benefits, old age security, pensions, and social housing. These and other policies significantly reduced social, economic, and political inequality and made the country more prosperous and democratic. While welfare state policies were most central to the platforms of the New Democratic Party and its predecessor, the Co-operative Commonwealth Federation, they were also to varying degrees supported by Liberal and Conservative governments during the period.

For the past forty years, however, employers and neoliberal governments have attacked and weakened this progressive policy direction.

Workers, their families, communities, the labour movement, and allies have often been divided and defensive. Yet as the evidence in this chapter suggests, we may be entering a new period in which workers, social movement allies, and communities are developing new forms of power in the workplace and in the political system.

Today, to win key demands for public policies to build a more socially just, prosperous, environmentally sustainable, and genuinely democratic Canada, increasing numbers of workers and their allies are building overlapping, reinforcing solidarity in their unions and neighbourhoods, and in their political organizations and social movements.

Innovative organizing strategies and labour-community coalitions illustrate not only resilience and creativity but also a growing organizing capacity. These continuing struggles will shape our future as workers, as members of families and communities, and as citizens. They will be central to the kind of Canada and world we inhabit.

ACKNOWLEDGMENTS

Thanks to scholars, activists, and union staff including Gabriel Alladua, Alex Diceanu, Roxanne Dubois, Mathieu Dupuis, Pam Frache, Euan Gibb, Ella Haley, Deena Ladd, Jane McAlevey, John Peters, Chris Ramsaroop, Kevin Shimmin, Terri Szymanski, and Fred Wilson for providing me with valuable insights and authoritative information about key examples of alt-labour discussed in this chapter.

ADDITIONAL RESOURCES

Adler, Lee, Maite Tapia, and Lowell Turner. *Mobilizing against Inequality: Unions, Immigrant Workers, and the Crisis of Capitalism.* Ithaca, NY: Cornell University Press, 2014.

Bernhardt, Annette, and Paul Osterman. "Organizing for Good Jobs: Recent Developments and New Challenges." *Work and Occupations* 44, no. 1 (2017): 89–112.

McAlevey, Jane. *A Collective Bargain: Unions, Organizing, and the Fight for Democracy.* New York: Ecco Press, 2020.

Tattersall, Amanda. *Power in Coalition: Strategies for Strong Unions and Social Change.* Ithaca, NY: Cornell University Press, 2010.

NOTES

1   Sheila Block and Grace-Edward Galabuzi, *Persistent Inequality: Ontario's Colour-Coded Labour Market* (Toronto: Canadian Centre for Policy Alternatives, 2018).

2   Jasmin Thomas, *Trends in Low-Wage Employment in Canada: Incidence, Gap and Intensity 1997-2014* (Ottawa: Centre for the Study of Living Standards, 2016).

3   Joel Harden, *The Case for Renewal in Post-Secondary Education* (Ottawa: Canadian Centre for Policy Alternatives, 2017).

4   Charles W. Smith, "Class, Power, and Neoliberal Employment Policy," in *Divided Province: Ontario Politics in the Age of Neoliberalism*, ed. Greg Albo and Bryan Evans (Montreal and Kingston: McGill-Queen's University Press, 2019), 275-306; Charles Smith and Andrew Stevens, "The Architecture of Modern Anti-Unionism in Canada: Class Struggle and the Erosion of Workers' Collective Freedoms," *Capital & Class* 43, no. 3 (2018): 459-81.

5   Judy Fudge, "Making Claims for Migrant Workers: Human Rights and Citizenship," *Citizenship Studies* 18, no. 1 (2014): 29-45.

6   Simon Black, "Community Unionism and Alt-Labour in Canada," in *Rethinking the Politics of Labour in Canada*, eds. Stephanie Ross and Larry Savage, (Halifax: Fernwood Publishing) 186-88.

7   Simon Black, "Community Unionism: A Strategy for Organizing the New Economy," *New Labor Forum* 14, no. 3 (2005): 24-32; Cynthia Cranford and Deena Ladd, "Community Unionism: Organizing for Fair Employment in Canada" *Just Labour* 3, 46-59; Christian Lyhne Ibsen and Maite Tapia, "Trade Union Revitalisation: Where Are We Now? Where to Next?" *Journal of Industrial Relations* 59, no. 2 (2017): 170-91; Maite Tapia, "Not Fissures but Moments of Crises that Can Be Overcome: Building a Relational Organizing Culture in Community Organizations and Trade Unions" *Industrial Relations* 58, no. 2 (2019): 229-50.

8   Michele Campolieti, Rafael Gomez, and Morley Gunderson, "Managerial Hostility and Attitudes towards Unions: A Canada-US Comparison," *Journal of Labor Research* 34, no. 1 (2013): 99-119.

9   David Weil, *The Fissured Workplace: Why Work Became So Bad for So Many and What Can Be Done to Improve It* (Cambridge, MA: Harvard University Press, 2014).

10   Maite Tapia and Lowell Turner, "Renewed Activism for the Labor Movement: The Urgency of Young Worker Engagement," *Work and Occupations* 45, no. 4 (2018): 391-419.

11   Ruth Milkman, Joshua Bloom, and Victor Narro, *Working for Justice: The LA Model of Organizing and Advocacy* (Ithaca, NY: Cornell University Press, 2013).

12   Luis Aguiar and Shaun Ryan, "The Geographies of the Justice for Janitors," *Geoforum* 40, no. 6 (2009): 949-58.

13   Larry Savage, "Building Union Muscle: The GoodLife Fitness Organizing and First Contract Campaign" *Labour/Le Travail* 84 (2019): 167-97.

14   Steven Tufts, "Community Unionism in Canada and Labor's (Re)organization of Space," *Antipode* 30, no. 3 (1998): 227-50.

15   Fred Wilson, Unifor (October 4, 2019), and Roxanne Dubois, Unifor (October 7, 2019), interviews by author.

16   Michael Sainato, "Strikes Erupt as US Essential Workers Demand Better Protection amid Pandemic," *The Guardian*, May 19, 2020, www.theguardian.com.

17   Jeremy Brecher, "Striking in the Coronavirus Depression," *Portside*, September 14, 2020, www.portside.org.

18   Jeremy Brecher, "Workers vs. the Coronavirus Depression," Labor Network for Sustainability, *Strike! Jeremy Brecher's Corner* podcast, September 17, 2020, www.labor4sustainability.org.

19   Staughton Lynd and Daniel Gross, *Solidarity Unionism at Starbucks*, PM Press Pamphlet Series no. 0009 (Oakland, CA: PM Press, 2011). Labour organizations advocating this model of unionism include the Industrial Workers of

the World (iww.org) and Labor Notes (www.labornotes.org).

20 IWW Member X364139, "Escalating a Picket Line: Learning from the Porter Airlines Strike," *Briarpatch*, September 30, 2013, https://briarpatchmagazine.com. Thanks to Alex Diceanu for this example.

21 Don Wells, "Living Wage Campaigns and Building Communities," *Alternate Routes: A Journal of Critical Social Research* 27, no. 1 (2016): 235–46.

22 Ruth Milkman, "Back to the Future? US Labour in the New Gilded Age," *British Journal of Industrial Relations* 51, no. 4 (2013): 645–65.

23 Bryan Evans and Carlo Fanelli, "A Survey of the Living Wage Movement in Canada: Prospects and Challenges," *Interface: A Journal for and about Movements* 8, no. 1 (2016): 77–96; Edmund Heery, Deborah Hann, and David Nash, "The Living Wage Campaign in the UK," *Employee Relations* 39, no. 6 (2017): 800–14.

24 Annette Bernhardt and Paul Osterman, "Organizing for Good Jobs: Recent Developments and New Challenges," *Work and Occupations* 44, no. 1 (2017): 89–112.

25 Fiona Jeffries, "Getting to $15 and Fairness: How Large Numbers of Society's Most Vulnerable Organized and Won a Historic Victory," *The Monitor*, Canadian Centre for Policy Alternatives, July 1, 2018, https://monitormag.ca.

26 Wayne Lewchuk, Michelynn Laflèche, Stephanie Procyk et al., *The Precarity Penalty: The Impact of Employment Precarity on Individuals, Households, and Communities – and What to Do about It* (Hamilton, Ontario: PEPSO, McMaster University, and United Way of Greater Toronto, 2015.

27 Fay Faraday, *Demanding a Fair Share: Protecting Workers' Rights in the On-Demand Service Economy* (Ottawa: Canadian Centre for Policy Alternatives, 2017).

28 Daniel Tencer, "Temporary Foreign Workers Subject to 'Quasi-Indentured Status' Jason Kenney Says," *Huffington Post Canada*, September 20, 2014, www.huffingtonpost.ca.

29 Janet McLaughlin, Don Wells, Aaraón Mendiburo, André Lyn, and Biljana Vasilevska, "'Temporary Workers,' Temporary Fathers: Transnational Family Impacts of Canada's Seasonal Agricultural Worker Program," *Relations Industrielles/Industrial Relations* 72, no. 44 (2017): 682–709.

30 Deena Ladd, and Sonia Singh, "Critical Questions: Building Worker Power and a Vision of Organizing in Ontario," in *Unfree Labour? Struggles of Migrant and Immigrant Workers in Canada*, ed. Aziz Choudry and Adrian Smith (Oakland, CA: PM Press, 2016), 123–39.

31 Joey Calugay, Loïc Malhaire, and Eric Shragge, "A Jeepney Ride to Tunisia – From There to Here, Organizing Temporary Foreign Workers," in *Unfree Labour?* 141–56.

32 Loïc Malhaire, Lucio Castracani, and Jill Hanley, "La défense des droits des travailleuses et travailleurs: Enjeux et défis d'une mobilisation collective à Montréal," *REMEST* 11, no.1 (2018): 32–59.

33 Thanks to Mathieu Dupuis for providing examples of this and other campaigns in Quebec.

34 Geraldine Pratt, "Organizing Filipina Domestic Workers in Vancouver, Canada: Gendered Geographies and Community Mobilization," *Political Power and Social Theory* 35 (2018): 99–119.

35 Carrie Sinkowski, "Advocates with Status: A Snapshot of Three NGOs in the Canadian Migrant Agricultural Workers' Movement," in *Civil Society Engagement – Achieving Better in Canada*, ed. Patricia Daenzer (New York: Routledge, 2018), 137–43.

36 Jane McAlevey, *No Shortcuts: Organizing for Power in the New Gilded Age* (New York: Oxford University Press, 2016); Barry Eidlin, *Labor and the Class Idea in the United States and Canada* (New York: Cambridge University Press, 2018); Christopher Hermann and Jörg Flecker, eds., *Privatization of Public Services: Impacts for Employment, Working Conditions, and Service Quality in Europe* (New York: Routledge, 2012); Giulano Bonoli, *The Origins of Active Social*

Policy: *Labour Market and Childcare Policies in a Comparative Perspective* (Oxford: Oxford University Press, 2013).

37   Simon Black, "Community Unionism without the Community? Lessons from Labor-Community Coalitions in the Canadian Child Care Sector," *Labor Studies Journal* 43, no. 2 (2018): 118–40.

38   Stephanie Ross and Larry Savage, eds., *Public Sector Unions in the Age of Austerity* (Halifax: Fernwood Publishing, 2013); Amanda Tattersall, *Power in Coalition: Strategies for Strong Unions and Social Change* (Ithaca, NY: Cornell University Press, 2010), 104–41.

39   Jean-Noël Grenier and Marie-Michelle Audet-Tremblay, *La représentation collective et le défi de la qualité des emplois: Les expériences des syndicats des secteurs public et parapublic québécois* (Quebec City: Université Laval, Alliance de recherche universités-communautés, Innovations, travail et emploi, 2014).

40   Martine August, "The Coronavirus Exposes the Perils of Profit in Seniors' Housing," *The Conversation*, July 26, 2020, theconversation.com.

41   Pat Armstrong and Hugh Armstrong, *About Canada: Health Care*, 2nd ed. (Halifax: Fernwood Publishing, 2016).

42   Rianne Mahon, "Canada's Early Childhood Education and Care Policy: Still a Laggard?" *International Journal of Child Care and Education Policy* 3, no. 1 (2009): 27–42; Martha Friendly, Laura Feltham, Sophia Mohamed, Ngoc Nguyen, Rachel Vickerson, and Barry Forer, *Early Childhood Education and Care in Canada 2019* (Toronto: Childcare Resource and Research Unit, 2020).

43   Families with children in private childcare centres and home-based care receive a tax credit to cover their tuition fees.

44   Rachel Langford, Patrizia Albanese, and Susan Prentice, *Caring for Children: Social Movements and Public Policy in Canada* (Vancouver: UBC Press, 2017).

45   Martha Friendly, "Why Women Still Ain't Satisfied: Politics and Activism in Canadian Child Care, 2006," *Canadian Woman Studies* 25, no. 3–4 (2006): 41–46.

18 In Search of a New Politics of Labour

Stephanie Ross and Larry Savage

CHAPTER SUMMARY

If labour unions and popular democratic movements are to develop from defensive or merely local positions to more assertive and international ones, they need new alliances and new vision. This chapter surveys some of the initiatives designed to move in that direction.

After describing various political and organizational challenges that unions face today, this chapter addresses electoral, new social movement, and judicial strategies. The chapter makes the case for unions to shift their political tactics and priorities. After reviewing a range of union strategies, it argues for a more inclusive and integrated approach that leverages union power in a way that promotes working-class interests more broadly, builds union members' capacities to challenge capitalist power, and contributes to a more genuinely democratic politics in Canada.

Approaches that strategically integrate electoral, social movement, and judicial strategies and link worker, community, and other civil society organizations in the pursuit of more democratic, egalitarian, and sustainable futures are the way forward.

KEY THEMES

This chapter will help you develop an understanding of:

- the current political and social challenges facing unions
- how and why Canadian unions are pursuing alliances with community organizations and social movements
- why Canadian unions are mounting legal challenges in the pursuit of labour law reforms
- the difficult choices for workers and unions trying to renew their organizations and expand their influence on governments and employers.

LIKE ITS COUNTERPARTS around the globe, the labour movement in Canada is under attack on several fronts. Beyond the pandemic, the combined long-term impacts of neoliberal trade and investment regimes, privatization, marketization, and government austerity policies have severely eroded union power across the board. The economic power of corporations in the form of international mobility, and political power expressed through electoral and lobbying activities, has undermined unions' capacity to preserve existing labour rights and standards, working conditions, and pay, let alone to bargain gains for their members. And a so-called taxpayer backlash against public-sector unions – fanned by right-wing populist ideology that frames labour unions as establishment insiders working against the interests of the people – has led to calls for greater restrictions on the right to strike.

At the same time, the traditional political strategies employed by organized labour have failed to stem a growing tide of anti-union and right-wing populist sentiment. This reversal in political culture became more apparent following the 2007-8 recession and has now found institutional expression in right-wing political parties and movements such as Yellow Vests Canada, the Proud Boys, the Freedom Convoy, and any number of localized anti-mask and anti-vaccine groups that emerged during the COVID-19 pandemic.

More generally, the entrenchment of neoliberalism as a political project, combined with the weakness of genuinely anti-neoliberal, anti-austerity electoral alternatives, has undercut support for collectivist solutions to social problems and made working-class voters vulnerable to populist right-wing appeals. This trend has reinforced a politics that says we can deal with economic anxiety only through strategies of self-reliance and social exclusion of others, especially racialized immigrants.

In this context, organized labour has struggled to re-establish political power and rally people to progressive alternatives. Labour movements have been experimenting with many approaches to restoring power, but for the most part their political tactics - whether electoral, judicial, or based on social movements - have remained narrowly focused and defensive.

In general, unions have not effectively integrated different strategies in ways that maximize their potential leverage over political decision makers. Even when unions have combined various approaches, their relative strength has still been less than that of the allied corporate and political interests that seek to diminish the power of workers and their organizations.

LABOUR'S RESPONSE TO CONTEMPORARY CHALLENGES

Any discussion of labour politics must begin with an acknowledgment that not all problems workers face in a capitalist society can be resolved at the workplace. Housing affordability, childcare needs, and racial discrimination are all issues affecting daily life that can seriously be addressed only through broader political, economic, and social change. Many historical achievements of the labour movement, such as a shorter workday and the adoption of a minimum wage, were ultimately accomplished outside the workplace through political action. The push by some labour organizations for universal and permanent paid sick days in the wake of COVID-19 is a good example of a contemporary political demand that has gained national media attention. These broader social and economic issues, and others like them, are political matters in which unions and their members have a direct interest. To effectively defend these interests, unions need to act politically.

Although most unions engage in political activities outside their immediate workplaces, the strategies and tactics they use and the purposes behind those activities vary widely. Unions provide workers with the potential to strengthen their collective voice in the political sphere through a combination of traditional **electoral politics**, social movement activities, and **legal activism** through the courts.

Historically, many unions in Canada have been aligned with the social democratic New Democratic Party (NDP). While accepting the framework of a capitalist economy, social democratic politics has focused on using state policy to curb the harmful effects of corporate power on workers, to foster economic growth and full employment, to redistribute wealth more equally through the expansion of universal social programs such as public health care and public education, and to promote social justice more generally.

By the 1980s, ties between unions and the NDP had begun to fray in the face of economic crisis, opening space for neoliberal politics in the form of free market policies such as corporate-oriented international trade and investment agreements, privatization, economic deregulation, corporate tax cuts, and a general weakening of universal social programs (chapters 4 and 5). The ascendancy of neoliberalism has shifted the centre of the political spectrum to the right in Canada and other countries, dragging social democratic parties along with it.

As social democratic parties have internalized some neoliberal ideas and policies, union electoral support for social democracy has produced diminishing returns. Moreover, the dual role that social democratic governments play as both union allies and public-sector employers has complicated their relationship with the labour movement, especially given how dominant public-sector unionism has become in Canada.[1]

In response to the limits of the labour movement's electoral strategies, social movement-based organizations, such as union–community coalitions, workers' centres, and campaigns to increase the minimum wage have emerged (Chapter 17). These efforts have galvanized significant energy and support, especially beyond the confines of union membership, and have won important public policy improvements. However, defending these gains for working-class people requires a level of political mobilization that has proven difficult to sustain, particularly when movements do not seek state power.

More recent union strategies have attempted to bypass parties and movements altogether by focusing on the courts. Once strictly a defensive strategy to preserve workers' rights and freedoms, judicial tactics have become increasingly sophisticated, designed to advance the interests of labour through the legal system. This strategic approach has been criticized for its tendency to demobilize unions and reduce their political capacity to act outside the strict confines of the law.[2]

At various times, one or another segment of the Canadian labour movement has practised each of these strategic approaches. Indeed, heated differences over how best to engage in politics have helped to keep the union movement in Canada divided.[3] These divisions are often shaped by political ideologies about what unions should do and how they should express and act in their members' interests. **Business unionism** and **social unionism** are often seen as the two main competing archetypes of union political orientations.

Business unionism is narrowly focused on the economic role of unions in the workplace and therefore places priority on the key union functions of collective bargaining (wages, benefits, work hours, etc.) and workplace representation. Business unionists typically emphasize political action to increase union influence and bargaining power by promoting pro-union labour legislation and lobbying for government policies that support sectors of the economy in which their members work. Business unionists tend to pursue these goals in non-partisan, non-ideological ways, rather than attaching themselves permanently to a particular party.[4] Instead, their relationship with political parties reflects the maxim expressed by former American Federation of Labor president Samuel Gompers: "Reward your friends and punish your enemies."

Social unionism has a more expansive view of unions' purpose, and therefore of the role and types of political engagement appropriate in the labour movement. Social unionism is premised on the view that, because workers' interests lie both inside and outside the workplace as citizens and not just as wage earners, unions should engage in strategies that are more broadly political.[5] For instance, many unions champion the protection of universal public health care. Because social programs are not direct workplace bargaining issues, however, workers need strategies and organizational forms that transcend the workplace in order to fight for these issues.

Social unionists also emphasize arrangements that create more economic and social equality in their communities. In that sense, social unionists are more open to partisan affiliation, because they recognize that political parties have different visions and priorities, and that some parties are clearly more progressive or egalitarian than others. Social unionism also holds that the organizational strength of the labour movement should be used to support working-class people who have been unable to create effective collective organizations.

Neither business nor social unionism are strategies in and of themselves. Very few unions conform to either ideal type. Rather, most labour organizations are complicated hybrids, reflecting unique historical trajectories, shifting sources of leverage, the varying cultures and histories of their members, and the influence of particular leaders.[6]

It would therefore be a mistake to associate one particular orientation with one particular strategy, since all strategies can be deployed, shaped, or framed in a way that suits either social or business unionist orientations. Separate and apart from these orientations, unions' concrete political strategies tend to be organized into three major categories: electoral, social movement, and judicial. The possibilities and contradictions in each are examined below.

UNION ELECTORAL STRATEGIES

The fable of Mouseland, made famous by former Saskatchewan NDP premier Tommy Douglas, is key to understanding why working people and union activists formed the NDP. In the fable, working people – the mice – face an empty choice between two competing political parties made up of cats distinguished only by their colour: the Liberal and Conservative parties, respectively. After successive governments made up of black cats or white cats have been elected, it becomes clear that neither is working in the interest of mice. One mouse wonders aloud why mice don't get together and elect a party of their own. The mouse is immediately imprisoned for proposing such a revolutionary idea, and the fable concludes, "You can lock up a mouse or a man, but you can't lock up an idea."

Despite this, union engagement with electoral politics in Canada varies greatly, ranging from institutionalized partisan links to formal non-participation and non-partisanship. Some unions run educational campaigns designed to make their members aware of the benefits and disadvantages of government actions and policies, to encourage them to be politically active, and to mobilize them around elections and lobbying activities. In Quebec, unions generally reject formal partisan ties, though they do occasionally endorse or align themselves with left-leaning sovereigntist parties.

While many unions continue to promote support for the NDP as the party of working people, and to commit personnel and money to its electoral efforts where campaign finance law permits, the party's uneven, sometimes anti-union record while in government has generated a debate about how organized labour ought to do electoral politics.[7] Across Canada, that debate goes back to the 1870s. The issue appeared to be settled with the creation of the NDP in 1961, but the inability of the party and of social democracy more generally to respond adequately to changing economic circumstances since the 1980s has opened the question again and split the labour movement.

The NDP resulted from a partnership between the Co-operative Commonwealth Federation (CCF), the party's predecessor, and the Canadian Labour Congress (CLC), the largest central labour organization in Canada. The NDP's founders hoped the emergence of a social democratic labour party would challenge the long-standing electoral dominance of the Liberal and Conservative parties by realigning Canadian politics on a left-right basis, as had occurred in Britain after the creation of the Labour Party.[8]

While the NDP has had some sustained electoral success in provincial politics, particularly in Saskatchewan, Manitoba, and British Columbia, it has struggled to break out of third-party status in federal politics.[9] Vigorous disagreements have arisen over whether the failure to establish the party as a consistently significant federal force rests primarily with the party itself, with organized labour, or with a lack of working-class consciousness among Canadian voters.[10] However, the institutional NDP-union link has always been relatively weak, with formal union affiliation to the party covering just 15 percent of unionized workers at its peak shortly after the party's creation.[11]

NDP provincial governments have shown both the possibilities and the limits of social democratic electoralism. In the 1970s, NDP governments in Manitoba, Saskatchewan, and British Columbia introduced relatively strong labour legislation, including substantial gains in both occupational health and safety and workers' rights. These governments served working-class interests relatively well, thus justifying union support.

A rising tide of neoliberalism in the 1980s initially dented support for the traditional Keynesian redistributive policies promoted by the NDP, but by the early 1990s, many voters were looking for alternatives to the new norm of neoliberal economic restructuring, personified by Progressive Conservative prime minister Brian Mulroney. As a result, NDP governments were elected in Ontario in 1990, in British Columbia and Saskatchewan in 1991, and in the Yukon in 1992. More than half of Canada's population was governed by NDP governments during this period and union activists were thrilled at the possibilities.

Those hopes were soon dashed, however, as the party proved incapable of resisting the pull of neoliberalism. The political terrain continued to shift to the right and pulled NDP governments along with it.[12] Despite introducing some pro-labour legislation, all the NDP governments in the 1990s alienated the labour movement to some degree. Rather than challenging neoliberalism in the interests of working people, they accommodated their policies to its demands, implementing cutbacks that made provincial NDP governments little different in practice from governments led by other parties.

The problem confronting most NDP governments elected in the 1990s and since has

BOX 18.1 THE SOCIAL CONTRACT

In 1993, Bob Rae's Ontario NDP government imposed the Social Contract Act on public-sector unions. It effectively removed the right of free collective bargaining for public-sector workers in a bid to reduce government expenditures while avoiding layoffs. The legislation forced the reopening of existing public-sector collective agreements and imposed unpaid days off – dubbed Rae Days – to cut costs.

Although it is widely accepted that poor economic conditions narrowed the room to manoeuvre politically, the decision to implement the so-called Social Contract was met with fierce resistance by public-sector unions and had negative repercus-

sions for union–party relations across the country. Public-sector union leaders pleaded with Rae to explore more progressive alternatives, like raising corporate taxes, but he refused.

The now infamous Social Contract created deep divisions within the Ontario labour movement. Some unions, especially in the private sector, continued to support the government despite the legislation, but for many others the law negated any good the party had done in the field of labour relations and led to a fundamental re-evaluation of the traditional link between organized labour and the NDP.

been their tendency to define their governing strategy by the demands of their traditional enemies. They have gone out of their way not to offend powerful corporate interests. Thus, their improvements to labour and social legislation are meek, making them increasingly indistinguishable from other parties and provoking disillusionment and cynicism within much of their traditional working-class base.[13]

Disappointment with NDP provincial governments throughout the 1990s contributed to the unravelling of the traditional party–union relationship and prompted some segments of the labour movement to embrace strategic voting to block the re-election of explicitly anti-union parties. Strategic voting occurs when an elector consciously decides to vote for a candidate or party that is not their first choice, based on the belief that their vote could be decisive in affecting the outcome of the election.

With respect to organized labour, contemporary strategic voting campaigns are designed to prevent vote splitting among non-Conservative parties. So, for example, in a riding where

the Liberal and Conservative parties are competitive but the NDP is not, union members and allies who identify most closely with the NDP might opt to vote strategically for a Liberal candidate (their second choice) with the ultimate aim of defeating the Conservative. The utility of strategic voting has been hotly debated, but whether effective or not it has become a key electoral tactic for a growing number of unions, reflecting both disenchantment with the NDP and an increasingly defensive stance in relation to employers and the state.[14]

Beyond either strategic voting or electoral loyalty to a single political party, more and more unions have embraced a pragmatic strategy of rewarding political friends and punishing political enemies. These more narrowly instrumental efforts to influence government policy have also produced mixed results. On the one hand, some unions have extracted sector-specific improvements to labour legislation and employment standards, and sometimes subsidies for their employers or industries in an effort to protect jobs. On the other, these temporary electoral pacts tend to produce policies that benefit only a narrow slice of union members, thus reinforcing business unionist impulses, sowing seeds of division between unions, and lowering expectations of what can be achieved for all workers through government.

Overall, however, the labour movement in Canada has no uniform electoral strategy (Chapter 5). Various strategies are often employed simultaneously, and sometimes at cross-purposes, even within a single province. These divisions are both regionally and ideologically rooted. This has made it very difficult to achieve a firm political basis for party-union solidarity in a country as regionally and linguistically polarized as Canada.[15] For that reason, some unions have turned to social movement-based political action outside the parliamentary framework.

MOVEMENT-BASED STRATEGIES

On February 14, 2017, students at university campuses across Ontario participated in a province-wide Valentine's Day of Action in support of a campaign for decent work. Drawing links between bad jobs with poverty wages and student debt, students at Queen's, Carleton, Wilfrid Laurier, Nipissing, Brock, McMaster, York, Toronto Metropolitan, and the University of Toronto mobilized their peers to fill out heart-shaped petitions declaring, "It's time to show workers some love!" The students were part of the broad and growing Fight for $15 and Fairness campaign that had been working hard to convince the provincial government to raise the minimum wage and pass sweeping reforms to Ontario's Employment Standards Act that would grant workers more rights and greater benefit entitlements.

Their advocacy appeared to pay off when in May 2017, Premier Kathleen Wynne announced that her Liberal government would boost the general minimum wage from $11.40 to $14.00 per hour on January 1, 2018, and then by an additional dollar to $15 in 2019 (Chapter 3). The government also announced several reforms, including two paid sick days, increased minimum vacation entitlements, equal pay for equal work for full- and part-time workers, an expansion of personal emergency leave, and fairer rules for scheduling. The announcement represented a stunning victory for the campaign, which was backed by a coalition of unions and community organizations.

In the wake of the 2018 Ontario provincial election, however, which saw the anti-union Progressive Conservative government of Doug Ford come to power, the business community successfully lobbied the premier to repeal most of the employment standards improvements and to cancel the minimum wage increase for 2019, thus watering down or eliminating the key victories of the Fight for $15 and Fairness campaign.

Movement-based strategies like the Fight for $15 and Fairness campaign are designed to challenge and influence government policies and actions independently of political parties or elections. Some unions have historically used such efforts to supplement the election of labour-friendly governments, since there is always a need to make sure politicians fulfill their commitments between elections.

They typically involve organizing and participating in public demonstrations, public awareness or pressure campaigns, and union-community coalitions (Chapter 17). Such tactics sometimes focus on arguments for why those with decision-making power should take a certain position. At other times they are designed to disrupt normal routines, typically through sit-ins or mass demonstrations, and to raise awareness of and convince the public to support a particular cause.

Such movement-based strategies and tactics are often characterized as the repertoire of the excluded: the relatively less powerful groups in society that must mobilize outside the established political system to press their concerns. Over the last several decades, there has been a growing sense in some quarters that electoral politics does not produce enough influence over the policy-making process, especially for working-class people. After having secured unprecedented legitimacy as part of the postwar labour relations framework, the labour movement has been pushed to the margins of policy making in recent decades. In contrast to large corporations and employer organizations, significant segments of the labour movement feel like – and are – political outsiders.[16]

In response, central labour organizations and individual unions have developed campaigns and coalitions, often with like-minded social movements or community organizations, to reassert labour's political strength. For example, there exists a strong partnership between labour and the Ontario Health Coalition, which actively campaigns against the privatization of health services. Similarly, Blue Green Canada is an alliance between unions, environmental organizations, and civil society groups to advocate for good green jobs across the country.

In Canada, movement-based strategies took off during the free trade battles of the late 1980s and have expanded over the years to include myriad coalition partners, including the student, anti-globalization, feminist, racial justice, environmental, Indigenous rights, antipoverty, and queer rights movements. Labour has been influenced by the tactical repertoires of protest action of its coalition partners. For instance, direct action – in the form of mass protests, occupations of public space, and nonviolent civil disobedience – was used in the struggle against new global free trade agreements and to defend workers and communities after the 2008 global financial crisis.[17]

Unions have also provided financial support to efforts led by coalition partners, such as the Occupy movement against inequality and the Idle No More movement for Indigenous rights and against environmental destruction.[18] Often, disruptive tactics produce positive results because they directly pressure decision makers, who may fear threats to their re-election or the ire of a public angered by their inaction.[19]

Movement-based strategies often rely on the development of strong union–community coalitions designed to facilitate the joint pursuit of common aims.[20] Coalition strategies reduce the isolation of individual labour organizations, widen the activist base, and raise the public profile of the issues that unions and their allies champion.

Nevertheless, union–community coalitions are not without their problems. Unions typically bring the lion's share of financial resources to the coalition table, which tends to give them greater decision-making authority. This can

---

BOX 18.2 THE ONTARIO HEALTH COALITION

Formed in the late 1990s in response to the then Progressive Conservative government's efforts to restructure public health care to the benefit of private business interests, the Ontario Health Coalition brought together unions, community groups, and seniors' organizations as part of a union–community coalition to advocate for the defence and expansion of public health care. The coalition hosted province-wide town halls and launched municipal referendums opposing privatization and the higher costs and poorer care that would result.

The Ontario Health Coalition is one of the most successful examples of a union–community coalition, demonstrating how the power of working together helps to reduce isolation and build political power.

alienate social activists who resent the idea that labour gets to call the shots.[21] Moreover, movement-based strategies can involve significant risks. Direct action tactics such as street protests, blockades, or sit-ins may unduly inconvenience the very public whose support is being courted, thus potentially undermining the effectiveness of the strategy. Many people, including union members, are reluctant to engage in direct action because they fear how they will be perceived, are unwilling or unable to risk arrest, or have little attachment to the cause prompting the action.

Finally, despite their significant achievements, social movements do not seek state power as such. The exercise of state power, particularly to shift social and economic relationships to the advantage of unions and working-class people more broadly, generally requires a powerful political party. Some social movements do become integrated into political parties or engage with sympathetic parties in order to have their interests and priorities enacted in legislation. Others are deeply suspicious of state power, not least because of the dangers of being dominated by state elites. Movement-based strategies thus court the possibility of having their achievements undone when unsympathetic governments are elected.

JUDICIAL STRATEGIES

On January 30, 2015, Saskatchewan Federation of Labour (SFL) president Larry Hubich celebrated a stunning Supreme Court victory. Seven years earlier, the conservative Saskatchewan Party government had removed the right to strike for certain public employees, prompting the SFL and other labour organizations to challenge the constitutional validity of the decision. The Supreme Court issued a landmark ruling in *Saskatchewan Federation of Labour v Saskatchewan*, determining that the Charter of Rights and Freedoms protects workers' right to strike. The ruling validated the union's claim that the government had acted unconstitutionally and reinforced a growing chorus of activists advocating for a labour-rights-as-human-rights approach to politics.

Ironically, unions were suspicious of the Charter when it was introduced as part of the Constitution in 1982, expressing reservations about its impact on labour and employment relations. Underpinning this wariness was the reality that the courts had usually not been kind to workers' organizations, having sided almost exclusively with employers in pre-Charter legal disputes.[22]

When federal and provincial governments began to mount an aggressive anti-union legislative assault in the 1980s, however, the labour movement overcame its historical judicial phobia to test the constitutional guarantee of freedom of association. A trio of anti-union Charter decisions in 1987 declared there was no constitutionally protected right to collectively bargain or to strike. These court decisions seemingly confirmed union fears that the courts would interpret the Charter in ways that would help employers and individual anti-union workers to dismantle hard-fought union rights and freedoms.[23] Yet the crisis in social democratic electoral strategies in the 1990s and the limits of social movement approaches to contesting state power gave unions few political opportunities to challenge neoliberal restructuring effectively. Some unions drifted back toward the judicial arena in hope of shielding themselves from further attacks.

The timing of this strategic shift coincided with a period of growing flexibility in the Supreme Court's interpretation of the Charter. At the turn of the twenty-first century, a significant change in the court's approach to interpreting Charter guarantees of freedom of association and expression gave unions hope that the Charter could be used to defend and even enhance unions' economic and political power. A string of Charter victories securing constitutional rights to secondary picketing and collective bargaining rights reinforced this new hope and encouraged some unions to use the language of human rights more explicitly to frame their claims for increased constitutional protection of workers' rights.[24]

Nevertheless, the outcomes of the labour movement's human rights-based legal strategies have also been mixed. Unions have scored several important defensive victories at the Supreme Court, but union leaders cannot take these pro-union legal rulings for granted. Indeed, a Supreme Court ruling in 2015 granting constitutional protection for the right to strike has not prevented governments from continuing to use back-to-work legislation to end public-sector labour disputes.[25]

If unions lack sufficient capacity to mobilize or opportunity to advance workers' interests successfully through electoral or social movement-based activity, they are forced to fall back on judicial-based strategies to defend or assert their rights in court. At their best, legal strategies can overturn anti-worker legislation, but positive results are far from guaranteed. Judicial approaches are also expensive and lengthy and can leave workers demobilized and vulnerable, especially if the outcome is negative. Contracting out labour's political struggle to legal experts causes grassroots political muscle to atrophy.

Constitutional challenges take the struggle away from the workplace and the electoral political realm, out of the hands of workers and into those of judges and lawyers. Over-reliance on judicial strategies also reinforces the legalism of the postwar labour relations framework. Moreover, while current constitutional jurisprudence holds that the Charter of Rights and Freedoms protects workers' rights to organize

into unions, to bargain collectively, and to strike, this was not always the case. And it may not always be the case. There is no substitute for ongoing political struggle.

WHICH WAY FORWARD FOR LABOUR?

Unions are both a product of and a reaction to capitalism. As such, their relationship to the economic system is complicated. Political and economic elites first attempted to contain militant and anti-capitalist currents in Canada's working class by more fully integrating unions into the country's labour relations framework in the mid-twentieth century. Toward the end of the twentieth century, once class forces had become so unequally balanced that unions were no longer seen as a threat to management control or to the capitalist order, dominant economic and political elites jettisoned any notion that adversarial unions needed to be tolerated, let alone accommodated.

Ill-equipped to shield themselves from state and employer attacks on workers' hard-won rights and freedoms, unions went into retreat in all capitalist democracies in the Global North as neoliberal restructuring took hold in the 1980s and '90s. They have not yet recovered.[26]

It's too early to tell if the economic and political tumult caused by the COVID-19 pandemic will precipitate renewed militancy on the part of the Canadian labour movement. While the pandemic certainly exposed holes in the social safety net and drove more workers to seek union representation in order to defend their interests, it also reinforced the business unionist impulses of labour organizations desperate to address the immediate needs of their members in the face of economic and public health crises. The fact that some employers and governments used the pandemic as a cover to gut workers' rights only reinforced many unions' decision to turn inward rather than go on the offensive as part of a broader class-based movement.

Given the multifaceted nature of the attacks they face, unions must fight on several fronts. Each of the three political strategies (electoral, social movement, and judicial) outlined in this chapter holds promise but also has limitations. Strengthening the labour movement requires a more comprehensive and integrated approach to political power. Rather than seeing these strategies as mutually exclusive, unions must pursue them simultaneously, leveraging the power from one approach to make up for deficiencies in the others. Social movement mobilizations need sympathetic legislators to transform popular demands into actual policy. Defiance of unjust laws through direct action is often necessary to create the conditions for successful court challenges. In other words, the labour movement cannot place all its eggs into one strategic basket.

Bringing strategic orientations together requires a strong labour movement with a clear vision. And reviving the labour movement depends, in part, on the development of a new politics of labour that breaks with the singular focus of business unionism on workers' immediate economic interests at the expense of broader working-class interests and solidarity. Although limited conceptions of solidarity have benefited some unions and their members, the effectiveness of this approach is in decline. Unions face diminishing returns as they become increasingly isolated and resented by other working people who are being left behind.

Prioritizing the interests of one's own membership is part of union DNA. Each union has a legal mandate to represent only its own members in collective bargaining, constraining strategic political decisions. Furthermore, the weight of habit, union culture, and earlier strategic choices are reinforced by specific union structures and practices.[27] Changing these ways of thinking and doing involves cultural shifts, internal union education, and solidarity across unions and the broader working class. Such transformations require great political will.

The interests of organized labour are not uniform. Political power for one union may mean something very different for another. Unions in Canada have been at odds over many issues, from constitutional questions related to national unity to environmental issues, such as pipelines, nuclear power, and climate change.[28] The prospect of a uniform political strategy or orientation is unlikely.

While barriers persist, however, there are also opportunities to establish a new politics of labour. Student strikes, Indigenous uprisings, Black Lives Matter, and alt-labour organizations are building power in multiracial working-class communities. In some places, the crisis of social democracy is generating electoral alternatives that reject neoliberalism. Consider the rise of democratic socialist and pro-labour politicians in the United States, most notably Bernie Sanders and Alexandria Ocasio-Cortez, whose candidacies would have been unthinkable before the global financial crisis of 2008. Similarly, movements pulling established labour parties to the left (notably the Labour Party in the United Kingdom while Jeremy Corbyn was its leader) or creating leftist electoral alternatives (Québec solidaire in Canada and Die Linke in Germany) have expanded their bases and their presence in legislatures. While English Canada has not yet seen similar dynamics, opportunities for such politics are constantly opening, closing, and reopening.

Labour movement renewal goes well beyond tinkering with union organizational structures and processes, or leadership. A new politics of labour must overcome its own isolation and speak to the needs of an increasingly diverse working class, most of whom are not formally represented by organized labour. Unions need to break down enduring barriers that keep the vast majority of workers out of the labour movement and out of the leadership of their organizations. If they fail to do so, union appeals to become part of a labour-led political project will find no resonance with workers and community members. As Donald Swartz and Rosemary Warskett argue, "Any revival of the labour movement rests on the construction of a qualitatively different culture of solidarity with a capacity for collective struggle that can challenge the far-reaching changes in the organization of production, the labour market, the role of finance, and the individualist culture of the global capitalist order."[29]

Given the political and economic climate, it's no surprise that some union activists believe more radical and militant political strategies are needed to defend and advance workers' interests. But there's nothing inherently radical or militant about Canadian working-class politics. Renewed political vision and strategic direction will not emerge automatically from lived experience; they must be consciously constructed and fought for. If unions are to evolve from adopting defensive or self-preserving strategies to becoming more assertive and inclusive, they will need new alliances, new politics, and an eye to the future.

ADDITIONAL RESOURCES

Camfield, David. *Canadian Labour in Crisis: Reinventing the Workers' Movement*. Halifax: Fernwood Publishing, 2011.

Fine, Janice. *Worker Centers: Organizing Communities at the Edge of Dream*. Ithaca, NY: Cornell University Press, 2006.

Kumar, Pradeep, and Christopher Schenk. *Paths to Union Renewal: Canadian Experiences*. Peterborough, ON: Broadview, 2006.

MacDonald, Ian Thomas, ed. *Unions and the City: Negotiating Urban Change*. Ithaca, NY: Cornell University, 2017.

Ross, Stephanie, and Larry Savage. *Building a Better World: An Introduction to the Labour Movement in Canada*, 4th ed. Halifax: Fernwood Publishing, 2022.

Savage, Larry, and Charles Smith. *Unions in Court: Organized Labour and the Charter of Rights and Freedoms*. Vancouver: UBC Press, 2017.

NOTES

1 Larry Savage and Charles Smith, "Public Sector Unions and Electoral Politics in Canada," in *Public Sector Unions in the Age of Austerity*, eds. Stephanie Ross and Larry Savage (Halifax: Fernwood Publishing, 2013), 52.

2 Larry Savage and Charles Smith, *Unions in Court: Organized Labour and the Charter of Rights and Freedoms* (Vancouver: UBC Press, 2017).

3 Stephanie Ross, Larry Savage, Errol Black, and Jim Silver, *Building a Better World: An Introduction to the Labour Movement in Canada*, 3rd ed.

(Halifax: Fernwood Publishing, 2015); Janine Brodie and Jane Jenson, *Crisis, Challenge and Change: Party and Class in Canada Revisited* (Ottawa: Carleton University Press, 1988).

4 Stephanie Ross, "Business Unionism and Social Unionism in Theory and Practice," in *Rethinking the Politics of Labour in Canada*, eds. Stephanie Ross and Larry Savage (Halifax: Fernwood Publishing, 2012), 37.

5 Pradeep Kumar and Gregor Murray, "Innovation in Canadian Unions: Patterns, Causes and Consequences," in *Paths to Union Renewal: Canadian Experiences*, eds. Pradeep Kumar and Christopher Schenk (Peterborough, ON: Broadview, 2006), 82.

6 Stephanie Ross, "Varieties of Social Unionism: Towards a Framework for Comparison," *Just Labour: A Canadian Journal of Work and Society* 11 (2007): 16–34.

7 Bryan Evans, "The New Democratic Party in the Era of Neoliberalism," in *Rethinking the Politics of Labour*, eds. Ross and Savage, 48–61; Larry Savage, "Contemporary Party–Union Relations in Canada," *Labor Studies Journal* 35, no. 1 (2010): 8–26.

8 Dennis Smith, "Prairie Revolt, Federalism and the Party System," in *Party Politics in Canada*, 2nd ed., ed. Hugh G. Thorburn (Toronto: Prentice Hall, 1967), 190.

9 The NDP has formed governments in six provinces (Saskatchewan, Manitoba, British Columbia, Ontario, Nova Scotia, and Alberta) and one territory (Yukon).

10 Keith Archer and Alan Whitehorn, *Political Activists: The NDP in Convention* (Toronto: Oxford University Press, 1997); Brodie and Jenson, *Crisis, Challenge and Change*; Neil Bradford, "Ideas, Intellectuals and Social Democracy in Canada," in *Canadian Parties in Transition: Discourse, Organization, Representation*, eds. Alain Gagnon and Brian Tanguay (Scarborough, ON: Nelson, 1989), 83–110.

11 Archer and Whitehorn, *Political Activists*, 50.

12 Evans, "The New Democratic Party."

13 Ross et al., *Building a Better World*.

14 Larry Savage, "Organized Labour and the Politics of Strategic Voting," in *Rethinking the Politics of Labour*, ed. Ross and Savage, 75–87; Larry Savage and Nick Ruhloff-Queiruga, "Organized Labour, Campaign Finance, and the Politics of Strategic Voting in Ontario," *Labour/Le Travail* 80 (2017): 247–71.

15 Savage, "Contemporary Party–Union Relations."

16 Bryan Evans and Stephanie Ross, "Policy Analysis and Advocacy in the Canadian Labour Movement: When the Force of Argument Is Not Enough," in *Policy Analysis in Canada: The State of the Art*, 2nd ed., eds. Laurent Dobuzinskis, David Laycock, and Michael Howlett (Bristol: Policy Press, 2018), 331–50.

17 Ross et al., *Building a Better World*. One such wave of direct action protests in North America peaked between 1998 and 2001, during which period it registered a series of successes. Following the derailing of the Multilateral Agreement on Investment (MAI) in 1998, giant demonstrations were organized against meetings of the World Trade Organization (WTO) in Seattle in 1999 and the Free Trade Area of the Americas (FTAA) in Quebec City in 2000.

18 Joel Harden, *Quiet No More: New Political Activism in Canada and around the Globe* (Toronto: James Lorimer and Company, 2013).

19 Frances Fox Piven and Richard Cloward, *Poor People's Movements: Why They Succeed, How They Fail* (New York: Vintage, 1977).

20 Steven Tufts, "Community Unionism in Canada and Labor's (Re)Organization of Space," *Antipode* 30 (1998), 227–50.

21 Ross et al., *Building a Better World*.

22 Savage and Smith, *Unions in Court*.

23 Leo Panitch and Donald Swartz, *The Assault on Trade Union Freedoms: From Consent to Coercion*, 3rd ed. (Toronto: Garamond Press, 2003).

24 Secondary picketing refers to picketing a firm that does business with a struck employer but is

not otherwise involved in the labour dispute. Roy Adams, "Voice for All: Why the Right to Refrain from Collective Bargaining Is No Right at All," in *Workers' Rights as Human Rights*, ed. James A. Gross (Ithaca, NY: Cornell University Press, 2003), 142–59; Larry Savage, "Labour Rights as Human Rights: Organized Labor and Rights Discourse in Canada," *Labor Studies Journal* 34, no. 1 (2009): 8–20.

25 Since the *SFL v Saskatchewan* decision in 2015, back-to-work legislation has been used twice in Ontario (in the 2017 Ontario college professors' strike and in the 2018 strike by teaching assistants and contract faculty at York University) and federally in the CUPW/Canada Post dispute in late 2018.

26 Panitch and Swartz, *The Assault on Trade Union Freedoms*.

27 Rosemary Warskett, "Federal Public Sector Unions in Times of Austerity: Linking Structure and Strategic Choice," in *Public Sector Unions*, eds. Ross and Savage, 126–38.

28 Larry Savage, "From Centralization to Sovereignty-Association: The Canadian Labour Congress and the Constitutional Question," *Review of Constitutional Studies* 13, no. 2 (2008): 67–95; Derek Hrynyshyn and Stephanie Ross, "Canadian Autoworkers, the Climate Crisis, and the Contradictions of Social Unionism," *Labor Studies Journal* 36, no. 1 (2010): 5–36; Larry Savage and Dennis Soron, "Organized Labor, Nuclear Power, and Environmental Justice: A Comparative Analysis of the Canadian and U.S. Labor Movements," *Labor Studies Journal* 36, no. 1 (2011): 37–57; Larry Savage and Dennis Soron, "Organized Labor and the Politics of Nuclear Power: The Case of the Canadian Nuclear Workers Council," *Capitalism Nature Socialism* 22, no. 3 (2011): 8–29.

29 Donald Swartz and Rosemary Warskett, "Canadian Labour and the Crisis of Solidarity," in *Rethinking the Politics of Labour*, eds. Ross and Savage, 18–32.

Glossary

Aboriginal people. Members of any of the legally defined culture groups Métis, Inuit, and First Nations in Canada who self-identify as such.

alt-labour. Non-union, alternative forms of labour organizing. Alt-labour practices often particularly help younger, racialized, and immigrant workers through broad activist campaigns to raise minimum wages, pressure governments to enforce economic and workplace rights, and raise public awareness of anti-worker labour practices and inadequate labour policies and regulation. Notable alt-labour initiatives include the Fight for $15 movement and worker centres for immigrant and low-wage workers.

automation. A manufacturing practice long associated with the use of technology to mass produce standardized goods. Assembly lines with unskilled or semi-skilled workers are an example. More recently, non-manufacturing sectors such as banking, shipping, trade, and retail are being transformed by automation using information and communication technologies and artificial intelligence.

bad job. Typically a job with low pay, little or no employment security, and severely constrained opportunities for advancement or pay rises. Many bad jobs - because they are temporary or have no permanence - leave workers without access to basic social benefits (such as pensions or unemployment insurance). Bad jobs are also generally characterized by workers having little protection from major risks such as unemployment, termination, or accidents, as they are excluded from legislative protection such as employment standards regulations in Canada. See also **precarious employment.**

bargain in good faith. A genuine willingness by both employers and unions to reach an agreement when negotiating a new collective agreement during the process of collective bargaining.

build back better. A set of policy strategies to improve the well-being of people in the wake of the COVID-19 pandemic or future disasters. The concept outlines policies to address catastrophes and create more sustainable economies and communities. Key principles are government recovery plans to promote fairness and equity, measures to reduce climate risk and build resilience, and new public efforts to address long-term community needs such as public health and social protection.

business unionism. An approach to unionism that emphasizes the material interests of union members in terms of higher wages and better benefits and working conditions. Unions that focus primarily on collective bargaining as the strategy to further those interests with little regard to wider community issues are said to practice "business unionism."

Canada Emergency Response Benefit (CERB). A federal policy response to support unemployed Canadians and the wider economy during the

COVID-19 pandemic. CERB was introduced in April 2020, when only 38 percent of unemployed people were eligible to receive income support. It removed certain eligibility requirements of the former employment insurance program, increased the benefit rate, and extended the number of weeks for which recipients could draw benefits. In September 2020, CERB was replaced with a revamped Employment Insurance program and two new temporary programs: the Canada Recovery Benefit (CRB) for self-employed workers, and the Canada Recovery Caregiving Benefit (CRCB) for those staying off work due to COVID-19.

Canada Health Act. Legislation introduced in 1984 to establish national conditions and criteria that provinces must meet in order to receive federal funding for public health insurance plans, although the provision of services is largely in the private sector. The criteria require provinces and territories to establish a publicly administered, universal health insurance system that provides eligible residents with access to a comprehensive range of services and ensures that coverage is portable within Canada, outside one's home province.

Canada Labour Code. An act governing industrial relations (Part 1), occupational health and safety (Part 2), and labour standards (Part 3) in the federally regulated private sector.

Canadian Auto Workers (CAW). Former leading private-sector union. Formed in 1985 after Canadian autoworkers left the US-headquartered United Auto Workers (UAW), the CAW was the primary union representing autoworkers in Canada until 2013 and played a key economic and political role nationally. The CAW merged with the Communications, Energy, and Paperworkers in 2013 to create Unifor. *See* **Unifor.**

Canadian Labour Congress (CLC). A national body composed of provincial and territorial federations of labour and approximately 130 community labour councils. Founded in 1956, the CLC organizes member education services and issue-focused campaigns, with health care being a long-standing priority. The

organization unites more than three million private- and public-sector workers to fight for improvements in working and living standards.

carbon emissions. *See* **greenhouse gas (GHG) emissions.**

carbon footprint. The amount of carbon dioxide and other greenhouse gases emitted due to the use of fossil fuels by a particular industry, sector, building, person, place, product, etc.

care provision. A system of care provision for people's physical, emotional, mental, and social well-being. The system may be based on care within the family, care privately paid for by the family or individual, care publicly funded through taxes, or a mix of these three approaches.

care work. Activities to meet the physical, emotional, and mental health or social needs of others. The work may be unpaid care by family or community members, or professionalized and relatively well paid, such as care by nurses or social workers. The proportion of paid and unpaid care work carried out in a society depends on the approach reflected in public policies.

Charter of Rights and Freedoms. A bill of rights entrenched in the Canadian Constitution that protects equality rights and other fundamental rights, such as freedom of expression, freedom of assembly, and freedom of religion. The Charter applies only to government laws and actions – including the actions of public institutions such as hospitals, police, and universities – not to the activities of private businesses.

climate adaptation. A set of policies designed to adjust societies to withstand the impacts of climate change such as sea-level encroachment, extreme weather events, and food insecurity. Adaptation strategies that can curb climate change and help societies cope with its impacts include: protection of coastal wetlands, agricultural diversification, improved forest and land management, and the protection and redesign of energy and public infrastructure.

climate bargaining. Negotiations between unions and employers on how to lower the climate footprint of work and workplaces.

climate change. A significant and lasting change in the statistical distribution of meteorological elements (e.g., wind speeds, temperatures, precipitation) as well as ecological features (ocean acidification, biodiversity loss, air pollution, and the destruction of natural habitats for plants and animals) calculated for different periods in global history. Climate change can result from natural factors such as changes in solar activity. Climate change occurring through the burning of fossil fuel use is formally known as "anthropogenic" climate change. The widespread use of fossil fuels has increased concentrations of greenhouse gases (GHGs), triggering a greenhouse gas effect with more extreme and erratic weather conditions with important implications for public health, environmental sustainability, and working conditions. The consequences of climate change are often devastating, ranging from severe heat waves, hurricanes, extreme rainstorms, floods, and mudslides to change in sea levels, the loss of certain species and ecosystems, as well as major crop failure and reductions in yield of desirable crops. See also **climate adaptation, climate mitigation,** and **greenhouse gas emissions.**

climate literacy. Understanding of essential principles of Earth's climate system including impacts of human societies on the climate and impacts of the climate on human societies.

climate mitigation. Policies to limit the further release of greenhouse gases into the atmosphere by cutting back and eventually ending the use of fossil fuels across the global economy. Key mitigation measures include: the building of 100 percent clean and renewable energy systems; the development of zero-emission transportation; increased building efficiency, and the transition of manufacturing onto clean and renewable sources of energy. The International Energy Agency (IEA) estimates that reforms to these four sectors alone offer the possibility of reducing GHGs by 85 percent by 2050.

collective agreement. A collective agreement is a written contract between an employer and a union that outlines many of the terms and conditions of employment for employees in a bargaining unit, workplace, or sector. It is the result of collective bargaining, with collective agreements typically setting out the wages, benefits, and duties of the employees as well as the duties and responsibilities of the employer or employers. See also **collective bargaining.**

collective bargaining. A legal right secured by trade unions in the early twentieth century as well as in the aftermath of World War II. By securing these economic rights after decades of opposition, workers were guaranteed the right to negotiate wages and other terms of employment, and to engage in legal strikes. In Canada, with the establishment of national or provincial legal frameworks for collective bargaining, legislation typically set out the rights of workers to unionize by holding elections. Legislation also provided procedures for the bargaining of new collective agreements; the terms and conditions for employers to opt out of collective bargaining, and for workers to conduct strikes; as well as mechanisms of dispute resolution. Through collective bargaining over the past half century, workers and their unions have been able to negotiate the terms of their employment, including wages, benefits, hours, leave, and health and safety policies. See also **collective agreement.**

collective bargaining coverage. Labour laws and institutional mechanisms ensure workers the right to bargain with employers and extend the wages, benefits, and working conditions negotiated across workplaces, sectors, or national industries. In Canada and the United States, collective bargaining coverage extends only to the proportion of unionized workplaces whose terms of work are governed by a collective agreement. By contrast, in many West European countries, collective agreements can be extended to cover a wider proportion of the labour force including workers in non-unionized workplaces. *See also* **union density.**

community unionism. A form of unionism that broadens the social and political basis of unions and the labour movement by building coalitions with immigrant, faith, gender, and other groups and networks in their geographic communities. Community unionism helps to address problems that affect many workers, such as poverty, housing, health care, and discrimination based on immigration status, gender, race, sexuality, faith, and other issues workers face inside and outside their workplaces.

complex poverty. Poverty caused by a complex set of related factors including poor housing, poor health, low levels of education, unemployment or precarious employment, living in a neighbourhood where violence is common, and experiencing racism and/or colonialism. Those experiencing complex poverty often blame themselves and suffer low self-esteem, low self-confidence, as well as feelings of hopelessness.

compulsory arbitration. Mandatory process to settle a labour dispute when the employer and union fail to reach a settlement through collective bargaining. Such arbitration can include automatic access to employers or unions, the provision of arbitration at the discretion of the labour board, or even imposition of the first contract. Some labour contracts make specific provision for compulsory arbitration. *See also* **collective bargaining.**

contracting out. Transfer of work to workers not employed by the employer, usually outside the employer's establishment. An important example is the shifting of care services and other service work out of the public sector and into the private and non-profit sectors. Governments save costs on wages and overhead, and they transfer the risk and responsibility of running these often underfunded services to non-government (and often non-union) service providers. *Also known as* **outsourcing.**

duty of fair representation. The obligation of unions not to act in a manner that is arbitrary, discriminatory, or in bad faith in representing employees. For example, unions are obliged to represent all workers covered by a union collective agreement, regardless of whether or not all the workers in the union choose to sign their union membership card.

electoral politics. In Canada, national electoral politics centres on elections to Parliament through an electoral system in which the candidate with the most votes in a riding represents the constituents of that riding in Parliament.

employee misclassification. Employee misclassification occurs when an employer does not treat someone who is an employee as an employee. Such misclassification occurs, for example, when an employer classifies a worker as an independent contractor or a self-employed contractor even though the worker is in a dependent employment relationship with the employer and lacks control over how and where their work is performed. *See also* **solo (or bogus) self-employment** and **gig economy.**

employment standards. Legislated minimum standards that establish the rights and responsibilities of workers and employers. These laws cover national or subnational jurisdictions and structure requirements such as minimum wages, hours of work, and benefits. Employment standards typically set the rules and floors for all non-unionized workers, although they often exclude the self-employed.

federally regulated private sector (FRPS). Collectively, all industries and private-sector employers whose business operations fall under the regulatory jurisdiction of the federal government. Some areas are air transportation, banks, grain elevators, feed and seed mills, fisheries, certain First Nations band council activities, marine shipping, ferries, pipelines, ports, postal and courier services, radio and television broadcasting, interprovincial rail and road transportation, uranium mining, and other industries in the national interest.

financialization. The term used to describe major shifts in advanced industrial economies in recent decades. Financialization characterizes how many economies have transitioned away from manufacturing and are now led by their financial sectors, with private financial actors, markets, and credit playing leading roles in, for example, housing markets and real estate, manufacturing, and agriculture, as well as in the growth of new information technologies. Financialization also characterizes how companies in the "real" economy – that is, firms that create goods – have become tied to financial owners and markets, and have turned much of their attention away from earlier concerns with making productive changes and investing long-term in machinery and workers, and instead prioritize finance to maximize short-term profits and financial returns.

First Nations. Indigenous peoples of Canada who are ethnically neither Métis nor Inuit. A First Nation can refer to a band, a reserve-based community, or a larger tribal grouping, or to status Indians who live either in or outside First Nations communities.

fissuring. Processes whereby businesses rely on various forms of outsourcing, subcontracting, and temporary agencies in supply chains to reduce the number of their direct employees as well as fragment statutory responsibility for their workforces.

General Agreement on Tariffs and Trade (GATT). An agreement signed in 1947 to promote international trade by reducing or eliminating trade barriers such as tariffs or quotas. Superseded by the World Trade Organization (WTO) in 1995.

gig economy. The arrangement of flexible work in temporary or contract positions that connects workers to tasks and customers through digital platforms (e.g., Uber). The gig economy undermines traditional employment by making it more difficult to define employees and employers within the work relationship. *Also known as the* **platform** economy.

globalization. Processes of global integration of economies, cultures, and populations brought about by massive increases in corporate size, cross-border trade in goods and services, and in flows of investment, technologies, people, and information.

golden age of capitalism. A period of high employment, economic growth, and productivity running from 1945 to 1975. The period is identified with the growth of the middle class. It is also associated with the massive rise of strong industrial unions and the expansion of public services such as education and health care allowed. This expansion of unionized workforces and public services helped lower inequality and raise living standards for the vast majority of citizens for the first time in history – hence a "golden age."

good job. A job typically offering at least living wages and providing safe working conditions, predictable schedules, job security, and other benefits such as paid time off. Good jobs often provide longer-term economic security with a greater degree of permanence. With the support of public policies and statutory protections, those in good jobs have higher degrees of security and assistance when they experience unemployment, sickness, disability, and retirement. In addition, to reduce the risk of workers being trapped in low-quality jobs or joblessness, governments can help ensure good jobs through the provision of public services that develop, maintain, and upgrade skills and training at all ages.

green economy. A transformative economic change incorporating principles of social justice in which economic activity is no longer primarily based on burning fossil fuels and the unsustainable use of resources. Green economies promote economic systems that are sustainable and have higher clean energy requirements. Green economies also highlight the importance of re-using, repairing, refurbishing and recycling existing materials and products, as well as better eco-design of products with longer life cycles that provide much greater durability, reparability, recyclability, and waste prevention.

Green New Deal and Just Transition. The Green New Deal is a package of public policies (and now international policy model) to cut greenhouse gas emissions in half by 2030 while creating many more good jobs and expanding public services, including public transit, health care, affordable housing, and postal services. Central to the Green New Deal is a Just Transition developed in conjunction with the labour movement to provide workers, their families, unions, and communities participation in policymaking to ensure that they have the income, training, employment, and other supports they need to participate successfully in the transition to a low-carbon economy. *See also* **green recovery.**

green recovery. To address the climate crisis and ensure long-term sustainable growth, the International Labor Organisation (ILO), the Organisation for Economic Co-operation and Development (OECD), and many trade unions have recommended that governments enact policy reforms to ensure environmentally sustainable and socially inclusive production in the wake of the COVID-19 pandemic. A green recovery policy initiative involves governments fast-tracking clean energy and zero-emission transport investments, and in providing income and training for workers so that countries can achieve decent work and environmental sustainability. *See also* **green economy.**

greenhouse gas (GHG) emissions. The burning and extraction of fossil fuels accounts for 80 percent of carbon dioxide emissions and is a key source of other gases such as methane. These gases trap heat in the atmosphere and contribute to calamitous climate changes that endanger all life on the planet.

hazard. In the context of the workplace, any source of potential damage, harm, or adverse health effects on a worker. Hazards created by work organization can be physical, chemical, biological, or psychosocial. Psychosocial hazards are the most prevalent. *See also* **psychosocial hazard, risk.**

health and safety movement. The historical and contemporary roles that organized workers, community groups, unions, and allies play in improving occupational health and safety.

independent contracting. The provision of services by a person or business on a term-limited contract basis. In the case of labour, this often entails providing work to a firm outside of an employment relationship, depriving the worker of labour standards protection and other social entitlements.

Indigenous peoples. In Canada, Indigenous peoples include First Nations, Inuit, and Métis peoples who are descendants of the original inhabitants of the land that is now Canada.

industrial wage. The wage of a worker in the industrial and manufacturing sector. The average industrial wage has generally been used as a measure of a good wage more broadly, because traditionally higher rates of unionization in the industrial sector typically translate into higher wages, job security, access to benefits, and permanent employment.

Intergovernmental Panel on Climate Change (IPCC). A United Nations body established in 1988 to provide policy makers with up-to-date scientific assessments of climate change developments and implications and to offer adaptation and mitigation strategies. *See also* **climate adaptation, climate change, climate literacy, climate mitigation.**

International Labour Organization (ILO). A United Nations agency established in 1919 with the mandate to promote social justice and internationally recognized human and labour standards. Bringing together governments, employers, and workers of UN member states, it is the body's only tripartite agency. The ILO also tracks major developments related to COVID-19, provides regular updates, and offers policy advice to promote safe and secure work.

Justice for Janitors.   Initially a campaign strategy of the Service Employees International Union (SEIU) to organize janitorial workers in the United States in the 1980s. Justice for Janitors has become a model for organizing workers who face strong barriers to unionizing, especially low-wage, service-sector employees. The model develops alliances with community organizations and social movements, and uses innovative tactics such as street theatre, protests, and publicity focused on employers' corporate reputations.

Kyoto Protocol.   The first major international climate treaty, adopted in 1997. The protocol put the 1992 United Nations Framework Convention on Climate Change into operation by committing industrialized countries and economies in transition to reducing greenhouse gas emissions according to stated targets.

labour market deregulation.   A set of policies and reforms intended to help business boost employment and profitability by lowering labour costs and increasing the flexibility of the labour force through part-time and temporary jobs. Deregulation involves labour law and regulatory reform, and the recasting of social security policies to emphasize business priorities over social protections.

labour market flexibility.   A neoliberal policy model focused on giving employers more choice to worsen various working conditions and lower labour costs. The flexibility of the labour market increases with lower statutory minimum wages and the reduction of employer contributions to social programs. Employers also seek more freedom to hire and fire workers quickly and easily, to use non-standard employment, and fewer fines and enforcement of labour and employment laws.

labour market reform.   The active dismantling and/or overhaul of key labour laws related to those related to union organizing in new workplaces, employers' power to intervene in union certification and labour disputes, and collective bargaining rights in the public sector.

labour precarity.   *See* **precarious employment.**

labour regime.   The set of labour laws, regulations, and social policies intended to stabilize wages and provide income and social security for workers in national labour markets. In Canada, the United States, and Western Europe, broad labour regimes first emerged in the wake of the Second World War. Recent deregulation efforts seek to make these regimes more favourable to employers while restricting collective labour protections for jobs, wages, and social security.

labour relations board.   An independent body responsible for adjudicating and resolving labour-management disputes.

layering-in.   The introduction of public policies and labour laws that circumvent existing policies and standards. For example, governments can foster low-wage, flexible labour markets by permitting employers to hire more temporary foreign workers, who are largely unable to access core employment rights. Government initiatives to increase low-wage work by subsidizing employers who hire low-skilled workers on social assistance are another example.

legal activism.   An approach to political and social change that emphasizes the use of courts. Legal suits launched to defend or expand workers' rights by challenging the constitutionality of anti-labour government legislation are an example.

living wage.   An hourly wage a worker needs to earn in order to pay their basic expenses and participate in their community.

low-carbon economy.   An economy based largely on renewable energy sources that produce low levels of greenhouse gas (GHG) emissions. See **net-zero carbon economy** and **zero-carbon economy**.

manufacturing value-added. The difference between the cost of producing a product and the price to the consumer.

measure of poverty. An indicator assessing a person's ability to achieve a minimally acceptable standard of living in a given society. No matter which measure is used, the poverty line highlights an income level at which people face considerable hardships in trying to secure the basic necessities of life in their societies.

minimum wage. The minimum that can legally be paid to a worker. Minimum wages are set by governments and typically bear no relation to what is needed to survive and thrive.

National Health Service (NHS). An umbrella term for the health systems of England, Scotland, Wales, and Northern Ireland that provide publicly funded comprehensive and universal health services. Established in 1946, the program is a model that many countries have emulated.

neoliberalism. An ideology and set of political practices and policies that emphasize and reinforce competition in human relations. The primary goals of neoliberalism are to transfer economic power from the state to corporations and banks, while increasing the profitability of firms. Key neoliberal policies include international free trade and investment agreements, privatization of public services, the reduction of corporate and personal taxes, and the elimination or significant weakening of regulations that protect workers.

net-zero carbon economy. An economy that achieves a balance between carbon it emits into the atmosphere and carbon it removes from the atmosphere by, for example, using carbon capture technologies or planting trees. See **low-carbon economy** and **zero-carbon economy**.

new public management. A model of public-sector management that requires public and contracted-out services to adopt strict measures of cost reduction and efficiency performance. This private-sector-like system tends to standardize work, removing and reducing hard-to-measure activities that enhance care, such as more open-ended and holistic relationships. In care work, standardization breaks complex tasks into small, repetitive, highly scripted tasks, which intensifies the work and makes it easier to replace higher-credentialled, higher-paid workers with lower-credentialled, lower-paid workers or volunteers.

non-standard employment. Part-time work, temporary employment, self-employment, holding multiple jobs, and work involving a disguised employment relationship. *See also* **employee misclassification** and **solo (or bogus) self-employment.**

occupational health and safety (OHS). The conditions and processes of work in relation to its impact on workers' health and safety. OHS processes seek to identify and characterize hazards created by work organization in order to control or prevent them at the source. Workers have the right to raise concerns about OHS, the right to know the hazards they face, and the right to refuse unsafe work.

occupational violence. *See* **workplace violence.**

Order in Council P.C. 1003. An order issued in 1944 to officially adopt the Wartime Labour Relations Regulations. Implemented after a wave of strikes in Canada, the legislation granted workers the right to form unions and required employers to recognize unions chosen by a majority of workers.

Organisation for Economic Co-operation and Development (OECD). An international organization comprised mainly of high-income countries that conducts research and coordinates international and domestic policies. Its reports include analyses of economic challenges, labour market policies, energy transitions, sustainable recovery plans, and the COVID-19 pandemic.

outsourcing. *See* **contracting out.**

own-account self-employment. *See* **solo (or bogus) self-employment.**

permanent residency. The right of someone who is not a Canadian citizen to live, study, and work in Canada without a time limit. Permanent residents have the same social benefits as citizens, such as universal health care, but not the right to vote or to run for public office. Permanent residents may apply for citizenship after a specified period of residence in the country.

platform economy. *See* **gig economy.**

policy drift. Changing the effectiveness of a policy by failing to update it to reflect changing circumstances. For example, minimum wage policies are less effective when the minimum wage (in contrast to a **living wage**) is not increased in line with increasing costs of living.

populism. Most often defined as a political appeal to the people as actors who have been disregarded or exploited by the so-called economic, political, and cultural elites who are seen to hold excessive power. Waves of populism ebb and flow over time. *See also* **populist moment.**

populist moment. A period in which populism of either the right or the left is on the rise. *See* **populism.**

post-democracy. A term coined by political scientist Colin Crouch to describe liberal democratic states, such as the United Kingdom and the United States, that are increasingly controlled by politico-economic elites. In the context of ongoing transformative changes such as globalization and large-scale privatization, legislatures, political parties, and public administration, continue to function but are increasingly hollowed out. In the process, political power shifts away from citizens, including organized labour and community groups, toward corporate and other powerful elites with concentrated political power.

precarious employment. Employment characterized by dimensions of labour market insecurity, such as uncertain job tenure, lack of control over the labour process, limited regulatory protection, variable hours and irregular schedules, low wages, and a lack or absence of benefits. *See also* **bad job.**

prepayment scheme. An arrangement in which individuals or groups voluntarily pay a predetermined amount of money (a premium) in return for access to defined health services. Prepayment (insurance) plans can be non-profit or for-profit. They are less equitable than public insurance schemes, which are funded through the income tax system.

private sector. That sector of the economy that is not under direct government control and instead is owned by private groups and individuals, including both for-profit and non-profit organizations.

privatization. The transfer of publicly owned assets to the private sector, increasingly represented by large, often transnational, corporations. In the health care sector, privatization involves the de-listing of services, such as physiotherapy, from public health insurance plans, thereby shifting the responsibility to pay to private insurers and/or consumers.

provincially regulated private sector (PRPS). Private businesses subject to the laws and regulations of the province in which they operate. Private-sector employers under the legislative authority of the Parliament of Canada, such as airlines, banks, and railroads, are in the **federally regulated private sector.**

psychosocial hazards. In the workplace, such hazards are linked to ways work is designed and/or managed that increase stress. They can cause psychological harm. *See also* **hazard, workplace stress, workplace violence.**

public health. Branch of medicine specializing in protecting and improving the health of communities through policies and programs that prevent and reduce disease and injury. Such policies and programs are normally regulated and funded by governments at international, national, and subnational levels.

public sector. All enterprises and services run and operated by governments whether at the national, provincial, or municipal level. It does not include private companies, voluntary organizations, or households. Major public-sector institutions include health care, education, municipal services, and public administration.

quantitative easing. A monetary policy used by a central bank, such as the Bank of Canada, that increases the money supply by buying government bonds, corporate debt, and other assets in order to stimulate greater lending and investment in the economy.

racism. Belief that a particular race is superior or inferior to another race based on biological or cultural characteristics. Racism can be exemplified through the actions of individuals or be embedded in institutions that, through policies and procedures, reproduce racial hierarchies that racist beliefs seek to justify.

Rand Formula. A feature of Canadian labour law that requires mandatory payment of union dues for those working under and covered by a collective agreement, regardless of the worker's decision to become a member of a union.

real wages. Wages that have been adjusted for inflation to reflect their current real power to buy goods and services.

risk. In the context of the workplace, the likelihood that damage, injury, illness, or death will occur as a result of exposure to a hazard. Risk is often mischaracterized by management as acceptable or reasonable without consideration of its acceptability to workers. *See also* **hazard, workplace stress.**

Royal Commission on Health Services (RCHS). Also known as the Hall Commission (after its chair, Justice Emmett Hall), the RCHS was established in 1961 to investigate the feasibility of establishing a public universal health care system. The commission report included recommendations for a comprehensive health services program whose cost would be shared by federal and provincial governments.

service sector. The part of the economy that provides services, or intangible goods, rather than the products of manufacture, mining, forestry, agriculture, etc. The definition is not without its contradictions as several service industries (e.g., restaurants) do produce something tangible (e.g., meals).

social democracy. A political orientation embodied in social democratic parties, such as the New Democratic Party in Canada. Social democratic parties operate within liberal democratic capitalist systems and typically support stronger labour movements, more equal distribution of income and wealth, and a greater state role to provide more comprehensive, egalitarian, and effective social services, such as public education, health care and social welfare. Social democratic politics today is particularly associated with key welfare state policies and collective bargaining institutions found in Nordic countries (Sweden, Finland, Denmark, Iceland, and Norway).

social movement politics. In addition to labour movement politics, social movement politics in Canada based on mass mobilization of social movements to advocate for political change and to strengthen social movements identities include Indigenous (e.g., Idle No More), anti-racist (e.g., Black Lives Matter), feminist (e.g., #MeToo movement), environmental (e.g., Schools Strike Movement), and student (e.g., Quebec Student Strike of 2012), among other politically mobilized social movements.

social unionism.   A type of unionism linking narrower, more immediate workplace issues, such as collective bargaining for better wages and work hours, to broader, longer-term working class political issues in society, such as racial and gender oppression, inadequate health care, the climate crisis, etc. As union members and as citizens, workers thus participate in a broader working-class politics that helps to link workplace and non-workplace collective action for progressive political change and social justice. *See, for example,* **Unifor**. *See also* **community unionism, solidarity unionism.**

social wage.   A measure of how people benefit from government social programs, such as pensions, unemployment insurance, and income transfers paid to parents of young children. The level of the social wage varies from country to country, generally inversely to poverty levels.

solidarity unionism.   Do-it-yourself organizing by rank-and-file workers to build their collective power to improve working conditions in their workplaces independently of union officials, particularly through direct action tactics. Such tactics include "slowdowns" in which workers reduce their output while appearing to do their job normally. Anti-oppression protests alongside other social movements are also common. Another tactic is the "sick in," where workers call in sick, so that they are collectively absent from their work, thus disrupting production. "Work to rule" is a tactic in which workers obey employers' formal work rules so strictly that production becomes chaotic. In "Sit-down strikes," workers occupy their workplaces to pressure their employers to resolve their grievances. Using such direct action tactics, workers collectively organize to build their workplace power to improve their jobs and working conditions.

solo (and bogus) self-employment.   A category of work in which a person does not directly work for an employer and does not employ anyone else. Also known as *own-account self-employment* or often as *bogus self-employment*, where employees are registered as self-employed, freelance, or temp but are effectively under the authority and responsibility of an employer. Such bogus self-employment has increased dramatically in recent years as employers have sought ways to circumvent employment and social policy legislation as well as avoid paying employer contributions to government programs such as the Canada Pension Plan, and avoid their obligations to comply with employment standards such as minimum wage and overtime rights.

standard employment relationship.   A full-time relationship in which a worker provides paid labour to a single employer, normally at a fixed worksite, and receives a full range of statutory and other job protections.

Tommy Douglas.   Premier of Saskatchewan from 1944 to 1961 and leader of the federal New Democratic Party from 1961 to 1971. Under his leadership, Saskatchewan introduced North America's first universal health care program.

trade union.   A formal organization of workers (historically belonging to specific trades) formed to advance the interests of members.

unemployment insurance.   Income benefit programs provided to the unemployed for financial assistance and income security. Established widely in North America and Western Europe after World War II, unemployment insurance programs support workers during periods of unemployment while also stimulating the wider economy during economic downturns. In 1996, Canada renamed its program "Employment Insurance," cutting government funding, lowering benefits, and restricting access to EI benefits for those in part-time or self-employment.

unfair labour practices (ULPs).   Conduct by employers, unions, or individuals that interferes with an employee's ability or right to decide whether to support a union, including when a union is being organized, during collective bargaining, and during a strike by employees or lockout by the employer.

Unifor. Canada's largest private-sector union, with more than 315,000 members across the country. Unifor has a commitment to promote broad social justice goals.

union advantage. Better pay, benefits, working conditions, and other gains, including due process protections in grievance and arbitration procedures, that usually accrue to workers who are members of a union or are covered by a collective bargaining agreement.

union density. The proportion of the labour force that belongs to trade unions and is covered by collective agreements in a particular industry or country. Union density indicates labour movement strength, with higher density often linked to a stronger and more coordinated labour movement that is more able to improve wages and working conditions. Higher density also often contributes to a better-resourced labour movement that has greater ability to pressure governments and political parties to introduce and uphold better labour and social policies. *See also* **collective bargaining coverage.**

union organizing. The organization (or certification) of a non-union company or worksite. In Canada, the process normally entails having workers sign union cards as proof that they want to join the union. When a card-signing campaign succeeds, it is usually followed by a secret ballot election. If a majority of employees agrees to union representation, the employer is legally obligated to recognize and to bargain in good faith with the union to achieve a collective agreement.

vertical disintegration. The organization of work or production in which formerly integrated tasks are broken into constituent activities and performed by separate companies or workforces.

Wagner Act. An informal name for the National Labor Relations Act of 1935 (written by Senator Wagner), which provided most workers in the US (excluding agricultural workers, domestic workers, among many others) the right to join unions, engage in collective bargaining, and take collective action, including strikes, under the protection of the National Labor Relations Board (NLRB).

whole worker approach. Holistic approach to worker organizing inside and outside the workplace espoused by Jane McAlevey in *No Shortcuts: Organizing for Power in the New Guilded Age.* This organizing approach emphasizes the untapped organizing potential "whole workers" have not only as workers but also as family members, neighbours, volunteers, friends, members of faith organizations, and other important social roles that make up their lives.

worker voice. Ability of workers, individually and collectively, to have a formal or informal role in workplace decisions that affect them. Trade unions and collective bargaining regimes raise the influence of worker voice in the workplace and often in politics and public policy more generally. In addition, institutions such as health and safety committees and pay equity committees, as well as works councils and co-determination (found in countries such as Germany) where worker representatives sit on corporate boards, are also used to provide employees with information on business decisions as well as offer the opportunity for employees to offer alternative approaches to production, employment, and sustainability initiatives. Employee surveys and feedback provide weaker forms of employee input and participation. With the decline of trade unions and supportive institutions in recent decades, worker voice over business decisions has been weakened or divided.

workplace stress. Harmful physical and emotional responses linked to conflicts between job demands placed on an employee and the amount of control the employee has over meeting those demands. Described as the result of an effort and reward imbalance, workplace stress can result in mental illness, musculoskeletal injuries, violence, and increased risk for the worker. *See also* **hazard, risk, workplace violence.**

workplace violence. Act or threat of physical violence, harassment, intimidation, or other disruptive behaviour at a workplace.

zero-carbon economy. An economy that achieves no carbon emissions by using renewable energies such as wind, geothermal, hydro, and solar energy sources. See **low-carbon economy** and **net-zero carbon economy.**

Contributors

JOHN PETERS is a research fellow at the Inter-university Research Centre on Globalization and Work at Université de Montréal.

DON WELLS is professor emeritus at the School of Labour Studies and Department of Political Science at McMaster University.

Donna Baines is a professor of social work at the University of British Columbia.

Yale Belanger is a professor of political science at the University of Lethbridge.

John Calvert is an associate professor in the Faculty of Health Sciences at Simon Fraser University.

Bryan Evans is a professor in the Department of Politics and Public Administration at Toronto Metropolitan University.

Carlo Fanelli is an assistant professor in the Department of Social Science at York University.

Colleen Fuller is an independent health policy researcher in Vancouver, British Columbia.

Rafael Gomez is director of the Centre for Industrial Relations and Human Resources and an associate professor at the University of Toronto.

Jennifer Harmer is a PhD candidate at the Centre for Industrial Relations and Human Resources at the University of Toronto.

Rebecca Hii is a PhD candidate in the Department of Sociology at Toronto Metropolitan University.

John Holmes is professor emeritus in the Department of Geography and Planning at Queen's University.

Phillip Kelly is a professor in the Department of Geography at York University.

Adam King is a senior researcher in the Social and Economic Policy Department at the Canadian Labour Congress.

Andrew King was the department leader for Health and Safety for the United Steelworkers Union Canada (retired). He is now a researcher in residence at McMaster University.

Stephanie Luce is a professor at CUNY School of Labor and Urban Studies at the City University of New York.

Janet McLaughlin is an associate professor of health studies at Wilfred Laurier University.

Andrea M. Noack is an associate professor in the Department of Sociology at Toronto Metropolitan University.

Stephanie Ross is an associate professor and director of the School of Labour Studies at McMaster University.

Larry Savage is a professor of labour studies at Brock University.

Jim Silver is professor emeritus of urban and inner-city studies at the University of Winnipeg.

Mark Thomas is a professor of sociology at York University.

Steve Tufts is an associate professor in the Department of Geography at York University.

Leah Vosko is a professor of political science and Canada Research Chair in the Political Economy of Gender and Work at York University.

Index

254; governments and, 102; green recovery plan and, 38; influence of, 4, 10, 92–93; and labour laws, 4; and labour market deregulation, 290; and liberal democracies, 4; and lobbying, 93–95; NDP and, 311; neoliberalism and, 8; and OHS, 290; and paid sick leave, 82; and political parties, 79, 94–95; and progressive change, 38; provincial governments and, 92, 94–95, 97–98, 102; and public interest, 93; and public policy, 4, 10, 11, 92–93, 94–95; and research institutions, 94; and right-wing cultural appeals, 92; and social programs, 225; and unions, 299–300; and welfare state policies, 225. *See also* profit(s)

business unionism, 308–9, 312, 316

Buy American policy, 217

California Assembly Bill (AB5), 118

Cameron, Barbara, 109

Campbell, Archie, 150

Canada Assistance Plan, 180

Canada Child Benefit (CCB), 175

Canada Child Tax Benefit, 175

Canada Emergency Wage Subsidy (CEWS), 31, 33

Canada Health Act (CHA) (1984), 236, 238, 239, 241, 244

Canada Labour Code, 110, 111, 115, 118, 120, 196(box)

Canada Pension Plan, 176, 180

Canada Post, 280(box), 293

Canada Recovery Benefit (CRB), 180; Canada Emergency Response Benefit (CERB), 4, 10, 12, 31, 33, 82, 101, 180, 183, 199; Canada Recovery Sickness Benefit (CRSB), 35, 101–2

Canada's Building Trades Unions (CBTU), 279; *Jobs for Tomorrow: Canada's Building Trades and Zero Emissions,* 280–81

Canada–United States Free Trade Agreement, 45–46

Canada–United States–Mexico Agreement (CUSMA), 217. *See also* North American Free Trade Agreement (NAFTA)

Canadian Agricultural Human Resource Council (CAHRC), 157–58, 162

Canadian Auto Workers (later Unifor) (CAW), 96, 213, 215

Canadian Centre for Policy Alternatives, 297

Canadian Chamber of Commerce (CCC), 94

Canadian Federation of Nurses Unions, 151

Canadian Freelance Union (CFU), 294

Canadian Injured Workers Alliance (CIWA), 145

Canadian Labour Congress (CLC): and climate crisis, 281; and environmental movement, 284; Green Economy Network (GEN), 284–85; and health care, 240; on health care, 238; Just Transition Task Force for Canadian Coal Power Workers and Communities, 282–83; and migrant workers, 298; and NDP formation, 310

Canadian Manufacturer Association, 94

Canadian Manufacturing Coalition, 205

Canadian Medical Association, 238

Canadian Sickness Survey, on low-income earners, 237

Canadian Union of Postal Workers (CUPW), 280(box); community organization, 293; #FoodstersUnited campaigns, 191(box)

Canadian Union of Public Employees (CUPE), 131(box), 300

cannabis dispensary workers, 293

capital: union relationship with, 315; worker relationship with, 123

capitalism: changes in relationship with democracy, 10–11; democracy vs., 92; golden age of, 68; home-based tasks and, 191(box); and low-wage work, 68; NDP and, 308; regulation of, 76; social democracy and, 308

carbon: budgets, 37; climate mitigation and, 275; concentration of, 274; emissions, 5; footprint, 277; low-carbon economy, 38, 218, 277, 283; zero-carbon economy, 16, 217; zero-emission economy, 37, 278, 281, 285. *See also* greenhouse gases (GHGs); just transition to low-carbon economy

care provision: community services and, 223; COVID-19 and, 119; within families, 222(box), 223, 224; Indigenous peoples and, 223; individual responsibility for, 224, 231; LCP and, 163–64; nature of, 226; neoliberalism/privatization/re-individualized risk era, 222, 225–26; pre-welfare state/family era, 222, 223–24; public policy/policies in, 222, 223–26; shifting from hospitals to community-based,

244; social action and, 229–30; TFWs in, 100; unpaid, 223, 229, 230–31; value of, 230–31; wealthy and, 223; welfare state/publicly shared risk era, 222, 224–25; women and, 12, 223, 224. *See also* childcare; home-based care

care sector: collective agreements in, 229–30; contracting out in, 226; COVID-19 and, 222, 230; in COVID-19 recovery plan, 16; gender in, 230; governments and, 223–26; green recovery plan and, 38; institutions in pre-welfare state era, 223; national differences in investment in, 38; precarious employment in, 226–28; privatization/defunding of services and, 226; social movements for, 231; and stockholder dividends, 226; women in, 224. *See also* long-term care (LTC)

care work: cash-for-care model, 227–28; COVID-19 and, 195; COVID-19 and aides/nurses in LTC facilities, 283; gig economy in, 231; gig/on-demand platform work in, 228; in-home vs. nursing home, 222(box); ideology of, 222; job losses, 225; neoliberalism and, 228, 229, 230, 231; NPM in, 226–27, 229; outsourcing, 229; political choices and, 228–29; as precarious employment, 231; in pre-welfare state/family era, 228; in private realm, 222, 230; privatization of, 13, 229; in public sector, 224; Resident Assessment Instrument in, 227; and social justice, 227; unions and, 229–30, 231; wage levels, 225; welfare state and, 228, 230; women and, 222; working conditions, 222, 226–27

care workers: during COVID-19, 230; pay equity and, 224–25; unpaid care work, 229; wage levels, 230; working conditions, 223

care workers: abuse of, 164, 165; activism, 164–65; advantages of, 158; campaigns for, 298–99; children of, 165, 166(box); COVID-19 and, 164; families of, 164, 165, 166(box); hours of work, 165; numbers of, 164; open work permits, 164; and permanent residency, 163–64; and social services, 164; and union rights, 164; West Indian Domestic Scheme, 163; women as, 158. *See also* temporary foreign workers (TFWs)

Caregiver Program (CP), 163

Caregivers Action Centre, 164

Cargill High River meat-processing plant, 90, 150

Caribbean people: men and agricultural work, 159; women and domestic work, 159

C.D. Howe Institute: on First Nations reserve education, 262; national media coverage, 94

Centre des travailleuses et travailleurs immigrants (Immigrant Workers Centre), 298

CEOs. *See* corporate executives

Charter of Rights and Freedoms: on collective bargaining, 315; on freedom of association, 127, 242, 243, 314–15; and Health and Social Services Delivery Improvement Act (BC), 242, 243; and labour law, 127–28; and Labour Trilogy/New Labour Trilogy, 314, 315(box); occupational stress and, 142; on right to strike, 314, 315(box); and unions/unionization, 127–28, 314–15

Chevron, 49

childcare: Caregiver Program and, 163; COVID-19 and, 33–34, 35; expenses, 173; federal government and, 35; labour-community coalitions and, 300–1; male workers in, 225; national program, 183, 301; need for employment in, 278; privatization of, 299; provincial governments and, 34, 35; subsidization of, 158; TFW caregivers and, 158; as underpaid, 225; universal, 8, 33–34, 35, 224; women and, 193; and women's employment, 301; women's responsibilities for, 199

children: child welfare/foster care systems and, 259; entrenched lifestyles and, 259; Indigenous/First Nations, 177, 254, 259; infant mortality rate, 237; life circumstances and later outcomes, 258–59; poor families and, 177; in poverty, 176–77; poverty of opportunity and, 177; precarious employment and, 176–77; of SAWP workers, 161; social policies and, 176–77; of TFW caregivers, 164, 165, 166(box)

China: automotive industry in, 13; COVID-19 in, 30; labour standards in, 13; low-wage employment in, 13; WTO membership, 210

Chrétien, Jean, 241

Chrysler, 212, 216. *See also* Fiat Chrysler Automobiles (FCA) (later Stellantis)

citizenship rights: and labour rights, 297; migrant workers, 297; SAWP workers and, 159; TFWs and, 156, 290, 297

civic participation. *See* public participation

Climate Action Network, 284

climate change: citizen concern regarding, 17; citizen mobilization regarding, 82; and climate adaptation, 275; and climate literacy, 281; climate mitigation of, 275; and climate resilience, 37; COVID-19 and, 5, 275; in COVID-19 recovery plan, 16; democratic approach to, 285; effects, 274–75; federal government and, 275–77; governments and, 36; human activity and, 274; manufacturing sector and, 217–18; responses, 275; skilled workers and, 37; and sustainable economy, 24; threat of, 274; and workplaces, 278. *See also* carbon; global warming; green economy; greenhouse gases (GHGs)

Coalition Avenir Québec, 97

Coalition Main rouge (Red Hand Coalition), 300

Coalition opposée à la tarification et la privatisation des services publics (Coalition against Pricing and Privatization of Public Services), 300

Coalition to Save Home Care, 244

Code Blue for Childcare, 301

collective agreements: in agricultural work, 162; in automotive industry, 212; in Canada Labour Code, 110; in care sector, 229–30; and contracting out, 242; and employment standards, 67; ILO and, 67; and just transition to low-carbon economy, 279; and minimum wages, 67; in Nordic countries, 8; opting out of, 81; and precarious workers, 291; public policy and, 126–27; and rule of law in workplace, 67–68; between UFCW and Loblaws, 196–97; worker numbers covered by, 125

collective bargaining: across industries/sectors, 77; advantages of, 135; in agricultural work, 162; in automotive industry, 212; business unionism and, 308–9; Charter of Rights and Freedoms and, 315; climate bargaining in, 280(box); decline in, 123; federal government and, 108; in FRPS, 108, 109; ILO and, 67; at individual workplace level, 197; in individual workplaces, 123; international comparisons, 62; and just transition to low-carbon economy, 279; and low-wage work, 62; multi-establishment/regional units, 133–34; neoliberalism and, 81; and non-union workers, 127; and non-union workers and, 128; Order in Council P.C. 1003 and, 108, 109; and postwar class compromise, 67; in PRPS, 119; in public sector, 76–77; sectoral, 127; universal, 134; Wagner Act and, 123. *See also* Order in Council P.C. 1003

commission on fairness at work (2004–06), 108

commodification: of health services, 236, 243; of labour, 59, 123

community unionism, 291–93

Compass Group, 241

Confédération des syndicats nationaux (CSN), 298

Conference Board of Canada: on agricultural mechanization, 162; on child poverty, 176–77; and tax avoidance gap, 48

Conference of the Parties to the United Nations Framework Convention on Climate Change, 276; "Solidarity and Just Transition: Silesia Declaration," 283–84

Congress of Aboriginal Peoples (CAP), 261

construction sector: employment growth, 190; job creation in renewable energy, 280–81; and transition to low-carbon economy, 279, 280–81, 285

Consumer Price Index, 115

contracting out: in care sector, 226; collective agreements and, 242; contract flipping, 196(box); corporate restructuring and, 49; in-home care, 243–44; of hospital services, 241–42; and private health insurance/care companies, 244; vertical disintegration and, 113; and wage levels, 226; and work force reduction, 49; and working conditions, 226. *See also* independent contracting

Cook, Tim, 48(box)

Co-operative Commonwealth Federation (CCF): and NDP formation, 310; and social justice, 75; and universal health care, 236; welfare state and, 302

Corbyn, Jeremy, 317

corporate executives: buyback strategies, 50; COVID-19 and, 32, 50; hourly wages vs. average, 179; short-term stock market performance and, 47

corporations: COVID-19 pandemic aid to, 32, 50; Crown, private power corporations vs., 282; minimum wages in small, 94; restructuring, 45, 48–49, 50, 51, 113–14; size, and employment standards, 94, 114, 209; size, in FRPS, 114; and taxation, 47–48, 181. *See also* business interests

Corus Entertainment, 50

COVID-19 pandemic: activism during, 246; building back better from, 15, 24, 34–36, 38–39; business interests and, 33, 38; and business unionism, 316; case numbers, 24, 29, 31; and citizen mobilization, 82; and climate change, 5, 82, 275; contact tracing, 30–31, 34, 35; in Denmark vs. Canada, 3–4; and economic crisis, 4–5; and economy, 24, 25–26, 29(t), 31–32, 50; effects of, 4–5; and elderly people, 245; emergency measures, 5; as endemic disease, 24, 25, 35; and families, 34; federal government and, 31, 33, 35, 38, 101–2, 263; and Filipino community, 164; financial sector and, 31–32; and food banks, 178; food delivery services during, 191(box); and government debt, 31–32; Great Depression compared, 5, 26, 50; green recovery from, 4; human-centred recovery from, 68–69; impacts of, 24–26; income support during, 5, 33, 82, 101, 217; and Indigenous communities, 245; and inequality/inequalities, 5–6, 26–27, 31, 73, 90, 179, 245; and investment in markets/corporations vs. jobs, 90; and living conditions, 178; Marshall Plan for, 230; mortality rates, 24–25, 28, 29–30, 238, 239, 245–46; national differences in performance regarding, 38; and neoliberalism, 63, 244–45; official national responses to, 28–31; and platform economy, 134; and populism, 199; and poverty, 27, 174, 175, 178; precautionary principle toward, 150–51; and private vs. public/non-profit health care, 246; and profits, 55; protest movements, 307; provincial governments and, 31, 33, 35, 38, 92, 101–2; and public policy, 4–6, 28–31; public support for government intervention in, 230; and quantitative easing, 32; and racialized groups, 63, 90, 177; recovery plan, 15–18; reopening, 5, 34, 35; and schools, 34, 35, 150; social solidarity during, 230; subsidies to corporations, 50; and supply chains, 50, 205, 217; and sustainable environment, 15; sustainable green economy recovery from, 28, 34, 36–38; testing, 30–31, 34, 35; as turning point, 6; and unions/unionization, 17, 27, 53, 83, 119, 217; vaccines, 5, 25, 29, 34, 35; variants, 5, 25, 34; and vulnerable people, 26–27, 245; and wealth inequality, 50; WHO on, 244; and women, 63–64, 193, 198–99; and young people, 176; zero-tolerance mobilization vs. slowing of, 28, 30, 33. *See also under names of individual industrial sectors*

COVID-19 pandemic, and employment: and agricultural work, 36, 157(box); aid for workers, 50; and bad jobs, 52–53; and care sector, 119, 140, 164, 195, 222, 230; and class divide between professionals vs. low-paid precarious workers, 83; and essential services, 27, 35–36, 55, 102, 150, 198, 217, 230, 283; and fragmented service labour market, 193; in FRPS, 116–17, 119; gig economy, 33; and government protections of workers, 83; and health care workers, 140, 195; high-risk worker groups, 150; and hours of work, 27; and Indigenous employment, 262–63; and job insecurity, 73; job losses during, 175, 198, 205; job retention schemes, 5, 26, 81, 101; and labour market deregulation, 101–2; layoffs during, 5, 26, 27, 33, 90; and loss of working hours, 198; and low-wage employment, 27, 33, 63–64, 198; and manufacturing employment, 205, 211; and meat-processing-plant workers, 73, 90, 150, 283; and migrant workers, 27, 36, 140, 150; and non-standard employment, 32; non-unionized vs. unionized workers and, 55, 64; and OHS, 102, 140, 145, 150–51, 152; and pay increases, 198; personal support workers (PSWs) and, 135–36; and precarious employment, 10, 33, 64, 68, 82, 117, 263; public health response and risk, 135–36; and racialized workers, 27, 198; and SAWP workers, 160; self-employed, 33; and sick leave, 33, 35, 101–2, 119, 140, 151, 173, 200, 217; and social wage, 180; and strikes, 295; and unemployment, 5, 26, 33, 63–64; and vulnerable workers, 283; and women, 34; worker control over own work during, 152; and worker–capital relationship, 123; and workers' rights, 152, 316; working from home vs. in workplace, 27, 278; and working poverty, 173; and workplace closures, 26; workplace transmissions, 151; and young workers, 54

Coworker.org, 295

Criminal Code (Canada), 145

crises: and changes for better, 82; community services and, 223; market primacy/business profitability and, 82; urgency, and government action, 16

Crown–Indigenous Relations and Northern Affairs Canada (CIRNAC), 253

employment relations. *See* industrial relations

employment standards: business interests and, 312; Canada Labour Code and, 110, 111; collective agreements and, 67; courier firms and, 293; defined, 108; destruction of union-based industrial relations system and, 94; federal government and, 109; firm size and, 114; in FRPS, 108, 109, 110, 111; globalization and improvement in, 93; liberal market economies and, 61; minimum, 297; policies, 14; and private service sector, 197; provincial governments and, 100, 110; small businesses and, 94; social minimums in, 110; unevenness between provinces, 109; union certification and, 64; weakening of, 10, 11, 81, 99

Employment Standards Act (ESA) (Ontario), 110, 197, 298, 312

employment/unemployment insurance, 99; CERB replaced by, 101; COVID-19 and, 101; economic slowdown of 2020 and, 81; Employment Insurance (EI), 180; erosion in, 181; federal–provincial division of powers and, 109; New Deal (Canada) and, 109; program reduction, 81

energy conservation, 277–78

environment: CLC and environmental movement, 284; COVID-19 and sustainability of, 15; free trade agreements and protections of, 46; policies for sustainability of, 15; and Site C dam, Peace River, 280. *See also* green economy; renewable energy

equality: restoration of, 82–83; social unionism and, 309; universal health care based on, 236

essential services/workers, 278; agricultural, 157(box); COVID-19 and, 27, 31, 35–36, 55, 150, 198, 217, 230, 283; federal legislation and, 102; and hours of work, 27; provincial legislation and, 102; temporary migrant farm workers as, 27; wages, 217; women as, 198; working conditions, 135

Eugenio-Romero, Bonifacio, 157(box)

European Trade Union Institute, 277

European Union (EU): Build Up Skills, 277; low-wage jobs across, 60; and manufacturing sector, 210

ExxonMobil, 49

Fair Workplaces, Better Jobs Act (2017) (Ontario), 66(box), 197, 297

Fairness movement (later Justice for Workers: Decent Work for All), 17

families: care provision within, 222(box), 223, 224, 244; COVID-19 and, 34; family policies/benefits, 33, 34; household income disparities, 91; poor, and child poverty, 177; of SAWP workers, 161, 162; of temporary foreign agricultural workers, 159, 162; of TFW caregivers, 164, 165, 166(box); transnational, 161; types, and poverty, 175–76. *See also* children

Faraday, Fay, 159

federal government: anti-poverty strategy, 182; anti-union stance, 314; and childcare, 35; and climate change, 275–76; and collective bargaining, 108; and COVID-19, 31, 33, 35, 38, 82, 101–2, 263; and employee misclassification, 118; and equal pay for equal work, 118–19; essential worker legislation, 102; and Indigenous employment, 256; jurisdiction, 109–10; labour market reshaping, 12; and labour relations/standards, 108, 109; and labour rights, 11; and minimum wage, 115; as model employer, 11; NDP and, 310; and neoliberalism, 78–79; and occupational health and safety, 108; and OHS statistics, 140; "Pan-Canadian Framework on Clean Growth and Climate Change," 276; and pay equity, 225; and precarious employment, 118; and public health, 245; responsibility for federal employment sector, 143; and sick leave, 35; social program spending, 174, 180; and standard employment relationship, 117–18; and unions, 108; and universal hospital insurance, 237–38; and workers' rights, 108; workforce responsibility, 143

Federal Labour Standards Review, 65

Federal Public Sector Labour Relations and Employment Act, 111

federally regulated private sector (FRPS): Canada Labour Code and, 110, 120; collective bargaining in, 108, 109, 119; COVID-19 and, 116–17, 119; disadvantaged social group employment in, 120; employee profile, 110–13; firm size in, 114; independent contracting in, 113–14; industrial restructuring and, 113–14; job quality in, 118; job security in, 108; job tenure in, 114; labour standards in, 108, 109, 110, 111; low-wage work in, 115; minimum wage in, 115; numbers of employees, 111; permanent full-time jobs in, 113; precarious employment in, 11, 108, 113-16, 120; provincial distribution of employees, 111-12; provincial distribution of industries, 111-12; PRPS compared, 108, 112-13, 120; public sector employment compared, 108, 111, 113; self-employment in, 118; shifts in, 11; sick leave in, 119; solo or bogus self-employment in, 114; standard employment relationship in, 108, 113, 117; union coverage in, 115; working conditions in, 108

federal-provincial division of powers, 109; Constitution and, 108, 109; Great Depression and, 109; and New Deal, 109; Second World War and, 109

Federation of Sovereign Indigenous Nations (FSIN), 260(box)

Feed Ontario, 182(box)

Fiat Chrysler Automobiles (FCA) (later Stellantis), 211, 213; and electric vehicles, 218

Fiera Foods, 148

Fight for $15 (US and other countries), 91-92

Fight for $15 and Fairness (Canada), 17, 91-92, 196(box), 200, 291, 297, 312

Filipina women: as caregivers, 298-99; and domestic work, 159; in LCP, 163-64

financial crisis of 2008-09. See global financial crisis of 2008-09

financialization: and automotive industry, 215-16; in automotive industry, 215; and corporate restructuring, 48; governments and, 47; influence of, 10; neoliberalism and, 46; and shareholder value maximization, 215; and unequal global economy, 50

Finland: collective bargaining in, 62; COVID-19 in, 29-31, 33, 35; income inequality in, 8; low-wage work in, 63; neoliberalism in, 8; social spending in, 63; unions/workers as social partners in, 135; wages in, 59; workplace-related deaths in, 142

firms. See corporations

First Nations: autonomy, 254; casinos, 260(box); defined, 264n2; federal transfer payments and, 258; reserve schools, 262; reserves, 254, 257-58; residential schools, 254, 256, 262; and Site C dam, Peace River, 280; and social benefits, 258; transition to green energy and job offers to, 282; unemployment, 257, 258; urbanization, 255, 262. See also Indigenous peoples

First Nations employment, 256-58; alternative land management options and, 258; anti-discrimination/anti-harassment policies and, 262; available work and, 259; benefits of, 263-64; casino employment, 15; complexity of, 253; concentration within reserve administration, 258; co-op/internship programs, 261; earnings, 257; educational responses, 262; employer discrimination and, 13, 15; and health, 259; improvement to, 260-62; income disparities, 256; Indigenous organization responses, 260-61; investment in employment initiatives, 253; labour exclusion vs., 258; layoffs and, 262; as low-wage, 258; off reserve for reserve residents, 258, 262; participation rates, 257(t), 258; policy responses, 261-62; as precarious, 254, 255-56, 263; and primary, resource-based industries, 254; public policy and, 254-55; skills training, 256; stereotypes regarding, 254; stressful conditions, 259; as unsafe, 258; urbanization and, 258; and workplace inequities as systemic barriers, 261-62. See also Indigenous labour

Fischer, David, 54(box)

fissuring of workplaces: and bad jobs, 52; in care work, 226, 227; contracting out and, 49, 226; COVID-19 and, 53; effects of, 9; of employment relations, 93; in hospitality sector, 93; independent contracting and, 194; labour market flexibility and, 51; in manufacturing employment, 211; neoliberalism and, 108; outsourcing and, 291; in service sector, 93; temporary employment and, 194; unionization vs., 119

5-10-15, 297

flexible employment: and economic change, 181; and employment benefits, 60; labour costs and, 60; labour market deregulation and, 60; neoliberalism and, 108; non-standard employment and, 193; and precarious employment, 181; in public sector, 52; and unionization, 61. See also labour market flexibility

Floyd, George, 295

food/food services sector: banks, 54(box), 178; COVID-19 and, 198, 199; delivery, 191, 291; Food Banks Canada, 178; insecurity, 181; loss of working hours during COVID-19, 198; prices, 181; store workers,

198, 283; sustainable vs. unsustainable production, 37; unionization of, 191

Ford, 49, 211; and electric vehicles, 218

Ford, Doug, 66(box), 190, 197, 199, 218, 312

Ford, Henry, 214

Foreign Domestic Movement, 163, 164

Foroohar, Rana, 48(box)

fossil fuels: elimination of reliance on, 277–78; market domination of sector, 17; oil and gas sector transnational corporations, 49; pollution cutting, 37; primary economic role of coal/oil/gas production, 277; tar sands subsidization, 276

Fraser, Nancy, 223

Fraser Institute, 94; in BI system, 183; on minimum wage, 66(box)

free market(s): and automotive industry job losses, 214; democratic politics vs., 17; inflation and, 60; and labour markets, 59; neoclassical economic theories, 80; neoliberalism and, 78; think tanks, 94

free trade agreements: direct action struggle against, 313; movement-based strategies against, 313; neoliberalism and, 45–46

freelance workers, 294

French revolution, 73, 74

Friedman, Milton, 8

full-time work: in manufacturing sector, 205; as precarious, 194; unionized workplaces and, 68

GABRIELA, 165

Galabuzzi, Grace-Edward, 177

Galgóczi, Bela, 277

gender: in care sector, 230; low-wage employment, 195; and manufacturing wages, 208; in non-standard employment, 195; in precarious employment, 195; in service sector, 191; social program cuts and, 182; in standard employment relationship, 113; and TFWP creation of minorities pockets, 165; and wage inequities, 224–25. See also women

General Agreement on Tariffs and Trade (GATT), 210

General Motors (GM): bankruptcy protection restructuring, 212, 215, 216; Canadian government aid to, 216; Delphi bankruptcy restructuring, 215; and electric vehicles, 218; in GLR, 211; as international corporation, 49; Oshawa plant closure, 213

Germany: health care sector in, 247; heavy industry/coal phasing out in Ruhr, 277; job retention schemes, 101; Die Linke, 317; low-wage work in, 60, 63; social spending in, 63; unemployment insurance in, 101; union coverage vs. density in, 124; unions/workers as social partners in, 135; wages in, 59; worker voice and efficiency in, 128; works councils in, 134

gig economy, 191; in care work, 228, 231; COVID-19 and, 33. See also platform economy; self-employment; solo or bogus self-employment

Gini coefficient, 92(box)

Glencore, 49

global financial crisis of 2008–09: 2020 economic slowdown compared, 81–82; and automotive industry, 212, 216; direct action struggle against, 313; financial deregulation and, 46; and insufficiency of austerity/small measures, 55; lack of job market recovery since, 45; and low-wage work, 60; and manufacturing sector, 206, 207–8, 210; and pro-business government intervention, 82; and unemployment, 63; and US pro-labour politicians, 316–17

Global Gender Gap Report, 176

Global Skills Strategy (GSS) program, 100

global supply chains. See supply chains

global warming: and climate adaptation, 275; costs/damages resulting from, 36–37; effects, 274–75; GHGs and, 274; IPCC and, 274; irreversible tipping points, 275; policy agenda for, 16; and wildfires, 37. See also climate change

globalization: and bad vs. good jobs, 51; and climate crisis, 5; and employment standards improvement, 93; history, 45; and labour laws, 93; and low-cost employment, 93; and manufacturing employment, 210–11; neoliberalism and, 78–79; and OHS, 145; and private-sector unionization decline, 125; and right-wing populism, 200; and service sector, 199; and workers' compensation, 145; and zoonotic diseases, 24

Gompers, Samuel, 309

good jobs: bad jobs vs., 4, 51–52, 54; and economic growth, 61; education and, 290; factory work as, 142; frontline workers and, 52–53; green, 313;

knowledge-based world and, 190; loss of, 205–6; in manufacturing sector, 205; precarious employment vs., 5; scarcity of, 59; service-sector employment and, 190; in sustainable industries, 37. *See also* job quality

GoodLife Fitness, 17, 292–93

governments: actions as problem, 78; and business interests, 102; business/union cooperation/coordination in Nordic countries, 61; and care sector, 223–26; and COVID-19, 150; crisis responses, 16; and democracy, 73; distrust of, 90, 97; enforcement of OHS laws, 147; and financialization, 47; and fossil fuel sector, 36; and income inequality, 90–91; and just transition, 281–82; and long-term care, 226; and poverty, 173; role in labour markets, 80(t); and social wage, 173, 180–82; worker protection action during COVID-19, 83. *See also* federal government; provincial governments

Great Depression: and citizen mobilization, 16–17, 82; COVID-19 compared, 5, 26, 50; effects of, 223; and federal–provincial division of powers, 109; and health services, 237; and Indigenous wage labour, 254; Keynesianism and, 76; and unemployment, 254; unemployment during, 63; and Wagner Act, 127(box)

green economy: and climate mitigation, 275; costs of, 37–38; Green Economy Network (GEN), 284–85; Green New Deal, 16, 83, 183, 200, 283; green recovery plan and, 28, 34, 36–38; and job creation, 38; renewable energy sources and, 282; taxation and, 37–38; worker opportunities in, 38; zero-emission economy, 37, 281, 285; zero-net energy use, 278. *See also* environment; renewable energy

greenhouse gases (GHGs), 37, 282(box); climate mitigation and, 275; concentration of, 274; COVID-19 and, 5; emissions reduction/targets, 15, 36, 276; and global warming, 274; projects cutting, 38. *See also* carbon

guaranteed annual income (GAI), 183

Guaranteed Income Supplement to Old Age Security, 176, 180

Ham Commission, 144

Hansen, James, 274

Harper, Stephen, 275

Harris, Mike, 78, 100(box)

Hauglie, Anniken, 243

Hayek, Friedrich, 8

Hayter, Susan, 68

hazardous materials, 141, 143–44

hazards: of agricultural work, 160; psychosocial, 143, 149, 151; work and, 140; and workers' rights, 144

health care: commodification of, 236; commodification of services, 243; community-based, 237–38; and democracy, 241; expenditure as share of GDP, 239; health coalitions, 300; history, 236–38; as human right, 236, 237, 240; labour intensivity, 241; market operating principles, 239; in private realm, 236; privately funded expenditure, 239; privatization of, 242, 246; as public service, 238; universal, 236, 237, 238. *See also* public health care systems

health care sector: allied health services in, 240; ancillary services, 240; COVID-19 and, 150, 245; and democracy, 247; focus on in-patient hospital/physician services, 239–40; government–employer–union partnership model, 243; neoliberalism and, 240–43, 246, 247; NPM in, 13; nurse numbers, 240; physician numbers, 240; precarious employment in, 247; privatization of, 313; size, 240; social solidarity and, 247; unionization in, 240, 243, 247; in US vs. Canada, 62; women in, 240; worker voice in, 247; working conditions in, 247

health care workers: COVID-19 and, 140, 195, 198; emergency responders, 150; refusals by, 151; SARS and, 150; unionization of, 240, 247; universal health insurance and, 240; wage cuts, 242; women as, 240; and workplace violence, 149

Health Employers Association of BC (HEABC), 243

health insurance: and Canadian Medical Association, 238; employer-sponsored, 238; Hall Commission and, 238; prepayment schemes, 236–37; SAWP workers and, 162; universal, and health care workers, 240; in US, 238–39

heating, ventilation, and air conditioning (HVAC) systems, 282(box)

Henwood, Doug, 45

Home Child Care Provider Pilot, 164

Home Support Worker Pilot, 164

home-based care: contracting out in, 243–44; COVID-19, and workers, 140; need for employment in, 278; outsourcing in, 243–44. *See also* care provision; long-term care (LTC)

Homeless Hub, 182(box)

Honda, 49, 211

Hong Kong, COVID-19 in, 28, 30

Hospital and Diagnostic Services Act (1957), 236

Hospital Employees' Union (HEU), 242–43

hospitality sector. *See* accommodation sector; food/food services sector

hospitals: care shifting to community-based care, 244; closures/bed closures, 241, 300; contracting out/outsourcing of services, 241–42; core providers, 241; delayed admission/early discharge policies, 243; downsizing, 247; history of, 223; non-core functions, 241–42; NPM and, 13; prepayment schemes, 236–37; privatization of, 300; unionization in, 243; universal insurance, 237–38; workforce reductions, 241

hotels. *See* accommodation sector

hours of work: caregivers (TFW) and, 165; COVID-19 and, 27; essential workers and, 27; flexible, 162; living wage, and reduction in, 66; loss, during COVID-19, 198; low-wage workers and, 27; New Deal (Canada) and, 109; in private service sector, 196–97; SAWP workers and, 162; of TFWs, 156

housing: COVID-19, and prices, 178; prices, and poverty, 178; strategy for social, 183

Howe, Eric, 262

Hubich, Larry, 314

human capital theory, 192

human rights: caring/egalitarian politics and, 38; COVID-19 pandemic and, 53; health as, 237; health care as, 236, 240; labour/workers' rights as, 314, 315; OHS as, 149; United Nations Universal Declaration of Human Rights, 237; work and, 290

Hyatt, 291

Idle No More, 313

immigrants: community unionism and, 291–92; East Danforth Community Chapter and, 294; and First Nations unemployment, 258; and Indigenous peoples, 253; in non-standard employment, 124; rights, and populism, 200; in service-sector employment, 192, 193. *See also* migrant workers

income equality: and economic growth, 90; labour law reforms and, 95; labour protection extension to non-unionized workers and, 61; progressive policies for, 4

income inequality: in average household incomes, 91; consequences of, 90–91, 179–80; COVID-19 and, 50, 53, 90, 179; democracy and, 73, 90, 91; and democratic participation, 180; and distrust of government, 97; between First Nations and Métis/Inuit, 256; between First Nations on vs. off reserve, 256; governments and, 90–91; and health care privatization and service accessibility, 247; increase in, 90, 179–80, 290; indicators, 92(box); between Indigenous men and women, 256; between Indigenous peoples and non-Indigenous Canadians, 255; across labour market, 13; living wage and, 67; low-wage employment and, 90; neoliberalism and, 8; non-standard employment and, 90; in non-standard vs. standard employment, 91; in post-democracy, 96–97; and power concentration, 180; powerlessness toward, 90; private health insurance market and, 240; provincial governments and, 90; public policy and, 91; racialized women and, 177; and racialized workers/visible minorities, 90; and redistribution variations among countries, 77; between rich and rest of population, 6, 73, 91; between richest 1% and low-wage earners, 91, 92(box); and social determinants of health, 180; union decline and, 125; and voter turnout, 97. *See also* poverty; wealthy

income security: individual responsibility for, 81; insecurity among advanced industrial countries, 91; laws and, 76; neoliberalism and, 79; OHS and, 76; program reduction, 81; variations among countries in, 77

income support: COVID-19 and, 5, 33, 82, 101, 217; On-Reserve Income Assistance Program, 263; restriction of access to, 81. *See also* social supports

independent contracting: of couriers, 293; employees vs. contractors in, 130; and fissured workplaces, 194; in FRPS, 113–14, 118; and gig economy, 191(box); neoliberalism and, 108; in postal delivery services,

293; and precarious employment, 110. *See also* contracting out

ability and, 290; provincial governments and, 97–101, 102–3; and reshaping of labour market, 12; and right-wing populism, 200; risk for workers, 12; and unionization, 217; and working conditions, 93

labour market flexibility: about, 50–51; and bad jobs, 12; and job quality, 12; labour market deregulation and, 60; neoliberalism and, 50; and profit maximization, 50; provincial governments and, 99–100; public policies and, 12; shift of employment risk to workers, 51. *See also* flexible employment

labour markets: dual/split, 192; free market and, 59; government role in, 80(t); provincial governments and reform of, 97, 98–99; secondary, 192; segmentation, 191–93, 200

labour movement(s): attacks on, 307; in Canada vs. US, 64; fragmentation of, 77; and policy making, 313; and political change, 301; and political/economic/social change, 307; revival of, 315–17; and social movements, 301; strategic voting by, 311. *See also* unions

Labour Party (UK), 224, 310, 317

labour policy/policies: market/business priorities and, 80; politics of, 10–12; and standard employment relationship as norm, 113

labour protections. *See* employment protection(s)

labour regimes, development of, 76–78

labour relations. *See* industrial relations

labour rights: citizenship rights and, 297; COVID-19 pandemic and, 53; equal, 290; federal government and, 11; as human rights, 128, 129, 135, 314; labour regime development and, 76; and OHS, 149; provincial governments and, 11; SAWP workers and, 161; weakening of, 10. *See also* workers' rights and; workplace rights

labour standards. *See* employment standards

labour unions. *See* unions

labour-community coalitions: and childcare, 300–1; and social programs, 299

Lashley, Phillip, 262

Law Commission of Ontario, 52

layoffs: COVID-19 and, 5, 26, 27, 33, 53, 90; First Nations workers, 262; in manufacturing employment, 205–6; racialized workers/visible minorities and, 90; sick leave and, 82; and stock prices, 47

liberal democracies, 4, 74

liberal market economies, 61, 62–63

Die Linke (Germany), 317

Live-In Caregiver Program (LCP), 100–1, 163–65, 166(box)

living conditions: COVID-19 and, 178; and health, 178; labour market deregulation and, 93; low-wage employment and, 93; and poverty, 178; of SAWP workers, 159, 161

Living Wage for Families Campaign, 52

living wage(s), 52, 65; arguments against, 66–67; benefits, 65–66, 67; campaigns, 17, 52, 91–92, 200, 291, 296, 297, 301, 312; and job losses, 66; minimum wages vs., 65–67; and redistribution of wages, 67; and rich–poor gap, 67; in US, 65–66; and working poverty, 67; and younger workers, 66–67. *See also* minimum wage(s)

lobbying, 93–95, 312

Loblaws, 32, 197

lone-parent families. *See* single-parent families

long-term care (LTC): Angus Reid poll on, 226; contracting out, 243–44; COVID-19 and, 26–27, 195, 226, 245–46; COVID-19 deaths in for-profit vs. publicly-funded facilities, 300; deaths in, 140; for-profit, 245; funding cuts for, 245; government intervention in, 231; governments and, 226; illness among workers, 140; low-wage workers in, 245; need for employment in, 278; nursing home care, 222(box), 223; personal care workers and, 244; profit in, 246; public expenditure as share of GDP, 228; public home care system in Manitoba, 244; quality of, 244; racialized workers in, 245; staffing shortages, 227; wage levels in, 230; working conditions in, 246. *See also* home-based care

low-cost employment: agricultural producers and, 94; global competition and, 80; globalization and, 93; immigration regulations and, 100; and living/working conditions, 93; technological changes and, 80. *See also* labour costs; low-wage employment

low-income people. *See* poverty

low-wage employment: capitalism and, 68; CERB and, 199; collective bargaining coverage and, 62; COVID-19 and, 27, 33, 63–64, 198; definition, 10; disability days, 237; education levels and, 290;

employer exit options in, 99; First Nations and, 258; in FRPS, 115; gendered division of labour and, 195; global financial crisis of 2008-09 and, 60; globalization and, 93; growth in, 12; and hours of work, 27; and income inequality, 90; Indigenous peoples and, 223; international comparisons, 59, 60-63; labour commodification and, 59; labour market deregulation and, 10; labour protection extension to non-unionized workers and, 61; living wage campaigns and, 67; in long-term care sector, 245, 246; minimum wage and, 65; neo-liberalism and, 68; OECD and, 60, 92(box), 115; part-time employment as, 173; as precarious, 115-16, 194-95; prevalence of, 73; in private service sector, 197-98; profitability and, 292; in PRPS, 115; public policy and, 59-61; in public sector, 115; racialized workers and, 159, 173, 177, 195; richest 1% of income earners vs. low-wage earners, 92(box); in service sector, 193-95; social programs and, 62-63; temporary agency workers and, 52; TFWs in, 100, 156; and unemployment, 63; and union density, 62; women in, 173; workers' rights and, 197-98; as workforce percentage, 59; and working/living conditions, 93; and workplace stress, 146. *See also* labour costs; low-cost employment

Lütke, Tobias, 32

Manitoba: basic income experiment in Dauphin, 183; First Nations casinos in, 260(box); First Nations child poverty in, 177; Indigenous unemployment in, 177; NDP governments, 310; public home care system, 244; SAWP workers in, 162

Manitoba Government Employees' Union (MGEU), 244

manufacturing employment: automation/technologies and, 209, 211; in automotive industry, 211; benefit packages in, 205; climate change and, 278; COVID-19 and, 205, 211; decline in, 206, 207-11; education levels in, 205, 206, 208, 209, 211; fissuring in, 211; as full-time, 205; and GDP, 207(f); gender, and wages, 208; globalization and, 210-11; as good jobs, 205; good vs. bad jobs in, 52; growth in, 190; hourly wages in automotive sector vs., 214-15; by industries, 206, 208; job location, 210(f); job

losses in, 79, 199, 205-6, 217; and labour costs, 205, 210; labour market deregulation and, 13; layoffs in, 205-6; lower job availability, 205; networked forms of industrial organization and, 209; OHS in, 205, 217; outsourcing and, 209; pension plans in, 205; productivity, and value-added, 208; service-sector employment vs., 205, 207; union density in, 205, 210-11; unionization in, 205, 208, 211(f); unskilled/semi-skilled workers in, 205; wage stagnation, 205, 208, 209; wages, and middle-class lifestyle, 205

manufacturing sector: assembly line production, 209; automotive industry value-added, 206; climate change and, 217-18, 278; COVID-19 and, 217; economic importance, 205; global financial crisis of 2008-09 and, 206; and just transition to low-carbon energy, 281-82; multinationals in, 13; offshoring in, 49, 210; outsourcing in, 49, 209; plant closures, 205; service sector and, 125, 199, 206; spinoff effects, 205; supply chains, 205, 217; technology in, 206; transnational corporation branch plants in, 210; trends, 206-7; unions in, 143; value-added, 206, 208. *See also* automotive industry

Marchildon, Greg, 239

Marriott, 291

McDonald's, 291, 295, 296

McGuinty, Dalton, 100(box)

McMaster University, 297

McNeil, Stephen, 135

Medical Care Insurance Act (1966), 236, 238

medicare, 180, 224, 236

Mendelson, Michael, 262

mental health/illness: Indigenous peoples and, 259; occupational stress and, 141-42; SAWP workers' families and, 161; workplace violence and, 149-50

Métis: defined, 264n2; unemployment, 257; wages, 256

Métis Centre of Excellence, 261

Métis National Council (MNC), 261

Métis Scholar Awards, 261

Métis Training to Employment (MTE) program, 262

Mexico: agriculture in, 160; automotive industry in, 13, 210, 214, 215, 217; labour costs in, 210, 214;

governments, 77; formation of, 309, 310; and Keynesian redistributive politics, 310; labour reform bill in Ontario, 94; later reversal of pro-labour legislation, 98; organized labour and, 95–96; provincial governments, 310-11; in provincial vs. federal politics, 310; size of donations to, 95; as social democratic party, 6, 64, 310; and social justice, 75, 308; Unifor and, 96; unions and, 299, 308, 310; and welfare state, 302

new public management (NPM), 13, 226-27, 229

New Zealand, COVID-19 in, 28, 29-30

newcomers. *See* immigrants

Newfoundland and Labrador: manufacturing job losses, 207; provincial party financing in, 95

non-financial companies (NFCs), assets of, 46, 47(f)

non-standard employment: categories of, 52; COVID-19 and, 32; earnings gap with standard employment, 91; and flexibility, 193; gendered division of labour and, 195; growth in, 12, 124, 193, 255–56; ILO on, 52; and income inequality, 90; increase in, 52; labour market deregulation and, 10, 80; newcomers in, 124; precarious employment compared, 113, 194; in private-service sector, 13; proportion of workers in, 10; provincial governments and, 97; racialized workers and, 124, 195; in service sector, 193, 194; union decline and, 123; unionization and, 124; young workers and, 124. *See also* bad jobs; job quality; precarious employment

Nordic countries: collective agreements in, 8; cooperation/coordination between business, government, unions, 61; COVID-19 in, 30; health care sector in, 243; poverty rates, 173; social programs in, 8; social wage in, 173; unions in, 8. *See also* Denmark; Finland; Norway; Sweden

North American Free Trade Agreement (NAFTA), 45–46; and manufacturing sector, 210, 214; and Mexican agriculture, 160; Trump's promise to renegotiate, 217. *See also* Canada–United States–Mexico Agreement (CUSMA)

Northern Business Relief Fund, 263

Norway: care work in, 228, 229; COVID-19 in, 29-30, 35; health care sector government–employer–union partnership model, 243; health expenditure in, 239; income inequality in, 8; labour movements in, 77; neoliberalism in, 8; unionization of health care workers in, 247; unions/workers as social partners in, 135

Nova Scotia: First Nations casinos in, 260(box); health services system, 237; manufacturing job losses, 207; Provincial Workers' Association, 237

nurses, 240; unionization rates, 243

Obama, Barack, 216

Ocasio-Cortez, Alexandria, 316-17

occupational health and safety (OHS), 12; in agricultural work, 160; assembly line work and, 213; behaviour-based safety, 146(box); Canada Labour Code and, 110; COVID-19 and, 102, 140, 145, 150–51, 152; employment insecurity and, 146; enforcement limits, 146–48; federal government and, 108; federal-provincial joint laws, 143; globalization and, 145; Ham Commission and, 144; health and safety movement history, 143–44; health and safety training for SAWP workers, 163; history, 142–45; as human right, 149; and income security, 76; individual responsibility and, 145; inspection of workplaces and, 143, 144, 145, 147–48, 197; international comparisons, 142; IRS and, 144; joint health and safety committees, 150; labour laws and, 143; in manufacturing employment, 205, 217; NDP and, 310; neoliberalism and, 140, 143, 144, 145, 151; permanently disabled workers, 144; policies, 14; precautionary principle, 150–51; preventative strategies, 140; profitability and, 290; prosecutions, 148; and public health/safety, 148; statistics regarding, 140; strikes, 144; as struggle between workers and employers, 143; TFWs and, 156; union campaigning for improved monitoring/compliance, 83; unionized workplaces and, 68; unions and, 143–44, 148, 217; voluntary compliance, 146–47; worker carelessness myth, 145–46; worker discipline for raising concerns, 144, 148–49; worker representatives, 150–51; worker voice and, 148–49; workers' rights and, 140, 149. *See also* hazards; injuries, workplace; stress; workplace violence

Occupy movement, 313; Occupy Wall Street movement, 190

Offert, Rose, 262

right-wing, 190, 197, 307; service sector and, 199–200; social unionism vs., 134; union decline and, 125

postal service, 293

post-democracy, 90, 92; citizenship in, 96–97; effects of, 96–97; income inequality in, 96–97; and labour market deregulation, 97–101; political polarization in, 96; provincial governments and, 93; public power and, 103; trends of, 93; union–political party relations and, 96

poverty: anti-poverty strategy, 182–83; basic income and, 183; causes of, 173; complex, 178–79; cost of, 182(box); COVID-19 and, 27, 174, 175, 178; and democratic participation, 180; family types and, 175–76; and food banks, 178; gap, 181; governments and, 173; guaranteed annual income and, 183; and health, 178; health care and, 236; housing prices and, 178; Indigenous peoples and, 177–78; AT LICO (after-tax low-income cut-off), 174, 175; AT LIM (after-tax low-income measure), 174, 175, 176; line, 173–74, 182(box); and living conditions, 178; living wage and, 66; MBM (market basket measure), 174, 175; of opportunity, 177; part-time employment and, 173; pensions, employee and, 176; people with disabilities and, 176; precarious employment and, 173; racialized groups and, 177–78; recessions and, 174; of SAWP workers' families, 162; self-employment and, 173; seniors and, 176; single individuals and, 175–76; single-parent families and, 173, 176; size of gap, 175; social determinants of, 178; social investment vs., 183; social policies/programs and, 173; social spending and, 174, 176; social wage and, 173; temporary employment and, 173; temporary vs. complex, 179(box); trends in Canada, 174–75; wages, 53, 64; women and, 176; young people and, 53, 176, 178. *See also* income inequality; working poverty

precarious employment: basic income and, 183; in care sector, 226–28, 231; characteristics of, 113; and child poverty, 176–77; COVID-19 and, 10, 33, 64, 68, 82, 117, 263; criteria for, 115–16; definition, 52, 193–94; federal government and, 118; in federally regulated private sector, 11; firm size and, 114; First Nations and, 254, 255–56, 263; flexible labour force and, 181; and food bank usage, 178; frontline workers in, 53; in FRPS, 108, 113–16, 120; full-time work as, 194; gendered division of labour and, 195; good jobs vs., 5; in health care sector, 247; Indigenous employment as, 15, 177, 254, 255, 258–60; industry variations, 116; and job insecurity, 256; job tenure and, 114; and labour conflict, 190; lack of worker voice in conditions and, 195; living wage campaigns and, 67; low wages and, 115–16, 190, 194–95; marginalized groups in, 192; neoliberalism and, 68; non-standard employment and, 113, 194; political action/citizen mobilization against, 83; populism and, 190, 200; and poverty, 173; prevalence of, 73; in private-service sector, 13; in PRPS, 114(f), 115, 116, 120; in public sector, 114(f), 115, 116; racialized workers and, 195; in road transportation, 116; sectoral bargaining vs., 119; self-employed contractors and, 110, 293; in service sector, 190, 193–95, 200; and social programs, 100; temporary employment and, 194; TFWs and, 100, 156; and tuition costs, 178; UFCW and, 293; unionization and, 123, 194, 291; vertical disintegration and, 108, 110; working conditions in, 194; and workplace stress, 146. *See also* bad jobs; non-standard employment

private sector, unionization in, 95, 96, 125

private service sector. *See* service sector

privatization: of care work, 13, 229; of childcare, 299; defined, 60; of health care, 242, 246, 313; of hospitals, 300; labour–community coalitions and, 299; neoliberalism and, 8, 226; social action against, 229; of social programs, 241

profit(s): COVID-19 and, 55; efficiency and, 80; from financial sector vs. sale of goods and services, 46; health care systems and, 239; hospital services outsourcing and, 241; inflation and decline of, 79; labour laws and, 4; labour market deregulation for, 290; labour market flexibility and, 50; and long-term care, 246; and lower tax jurisdictions, 48; neoliberalism and, 50; OHS and, 290; public policy and, 4; social wage and, 173; TFWs and, 157; and wages, 50, 292; welfare state vs., 181. *See also* business interests; shareholder value maximization

protests. *See* social action/movement(s)

provincial governments: anti-union stance, 314; business interests and, 94–95, 97–98, 102; and Charter notwithstanding provisions, 127–28; and childcare, 33, 34, 35; and COVID-19, 31, 33, 35, 38, 92, 101–2; and employment policy, 77; and employment standards, 100, 110; and essential worker legislation, 102; funding transfers to private medical sector, 300; health care spending cuts, 241; and income inequality, 90; industrial disparities among, 110; and injured workers' benefits, 145; and labour laws/regulations, 77, 92, 93; and labour market deregulation, 97–101, 102–3; labour market reshaping, 12; and labour rights, 11; NDP, 310–11; and needs of poor, 97; and neoliberalism, 78–79; and non-standard employment, 97; "open for business" legislation, 92; policy drift, 99–100; policy layering-in, 100–1; and post-democracy, 93; and public health, 245; responsibilities of, 93; reversal of pro-labour legislation, 98–99; and sick leave, 35; social spending cuts, 181; and TFWs, 100–1; unions and, 95–96, 98–99; and university costs, 178; and workers' rights, 143

Provincial Nominee Program (PCP), 101

provincially regulated private sector (PRPS): disadvantaged social group employment in, 120; employees compared with FRPS, 112–13; FRPS compared, 108, 113, 120; independent contracting in, 118; job tenure in, 114; low-wage work in, 115; minimum wage in, 115; precarious employment in, 114(f), 115, 116, 120; standard employment relationship in, 108, 117; union coverage in, 115, 119

psychosocial hazards, 143, 149, 151

public health: COVID-19 and, 35, 244–46, 283; in COVID-19 recovery plan, 16; federal/provincial/territorial responsibility for, 245; goals of, 245; incorporation into just transition, 283; structural weakness, 245

Public Health Agency of Canada, 245

public health care systems: cost effectiveness of, 239; COVID-19, and private vs., 246; COVID-19 and, 150; universal, 309. *See also* care sector

public participation: and democracy, 97; history of, 74; income inequality and, 180; and public policy/policies, 97; union decline and, 125; union marginalization from, 79; welfare state and, 225

public policy/policies: business interests and, 4, 7–8, 10, 11, 92–93; capital vs. labour in, 79; in care provision, 222, 223–26; climate change and, 276–77; and collective agreements, 126–27; COVID-19 and, 4–6; drift in, 99–100, 256; importance of, 6–7; and Indigenous/First Nations employment, 15, 254–55, 256, 261–62; influence of wealthy on, 97; and labour market flexibility, 12; layering-in, 100–1; liberal economic principles in, 8; and low-wage work, 59–61; neoliberalism and, 8; permanent austerity in, 227; and profits, 4; public participation and, 97; responses to COVID-19, 28–31; social movement mobilizations and, 316; and unionization, 123, 126–27; voter turnout decline and, 97; and wealth gap, 91; and welfare state, 228, 301–2

public sector: back-to-work legislation in, 99, 315; care employment in, 224; collective bargaining rights, 76–77; FRPS compared, 108, 111, 113; good job undermining in, 13; job tenure in, 114; labour flexibility in, 52; low-wage work in, 115; minimum wage in, 115; precarious employment in, 114(f), 115, 116; right to strike in, 126; shrinking of, 98; Social Contract and, 311(box); taxpayer backlash against unions, 307; temporary workers in, 52; unions/unionization, 111, 115, 125, 190, 224, 308, 315; women in, 182; workplace violence in, 142

public services: in COVID-19 recovery plan, 16; health care as, 238; labour–community coalitions and, 299

Public Services Employment Act, 111

Quebec: back-to-work legislation in, 99; childcare program in, 34, 163, 300; COVID-19 in, 34, 150; living wages in, 297; long-term care homes in, 226; manufacturing employment in, 206, 207; minimum employment standards in, 297; minimum wage in, 297; SAWP workers in, 162; social unionism in, 134; union partisan ties in, 310

Québec solidaire, 317

racialized people: COVID-19 and, 63, 177; demographic growth, 178; and poverty, 177–78

racialized workers: COVID-19 and, 27, 90, 198; employment equity and, 225; filling labour shortages, 158;

service sector employment: automotive industry knock-on effects on, 213; bad jobs in, 52, 194; benefits in, 194; emotional labour in, 195; employment standards and, 197; fissuring in, 93; flexible work arrangements in, 13; gendered labour market segmentation, 191; growth of, 190–92, 207; immigrant workers in, 192, 193; Indigenous workers in, 177, 192, 193; low-wage, 193–95, 197–98; manufacturing outsourcing and, 209; manufacturing vs., 205, 207; non-standard nature of, 13, 193, 194; part-time, 194; precariousness in, 13, 193–95; racialized labour market segmentation in, 191; racialized workers, 177, 192, 193; racialized workers in, 192; scheduling in, 196–97; self-presentation of worker in, 195; as socially interactive, 195; students and, 177; temporary employment in, 194; temporary work agencies in, 99; unevenness of conditions in, 191; unionization in, 190–91, 196–97; women in, 192; working conditions, 196, 197–98

Seven Years' War, 253

Severe Acute Respiratory Syndrome (SARS), 150–51

shareholder value maximization: in automotive industry, 215; care sector and, 226; for-profit health facilities and, 300; short-term stock market performance and, 46, 47. *See also* profit(s)

Shell, 49

short-term stock market performance: and CEO/top manager remuneration, 47; long-term investments vs., 47; and shareholder value maximization, 46, 47; and stock prices, 47

sick leave: COVID-19 and, 33, 35, 101–2, 119, 140, 151, 173, 200, 217; FRPS and, 119; and layoffs, 82; paid vs. unpaid, 35; union campaigning for, 83

single-parent families: and childcare expenses, 173; and poverty, 173, 176

single-person households: food bank use, 178; and poverty, 175–76

Site C dam, Peace River, 280

skills: climate change and, 37; development of new, 278; in First Nations employment, 37; Global Skills Strategy and, 100; industrial unions and, 212; levels in union system, 212; and loss of working hours during COVID-19, 198; low-skill programs, 100; low-skilled workers, 156, 198; skilled workers, 37,

100; TFWs and, 100, 156; training, 37, 256, 277; in transition to low-carbon economy, 277, 278, 279; unionization of unskilled/semi-skilled, 205; unskilled workers in assembly line production, 209; unskilled/semi-skilled workers in manufacturing, 205

social action/movement(s), 291; during 1960s/70s, 299; after Great Depression, 16–17; after Second World War, 17; for care sector, 229–30, 231; regarding climate change, 82; community unionism and, 292; COVID-19 and, 82, 83, 246; direct action tactics, 313, 314, 316; Great Depression and, 16–17, 82; labour movements and, 301; and political parties, 314; against precarious employment, 83; against privatization, 229; and public policy/policies, 302, 316; right-wing, 307; Second World War and, 17, 82; social movement politics, 299–300; social wage, 180; and state power, 314; union–community coalitions, 308; unions and, 299, 308. *See also* alt-labour activism; strikes

social democracy: and capitalism, 308; crisis of, 316–17; golden age of capitalism and, 68; influence in Denmark vs. Canada, 6–7; NDP and, 7, 310; and social justice, 308; unions and, 308

social democratic parties/governments, 77; and neoliberalism, 308; rightward political shift and, 308

social determinants: of health, 180; of poverty, 178

social justice: alt-labour activism and, 291; care work and, 227; community unionism and, 292; labour law reforms and, 297; NDP and, 308; neoliberalism and, 144; OHS and, 149; social policies and, 76; social unionism and, 134; union activism and, 290

social media, 293, 294–95

social movement(s). *See* social action/movement(s)

social policy/policies: COVID-19 and, 101–2; democracy and, 73; and labour costs, 61; market/business priorities and, 80; need for better, 69; neoliberalism and, 79; and poverty, 173; and rights/services, 76; and social justice, 76; unions, and expenditures on, 62

social programs: basic income and elimination of, 183; business interests and, 225; cost sharing, 224; economic policies supporting, 76; federal government spending per GDP, 180; and income transfers,

76; international comparisons, 62–63; and job quality, 62; and labour costs, 61; labour–community coalitions and, 299; in liberal market economies, 62–63; low-wage work and, 62–63; neoliberalism and, 241; in Nordic countries, 8; in Nordic countries vs. liberal market economies, 61; and poverty, 173; precarious employment and, 100; privatization of, 241; reductions in, 12; and risk reduction, 61; social unionism and, 309; spending per GDP, 12, 180; spending reduction, 241; targeted, 224; TFWs and, 100; unions and, 95; universal, 12, 224, 308; wealthy and, 97; women and, 12; and women's employment, 224. *See also* social supports

social security. *See* social supports

social solidarity, 302; CUPW and, 293; and health care sector, 247; union activism and, 290; universal health care based on, 236. *See also* social action/movement(s)

social supports: COVID-19 and, 26, 33–34, 245; First Nations and, 258; Indigenous peoples and, 255; policies, 14; and risk reduction, 61; spending on, 174, 176; TFW caregivers and, 164; variations among countries, 26, 77. *See also* income support

social unionism, 134, 308, 309

social wage: COVID-19 and, 180; in essential services, vs. basic income, 183; governments and, 173, 180–82; neoliberalism and, 173, 180; organization for, 180; postwar economic boom and, 180; and poverty, 173; and profits, 173; tax avoidance and, 181; unions and, 95

Sodexo, 241

"Solidarity and Just Transition: Silesia Declaration" Conference of the Parties to the United Nations Framework Convention on Climate Change (COP 24), 283–84

solo or bogus self-employment: in FRPS, 114; prevalence of, 10; in private postal service industry, 116; in road transportation, 116; in service sector, 193. *See also* self-employment

South Korea: COVID-19 in, 30; health care sector in, 247

Spain: COVID-19 in, 33; low-wage jobs in, 60

stagflation, 79

standard employment relationship: definition, 108; earnings gap with non-standard employment, 91; federal government and, 117–18; FRPS and, 108, 113, 117; gender in, 113; as norm, 113; PRPS and, 117. *See also* non-standard employment

Starbucks Partners, 295

Stellantis (formerly FCA), 49, 211

stress: in care work, 228; Charter of Rights and Freedoms and, 142; of First Nations employment conditions, 259; job insecurity and, 258; as major concern, 140; and mental health, 141–42; and physical injuries, 141; precarious employment and, 146; rates of, 141–42; workplace violence and, 149–50

Strike for Black Lives, 295

strikes: Amazon, 53, 295; COVID-19 and, 295; direct-action tactics and, 295; Elliot Lake uranium mines, 144; first contract negotiation and, 132; against Health and Social Services Delivery Improvement Act (BC), 242–43; history of consequences, 74–75; McDonald's, 295; and Order 1003, 109; personal care workers, 244; rarity of, 95; right to, 126, 314, 315(box); Saskatchewan doctors, 238; student, 300; TACW and, 295; teachers, 200, 300; United Auto Workers (1946), 126; Whole Foods, 295; wildcat, 291, 295; Winnipeg General Strike (1919), 125

supply chains: in automotive industry, 13, 213; COVID-19 and, 50, 205, 217; in manufacturing sector, 217; offshoring and, 49; trade liberalization and, 210

Supreme Court of Canada: on collective bargaining rights, 99; and Health and Social Services Delivery Improvement Act (BC), 243; and Rand Formula, 126; and right to strike, 315; *Saskatchewan Federation of Labour v Saskatchewan,* 314, 315(box); and Saskatchewan Public Service Essential Services Act, 98(box); and unions, 315; and Walmart unionization, 129(box)

Supreme Court of the United States: *Janus v American Federation of State, County, and Municipal Employees* (2018), 126; and Wagner Act, 126

Sustainable Development Goals (UN), 284

Suzuki, David, 285

Swartz, Donald, 317

Sweden: care work in, 228, 229; collective bargaining in, 62, 77; COVID-19 in, 35; health/social security program spending, 77; income equality in, 61; labour movements in, 77; low-wage work in, 63; poverty rates, 173; social wage in, 173; unions/workers as social partners in, 135; wages in, 59, 61; worker voice and efficiency in, 128; workplace-related deaths in, 142

Taiwan, COVID-19 in, 28, 30
Task Force on Agricultural Labour Relations (Ontario), 162
TaskRabbit, 134
taxation: avoidance, 48, 48(box), 181; corporations and, 181; evasion, 46; and green economy, 37–38; havens, 48; and individuals vs. corporations, 181; international investment and, 46; reduction, 46; and social programs/benefits, 61; and social wage, 181
teachers: additional hiring, 38; COVID-19 and back-to-school recommendations, 35, 151; funding for, 35; strikes, 200, 300; and student violence, 149. *See also* education
technologies: automation, 209; change, and Indigenous employment, 255; and education levels, 206, 211; and job losses, 206; in manufacturing sector, 206, 209, 211; and worker education levels, 209
temporary employment: agency lack of regulation, 99; in automotive industry, 13; and fissured workplaces, 194; growth in, 12; low-wage agency workers, 52; and poverty, 173; and precarious employment, 194; prevalence of, 10; in public sector, 52; in service sector, 193, 194; women and, 173; workplace deaths in, 148
temporary foreign worker program (TFWP), 12, 156, 157, 298–99; creation of gendered minorities pockets, 165; creation of racialized workers, 165; expansion of, 101; history, 100; as policy layering-in, 100; Provincial Nominee Program within, 101; and temporary migrant workers, 12
temporary foreign workers (TFWs), 290; and citizenship rights, 156, 290, 297; COVID-19 and, 27, 150; disadvantages of, 158; employer power over, 156; employment protections and, 290; as essential workers, 27; freer employment contracts and use

of, 81; in low-skill programs, 100; in low-wage employment, 100, 156; numbers of, 156, 297; numbers of permits, 157; numbers of positions, 156; occupational health and safety, 156; and permanent residency, 156; and precarious employment, 100, 156; and profitability, 157; provincial governments and, 100–1; and social programs, 100; as whole workers, 165; and workers' rights, 156; working conditions, 150, 156, 158. *See also* agricultural workers; care workers; migrant workers
Thatcher, Margaret, 8, 45, 68, 78
Tim Hortons, 47, 66(box), 291
Toronto Airport Workers' Council (TAWC), 196(box), 295
Toronto Stock Exchange, 32
Toyota, 49, 211, 216
trade unions. *See* unions
transnational corporations: branch plants in Canadian manufacturing sector, 210; foreign affiliates, 49; growth of, 49; sector control, 49
transportation sector: COVID-19 and, 117; fuel amounts used in, 277; precarious employment in road sector, 116; in transition to renewable energy, 285. *See also* air transportation
Trudeau, Justin, 31
Trump, Donald, 28–29, 190, 217
Trumper, Ricardo, 159

Uber, 134, 191(box), 291
underemployment: COVID-19 and, 33; of Indigenous peoples, 255; young workers and, 53
unemployment: Aboriginal people and, 256–57; in Canada among advanced industrial countries, 91; COVID-19 and, 5, 26, 33, 53, 63–64; in Europe, 63; First Nations and, 257, 258; Great Depression and, 63, 254; and health inequality, 259; Indigenous peoples and, 177, 255, 259; inflation and, 60; insurance, 81, 101, 109; low-wage workers and, 63; Métis and, 257; recessions and, 63; young workers and, 53, 176
unemployment insurance. *See* employment/unemployment insurance
Unifor (formerly Canadian Auto Workers (CAW)), 83; and community chapters, 293–94; and COVID-19,

36; and electric vehicles, 218; strategic voting vs. for NDP, 96; and UAW two-tier system, 216, 217

union activism. *See* alt-labour activism

union certification: about, 130–31; in Canada Labour Code, 110; decertification and, 129–30; difficulty with, 291; employee eligibility/status and, 130; and employment standards legislation, 64; fitness instructors, 292–93; labour relations legislation and, 128–29; membership card signing (card check), 130; negotiating first contract, 131–32; restrictiveness of, 64; weakening of, 11–12; workplace elections, 130

union coverage: decline in, 123; in FRPS, 115; of manufacturing workers, 205; in PRPS, 115; in public sector, 115; union density vs., 124; variations among countries, 77

union density: in automotive employment, 215; community chapters and, 294; decline in, 60, 95, 123; in FRPS, 119; international comparisons, 60; low-wage work and, 62; in manufacturing employment, 210–11; in manufacturing sector, 205; in OECD countries, 124; in private sector, 95; in PRPS, 119; rates, 77; union coverage vs., 124; and union membership dues, 124; variations among countries, 77

union membership: agency shop/dues check-off, 126; closed shop, 126; COVID-19, and losses to, 83; dues paycheque deductions, 126; eligibility for, 135; losses in, 55, 95; union density and, 124

union–community coalitions, 308, 312–14

unionism: and communications technology, 134; free rider problem, 126; and marginalized groups, 134; social, 134; solidarity, 294–95; and worker voice, 133

unionization: bringing unionized/non-unionized workers together, 17; Charter of Rights and Freedoms and, 127–28; and compensation in workplaces, 67–68; COVID-19 and, 55; COVID-19 and rate of, 27; decentralization of, 127; duty of fair representation, 131; employer resistance to, 77, 129, 132–33, 136, 291; employer vs. employee freedoms and, 132; fissuring vs., 119; flexible workforces and, 61; and good vs. bad jobs, 54–55; history of, 125–28; hurdles to, 77, 128–30; and Indigenous employment, 259; at individual workplace level, 77, 124, 127, 128, 129, 197; by industry, 190(f); innovative forms of organizing, 17; internal non-union workplace committees vs., 131(box); labour laws and, 123, 124; labour market deregulation and, 217; neoliberalism and, 8; and non-standard employment, 124; and non-union/no-voice default workplace status, 128; platform economy and, 134; political/legal structure of, 128–29; postwar, 301; and precarious employment, 194; public policies and, 123, 126–27; right-to-work laws and, 126; and safety, 68; steps in, 130–33; unfair labour practices and, 126, 132; union advantage, 119; and wage gap, 68; and wages, 54–55; Wagner Act and, 124; of WestJet, 131(box); and workplace rights, 124. *See also under names of individual industrial sectors*

unions: and attacks on workers' rights, 315–16; automotive industry concessions, 214–17; and bad vs. good jobs, 51; benefits of, 128; business interests and, 77, 299–300; and Charter of Rights and Freedoms, 314–15; and clean energy economy, 83; climate education programs, 281; and co-determination, 77–78; conceptions of solidarity, 316; concessions, 214–17, 290; and contingent compensation vs. annual increases, 213, 215; cooperation/coordination with business interests/government in Nordic countries, 61; COVID-19 and, 53, 83, 119, 217; craft, 134, 212; declining political power, 95–96; and democracy, 90, 95; destruction of industrial relations system based on, 94; division by American vs. Canadian allegiances, 77; educational campaigns, 309–10; and efficiency, 128; and electoral politics, 308; electoral strategies, 309–12, 316; and employment benefits, 55; erosion of power, 307; federal government and, 108; financial/staff resources, 95; First Nations outreach program, 261; and First Nations/Indigenous employment, 261; formation of industrial, 205; and fossil fuel sectors, 17; French–English divide in, 77; and Green New Deal, 283; innovative organizing strategies, 301, 302; integration in labour relations framework, 315; and international climate efforts, 283–84; and job security, 55; joint union–employer committees, 279; judicial strategies, 308, 314–15, 316; and just transition, 278–79, 280, 283, 285; and labour law reforms, 95; and labour–capital balance, 135; lack of uniformity of interests, 316; and legal activism,

in, 142. *See also* Supreme Court of the United States

United States–Mexico–Canada Agreement, 46

United Steelworkers (USW), 83, 144; Stop the Killing!, 145

United Voices of the World (UVW), 295

United Way of Greater Toronto, 297

UNITE-HERE, 196

Vale, 49

Valentine's Day of Action, 312

vertical disintegration, 108, 110, 113

Vietnam, COVID-19 in, 28, 30

violence. *See* workplace violence

visible minorities. *See* racialized people

Visser, Jelle, 68

voting: income inequality and, 97; rights, 74; voter turnout decline, 97

wage levels: in automotive industry, 206, 212–13; in automotive vs. all manufacturing sectors, 214–15; in care work, 225, 230; of CEOs vs. average, 179; contingent compensation vs. annual increases, 215; contracting out and, 226; cuts for health care workers, 242; Equal Pay Day, 176; equal pay for equal work, 118–19; equality, 243; equity, and health care workers, 242; inflation and, 79; in long-term care, 230; in manufacturing sector, 205, 208; in non-standard vs. standard employment, 91; productivity growth and, 212; provincial differences in median, 115; racialized women and, 177; and SAWP workers, 162; TFWs and, 158; tiered for new hires, 215–17; unionized workplaces and gap in, 68

wages: contingent compensation vs. annual increases, 213, 215; essential workers, 217; gender inequities/equity, 224–25; increases in average, 52; Indigenous peoples and industrial wage labour, 253–54, 259–60; market determination of, 59; neoliberalism and decline in real, 68; sectoral level negotiation, 61; subsidies, 6; unionized workers and, 54–55

Wagner, Robert F., 127(box)

Wagner Act (1935) (US), 123, 125–26, 127(box), 129, 130, 133

Wall, Brad, 98(box)

Walmart, 129(box), 136, 296

Warskett, Rosemary, 317

We Care, 244

wealth gap. *See* income inequality

wealthy, 199; and care provision, 223; COVID-19 and, 32; and democracy, 93; influence of, 4, 7, 97; limiting power of, 75; motivations, 96; neoliberalism and wealth concentration, 59; priorities of, 97; and social programs, 97; us vs. them identity, 96. *See also* income inequality

Weil, David, 49, 113

welfare state: business interests and, 225; and care provision/work, 224–25, 228, 230; cash-for-care model vs., 227; and civic participation, 225; and Co-operative Commonwealth Federation, 302; golden age of capitalism and, 68; NDP and, 302; neoliberalism and, 180, 240–41; postwar economic boom and, 181; pre-welfare state/family era, 223–24; profitability vs., 181; progressive public policies and, 301–2; public policy and, 228; and publicly shared risk, 224–25

West Indian Domestic Scheme, 163

WestJet, 117, 131(box)

Whole Foods, 295

Wilson, Chip, 32

Winnipeg General Strike (1919), 125

women: during and after Second World War, 224; and care provision, 12, 223, 224; in care sector, 222, 224; and childcare, 193, 199, 224, 301; COVID-19 and, 34, 63–64, 193, 198–99; employment equity and, 225; in health care sector, 240; and job losses, 198; in low-wage employment, 173; manufacturing employees, 208; maternal mortality rate, 237; and minimum wage, 176; part-time employment, 173, 176, 195; and poverty, 176; public-sector job cuts and, 182; retail workers during COVID-19, 198–99; service-sector employment, 192; social program employment, 224; social programs and, 12; social service cuts and, 182; in temporary employment, 173; as TFW caregivers, 158; transition to green energy and job offers to, 282; workplace violence and, 142, 149. *See also* gender

Wong, Lloyd, 159

work: hazards of, 140; and human rights, 290; valuation of, 290

worker voice: COVID-19 and, 150; in COVID-19 recovery plan, 16; efficiency vs., 11; in health care sector, 247; human resource management and, 125; in just transition to low-carbon economy, 278–79; labour laws and, 124, 133; lack of, in precarious employment, 195; in OHS, 148–49; and SARS, 150; unionism/unions and, 119, 128, 133, 229; worker-owned cooperatives and, 134; workplace democratization and, 133–35

Workers' Action Centre (WAC), 297, 298

workers' compensation: boards (WCBs), 143, 144; globalization and, 145; TFWs and, 156

workers' rights: for agricultural workers, 36; associations, 73; COVID-19 and, 152, 316; and democracy, 74; federal government and, 108; formal/paper vs. exercisable, 160; and hazards, 144; and health, 140; history of, 74; as human rights, 315; NDP and, 310; neoliberalism and, 151; provincial/territorial responsibilities for, 143; TFWs and, 156; unions, and attacks on, 315–16. *See also* labour rights; workplace rights

Workers United Canada Council, 292-93

working conditions: of agricultural TFWs, 159, 160, 161; in care work, 222, 226-27; contracting out and, 226; in Crown vs. private corporations, 282; in FRPS, 108; in health care sector, 247; labour market deregulation and, 93; in long-term care sector, 246; low-wage employment and, 93; of migrant workers, 150; in precarious employment, 194; in service sector, 196, 197–98; of TFWs, 150, 156, 158. *See also* workplace violence

working poverty, 65; COVID-19 and, 173; incidence of, 290; living wage and, 67; minimum/living wage and, 295–96; numbers in, 4; precarious employment and, 173; rates, 183; social wage reduction and, 173. *See also* poverty

workplace rights: for low-wage service workers, 197–98; politicization of, 124; San Francisco bill of rights, 197–98; unionization and, 124; weakening of, 290

Workplace Safety and Insurance Board (Ontario), 144

workplace stress. *See* stress

workplace violence, 140, 142, 149–50

WorkSafeBC, 144

World Bank: on COVID-19 and economy, 50; and self-regulated free markets, 78

World Health Organization (WHO): on affordable housing, 259; on COVID-19, 244; declaration of global pandemic, 28; on health as human right, 237

World Meteorological Organization, 274

World Trade Organization (WTO): and Auto Pact, 214; and Chinese membership, 210

Wynne, Kathleen, 66(box), 312

younger people/workers: basic income and, 183; community unionism and, 291–92; COVID-19 and, 54, 176; insecurity, 73; job quality, 54; living wage and, 66–67; loss of working hours during COVID-19, 198; minimum wage for, 115; as NEETs, 53, 176; in non-standard employment, 124; in part- vs. full-time work, 53–54; and poverty, 176, 178; and poverty wages, 53; and precarious employment, 192; transition to green energy and job offers to, 282; underemployment, 53; unemployment, 53, 176; and workplace injuries, 146

Yukon, NDP governments in, 310

Yussuff, Hassan, 283

zoonotic diseases, 24, 34, 37, 150, 275